The Illuminated Life

Abe Arkoff
University of Hawaii at Manoa

ALLYN AND BACON
Boston • London • Toronto • Sydney • Tokyo • Singapore

Copyright © 1995 by Allyn and Bacon
A Simon & Schuster Company
Needham Heights, MA 02194

Executive Editor: Laura Pearson
Vice President, Publisher: Susan Badger
Editorial Assistant: Sarah Dunbar
Marketing Manager: Joyce Nilsen
Editorial-Production Service: Trinity Publishers Services
Text Designer: Donna Chernin, DMC & Company
Cover Administrator: Linda Knowles
Manufacturing Buyer: Megan Cochran

Library of Congress Cataloging-in-Publication Data

Arkoff, Abe.
    The illuminated life / Abe Arkoff.
       p.   cm.
    Includes bibliographical references and indexes.
    ISBN 0-205-15008-X
    1. Conduct of life.   2. Adjustment (Psychology)   I. Title.
  BF637.C5A65   1995
  158—dc20
                            94-9590
                            CIP

Printed in the United States of America
10 9 8   01

For Susan, Amy, and Ty, with love

Overview

Contents

To the Reader

"The unexamined life is not worth living." So Socrates said, but many of us don't know how to examine our lives in a helpful way, or we don't take time to do so. Instead, we muddle through.

Carl Jung assiduously examined his own life and spent his long lifetime in the study of human nature. He concluded that the "art of life" is of all the arts the most distinguished and also the rarest: "Only a few persons are artists in life. . . . So for many people too much unlived life remains over."

A similar observation had been made by Henry David Thoreau when he removed himself to the hut he had built by the side of Walden Pond. He wrote, "We lead but a fraction of our lives." Thoreau cautioned his readers not to follow in his footsteps but to find their own lives—to march to whatever drummer's music they heard, "however measured or far away." And indeed he marched away from the pond himself, because he decided that he had more lives to lead and no further time for that one.

Oscar Wilde, who himself stepped to a different drummer—which marched him into Reading Gaol—wrote, "One's real life is often the life one does not lead." It was because my father, at least as I saw it, did not lead his own life, his real life, that I was drawn to the study of lives. I was very close to my father. He was a dear man, a troubled man, a brilliant man; but at his death it might have been said that he never came fully into his own, that much of his life was unspent.

In my over forty years as a clinical psychologist, I have found many persons whose lives are not so different from my father's. There are many who have trouble finding their lives and living them fully. There are many who have trouble finding themselves or making all that they could of themselves or becoming the persons they hunger to be.

This book was written to help you *illuminate* your life. In it, you are asked to pursue answers to fourteen basic questions concerning yourself. In doing so, you may clarify and come to terms with your past; find more joy, purpose, and peace of mind in the present; and obtain assurance and direction for the future.

Life has been described as a journey, and your travel through this book might also be thought of as one. The chapters have been arranged to move you along in both journeys. The first chapter will help you get your *bearings,* and the next two will help you appraise your relationship to your *self,* and the *beliefs* that guide your life. Next, to gain perspective, you will trace the crucial *turning points* in your journey; then, in the chapters on *significant others* and *love,* you will consider those who have journeyed with you. To complete the first half of the book, you will reflect on the *ultimate point*—death—an event that intrudes on all of life.

In the chapters of the last half of the book you will move ahead, considering your *potentiality* (what's possible for you), your *values* (what's important to you), and the *goals* stemming from these values. You will examine the *coping* strategies, personal *assets,* and *commitments* that assist you in reaching your goals and moving your life along. In the last chapter, standing on the *threshold,* you will look back to see what you have learned and look forward for a vision of the future.

From time to time in this book, I will have occasion to refer to my life as well as to the lives of others. In the application items and explorations that conclude each chapter, you will have the opportunity to work on your own life. As you do so, I hope that you will find others with whom you can share your responses and who will share their responses with you. I think the stories of our lives, candidly told and empathically heard, are among the most precious things we can share.

All the best to you on your journey through this book, and all the best to you on your journey through life.

Aloha,

Abe Arkoff

Thanks

I am grateful to my many students and clients who over the years have shared their lives with me and helped me develop the materials that appear in this book. I am also grateful to the instructors who have reviewed these materials for me or used them in a prepublication draft and offered helpful suggestions based on their experience. These instructors include Denise Lajoie, Kapolani Community College; Larry Fujinaka, Leeward Community College; Otome Myers and Langley Frissell, Windward Community College; Michael Wiesner, Mid-Pacific Institute; Loren Ekroth and Earle Schmitz, University of Hawaii at Manoa; Steven Coccia, Orange County Community College; Jackie Gerstein, Georgia College; John Long, Mt. San Antonio College; Barbara Elicker, Sinclair Community College; Kathryn Goddard, California State University at Long Beach; and Victor Messier, University of New Hampshire.

My thanks to the editorial and production staff of Allyn and Bacon and also to John and Evelyn Ward of Trinity Publishers Services. My warmest aloha of all to Dorothy Conway, who was described to me as a "superb copyeditor" and proved this to be an understatement.

About the Author

Abe Arkoff is professor emeritus of psychology at the University of Hawaii at Manoa, where he continues to teach on a part-time basis. His present students include both the youngest on campus and the oldest—those in the Freshman Seminar Program, which he created and directed for many years, and those in the Elderhostel program, which he brought to the Manoa campus and coordinated. He has won two awards for excellence in teaching.

Abe is a licensed, board-certified clinical psychologist (ABPP) who has practiced in various settings. For ten years he was a volunteer working with terminally ill persons and their families. He is currently working to establish a self-help network of persons interested in sharing their lives and facilitating their own personal growth.

Abe has taught courses in adjustment and personal growth almost every semester since 1951. In these courses and also in his "The Illuminated Life" workshops, the materials in this book originated and reached their present form. Abe has written widely in this area, and his recent publications include *Psychology and Personal Growth* (now in its fourth edition).

Question 1

Bearings

Where Am I Now in My Life?

One summer some years ago, psychotherapist Sheldon Kopp spent many hours alone, huddled, brooding on an empty beach. He was taking stock of his life and finding it a poor thing. The preceding winter, he had undergone surgery for a brain tumor that could not be wholly removed. He was infirm and in pain, and his future was ominously uncertain. He was trying to decide whether to swim out as far as he could and leave his painful life on the shore. Instead, he sought help, got his bearings, and decided he would live out the years he had left, enjoying what he could and being what he might be to the persons he loved (Kopp, 1976).

One autumn some years ago, writer Nancy Kelton sat down to take stock of everything that was right with her life. Recent years had not been easy; she had gone through an unpleasant marriage and divorce and was now on her own raising her daughter (with a biweekly dad). But she found she had a lot of reasons to be grateful—some light and some serious—and they all appear in Box 1.1. Kelton remembered something her father had told her: "It's not what you have that matters; rather, it is what you *think* you have." After taking stock, she wrote, "I *think* I have a lot."

Kopp spoke of his life as a pilgrimage, and poets and writers have often described life as a journey. I can think of my own life that way. There have been hills to climb (some have seemed more like mountains), high plateaus, and an occasional peak. I haven't fallen off any cliffs, but I've tumbled down some slippery slopes into dark valleys. I have usually been fortunate and traveled quickly, but there were times when I barely crept along and times when I seemed to lose my way.

It may be only when we get stuck or when things threaten to fall apart that we give some serious thought to our lives and try to get our bearings. Perhaps at such times we will, like Kopp, huddle with ourselves and wonder whether life is worth it. Perhaps, like Kopp, we will seek help and find new courage, direction, or resolve. (More about Kopp's life and resultant philosophy later in this book.)

1

Box 1.1

Thirty-One Reasons I'm Thankful

by Nancy Kelton

1. I am thankful celibacy isn't a terminal disease.

2. I am thankful my daughter Emily thinks my very best chicken dish is almost as good as the school hot lunch.

3. I am thankful for Woody Allen, Russell Baker and Nora Ephron, as well as the person who said, "And this, too, shall pass away."

4. I am thankful that Emily is healthy and thriving.

5. I am thankful that, last week when I went to a college gym to work out, the fellow doing sit-ups next to me asked what I was majoring in.

6. I am thankful that I have the strength to do 13 push-ups.

7. I am thankful for my friend and neighbor Judy, whose daughters play with my daughter—usually at Judy's house.

8. I am thankful Judy is a fashion designer and I am her sample size.

9. I am thankful that the single father I see at the PTA has started asking me out.

10. I am thankful that the whiny podiatrist whom I couldn't avoid meeting at a party has finally stopped.

11. I am thankful Emily has come to terms with my divorce.

12. I'm thankful Aunt Rose has too.

13. I am thankful that my parents, both in their 70s, still play 18 holes of golf three times a week.

14. I am thankful Emily has learned to discuss her feelings openly with me.

15. I am thankful she has learned not to discuss them before my morning coffee.

16. I am thankful for my friend Cindy, who always finds two hours to listen.

17. I am thankful for chocolate egg creams.

18. I am thankful for chocolate anything.

19. I am thankful my former in-laws still have a relationship with Emily.

20. I am thankful that one way they do so is with presents of clothing, and checks that get bigger every year.

21. I'm thankful I've learned to enjoy New Year's Eve without male company.

22. I am thankful I have the luxury of enjoying New Year's Day without male company and without the Orange, Rose, Cotton and every other Bowl.

23. I am thankful for the friends who helped me through moments of despair.

24. I am thankful that the moments of despair are almost always followed by moments of joy.

25. I am thankful that sardines are the only food I must get to with a key.

26. I am thankful for all the warm and loving people who have touched my life.

27. I am thankful I no longer feel guilty about buying myself something frivolous—unless it's also expensive.

28. I am thankful I no longer feel guilty about occasionally calling my parents collect.

29. I am thankful that although I sometimes yell and nag and lose patience with my daughter, she says she doesn't want to trade me.

30. I am thankful that although she sometimes whines and sulks and is willful and challenging, my kid is totally terrific most days.

31. I am thankful that if I had to live my life again, I'd be happy to live it pretty much the same.

(From Kelton, 1984, p. 220)

Major points of change can force us to take stock and get our bearings, but some unhappy points come about because we have paid too little attention to how we are living our lives. I remember seeing a house whose roof was sagging (the rest of it was not much better). The real-estate agent described it as a case of "deferred maintenance." It needed, she confessed, a little attention. We didn't buy the house, but I appropriated the term, because it seemed to be an apt description of what is wrong with many lives.

When I was a youth, the coming of each new year was the time to take stock of one's life and to resolve to change what needed changing in the year to come.

Although the custom of making New Year's resolutions survives to this day, it seems to be taken less seriously. Psychotherapist Richard Frank (1977) finds it helpful to ask himself several times a week how he would behave if he had infinite courage. That's a provocative question. (It's not sheer audacity that Frank has in mind but rather what would be in his "best moral interest.") You might consider what your own answer would be. Stop right now and ask yourself how you would complete this statement:

If I had infinite courage, I would . . .

And you might consider an alternative approach (also suggested by Frank) that asks how you would live your life if you were bereft of courage. How would you complete this statement?

If I were an infinite coward, I would . . .

Frank writes that these questions help him and his patients put their lives in perspective. They can see where on the battlefield of everyday life they have shown valor and where they are hunkering down in their foxholes.

Eda LeShan (1988) asked herself some similar questions in reviewing what was unlived in her life. She noted that in her adolescence she had been terrified by the "restless adventurer" she felt within herself, and to deal with that terror she had clipped her own wings. She wrote, "I can't forgive myself for the fact that I was a coward; that I didn't have the guts to fight harder to be free, when that's what I should have been doing" (p. 474).

In making resolutions, we generally focus on what's wrong in our lives that needs to be made better, but it is just as important to focus on what's right in our lives that needs to be remembered, acknowledged, and affirmed. Nancy Kelton did that in constructing her list, and the occasion was—as you might have guessed—Thanksgiving. On Thanksgiving, some of us forget the thanks-giving part and simply dig into the turkey and stuffing. I remember being a Thanksgiving dinner guest of a large family whose custom it was to begin by having everyone in turn tell what he or she was thankful for. By the time we all had had our heartfelt say (including the 4-year-old), there were more than a few tearful eyes.

There are many places that one can get lost or stuck on life's journey. Many of us seem to have no map or plan (or even a plan not to have a plan). As psychologist James Coleman (1979) observes, we simply "muddle through." He writes, "Most people would consider it sheer folly to attempt to climb a high mountain peak without studying the possible routes, obtaining a clear understanding of the hazards, and procuring the necessary equipment. Yet many people expect inadequate information, competencies, and values to carry them successfully through the journey of life—a far more difficult undertaking than the conquest of a mountain peak" (pp. 14–15).

Coleman points out that the cost of muddling through is ordinarily a high one. We wind up with the wrong job and the wrong mate and the wrong number of kids. We wind up frustrated, unfulfilled, and in the wrong life. We validate Oscar Wilde's observation that "One's real life is often the life one does not lead."

After thirty years of listening to his clients talk about their lives, psychotherapist James Bugental (1976) concluded that although each had engaged in endless rumination, not one knew how to reconsider her or his own life fully and candidly. And Bugental found this same "curious lack of ability to take stock in one's own being" (p. 65) in other groups of people, his colleagues, his friends, and even himself.

"Where am I now in my life?" This question, which is suggested by the work of Ira Progoff (1975), asks you to take stock, get your bearings, and determine

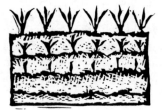

Bearings: Where Am I Now in My Life?

Seedthoughts

A *seedthought* is a thought that provokes us to think of something in a new or deeper way. It is a seed for thought and further thought. As we turn it over in our minds, it offers new insight or understanding. Someone has said that one possible difference between good poetry and *great* poetry is this: when we hear good poetry, we say, yes, I have felt that way. But when we hear great poetry, we say, I have felt that way, but I never fully realized it until now. Some seedthoughts help us express the feelings and insights that we may never have been able to put into our own words. Below are some quotations that may serve as seedthoughts on the first life question, "Where am I now in my life?" As an exercise, you might select one that speaks to you and your life and think about it, and then write about it.

1. You can't steal second base and keep one foot on first.
   —*unidentified aging junior executive*

2. We are always getting ready to live, but never living.
   —*Ralph Waldo Emerson*

3. Our life is frittered away by detail. . . . Simplify, simplify.
   —*Henry David Thoreau*

4. Bad times have a scientific value. These are occasions a good learner would not miss.
   —*Ralph Waldo Emerson*

5. It's good to fail now and then—you learn a lot more out of failure than you do out of success.
   —*Ian Hunter*

6. A man is a success if he gets up in the morning and goes to bed at night and in between does what he wants to do.
   —*Bob Dylan*

7. I have learned that success is to be measured not so much by the position one has reached in life as by the obstacles which he has overcome trying to succeed.
   —*Booker T. Washington*

8. If your daily life seems poor, don't blame it; blame yourself . . . that you are not poet enough to call forth its riches.
   —*Rainer Maria Rilke*

9. There are only two ways to live your life. One is as though nothing is a miracle. The other is as though everything is a miracle.
   —*Albert Einstein*

10. A man said to the universe:
    "Sir, I exist!"
    "However," replied the universe,
    "The fact has not created in me
    A sense of obligation."
    —*Stephen Crane*

11. My candle burns at both ends:
    It will not last the night;
    But ah, my foes, and oh, my friends—
    It gives a lovely light!
    —*Edna St. Vincent Millay*

where you are now on life's journey. Is your life a success? Do you like yourself? Do you have good relations with others? Do you have a sense of purpose? Are you growing? Are you choosing your life? The material in this chapter may help you address these questions a little better.

Is Your Life a Success?

Reviewing his life in 1986, country singer Joe Diffie pronounced it a failure. It was, he said, a year filled with low points, and they are vivid in his memory: "I lost my job, got divorced and lost my family, and got a tax audit."

Over the centuries, philosophers have thought deeply about the nature of "the good life." What would a "successful" life be? Here is how the American essayist and poet Ralph Waldo Emerson defined success:

What is Success?

To laugh often and love much;
To win the respect of intelligent
  persons and the affection of children;
To earn the approval of honest critics
  and endure the betrayal of false friends;
To appreciate beauty;
To give of one's self without the
  slightest thought of return;
To have accomplished a task, whether
  by a healthy child, a rescued soul, a
    garden patch or a redeemed social condition;
To have played and laughed with
  enthusiasm and sung with exaltation;
To know that even one life has
  breathed easier because you have lived;
This is to have succeeded.

Is your life a success? What would you say if you were asked this question? Stop reading for a moment and try to arrive at an answer.

In a poll at my school, the University of Hawaii at Manoa, the students were asked to grade themselves on all the course work they were doing at that point in the semester; the results were A 29 percent, B 50 percent, C 19 percent, D 1 percent, and F nobody (Chung, 1991). It might be interesting for all of us to try to grade our own lives in the same way. If your life were to end today, what grade could be inscribed on your headstone or written in red on your box of ashes? If you knew you were to be graded, you might prefer simply to audit life (some seem to do this anyway) or perhaps to enroll on a credit–no credit basis.

A call to evaluate one's life is a feature of many near-death experiences. A physican interviewed a number of persons who had been clinically "dead" but then revived. They commonly reported an encounter with a being of light, who asked them to review and determine the sufficiency of their lives. The request was made lovingly—not critically—to get them to reconsider what they had done with their years. One of the most important lessons they brought back from this close encounter with death was the need to love others more acceptingly, more deeply, more profoundly (Moody, 1975).

In 1987, the *Wall Street Journal* (*The American Dream,* 1987) commissioned a poll in which the respondents were asked to indicate how important various items

POT-SHOTS NO 800

INCREDIBLE AS IT SEEMS,

MY LIFE IS BASED ON A TRUE STORY.

were to their idea of success. Relatively few of these respondents designated the conventional criteria of success—money, power, fame—as very important. Instead, the item that was most often highly rated was success in social relationships: being a good parent, having a happy marriage, having a happy relationship with another person, and having friends who respect one. Being well educated and excelling at one's job were also high on the list of very important elements.

Interestingly, these several sets of data validate an observation made many years ago by Sigmund Freud, the founder of psychoanalysis. Freud was asked what a person should be able to do well. It is a question to ponder, and a ponderous answer might have been expected. But Freud's response was brief. "Lieben und arbeiten," he answered. What should one be able to do well? One should be able to love and to work (Erikson, 1963).

Despite the influence of Freud, the ability to love or the ability to work is not the most commonly cited criterion of success in life; rather, it is happiness or subjective well-being. A century and a half ago, Henry David Thoreau observed, "The mass of men lead lives of quiet desperation." In 1993, a National Institute of Mental Health research team concluded that more than one in four American adults suffer a mental or addictive disorder at some point in any one year (Regier et al., 1993). Nevertheless, the masses these days appear pretty happy; at least, that is what we report when we are surveyed. The findings of a National Opinion Research survey (*General Social Surveys*, 1991) are typical. The respondents were asked, "Taken all together, how would you say things are these days—would you say you are very happy, pretty happy, or not too happy?" Nearly six in ten of the respondents described themselves as pretty happy, three in ten as very happy, and only one in ten as not too happy.

Think about your own happiness or satisfaction with life. Immediately below is a question for you. Please respond before reading on.

In general, are you satisfied or dissatisfied with the way things are going in your own personal life? (check one)

_____ satisfied _____ dissatisfied

The above question was asked early in 1992 in a national Gallup poll (Hugick, 1992). About eight in ten of the respondents said they were satisfied with the way things were going in their personal lives; only two in ten were dissatisfied. Interestingly, when this same group was asked if they were satisfied or dissatisfied with the way things were going in the United States, the results were almost

©ASHLEIGH BRILLIANT '983

POT-SHOTS NO 2844.

WITH PSYCHIATRIC HELP SO EXPENSIVE AND TIME-CONSUMING, I CAN'T AFFORD TO BE MORE THAN SLIGHTLY UNHAPPY.

exactly reversed; about eight in ten were dissatisfied—not an auspicious omen for the reelection campaign of then President Bush.

Think some more about your own happiness or satisfaction with life. Below are some faces expressing various feelings. Which face comes closest to how you feel about life as a whole? (Circle one letter.)

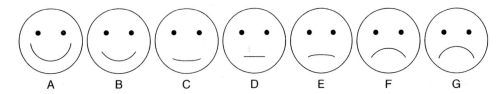

The above item was included in a national survey conducted several decades ago (Andrews & Withey, 1976). The percentage of respondents choosing each face is indicated below. Also indicated are the percentages for the seventy-eight freshmen and sophomores in one of my personal growth courses in 1993. As you can see, almost all of the respondents in both surveys managed to crack something of a smile. The national data were collected in interviews and may paint a somewhat rosy picture, because people tend to put on a good face in public. The student data were gathered in a self-administered survey that was anonymous except for certain demographic information.

	A	B	C	D	E	F	G
1976 national survey	20%	46%	27%	4%	2%	1%	0%
1993 student survey	10	56	28	4	0	0	1

What are the causes or sources of happiness? What makes us happy? And what doesn't make us happy? Research indicates that wealth (beyond a certain minimum), age, and gender are relatively unimportant factors. What appears to be most important are social relationships (Argyle, 1987). In his book *The Pursuit of Happiness,* David Myers (1992) reviews the research evidence and concludes that the following things "enable" happiness:

Supportive friendships that enable companionship and confiding

A socially intimate, sexually warm, equitable marriage

A faith that entails communal support, purpose, acceptance, outward focus, and hope

Challenging work and active leisure, punctuated by adequate rest and retreat

Positive self-esteem, feelings of control, optimism, outgoingness

Realistic goals and expectations

A fit and healthy body

Not everyone agrees that happiness is important. Is it? Many vigorous (although perhaps unhappy) individuals vigorously assert that it is not. Some feel that happiness is a trifling and insignificant emotion, others that it is unworthy, and still others that its pursuit may be incompatible with the attainment of more meritorious goals. Political scientist John Schaar, critic George Jean Nathan, and physicist Albert Einstein are among those who have taken a dim view of happiness. Schaar believed that happiness might be a goal unworthy of a great nation or a great person. Nathan held that no happy person ever produced a first-rate piece of painting, sculpture, music, or literature. And Einstein seemingly dismissed the whole subject when he wrote, "Well-being and happiness are such trivial goals in life that I can imagine them being entertained only by pigs."

Schaar's essay (1970) on happiness is thoughtful and compelling. He pointed out that the persons we admire most are not necessarily the happiest ones. He also noted that the purpose of many of our actions is not to make our lives happy but, rather, to make them challenging and worthwhile. In fact, "Willingness to sacrifice happiness and pleasure for other things seems at least as basic to human life as happiness" (pp. 25–26).

Psychologist Carol Ryff (1989) argues that the use of happiness as a single criterion of psychological well-being neglects other, theoretically richer, criteria of positive functioning. In her estimation, these other criteria include self-acceptance, positive relations with others, purpose in life, personal growth, autonomy, and environmental mastery. The first four of these criteria are described in Box 1.3 and are included in the discussion that follows; the remaining two pertain to the power to make choices in one's life or to exercise control over it and are subsumed in the discussion of that concept.

Do You Like Yourself?

Suppose you just met yourself and got to know you. Would you like yourself? Would you think that you're a person with whom you would like to spend twenty-four hours a day, every day, for the rest of your life? Stop for a moment before reading further and decide how you would answer these questions.

I'm reminded of a cartoon of a duckling that has just emerged from its shell. It is looking downward and downcast (or maybe just startled) and saying, "My god, webbed feet!" Do you have some webbing to accommodate or get used to?

Psychologists are more apt to use the concept *self-acceptance* than *self-liking,* but these two concepts are pretty much the same. Ryff presents good definitions of self-acceptance and its opposite, self-rejection; these definitions appear as anchor points for this dimension in Box 1.3.

Before we consider self-acceptance more fully, it may be helpful to look at self-rejection—all the things self-acceptance is not. Following is a checklist of behaviors seen in those who find themselves personally unacceptable. This list, which is adapted from larger listings by Dyer (1976) and Bloomfield and Kory (1980), is presented here just to get you thinking about yourself; it is not a deep or definitive device. As you think and read, answer each item "yes" or "no."

_____ 1. Do you feel embarrassed by your abilities or accomplishments?

_____ 2. Do you give credit to others when you really deserve it yourself?

_____ 3. Do you put others above you when you are really their equal or superior?

_____ 4. Do you fail to stand up for the things you really believe in?

_____ 5. Do you put yourself down when you have made a mistake?

_____ 6. Do you let others put you down?

_____ 7. Do you have a cute name for yourself that reduces you in some way?

_____ 8. Do you depend on others to bolster your opinions?

_____ 9. Do you believe others cannot possibly find you attractive?

_____ 10. Do you believe others are being kind out of charity or some ulterior motive?

Box 1.3

Criteria of Well-Being

"Happiness Is Everything, or Is It?" That's the title of a research paper by Carol Ryff (1989). Her answer is that happiness is far from everything; there are other, theoretically richer, criteria of well-being to consider in the evaluation of lives. In her research, these criteria are measured by multi-item scales, but in the material below, four of her sets of criteria have been adapted to anchor simple rating scales. Circle a number on each scale to indicate your rating of yourself. (Note: The more fully you meet a particular criterion, the more to the right your circled number will be.)

Self-acceptance

1   2   3   4   5

Feels dissatisfied with self; is disappointed with what has occurred in past life; is troubled about certain personal qualities; wishes to be different than what he or she is.

Possesses a positive attitude toward the self; acknowledges and accepts multiple aspects of self, including good and bad qualities; feels positive about past life.

Positive relations with others

1   2   3   4   5

Has few close, trusting relationships with others; finds it difficult to be warm, open, and concerned about others; is isolated and frustrated in interpersonal relationships; is not willing to make compromises to sustain important ties with others.

Has warm, satisfying, trusting relationships with others; is concerned about the welfare of others; is capable of strong empathy, affection, and intimacy; understands give and take of human relationships.

Purpose in life

1   2   3   4   5

Lacks a sense of meaning in life; has few goals or aims, lacks sense of direction; does not see purpose of past life; has no outlook or beliefs that give life meaning.

Has goals in life and a sense of directedness; feels there is meaning to present and past life; holds beliefs that give life purpose; has aims and objectives for living.

Personal growth

1   2   3   4   5

Has a sense of personal stagnation; lacks sense of improvement or expansion over time; feels bored and uninterested with life; feels unable to develop new attitudes or behaviors.

Has a feeling of continued development; sees self as growing and expanding; is open to new experiences; has sense of realizing his or her potential; sees improvement in self and behavior over time; is changing in ways that reflect more self-knowledge and effectiveness.

_____ 11. Do you find it hard to say "no" to a request because of what the person might think of you?

_____ 12. Do you find it hard to complain about poor treatment because you are afraid of making a fuss?

Because the items in the preceding list reflect self-rejection, each item that you answered "yes" suggests an area for you to work on to change the "yes" to "no." But don't put yourself down for your "yeses"—that would be another bit of self-rejecting behavior.

Following is a checklist, adapted from a larger listing by Hamachek (1978), describing self-accepting persons, those who have a healthy, positive self-image. Such persons are at home with themselves and at home in the world because they see themselves and their world in an affirming way. This list, like the one on self-rejecting behavior (with which you might compare it), is presented to help you think about yourself; it is not intended to be a deep or definitive device. As you think and read, answer each item "yes" or "no."

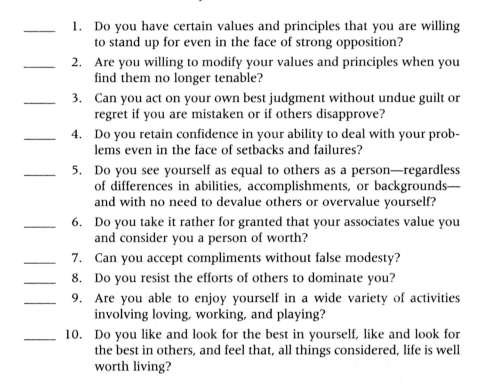

_____ 1. Do you have certain values and principles that you are willing to stand up for even in the face of strong opposition?

_____ 2. Are you willing to modify your values and principles when you find them no longer tenable?

_____ 3. Can you act on your own best judgment without undue guilt or regret if you are mistaken or if others disapprove?

_____ 4. Do you retain confidence in your ability to deal with your problems even in the face of setbacks and failures?

_____ 5. Do you see yourself as equal to others as a person—regardless of differences in abilities, accomplishments, or backgrounds—and with no need to devalue others or overvalue yourself?

_____ 6. Do you take it rather for granted that your associates value you and consider you a person of worth?

_____ 7. Can you accept compliments without false modesty?

_____ 8. Do you resist the efforts of others to dominate you?

_____ 9. Are you able to enjoy yourself in a wide variety of activities involving loving, working, and playing?

_____ 10. Do you like and look for the best in yourself, like and look for the best in others, and feel that, all things considered, life is well worth living?

Because the items in the preceding list reflect self-acceptance, each item you answered "yes" is evidence of a healthy, positive sense of self. Give yourself a pat on the back for your "yeses" and resolve to work on any item that wasn't answered in the affirmative.

If we found ourselves acceptable to our parents, it's easier for us to accept ourselves. Psychologist Nathaniel Branden (1985) often tells parents, "Be careful what you say to your children. They may agree with you" (p. 28). Children may be convinced that they are indeed "bad," "stupid," or whatever it was they were told over and over again. Worse yet, they may be convinced that whatever they are, they are not acceptable—they are not enough. Branden writes:

In considering the many parental messages that may have a detrimental effect on a child's self-esteem, there is probably none I encounter more often in the course of my work than some version of "You are not enough." Unfortunately, early in life all too many of us receive this message from parents and teachers. You may have potential, but you are unacceptable as you are. You need to be fixed. ("Here, let me adjust your hair," "Your clothes aren't right," "Smile," "Let me rearrange your posture," "Stand straighter," "Lower your voice," "Don't be so excited," "Don't play with that toy, play with this toy," *"What's the matter with you?"*) One day you may be enough, but not now. You will be enough only if and when you live up to our expectations. (pp. 25–26)

If we accept the judgment that we are not enough, we may spend our lives in the exhausting pursuit of "the Holy Grail of enoughness." As Branden notes, this pursuit can take many pathways: "If I make a successful marriage, then I will be enough. If I make so many thousands of dollars a year, then I will be enough. One more promotion, and I will be enough. One more sexual conquest . . . one more person telling me I'm lovable . . . " (p. 26). Branden warns us that the battle for acceptability or enoughness can never be won on these terms; in fact, the battle is lost the moment we concede that there is something that needs to be proved, and we can free ourselves from this endless pursuit only by rejecting this premise.

Not all professed self-rejection is what it appears to be. A psychologist who made a study of those of his clients who continually put themselves down found that they made their "I'm no good" statements not just because they felt inferior but also to accomplish something. Some constantly criticized themselves to pressure themselves to improve, to avoid responsibility, or to ward off the criticism of others by beating them to the punch. Some were overly tough on themselves to evoke sympathy and to invite others to reassure them of their worth (Driscoll, 1982).

Do You Have Positive Relations with Others?

Most probably you are going to live to a ripe old age, but suppose that you had died several days ago and your funeral was held yesterday. And suppose everyone came who cared about you and with whom you had good relations. Who would have been there to sincerely pay their last respects? How many would there have been?

Psychologist Shelley Taylor (1989) has written about Emily and Linda, who were included in a study she and her colleagues did concerning women who had been diagnosed with advanced breast cancer. Emily and Linda were remarkably similar in many ways and lived just a few blocks apart in Los Angeles. They were both middle-aged, had three grown children, and were in roughly comparable financial situations. They also had similar medical profiles: both had had surgery and chemotherapy and were symptom free at the time of the interview. But there was an essential difference.

It was not easy interviewing Emily. During the interview, which was conducted at her home, the phone rang many times, and her three children (all of whom lived nearby) were in and out of the house, dropping things off and kissing her as they dashed away to their other activities. Two large dogs were also in attendance, greeting each visitor with unrestrained enthusiasm. And not to be left out, her husband called in from his office and interrupted the interview to have a chat. Taylor writes, "Despite her difficulties with cancer, Emily seemed a serene and contented person, basking in the warmth of her family" (p. 140).

The interview with Linda revealed quite a different situation. There were no interruptions. Her husband had died suddenly when he was in his forties, her children had scattered, and she had lived alone for five years. One daughter was in Atlanta, the other in Boston; and her son, who was traveling in Europe, was intending to relocate to Oregon upon his return. Linda was hoping to find a male companion to relieve her loneliness and as the solution to her problems, but she was not finding this search an easy one.

Three years later, in a follow-up interview, Emily was found to be flourishing and even happier than at the time of the first interview. The follow-up was not possible with Linda; she had died two years before.

Almost all of us need privacy, but we also seek intimacy and community. We need periods of solitude—times to be away from others and in communion with ourselves; even when we are with others, we need a certain amount of personal space and things that are only ours. But on the other hand, we need intimacy— a deep closeness and sharing with one or more persons. And we need a sense of community—a supportive network of others with whom we share common pursuits or goals.

The need for intimacy and community is often unmet. Loneliness is a common problem in our society. Some years ago, a national survey found that 26 percent of the respondents answered "yes" when they were asked if during the past few weeks they had ever felt "very lonely or remote from other people" (Bradburn, 1969). A later survey, by *Psychology Today* (the respondents were predominantly unmarried, well-educated adults between 18 and 34 years of age) showed that 67 percent felt lonely "sometimes" or "often" (Parlee & Editors of *Psychology Today*, 1979).

Too many of us are leading lives narrowed to ourselves; that's the opinion of psychologist Martin Seligman (1991). He points out that the institutions of marriage and family are in disarray, and there is a diminished sense of community. Individualism, Seligman maintains, makes for a selfish, meager, and also meaningless life, because meaning comes from attachment to something larger than oneself. In his view, individualism also makes for a life vulnerable to depression— a heightened possibility if we invest everything in ourselves and then come up short.

The more individual our pursuits, the more we are separated from social support, and social support has been shown to be a prime factor in the maintenance of psychological and physical health. Although it is impossible to say for certain that the difference in social support contributed to the difference in outcomes in the cases of Emily and Linda, there is considerable evidence that those of us with social ties—spouses, children, other relatives, friends, neighborhoods, communities, church and other groups—are healthier physically and psychologically than those who are isolated or have little social support (Justice, 1988). Our support persons and groups stand by us, assist us, and give us a sense of permanence and continuity.

It is only fair to note that some of the ties that bind may simply bind without providing help, and some may actually be harmful. Whether or not support is helpful depends on the context in which it is given and on how we perceive and use it (Justice, 1988). The support we receive may keep us from taking active measures on our own that might be helpful. The group may be a negative influence (for example, by supporting our prejudices or use of drugs) or saddle us with its own internal demands or problems.

Some of us are separate or disconnected because we want to be; others are separate because they have difficulty in making or maintaining connections. Communications experts Gerald Phillips and Nancy Metzger (1976) declare, "Our society is filled with people who are ineffective in the way they deal with others." Political scientist Benjamin Barber (1985) agrees. "Americans," he writes, "are good at joining, but lousy at doing things together" (p. 36).

A surprising fact is that after three million years of talking to each other, our species still doesn't communicate very well. My closest friend, a retired professor of speech, tells me that all human communication is imperfect and sometimes on purpose. We often don't say what we want to say or what we need to say.

Writes psychologist Gerald Goodman at the beginning of his *Talk Book* (Goodman & Esterly, 1988): "Here's my position: Improve one way of communicating and watch all your relationships improve." To me, two of the most important and most imperfect communication skills involve what I call being "a caring presence" and "a caring discloser." These skills are especially important for persons who are interested in illuminating their lives and drawing closer to others, so I would like to give them special attention.

A caring presence is a person who makes time for us, makes no assumptions that would interfere with hearing all we have to say, empathizes with us, and respects our ability to help ourselves. (See Box 1.4 for a fuller description.) We are often called upon to help another, and often the best way to help is simply to listen. Instead, we may be so caught up in our own world that we fail to truly hear the person, or we rush in to advise or rescue or do the other's work ourselves. Simply listening is not as simple as it sounds. We have been taught how to speak but not how to listen.

A caring discloser is an individual who can reveal herself or himself in a way that does not burden the listener and whose manner encourages the listener to do the same. To disclose oneself—to share one's private thoughts and feelings with another—is a basic requirement of true friendship. As we share ourselves with others and they share themselves with us, we feel less alone and more connected. Without this mutual sharing, we remain only acquaintances. (More about self-disclosure appears in the next chapter.) When persons who know how to be both caring presences and caring disclosers come together, something very special can happen. I hope you have had this experience or will come to have it as you pursue answers to the questions posed in this book.

Does Your Life Have Purpose and Meaning?

Psychiatrist Viktor Frankl (1985) sometimes asks a patient, "Why do you not commit suicide?" That's a provocative question. Let's ask it a little more gently. "What gives purpose and meaning to your life?" "What is it that makes you want to jump out of bed in the morning?" "What is it that you are eager to do?" "What is it that you look forward to?" Stop for a moment and see what answers (or what blanks) come to mind as you ponder these questions.

Frankl lived through three years of imprisonment at Auschwitz and Dachau, where each day was a struggle to survive. During those terrible years Frankl was stripped of almost everything of importance. His father, mother, wife, and brother all died in concentration camps. His own survival, he later reported (and others who have survived such extreme conditions have said the same), depended upon his finding something worth living for. In Frankl's estimation, the minimum essential for survival is a "what for" or a "whom for" (1979, p. 35).

It might be said that life consists of two great quests. The first quest is the pursuit of the means to live. The second pursues meaning to make life worth living. Concerning these two quests, Frankl (1979) notes, "Ever more people today have the means to live, but no meaning to live for" (p. 21).

Without a "what for" or a "whom for," life can be bleak even outside of concentration camps. If life lacks meaning, we can be precipitated into great despair. Frankl (1979) takes note of a study of sixty university students who attempted suicide but lived and were later interviewed: 85 percent reported that they had attempted suicide because their lives seemed meaningless.

Box 1.4

The Caring Presence

This book invites you to explore and illuminate your life by pursuing answers to fourteen questions. As you do, you may find it very helpful to share your responses with others and to have others share their responses with you. The richness of this sharing will depend on your skill in both listening and self-disclosure.

Listening is the most important element of interpersonal communication. One study of a varied group of adults found that these persons spent, on the average, 70 percent of their waking day in verbal communication. Of this time, 9 percent was spent writing, 16 percent reading, 30 percent talking, and 45 percent listening (Rankin, 1939).

Despite the importance of listening, most of us have had little training in this skill. We have been taught to read and write, but not how to listen. Many of us listen poorly. Extensive testing led two communications experts to conclude that immediately after an average person has heard someone talk, he or she remembers only half and two months later, only one-quarter (Nichols & Stevens, 1957).

The great psychologist Carl Rogers wrote, "Very early in my work as a therapist, I discovered that simply listening to my client, very attentively, was an important way of being helpful. So when I was in doubt as to what I should do in some active way, I listened. It seemed surprising to me that such a passive kind of interaction could be so useful."

In the course of our lifetime, many persons will need our help, and we can help a large proportion of these by simply listening—if we know how. A truly helpful listener is "a caring presence"—someone who can be trusted, who is very much there for the other and cares for the other but does not intrude or impose. Here are some pledges that a caring presence demonstrates as he or she listens:

1.   I have made this time for you.

Have you ever gone to someone for help and found that that person wasn't completely there for you? You wanted to sit back and tell your story; instead, you felt rushed or made to share the time with everything else that was going on. Or perhaps the other person took over, and it became her or his story but not your story.

Persons who are caring presences show us that they have made time for us and don't begrudge us this time. They don't ask us to share this time with anyone else or anything else. They don't try to seize the stage to tell about

© PEANUTS reprinted by permission of UFS, Inc.

Carl Jung (1966) found that about one-third of his therapy cases were suffering not from a clinically definable neurosis but rather from the aimlessness and senselessness of their lives. Frankl (1972) diagnosed a crisis of meaninglessness in over 50 percent of his hospital patients. And Irvin Yalom (1980) noted that virtually all his hospital patients showed concern about the lack of meaning in their lives.

A number of observers have written of the "existential crises" many of us face when our lives—although possibly filled with things we have worked for and thought important—seem unfulfilling and without real meaning. In his work *Confession* (written between 1879 and 1882), the great Russian novelist Leo Tolstoy described such a crisis in his own life. Questions arose within him regarding what his life was for, what it would lead to, and what good would come of it. These questions became more frequent, more insistent, and demanded answers.

Amid the thoughts of estate management which greatly occupied me at that time, the question would suddenly occur: Well, you will have 6,000 desy-

Box 1.4

themselves. They are quiet, listen carefully to everything we have to say, and hear us out.

2. I have cleared my mind.

It seems to be human nature to form oversimplified hypotheses about others and then look for evidence that confirms these assumptions. It may be hard for another to truly hear us because he or she is captured by past history or preconceptions about us or our "kind." A first-rate mind keeps an open house.

Caring presences communicate that they have made no assumptions that will keep them from hearing everything we have to say. They have formed no conclusions about who we are or what we should be thinking or feeling or doing. No matter how well or how unhappily acquainted we may be, they do not let past experiences interfere with their listening in this instance.

3. I will try to understand your world.

There is an old saying, "Never judge someone until you have walked a mile in his moccasins." There are some persons whom we may want to hold at a distance; perhaps their world seems strange to us or threatening to our sense of order or control. For example, some adolescents and their parents seem to live in very different worlds and are very misunderstanding of each other.

Persons who are caring presences for us try to put themselves in our place and see the world through our eyes. They empathize but they don't pity us or put themselves above us or apart from us. At the same time, they keep one foot in their own world and don't overidentify; this can give them a useful broader perspective.

4. I will respect your ability to help yourself.

There are times in our lives when we need advice or someone to step in and do something for us. But we also need to learn to do things for ourselves, and at times like these it can be helpful and comforting to have someone who is simply there, someone who cares for us and believes in us.

Caring presences do not try to advise us or rescue us or fix us. They do not take our burdens upon themselves. They show us by their attitude that they value us and our ability to help ourselves. They help us summon our own insights and strengths, so that we can take pride in what we have done ourselves.

© PEANUTS reprinted by permission of UFS, Inc.

atinas of land in Samara Government and 300 horses, and what then? . . . Or when considering plans for the education of my children, I would say to myself: "What for?" . . . Or when thinking of the fame my works would bring me, I would say to myself, "Very well; you will be more famous than Gogol or Pushkin or Shakespeare or Molière, or than all the writers in the world—and what of it?" And I could find no reply at all. The questions would not wait, they had to be answered at once, and if I did not answer them it was impossible to live. But there was no answer. ([1882] 1978, pp. 676–677)

Just as Tolstoy arrived, as he wrote, "at the necessity of suicide," he underwent a transformation. He came to see that the purpose of his life was to be found in spiritual pursuit. But did Tolstoy ever find the purpose and meaning he sought? This is the way that David Patterson (1983), a Tolstoy scholar, answers that question:

Whatever is said in this regard, it is clear that [Tolstoy] continued his search until his death in 1910: his was a life characterized as much by seeking as by finding. Indeed, the meaning he was striving for reveals itself more in the search than in the discovery, and asking the question of life is more vital than answering it. For it is by raising the question that the spirit engages in its struggle for voice, a struggle that finds its expression in works such as the *Confession*. (pp. 8–9)

Are You Growing?

A story is told (in fact, it has been told in a number of ways) about a 70-year-old man who decided to take up flying and went to apply for a medical certificate. In taking this man's history, the doctor asked him at what age his father had died. Well, said the man, his father didn't appear to be dead. In fact, his dad had just had a double celebration: his ninety-second birthday and his graduation from college. In that case, said the doctor, how old was his father's father when *he* died? The man replied that his grandfather also appeared to have a bit a life left in him; he was 112 and getting married again next Tuesday.

As the instructor of a life-review workshop for older persons, I can testify that the above story is not far from the truth. But then, by contrast, there is a completely true story told to me recently by a troubled undergraduate. He came to see me because he was concerned about his 44-year-old father, who had lost his job last year and shortly thereafter all his zest for life as well. Now his dad just sat around the house all day and watched television.

All of life is growth, or at least it can be. As we observe young children, we quickly see how eager they are to exercise each new capacity and make the most of it. Each of us will be able to remember our own joy in finding ourselves able to do new things and learn new things. We may remember certain periods of our lives that were particularly growth filled and, by contrast, times when we felt stuck and unable to progress at all. We desire to make the most of ourselves, but there are growth-discouraging forces as well as growth-fostering forces in each person. Both growing and not growing have advantages and disadvantages. Growth holds promise but often entails considerable effort, sacrifice, and risk. Not growing or just standing pat can seem easier and safer but may trigger boredom and guilt (Maslow, 1968, 1972).

Our seemingly mundane everyday lives are filled with growth adventures that provoke anxiety and require courage. Sometimes we rise to the challenge to grow, and sometimes we don't. Amy Gross (1993) describes the plight of a woman she knows who has a long commute each day to the hospital where she works:

> She hears about a job opening at a better hospital, only ten minutes from home; the job is bigger than hers, and so is the salary. This is terribly upsetting news. She asks everyone what she should do, apply or not. Of course, everyone tells her to apply. But she argues, what if she got the job and then couldn't do the work? A challenge like hers, when unmet, is obsessing. She talks and talks about applying. Finally, the decision is made for her—she hears the job is taken.
>
> When people asked her, "What do you have to lose?" she thought they didn't understand what was at stake. Her definition of herself, her "ego" as she put it. She has a bank of negative statements and if she were to apply and not get the job, or get the job and then be fired, all those judgements would be confirmed. Once and for all she would know herself—and the world would know her—to be a failure. (p. 245)

I understand this woman's experience because I can recall a number of times in my own life when I shrank from a challenging opportunity. As I look back, I think "I could have done it. *I could have done it.*" And I remind myself of that when new opportunities present themselves.

Are you growing as a person? *Growth*, as the term is used here, is simply change in a desired direction. What is it that you desire to have or be or become? Are you making progress toward your goals? Are you becoming more and more the person you want to be? Are you making your life more and more the life you want to live? Are you showing an increasing skill at enjoying the good things of life and also an increasing skill at dealing with the things that are not so good—even those things that are far from good? Stop for a moment and try to arrive at answers to these questions.

Are You Choosing Your Life?

Lives are filled with choice, and in a sense, each person's life is the sum total of the choices he or she has made. Someone not totally in agreement with this statement is little Linus; he concludes at the end of a *Peanuts* strip that "Life is full of choices, but you never get any!"

Are you choosing your life? Or, to ask the same question in another way, are you in control of your life? Are you making your life happen? Or are you standing by while your life is happening to you? To help you think your way to some answers to these questions, take the brief test in Box 1.5 before continuing to read in this section.

Some of us may believe we are not responsible for our lives; we are leading the lives we *have* to lead, whether we like it or not. Others among us believe we are leading the lives we *choose* to lead; our lives are ours to change if we wish or to affirm. Finally, some of us take an intermediate position, regarding our lives as a combination of have-tos and choices. For example, our life at work may be beyond our control—we're a cog in the machine—but at home we can call the shots. Or maybe it's the other way around: although we're movers and shakers at work, we feel powerless to do anything to make a bad home situation better.

According to one theoretical point of view, all human behavior is determined; that is, our every action is dictated by inherited or environmental influences. Looked at in this way, human beings are not much more than machines or robots. An opposing view holds that human beings are free to act and free to choose how to act; that is, humans have free will or free choice. Rather than being determined by forces beyond their control, they are self-determining. According to this orientation, we are always free agents. There may be situations that we are not free to change or that we do not have the power to change. But we are always free to choose how we will regard these situations, what our attitude will be toward them, and what stance we will take concerning them. If we do not create our world, we can at least create ourselves, and we do so in the choices we make.

Freedom, of course, brings responsibility. Being in charge of our own lives can be exhilarating or burdensome. Erich Fromm (1941) and others have written that many try to escape from freedom. These fugitives from freedom deceive themselves that what they do is dictated by powers larger than their own—by Society, Nature, or God. But the opposing view holds that each of us has a life to lead if indeed we have the courage to do so.

Perceived locus of control, a concept considerably studied by psychologists, refers to the beliefs people have concerning the source (locus) of control over what befalls them. Those who believe there is a causal relationship between what they do and what happens to them—that they exercise control over their lives—are called *internals* or are said to have *internality* or *internal locus of control*. Persons who

Box 1.5

Who's in Control of Your Life?

Indicate the strength of your agreement or disagreement with each of the items below by placing a check in the appropriate column.

	Strongly agree	Agree	Disagree	Strongly disagree
1. I often feel helpless in dealing with the problems of life.	____	____	____	____
2. What happens to me in the future mostly depends on me.	____	____	____	____
3. I have little control over the things that happen to me.	____	____	____	____
4. There is really no way I can solve some of the problems I have.	____	____	____	____
5. I can do just about anything I really set my mind to.	____	____	____	____
6. Sometimes I feel that I'm being pushed around in life.	____	____	____	____
7. There is little I can do to change many of the important things in my life.	____	____	____	____

The preceding items have been included in a research instrument to measure the extent to which persons have a sense of mastery and control over their lives. Agreement with Items 2 and 5 and disagreement with the remaining items indicate an *internal locus of control*—that is, the belief that one is in control of and responsible for what happens to one. Disagreement with Items 2 and 5 and agreement with the remaining items indicate an *external locus of control*—the belief that what happens to one is determined by chance or by powers beyond oneself (Pearlin & Schooler, 1978; Folkman, Lazarus, Gruen, & DeLongis, 1986). These items, as they are presented here, cannot be considered a definitive test of your locus of control, but they can help you think about your own sense of mastery and control.

see little relationship between their own efforts and outcomes or who attribute the control of their lives to forces external to themselves—to luck, chance, fate, powerful others, or society—are called *externals* and are held to have *externality* or an *external locus of control.*

The research evidence suggests that internals are better at grappling with and mastering their environment. They acquire more information on matters relevant to themselves and make better use of it. Internals are more self-reliant, independent, and less easily influenced.

Social standing appears to be correlated with locus of control. In general, higher externality has been found in those whose milieu is less fortunate and less responsive to their needs. There is also higher externality in those who are low in power. As might be inferred, disadvantaged or denigrated groups, classes, and races tend to score high in externality (Lefcourt, 1982, 1983, 1984).

In his book *Who Gets Sick* (1988), Blair Justice reviews the evidence concerning how beliefs, moods, and thoughts affect health. He concludes that a sense of personal control is a powerful force for maintaining or regaining health: whatever gives us an increased sense of control "seems to mobilize our self-healing systems. . . . if we become convinced that we can control our lives, our bodies or our health, we apparently gain access to our self-healer" (p. 309). Similarly, another set of reviewers concluded that individuals who believe they can influence their

POT-SHOTS NO 2992.

I WOULD LIKE TO SPEAK TO WHOEVER IS IN CONTROL OF MY LIFE,

AND SUGGEST SOME IMPROVEMENTS.

©ASHLEIGH BRILLIANT 1983.

own lives act accordingly; if we think we can, we get busy and try (Kobasa & Maddi, 1977).

The goal of some training and therapy programs is to help people revise their beliefs so that they can gain control of their lives. Some programs work the other way around: they prompt individuals to get busy in their lives so that their beliefs about themselves will change. Implicit in both approaches is the idea that our lives can be ours to live.

When Marie Ragghianti was 10, her mother suffered a spinal tumor that—although benign—left her paralyzed. Yet her mother went on to lead a remarkably full existence, including for a time teaching creative writing to inmates of a penitentiary and then later corresponding with them. Below is a letter she wrote to a prisoner named Waymon. It was included in an account which Marie wrote about her mother that had the remarkably appropriate title "The Life My Mother *Chose*" (my italics).[1]

Dear Waymon,

I have been thinking about you often since receiving your letter. You mentioned how difficult it is to be locked behind bars, and my heart goes out to you. But when you say I can't imagine what it is like to be in prison, I feel impelled to say you are mistaken.

There are two different kinds of prison, Waymon.

When, at age 31, I awoke one day completely paralyzed, I was overwhelmed by a sense of being imprisoned in a body that would no longer allow me to run through a meadow or dance or carry my child in my arms.

For a long time I lay there asking myself whether life was worth living. It seemed I had lost everything that mattered.

But then one day it occurred to me that I still had the freedom to make choices. Would I smile when I saw my children, or weep? Would I rail against God—or would I ask him to strengthen my faith? In other words, what would I do with the free will that was still mine?

I decided to live as fully as I could, to look for ways to transcend my physical limitations by expanding my mental and spiritual boundaries. I

---

[1]   Reprinted with permission from Parade, copyright © 1988. Reprinted by permission of the author and the author's agents, Scott Meredith Literary Agency, Inc., 845 Third Avenue, New York, New York 10022.

could choose to be a role model for my children, or I could wither and die, emotionally as well as physically.

There are many kinds of freedom, Waymon. When we lose one kind, we must look for another.

You can look *at* your bars, or you can look *through* them. You can be a role model for younger inmates, or you can mix with trouble-makers. You can love God and seek to know him, or you can turn your back on him.

To some extent, Waymon, we are in this together. (Ragghianti, 1988, p. 5)

Many students of human nature would agree with these often quoted lines of John Milton: "The mind is its own place, and in itself/Can make a heav'n of hell, a hell of heav'n." In general, it is not the events of our lives that upset us but rather the meanings and interpretations that we give to these events (Ellis, 1992). We all can use a bit of help now and then, but what we make of our lives is up to us. A conclusion that seems warranted from the study of lives is that a successful life is often created in very difficult circumstances while the most favorable circumstances do not guarantee success or happiness. A case in point was Abd-er-Rahman III of Spain, who seemed to have been given every advantage. Even so, this is the assessment he is reputed to have made of his life: "I have now reigned about fifty years in victory or peace, beloved by my subjects, dreaded by my enemies, and respected by my allies. Riches and honors, power and pleasure, have waited on my call, nor does any earthly blessing appear to have been wanting to my felicity. In this situation I have diligently numbered the days of pure and genuine pleasure which have fallen to my lot; they amount to fourteen."

A sharp contrast is provided by Jill Kinmont, who was once the country's top female skier. She became a quadriplegic when she fell and severed her spine in a race before her twentieth birthday. When she was 41, she was asked what accounted for her bright and positive outlook on life. Was it, the questioner suggested, because she had had nineteen great years in the beginning? "I beg your pardon," she replied. "I've had 41 great years" (Pesmen, 1977).

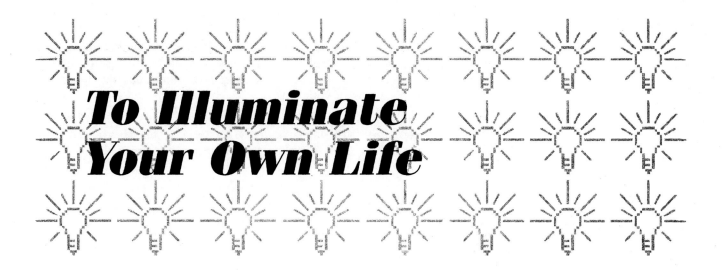

To Illuminate Your Own Life

This book, particularly the anchor-and-apply items and the exploration items that are included in each chapter, is designed to help you illuminate your life. Sharing can be an important part of the illumination process, but each sharer must be a "caring discloser" (see Box 2.4) and also a "caring presence" (see Box 1.4). The guidelines presented in this book for these two roles need to be carefully followed. Furthermore, as a general rule, whether the sharing is with one person or a group of persons, share only what you wish to share or what you are comfortable in sharing. A set of ground rules for sharing in small groups is presented in Appendix B.

Anchor and Apply*

1. How would you live your life if you had infinite courage? How would you live your life if you were an infinite coward? Answer these questions and discuss the insights your answers provoke.

2. Is your life a success? What letter grade would you give yourself in living? Why?

3. Would you say you are very happy, pretty happy, or not too happy? What are the sources or causes of your happiness or unhappiness?

4. Do you like yourself? Why or why not? Discuss something about yourself that you particularly like and something that you particularly dislike.

5. Do you have positive relations with others? Answer and give your evidence.

6. Are you a caring presence? If you are, give your proof. If you aren't, indicate what steps you need to take and will take—beginning today—to become one.

7. Does your life have purpose and meaning? Answer and give your evidence.

8. Are you growing? Answer and give your evidence.

---

* These "anchor and apply" items are designed to help you use the concepts of the chapter as stimuli to prompt new or deeper or clearer insights into yourself and your life. To respond to an item, first find the material in the chapter that is most relevant to the item *and* yourself; that's called "anchoring." Second, think about this material in relationship to yourself and your life and keep thinking about it until you arrive at a new or deeper or clearer understanding; that's the "apply" or application part. When you write or present your response to the item, be sure to include both parts, that is, both the anchor material and the application. You can know you are successful on an item if, in completing it, you truly learn something new or understand something better.

9. Are you in control of your life? And how much control do you have over the various areas of your life (for example, at home or in important relationships, at school, in work, in leisure-time activities, in government or politics, and so on)? Discuss this aspect of your life.

10. Are you leading the life you *choose to* lead or is it the life you *have to* lead? Answer and give your evidence.

Where Am I Now in My Life?

"Where am I now in my life?" How would you answer this question? It asks you to take stock and determine exactly where you are on your path in life. Here is how a venerable Chicano woman—one of Robert Coles's *Old Ones of New Mexico*—took stock of her life at the age of 90:

> My life is not mine; it belongs to God. I am afraid to die. I do not want to die. I cannot persuade myself to like being old. I am no magician who can make a trance for herself, and end up welcoming what is a fearful moment: the last breath. But I have been given ten years short of a century already, and I don't seem to be leaving yet, for all my aches and pains. I am rich with years, a millionaire! I have been part of my own generation, then I watched my children's generation grow up, then my grandchildren's, and now my great-grandchildren's. Two of my great-grandchildren are becoming full-grown women now; they come visit me and will remember me. Now, I ask you, how much more can a woman expect? My great-granddaughter told her teacher I was a barber fifty years ago, and the teacher wanted to send my name to Santa Fe, and they would honor me as a pioneer among women. Well, imagine that! I said no. I have been honored already—all this life I've been given is an honor God has chosen to offer. It is a big achievement, if I say so myself, to have accumulated all these years. And as I look back and think, I decide that I wouldn't have done things any different, not for the most part anyway. (1989, p. 59)

"Where am I now in my life?" When I pose this question to my students, I answer it along with them. This is a part of my most recent answer, written just after my seventy-first birthday:

> I am at a time when I am beginning to feel quite old. "Old" to me is a good word. Old books. Old wine. Old friends. For the most part, I have enjoyed each of my ages. I enjoyed most of my childhood. Most of my adolescence. Most of my young adulthood and middle age. Now I'm enjoying my old age. I've met some people my age who seem determined to be middle-aged forever. Even if they were able to finesse old age, it would be a shame to miss such an important season of life; it would be like repeating the second

---

* The explorations in this book are designed to extend the material of the chapter and to help you find your own answers to the fourteen life questions. In completing an exploration, you will learn more and enjoy yourself more if you do not read ahead, because there are some unexpected turns and surprises. However, unless there are instructions to the contrary, you may modify an exploration or add to it in any way that might be helpful for you. And add another sheet of paper whenever you would like more space than is provided for your response. This first exploration is suggested by the work of Ira Progoff (1975) and Joseph E. Shorr (1977).

act of a play and never getting on to the third act, where there is a chance for resolution and perspective.

I'm grateful. I have a good life, and I have no wish to change it. I continue to do everything I have been doing except now I do less of it and I do it slower, but then I am no longer in a hurry to get some place. Some parts of me don't work as well as they used to, but because I have grown more tolerant of things that are as they are, I complain only on Mondays. I remind myself of the words of the third Zen patriarch: "The Great Way is not difficult for those who have no preferences." I still have preferences, but I hold them more lightly than I once did.

When I visited my Iowa hometown, I wondered how it would have been to have lived my whole life in those familiar, friendly surroundings. Instead, the Manoa campus has become my familiar, friendly village—one in which I am now beginning my forty-third year. I have watched my colleagues grow and age along with me; some have retired and some—including one of my dearest friends—have died. Occasionally, students appear in my office to convey the regards of their parents who were themselves my students. (I used to tell these sons and daughters to ask their parents for their old notes because I haven't changed my lectures; however, I have stopped saying this because some seemed to half believe me.) One of these days, a grandchild of my first generation of students should appear.

Working for a decade as a volunteer with people with life-threatening illnesses has given me a real sense of the precariousness and preciousness of life. I want to make the most of the years that are left to me—to wear out, not rust out. A leisurely retirement and trips around the world are not for me. I don't want to see new places. I want to do new things that pull me out of my comfort zone and keep me growing.

"Where am I now in my life?" Here is an answer (somewhat condensed) written by a former student of mine, a woman, 45 years of age:

I am at a time when all things no longer seem possible. I have passed the midpoint of my life, and the end is in sight. I am surprised that this prospect no longer frightens me. I suspect that we learn, over time, to accept more or less gracefully the inevitability of all endings, including our own.

Perspective tells me that on the whole my life has been, and is, a good one. It is in my marriage that I have been most blessed. How fortunate a choice I made here is evident to me each day. A life partner who supports efforts at growth is not something everyone can take for granted. After almost twenty-three years, my heart still gladdens when I see his car turn into the driveway, hear his voice on the phone, or feel his touch. There is no one with whom I would rather share the rest of what may turn out after all to be a rather mundane life.

I married at 23, and (surprise!) eleven months later was a mother. The three closely spaced children, whose adulthood it seemed would never come, are out of the house, and only the fourth remains; ten years younger than her next sibling, she is almost like a second family.

For years, the caregiver role was paramount in my life. Now I play a peripheral role in the lives of the three older offspring. With the remaining child, a girl of 8, I am content to be what Bruno Bettelheim terms "a good enough parent." With the others, I tried so hard (and failed) to be perfect although they turned out reasonably well.

Yes, I have worked. For a year, I taught. Other jobs followed, on and off, most recently as a technical writer, trainer, and in administration. My last job was the best, but the company I worked for fell upon bad times, and I was let go.

Finding another job worth having has been harder than I anticipated. Though I am good at what I do, I have few formal credentials, and I am thinking of returning to school to get them. While I am fortunate to have no financial pressure to return to work, an internal pressure is there: I miss having a work-based identity and interesting problems with which to concern myself. For me, wife, mother, daughter, and friend are not sufficient roles in themselves.

But back to the question: Where am I now in my life? My life seems rather turned around. Now that my family is nearly raised, I can ask myself "What do I want to be when I grow up?" and go to school to find the answer.

"Where am I now in my life?" This is the response of a young man, a college senior, 21 years old:

I am at a time when there are some clouds on the horizon, but all in all I have a good life. I would rate my life about 8 on a scale of 10. I have a nice family that I appreciate all the more when I hear my friends talk about their problems at home. My dad keeps saying how lucky he is to have such a good job, such a good wife, and such good kids. My mom's really sweet; she comes right out and says that I'm her favorite, but then I am also the youngest. And I have had the same girlfriend for the past two years.

One cloud is that I don't know if I can realize my ambition, which is to get into the state air guard. Since I was a little kid, I have wanted to be a pilot (my father works for an airline), and I have my commercial license (with some restrictions). Only about one in fifty applicants is accepted by the air guard; it's important to have a recommendation from somebody already in the guard, but I don't know anyone. My second preference would be to find work with a small commuter airline, but nothing has turned up yet. If I don't fly, I don't know what I will do—my whole life has been focused on that.

A second cloud is that I don't know what will happen to my relationship with my girlfriend. We have been very close, but marriage is out for the foreseeable future. Being married would jeopardize my eligibility for the guard, and working for a small commuter airline or maybe just flying night cargo would not be a secure way of earning a living—such jobs come and go. My girlfriend seems to understand, but then there are the times when she wonders about continuing a relationship that's not going anywhere.

I still live at home, which is fine with my folks, but sometimes I feel—not trapped—but restricted. Home's a comfortable nest, but it seems like it's time for me to head out and find a place of my own. I used to be kind of a loner and a little shy, but I am becoming more and more sure of myself. This is happening just in time, because my life is going to get more complicated. I have been traveling a well-marked road, but there are some uncertain stretches ahead. Whatever comes, I can't complain because I haven't had much hard traveling so far.

"Where am I now in my life?" Here's the answer of a young woman, a sophomore, 20 years old:

I am at a time when my life is total chaos. I recently changed my major from accounting to nursing, and I have to start all over taking appropriate courses. Although I have changed my major, I am still confused about what I want to really be.

Sometimes I wish that I could just quit school and work. But then I would be a college "dropout" and on the treadmill to nowhere. And besides I don't think that I could face my family or friends. I just wish that I had a definite goal in life.

I don't think that my life has changed much in college. I study harder but otherwise it's pretty much the same as high school. The same friends, study, work, go out on the weekends, and then here's another week like the last one. Coming to college, I thought I would be more like an adult, but I am just the same as I was at 17.

I just wish I was more sure about myself and my life. I know that I need to take more responsibility for my life. It's up to me to get up and go, but go where? I don't know where I want to go. I only know that where I am is not where I want to be.

Your work in this exploration will be in two parts. First, as a brief survey, complete each of the six incomplete statements below.

Where am I now in my life?

1. *At this time in my life, I need . . .*

2. *At this time in my life, I regret . . .*

3. *At this time in my life, I fear . . .*

4. *At this time in my life, I hope . . .*

5. *At this time in my life, I take pride . . .*

6. *At this time in my life, I'm determined . . .*

Prompted by one or more of your just completed statements and by the examples given by other people at the beginning of this exploration, compose a larger answer (perhaps four paragraphs or longer) to the question "Where am I now in my life?" Write your answer in the space below and begin it with the words "I am at a time when . . ."

Where am I now in my life? I am at a time when . . .

E x p l o r a t i o n

1B

The Balance Sheet

Life is, as we soon come to understand, a bittersweet mixture of ups and downs, sun and shadows, good and bad. Even so, there are times when we may focus more on what's wrong about our lives than on what's right. Here's our opportunity to focus on the good as well as the not so good.

Below, in the column on the left, list (numbering each item as you go) everything you are thankful for at this time in your life—all the pluses. (Before you begin, you might reread the list in Box 1.1, Nancy Kelton's reasons for being thankful.) In the column on the right, list everything you are *un*thankful for—all the minuses. Afterward, at the end in "the bottom line," write what you learned from this exploration or what thoughts, feelings, or conclusions resulted from it.

What I'm thankful for	What I'm *un*thankful for

(continued)

From: *The Illuminated Life,* by Abe Arkoff. Copyright © 1995 by Allyn and Bacon.

What I'm thankful for	What I'm *un*thankful for

The Bottom Line:

The Life Ladder*

Below is a picture of a ladder. Suppose the top of the ladder represents the best possible life for you, and the bottom represents the worst possible life for you.

10	Best possible life for me
9	
8	
7	
6	
5	
4	
3	
2	
1	
0	Worst possible life for me

Answer each question below by writing a number on the line before it. Then turn to the next page.

_____ On which step of the ladder do you stand at the present time?

_____ On which step were you five years ago?

(Note: If it would be more meaningful, use a different interval of time for this item and/or the next item; for example, you might use three years instead of five years.)

_____ On which step do you think you will be five years from now?

* This ladder technique is based on the work of Hadley Cantril and his associates (Cantril, 1965).

In 1985, the Gallup Organization surveyed a representative sample of American adults, asking them (1) where they personally were on the ladder at that time, (2) where they were five years earlier, and (3) where they expected to be five years from then. The respondents were also asked to surmise the same information for the nation as a whole. The results, shown below, suggest that the respondents generally felt pretty good about their lives. They believed that their lives were getting better and also that their lives were better than for the nation considered as a whole. (Interestingly, this finding suggests that the average American believes her or his own life is better than average.)

	For self	For nation
Five years ago	5.7	5.3
Present	6.4	5.9
Five years hence	7.6	6.6

1. Is your life at present better or worse than it was before? What accounts for any change or lack of change?

2. Do you anticipate a future better than the present? Why or why not?

3. Describe something you could do beginning today to make your life better. Will you do it? Why or why not?

Question 2

Self

What Is My Relationship to Myself?

John Vasconcellos is a highly esteemed member of the California legislature, but he speaks candidly about his own early failure to value himself and of many later years of therapy to develop his self-esteem and personhood. Recalling his own long trek to a better sense of self, he wrote:

> In school, I was a high-achiever, receiving awards and excellent grades. In adulthood, I became a prominent lawyer in a prestigious firm. My first campaign for a seat in the state legislature in 1966 was successful, and I have now been reelected eleven times.
>
> Yet, through it all, I had almost no sense of my self, no self-esteem. I worked for my successes only in a constant attempt to please others. My intellect functioned superbly, but the rest of my self barely functioned at all. I had been conditioned to know myself basically as a sinner, guilt-ridden and ashamed, constantly beating my breast and professing my unworthiness. I had so little self-esteem that I lost my first election (running for eighth-grade president) by one vote—my own. (Vasconcellos, 1989, pp. xiv–xv)

Personal experience has taught Vasconcellos the importance of valuing oneself. As a result, he has sponsored legislation creating the California Task Force to Promote Self-Esteem and Personal and Social Responsibility, whose aim is to promote the well-being of the individual and society as a way of preventing rather than just reacting to serious social ills.

As a clinical psychologist, I have worked with many people who have come to me for help. Some were deeply troubled. Of these, I cannot recall a single one who had a good relationship with herself or himself. Not one was her or his own best friend. When they began to like themselves and trust themselves, I knew they were getting better. When they began to take some pride in themselves, I knew they were getting well.

Not long ago I heard a comedienne ask a group this question: "How many of you know how it feels to be the only person in a relationship?" This got a laugh,

33

but my clinical experience with human beings has made clear to me that the most important relationship we each have is the one with ourself. How strange that most of us do not think of this as a relationship at all! How strange that in this relationship we sometimes appear at our least humane, treating ourselves in a way we would never treat somebody else!

Think about your own relationship to yourself. You are always in your own presence, and just as you are aware of the world around you, you are aware of yourself. You think, you feel, you act. You also observe yourself thinking and feeling and acting. You reflect on yourself and come to know yourself. You have *reflective awareness*—the ability to consider your behavior as you observe it. Because you have the power of reflective awareness, you are both actor and audience in your life. You perform and at the same time watch yourself perform. But you are not a passive audience. You, the audience, attend and consider. You weigh and evaluate. Sometimes you applaud, sometimes you hiss or jeer, sometimes rise and command. You the actor are influenced by you the audience, just as you the audience are influenced by you the actor.

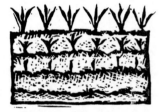

Box 2.1

Self: What Is My Relationship to Myself?

Seedthoughts

1. No one can make you feel inferior without your consent.

    —*Eleanor Roosevelt*

2. Self-acceptance means that the individual fully and unconditionally accepts himself whether or not he behaves intelligently, correctly, or competently, and whether or not other people approve, respect, or love him.

    —*Albert Ellis*

3. Do I contradict myself?
    Very well then, I contradict myself.
    (I am large. I contain multitudes.)

    —*Walt Whitman*

4. Learn to forgive yourself, again and again and again and again . . .

    —*Sheldon Kopp*

5. Of all the judgments that we pass in life, none is as important as the one we pass on ourselves, for that judgment touches the very center of our existence.

    —*Nathaniel Branden*

6. The greatest evil that can befall man is that he should come to think ill of himself.

    —*Goethe*

7. Why must I suffer for not being perfect when I can be good enough.

    —*Sheldon Kopp*

8. It seems to me that a woman's powers of attractiveness are largely based not on her physical equipment but on the peace she has made with herself.

    —*Holly Brubach*

9. . . . the essential core of healing is how we can *be* with ourselves rather than anything we can *do* to change or improve ourselves.

    —*John Welwood*

10. In real life it only takes one to make a quarrel.

    —*Ogden Nash*

11. All of the truly important battles are waged within the self.

    —*Sheldon Kopp*

12. I stand and listen, head bowed
    to my inner complaint.
    Persons passing by think
    I am searching for a lost coin.
    You're fired, I yell inside
    after an especially bad episode.
    I'm letting you go without notice
    or terminal pay. You just lost
    another chance to make good.
    But then I watch myself standing at the exit,
    depressed and about to leave,
    and wave myself back wearily,
    for who else could I get in my place
    to do the job in dark, airless conditions?

    —*David Ignatow, "Self Employed"*

13. I exist as I am—that is enough;
    If no other in the world be aware, I sit content;
    And if each and all be aware, I sit content.

    —*Walt Whitman, "Song of Myself"*

Of course, there are other people in the audience, too—parents, siblings, teachers, friends, etc. In their response to you, they tell you who they think you are and what you can and can't do and should and shouldn't do. You observe these others and observe them observe you, and you observe yourself. Out of all these observations, you shape and reshape the idea of who you are, and you shape and reshape your relationship to yourself. Your relationship to yourself could be called "the basic relationship," because how you come to see and regard yourself becomes a fundamental force in your life.

Why Is Your Self-Image Important?

Take a look at yourself in a mirror. What do you see? More important, what do you think of the person you see there? Your conception of yourself—your *self-image*—is the most important image in your world. In fact, how you perceive yourself greatly affects the way you perceive your world. And how you perceive yourself and your world greatly affects the way you behave in it. To give a simple example, persons who think that they're not much or persons who have to prove to themselves that they are okay move about in their worlds less easily than those who believe they are first-class citizens with a ticket to ride.

Much of our behavior can be attributed to our need to maintain and to enhance our perception of ourselves. Stop for a moment and think about that statement. It means that we are most comfortable when our behavior is consistent with our picture of ourselves and also with the picture of the person we would like to be. Of course, these may be quite different pictures.

The urge to maintain our conception of ourselves is strong. Our self-image serves us as basic frame of reference—as a foundation and guide for our actions. We would be lost without it, and therefore we defend it against change. When we are resistant to growth or positive movement in our lives, we may simply be trying to remain true to ourselves.

Although the urge to maintain our conception of ourselves is strong, so is the urge to enhance it. Every living thing wants to grow. We want to do more and be more. And the more positively we see ourselves, the more we attempt and achieve.

When we believe something to be so, we tend to behave in a way that makes it so; this is called a *self-fulfilling prophecy*. If we see ourselves in a positive light, we are apt to try harder, because we think our efforts will pay off; and we are more likely to succeed or to define the outcome as successful. If we have a low opinion of ourselves, we may avoid a situation or approach it halfheartedly, and we are more likely to fail or to interpret the results as failure (Langer & Dweck, 1973).

If we like and accept ourselves, we tend to accept others (Berger, 1952; Pirot, 1986), and we also expect others to accept us (Baron, 1974; Walster, 1965). And, of course, when others are approached in this light, they are likely to respond favorably. If we dislike or reject ourselves, we are likely to view and treat others in the same way, and consequently our relations with others will suffer. Psychologist Don Hamachek (1978) suggests some personal research one can do on this point: "Pay particular attention to your feelings about yourself for the next three or four days and note how they influence your behavior toward others. It may be that it is not our friend or our loved one or our children we are mad at; it is ourselves. What we feel toward ourselves gets aimed at others, and we sometimes treat others not as persons, but as targets" (p. 46).

We tend to form relationships with persons who are similar to us, who see us as we see ourselves and who confirm our own positive self-impressions (Swann, 1984; Taylor & Brown, 1988). It's hard for us to rest easy in the company of those who don't see us as we wish to be seen. The French philosopher Joseph Joubert understood this prime requisite of friendship. "When my friends are one-eyed," he wrote, "I look at their profile."

How Many Selves Are You?

Take another look at yourself in the mirror. And suppose you had taken a look yesterday morning when you got up on the wrong side of the bed, ready to tear the world apart, and another look last night after that great evening with friends. What if you had monitored yourself in this way during the past week or month? How many selves would you have seen?

One of Shakespeare's most famous lines (part of the counsel that Polonius gives his son Laertes in *Hamlet*) reads, "This above all: to thine own self be true." Kenneth Gergen (1972), a psychologist who has made an extensive study of the self-concept, calls this advice "poor psychology." He believes we are unlikely to find a single self to be true to. Gergen's research suggests that we are considerably affected by the situations in which we find ourselves—the self we are in one situation may be very different from the self we are in another. Different environments may prompt different thoughts and feelings about ourselves and therefore different behaviors. When we are talking to someone who is in a superior position, our self-relevant thoughts and feelings may be quite different from our thoughts and feelings when we are with a subordinate. When we are standing up to a group, we may see ourselves differently than when we have reluctantly decided to go along with it (Markus & Kunda, 1986).

Gergen questions an assumption made by many psychologists and laypersons: that it is good—or even normal—to have a firm and coherent sense of self. In fact, he suggests that we should become concerned when we become too comfortable with a self or set in a particular identity, because we may simply have settled into a rut—a routine in which the same situations call forth the same old responses.

Gergen concludes that "we are made of soft plastic and molded by social circumstances," but other research suggests that the self-concept is not all that malleable. Taken together, the evidence supports the conclusion that the self-concept is *both* stable and malleable. We have a certain core of ideas about ourselves, and we resist information that challenges this core. At the same time, we are influ-

Drawing by Lippman; © 1972 The New Yorker Magazine, Inc.

enced by the situations in which we find ourselves. How we see ourselves in a particular situation results from self-conceptions prompted by this core, as modified by those called forth by that situation (Markus & Kunda, 1986). It can be trying when a core conception is challenged—for example, when we pride ourselves on our honesty but also see that we are sorely tempted to lie or cheat to gain an important end.

Subpersonalities

Not all psychologists who agree that we may not be a single self are willing to concede that we shouldn't try to be. Whereas Gergen attributes our variability to the varying situations in which we find ourselves, John Vargiu (1980) attributes it to a number of *subpersonalities*—semiautomous personages within us—all striving for expression. He holds that we need to understand these subpersonalities better and bring them into harmony with each other; doing so, we become a single harmonized self.

St. Augustine eloquently described the struggle between two of his subpersonalities—the "animal man" and the "spiritual man." Recalling this struggle in his *Confessions*, he wrote, "My inner self was a house divided against itself." Ted Kennedy was described in a 1991 *Time* magazine profile as seemingly a person of several sets of selves. One set: statesman, serious lawmaker, family patriarch. The other set: overage, drunken frat-house boor and party animal. The profiler suggested, "A man with Kennedy's temperament and past may need a sort of unofficial self that he can plunge back into now and then—a rowdy, loutish oblivion where he feels easy, where he takes a woozy vacation from being a Kennedy" (Morrow, 1991, p. 27).

You may recall seeing an acquaintance behave in a quite uncharacteristic way. You wonder, "What's got into him?" Or you think, "She's not herself today." Of course, she *is* herself—but a different one of her selves or subselves or subpersonalities.

Consider your own inconsistencies or subpersonalities. Do you sometimes seem to get caught up in a particular way of being and behaving? You recognize it and could even give it a label, since it is so salient and you have been caught up in it before. When you are under its spell, you see yourself and your world differently and behave differently, perhaps in a way you like or don't like. You may be able to identify a number of these subpersonalities in yourself, some in harmony and some in conflict with each other.

You might find it useful to study these subpersonalities. When I recently tried to identify and study my own subselves, these were the most salient ones: The Creative but Tiring Soul (a subself that enjoyed creating something new or different and watching it develop—for a while), Dad (a caring, helpful subself), The Relentless Searcher (a subself that was always looking for something better but never quite finding it), and The Wise Old Man (an emerging subself, one with the ability to understand, accept, and enjoy things as they are). I was pleased to note that The Examiner (a subself that was constantly scrutinizing things to see if they measured up) had been largely decommissioned.

We should not confuse the concept of "subpersonalities," which applies to normal behavior, with that of "multiple personality," which is a serious and disabling disorder (Rowan, 1990). This latter condition is rare—better known to Hollywood and television script writers than to psychiatrists or psychologists. The added personalities in multiple personality disorder are quite autonomous, even with differences in handedness (left or right dominance) and in patterns of handwriting and brain waves (Putnam, 1984) and usually operate without the awareness of the original personality.

Possible Selves

Some psychologists have been interested in the concept of *possible selves*—the images we have of the persons we might be in the future (Markus & Kunda, 1986; Markus & Nurius, 1986). These images—the selves we expect to be, the selves we desire to be, and also those we fear we might become—function as incentives and serve to guide us toward certain kinds of behaviors and away from others. For a person struggling to keep her or his weight within bounds, a desired self may be a thin self and the feared self may be a fat one. For a student doing marginal work in college, the desired self may be a lawyer self or a doctor self or some other vocational image, and the feared self may be a dropout stuck in a dead-end job. For some of us, one or other of our parents may provide an image of what we desire to be or what we fear we might become.

We seem to get more satisfaction by establishing distance from our feared selves than we do by achieving closeness to our desired selves. Researcher Daniel Ogilvie says, "The ideal self is so abstract that we never quite know if we're there or not. And it's a continually receding goal; whenever we feel we're getting near it, we raise the ideal a bit. It serves to motivate us, to keep us striving." Ogilvie believes that our feared selves are less vague than our desired selves; we know exactly what we don't want to be: "People seem to use their undesired self as a marker to judge how their life is going; it gives us a navigational cue" (quoted in Goleman, 1991, p. 114).

Our repertory of possible selves is influenced by our individual histories and also by developments in society. Social advances such as increased opportunities for women and blacks create new hoped-for possible selves among these groups. New or exacerbated social problems create new dreaded possible selves, such as the AIDS-afflicted self, the drug-dependent self, the bag lady, or the street person.

How Do Your Looks and Gender Affect Your Self-Esteem?

Take one more look at yourself in the mirror. Are you looking at a person you consider attractive? We live in a society in which looks are important. In many areas of our lives, attractive people fare better than those who are unattractive (Allen, 1990; Hatfield & Sprecher, 1986). One would expect good-looking persons to feel better about themselves than do those who are homely. But a review of pertinent research indicates that there is little connection between what we actually look like (as determined by objective judges) and our overall self-esteem (Hatfield & Sprecher, 1986).

While self-esteem is largely unrelated to what we *actually* look like, it is positively related to what we *think* we look like. Persons who are satisfied with their bodies are likely to have a positive self-concept and to be satisfied with themselves generally. Persons dissatisfied with their bodies tend to have less favorable general impressions of themselves. Evidently, if we like our looks, we like ourselves; or if we like ourselves, we like our looks (Hatfield & Sprecher, 1986).

"How can beautiful people end up with low self-esteem? How can physically unappealing men and women manage to maintain their self-regard?" These are questions posed by Hatfield and Sprecher. They found evidence that beautiful men and women were much more interested in appearance than were homely individuals; if beautiful folks bank their self-esteem on their looks, and surround themselves with or compare themselves to other beautiful people, their self-esteem could suffer, for there is almost always someone superior somehow (and, of course, there is the awareness that beauty in time can be a depreciating asset). On the other hand, homelier folks may be less likely to move in beautiful circles or circles where beauty is highly valued or where unfavorable comparisons might be drawn, and they may be more likely to develop their other attributes. These other attributes can be more enduring than physical beauty.

In much of the world, gender as well as beauty can grant status, and it can be a considerable advantage to be male. Males are generally more privileged and have more power. A study of stereotypes in thirty countries showed that in most countries stereotypes of males are more positive than those of females (Williams & Best, 1982). It doesn't come as a surprise that a review of twenty-nine studies between 1975 and 1985 showed that men generally have higher self-esteem than women (Skaalvik, 1986).

Research also indicates that women are less confident than men. Men tend to attribute their successes to internal factors—their own effort and ability—while women tend to attribute success to external factors—luck, fate, or the ease of the task. For failure, it's just the other way around: women who before sacrificed the credit suddenly turn internal and shoulder the blame (Tavris & Wade, 1984). However, married women who are employed outside the home seem to have higher self-esteem than those who are not (Birnbaum, 1975; Coleman & Antonucci, 1983). Outside employment apparently provides a sense of autonomy and mastery. Such employment can also provide women with more power in the family; and the greater the earnings, the greater the power.

Tavris (quoted in McCarthy, 1990) believes that research in this area is flawed because it assumes that the male is the norm and males are used as the basis of comparison. In this biased approach, Tavris says, "Women have lower self-esteem than men do; women do not value their efforts as much as men do; women have more difficulty in developing a 'separate sense of self'" (p. 33). If the bias had been reversed and women had been used as the basis of comparison, Tavris points out these might have been the conclusions: "Men are more conceited than women; men are not as realistic as women in assessing abilities; men have more difficulty in forming and maintaining attachments" (p. 33).

How Can You Improve Your Relationship to Yourself?

If you want to improve your relationship to yourself, you can take a big step forward by getting to know yourself better and by allowing others to know you. You can also learn to prize yourself and to become yourself. These steps are discussed in the material that follows.

Knowing Yourself

"Know thyself" has been the continuing advice of philosophers and poets down through the centuries. It is fairly stock advice of clinical psychologists and psychiatrists today. But is it a good idea to focus our attention on ourselves? And if we do, do we really want to find out the truth, the whole truth, and nothing but the truth?

Self-Focus. Socrates said, "The unexamined life is not worth living." But there is a difference of opinion on this subject. In her book *What I Saw at the Revolution* (a memoir of the Reagan White House), presidential speech writer Peggy Noonan called her boss the "least introspective of men . . . living proof that the unexamined life *is* worth living" (1990, p. 160). The late actor Peter Sellers, known as "the great impersonator" and as someone who vanished into his roles, told an interviewer that he got to where he was by not following Socrates' advice. "To me," he said, "I'm a complete stranger" (Ansen, 1980, p. 43). In 1989, tycoon Donald

©ASHLEIGH BRILLIANT 1982.   POT-SHOTS NO. 2498.

**HOW LITTLE
I KNOW
ABOUT
MYSELF!**

ALTHOUGH
I'M CONSIDERED
A LEADING AUTHORITY
ON THE SUBJECT.

*Ashleigh
Brilliant*

Trump told an interviewer that he didn't want to be examined in any depth by anyone, including himself. "When you start studying yourself too deeply," Trump said, "you start seeing things that maybe you don't want to see" (Friedrich & McDowell, 1989, p. 54). Subsequent events have shaken his financial empire and suggest that he might want to review this strategy.

In this book the reader is encouraged to make herself or himself the object of study. Is this entirely a good thing? How much of our attention should be focused externally, on the world around us? How much should be *self-focused*—that is, concentrated internally on ourselves? Rick Ingram (1990) believes that "a relatively even balance is optional for psychological functioning" (p. 168). Researchers have found a heightened degree of self-focused attention in people with various clinical disorders, such as depression, anxiety, and alcohol abuse; but there is no conclusive evidence that one is the cause of the other. In pathological states of functioning, Ingram suggests, one is not just self-focused but *self-absorbed*, a condition in which internal attention is not only excessive but also sustained and rigid.

An important insight concerning self-focus is provided by the work of Ingram and Smith (1984). Among their subjects (university students in introductory psychology), those with higher scores on a depression inventory had self-focused thoughts that were equally positive and negative; in constrast, similar thoughts in students with lower depression scores were largely positive. These findings are consistent with what has been called "the power of non-negative thinking." They suggest that self-focused attention can have positive consequences when it is positively directed and employed in the service of constructive change.

Self-Deception. Finding out the truth about ourselves is not all that easy. Miguel de Cervantes wrote, "Make it thy business to know thyself, which is the most difficult lesson in the world." We human beings are masters at self-deception. Textbooks on adjustment and personal growth commonly contain long lists of defense mechanisms that we use to protect ourselves from facts about ourselves that might cause us anxiety or guilt. One book on such mechanisms listed fortynine different defenses (Laughlin, 1979). For a briefer but typical list, see Box 2.2.

Both research and common sense suggest that it's not so easy for us to see what we don't want to see. As psychologist Anthony Greenwald (1980) persuasively argues, our knowledge of ourselves is distorted by three self-serving biases. First, we are *egocentric* and tend to overestimate our influence in a situation or the extent to which we are the target of attention. We like to be important. Second, we are subject to *beneffectance*, a word coined by Greenwald to describe

Box 2.2

Some Common Defense Mechanisms

If we don't like or are threatened by what we see in ourselves or in the world about us, we may protect ourselves through various strategies called *defense mechanisms*. To the extent that a mechanism prevents our full awareness of a reality, it can be said to be a self-deception. Below are brief definitions and examples of some common defense mechanisms.

Name	Definition	Example
Denial	Refusing to admit a threatening reality	A woman refuses to accept the fact that she is terminally ill.
Suppression	Deliberate inhibition of threatening stimuli	A cigarette smoker quickly turns the page when he sees an article about lung cancer.
Repression	Automatic inhibition of threatening stimuli	A student has trouble remembering the name of an instructor who failed her last year.
Rationalization	Interpreting behavior in personally and socially acceptable ways	A parent convinces himself that his abusive disciplinary policies are for his child's "own good."
Adjustment by ailment	Noninsightful use of illness, imaginary or real, as a way of avoiding anxiety	A woman develops a severe headache whenever she is confronted by an unpleasant task.
Fixation	Continuation of patterns of behavior that have become immature or inappropriate	A young man remains tied to his mother's apron strings.
Regression	Return to patterns of behavior that have become immature or inappropriate	A young wife runs home to mother at the first sign of marital discord.
Projection	Attributing one's own qualities to others	A man who is tempted to be unfaithful shows unwarranted concern about his wife's flirtations.
Displacement	Shifting a thought, feeling, or action from one object to another	A little boy, mad at his mother, tramples her flower beds.
Reaction formation	Inhibiting, masking, or overcoming threatening impulses by emphasizing opposite ones	A man who feels weak and inadequate affects a tough, hard-boiled stance.
Compensation	Substitution of achievement in one area to make up for failure in another	A classroom dunce becomes the playground bully.
Sublimation	Expression of frustrated motives in socially sanctioned ways	A teacher, frustrated in the desire for a family of her own, lavishes affection on her pupils.
Undoing	Making amends or atoning for guilt-producing thoughts, feelings, and actions	A rejecting parent lavishes material things on a child.

(Adapted from Arkoff, 1968)

our tendency to take credit for what proves good but not the responsibility for what proves bad. We like to be well regarded. For example, winners in almost any enterprise are more willing to accept the praise than losers are to accept the blame. Third, we tend to show *cognitive conservatism*; that is, we tend to manage new information so that it accords with what we already know or think we know. We like to appear right. Therefore, we may cling to old ideas about ourselves despite new facts, or we may revise our memories to make them agree with the new information.

We filter incoming information, and distort it to enhance ourselves, in various ways. As noted earlier in this chapter, we select associates who see us as we see ourselves and, indeed, are somewhat like ourselves—thereby reinforcing our conviction that our beliefs, attitudes, and attributes are correct (Swann, 1984; Taylor & Brown, 1988). Incoming information is further distorted by the human tendency to give and receive mostly positive feedback; negative feedback is withheld or muted or put in euphemistic terms, making it ambiguous (Goffman, 1955).

In her book *Positive Illusions* Shelley Taylor (1989) makes a strong case for "creative self-deception." *Self-deception* refers to our efforts to hide the truth from ourselves, whereas *creative self-deception* concerns our attempts to exaggerate the positive aspects of a situation. In Taylor's view, a perfectly accurate knowledge of oneself and one's world is neither usual nor even desirable, and most persons possess unrealistically (but not outlandishly) positive self-impressions. For example, we are more aware of our strengths than our weaknesses; we see ourselves as better than average and better than others see us; and we have exaggerated notions of our capacity to control the important events in our lives and are overly optimistic about the future.

These positive illusions are generally kept modest and in check by feedback from the environment; they help rather than sabotage our coping efforts; and they foster a positive mood and promote happiness and contentment. As a result, other aspects of mental health—our ability to care for and care about others, our self-confidence, and our capacity to engage in creative and productive work—are enhanced.

Taylor makes an important distinction between positive illusions, which are often operative in our daily lives, and mechanisms such as denial and repression (see Box 2.2), which come into play when we defend ourselves against threat. Denial and repression cause us to distort or hide the facts, whereas positive illusions only mute or blunt the facts (which are often ambiguous anyway) and lead us to interpret them in the best possible light. Positive illusions encourage an optimistic outlook and work to promote mental and physical health. A good deal more will be said about both denial and optimism in the last chapter in this book.

A major limitation of some self-deception is that it can keep us from owning our problems or deficiencies and working on them. Self-deception is least likely to be harmful and most likely to be useful (1) when it is temporary, (2) when it is reserved for what otherwise might be an overwhelming situation, and (3) when it maximizes the positive and minimizes the negative content of a situation without grossly distorting the facts or preventing actions essential to well-being. But an inflated notion of self can encourage persons to ignore risks that need to be considered, disregard steps that should be taken (for example, in matters of health), persevere at impossible tasks, pursue careers for which they are unsuited, and fail to prepare for likely catastrophic events. Furthermore, unquestioning faith in the absolute rightness of one's beliefs can lead a person to trample on the rights of others (Taylor & Brown, 1988).

Self-Insight. During one period of his life, Sigmund Freud spent the last half hour of each working day analyzing himself. In one of my workshops, I share some things I have learned about myself from living with myself all these years and then ask my students to make up a list of things they have learned about themselves. At first, some are a bit dumbfounded, but once they have set themselves to the task, most find they have quite a bit to write down. As you work your way through the fourteen questions posed by this book, you will have many opportunities to gain personal insight.

If you are working on your life by yourself, there are a number of techniques that can be quite helpful. One is called "the evening review" and it is just that; you sit down each evening, at a regular time and in a regular place, to think and write about your day. Regular practice will prompt you to be more observant during the day and to take mental notes for later reviews.

A somewhat more elaborate approach is keeping a personal journal. This approach, when properly used, provides you not only with knowledge about yourself but also with a way to lend yourself support and to work on current issues in your life. A good journal is not a log that simply records the events of the day; it is a life workbook—a book in which you work on your life. For those who would like to learn how to keep a personal journal, I recommend *The New Diary* by Tristine Rainer (1978) and *At a Journal Workshop* by Ira Progoff (1975). Various courses in the use of a personal journal are available, including some by Progoff and his staff.

An evening review or a personal journal can be devoted to anything in our behavior that surprises or mystifies us or suggests an area that needs attention. One master of the art of self-reflection is Hugh Prather. In his notebooks, he carefully observes himself and candidly shares these observations with his readers. The following brief example from his book *Notes to Myself* shows him in his watchful but positive, nurturant pursuit of self-knowledge:

> One kind of lie that I tell pops out in conversation and takes me by surprise. Sometimes I like to correct these lies right on the spot, and when I do I find that most people don't think less of me. This kind of lie, when I notice it, usually helps me see where I feel inadequate—the areas where I could be more acceptant of myself. (1970)

In their book *Self-Directed Behavior*, David Watson and Roland Tharp (1993) suggest that a "structured diary" can help people track behavior they want to learn more about and change. The diary has three columns: A, B, and C. In the B column, the diarist notes each instance of the problem behavior (thought, feeling, and/or action) as soon after it has occurred as possible. Then, in the A column, he or she enters the antecedents or events that preceded it and, in the C column, the consequences that followed. A later study of these entries can provoke some helpful questions and insights. Box 2.3 shows how one person made use of this technique to gain information about her lack of assertiveness.

Disclosing Yourself

Do you have a confidant or someone who is a caring presence for you? Is there someone with whom you can share some of your innermost thoughts and feelings?

As noted in the last chapter, *self-disclosure* is the process of sharing our private thoughts and feelings with others (Jourard, 1971).[1] In disclosing ourselves, we come to know ourselves better. When we put our thoughts and feelings into words, they become clearer to us and even take on new or fuller meaning. We receive feedback from others, and this helps us to refine and validate our own self-awareness.

Psychologist Sidney Jourard (1971), who pioneered this area of research, considered self-disclosure to be an important component of mental health. Jourard became interested in self-disclosure because many of his clients told him that he was the first person with whom they had ever been completely honest. He wondered if there was some connection between their reluctance to confide in a relative or friend and their need to see a psychotherapist. Mentally healthy persons, he concluded, have the ability to make themselves known to at least one significant other. By contrast, less healthy persons are unable or unwilling to drop their guard.

None of us is completely transparent or completely opaque, nor should we be. Too much disclosure, like too little, can have negative effects. Disclosure requires the appropriate time and place and pace and person. In a comfortable

---

[1] Self-disclosure and other key concepts will appear from time to time in different contexts. Human nature is too interestingly complex to be neatly factored into chapters.

Box 2.3

Use of the Structured Diary for Self-Knowledge and Goal Setting

Evelyn, a young college student, felt that she needed to be more assertive, but she wasn't sure when and in what situations. She recorded in her diary the times she thought she *could* have been assertive but was not, and the times she *was* assertive.

Antecedents (A)	Behaviors (B)	Consequences (C)
11:30 p.m. I am about to fall asleep. Ed telephones. He starts to ramble.	I'm angry, it's late, and he is boring, but I don't say anything.	He talks about 20 minutes.
Noon the next day. Walking to work, I see Ed, try to avoid talking to him. He calls me. I keep on going. He grabs my arm. He asks me to lunch.	I look away, say "I don't know . . . (pause) ok."	We have lunch. He asks me out again.
Polly wants me to see a movie I swore I would not see. She complains that I haven't been to a movie with her in a long time.	I say, "I really shouldn't, I need to get some rest." But I give in and go.	The movie was gross.
1:00 p.m. Went to meet Jill. We were supposed to go jogging, but she wants to do it later in the day.	I tell her I can't go later. I have to work.	
6 p.m. My sister comes over to ask me to baby-sit.	I tell her I can't. I have other plans. A bunch of us are going out.	

Several days of this kind of observation revealed a pattern: When other people asked Evelyn to go places with them and she had nothing else specifically scheduled, she usually went, even if she didn't want to. If they asked but she had something specifically scheduled, she didn't go with them. "But," she wrote, "why should I have to have something scheduled before I feel I can say no? Isn't the need to go to sleep enough? I need to be able to refuse even when I have no specific activity planned but just don't want to do it." Once we've pointed it out to you, Evelyn's goal seems obvious, but it was not apparent to her until she began keeping a structured diary.

(From Watson & Tharp, 1993, pp. 67–68)

setting, we tell someone we trust something from within ourselves. That person listens without judging or giving advice—just being there with us. Then perhaps he or she shares something with us as we listen. In this way, we continue back and forth, learning about each other and at the same time learning about ourselves.

We can be uncomfortable with those who share too much too soon, just as we can be with those who refuse or are unable to share themselves at all. Each person must consider the effect of the disclosure on the other. Morton Hunt (1993) writes that the persons we pick to confide in should not be ones who might be wounded by what we reveal. For example, nagged by guilt concerning an affair, an unfaithful husband may confess and ask forgiveness, but in doing so, he may transfer the pain to his mate. Hunt suggests that disclosures of this kind might better be made to professional counselors, along with certain confessions that tumble out and later are regretted. Concerning the latter, he gives this example:

Consider a woman with whom I had been friendly for years, who once wrote me a long and incredibly revealing letter when I was gathering data

POT-SHOTS NO. 2471.

IF WE ALL
CONCEAL OUR
EMBARRASSING
PECULIARITIES,

WE'LL NEVER
KNOW
HOW MANY OF US
HAVE THEM.

©ASHLEIGH BRILLIANT 1982.   *Ashleigh Brilliant*

for a book on the problems of American women. Writing late at night when she was feeling sorry for herself, she told me that she often bitterly regretted having children. They had brought her far less joy and far more emotional upset than she'd ever expected, and, while she often loved them, quite often she hated them. A day after I received the letter, she sent a telegram asking me to burn it. Though she and her husband were longtime friends of mine, I have not seen or heard from them since. Friendship, though it flourishes on the nutrients of sharing and intimacy, can be killed altogether by an overdose. (p. 325)

Self-disclosure can enhance interpersonal relationships (Berg, 1987; Berg & Derlega, 1987; Jourard, 1971). The more appropriately self-disclosing we are with others, the more they like us and the more they disclose themselves to us. Hiding ourselves from others can be not only hard work, as Jourard notes, but also a lonely business. Some of us equate silence with strength, but it takes strength to risk revealing ourselves to another.

James Pennebaker and his colleagues (1986, 1988, 1990) have been studying the consequences of confiding versus not confiding traumatic events. Their results indicate that individuals who confront and work through previously inhibited experiences reap physiological, psychological, and social benefits. Physiologically, the disclosure leads to reduced stress-related bodily changes and improved immune function and physical health. Socially, the disclosure usually strengthens the bond between disclosers and those they confide in. Psychologically, the disclosure divests the event of its emotional charge. For example, in a study (Pennebaker, Kiecolt-Glaser, & Glaser, 1988) that asked the subjects to write on four consecutive days their deepest thoughts and feelings concerning the most upsetting experiences of their life, a gradual change in perspective was noted in several participants who concentrated on a single trauma.

One woman, who had been molested at the age of 9 years by a boy 3 years older, initially emphasized her feelings of embarrassment and guilt. By the third day of writing, she expressed anger at the boy who had victimized her. By the last day, she had begun to put it in perspective. On the follow-up survey 6 weeks after the experiment, she reported, "Before, when I thought about it, I'd lie to myself. . . . Now, I don't feel like I even have to think about it because I got if off my chest. I finally admitted that it happened. . . . I really know the truth and won't have to lie to myself anymore." (p. 244)

Emotional openness has been found to be a more affecting kind of self-revelation than informational disclosure. In one study, persons who wrote about their deepest thoughts and feelings surrounding a trauma felt much worse immediately afterward than those who just wrote about the facts of a trauma or about trivial topics. However, in the five and a half months after the experiment, the former group, unlike the latter, showed a considerable decline in illness visits to the student health center (Pennebaker & Beall, 1986).

According to Robert Ornstein and David Sobel (1989), a case can be made for maximizing the positives and ignoring the negatives of life, but there is a limit and a principle. The principle (which states the limit) is this: If the trauma is relatively small, it may be best to minimize, ignore, or deny it. But if the trauma is very upsetting, it will be better and healthier in the long run to face it and work it through.

Learning appropriate self-disclosure is an important social skill. We can learn to disclose ourselves. In the warmth and security of certain relationships, we can dare to be who we are. We let down our guard and let others see us, and we see ourselves more clearly.

Chapter 1 called attention to the importance of our ability to be a "caring discloser" as well as our ability to be a "caring presence" as we seek to illuminate our lives. How to be a caring presence was explained in Box 1.4, and for a discussion of what it means to be a caring discloser, see Box 2.4.

Prizing Yourself

Since you are going to be spending your life with yourself, it's important that you regard yourself as someone special. Do you?

The last chapter noted the importance of liking ourselves or accepting ourselves. To *accept* ourselves means we believe we are okay. That's a good beginning. To *prize* ourselves means we have a high regard for ourselves and even think we're special. That's even better, especially if it creates a quiet inner pride. I'm indebted to Carl Rogers for this use of the word *prize*, but others have written in much the same way about the importance of "self-esteem" or "honoring" oneself or "befriending" oneself.

Strictly speaking, *self-esteem* is the evaluation we make of ourselves. As the term is commonly used, to have self-esteem—or, more exactly, to have high self-esteem—means we place a high value on ourselves. We feel we are worthy. We take pride in ourselves.

Box 2.4

The Caring Discloser

We disclose ourselves to others who care for us, but because we also care for them and for the sharing process, we monitor our disclosure. We can know that our exchange is caring disclosure if it meets the criteria below (partly based on Goodman & Esterly, 1988; Johnson, 1993).

1. *Caring disclosure involves persons who are appropriately paired.*

This means we share some common ground, have concern for each other, and trust each other. It also means we have the capacity to open ourselves to and empathize with each other.

Promiscuous disclosure, by contrast, is that which is broadcast or nearly so, made to a number of persons seemingly without discrimination or selection or any setting of the stage. Such disclosure may not be disclosure at all but ploys to create an image, carry out a personal crusade, or even to block true sharing through erecting a façade. Promiscuous disclosure, like promiscuous sexuality, can sabotage any chance there may be for a durable intimacy.

2. *Caring disclosure is paced and reciprocated.*

In such disclosure, we take turns, matching the depth of our disclosures to each other, going deeper little by little as we learn to trust each other and ourselves. This measured sharing is in contrast to premature, flooded, and constrained disclosure.

Premature disclosure comes too early in an exchange. It is out of sequence, appearing before sufficient intimacy and trust have been established. Such disclosure can interfere with the sharing process, possibly alarming or frightening the listener and causing her or him to draw back or away.

In *flooded disclosure,* one person's thoughts and feelings rush out and spill over, so that the outpouring dominates the exchange and inundates the listener. Some of us tend to be heavy-duty flooders who bore, annoy, crowd out, and turn away our listeners. Flooding can disrupt the give and take of true intimacy and even be a defense against it, but letting it all out on certain occasions may be an important and even necessary kind of cleansing or catharsis.

In *constrained disclosure,* the opposite side of the continuum from flooded disclosure, the person refuses or is unable to share in appropriate measure. Since intimacy and trust are built though escalating and mutual exchange, constrained disclosure can bring the process to a halt. In disclosure there is sometimes concealer's regret and discloser's remorse. The concealer can in retrospect regret a missed opportunity to share, just as a discloser who rushes the pace may have second thoughts about the wisdom of sharing so much so soon.

3. *Caring disclosure takes into account the effect that it has on the listener.*

It does not ask the listener to be more than a listener. It does not shift the work of the discloser to the listener. It does not convey information that will be hurtful to the listener under the guise of concern for the listener.

Burdening disclosure, by contrast, wittingly or unwittingly attempts to shift the burden to the listener. It may seek to make the listener assume a role or respond in a particular way—to judge, advise, rescue, reassure, or ally against another. It may make the listener aware of information that may compromise his or her position or peace of mind.

4. *Caring disclosure leads to deeper insight and personal growth.*

It is sharing for the purpose of growth, but it is not a substitute for necessary actions. As we learn to trust others and trust ourselves, our defenses fade, and we arrive at deeper understanding of our lives and what we need to do to move them along.

Spurious disclosure is a counterfeit of the growth process. Such disclosure may be well-rehearsed material that involves no risk and plumbs no depths. It may be material shared over and over, which—like some kinds of promiscuous disclosure—is designed for effect on the listener rather than for work on ourselves. The most growth-provoking disclosure involves material we need to work on, and indeed we work on it as we attempt to put it into words and share it with another.

Not one to hide pride under a bushel, Nathaniel Branden (1985) has written a book with the title (and on the subject of) *Honoring the Self.* "Honor thyself" might almost be an addition to the Ten Commandments. Logically, it might precede the Fifth Commandment, "Honor thy father and mother," because, as Branden writes, the evidence is overwhelming that the higher our self-esteem, the more likely we will treat others with respect, kindness, and generosity. There is also evidence that the higher our self-esteem, the better our physical and psychological health (Coopersmith, 1967; Turner & Vanderlippe, 1958).

To take pride in oneself or to honor oneself will be for some a troubling notion. We may have been taught to be modest and humble. We may have been

©BRILLIANT ENTERPRISES 1973   POT-SHOTS NO. 433

I MAY NOT BE TOTALLY PERFECT, BUT PARTS OF ME ARE EXCELLENT.

warned against the sin of pride. We may have been cautioned that excessive pride can result in arrogance or prejudice (Tavris, 1985), but pride can be either harmful or healthy. It can be arrogance toward others or a respect for self that makes arrogance unnecessary (Lynd, 1958; Rosenberg, 1979).

The efforts by some state and educational bodies to increase self-esteem in various groups have recently come in for some hard knocks and even attempts at ridicule (Adler, 1992). Some critics of these efforts seem worried that persons who are encouraged to feel good about themselves will become conceited ("I'm terrific!") and complacent and be in for some rude shocks in the real world. These critics maintain that effective functioning must precede a belief in oneself: First, you prove what you can do, and then you know you're good. But one can follow several routes to becoming more effective. Our opinion of ourselves indeed rises when we see what we can do; but when we are encouraged to raise our opinion of ourselves, we are willing to try more and become able to do more. Psychologist Andrew Sappington (1989) reviews the evidence and concludes, "Effective functioning can raise self-esteem, and high self-esteem can increase the chances of effective functioning" (p. 202).

Some critics of self-esteem movements believe in a kick in the pants (or the ego) to make us improve, but what about a pat on the back (and a sense of quiet pride) for who we are right now? Whoever we are, it helps to feel good about our race and ethnic origins, about our age and gender and sexual orientation, about our bodies. TV talk host Jenny Jones has had her original silicone implants replaced five times; her hardened breasts have no feeling, and the silicone leakage cannot be removed. "Learn to love yourself," she said in an interview. "If I could have learned that, I wouldn't have had to suffer these 11 years of torture" (Beck, 1992, p. A14).

To accept, to prize, to honor, to *befriend.* Much of what has been written about self-regard in these first two chapters comes down to this: Be a good friend to yourself. That means treating yourself as nicely as you would a highly valued friend. A friend like that is someone you can always count on for support. Can you count on yourself for support? The brief quiz in Box 2.5 may help you answer this question.

Becoming Yourself

Have you become yourself? Or are you somebody else's invention? Have you been persuaded by your parents or teachers or other forces to be someone you're not or someone you don't want to be (Jourard, 1975)? If this has happened to

Box 2.5

"Support Your Local Self"

If a statement below is true or mostly true concerning yourself, circle T.
If a statement is false or mostly false, circle F.

T   F   1. When I do something right, I take time to feel good about it.
T   F   2. I rarely meet the high standards I set for myself.
T   F   3. I get through hard things by planning treats or rewards for myself afterward.
T   F   4. I silently praise myself for even small achievements.
T   F   5. When things go wrong, I am quick to blame or criticize myself.
T   F   6. I achieve my goals by rewarding myself at every step along the way.
T   F   7. Any activity can provide some pleasure or satisfaction regardless of the outcome.
T   F   8. I think less of myself if I don't do the best possible job.
T   F   9. Even when I fail at something, I am still able to feel good about myself.
T   F   10. My happiness depends on me more than it does on other people.

Harry Browne writes that when it comes to your happiness, you should be your own best provider. "Give to you" is Browne's advice. "Support your local self" (1974, p. 64). Psychologist Chris Kleinke suggests this question as a test: "Who is your best friend?" Your answer should be "I am" (1991, p. 40).

We can't always count on others for support, so we need to be able to count on ourselves. Unfortunately, some of us fail to provide such assistance. We ask too much of ourselves, and we are too slow to feel good about ourselves or to reward ourselves for what we have accomplished. We are too quick to criticize ourselves or too slow to support ourselves when we need a boost.

The ten statements above are adapted from a larger instrument developed by psychologist Elaine Heiby (1983a).

Heiby has found that depressed persons less frequently reinforce or reward themselves than do those who aren't depressed; similarly, persons who are low reinforcers are more likely to become depressed when external sources of reinforcement are lost (Heiby, 1981, 1983b, 1983c). This finding suggests that those of us who "support our local self" will be less likely to become depressed and more able to get through difficult times when there is little or no help from others.

Circling T for Items 1, 3, 4, 6, 7, 9, and 10, and circling F for Items 2, 5, and 8 would suggest the presence of a good self-reinforcement or self-support system. These items, as they are presented here, cannot be considered a definitive test of this quality, but they can help you think about this aspect of yourself.

you, you may want to rescue yourself from your miscasting, assume your own character, and plot out your own life story (Kopp, 1987).

We are each unique, and each of us has a life like no other life. There are general laws, but, as Danish theologian Søren Kierkegaard wrote, every person is an exception, and every person has something exceptional to offer. To quote the words Nikos Kazantzakis put in the mouth of his Zorba the Greek: "When I die, the whole zorbatic world dies with me."

Carl Rogers (1961) noted that each person coming to him for therapy appeared to be asking the same questions: "Who am I, *really*? How can I get in touch with this real self, underlying this surface behavior? How can I become myself?" (p. 108). Rogers theorized that each of us is born with a tendency to make the most of our own unique potential. We each have an inherent wisdom allowing us to distinguish those experiences or pathways that lead to fulfillment from those that lead to stagnation or destruction. Each of us struggles (and here Rogers quotes Kierkegaard) "to be that self which one truly is" (p. 110).

Being ourselves proves not to be an easy task. The poet E. E. Cummings wrote, "To be nobody but yourself in a world which is doing its best, night and day, to make you everybody else, means to fight the hardest battle which any human being can fight, and never stop fighting."

Psychotherapist Lawrence LeShan has worked with cancer patients for over thirty-five years. What he notes in long-term individual therapy with these patients is a chronic despair, but it is a despair that *predates* the appearance of cancer by many years and arises from a dilemma. Such patients come to believe they can be loved only if they give up being who they truly are, but to them this is unacceptable and unworkable. LeShan advises those caught up in this dilemma that the solution is to become "more and more the self you are."

> The more this becomes your path and goal, then the more those who approve of the person you really are can recognize you and move toward you. By and large, these will be the kind of people *you* like, although there will be exceptions. Only after people in despair have had the courage to show their true face can these others recognize and respond with liking and love. And it is only after this—after finding and showing your true being—that love can be accepted and believed in. (1989, p. 110)

Showing one's "true face" even to oneself can be a difficult task when it is a face that one has somehow come to think is wrong or even evil. Some lesbians and gays have written of their confusion or consternation at discovering their sexual orientation and of their struggle to "come out of the closet" and be who they truly were. In one study (Jay & Young, 1979), a woman reported that she didn't realize she was a lesbian until she was 20, and her coming out was traumatic. "I used to look at myself in the mirror and cry. I couldn't believe what I was. How could a good girl like me be something as wicked as a lesbian? Once I found the gay bars and gay community I found that there were many 'good girl' lesbians" (pp. 55–56). She noted that since then her self-image had improved each year, and now she wouldn't want to be anyone other than who she is.

The experience reported by a gay man was somewhat similar. Being in the closet, he wrote, was a nightmare that lasted about ten years. He had known he was gay since his sexual awakening at age 13, but he tried to pretend that he was "normal":

> I remember constantly lying in order to keep a front of heterosexuality protectively between me and the heterosexual world around me. I remember talking myself into love with a teenaged woman, but only carrying the relationship so far in order to avoid anything sexual. Finally, at age 21, after the army and before college, I lost grasp of the world, plunged into a depression, and finally lifted myself out of it by coming out. Coming out was an either/or decision for me: either go insane and live a miserable lie all my life, or buck the system, outrage those around me, and be honest with myself. Not having the political analysis nor the support of other gay people available, it was a difficult decision, but I now know that I made the right one—the only one. (p. 110)

We must constantly seek to understand ourselves if we are to become ourselves, but the understanding does not come once and for all. It comes little by little as we observe ourselves in every new situation. We can learn to tell whether we are being genuine and true to ourselves, or phony and inauthentic (Friedman, 1967).

As a hospice volunteer, I have worked closely with a number of persons as they faced death. I've come to believe that dying has been hardest for those who never really lived their lives—those who were losing both life and their last chance to become themselves. I am reminded of the story told about Rabbi Zusya as he approached death. Rabbi Zusya said that when he met the Holy One, he would not be asked, "Why were you not like Moses?" No, he would be asked, "Why were you not like *Zusya*?" And Zusya added, "It is for this reason that I tremble."

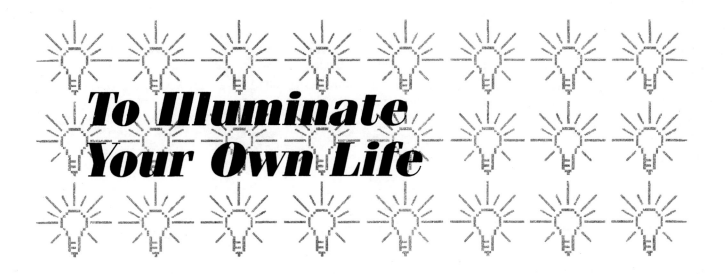

To Illuminate Your Own Life

Anchor and Apply*

1. What kind of a relationship do you have with yourself? Describe this relationship as it seems to you.

2. What subpersonalities can you detect in yourself? Name and describe each one and its influence on you.

3. How does your self-image affect your behavior? Discuss this aspect of yourself. Give examples and be as specific as you can.

4. Discuss the relationship between your body image and your self-image and self-esteem.

5. Discuss the relationship between your gender and your self-image and self-esteem.

6. Do you tend to focus your attention on your own thoughts and feelings too much? Too little? Discuss this aspect of yourself.

7. Have you become aware of any of your own "positive illusions" or self-deceptions? If so, discuss this aspect of yourself.

8. How much insight into yourself do you have? How much of a puzzle are you? Discuss an important aspect of yourself that remains a mystery to you.

9. How much insight into yourself do you have? How much of an open or opening book are you? Discuss a recent situation or event that provided some important insight.

10. Do you tend to disclose too much? Too little? Appropriately? Inappropriately? And to whom? Discuss this aspect of yourself.

11. Do you have a confidant—a close friend to whom you disclose your deeper feelings and problems? Discuss the effect on you of having or not having such a person.

---

* These "anchor and apply" items are designed to help you use the concepts of the chapter as stimuli to prompt new or deeper or clearer insights into yourself and your life. To respond to an item, first find the material in the chapter that is most relevant to the item *and* yourself; that's called "anchoring." Second, think about this material in relationship to yourself and your life and keep thinking about it until you arrive at a new or deeper or clearer understanding; that's the "apply" or application part. When you write or present your response to the item, be sure to include both parts, that is, both the anchor material and the application. You can know you are successful on an item if, in completing it, you truly learn something new or understand something better.

12. Are you a good friend to yourself? Can you count on yourself for support? Discuss this aspect of yourself.

13. Are you your real self—your true self? Do you show your true face to others? Discuss this aspect of yourself.

Three Images

Self-Image

Your *self-image* is the concept or picture you have of yourself. It is the way you see yourself. It is what you think yourself to be. It is your answer to the question "Who am I?"

Lyndon B. Johnson might well have been answering the question "Who am I?" as he described himself on an occasion before he became president. He said that he was "a free man, an American, a United States Senator, a Democrat, a liberal, a conservative, a Texan, a taxpayer, a rancher, and not as young as I used to be nor as old as I expect to be."

We often see ourselves in terms of the roles we play, and we may become a captive of these roles. The protagonist in the movie *Shirley Valentine* is a middle-aged English housewife caught up in a routine life with a demanding, unappreciative husband and adult daughter. Fate contrives to send her off on a vacation to Greece, and her experience there frees her from her role-locked image of herself. Her husband, who flies to Greece in an attempt to take his fugitive wife back into custody, barely recognizes her, and she tells him with a sure sense of her regained identity: "I used to be the mother. I used to be the wife. But now I'm Shirley Valentine again."

Erik Erikson has been called the "dean of American psychoanalysts" and his theory of development through the life span has been highly influential. His theory calls attention to the importance of identity. Speaking of his own life, he once said, "Every adult needs a rock, a ground, for his identity—something he truly knows, something he can do no matter what. For me, the ground is this: I am a psychoanalyst" (Keniston, 1983, p. 29).

Many of us do not have a salient rock on which to stand, and there may be times when we feel as though we have no rock or identity at all. This is the situation described by Lida G. Chase in her poem entitled "Identity Crisis":

Who am I?

I am a cloud—wispy, of no substance, easily fragmented, and moving relentlessly.

I am a stone being hurled across the surface of water. The force which drives me is greater than me. I touch only lightly upon the surface, yet each time I contact the pool I feel a sting.

I am a tree on a windswept hill; I am barren and dead. There is no whisper of life in me. Even my roots have withered. The wind rushes past; it has no desire to caress my stark branches. The sun does not bathe me with warmth; it beats down unmercifully and speeds my destruction.

Who am I?

Contrast the above image of self with that of an octogenerian in a poetry workshop at a rehabilitation center (Ratner, 1984):

I am 82
Still going strong
Broke my hip
Still going strong
Had it mended
And still going strong
You can't keep a woman like me down

One instrument used to measure identity or self-image is the WAY Test, in which the person is simply asked to answer the question "Who are you?" and sometimes the question "Who are you not?" A similar but more structured test is the TST or Twenty Statements Test, in which the person lists twenty answers to the question "Who am I?" or "Who am I not?" Here are the TST answers given recently by a good friend of mine—a creative, spirited woman, 71 years of age and now undergoing intensive treatment for cancer:

Who am I? I am . . .

1. an individualized expression of the energy I call God.
2. a cosmic dancer, dancing through the Valley of the Shadow of Death.
3. a constantly evolving pilgrim on a spiritual path.
4. a risk-taking, curious adventurer.
5. a believer in fairies, elves, gnomes, magic, miracles, and the Land of Oz.
6. a creative artist.
7. a loyal friend.
8. a nourishing mother.
9. a devoted wife.
10. a fun and wise grandmother.
11. a generous but prudent giver.
12. energy living in a human body.
13. a vital lover of living.
14. ME, Mary Elaine, who likes being a living, loving woman.

This woman stopped at fourteen answers. She said that these responses were central to who she was at this moment in her life. Further responses that came to mind—such as gardener and swimmer—were more peripheral, and she preferred not to include them in her list. Her answers to the question "Who am I not?" were terse and to the point:

Who am I not? I am not . . .

1. a grouch.
2. lazy.
3. boring.

From: *The Illuminated Life*, by Abe Arkoff. Copyright © 1995 by Allyn and Bacon.

    4. skinny.

    5. timid.

    6. uninvolved.

    7. conservative.

    8. asexual.

    9. undependable.

  10. ugly.

  11. fearful.

In the space provided on the next page, construct something to describe your own self-image—the concept or picture that you have of yourself. Your construction can be your own twenty or so answers to the question "Who am I?" and/or "Who am I not?" Or your construction can be a poem, painting, drawing, essay, collage, or anything. If you decide to construct a collage, you might proceed in this way (which can lead to some new or unexpected insights): leaf through some old magazines without a preconception of what you are looking for. Be passive and let the materials in the magazines nominate themselves for inclusion in your collage. As they do, cut them out, and when your search is complete, cull and synthesize them. Whatever your construction, don't overcrowd it; eliminate peripheral ideas, and just include those most central and important to your conception of yourself.

My Self-Image

Feared Self

A story is told of a holy man so renowned for his good deeds that the ruler of the kingdom ordered his portrait painted to hang in the great hall. But when the portrait was unveiled, the face it depicted was cruel, brutish, and morally depraved. The king was outraged, but the holy man said that the portrait was true. It was, he explained, the picture of the person he had struggled all his life not to be (Viorst, 1987).

Your *feared self* is the concept or picture of the person you are afraid you might become. This image can be rational in that what it portrays is likely to occur, or it can be far-fetched or completely irrational. I think my own interest in psychology was partly prompted by a depression suffered by my father when I was in my teens; I was close to my father, but I felt unable to understand what he was going through and fearful that the same condition might be ahead for me.

In an essay entitled "Night Terrors of a Middle-Class Sort," safely middle-class Barbara Ehrenreich (1986) discusses her own fear that she will one day become destitute; she writes that many women share the same fantasy, so many that it has even been given a name—the "bag lady syndrome." Another widely shared feared self is movingly described by Florida Scott-Maxwell (1968) in her notebook, written when she was 82 and in poor health:

> I don't like to write this down, yet it is much in the minds of the old. We wonder how much older we have to become, and what degree of decay we may have to endure. We keep whispering to ourselves, "Is this age yet? How far must I go?" For age can be dreaded more than death. "How many years of vacuity? To what degree of deterioration must I advance?" Some want death now, as release from old age, some say they will accept death willingly, but in a few years. I feel the solemnity of death, and the possibility of some form of continuity. Death feels a friend because it will release us from the deterioration of which we cannot see the end. It is waiting for death that wears us down, and the distaste for what we may become. (p. 138)

A dread of becoming their feared fat self is present in many persons in our culture. This fear can be carried to life-threatening extremes in certain eating disorders. One woman described her fearful fantasy that she would become fatter and fatter—like her fat mother, like her fat aunt, like her fat sister. All had once been slim and ambitious until they got married, had babies, and let themselves go (Chernin, 1985). An only slightly overweight male once told me, as he wiped his plate clean with the last roll, that he was in a constant battle with the fat man inside him who was trying to get out.

Carl Jung (1953, 1959) noted that both sexes have a masculine and a feminine side and the recognition of both makes for completeness. Males in our society are under pressure to avoid any behavior that might be considered feminine, and they can become concerned that they possess or are seen as possessing feminine qualities that may reflect negatively on them (O'Neil et al., 1986). For some males, this fear of femininity may create a feared homosexual self along with an abhorrence of and intolerance for any behavior that might be considered homosexual. It has been suggested that the fear of femininity crests in young adulthood and then diminishes (O'Neil et al., 1986).

People who feel particularly vulnerable to a devastating or possibly fatal disease may develop a feared image of the diseased person they might become. I knew a woman whose family had a history of susceptibility to a debilitating disorder. She had seen one parent and two siblings fall ill, and she had recurrent nightmares in which she saw herself as afflicted; fearing the worst, she reined in her life and decided not to marry. Graphic descriptions of illness and death from AIDS of well-known persons have created a sizable proportion of "worried well"—persons who are healthy but fear they are not.

In the space provided on the next page, construct something to describe a feared self—a self that you fear you might become. Proceed in any way you like (you might read again the suggestions made for the first construction in this exploration).

My Feared Self

Desired Self

Your *desired self* is the concept or picture of the person you would like to be. Most of us want to be more than we are—perhaps smarter, richer, healthier, better looking, more competent, more powerful, more serene, or more loved. Some of us want to be less than we are—at least, on any particular day, a large number of Americans are on a diet or thinking about going on a diet or just coming off of a diet.

Some of us just want to be who we truly are—which sometimes proves not an easy thing to be. I am reminded of a conversation I had with a psychiatrist on this subject. He recalled asking an adolescent boy who he wanted to be, and without hesitancy the boy replied, "I would like to be myself—if I thought I could get away with it."

Your desired self can help or hurt you. It can be an image that inspires and guides you. Or it can be one that tyrannizes you because it asks so much or seems so far beyond your reach.

Your desired self can be a moral image—a self you should be (or else you feel guilty) or a self you have to be (or else you are nothing). Some desired selves are idealized images of nearly flawless perfection. One day while she was writing in her personal journal, Christina Baldwin (1977) titled a page "Expectations of Myself" and made up the following list:

My Expectations

Be perfect
Always be sensitive
Take care of others whenever they need it
Be loving, gentle, kind, good, responsible
Be smart
Be articulate
Be original
Be creative
Be able to synthesize experience at all times, under any conditions
Be able to cope with experience at all times, under any conditions
Be trusting and trustworthy
Be sexually active, and also true to my spiritual-sexual needs
Be the ideal feminist, Amazon, model woman
Be open to men, their graceful lover
Be open to women, their true friend
Be always full of energy
Succeed: be a successful writer
       be a successful counselor
       be a successful person
Be strong
Keep active
Have faith (pp. 43–44)

Looking back on her list of desired qualities, Baldwin realized that it could keep her in a state of self-worthlessness and prevent her from growing. But by "disgorging" these expectations in her journal, she became more fully aware of her impossible striving and better poised to release herself from them. (You might try making up a similar list of self-expectations.)

In his autobiography, Theodore Roosevelt described how he had achieved an important aspect of his own desired self. His ideal was to be fearless, but he had been a sickly and awkward boy and was distrustful at first of his prowess as a young man. To master fear, he pursued a strategy described in a passage of a book that had impressed him:

> In this passage the captain of some small British man-of-war is explaining to the hero how to acquire the quality of fearlessness. He says that at the outset almost every man is frightened when he goes into action, but that the course to follow is for the man to keep such a grip on himself that he can act just as if he was not frightened. After this is kept up long enough it changes from pretense to reality, and the man does in very fact become fearless by sheer dint of practicing fearlessness when he does not feel it. . . . This was the theory upon which I went. There were all kinds of things of which I was afraid at first, ranging from grizzly bears to "mean" horses and gun-fighters; but by acting as if I was not afraid I gradually ceased to be afraid. ([1913] 1946, p. 52)

Linda Hunt, who won an Academy Award for playing the dwarf Eurasian photographer in the film *The Year of Living Dangerously*, has a commanding presence despite her diminutive height. This presence is the manifestation of a desired self that Hunt began to practice early. An interviewer (Zarin, 1990) asked Hunt, "Does it surprise you that people recognize your authority?" Hunt's reply:

> No, because that's what I developed to survive. To survive what I was— how I was different from everyone else. I had this perception in the air around me that there was something wrong with me, and I knew that what was wrong with me *wasn't* wrong with anyone else. And I saw that if you talk in a loud voice people will think you have something to say, so I cultivated a loud voice. And I learned to say all my vowels and consonants. I developed grandeur at a very early age. Say, four. I saw my parents as safe and secure, and I realized that if I could only get to be a grownup I would be safe and secure, too. But I knew that for me it wasn't going to be enough to be a grownup. I was going to have to be a duchess. (p. 43)

In her book *Revolution from Within: A Book of Self-Esteem*, Gloria Steinem (1992) writes of her failure to value herself and also of a time when she had the first inkling of a healthier self within her, waiting for encouragement. Her therapist helped her visualize this "future self"—the self she wanted to become. What Steinem visualized was a shadowy figure but one that somehow had strength. "Only one detail was clear: this figure's feet were planted firmly on the ground and, more than that, *felt* the ground" (p. 192). Imaging herself in the body of this future self, Steinem felt sure-footed, stronger, wiser. She was gratified to find that this felt sense of her future self could be recalled to assist, guide, and inspire her.

In the space provided on the next page, construct something to describe a desired self—a self that you would like to be. Proceed in any way you like (you might read again the suggestions made for the first construction in this exploration). When you have finished your description on the next page, turn to the page that follows for final instructions for this exploration.

My Desired Self

Research on possible selves (Oyserman & Markus, 1986; Markus & Nurius, 1986) suggests that such images are important because they function as incentives—they are selves to be sought or avoided. In the space immediately below, discuss (1) the meaning of each of your three constructions—that is, what each has to say about you—and (2) the way each image affects you and your life.

The Positive Self

Imagine that you are talking to yourself, telling yourself everything that is wrong with you. Write your name in the blank space below, and then go ahead and list every negative thing about yourself that comes to mind. Number each item as you put it down. When you have finished this list, turn to the next page.

The trouble with you, _____, is . . .

Now imagine that you are talking to yourself, telling yourself everything that is good about you. Write your name in the blank space below, and then go ahead and list every positive thing about yourself that comes to mind. Number each item as you put it down. When you have finished this list, turn to the next page.

What I like about you, _____, *is . . .*

Important: Read the following paragraphs carefully, so that you can carry out the instructions at the end of this page and also the instructions on the next page.

Research has shown that persons who view themselves positively are favored in a number of ways. Compared to those with lower self-esteem, positive individuals have more self-confidence; they expect to be successful in their undertakings and are more likely to be so. They get along well with others, since they accept others as they accept themselves; they don't feel inferior, and they don't need to feel superior. Positive persons are not threatened by risk or put down by failure, since their opinion of themselves is not in question.

Self-condemnation problems have been held to be at the root of most human suffering (Ellis, 1973b; Lazarus, 1977). Of course, no one can excel in all situations, and almost everyone has some feelings of inferiority. A study on college students found that 88 percent felt inferior in some way (Allport, 1961). Nonetheless, if you have a very low opinion of yourself, you make yourself miserable and less able to function effectively.

One way to improve your self-image is to change the way you talk about yourself (Bower & Bower, 1991). In your internal dialogues, you frequently tell yourself what you think of yourself. The self-talk of those with low self-esteem is often full of negative statements or "downers." In fact, one may become obsessed with some personal defect or limitation, exaggerate it out of all proportion, and make oneself miserable. To improve your self-image, you can say more good things about yourself and fewer bad things. You can concentrate on your good points and constantly recall them to yourself. ("I work hard." "I am a good tennis player." "I speak well.") You can stop yourself when you begin to dwell on a negative point and even reverse yourself. ("I can't assert myself" becomes "I *can* assert myself" or "I *will* assert myself" or "I *do* assert myself.")

A second way to improve your self-image is to change the way you evaluate yourself. During your lifetime you are frequently appraised and compared with others, to see if you measure up, and you soon learn to evaluate yourself in much the same way. Langer and Dweck (1973) suggest that you check your reference group to make sure you're comparing yourself to the right people; if you are not, then choose a more appropriate group. If you are a beginner, compare yourself to other beginners, not to gold-medal winners or those with ten years of experience. (However, champions may be good models.)

To gain some insight into your ability to view yourself positively, compare the number of items in your negative list with the number in your positive list. On the last line on this page, give yourself a rating of "Great!" if your positive list is at least twice as long as your negative list. Give yourself a rating of "Good!" if your positive list is longer than the negative one although not twice as long. You don't need to get a lower rating, because you can keep adding items to your positive list until you merit "Good!" or even "Great!" (If a particular item on either list is especially important, you can give it double or even greater weight.)

This is my rating of my ability to view myself positively: _____

1. How positive are you generally about yourself? How often do you compliment yourself and give yourself a boost? Do you treat yourself as nicely as you treat others? Discuss this aspect of your behavior in the space immediately below and indicate its effects on you.

2. To whom do you usually compare yourself? What qualities are you concerned about in your comparisons? Discuss this aspect of your behavior in the space immediately below and indicate its effects on you.

E x p l o r a t i o n

2C

Quiet Pride

Psychotherapist John Welwood (1980) writes that the essential core of his healing practice is teaching his clients how to "be" with themselves. He recalled one of his clients who was simply unable to let himself feel good. We like to be with people who help us feel good about ourselves, and we avoid those who don't, but we may not have thought about our own company in this way. How are we with ourselves? Do we help ourselves feel good?

Mark Twain wrote that no one can be comfortable without his own approval, and yet that may be harder to get than the approval of others. Many of us have within a negative, critical, hurtful voice dragging us down. That's what George Bach and Laura Torbet (1983) write in their book *The Inner Enemy*. This enemy is the voice inside us that asks accusingly, "Who do you think you are, walking upright, trying to be successful, to be content, to be loved and lovable, trying to have a good time? You've got a lot of nerve. I'll show you" (pp. 29–30).

We need to learn—if we haven't already—to be our own ally and friend. We need to be at peace with ourselves, to be good to ourselves, to accept and—more than that—prize ourselves. Each of us needs to have a quiet pride in who we are. Not a noisy "pride" that needs to announce itself to the world. Not an embarrassed "pride" that is self-conscious and disconcerted. Neither of those is truly pride. Just a simple, confident, quiet pride.

Sometimes our sense of pride will be enhanced by our successes; these may be large or small, known to everyone or perhaps only to ourselves. At other times, we will find reason for pride in our failures; it will come from knowing we tried or fought a good fight or weren't kept down by defeat. We will realize that we must fail in order to succeed; we learn through our failures how to succeed.

This is a simple exercise to test your ability to show a quiet pride in yourself. In the list below, find three items that are appropriate for you in that you recall such times or events in your own life. Draw a circle around the number in front of each of these three items. Then write a full account of each on page 71, taking a quiet pride in yourself as you do. A simple, confident, quiet pride.

1. Recall a time when you were looked up to.
2. Recall a time when somebody was proud of you.
3. Recall a time when you lost but weren't defeated.
4. Recall a time when you found you had influence.
5. Recall a time when you succeeded in your struggle.
6. Recall a time when you survived a difficult situation.
7. Recall a time when you felt you had done a good job.
8. Recall a time when you knew you had shown courage.
9. Recall a time when somebody was glad you were there.

From: *The Illuminated Life*, by Abe Arkoff. Copyright © 1995 by Allyn and Bacon.

10. Recall a time when what you did made an important difference.
11. Recall a time when you made something good out of something bad.

1.In the space immediately below, describe the incident involved in the first item you circled on the previous pages and also describe your present feelings as you recall it.

2. In the space immediately below, describe the incident involved in the second item you circled on the previous pages and also describe your present feelings as you recall it.

3. In the space immediately below, describe the incident involved in the third item you circled on the previous pages and also describe your feelings as you recall it.

Question 3

Beliefs

What Truths and Rules Govern My Life?

Whether we know it or not, each of us is a philosopher. We have arrived at a philosophy of life or a system of motivating beliefs that influences our feelings, thoughts, and actions. Our philosophy includes our *values*—our beliefs about what is worthwhile—but it includes many other kinds of beliefs as well. These beliefs lead us to adopt certain attitudes and to set up certain rules for living.

A *belief* is an assumption or a conclusion that something is factual. It is our idea that something is true or false. It is the acceptance of a proposition or a teaching. For example, I may believe that my world is a reliable and friendly place and that I may attain what I need and wish in life. Or, by contrast, I may believe that my world is unreliable or hostile and that there is no assurance my needs and wishes will be met.

"At the age of twenty-two I believed myself to be unextinguishable," Siegfried Sassoon wrote in his memoirs. That's a central belief to sustain one. In my clinical practice I have worked with some persons who had an opposite belief: that they were losers or vanquished by life—although perhaps not completely or they wouldn't have shown up at my office.

Some famous people have much-quoted beliefs. Baseball's combative Leo Durocher fervently believed in a bit of fierceness; concerning an unfierce team he tersely remarked, "Nice guys finish last." Football's Vince Lombardi held a similar belief: "Winning isn't everything. It is the only thing." One of "Yogi" Berra's beliefs—"It ain't over till it's over"—has kept many a contender contending to the end.

Stop for a moment and think of the beliefs you have that influence the way you live your life. Do you believe in God? In a life everlasting? In sticking up for your rights no matter what? In saving your money for a rainy day? In always doing the best you can? Do you believe that honesty is the best policy? That people are basically good? That life is truly what you make it?

Not all our beliefs are supported by objective facts; some are supported only by our feelings or intuitions (Sappington, 1990). We sometimes say we can't prove something, but we have "a gut feeling" that it is so, or perhaps it is something we believe "in our bones." Our fact-supported and feeling-supported beliefs may agree with each other or be at considerable variance. For example, we may not feel comfortable associating with a person who has a particular disease although we know for a fact we are in no danger.

Beliefs may be distinguished from attitudes. An *attitude* is an evaluation of something or a stance that is taken in reference to it. In our attitude, we show whether we like or dislike something or consider it good or bad.

Beliefs and attitudes go hand in hand. For example, if I believe that mine is a good and provident world, my attitude will likely be one of trust or optimism. But if I believe my world to be threatening or unreliable, my attitude will probably be one of suspicion or pessimism (Erikson, 1982). If I believe my nature or human nature is basically good, I will make my way in my world differently than if I believe that I or human beings generally are fundamentally bad, hostile, or evil. (See Boxes 3.1 and 3.2.)

Box 3.1

Three Conceptions of Life

According to a French proverb: "Life is an onion, and one peels it crying." Not so, says a humanistic psychology textbook: "Life is a gift. Take it, unwrap it, appreciate it, use it, and enjoy it." What is your conception of life? Below, to help you think through your own beliefs, are three contrasting conceptions of life, which were deliberately chosen to be provocative.

1. Life is a staircase.

We all know where we want to be. We want to be rich, successful, ecstatically married to a beautiful woman or handsome man, have two gorgeous children, a job we are wild about, perfect mental and physical health, and read only good news in the paper. That's all at the top of the staircase. It's not easy to get there, but we are taught that it can be done if we work hard, are frugal, follow the laws of mental health, think positively, and persevere through adversity. And once we reach the top of that staircase, the world will be a wonderful golden room where we will live forever.

We learn in the fairy tales that once we triumph, we can live happily ever after. We learn in our theology that heaven (or the promised land) is permanent, unchanging perfect bliss. There will be pain along the way, and that is to be deplored; but at the end of the pain and at the top of the staircase, there is a nonchanging condition of perfect bliss, if only we find our way to it. Once we get to heaven or once we get to be a full professor, or once we marry the beautiful girl who is now unavailable, the strife is over and beauty will be ours forever.

2. Life is a roller coaster.

Life is a roller coaster. It goes up; it goes down. It goes rocketing around curves and creeping through straight places. It gives us extraordinarily breathtaking views of the amusement park and drags us through the depths where squalling kids are getting candied apples stuck in each other's hair. It never stops. It never runs backward. It never deviates a hair from the mysterious track laid out for it. We ride in the middle of the train and can't see what's ahead—at least, not very far ahead.

The roller coaster is on a journey of its own. We cannot affect that journey one iota. All we can do is go with it and ride differently in different parts of the cycle. We could get off if we wanted to, but we know what happens to people who get out of roller coasters in mid-trip. We can try to control it if we wish, but it's a futile and heartbreaking task which at best will put us in real danger. There is really nothing to do but sensitively gear our shouting and holding on and tension-relaxation patterns to the ride, and above all enjoy it. We're going to take the trip whether we want to or not, and so we may as well enjoy it. (Edited from Kahn, Kroeber, & Kingsbury, 1988)

3. Life is a path going nowhere (but hopefully one with a heart).

This question is one that only a very old man asks. My benefactor told me about it once when I was young, but my blood was too vigorous for me to understand it. I will tell you what it is: Does this path have a heart? All paths are the same: they lead nowhere. They are paths going through the bush, or into the bush. In my own life I could say that I have traversed long, long paths, but I am not anywhere. My benefactor's question has meaning now.

Does this path have a heart? If it does, the path is good; if it doesn't, it is of no use. Both paths lead nowhere; but one has a heart, the other doesn't. One makes for a joyful journey; as long as you follow it, you are one with it. The other will make you curse your life. One makes you strong; the other weakens you. (From Castaneda, 1968, p. 76)

Beliefs spawn rules. We are constantly acquiring beliefs or making assumptions about our world and adopting rules necessary to get by in it. Children's beliefs and rules can be overly absolute and overly inclusive. For example: Strangers are dangerous (belief), so never talk to strangers (rule). Or: Only bad people tell lies (belief), so always tell the truth (rule). As we grow, we move away from absolute and all-inclusive rules to those that take into account the circumstances of a situation (Beck, 1985).

We are heavily invested in some of our beliefs. They are "cherished beliefs," and we are reluctant to let them go, no matter what the facts seem to be. They comfort us and make us feel important or secure. For example, we may cherish the belief that we are better than someone else or that our group is superior to another, even though we have considerable evidence to the contrary.

One widely shared cherished belief is the *just-world hypothesis*, the belief that the world—or, at least, *our* world—is a just place where one gets what one deserves (Lerner, 1980). It's reassuring to think that in our world good things generally happen to good people (which we are) and that bad things are usually reserved for bad people (which we are not). When bad things happen to seem-

---

Box 3.2

Three Conceptions of Human Nature

Do you believe human nature is inherently good or inherently evil? Or are human beings born basically neutral, with the capacity for becoming either? Below are the contrasting views of three prominent psychologists: Sigmund Freud (founder of psychoanalysis), John B. Watson (father of behaviorism), and Carl R. Rogers (originator of person-centered personality theory, which was earlier known as nondirective and client-centered). (Adapted from Morris, 1990.)

1. Human nature as essentially evil.

. . . men are not gentle, friendly creatures wishing for love, who simply defend themselves if they are attacked. . . . A powerful measure of desire for aggressiveness has to be reckoned as part of their instinctual endowment. The result is that their neighbor is to them not only a possible helper or sexual object, but also a temptation to them to gratify their aggressiveness . . . to seize his possessions, to humiliate him, to cause him pain, to torture and to kill him. . . .

Anyone who calls to mind the atrocities of the early migrations, of the invasion of the Huns or by the so-called Mongols under Jenghiz Kahn and Tamurlane, of the sack of Jerusalem by the pious crusaders, even indeed the horrors of the last world-war, will have to bow his head humbly before the truth of this view of man.

—*Sigmund Freud,* Civilization and Its Discontents

2. Human nature as neutral.

In short, the cry of the behaviorist is, "Give me the baby and my world to bring it up in and I'll make it crawl and walk; I'll make it climb and use its hands in constructing buildings of stone or wood; I'll make it a thief, a gunman, or a dope fiend. The possibility of shaping in any direction is almost endless. Even gross differences in anatomical structure limit us far less than you think. Take away man's hand and I will make him write, use a typewriter, drive an automobile, paint, and draw with his toes. Cut off his legs and paralyze his trunk muscles so that he will be bedridden, but give me only his hands and arms, and I'll have him playing the violin, writing, and doing a thousand things. Make him blind and he can still play ice hockey, shoot with some degree of skill, read and write, model, and earn his living in a hundred different ways. Rob him of his ear at birth and I can teach him to carry on a conversation with you by watching you speak. Make him a deaf mute and I will still build you a Helen Keller."

—*John B. Watson,* The Ways of Behaviorism

3. Human nature as essentially good.

One of the most revolutionary concepts to grow out of our clinical experience is the growing recognition that the innermost core of man's nature, the deepest layers of his personality, the base of his "animal nature," is positive in nature—is basically socialized, forward-moving, rational and realistic. . . . The basic nature of the human being, when functioning freely, is constructive and trustworthy.

—*Carl R. Rogers,* On Becoming a Person

ingly good people, we may look for reasons to prove that they weren't all that good or that they brought the bad upon themselves. When bad things happen to us, we may search for the good within the bad—perhaps being grateful that the bad wasn't worse or using it as an opportunity to grow. Or we may undergo a "crisis in belief" and be forced to reexamine what we believed to be true (Barron, 1968).

In his widely read book *When Bad Things Happen to Good People*, Rabbi Harold Kushner (1981) discusses his own crisis when his first-born son succumbed to a disease that caused him to age rapidly and die in his teens. Out of this experience came Kushner's belief in a loving and compassionate but not omnipotent God. It is a God who cannot prevent misfortunes caused by the chaotic randomness of the world but who can give persons the strength to bear the pain and help themselves and others.

Research with a group of undergraduate "victims" (those who had suffered the death of a parent or sibling, incest, rape, accident resulting in serious disability, or fire destroying their home) found that they held more negative views of themselves and their worlds than did undergraduates without these experiences. These events had apparently served to disrupt the victims' assumptive worlds. Even though they had experienced the negative events many years before the study, the victims continued to regard their worlds as malevolent and themselves as vulnerable (Janoff-Bulman, 1989, 1992).

Some beliefs capture us, often without our full awareness or understanding; and these beliefs, as Dorothy Rowe (1982) writes, can "become an unseen power directing our choices and so determining our lives" (p. 112). As an example, Rowe suggests that we consider a child who is born into a world where no one wants him and where there seems to be no place for him as he is passed from home to home. He makes for himself what seems to be a sensible rule: "Trust nobody." Although this rule seems necessary for survival, in the long run it devastates his ability to form relationships. If he manages to go beyond his rule—to trust someone a little—mistrust may still lurk like a worm in a bud. Since he expects disappointment, he is quick to find it. Rowe continues:

> The axiomatic rules that we learn as children contain predictions of what our life would be. Some children learn to expect little. "Keep out of trouble and you won't suffer much pain" is the bleak rule on which many people fashion their lives, eschewing joy, and being thankful for an absence of pain. Some children learn to relish small pleasures and so find happiness in simple, unambitious lives. Some children are taught that if they meet certain standards of behavior, rewards will follow as night the day. For some fortunate children this proves to be the case. But not all children are so fortunate. Some parents, often loving, caring parents, set their children standards which are nearly impossible to live by. (p. 97)

A case discussed by James Bugental (1976, 1987) has much in common with Rowe's "trust nobody" child. "Kate," in psychotherapy with Bugental, had felt repeatedly abandoned (psychologically) by her parents as a child and grew up believing that she must be totally self-reliant. Two of her basic rules were "to need no one" and "to rigidly control her emotions since they were apt to undermine her other intentions" (1987, p. 6). "In therapy," Bugental writes, "she had to confront the futility of her tight, limited way of being and her long-suppressed hunger for relationships" (p. 6).

Quite early in our lives, we become aware that different people profess or follow different rules and that we can to some extent choose or make our own. Even so, some sets of rules acquire a not-to-be questioned quality, possibly because they emanated from very significant persons. Beryl, a woman studied by Rowe, recalled that—unlike her father, who was easygoing and affectionate—her mother never held and cuddled her. Her mother, immaculate and a perfectionist, expected Beryl also to be immaculate and perfect. When Rowe asked Beryl why she had accepted her mother's rules rather than her father's, she replied that she did so because her mother was the dominant figure and she wanted to please her. Thus, Beryl bound herself with the less friendly set of rules.

One way we have of distancing ourselves from significant others is to deny their beliefs and reject their rules. In her memoirs, Kitty Dukakis notes that her mother (whose hypercritical nature devastated her daughter's self-esteem) had two "guiding principles" or rules (which really seem to be just one): "Never show people what you are actually thinking; don't reveal yourself to others" (p. 45). Unlike Beryl, Kitty Dukakis (1990) did not bind herself to her mother's rules. In fact, one less than kind reviewer called her book, whose title is *Now You Know,* "a lung-bursting Bronx cheer directed at the very idea of decorous forbearance" (Ferguson, 1990, p. A14).

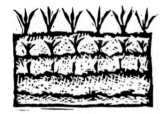

Box 3.3

Beliefs: What Truths and Rules Govern My Life?

Seedthoughts

1. We become what we contemplate.
   —*Alphonse de Chateaubrillant*

2. All that we are is the result of what we have thought.
   —*Dhammapada*

3. Your mind will be like its habitual thoughts: for the soul becomes dyed with the color of its thoughts.
   —*Marcus Aurelius*

4. There is nothing good or bad, but thinking makes it so.
   —*William Shakespeare,* Hamlet

5. The mind is its own place, and in itself
   Can make a Heav'n of Hell, a hell of Heav'n.
   —*John Milton,* Paradise Lost

6. Men are disturbed not by things, but by the views which they take of them.
   —*Epictetus*

7. The tendency to attribute unhappiness to external sources is widespread. It is one of the most serious psychological mistakes. People say: "His remark upset me!" "Her comments hurt me!" In reality, remarks, comments and statements do not hurt or upset people. They upset themselves over these statements or incidents.
   —*Arnold Lazarus and Allen Fay*

8. Sticks and stones may break my bones but words can never hurt me.
   —*old saying*

9. A mind stretched to a new idea never resumes its original dimension.
   —*Oliver Wendell Holmes*

10. Some things have to be believed to be seen.
    —*Ralph Hodgson*

11. My philosophy is: You can measure your life's worth by how many people you serve. If you work for your husband, you work for a single individual. If you work for your family, you are valued by that family. If you work for a community or society, you are precious to them. . . . How many people are you working for?
    —*Aye Saung*

12. My advice to you is not to inquire why or whither, but just to enjoy your ice cream while it's on your plate—that's my philosophy.
    —*Thornton Wilder,* The Skin of Our Teeth

Rational and Irrational Beliefs

We could not get along without our beliefs. To make our way in the world, we need to know what is true and what isn't true. But some of our beliefs may be manifestly false, and some may be firmly held even though they cannot be proven one way or the other.

Rational Beliefs

A *rational belief* is one that is logical or reasonable or capable of proof. However, in human affairs it is sometimes difficult to determine whether a belief is valid or not. Human beings not only discover reality; they create it. By fervently believing something, we may help make it so.

One of the tasks of psychotherapy is to help the person see that what he or she harmfully believes to be true is not true or need not be—that, for example, one is not a prisoner of one's past history if one chooses not to be. Albert Ellis, probably the most influential of current American therapists, writes, "My approach to psychotherapy is to zero in, as quickly as possible, on the client's philosophy of life; to get him to see exactly what this is and how it is inevitably self-defeating, and to persuade him to . . . profoundly change it" (quoted in Warga, 1988, p. 58).

We like to think that we are rational beings, that what we believe is true, and that the rules we make for ourselves are necessary rules. We feel comfortable in associating with people who have similar beliefs and rules. This agreement makes us feel we are right in what we profess, even though we may not be able to fully prove that we are.

Generally, rational beliefs are consensual or widely shared, but this is not always true. Today almost everyone believes the world is round, but there was a time when almost no one did.

Irrational Beliefs

An *irrational belief* is one that is adhered to although it has been disproved or is unreasonable, illogical, or manifestly wrong. Some irrational beliefs are consensual, or at least partly so, in that they are shared by a particular group of persons despite proof to the contrary. Many human fears are irrational in that the feared object or situation is manifestly harmless or nearly so.

Ellis (1990a) makes a special distinction between rational beliefs (which are reasonable, realistic, and have satisfying consequences) and irrational beliefs (which are unreasonable, unrealistically demanding, and have self-defeating consequences). Box 3.4 presents a list of thirteen beliefs that would qualify as irrational, but each is followed immediately with a rational replacement (which appears in italics). (Later in the chapter you will be encouraged to dispute your irrational beliefs and replace them with more rational ones.)

You will note that many of the irrational beliefs in Box 3.4 exhibit a "must" or "should" demandingness. Ellis writes that there are three "Major Musts" that afflict virtually all human beings to some degree:

I *must* (do well, be approved by people I find important, etc.)

You *must* (treat me fairly, treat me nicely, etc.)

The world *must* (give me what I want quickly and easily, keep me comfortable and free from major hassles, etc.)

Box 3.4

Irrational Beliefs and Their Rational Replacements

Psychologist Albert Ellis (1957, 1973a, 1977a, 1990a) makes a special distinction between "rational" and "irrational" beliefs. Rational beliefs promote feelings of well-being and adaptive behavior. Irrational beliefs produce dysphoric feelings and maladaptive behavior. Therefore, rational beliefs are self-enhancing while irrational beliefs are self-defeating.

The list of beliefs below has been drawn up from the work of Ellis as well as Walen, DiGiuseppe, and Wessler (1980) and Johnson (1993). The first item of each pair states a common *but irrational* belief—one that is self-defeating. The second item of the pair (the one in italics) is a rational replacement—one that is self-enhancing. To me, the second belief of each pair is clearly preferable to the first, but not all my students or clients agree; I tell them they *must* agree with me—it will be *awful* if they don't!

1. What I do I must do well.
   Having to always do well could keep me from doing many things that would be worthwhile; it's all right for me to be an imperfect, fallible human being.

2. I must always please others and live up to their expectations.
   I don't have to prove to myself that I am all right by getting everyone's approval; I only need my own approval and that of a few select others.

3. It's awful when things are not the way I would like them to be.
   Things are frequently not the way I would like them to be; I can use up my energies in bemoaning that fact or in making things better.

4. I need someone stronger than myself on whom I can rely.
   I can learn to rely on myself.

5. I must find perfect solutions to my problems.
   There are few perfect solutions in life, and endlessly searching for them can keep me from hitting on good-enough solutions that will let me get on with the business of living.

6. I must always be treated fairly.
   Life often isn't fair, and unless I see a way to make it fairer, I would better accept the fact and enjoy myself despite it.

7. Since I have always been this way, I will always be this way.
   I can change myself by believing in myself and working to change.

8. I must become upset about other people's problems.
   I can be concerned about others and try to help them if I wish without becoming upset; if I become as upset as they may be, I will not help anyone.

9. I should be very anxious about bad things that could happen.
   I will work to avoid bad things but accept them if they are inevitable, knowing I can manage whatever happens; constant worry won't help.

10. People (including myself) who behave badly toward others should be blamed and punished.
    What is important is seeing that wrong-doing doesn't continue, that restitution is made if possible, and that the same mistakes are not made in the future; I do not have to blame and punish myself or others for what is past.

11. I should be comfortable and without pain at all times.
    There is seldom gain without pain, and deadening myself to my problems is seldom a solution; I can tolerate some pain and discomfort although I don't like it.

12. My life must be free of major hassles or troubles.
    There is a myth that things are supposed to go right, but if anything can go wrong, it will; I can face, accept, and work on my hassles without being upset by them.

13. I must have someone to love with all my heart and who loves me in the same way.
    Human beings are imperfect and they love imperfectly; I can manage with an imperfect love or even without love, as indeed many persons do.

Making absolute demands of this kind is bound to lead to frustration. Ellis (who enjoys a bit of irreverence or mischief) calls this kind of demandingness "musturbation," and folks who constantly tell themselves what they must do or at least should do are said to be "shoulding on themselves." Whatever we call it, the frustration it engenders leads to four kinds of distorted or twisted and inevitably self-defeating thinking:

1. Awfulizing: It's awful, terrible, catastrophic that things are not as they must be or should be.

2. I can't stand-it-itis: I can't stand it that things are not as they must be or should be.

3. Damning of self and others: I and/or you must be rotten, etc. that things are not as they must be or should be.

4. Overgeneralizing: This proves that nothing will ever be as it must be or should be.

Ellis points out that one often starts with sensible and realistic observations but winds up with conclusions that do not follow and do not make sense. Suppose, for example, I start with the observation that it would be wonderful if Leslie loved me. But I proceed to the belief that Leslie *has* to love me. And furthermore: Leslie *must!* I find it *awful* if Leslie doesn't. More than that: I *can't stand it. Damn! Damn!* Life will never be worth living again.

A woman in one of my classes said that these four irrationalities were perfectly illustrated in her response to her divorce. When the possibility of divorce became apparent, she felt that the marriage *must* continue regardless of the circumstances; nobody in her family had ever had a divorce, and she was determined it would not happen to her. As her husband moved to make the divorce a reality, she began awfulizing, feeling that the situation was terrible and, more than that, unbearable; she felt as if she were on the verge of a nervous breakdown. Then she began to damn her husband for doing this to her and also to damn herself for whatever she might have done to contribute to the problem. She saw no future for herself.

Like the absolutistic beliefs of children, the irrational beliefs of adults often contain an element of truth, but one that is distorted or exaggerated. Consider a person who believes it's a hostile dog-eat-dog world in which the best rule is to get in the first bite (or at least show your fangs). It is true that people are sometimes hostile or difficult, and it may be necessary sometimes to come on strong or to be firm or blunt; but people who always anticipate the worst often see threat where none exists and create needless problems for themselves (Jakubowski & Lange, 1978).

Religious Beliefs

Some of our most important beliefs relate to our religious faith. Americans are firmly attached to religion. Recent national surveys show that about six in ten believe "religion can answer all or most of today's problems." About seven in ten Americans are church members, and four in ten attend religious services in a typical week (DeStefano, 1990; Gallup & Newport, 1990). Approximately nine out of ten Americans believe in the existence of God or a universal spirit (Gilbert, 1988; Greeley, 1989; Patterson & Kim, 1991). Respondents think of God chiefly as creator, but other dominant images include healer, friend, redeemer, father, master, and judge. Whatever their image, most respondents feel close to God (*General Social Surveys,* 1991). However, from their recent national survey, designed to produce candid responses and published as *The Day America Told the Truth,* James Patterson and Peter Kim (1991) conclude that more Americans are coming to think of God in abstract terms and less as a God who intervenes in human affairs.

In the last several decades, belief in the literal truth of the Bible has declined (Greeley, 1989). In a recent poll, approximately one-quarter to one-third of the respondents said that they believe the Bible is the actual word of God and to be accepted word for word. Approximately half said that they believe the Bible is inspired but not to be taken literally. The remainder regarded the Bible as a set of fables, legends, moral precepts, or history (Gilbert, 1988).

For some of us, our religious faith is what is most important in our lives. Our religious beliefs have the power to transform, guide, comfort, and sustain us. This is often true for those of us who have had a "born-again" experience. (In a 1987 *Los Angeles Times* poll, 43 percent of the respondents indicated that they had had such an experience.) Witness the testimony of this born-again Christian, Ernest Shippam (1968):

> Becoming a Christian was not just turning over a new leaf, going through a form of service, a brain-washing acceptance, or the mere resolution of emotional conflict.
>
> Becoming a Christian was not learning something, but experiencing something.
>
> Becoming Christian has meant for me a changed life, a life changed by the Holy Spirit, a life lived in the power of Jesus Christ himself.
>
> Becoming a Christian, I have discovered, is knowing a Person. That Person is Jesus Christ. (p. 191)

Our religious beliefs may also have the power to arouse anxiety, guilt, and self-condemnation. CNN's Ted Turner (1991) graphically describes the loss of his faith—a faith that had early convinced him he was born in sin and, unless he strived mightily, destined for hell:

> So, for quite a while, I thought I was going to be a missionary. I got permission to go to church on Wednesday nights *and* Saturdays, as well as Sundays, plus vespers and all that other stuff. I mean, I was into it, okay? Then my sister got terminally ill. It took her five years to finally pass away. It was real harsh, and I prayed for her—I prayed and prayed and prayed, and nothing happened. And I couldn't understand why this loving, wonderful God that I had been taught was so kind would allow someone to suffer so—someone small, someone who hadn't done anything wrong. I prayed and nothing happened, of course, and so I thought to myself, "I'm not sure that I want any part of this."
>
> Now, I hadn't said this to anybody, but if God is love and if he is all-powerful, then why does he allow these things to happen? And there's this interpretation that says, you know, it's his will. Well, if it's his will, I can't be enthusiastic about it.
>
> So, I began to lose faith. And the more I lost it, the better I felt. (pp. 12–13)

How much do our religious beliefs influence our lives? In some cases, like those of Shippam and Turner, they obviously have considerable effect. My father's Judaism was a powerful force in his life; I think he would have been lost without it. However, Christopher Morley passed along a comment made by his father concerning his Presbyterian faith—that it didn't prevent sin, it just took the fun out of it. Some partial support for this bit of cynicism has been provided by pollsters George Gallup, Jr., and Frank Newport (1990). They write, "Despite the stated beliefs of Americans in the transcendent, and their stated attachment to religion, survey findings on their depth of commitment are less impressive" (p. 33). The findings indicate several gaps, these among them:

> The "knowledge gap"—between Americans' professed faith and their lack of the most basic knowledge about that faith.

The "ethics gap"—between Americans' beliefs and how we like to think of ourselves, and how we actually are. Religious beliefs do not change people's lives to the degree one would expect from their level of professed faith. (p. 33)

When we know that an individual is a believer, what can we surmise about the likelihood that he or she is a caring, generous, loving, and helpful person? "Virtually nothing" is the answer of altruism scholar Alfie Kohn (1989, 1990). Summing up the many types of research (including one in which seminary students—some on their way to a talk on the parable of the Good Samaritan—walked right past a man slumped and groaning in a doorway), Kohn concludes that no connection has been found between religious affiliation or belief and activities taken voluntarily and intentionally to benefit another.

Gallup agrees with Kohn that the typical "churched" and "unchurched" are much alike, but his findings lead him to conclude that the most committed believers are a "breed apart": "When you get to the level of the truly, devotionally committed who live out their faith, they are dramatically different. They are more involved in charity, more tolerant, more ethical and much happier" (quoted in Cornell, 1992, p. A6). In the survey by Patterson and Kim (1991), respondents who described themselves as "very religious" scored higher in morality. They were more willing to die for their beliefs, more truthful, more committed to family. They were less likely to use drugs or commit petty crime. They were also more at peace with themselves and more satisfied with their lives. Other research has shown that, compared to nonreligious persons, those who are more religious are less involved in drugs and alcohol or in premarital and extramarital sex (Gorsuch, 1980; Spilka, Hood, & Gorsuch, 1985).

Being religious and attending church are correlated with better health, even with allowances made for demographic differences and health habits. Perhaps the social ties and support that religious groups provide their members and also the calming effects of faith and prayer are at least partly responsible for this finding. Specifically, regular church attendance has been found to be associated with lower blood pressure and a lower incidence of cardiovascular disease, cirrhosis of the liver, pulmonary emphysema, and abnormal cervical cytology (Comstock & Patridge, 1972; Graham et al., 1978). Among a large group of black Virginians, religious involvement provided significant protection against depression (Watts, Milburn, Brown, & Gary, 1985). In a group of elderly Connecticut residents who were poor both in pocket and in health, those with higher levels of religiousness were at reduced risk of dying (Zuckerman, Kasl, & Ostfeld, 1984).

The Power of Beliefs

Beliefs have power. We act upon our beliefs and our beliefs act upon us. The influence of religious beliefs was just noted, and other beliefs can be similarly influential. Current medical research suggests that beliefs can influence physiological reality and that people may sicken and die or get well and live because of what they expect or believe to be true.

A *placebo,* according to my *American Heritage Dictionary,* is "a substance containing no medication and prescribed or given to reinforce a patient's expectation to get well." Placebos can have considerable effect because, in stimulating expectations, they turn on the body's own pharmacy and self-healing mechanisms (Cousins, 1989; Justice, 1988). Summarizing the relevant research, psychologist Robert Ornstein and preventive-medicine physician David Sobel (1989) write, "What you believe and expect about your health may be more important than objective assessments made by your doctor. People who expect bad health get it; they die earlier and have more diseases than others who view themselves as healthy. Even sick people do better when they believe themselves to be healthy than when they believe themselves ill" (p. 30).

As noted in Chapter 2, our expectations can become self-fulfilling prophecies or beliefs. If we believe we're slated to fail, we're more likely to fail. If we believe we're going to succeed, we increase the chances that we will succeed.

When we believe in ourselves, we tend to work harder because we are certain our efforts will pay off; and this combination of belief and hard work increases our chances of succeeding. Whatever the outcome (many outcomes cannot be clearly labeled as success or failure), we are more likely to see success in it. We take success as a confirmation of our expectation and ability and feel confident of future success. Even failure need not be considered a setback since it can be seen as the source of helpful experience, information, and challenge.

When we don't believe in ourselves, we tend to avoid challenging situations or approach them halfheartedly, and this attitude is not likely to lead to success. We are set to interpret the results as a failure or, if successful, as a fluke. We are more likely to stick to sure things; but succeeding in such things, of course, is not very rewarding (Langer & Dweck, 1973).

When we believe something, we are disposed—sometimes even compelled—to behave in a particular way. If, for example, we see the hand of divine providence in every notable event, we may live our lives quite differently than if we believe that "God helps them who help themselves" (which appears to be a proverb in all languages). If we believe in marriage as a lifetime (even eternal) commitment, our approach will be very different from that of English author W. Somerset Maugham, who said, "Marriage is a very good thing, but I think it's a mistake to make a habit of it."

Not all beliefs are compelling. The "ethics gap" between what we profess and what we do was noted earlier. There are other gaps as well; for example, we may know for a fact that smoking may kill us and yet go on smoking. We may believe in the primary importance of the family but spend little time at home, or we may believe in the sanctity of marriage but stray occasionally into beds away from home.

Human beings like to be—even strive to be—consistent. When we have two cognitions (beliefs, thoughts, or attitudes) that are inconsistent, we feel uncomfortable and are motivated to reduce this inconsistency. This state of internal discord is called *cognitive dissonance* (Festinger, 1957). For example, if we believe that we should spend considerable time with our children and, on the other hand, are so dedicated to our careers that we spend little time at home, this inconsistency or dissonance can be upsetting. We can reduce dissonance by modifying one or both of the inconsistent cognitions or by adding a new cognition that remedies the inconsistency. For example, we may tell ourselves, "After all, our kids have lots of friends" or "Right now our devotion to our job is crucial to the family's welfare in the long run." Or we add a new cognition or belief: we decide it's quality—not quantity—that counts, and the time we spend with our kids is, of course, "quality time." (As an exercise, readers who believe it's bad to smoke but have been puffing away today, readers who believe they must lose weight but had sausage and waffles for breakfast or the double chocolate suicide cake at lunch, and those who believe they absolutely must study harder but instead watched TV last night might review their own dissonance reduction maneuvers.)

Our beliefs may retain their power over us even though we come to doubt them. We continue to subscribe to them and pay service to the rules they spawn because they have become part of us. Without them, we would not be who we are, and there would be nothing to hold on to. Better something we once believed in and now only half believe than nothing at all.

The real failure of the protagonists in a number of Arthur Miller's plays is their inability to face up to the truth of their situation. In an interview, Miller (1980) was asked why these individuals didn't face up to the truth. The playwright replied, "Because too much has been invested already; people make an investment in falsehood, invest a whole lifetime in it. It's not an inability to see the truth, it's an inability to start all over again. An age comes when it's impossible, so you continue on until the grave, to reinforce it, to justify it, because to overturn it is too painful or expensive."

Challenges to Beliefs

We change from instant to instant, and our world constantly changes too. But we cannot accommodate a constantly changing world, so we "freeze" it and ignore these changes until at some point we are forced to notice that our beliefs in ourselves and our worlds are disconfirmed and need reexamination. We grow when we acknowledge the changes that have occurred, allow the disconfirmed beliefs to shatter and disappear, and form new beliefs to accommodate the new reality (Jourard, 1968). But at times—despite the evidence—we try not to notice the changes in order to keep the disconfirmed beliefs from shattering. For example, we resist noticing the infidelities of our mate or the signs of the incipient failure of a crucial investment or business venture. We want to believe that our world hasn't changed.

Certain times or situations in life particularly challenge our belief systems. We may confront rapid change or devastating failure, or we may be brought into a new community that does not support our beliefs about the world or about ourselves. In their first year away at college, for example, students can find themselves exposed to peers and teachers with very different beliefs and rules from those that the students encountered at home. Belief in oneself can also be shaken as one suddenly seems to be a much smaller fish in a much larger pond. What Peter Madison (1969) has called "college shock" is evident in this senior's recollection of his freshman year (he had come from a small high school where he had excelled without working very hard):

For about the first two days, I had a pretty high opinion of myself, and from there on out for the rest of the year I felt like a midget among the giants. In high school I was a big man. I came down here with the thought that there would be no problems in college, and that I had a pretty good background;

when I got down here I found that this wasn't very true, academically, socially, just all around. Right from the first I would run into people who had definite ideas about politics, and I hardly even knew who the people they talked about were, and this sort of thing. It didn't seem like I knew very much; my confidence level wasn't very high. . . . It was a kind of an overwhelming situation." (pp. 98–99)

A participant in one of Warren Farrell's men's groups experienced a similar shock and challenge to belief. This participant, 41 years old, married, father of two children, a believer in the American Goddess Success, had put his family life and other activities on hold while he made his way to a senior partnership in a law firm. He had played the game according to what he thought was a standard set of beliefs and rules: you work hard and provide to show your family you love them. When he made it to the top, he found success flat; his relationship with his wife and children and even himself had been badly damaged along the way. Fighting back tears, he told the group: "I feel like I've spent 40 years of my life working as hard as I can to become someone I don't even like." He added, "What really gets me . . . what really gets me angry, is that I did everything I was supposed to for 40 years, did it better than almost any other man I know, and lost everyone I love in the process . . . including myself" (1984, p. 19).

As was noted earlier, we strive for consistency, and a serious problem can result when we are caught up in conflicting sets of beliefs, each challenging the other and each with its own hold on us. A friend of mine found himself torn between the fundamental religious beliefs and practices of his mother—a system in which he had been raised—and the more implicit humanistic philosophy of his father. The rituals and symbolism of his mother's faith had a strong emotional appeal that was not provided by his father's philosophy, but he found the latter more consistent with his scientific interests. "Gloria," a woman in therapy with James Bugental (1987), demonstrated a somewhat similar conflict.

> Gloria came from a deeply religious family in which all standards of conduct were based on interpretations of the Bible. She grew up to feel mistrust of her own impulses and dependence on the teaching of her church. As she matured and went away to college, she found herself in an emotionally wrenching conflict between a view of the world in which "good" and "bad" were sharply contrasted and a more relativistic view to which her intelligence was leading her. Relinquishing the traditional guide to her life seemed tantamount to "giving in to the Devil," but trying to live by that tradition became increasingly constricting.
>
> She came to therapy with complaints of unexpected bouts of temper, sleeplessness, and fear of suffocation. It was many months before the underlying conflict was evident to Gloria—and, of course, that conflict was only one of the more salient issues of her whole life situation. Working out a resolution to the contradictions in which she was enmeshed involved great anguish and struggle. Eventually she arrived at a way of being that gave space for her intellect's seekings while preserving some measure of value for her background. (p. 6)

We can protect our beliefs from challenge by refusing to consider conflicting ideas. One of my colleagues once had a sign on his desk that read: "My mind is made up. Don't confuse me with facts." Very opinionated persons are sometimes referred to as having a closed mind. Such persons are set in their beliefs. They don't receive and consider information that is at variance with what they already believe. A person who is not opinionated or who has an open mind is able to consider new information on its own merits.

Belief systems serve two powerful but conflicting systems at the same time: our need to know reality and our need to ward off the threatening aspects of reality (Rokeach, 1960). When the first need is predominant, we tend to be more open to all the data. As the second becomes stronger, our mind begins to close except to data that reduce the threat.

In his book *The True Believer,* Eric Hoffer (1951) holds that persons of closed minds, blind faith, and greatly depreciated self-worth often are drawn to mass movements: "Faith in a holy cause is to a considerable extent a substitute for lost faith in ourselves. The less justified a man is in claiming excellence for his own self, the more ready he is to claim all excellence for his nation, his religion, his race or his holy cause" (p. 14).

Modifying Beliefs

How can we change an irrational belief? The first step is to become fully aware of this belief and the part it plays in our lives. The second step is to dispute this belief and arrive at a rational replacement—one that is realistic and self-enhancing. We zero in on the irrational belief and then argue with ourselves and work on ourselves until our rational belief has fully replaced the irrational one.

Becoming Aware of Irrational Beliefs

Some of our beliefs are never formulated into words, so we may not be fully aware of them or of their effect on our lives. Sometimes the reason that seemingly "little" things upset us so much is that they rub against an important but not fully recognized assumption. The first step in modifying an irrational belief is to gain full awareness of it and of its hold on us.

Moments of surprising upset—when seemingly innocuous situations trigger extreme reactions—offer us the opportunity to gain some important insight. At those moments, we can check to see what we are thinking, what is going through our minds, what are we telling ourselves that is upsetting us so. This is not an easy task, because we are not accustomed to stop and think about our thinking; indeed, much of our thinking process consists of overlearned cognitive habits that have become automatic (Walen, DiGiuseppe, & Wessler, 1980). But by training ourselves to listen in, we can learn a lot about ourselves.

As we listen in and learn to pursue our thoughts, we may find that what we think has been upsetting us is only a distant reflection of a more basic belief. One technique for tracking down core beliefs is—when we are upset and awfulizing—to ask ourselves what is the worst thing that could happen and to keep asking it after each reply, so that we finally arrive at the ultimate worst. In the following interchange between a therapist and a client who is having trouble asserting himself with his wife, the client's core irrational belief—that he must have someone on whom he can depend—gradually is revealed.

> T: What's the worst that could happen if you stood up to your wife?
>
> C: She might leave me.
>
> T: What's the worst thing that could happen if your wife *did* leave you?
>
> C: I might not find another woman. My God!
>
> T: But let's suppose you never did find another woman. What's the worst that could happen then?
>
> C: I could get sick and no one would care for me.
>
> T: Well, what would be the worst thing about that?
>
> C: That would be the worst thing! That's so terrible I hate to even think about it. (Walen, DiGiuseppe, & Wessler, 1980, p. 90)

Another technique for getting at our more subtle irrational beliefs and the impossible rules and restrictions that they impose is to start with one of our musts or shoulds and to continue to ask ourselves "why" to each answer we give. This method is used by therapist Catherine Flanagan (1990), who describes a typical interaction between a therapist and a client who feels compelled to do something that he or she doesn't want to do:

> "I couldn't say no to his request, even though I wanted to."
> "Why?"
> "Because I would have felt guilty."
> "Why?"
> "Because people should be as obliging as possible."
> "Why?"
> "Because everyone should try to make everyone else as happy as possible."
> "Why?"
> "Because everyone should be as happy as possible all the time."
> "Why?"
> "Because when you are sad you waste time going over things, and you also bring others down, and these are both wrong."
> "Why?"
> "Because you shouldn't waste time. You should be on the go all the time, doing things that are useful and productive. You shouldn't bring others down, because it is wrong, and then you feel guilty."
> "Why?"
> "Because you should be in good spirits all the time." (pp. 106–107)

Reading through this chain of responses, one can see the unreasonable—even impossible—demands or beliefs that are involved. Converting all the pronouns to "I" and underlining all the shoulds and musts, one can see all the "shouldy" demands that this client is actually making on herself or himself: I *should* always be obliging, I *should* always be happy, I *should* never waste time, I *should* never bring others down, I *should* be on the go all the time doing useful productive things, I *should* be in good spirits all the time. Who could live up to that tall order?

Disputing and Replacing Irrational Beliefs

Once we become aware of a belief that is adversely affecting us, the next step is to refute or dispute this belief. We prove to ourselves that it is not true (or is wildly exaggerated) and that it is self-defeating. And we replace it with a more rational belief.

Albert Ellis (1977a) writes that we humans tend to attribute many of our responses to external stimuli, but this assumption is incorrect or partly so; rather, our beliefs largely determine what we feel and what we do in a situation. For example, there is an A (Activating experience or event); perhaps you get fired from a good job. This is followed by C (an emotional or behavioral Consequence); as a result of being fired, you feel very dejected and unable to look for another job. It could be erroneously assumed that A caused C, but actually C stemmed from B, your Belief about A. Your Belief may have been that you desperately need and must have that job, that it is awful that you lost it, and that you can't stand to be without it. If, instead, you told yourself that losing the job was unfortunate but not the end of the world, you would not have been so upset and unable to function.

Some two thousand years ago, the Greek philosopher Epictetus wrote that we are upset not by events but, rather, by the view we take of these events. Or, as Ellis writes, "A (Activating event) does not directly cause C (emotional or behavioral Consequence); B (your Belief about A) does" (p. 8). And, in many instances, it is our belief system that causes us to respond in one way rather than another; by changing our beliefs, we may bring about a considerable change in our lives.

Ellis recommends that when we detect irrational beliefs in ourselves, we Dispute them, prove to ourselves that they are not so, and surrender them so they can be replaced by more rational beliefs. The end result is that we wind up with a new Effect or philosophy that enables us to view ourselves, others, and the world in a more sensible way.

Let's use an example (and also see the diagram in Box 3.5). Suppose you want to try something new to add more dimension to your life, and suppose you are a perfectionist and are determined to do this new thing well, and suppose you find you are not too good at it and decide to give it up. That's the kind of situation that keeps many from having more fun in life. It could be charted like this:

A	Antecedent event:	I find I'm not doing well at this new thing.
B	Belief:	Whatever I do, I must do well.
C	Consequence:	I give it up.

The Consequence is due to my belief that I must do everything well. If I can successfully Dispute this Belief and replace it with a more rational one, I can produce a different Consequence for a new Effect. Suppose I convince myself that, although I want to do some things well, not everything needs to be done to perfection.

D	Dispute:	Having to do everything well can make everything into a test or a chore. This keeps me from new things that could make my life more interesting and more fun. Lots of people do lots of things and aren't all that good at everything they do. They seem to have more fun than I do. They don't seem to have to keep proving how good they are. Etc. Etc.
E	Effect:	I don't give up just because I'm not doing well. I worry less about how well I do. I have a richer, fuller, more enjoyable life.

Box 3.5

The ABCs of Ellis's ABCDE System

In Albert Ellis's rational-emotive system of psychotherapy, clients are persuaded to dispute their irrational beliefs in order to produce new and more rational effects.

As the first diagram indicates, if the belief triggered by an activating event is rational, the consequent feelings or experiences are rational. By contrast, if the belief is irrational, so are the consequent feelings or experiences.

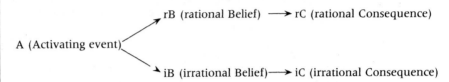

In the second diagram, an activating event has triggered an irrational belief. However, as the broken line shows, when this irrational belief is disputed and replaced with a rational one, a rational consequence is produced. Ellis calls this new consequence a new "effect" or E, thus completing his ABCDE.

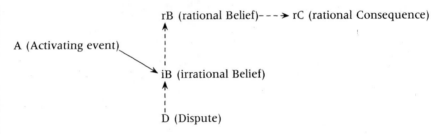

Ellis (1990a) advises his clients to keep seeking, discovering, and challenging their irrational beliefs. He tells them to take each irrational belief and keep asking themselves: "Why is this true?" Suppose their belief is: "I have to succeed in order to be a worthwhile person." They can then challenge themselves: "Where is the evidence that my worth to myself, and my enjoyment of living, utterly depends on my succeeding at something?" "In what way would I be totally unacceptable as a human if I failed at an important task or test?" (p. 97).

Psychiatrist David D. Burns (1990) has developed a technique called "Cost-Benefit Analysis" for disputing irrational beliefs and negative thoughts. Although most disputational methods are devised to show that irrational beliefs are not the truth, this method is calculated to show that an irrational belief is simply not a good deal, because its cost exceeds its benefits. Or, to say it another way, the belief has more disadvantages than advantages. Using this method, you simply list all the advantages of believing a particular belief in one column and all the disadvantages of believing it in another. Then you weigh the advantages against the disadvantages, allot each its fair portion of a total of 100 points, and possibly arrive at a new or revised attitude or belief. See Box 3.6 for an example of the use of this technique.

Once we dispute or challenge an irrational belief out of existence, we have implicitly arrived at a replacement, but it is helpful to make this new belief explicit. In many cases, the replacement belief will be just a softening or moderation of the old absolutistic or all-inclusive belief. In the example in Box 3.6, the old belief—that the person *must* have everyone's approval—becomes, in effect, that it

Box 3.6

Cost-Benefit Analysis

This technique for disputing irrational beliefs and negative thoughts, developed by psychiatrist David Burns, compares their advantages and disadvantages and awards each a certain portion of points out of a total of 100. The award of points is not made according to a formula; it is based on one's general impression. In the illustration below, the costs or disadvantages clearly outweigh the benefits or advantages, prompting the revision noted at the bottom of the form. Those wishing to work further on self-defeating thoughts would do well to read these books by Burns: *Feeling Good* and *The Feeling Good Handbook*.

COST-BENEFIT ANALYSIS*

The attitude or belief I want to change: __I must have everybody's approval__ __to be happy and worthwhile.__

Advantages of Believing This	Disadvantages of Believing This
1. It will feel good when people approve of me.	1. I'll feel lousy when people don't like me or approve of me.
2. I'll work hard to make people like me.	2. Other people will control my self-esteem.
3. I'll be very sensitive to other people's feelings.	3. People may not respect me in the long run if I don't stand up for what I believe in.
	4. I may be less sensitive to other people because I'll be so worried about criticism or conflict.

(35) —————— (65)

Revised attitude: __It can be great to have people like me and approve__ __of what I do. When people are critical of me, I can try to understand__ __their point of view.__

---

* Copyright © 1984 by David D. Burns, M.D., from *The Feeling Good Handbook*. New York: Plume, 1990.

would be great to have universal approval but one's failure to gain this approval isn't the end of the world; instead, it can provide an opportunity for insight.

Old, overlearned beliefs, like all old, overlearned habits, resist modification. Furthermore, beliefs that keep us from growing and moving along in our lives may still confer certain advantages that we are loath to give up. Consider a person who believes he is trapped by his past. Such a person may be comforted by the "fact" that he can't do anything about his life, because if nothing can be done, there is no need to try (Gillett, 1992).

We need to constantly keep working on irrational and self-limiting beliefs, stopping them, disputing them, and reinforcing their replacements. We tell ourselves that we do not choose to believe the old belief anymore or to be governed by the rules it spawns. Instead, it's a new ball game with new and better rules.

One useful kind of practice makes use of imagery. We imagine that we are in some situation that would ordinarily be upsetting, allow ourselves to experience that upset, and determine the assumptions or beliefs that caused it. What are we telling ourselves that is upsetting? Then, still imagining, we see our upset as diminishing—for example, our anxiety becoming simply concern—and note the cognitive shift that has occurred. What are we telling ourselves now that is acting to calm us? What new assumptions are we making? What new beliefs have we arrived at? Below, a group of therapists illustrate how this method works. Their hypothetical client is a familiar one—a person who believes he must be perfect:

> T: Now, I want you to close your eyes and imagine yourself back in the situation in which you felt so anxious yesterday. Can you do that?

Wait until clients indicate they have the image.

> C: Yes.
> T: Now, I want you to make yourself feel anxious right now, as you did yesterday. Signal me when you're feeling anxious.

Wait for the client's signal.

> C: (nods)
> T: OK, now tell me what thoughts are going through your head to make you feel anxious.

Wait for the client's response, which will be some form of irrational belief.

> C: I'm saying, "My God, suppose I goof up? He'll think I'm a jerk!"
> T: Now, I want you to change that feeling of anxiety to one of *mere concern*. Signal me when you have felt less anxious and now feel merely concerned—perhaps motivated to do something about the situation.

Pause until the client's signal.

> T: Now, what are you telling yourself so that you feel only concerned and not anxious?
> C: Well, if I goof, it's not the end of the world, and if he thinks I'm a jerk, that's too bad. I *do* make mistakes—everybody does—and I'm working at improving my performance all the time. I guess I'll be doing that as long as I live! (Walen, DiGiuseppe, & Wessler, 1980, p. 103)

The example just described makes use of both negative and positive imagery, but positive imagery alone can also be employed. You can imagine yourself as calm and relaxed in some situation in which you ordinarily would be anxious—for example, in speaking up in class, giving a talk, or going to a meeting with someone important. You close your eyes and picture yourself as you want to be in that situation, and then listen to what you are saying to yourself in order to be that way (Walen, DiGiuseppe, & Wessler, 1980).

To escape our irrational musts and shoulds, we can deliberately violate them to prove to ourselves that nothing awful happens and that we can stand whatever does happen. For example, a student who believes she just can't—somehow must not!—speak up in class takes a chance and speaks up. She tells herself and comes to see that it's not awful and she can stand it even if what she says isn't brilliant or well received. The earth's foundations do not depart, and life goes on.

Below are some practical "homework" assignments recommended by Bem Allen (1990). Such assignments are designed to show us that "skipping some 'must,' doing something feared, or failing at something isn't so bad after all" (p. 493).

1. Go to class with your socks mismatched and your shirt on backwards—or something similar. Note people's reactions and examine how you view their reactions. Was it all that bad?

2. Try to talk someone into a date who you are sure will not go out with you. Assuming you are turned down, what thoughts came to mind and how did it make you feel about yourself?

3. Pick out someone who irritates you to the *n*th degree and spend some time with that person. Were you able to stand it? Was it less repugnant than expected?

4. Say something foolish in class. Did the snickering and rolling of eyeballs cause you to think of yourself as rather totally foolish?

5. Say "no" to someone to whom you usually grant requests. Did the refusal change your relationship with that person?

6. Purposely be mildly mean to someone toward whom you have been unfailingly nice. How uncomfortable did you feel? Did your behavior change that person's feelings toward you? How?

7. Stand up to a person in authority. For example, ask the boss for a raise, or time off, or to come in late, or to leave early. Did something terrible happen?

8. Temporarily stop doing some social act you feel you must do. For example, if you feel that you must smile sweetly and say hello whenever you see someone you know, inhibit doing it for a few days. (p. 494)

Some Philosophies of Life

A *philosophy of life* is a system of motivating beliefs—that is, beliefs that prompt us to live our lives in a certain way or according to a particular set of rules. One goal of liberal education has been to help students formulate a meaningful philosophy

© PEANUTS reprinted by permission of USF, Inc.

of life or enduring guidelines for private and public conduct, but there is some question about how well colleges accomplish or even address this task. According to a continuing national survey, whose results will be presented more fully in a later chapter, only 43 percent of freshmen in 1991 (compared to 83 percent in 1967) believed it essential or very important to have a meaningful philosophy of life (Astin, Dey, Korn, & Riggs, 1992; Astin Green, & Korn, 1987).

Many of us embrace a set of religious beliefs as a philosophy of life and try to live our lives in keeping with these beliefs or our understanding of them. Some faiths are truly a way of life, with elaborate rules for day-to-day living. Other faiths are less prescriptive.

One of the best-known codes of conduct is the Ten Commandments, but this code has lost much of its force. In the recent national survey by Patterson and Kim (1991), only one out of ten Americans professes a belief in all of the commandments, and four out of ten believe in five or fewer.

Probably the simplest life philosophy is expressed in the Golden Rule. It is just one commandment: "Do unto others as you would have them do unto you." Or, in the ancient Judaic version: "What is hateful to yourself, do not do to your fellow-man." This statement was made by Rabbi Hillel in reply to an unbeliever's challenge that Hillel tell him the whole of the Torah (the first five books of the Bible) standing on one foot. After proving himself equal to the unbeliever's ploy, the good Rabbi added, "That is the whole of the Torah and the rest is but commentary. Go and learn it."

It would seem hard to argue with the Golden Rule. However, some have held that it might be a bit egocentric and have suggested that it be rewritten, "Do unto others as they wish done unto them." In my opinion, both versions are better than the revision offered by one of my students, which was "Do unto others *before* they do unto you!"

The Golden Rule, short as it is, is surpassed in brevity and simplicity (if not profundity) by Alfred E. Neuman's philosophy for living. As every reader of *Mad* magazine knows, this philosophy is expressed by the rhetorical question: "What, me worry?" And apparently Alfred never does.

A much more complex and thought-provoking philosophy of life has been set forth by psychotherapist Sheldon Kopp, who was introduced on the first page of this book. He calls his "laundry list" of beliefs "eschatological" because it deals with fundamental and final matters. Each point on the list presents a truth revealed to him on his own life's journey. The list is presented in Box 3.7.

There's more about Kopp's life in Chapter 11; also see Kopp's book *If you meet the Buddha on the road, kill him!* His book's title is a Zen Master's ironic warning to his disciple that a grown-up can be no one's disciple—or, as Kopp writes, "The most important things each man must learn no one else can teach him." In short, we each must arrive at our own "laundry list."

Kopp's philosophy is a very affecting one. Some find it dark and somber; others hear in it the ring of truth and find it affirming. In Box 3.8, for contrast, is a set of beliefs or rules composed by an anonymous philosopher. Prominent in this

Box 3.7

No Hidden Meanings—An Eschatological Laundry List

by Sheldon Kopp

1. This is it!
2. There are no hidden meanings.
3. You can't get there from here, and besides there's no place else to go.
4. We are all already dying, and we will be dead for a long time.
5. Nothing lasts.
6. There is no way of getting all you want.
7. You can't have anything unless you let go of it.
8. You only get to keep what you give away.
9. There is no particular reason why you lost out on some things.
10. The world is not necessarily just. Being good often does not pay off and there is no compensation for misfortune.
11. You have a responsibility to do your best nonetheless.
12. It is a random universe to which we bring meaning.
13. You don't really control anything.
14. You can't make anyone love you.
15. No one is any stronger or any weaker than anyone else.
16. Everyone is, in his own way, vulnerable.
17. There are no great men.
18. If you have a hero, look again: you have diminished yourself in some way.
19. Everyone lies, cheats, pretends (yes, you too, and most certainly I myself).
20. All evil is potential vitality in need of transformation.
21. All of you is worth something, if you will only own it.
22. Progress is an illusion.
23. Evil can be displaced but never eradicated, as all solutions breed new problems.
24. Yet it is necessary to keep on struggling toward solution.
25. Childhood is a nightmare.
26. But it is so very hard to be an on-your-own, take-care-of-yourself-cause-there-is-no-one-else-to-do-it-for-you grown-up.
27. Each of us is ultimately alone.
28. The most important things, each man must do for himself.
29. Love is not enough, but it sure helps.
30. We have only ourselves, and one another. That may not be much, but that's all there is.
31. How strange, that so often, it all seems worth it.
32. We must live within the ambiguity of partial freedom, partial power, and partial knowledge.
33. All important decisions must be made on the basis of insufficient data.
34. Yet we are responsible for everything we do.
35. No excuses will be accepted.
36. You can run, but you can't hide.
37. It is most important to run out of scapegoats.
38. We must learn the power of living with our helplessness.
39. The only victory lies in surrender to oneself.
40. All of the significant battles are waged within the self.
41. You are free to do whatever you like. You need only to face the consequences.
42. What do you know . . . for sure . . . anyway?
43. Learn to forgive yourself, again and again and again and again . . .

(From Kopp, 1970, p. 29)

philosophy is the idea that living is learning lessons. "If you are alive," it states, "there are lessons to be learned."

Robert Fulghum rewrites his personal statement of beliefs every spring, and he notes that in recent years the statements have gotten shorter and simpler. He claims that what's necessary to live a meaningful life isn't all that complicated—in fact, he learned all he really needs to know in kindergarten. "Wisdom was not at the top of the graduate-school mountain," he says, "but there in the sandbox." These are some of the things he learned:

Box 3.8

Rules for Being Human

1. You will receive a body.
   You may like it or hate it, but it will be yours for the entire period this time around.

2. You will learn lessons.
   You are enrolled in a full-time informal school called life. Each day in this school you will have the opportunity to learn lessons. You may like the lessons or think them irrelevant and stupid.

3. There are no mistakes, only lessons.
   Growth is a process of trial and error, experimentation. The "failed" experiments are as much a part of the process as the experiment that ultimately "works."

4. A lesson is repeated until learned.
   A lesson will be presented to you in various forms until you have learned it. When you have learned it, you can then go on to the next lesson.

5. Learning lessons does not end.
   There is no part of life that does not contain its lessons. If you are alive, there are lessons to be learned.

6. "There" is no better than "here."
   When your "there" has become a "here" you will simply obtain another "there" that will, again, look better than "here."

7. Others are merely mirrors of you.
   You cannot love or hate something about another person unless it reflects to you something you love or hate about yourself.

8. What you make of your life is up to you.
   You have all the tools and resources you need. What you do with them is up to you. The choice is yours.

9. Your answers lie inside you.
   The answers to life's questions lie inside you. All you need to do is look, listen, and trust.

10. You will forget all this.

—Anonymous

Share everything.

Play fair.

Don't hit people.

Put things back where you found them.

Clean up your own mess.

Don't take things that aren't yours.

Say you're sorry when you hurt somebody.

Wash your hands before you eat.

Flush.

Warm cookies and cold milk are good for you.

Live a balanced life—learn some and think some and draw and paint and sing and dance and play and work every day some.

When you go out into the world, watch out for traffic, hold hands, and stick together. . . .

Everything you need to know is in there somewhere. The Golden Rule and love and basic sanitation. Ecology and politics and equality and sane living. . . . Think what a better world it would be if we all—the whole world—had cookies and milk about three o'clock every afternoon and then lay down with our blankets for a nap. Or if all governments had a basic policy to always put things back where they found them and to clean up their own mess. And it is still true, no matter how old you are—when you go out into the world, it is best to hold hands and stick together. (1989, pp. 4–6)

Our philosophy of life constantly undergoes reformulation based upon new experience. However, some of our core beliefs are deeply held and undergo change slowly or not at all. It is helpful to stop occasionally on life's journey and examine our own philosophies or beliefs, so that we can see how well they serve us. Nadine Stair is a person who did so at the age of 85. Out of her review, she composed a prose poem to tell how she would live if she had her life to live over:

If I had my life to live over, I'd dare to make more mistakes next time. I'd relax. I would limber up. I would be sillier than I have been this trip. I would take fewer things seriously. I would take more chances. I would take more trips. I would climb more mountains and swim more rivers. I would eat more ice cream and less beans. I would perhaps have more actual troubles, but I'd have fewer imaginary ones.

You see, I'm one of those people who live sensibly and sanely hour after hour, day after day. Oh, I've had my moments and if I had it to do over again, I'd have more of them. In fact, I'd try to have nothing else. Just moments, one after another, instead of living so many years ahead of each day. I've been one of those persons who never goes anywhere without a thermometer, a hot water bottle, a raincoat, and a parachute. If I had to do it again, I would travel lighter than I have.

If I had my life to live over, I would start barefoot earlier in the spring and stay that way later in the fall. I would go to more dances. I would ride more merry-go-rounds. I would pick more daisies.

In looking back, Nadine Stair concluded that her philosophy of life had not served her well. There are many things she would change if she could live her life over. Rather than waiting and looking back when it is too late to change things, we might want to look ahead and imagine what our lives would be like if we continue with the same philosophy or observe the same rules we follow today. Which beliefs and rules serve us well? We can affirm them. Which ones serve us badly? We can change them. If we do this work well and do it now, we may be able to look back at the age of 85 or 95 or 105 and say: If I had my life to live over, I'd do it the same way again.

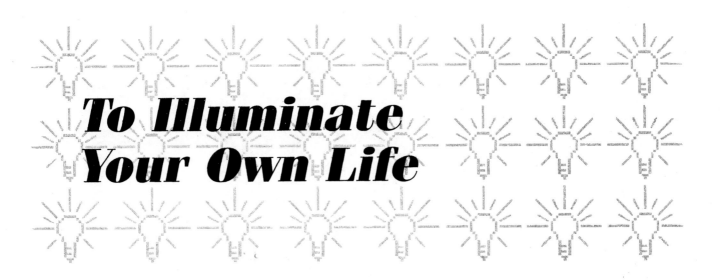

To Illuminate Your Own Life

Anchor and Apply*

1. Discuss (a) one of your beliefs that has spawned a rule that serves you well, and (b) one of your beliefs that has spawned a rule that serves you poorly. Or (c) discuss a belief that has spawned a rule that has proven both good and not so good.

2. Discuss your religious beliefs and indicate their effect upon your life.

3. Discuss a "crisis in belief" or "cognitive dissonance" currently present in your life, indicating how it affects you and what you are doing about it.

4. Discuss an important belief you have modified or abandoned, indicating how this change came about and the effect of this change on your life.

5. Discuss your own "musturbation" or "shouldy" behavior.

6. Discuss your own use of one or more of the kinds of distorted, twisted, or self-defeating thinking described in this chapter.

7. Pick out one of the homework assignments described in this chapter—one that would be hard but helpful and harmless for you to do. Do it, and write up the results.

8. Devise your own homework assignment—perhaps one similar to those described in this chapter. Discuss it with the instructor, to make sure you both agree that it would be hard, helpful, and harmless; then do it, and write up the results.

9. Compare or contrast your philosophy of life with one of those given in this chapter.

10. Suppose an anthropologist unobtrusively followed you around for a week, recording everything you said and did, with the intent of determining your philosophy of life—not from what you *said* it was but from what you *showed* it was. What would he or she report?

---

* These "anchor and apply" items are designed to help you use the concepts of the chapter as stimuli to prompt new or deeper or clearer insights into yourself and your life. To respond to an item, first find the material in the chapter that is most relevant to the item *and* yourself; that's called "anchoring." Second, think about this material in relationship to yourself and your life and keep thinking about it until you arrive at a new or deeper or clearer understanding; that's the "apply" or application part. When you write or present your response to the item, be sure to include both parts, that is, both the anchor material and the application. You can know you are successful on an item if, in completing it, you truly learn something new or understand something better.

Motivating Beliefs

A *motivating belief* is a belief that prompts us to live our lives in a certain way. One or more of our motivating beliefs may be considerably different from that of a significant other or different from the mainstream or even from what we used to believe or would prefer to believe. This discrepancy can have a profound effect on us.

When I think of my own belief system and contrast it with that of a very significant other, my wife, I note my financial philosophy has been "If you've got it, save it" but hers (wiser and overriding, as it's turned out) is "if you've got it, spend it, enjoy! enjoy!" Concerning myself and the mainstream: many people believe that you work to live, but I live to work (except that I don't believe my work is work). Concerning earlier beliefs: I used to believe in a personal deity that watched over the world and me, but now I believe I must find my own truths and make my own way. That's what I now believe, but I would like to believe (with the same religious fervor my father had) in a personal deity that indeed watched over the world and me.

To explore your own motivating beliefs and their effect on you, complete the four items below. (If you don't have a contrast for one or more of the remaining items, omit the item or items; but for each omission repeat Item 1, using a different significant other.)

1. Contrast your present motivating beliefs with those of a significant other by filling in the blanks immediately below:

My _____ *believes/believed* _____

_____

but I believe _____

_____ .

The effect of this difference in belief on me . . .

2. Contrast your present motivating beliefs with those of the mainstream:

   Many people believe _____

   _____

   but I believe _____

   _____ .

   The effect of this difference in belief on me . . .

3. Contrast your present motivating beliefs with those you had at some earlier time in your life:

   I used to believe _____

   _____

   but now I believe _____

   _____ .

   The effect of this difference in belief on me . . .

4. Contrast your present motivating beliefs with those you would like to have:

   I believe _____

   _____

   but I would like to believe _____

   _____ .

   The effect of this difference in belief on me . . .

Rules for Living

Beliefs spawn rules. Our beliefs tell us that the world is such and such a place, and we devise rules to get along in that kind of world. However, some of our rules have been introjected whole from our parents, our peer group, or society, and perhaps without much thought or questioning. Some of our rules, whatever their origin, serve us well, but others may be of little use or serve us poorly.

We may or may not know what our rules are, but they are implicit in everything we do (or don't do). If we *always* do something or *never* do something, there's likely to be a rule involved. As you'll recall, Nadine Stair wrote, "I've been one of those persons who never goes anywhere without a thermometer, a hot water bottle, a raincoat, and a parachute." The rule: *Never* take chances. It was a rule she regretted; for, as she wrote, if she had her life to live over, she would take more chances.

Another person, also addressing himself to what he would do if he had his life to live over, wrote in part: "I would have invited friends over to dinner even though the carpet was stained and the sofa was faded. I would have eaten popcorn in the 'good' living room and worried less about the dirt when someone wanted to light a fire in the fireplace. . . . I would have sat down on the lawn with my children and not worried about grass stains." The implicit rule: *Always* put up a good appearance.

Behind our inflexible rules, or our always and never rules, is often the fear that something terrible might happen if we don't follow them. Of course, this may be true in some cases; for example, something terrible might happen if we don't look both ways before crossing the street. But consider a woman who has a rule (that she probably hasn't thought of as a rule) never to refuse a request from a friend. Suppose she finally does say "no" to a request that would have truly inconvenienced her. Would that be a catastrophe? Her rule might seem to indicate that she thinks so. Consider another student who can never bring herself to go to a movie or a nice restaurant unless she has someone to go with. What terrible thing might happen if she did go alone?

Consider a young man who has never had a date because he has a rule (that he probably hasn't thought of as a rule) never to ask someone to go out with him. What is he afraid might happen if he did ask someone? Suppose he asked and the answer was no. Would that be a catastrophe? His rule might seem to indicate that he thinks so. Consider a person who always tries to sit in the back of a class or audience or on the aisle. If he has to sit in front or in the middle of a row, he feels very uncomfortable. What is he afraid might happen?

Consider the rules that govern your life that you aren't fully happy with—rules that some other people don't seem to have or need. What are you afraid might happen if you don't follow these rules? This exploration is designed to help you explore the fear behind one of your rules. To help you call to mind your own more inflexible rules, look through the "always" and "never" rules presented in

Box 3.9. Your own rule might not be so absolute—it might be "almost always" or "almost never." Whether it is on the list or not, select one of your rules and complete the three items below before proceeding to the next page.

1. *One of my rules that I might like to break or bend a little is . . .*

2. *The way this rule helps me is . . .*

3. *The way this rule hurts me is . . .*

Box 3.9

"Always" and "Never" Rules

Here are some "always" and "never" rules that my students and clients have reported. Mark Twain was not a student or client of mine, but if he had been, these lists would have included two rules he recommended. Slightly paraphrased, these are: "Always do right—this will gratify some people and astonish the rest." "Never do wrong when people are looking."

1. Always be a lady.
2. Always be clean and neat.
3. Always be concerned with what people think about you.
4. Always be on time.
5. Always be overprepared for what you do.
6. Always be prepared for the worst.
7. Always brush your teeth after every meal.
8. Always defend yourself.
9. Always do everything that needs to be done before having fun.
10. Always double-check the appliances before leaving the house.
11. Always do your best at everything that you do.
12. Always have a place for everything.
13. Always have a plan and follow it to the letter.
14. Always help others when they need help.
15. Always keep people guessing.
16. Always keep your cool.
17. Always put off facing a problem as long as possible.
18. Always put off unpleasant chores.
19. Always put up a good appearance.
20. Always put yourself last.
21. Always read the label before buying anything.
22. Always speak up in a group.
23. At all times be a man!

1. Never accept a compliment.
2. Never ask for help.
3. Never buy anything on credit.
4. Never call attention to yourself.
5. Never cry.
6. Never do what you don't do well.
7. Never get close to your boss.
8. Never get involved with people.
9. Never let an insult pass.
10. Never loan money to anyone.
11. Never lose control.
12. Never offend anyone.
13. Never refuse to help a friend.
14. Never show anger.
15. Never show weakness.
16. Never show your love.
17. Never spend money unless you have to.
18. Never talk to strangers.
19. Never take chances.
20. Never tell someone how you feel.
21. Never think about death or dying.
22. Never think about upsetting things.
23. Never throw anything away.
24. Never trust anyone.

One way to gain insight into a rule is to imagine in as much detail as possible all the things that might happen if this rule were ignored. What is there to be afraid of? In the space below, write a short story for *Terrible Tales* magazine. Your story is to describe an *imaginary* time—not a real one—when you abandoned your rule (the one you described on the previous page) and what happened as a result. Remember that the editor of this magazine only accepts made-up stories that portray really dreadful situations; therefore, in the story you concoct, graphically describe how, when you abandoned your rule, the situation went from bad to awful to terrible and even catastrophic. Really pour it on, making it the worst you can imagine. Then (assuming that you are still alive) turn to the next page.

My Terrible Tale

In the space below, answer these three questions: (1) What belief about yourself or your world might have spawned this rule? (2) How much of your Terrible Tale would be likely to happen if you broke or bent your rule? (3) What have you learned from writing and thinking about your Terrible Tale?

Lessons Life Has Taught Me

"You are enrolled in a full-time informal school called life. Each day in this school you will have an opportunity to learn lessons." So writes the anonymous philosopher whose "Rules for Being Human" are presented in Box 3.8.

The most notable lessons learned by Medal of Honor winner Vice Admiral James Stockdale (now retired) were taught him the hard way. They were deeply etched by nearly eight years of Vietnam captivity (four spent in solitary deprivation) when he was shot down after nearly two hundred fighter missions. Here is one of the lessons that Stockdale has learned from life:

> **Life is not fair.** The challenge of education is how to prepare young people to respond with grace when they don't succeed. They need to know that a failure is not the end of everything—how to not give up in the face of adversity.
>
> At the time I was shot down, I had the top job a Navy fighter pilot could hold. Suddenly, I was isolated and crippled, with my captors trying to tear apart my system of values. I was able to overcome the "why me?" feeling by recalling my studies of men who had successfully dealt with failure in our historical past. The biblical story of Job reminded me that life isn't always fair. Even honest and upright men can be tested by evil and must be prepared to deal with it (quoted in Santoli, 1990, p. 8).

Here is a lesson that one of my students, a young woman, a freshman, age 18, has learned from life:

> **I have learned to protect my independence.** In the past, I have bent over backwards to please my boyfriends. I would hang out with *his* friends, participate in *his* favorite sports, listen to *his* music. When we broke up, I would feel lost and lonely. I found I can't forfeit my own identity trying to please a guy. He is a person, but I am a person, too. I have come to appreciate guys who appreciate me and respect my talents and interests just as I appreciate theirs. It's okay for two people in a relationship to have differences. They don't have to lose themselves in each other. I know I am not going to lose myself again.

Here is a lesson by another of my students, a young woman, a sophomore, age 19:

> **I need to listen to listen to the authorities but decide for myself.** I have had arthritis since my junior year in high school. My rheumatologist has always given me medication to control the pain and maintains that diet would have little, if any, effect on my condition. However, I consulted a

naturopath, and following his suggestions concerning diet, I experience much less pain. I have learned that just because a person is an authority in a field doesn't mean he knows everything. I have learned it never hurts to ask questions, and if I am not satisfied with the answers, to keep searching until I am. In the end, I have to decide for myself.

Here is a lesson learned by a senior, a male, age 22:

Life has taught me to be a realistic idealist. When I was an adolescent, I was an idealist. I wanted my family, the world, and everything to be the way I thought they should be. Of course, they weren't—far from it. I am a member of a religious faith that taught me I was a sinner and should try to perfect myself. Of course, I fell short. Some of my friends became cynical when they saw their ideals go down the drain, but I have learned to be a realistic idealist. Hello and welcome to the real world. I still have my ideals, but they are goals to work toward—not things that have to take place tomorrow. I'm not as critical of things as I was at 16, but it's a lot easier living this way.

What lessons have you learned about life in life's school? Instruction is seldom as dramatic as that which James Stockdale underwent as a POW. You learn your lessons little by little, day by day; but once learned, they affect the way you live your life. If you have learned that happiness awaits at the top of life's staircase, you will live differently than if you have learned that what is important is how you ride life's roller coaster or how you journey along life's path going nowhere (see Box 3.1). If life has taught you that people are essentially evil or bad, you will make your way among them differently than if you have come to see them as essentially well-meaning or good (see Box 3.2).

In the space below (and add another page), write down three important lessons life has taught you. For each lesson, indicate (1) what the lesson is, (2) how you learned it, and (3) how the lesson influences your thoughts, feelings, and/or actions. One caution: In writing about the lesson, use the word "I," "me," "my," or "mine" rather than "you" or "your"; otherwise, you might sound like a preacher or even a psychologist.

Question 4

Turning Points

What Crucial Changes Have Brought Me to This Place in My Life?

What is life? My dictionary defines life as "the interval between conception or birth and death." But what is the interval? What is the course of life? Whatever the course, it doesn't appear to proceed smoothly.

I remember being in a large audience of adults—young, middle-aged, and old—and at one point the speaker asked for a show of hands in response to this question: "How many of you are still waiting for your life to settle down?" I looked around, and everyone I could see had a hand in the air. So did I.

The human body has marvelous homeostatic or self-regulating mechanisms that tend to keep it constant even when there are factors working to change it. But human life often seems to be more disequilibrium than equilibrium, and some theorists and observers see disequilibrium as the normal state (Wrightsman, 1988). In this view, we never "settle down."

"Life," Ralph Waldo Emerson wrote, "is a series of surprises." Not all students of human existence would agree. Some see a pattern of development common to all or most or many lives. Every life, indeed, is in some ways like every other life. But then again, every life is in some ways like no other life. In some ways, each of us is an original.

107

Box 4.1

Turning Points: What Crucial Changes Have Brought Me to This Place in My Life?

Seedthoughts

1. Below is an old story of a Chinese farmer who was the only one in his village to own a horse. The fragment of the story that appears here is all that is known; the beginning and end have been lost.

    One day the farmer's horse ran away. How unfortunate, the villagers said. But the village elder said, time will tell if it's good or bad.

    Several days later, the horse returned bringing a wild horse with it. How fortunate, the villagers said. But the elder said, time will tell if it's good or bad.

    While trying to tame the wild horse, the farmer's son was thrown off and broke his leg. How unfortunate, the villagers said. But the elder said, time will tell if it's good or bad.

    Soon after, the Emperor's press gang came to the village to seize recruits for the army but left the farmer's son behind as unfit. How fortunate, the villagers said. But . . .

2. Once upon a time there were two brothers who aroused the interest of a psychologist. One brother was an alcoholic, while the other hardly touched liquor at all. The psychologist, curious as to the "causes" of this difference, undertook to interview each man separately.

    To the alcoholic he said, "You've been an alcoholic for most of your adult life. Why do you suppose that is?" The man responded, "That's easy to explain. You see, my father was an alcoholic. You might say I learned to drink at my father's knee."

    To the man who hardly touched liquor at all the psychologist said, "You don't like to drink. How come?" The man responded, "That's easy to explain. You see, my father was an alcoholic. You might say I learned very early in life that alcohol can be poison." (Branden, 1985, p. 42)

3. A team of researchers compared the levels of happiness in twenty-two major lottery winners with those of a control group who were similar in other respects. Each group was asked how happy they were at present, had been earlier (for the winners, before winning; for the controls, six months earlier), and expected to be in a couple of years. They were also asked to rate how pleasant they currently found seven everyday activities: eating breakfast, reading a magazine, watching television, talking with a friend, hearing a funny joke, getting a compliment, and buying clothes. The results: (1) no significant difference of any kind in happiness between winners and controls; and (2) the winners found significantly less pleasure than the controls in the everyday activities (Brickman, Coates, & Janoff-Bulman, 1978).

Some human developmentalists have described the course of life as a progression through fairly predictable stages. Others have seen human life as the playing out of certain broad plans or themes that may have been learned early. And still others have felt that life's course is most affected by certain special events or turning points. In the material that follows, we will look briefly at the first two approaches and at some length at the last one.

Life as a Progression of Stages

An anonymous and cynical wag has described life as a sequence of three tablets: school tablet, aspirin tablet, stone tablet. A Chinese proverb presents a brighter progression (but then again it seems to be referring to "the good life"): Loving parents, happy marriage, good children, fine funeral.

What the two sayings have in common is the sense that the course of life for all its ups and downs is orderly and proceeds through a number of stages. Some years ago Gail Sheehy's *Passages: Predictable Crises of Adult Life* became a best-seller when it purported to unravel the mystery of adult development. As the subtitle indicates, the book held that adult life is predictable, and it went ahead to set forth the crises we all might reasonably expect. Sheehy wrote that "the older we grow, the more we become aware of the commonality of our lives" (1976, p. 19).

The most influential of all stage theorists is Erik Erikson, who proposes that there are eight psychosocial stages of life we pass through on our way from infancy to old age (Erikson, 1959, 1982; Erikson, Erikson, & Kivnick, 1986). Each stage gives rise to new capabilities and new responsibilities and is the focal point of a crisis or challenge that involves a potentially fruitful confrontation between seemingly contrary dispositions. If we deal with a particular crisis effectively, a new strength is forged, and we are better prepared to face subsequent crises.

In Erikson's view, we are never simply struggling with the tension generated by the challenge that is focal at the time. At every successive stage, we are anticipating tensions yet to become focal, and we continue to experience tensions that were inadequately integrated when they were focal or whose integration is no longer adequate. Erikson has considerably elaborated his theory in the four decades that he has been working with it, and a simple outline appears in Box 4.2. Research concerning his formulations has provided support for a number of aspects but not all (for a review, see Maddi, 1989).

Considerable objection has been raised to the stage conception of adult development, especially to the notion that there is a common pattern to adult lives. Anne Rosenfeld and Elizabeth Stark (1987), who mount a persuasive attack on stage theories, write, "Research on child development, begun earlier this century, has shown that children generally pass through an orderly succession of stages that correspond to fairly specific ages. But recent studies have challenged some of the apparent orderliness of child development, and the pattern of development among adults seems to be even less clear-cut" (p. 64).

Those opposed to stage theories insist that there is no universal timetable for adult development. For example, the midlife crisis identified by Sheehy and heralded by the popular media has been termed "more myth than substance" by Helen Bee (1987, p. 278), who reviews the evidence. Although midlife is not crisis-free, turbulence is no more likely there than at any other time of life (Costa & McCrae, 1980). In fact, it is probably less likely than among young adults, who are moving away from their families and trying to form new intimate relationships, families, and careers (Pearlin & Lieberman, 1979; Schlossberg, 1989). It seems we can choose our own time for our crisis or crises or forgo the "privilege" completely and still not be inconsistent with the research evidence.

Nancy Schlossberg, writer, researcher, and counselor-educator, holds that little can be predicted about a person on the basis of age alone. "Give me a roomful of 40-year-old women and you have told me nothing. Give me a case story about what each has experienced and then I can tell if one is going to have a crisis and another a tranquil period." Schlossberg explains: "What matters is what transitions she has experienced. Has she been 'dumped' by a husband, fired from her job, had a breast removed, gone back to school, remarried, had her first book published. It is what has happened or not happened to her, not how old she is, that counts" (quoted in Rosenfeld & Stark, 1987, p. 69).

Other workers in this field point out that any patterns found characteristic of one group of age cohorts (persons born in the same period) would not likely apply to another whose experiences and circumstances were different. Those who begin life in hard times may develop a different outlook from those having their start in a brighter era. Older persons today are healthier and wealthier than the elders of any previous generation, and therefore the meaning of old age has changed considerably (Dychtwald & Flower, 1989).

Box 4.2

Erik Erikson's Psychosocial Crises or Challenges

Erikson has proposed that in our lifetime we pass through eight stages, each the focal point of a crisis or struggle between two seemingly contrary dispositions. This opposition can be fruitful, for by arriving at an appropriate balance, we forge an essential strength and prepare ourselves for the crises to come. For example, if basic trust and mistrust are appropriately integrated (and this depends upon the care we receive as infants), we develop hope or a "belief in the benevolence of fate." Each of the eight crises is outlined below. (For a fuller exposition, see Erikson, 1982; Erikson, Erikson, & Kivnick, 1986.)

Stage	Crisis	Crisis Delineated	Strength
Infancy	Basic Trust vs. Basic Mistrust	Can I trust my world? (But not trust it too much or mistrust it and withdraw from it.)	Hope
Early Childhood	Autonomy vs. Shame, Doubt	Can I act autonomously? (Learn to do simple things myself so that I am not oppressed by shame or doubt and yet not be shameless or willful.)	Will
Play Age	Initiative vs. Guilt	Can I take initiative? (Learn to assert myself and also to limit myself without too much guilt or inhibition.)	Purpose
School Age	Industry vs. Inferiority	Can I be industrious? (Learn more complex academic and social skills without feeling generally incompetent or taking refuge in narrow virtuosity.)	Competence
Adolescence	Identity vs. Confusion	Can I establish an identity? (Find a way of being, a philosophy of life, and a system of values that fits me—one that is not confused or rigidly fanatic.)	Fidelity
Young Adulthood	Intimacy vs. Isolation	Can I achieve intimacy? (Develop the capacity for selective commitment, avoiding promiscuity or painful isolation.)	Love
Adulthood	Generativity vs. Self-Absorption, Stagnation	Can I be generative? (Show concern for and make a commitment to the next generation, taking care of what I truly care for.)	Care
Old Age	Integrity vs. Despair	Can I maintain my integrity? (Come to terms with the past, arrive at a non-presumptuous wisdom based on that experience, and not despair over the limitations of age or the prospect of death.)	Wisdom

---

Life as Fulfilling a Plan

We plan our days and weeks and what we are going to do on vacation. Do we plan our lives? Or might we live our lives according to a plan we do not even fully realize we have laid down for ourselves?

The Life Plan

One question that time-management expert Alan Lakein (1973) asks the persons he trains is this: "What are your lifetime goals?" Lakein reports that some of his trainees feel uneasy when they are confronted by this question. Some are embarrassed. Some are overwhelmed. But all manage to arrive at an answer. All seem to have some sort of a plan whether they are aware of it or not.

These trainees might more easily have told Lakein what they were planning to avoid in life than what they were planning to pursue. People who have had an unhappy past may be sure of only one thing: they don't want that to be their future as well. One young woman told me she was sure she didn't want a marriage like that of her parents or her three older sisters (two now divorced). Singlehood was an unappealing prospect, but still she had never really known a marriage that worked.

What are *your* lifetime goals? How would *you* answer this question? Do you have a plan?

Some people seem to "inherit" a plan. For example, some long-established family businesses appear to absorb practically all of the succeeding generations. I remember reading about one such absorbed family member who broke loose. He then established an identical business.

One of my students, who belongs to a religious order, told me that her plan from the time she had been a little girl was to be a nun. She had gone to a school where her teachers were nuns, one aunt was a nun, and she knew that was what her life was to be. Few of us will have so early and so clear a calling, but at the age of 4 or 5 many children have a ready response to the question "What do you want to do when you grow up?" They also have a ready explanation for the answer they gave. These early choices, of course, are usually wisps of fancy, but they will soon become more realistic (Ginzberg, Ginsburg, Axelrad, & Herma, 1951).

Whether we make big plans for ourselves or lesser plans is related to a number of factors. If we are from disadvantaged or lower socioeconomic groups, our vocational aspirations are likely to be lower than if we enjoy a higher status. We tend to be gender-bound, picking out occupations we see as appropriate to our sex, and we may be less confident of our chance for success in a career if we are female.

Almost all of us plan to marry and have children, but more of us are electing to remain single or marry later or have fewer children and have them later. In a study of low-income women of high school age, Kenkel (1985) found that those who planned to remain childless were those with higher aspirations; they were unwilling to become "simply" housewives, and they were not about to be caught in a "baby trap."

Through much of the history of this country, each succeeding generation has been able to anticipate and plan a more affluent life than the previous one, but that is not so true today. Many young couples are finding it hard to match their parents' standard of living. They have no assurance they will ever be able to afford a nice home, college educations for their children, or a measure of financial security for themselves. For them, it's a new and tougher ball game.

As Lakein notes, our lifetime goals or plans may not last a lifetime. Our plans change as we change and move along. We can gain some perspective on our lives by thinking back on what we wanted from life when we were children and adolescents, or when we were young adults or middle-aged.

The Life Script

One of the fundamental concepts of Eric Berne's (1961, 1964, 1972) transactional analysis, a system of personality theory and therapy, is that each person forms a life plan or script in early childhood. In this conception, young children are highly vulnerable and lacking in power, ability to handle stress, thinking capacity, information, and options. Therefore, they are very susceptible to the messages they receive from their parents. These messages are contained in the models presented by the parents and also in what the parents directly and indirectly tell the children they are and should be.

Some messages are positive and growth-enhancing; others are negative and growth-inhibiting. Positive messages communicate that the child is okay and give helpful information on how to live life. Negative messages tell the child he or she is not okay and may even suggest that the child has no right to think or feel or act or even to exist. In response to the messages received, a child makes a number of decisions that combine to form a life plan or script. Typically, we are not aware we are living a scripted life. We learn that script little by little and become the character by degrees.

An identifying characteristic of a life lived according to a script is its repetitive quality. Living out a script, we tend to repeat a pattern. To say it another way, a scripted life seems to have a theme. This theme can sometimes be expressed in a short phrase—one that might serve as the title of the person's autobiography. Is there a title for your autobiography in Box 4.3?

Some transactional analysts have criticized some of the assumptions of script theory (Allen & Allen, 1988; Cornell, 1988)—specifically, the notion that script

---

The Life Script

A personality theory called transactional analysis (TA) suggests that we may live our lives according to a script that is based on how we have come to see ourselves and our world. Our life script is the part we play out on life's stage. Unlike earlier TA theorists, who saw scripts as largely rigid and dysfunctional and set down in childhood, more recent writers have described scripts as either healthy or pathological constructions that are open to modification at any time in life.

Below are some common script themes. This list is an extension of one presented by Muriel James and Dorothy Jongeward (1971) in their book *Born to Win*. (This title itself could be considered a theme, as could its opposite, "Born to Lose.")

Losing My Mind	Succeeding then Failing
Coming to My Senses	Failing then Succeeding
Being the Best	Never Getting Anywhere
Settling for Second	Making It
Driving People Crazy	Saving for a Rainy Day
Being a Good Friend	Acting as If There Is No Tomorrow
Killing Myself by Degrees	Building Empires
Putting Myself Back Together	Losing My Shirt
Carrying My Cross	Being Miserable
Smelling the Flowers	Being Happy
Having a Ball	Walking on Eggs
By the Sweat of My Brow	Stomping Along
Trying Hard	Missing the Boat
Finding the Easy Way	Catching the Brass Ring
Bossing Others	Sorry for Being Alive
Doing What I'm Told	Grateful for Each Day
Stumbling but Recovering	Getting Stepped On
Watching My Step	Don't Tread on Me
Climbing the Staircase to Success	Looking for a Pot of Gold
On the Roller Coaster to Nowhere	Looking for the Worm in the Apple
Striving for Perfection	Completely Ruined by Yesterday
Getting By with Good Enough	On Hold for Tomorrow

decisions are made only at an early age and are resistant to change. These critics maintain that we can be the playwrights of our lives, and if we don't like the part we see ourselves playing, we can get busy and change it.

The Personal Myth

Some observers of human nature have concluded that there are a limited number of ways to live life, and they have all been catalogued in the world's myths, legends, and folk tales. Author Willa Cather summed up this position when she wrote, "There are only two or three human stories, and they go on repeating themselves as fiercely as if they had never happened."

Myths are traditional stories that attempt to explain or teach. Because these stories are generally made up, the word "myth" has sometimes come to mean something that isn't true, but there may be a larger truth in these stories. I like Jean Houston's definition of myth as "something that never happened but is always happening."

A *personal myth,* as Carl Jung used this term, is a set of truths by which one lives one's life. These "truths" are not necessarily true or even fully known to the person. Instead, the personal myth is largely below the level of consciousness and in fact stems from the "collective unconscious"—the inborn psychological heritage all humans share. Consequently, in our personal myths we reflect the central themes with which humans have struggled since the Garden of Eden.

Joseph Campbell (1968) found one myth, the hero's journey, common in the traditional stories of many countries. In myth, heroes (there is a scarcity of heroines) start their journeys to help their lands, which have fallen on bad times. On the path, they find assistance, master obstacles, grow in the process, and undergo a transformation. Upon their return they have what is necessary to heal their lands. Our lives could be thought of as journeys on which we encounter good times and bad times and sometimes respond heroically to the bad times—mastering obstacles with or without assistance and growing in the process. In fact, that pretty much is what a successful life—or personal growth—is all about.

Living according to a pattern dictated by a personal myth can give us a sense of identity and security, but this pattern can also limit and restrict us. It may tell us we are persons who thrive in one environment but not another, who can do certain things but can't do other things. It may lead us into the same cul-de-sac again and again or keep us stuck there once and for all. Psychotherapists Mary and Robert Goulding (1982) recall two of their life-stuck female clients, one 40, unmarried, and in an unsatisfactory career, who said she was "waiting for something to happen"; her favorite childhood story: *Sleeping Beauty.* The other, spending her life slaving for her ungrateful husband and children, was especially fond of *Cinderella.* Sam Keen and Anne Valley-Fox (1989) write, "To remain vibrant throughout a lifetime we must always be inventing ourselves, weaving new themes into our life-narratives, remembering our past, re-visioning our future, reauthorizing the myth by which we live" (p. xv).

Jung asked himself, "What is the myth *you* are living?" He found that he did not know, so he took it upon himself to find out. To Jung, this effort was "the task of tasks." He sought to make clear to his conscious mind the myth that was, as he said, "forming" him (Campbell, 1971). Following Jung's lead, workers who make the personal myth central in the growth process begin by encouraging individuals to become aware of their myth; then they are helped to affirm, revise, or supplant the myth as may be necessary, and finally weave it consciously and with commitment into their daily lives (Feinstein & Krippner, 1988; Keen & Valley-Fox, 1989).

Life as a Series of Turning Points

Life is a journey and an often uneven one. There are long stretches where little seems to happen and then places where everything seems to happen. Some of these happenings involve turning points. A *turning point* is a crucial change or shift in our lives. "Crucial" implies that the change is likely to shape future events.

Our use of the words "happen" and "happenings" in the previous paragraph requires some qualification. Psychologist Albert Bandura (1982) suggests that chance encounters are important in shaping the course of lives; as a case in point, he recalls his own experience in meeting his wife-to-be on the golf links where he had taken refuge from his graduate studies. But we humans are not simply receivers of life events. We take an active part in creating our lives. (After all, Dr. Bandura took himself to a place where harmonious young women were likely to be, but still—to be fair—if he had met and married another harmonious woman rather than that one, his life might have been considerably different.)

Rather than turning point, Ira Progoff (1975) uses the term "stepping stone." "The stepping stones," he writes, "are the significant points of movement along the road of an individual's life" (p. 102). One could think of life as a pond with various stones strewn in it. We pick our way across, stone by stone, moving this way, that way, until we have reached the far bank. By studying our stepping stones, we can begin to discern "lines of continuity" and "patterns of meaning" in our life.

Nancy Schlossberg's (1987) concept "transitions" is synonymous with turning points. She divides transitions into three categories:

1. *Anticipated transitions.* These are the expected or scheduled events of life. Most of us expect to leave our parents' home, find a job, get married, establish a home, have a child (or children), retire. We can anticipate these events and get ready for them.

2. *Unanticipated transitions.* These include the unexpected or nonscheduled events. They are unpredictable and often disruptive. Some examples: losing a job when our company is sold, destruction of our home by flood or earthquake, the death of a child or early death of our spouse, or our own disability through illness or accident. Some brighter examples (but possibly no less disruptive): winning a lottery or recovering from a "fatal" illness.

3. *Nonevent transitions.* These include the expected or scheduled events that didn't occur. We may anticipate marrying but never do so, or we may fail to complete our dissertation or publish that book. We may not have the child or grandchildren we wanted, or we may be unable to retire for financial reasons.

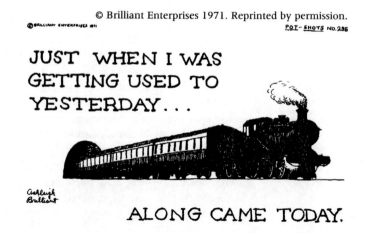

© BRILLIANT ENTERPRISES 1971   POT-SHOTS NO.255

JUST WHEN I WAS
GETTING USED TO
YESTERDAY...

Ashleigh
Brilliant

ALONG CAME TODAY.

Bernice and Dail Neugarten (1987) note that by the time we are adolescents we have developed a set of expectations about our major life events or transitions or turning points—what they will be and when they should take place. We develop an internal timetable or social clock that tells us whether we are on time or tardy. Although it may be not quite so true today, "most people still try to marry or have a child or make a job change when they think they have reached the 'right' age. They can still easily report whether they were early, late or on time with regard to one life event or another" (p. 33). The events that are anticipated and "on time" do not ordinarily precipitate life crisis. For example, the "empty nest" is not itself a problem for most middle-aged parents; rather, stress occurs when a child does not leave home at the appropriate time. Most men take retirement in their stride if it occurs at the expected age, and widowhood may be less of a crisis if it occurs in old age rather than middle age. In other words, "it is the events that upset the expected sequence and rhythm of life that cause problems" (p. 33). Problems occur when events are "out of sync," for example, when the death of a parent comes during one's childhood or adolescence, or when a child comes too early or too late, or when one is forced into premature retirement.

Support for the Neugartens was provided in a study of women in a large Eastern town. When these women were asked about the major turning points in their lives, only 20 percent mentioned marriage. Most frequently mentioned were unanticipated events such as divorce, which the majority of divorced women reported as a turning point. The second most mentioned category was common events that occurred at an unusual or "wrong" time (Baruch, Barnett, & Rivers, 1983). What appears to be a major event may not be a turning point if we have anticipated and prepared for it or if it does not bring about a change within ourselves.

Some turning points seem unrelated to any salient external happening; in fact, an inner change may come about because nothing seems to be happening in our lives. A burst of growth—a turning point—can "be triggered when goals and projects turn stale; when money can no longer buy anything that the person wants; when the fame that was once the person's glory has turned to ashes; and when the love of that woman, long-pursued, is now experienced as cloying, suffocating possessiveness" (Jourard, 1968, p. 155).

Turning-Point Resources

How well we manage a turning point or transition depends on the coping resources at our disposal. Schlossberg (1987, 1989) divides these resources into four categories, which she calls "the four S's": situation, self, support, and strategies. By taking a reading on the state of these resources, one can determine how well a person is equipped to deal with a transition. Here are the kinds of questions that Schlossberg asks (and that you might ask yourself if you are in a transition) in making an assessment:

1. Situation

   How do you see the situation? Is it desired or dreaded? Expected or unexpected? "On time" or "off time"? At a good time or the worst possible time? Voluntary or imposed? Surrounded by other stresses?

2. Self

   How do you see yourself as you go through transitions? Resilient? In control? Challenged rather than overwhelmed? An optimist rather than a pessimist?

3. Support

   What financial or emotional support or other assistance can you muster? From family, friends, and neighbors? From co-workers and colleagues? From groups, organizations, and institutions? And what usual sources of support and assistance may be disrupted by the transition?

4. Strategies

Do you have a variety of coping mechanisms to draw upon in a transition? Do these include some strategies for changing or modifying the transition? For changing the meaning of the transition when the situation itself can't be changed? For dealing with stress produced by the situation?

Transitions and the discomfort they cause are an integral part of life. Schlossberg (1987) notes that we cannot always control transitions or even anticipate them, but we can control our response to them: "By systematically sizing up transitions and our own resources for dealing with them we can learn how to build on our strengths, cut our losses—and even grow in the process. With a lifetime of practice, some people even get good at it" (p. 75).

Turning Points Illustrated

If we stop for a moment and think of our own lives, some of our turning points will come to mind. A young man in a group with me recalled that a major turning point in his life took place when his family moved from a small farm in the South to a Midwestern metropolis—his world changed and he changed. A middle-aged woman noted that for her an important turning point was the realization within herself that she no longer could depend on her husband and children to anchor her identity. For me, a salient point came in my mid-thirties when I became very dissatisfied with my bachelor life and entered psychotherapy.

In the following account, a young man—one of a number of students involved in Peter Madison's (1969) study of personality changes during the college years—attributes his decision to become a biologist to a turning point that occurred when he was 12 years of age:

One day when I was skin diving I remember seeing this group of snails and wanting desperately to watch them for a long period of time, and I remember just desiring that so intensely, and being filled with an incredible wonder at the way these things moved, and their shape. I was swimming about fifty or sixty feet from shore, and along the bottom I saw these beautiful snails, which, as I recall, I had thought beautiful on other occasions in the past; but here was a whole group of them, a whole bed of them, plowing this way and that. I dove down and got some of them and looked at them, and got a jar and put seawater in it, and took it home. And then I could see that this wasn't going to be enough; so I went to a drug store, got a mason jar, made an observation bottle, and then walked down to the beach again and filled it up with salt water and brought it back to keep these little snails in.

I have always dated the origin of my scientific interest in becoming a biologist from precisely that day, which is probably a mistake because there were precursors, but the precursors were never as crucial as the special experience. That day marked the beginning of my interest. There may have been things done previously like going skin diving, going swimming, but this was the origin of my being possessed, consumed with an interest in these things, and it came suddenly, just broke in that day. I am sure I was getting ready to develop such an interest, but this one day had about it an ecstatic feeling such as mystics are said to have; this day had a quality rather like that. (pp. 259–260)

The story that follows is told by Ellen Goodman (1979) in her book *Turning Points*. It concerns not the beginning of a love relationship but rather the end of one. After thirty years of marriage, "Lillian," age 52, finds she is losing her husband to a younger woman. Until she was "kicked out" of her traditional niche, Lillian had assumed she was coasting toward Social Security. Instead, she was confronted with a major point of change.

"I know, it's an old story," she remembers. "Most people don't even bat an eyelash. It's so horribly typical, almost ordinary. Middle-aged man meets thirty-year-old woman, has affair without wife knowing, wants to get rid of old wife to get young wife," Lillian says with bitterness. "I had read stories like that. But when it actually happens, well . . . it's the difference between reading about breast cancer and having it.

"There went everything . . . I suppose it's like the man who gets kicked out of the firm after thirty years. Twenty-seven years, my whole adult life, gone. It is still so astonishing to me. He left as if it had been nothing. I stood there while he was packing, saying, 'You can't just go . . . you can't just leave.' But, of course, he could and he did.

"He wiped out thirty years of me as easily as if he'd had a big eraser in his hand. There I was, a housewife without a husband. There's no such thing as a housewife without a husband, is there? Now the expression is a 'displaced homemaker.' I felt more like misplaced homemaker, something rather unimportant, something that could be misplaced somewhere or other without upsetting anyone.

"For the first six or seven months after he left, I really thought I was having a breakdown, and in a way I was. I became unsure of everything that I was or had done. All the right things I had done, so many of them well, I thought, how could they have been right when it all came out wrong? I had vertigo just wandering through my house. I'd keep setting the table for two. You know they say that after you have a limb amputated you can still 'feel' it for a long time. It was like that. . . .

"I never had much confidence, really. The only thing I had been sure of was how to run a house and keep a good marriage. Well, it was difficult to believe in that anymore. I no longer had any sense of confidence. I was a total failure. And I think I spent a lot of time wallowing in self-pity, putting a great deal of energy into the divorce settlement, and just generally being miserable.

"It was my daughter-in-law who forced me to see something. She is great, but she'll never win any points for tact. She is very, very direct. One day she drove over and said, 'Lillian, you're driving everyone crazy. You're driving yourself crazy. You can stay in this house with a black shawl over your head if you want to. But do you realize you've probably got thirty years of life left? That's a hell of a lot of time to spend looking at the walls.' Well, I went around the house saying, 'Thirty years, thirty years.' I thought, 'Lillian, either you kill yourself on the spot or you find some way out of this.' . . .

"I wasn't one of those women who had to get themselves back together. I had to start from scratch. At least I felt that way. Now I see some of the strengths that I must have had, way down deep, probably suppressed by my life, the priorities I had, all that.

"Finally, I was lucky. I was lucky in my friends and my family. My friend had opened that needlework shop a few years earlier without me. She offered me a job there." With some trepidation, Lillian learned to sell. Then she began to make needlepoint designs herself. Then, slowly, she learned about the running of a mail-order business out of the shop. Within three years, she and her friend have become partners in a modestly successful enterprise. (pp. 20–22)

Both of these accounts underscore a statement made earlier: a turning point is not just an event—it is a reconceptualization of oneself. In the first account, the young man's nascent biological interest was fanned into flames, and after that he was not the same as before. In the second account, Lillian—to continue in author Goodman's words—"changed in more ways than she would have believed possible." She not only took charge of her life but also became active in her community. She went from being a "victim of change" to an "agent of change." Caught up in her new concept of herself, Lillian said, "I cannot imagine going back to the way I was living before."

Turning Points as Autobiography

Each turning point introduces a new period or chapter of our lives. A period can be brief or long. It can be a period of growth and development, or consolidation, or deterioration and decline. It can be a relatively eventless time or one of many events. Ultimately, a larger event occurs—another turning point—that moves us into a new period and way of being. By linking our periods or chapters, we each arrive at our autobiography—the story of ourself as a person.

A chronological list of our most important turning points serves as a dramatic synopsis or outline of our life. Here is a list of turning points prepared by one of my students, a young woman 19 years old:

1. Age 3. My sister is born. I no longer am the baby of the family. I am now a "big girl." I hate not being the apple of my parents' eyes. This is my first experience of jealousy, and my first realization that I am not the center of the universe.

2. Age 11. Mom and Dad get a divorce. I had trusted my parents and felt that my family would be there for me forever. I now see that you can't trust adults, that there is no real safe harbor of security.

3. Age 11. Mom has a nervous breakdown and is hospitalized. I have to be strong for my little sister. I have to be strong for myself. I try to believe that I don't need anyone, that I can make it on my own.

© Ashleigh Brilliant 1981. Reprinted by permission.

© ASHLEIGH BRILLIANT 1981.   POT-SHOTS NO. 2328

MUST I LIVE THROUGH ALL THE DULL PARTS OF MY LIFE?

ISN'T THERE A CONDENSED VERSION?

4. Age 12. Dad remarries, and I go to live with him and my stepmother. She is young and pretty and really quite nice, but I hold her responsible for my parents' breakup. I hate her and I'm mean to her, but my feelings are all mixed up. I feel rebellious but also very vulnerable.

5. Age 16. My first sexual experience. I look to my boyfriend to provide a sense of safety and security. I try to think that in giving myself to him we become a family to replace the family I feel I no longer have at home.

6. Age 18. My high school graduation. This gives me my first real sense of achievement. I succeed almost in spite of myself. My parents were the ones who were determined that I finish high school. I was into drugs and other things and skipped school as much as I could. But in graduating, I feel something new—a feeling of empowerment. *I*—it's my decision this time—*I* decide to go to college.

Below is a list of turning points written by Jack Fincher (1975), who participated in one of Ira Progoff's journal workshops:

Creative, insecure son of an unhappy marriage

Alien resident of a new town

Lonely college student

Bitter draft bait passed over for coveted reporting job

Eager-beaver enlistee more at home in France than in his own country

Star cub

Disenchanted Francophile

Jilted suitor of the Bitch-Goddess Success

Competent craftsman

Middle-aged husband and father

Survivor (p. 20)

Concerning the process of constructing his list, Fincher recalled: "I wrote, tracing the contours of my life's journey from the American Southwest through Europe and New York City to the West Coast; from only child through air force recruit, college graduate, newspaperman, Fulbright fellow and magazine correspondent to freelance writer and family man. And as I wrote, the deeper, more telling outlines of my interior existence began to emerge in the shadowy landscape. They crept into the conscious train of my words unbidden and stayed there, refusing to be dislodged, communicating their own story" (p. 20).

As the list above shows, a set of turning points can reflect the movement or direction of a person's life. Here, as a last example, is a bare-bones but eloquent list of turning points read by another participant at a Progoff workshop:

I was born.

I loved.

I danced.

I wept.

I posed.

I suffered.

I was entranced.

I was humiliated.

I got lost.

I am trying to find my way. (Progoff, 1975, p. 111)

The Turning-Point Process

Turning points, Stanley Keleman (1974) writes, signal that an old way of living is coming to an end and a new way is beginning. He pictures each turning point as a loop, with the descending side representing the death of the old and the ascending side the birth of the new. Old boundaries (beliefs, feelings, action patterns, and/or relationships) are lost or modified, and new boundaries are formed. "Life," Keleman writes, "can be described as migration through many formative loops, many little dyings. Growth, change and maturing occur by deforming the old and forming the new" (p. 26).

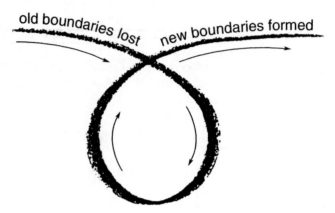

(From Keleman, 1974, p. 25)

The death of the old is not necessarily a sad event, and the birth of the new is not always joyous. We may be glad to see the old die or sad to see the new being born. In this regard, contrast the following accounts—one of regret, one of delight—related by two college women concerning their loss of virginity and initial reconceptualization of themselves:

My first experience with intercourse was a very painful one psychologically. I dated very little in high school so my first term freshman year up here was a new experience. I considered myself to be ugly and inferior to other girls, so when a really good-looking guy started paying attention to me I was swept off my feet. We went to bed soon after I met him (a week and a half). I was very inexperienced and he knew this. Afterwards he made a big joke out of the whole affair. This hurt me because I could not understand why he would joke about a matter so serious. After it was over I realized that he had just taken advantage of me and that I had just lost my virginity. I had many guilt feelings. I considered myself to be promiscuous and just a regular slut.

I lost my virginity at the age of seventeen. My hymen was "broken" by a guy named Don, whom I had planned to marry some day when we were both out of college. I went with him in high school until he moved to Alabama. During spring break of my freshmen year I went down to stay at his house for a few weeks. I must say, I was a little surprised when I felt what was happening. I guess we had just taken the petting a bit too far for him to handle. I wasn't about to wrestle with him because his parents were sleeping in their bedroom about twenty feet away and we were on the living room couch which was plastic. Needless to say, I didn't get much satisfaction out of it, but I didn't feel badly that it happened either. I guess I just didn't value being a virgin anymore and I did like him more than anyone else at the time. Wow! Did I ever feel like a real woman the next day! I can remember feeling that I must look different to other people. I felt so much older and prettier and sexier. (Morrison, Starks, Hyndman, & Ronzio, 1980, pp. 102–103)

In his insightful book *Transitions* (1980), William Bridges points out that culturally structured rites of passage, as well as those specific to individual lives, characteristically have three phases. There is the ending of the old, an intermediate "time in-between" phase, and then, at last, the beginning of the new.[1]

The Ending of the Old. Beginnings begin with endings. And endings begin when we note that we or our world has changed in some significant way. Change occurs all the time, but we experience it only at certain moments. Jourard (1968) writes that people "strive to construct a stable world, a world they can control and get their bearings in." They "freeze" the world "by pledging not to notice change until it has reached some critical degree, until it has gone so far that it can no longer be ignored" (p. 153).

The revelation of change may be a pleasant one—for instance, when we note that we have acquired some new skill or status or privilege. It may be decidedly unpleasant, as when we find that we have suffered a major loss and must downgrade our activities or aspirations or opinion of ourselves. Or it may be an occasion of mixed feelings, as when we discover that, eager as we are for the new, we are not quite ready to let go of the old—a condition in which many adolescents and more than a few new retirees find themselves.

Although a lifetime is filled with many endings, we often do not deal very well with them. We accumulate a lot of unfinished business: unexpressed grief, ungranted forgiveness, unburied regrets, wistful thoughts of what we might have done and what might have been. Why don't we put an end to the old and get on with the new? Why do we linger in the past?

One reason some of us get stuck is that we expect the world to be fair, but of course it often isn't—at least from our viewpoint. We remain too long at some delinquent debtor's door, pounding indignantly, demanding that he or she confess, pay up, make amends. By refusing to write off these bad emotional debts, we ironically incarcerate ourselves in a kind of creditor's prison.

Another reason for our stuckness is that it may give us an excuse for not moving into a bleak or intimidating present and future. By refusing to grieve, we may maintain the illusion that we are not bereft and alone. By being "victims of circumstance," we don't need to stir ourselves and become "movers." We have an excuse and a story to recite to everyone who will listen.

A third reason is that some of us simply haven't learned to do the often unpleasant work involved in tidying up our lives. The confrontations that are called for, the apologies that are in order, the restitutions that need to be made, the honest look at ourselves that is necessary if we are to learn from our mistakes—such things take determination, courage, and practice.

Our culture provides rituals to help us with some of our endings; for example, we have funeral and memorial rites to help us say good-bye to a loved one who has died. But for many important terminations, there are no rituals. There is a graduation ceremony that serves as a capstone to an educational process, but no ceremony when we flunk out or for some reason have to abandon a cherished academic and career goal. There is a marriage ceremony but no divorce ceremony. There is no ceremony when we lose a job to which we have given a good deal

---

[1] I acknowledge my considerable debt to William Bridges, upon whose work the following discussion of the phases in a transition is based. Readers who would like more help in understanding and coping with the turning points in their own lives would do well to read his book.

of our life or when we lose all our savings in a bad investment or when we suffer a major heart attack or stroke.

We need to pay attention to our endings and say good-bye to those things that are passing or lost. A proper good-bye keeps us from getting stuck in the past and helps us move on to give the present and future their due. With a proper good-bye, we don't need to weave our way gingerly around the untidy places we have made on life's path.

Today as I write this, by coincidence, an older woman who is an occasional student stopped by. "I have just got back from Las Vegas," she told me. "It's where I married my ex-husband, and I haven't wanted to return there to all those memories. But this time I got it all out of my system, and now Las Vegas is just Las Vegas."

The Time In-Between. Between the old ending and the new beginning, there is an intermediate phase that may be characterized by disorientation and nothingness. The old has disintegrated or been shattered, and the new has not yet formed. We may feel lost and confused or excited and intrigued or a little of both.

For those who are responding to a significant loss, this period can be one of great emptiness. What has been taken away has left a great vacuum that nothing else seems to fill. Life is seemingly without meaning or purpose. But, as Bridges (1980) points out, the seeming emptiness is an essential step between the old and the new, and it is one we need to understand and make time for. The emptiness is a kind of chaos, but it is not a mess. It is a primal state of energy and regeneration necessary to every new beginning. It is also a source of new perspective, for we come to see the old in a different light as we begin to glimpse the new.

In this intermediate phase, some persons report considerable difficulty in managing their everyday lives. They have trouble in getting their lives together. In fact, they seem to be "coming apart." In truth, there may be times when a person needs to fall apart in order to bring herself or himself together in a new way. Psychiatrist Frederic Flach (1974) has written eloquently about "the creative art of falling apart." Although many persons confuse this art with mental illness, weakness, helplessness, and vulnerability, Flach notes an essential difference. The former is a constructive experience leading to personal growth and readjustment. The person responds to the stress in a dramatic way, but is also able to put brakes on the upset and bring herself or himself together afterward.

In Flach's professional opinion, his clients who have mastered the art of falling apart are healthier than those who suffer the same stresses but bottle up feelings and try to stay stuck together no matter what. "The majority of people who have consulted me over the years, regardless of how much they have been suffering or how much they have been incapacitated at any particular moment, seem healthier mentally than many others I have encountered outside the consulting room. The latter, lacking insight, unmotivated to improve, blaming their problems on people around them, rarely if ever seek professional help. Working things out, to them, always depends on someone else's changing" (p. 17).

Bridges (1980) suggests a six-point program for those of us who find ourselves in an intermediate phase of a turning point. This program, he emphasizes, is not "a way out" but rather "a way in"—a way to amplify and make the most of this essential experience.

The first suggestion is that we find a time and place to be alone. In the middle of a transition, many are tempted to rush into the arms of others, but instead we may need to be more deeply with ourselves. Some of us sense this need to get away. We go backpacking or for long walks. We wander from cinema to cinema or simply drive, drive, drive with no seeming direction. Or we disappear within ourselves, leaving our external selves on automatic pilot. This is an important moratorium time in which we disengage ourselves from old stimuli and signals that keep us as we were. Instead, we tune into the new stirrings within ourselves.

Second, Bridges recommends that we keep a personal journal and record our experience during this phase. Hour by hour we seem lost in the forest, but in our observations set down day by day the pathway through the trees appears. A journal of this kind is not a simple ship's log of events; rather, we set down our feelings, fantasies, and dreams. We record surprises and puzzlements, and we search for connections. In our journal work we develop not only new insights but also a new appreciation of ourselves and a new way of being with ourselves.

The third suggestion is that we write our autobiography. Why? Bridges answers, "Because sometimes it is only in seeing where you have been that you can tell where you are headed. Because reminiscence is a natural impulse whenever something has just ended, as though you cannot really terminate anything without reviewing it and putting it into order. Because recollection is likely to turn up some useful information about other transitions in your past" (pp. 122–123). As we review the past from where we are in the present, we find that the past isn't quite what we thought it was; therefore, the present—built upon that past—isn't quite as it appeared either, and this discovery opens up some new futures.

Fourth, Bridges encourages us to use some of this intermediate time to discover what we really want. What we *really* want, surprisingly, may be something of a mystery to us. We may know what others want for us. We may know what we *should* want. We may know what almost everybody else seems to want. But what do *we* really want? To answer this question, psychotherapist James Bugental (1976) writes, we need to listen within ourselves—a kind of listening we may be unfamiliar with but can learn how to do. If we listen carefully, we can come to hear our own voice.

As a fifth step, Bridges writes, "Think of what would be unlived in your life if it ended today" (p. 126). Suppose you prepared two lists to show how you had dealt with all the years given you to date. On one list would be all the things you've done. On the other, all the things you didn't do. What would be on each list? Henry David Thoreau said that "we live but a fraction of our lives." How large a fraction of your life are you living?

As the sixth and last step, Bridges suggests that we devise our own "passage journey" to serve the function of "the rites of passage" that have been a structured part of traditional societies. This may be an elaboration of the first step, possibly spending a few days away from usual places, pursuits, and persons—a retreat into emptiness and receptivity. He cautions against anything foolhardy; this is to be a time of careful and conscious reflection on one's life and transition process.

The Beginning of the New. And then, at last, we come to the beginning. Out of the death of the old, out of the fallow, chaos, and realignment of the middle phase, a new energy arises, and something new begins to grow.

There is an Eastern saying to the effect that one doesn't need to seek a teacher because when the pupil is ready the guru will appear. When we are ready to begin again, opportunities will present themselves. Or we will find opportunities where none seem to have existed before.

As Bridges points out, our new beginnings are often not dramatic or impressive or even seemingly calculated. He suggests that we stop a moment and recall the important beginnings in our own past.

Think back to the important beginnings in your own past. You bumped into an old friend you hadn't seen for years, and he told you about a job at his company that opened up just that morning. You met your spouse-to-be at a party that you really hadn't wanted to go to and that you almost skipped. You learned to play the guitar while you were getting over the measles, and you learned French because the Spanish class met at 8:00 A.M. and you hated to get up early. You happened to pick up a book that totally changed your life because it was the only one lying on your friend's coffee table—and later you were astonished to find that you had once tried to read it before, but had found it dull and confusing. (pp. 135–136)

New beginnings are often rather rocky. Although we seek to shuffle off the old, we may also be reluctant to do so. Although we may seem to seek change, we may also resist it and be frightened by it. And those around us may also conspire to keep us as we have been. In the push and pull, we may become unsure of what we really want. So it's frequently two steps forward and one step back and, alas, occasionally one step forward and two back.

What can we do to help begin our beginnings? Bridges suggests four helpful tactics. First, put an end to getting ready. Timing is important, since until we are ready, we won't make a good beginning. But one can get ready endlessly and never be quite ready. "When the time comes, stop getting ready—and do it" (p. 146).

The second tactic is to begin to identify ourselves with the image of the person we wish to become. We act "as if" we are that person. "What is it going to feel like when you've actually done whatever it is that you are setting out to do? All right, then say it's done. There, you did it. You are the person who does that sort of thing" (p. 146). You are the person who picked himself up when the company folded and started a new one with absolute zero. You are the person who picked herself up after the devastating divorce, finished college, yes, with two kids in tow, and got a degree and a good position. You are the person who—disability, wheelchair, and all—made a good life, a full life.

The third tactic is to agree to proceed step by step—not leap by leap. Resist the siren song that says there is a better, faster, more exciting route. "Trudging from appointment to appointment, licking stamps, adding columns of figures, making reminder phone calls, and explaining your idea for the hundredth time—these are the trivia from which vital new ventures finally emerge" (p. 147).

The fourth and last tactic is to be mindful of the process and not preoccupied with the results. When we are focused on the goal, every interview that does not land a job becomes a *failure;* but when we are process oriented, every interview, whatever the result, can teach us something and deepen our understanding of ourselves. Goals come and go, things begin and end, but the process goes on and on.

Carl Rogers (1961) wrote that clients coming to him to mend their lives were likely to want to achieve some fixed state or become a fixed entity. They wanted to solve their problems once and for all. In therapy Rogers helped them see that human beings aren't products—they're processes; they are flowing rivers of change, streams of becoming. He showed them how to continue to discover new elements about themselves in the flow of their experience.

Out of Phase. Bridges takes care to note that the transition process, as it is lived, is frequently quite complicated; the phases do not stay lined up in their proper order—that is, (1) ending, (2) in-between or neutral zone, and (3) new beginning. The neutral phase may seem to precede the ending or even come after the supposed beginning.

You see the former case when someone "goes dead" at work or around the home. There has been no ending, no disengagement. The old job or the old relationship is intact. But the person is *not there.* He or she has become unplugged emotionally. Sometimes this happens because a decision has been made inwardly to end the situation. Emotionally, an ending has already taken place, although the outer circumstances remain unchanged. Or it may happen because of a great disappointment—the failure to get an expected promotion, for example. Again, a subtle inner ending takes place, although everything goes on as before on the outside. In such cases the neutral zone overlaps with the old life, and the person moves like a sleep-walker through a role that was once identified with. (pp. 129–130)

Bridges notes that the ending of the old and the beginning of the new often appear side by side without any of the internal work of the in-between zone. One moves across the country and immediately takes up a new life. One rushes into a new relationship with no alone and pondering time. "In such cases," Bridges writes, "one is likely to be well into the new beginnings before waking up to the fact that it is all strange and unreal" (p. 130). The inner reorientation must be accomplished, even though belatedly.

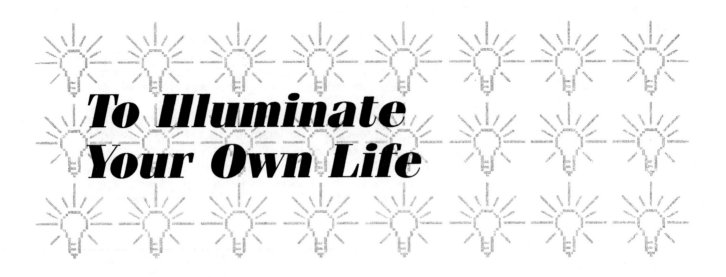

To Illuminate Your Own Life

Anchor and Apply*

1. Is there a particular Eriksonian crisis (see Box 4.2) that you have not managed well or are not managing well? Discuss this aspect of your development.

2. What are your lifetime goals? Or, to ask this question in another way, do you have a "life plan"? Discuss this aspect of your life, indicating what your plan is, how you arrived at it, why it's important to you, and how you will accomplish it.

3. Did you find a title for your autobiography in Box 4.3? If not, compose your own title. Does your life have a scripted quality, a repetitive pattern, or a theme? Discuss this aspect of your life.

4. Describe the similarities you see between your life and that of a character in a particular myth or legend or folk tale.

5. As you think of the turning points of your life, were those that were anticipated more easily managed than those that were unanticipated or nonevent transitions? Discuss this aspect of your life.

6. Make an assessment of a current or recent turning point, using Schlossberg's four S's—situation, self, support, and strategies.

7. Describe one of your turning points in terms of Bridges' three phases: the ending of the old, the time in-between, and the beginning.

---

* These "anchor and apply" items are designed to help you use the concepts of the chapter as stimuli to prompt new or deeper or clearer insights into yourself and your life. To respond to an item, first find the material in the chapter that is most relevant to the item *and* yourself; that's called "anchoring." Second, think about this material in relationship to yourself and your life and keep thinking about it until you arrive at a new or deeper or clearer understanding; that's the "apply" or application part. When you write or present your response to the item, be sure to include both parts, that is, both the anchor material and the application. You can know you are successful on an item if, in completing it, you truly learn something new or understand something better.

Exploration

Turning Points

A *turning point* is a crucial change or shift in our lives. "Crucial" implies that this change is likely to influence future events. A turning point is a significant point of movement. It is a gateway to a new chapter of our personal history or biography.

In their book *Watersheds: Mastering Life's Unpredictable Crises,* Robert and Jeanette Lauer (1989) tell about a young woman whose running became a turning point in her life. Her husband had begun to run and urged her to do so. She resisted because she had never exercised, was in terrible shape, and found running painful. But she didn't give up, and there was notable improvement—not only in her running but in the rest of her life as well. She said:

> It was a turning point for me. I was really tempted to stop. I could easily have gone back to being a slouch. But I kept on. I began to feel good physically and mentally. It boosted my confidence in myself. I lost weight. I had always been somewhat disappointed in my appearance and physical abilities, but now I was proud of them for the first time. And my husband and I became closer because of the new shared activity. (p. 187)

Although turning points are frequently associated with external events—for example, a death or birth or marriage or perhaps a change of location or job—it is the change within ourselves that is important. Psychologist Stanley Keleman (1974) recalls a change within himself arising from the time his father was ill, in pain, and fearful of dying:

> This experience was a major event, a turning point, a step in my life that galvanized me out of my childhood into the beginning of my manhood. I had just become bigger, older, wiser. The fragility of me, of those around me, and of our finiteness was born. I knew something. I thought differently. I felt differently. I had to realign myself to the world I knew, for it was no more. I became serious. A bit of melancholy stepped into my life. (p. 22)

A seemingly major external happening may leave us unmoved while an important change in the way we view ourselves or our world may occur without any specific observable event. For example, a divorce after many months or years of growing estrangement may not be a turning point. Instead, the turning point may have occurred much earlier, in the dawning realization that the marriage had too many problems to last or that there wasn't enough commitment to work out those problems.

What are the most significant turning points in your life? A question like this will not be fully welcomed by everyone. Some of us have difficulty in examining the past or have found little benefit from doing so, but reminiscence can be helpful. Rather than just rummaging in sometimes painful memories, we can use reminiscence to accommodate the past and build a better present and future. For more information on the beneficial use of reminiscence, see Box 4.4.

Creative Reminiscence

We are all historians. We record our experiences in the pages of our memories, where they await our reminiscence. The use we make of reminiscence can greatly affect our well-being.

Reminiscence as a doorway to personal growth has sometimes been criticized. One reason for this criticism is that we can get stuck in the past, endlessly retelling or reliving it but never learning from or using it to good purpose. Another reason is that a heightened preoccupation with the past can keep us from making the most of the present and future.

Creative reminiscence is the recollection and sharing of the past in a way that creates a better present and future. The Danish scholar Søren Kierkegaard wrote, "We live life forward but understand it backward." In creative reminiscence, we give ourselves an opportunity to reflect on what has been and relate it to the full sweep of the past and present. As we look at the past with more experienced, wiser eyes, we may gain new insight and obtain guidance for the present and future.

Through creative reminiscence, we can clear the past. We can finish unfinished business and deal with denial, regret, grief, and unfulfilled dreams. But we can also use creative reminiscence to commemorate and celebrate the past, making the most of what was good.

We learn about a nation by tracing its history. We learn about ourselves by tracing our development. In creative reminiscence, we get a new sense of identity. We also have an opportunity to maintain and affirm what we consider to be most positively and saliently us.

Sharing our recollections is an important part of creative reminiscence. As we share, we learn from observing ourselves—what was difficult to share and why, what brought unexpected tears of joy, what brought shame or pride, what brought pain or relief. And we welcome the response of others as we share ourselves with them; their response can give us a new perspective on ourselves and our lives.

© Ashleigh Brilliant 1987. Reprinted by permission.

Your work in this exploration is in two parts, but you can do both at the same time. For the first part, you are to identify the turning points of your life. Set the points down in chronological order (earliest turning point first, next earliest second, and so on). Include just your most important turning points but not less than six and not more than ten. Describe each point briefly in a phrase or one or two sentences.

For the second part of the exploration, you are to indicate why each turning point was indeed a turning point. To do this, clearly indicate in a few sentences or a paragraph the considerable, continuing, or lasting effect that this turning point had in your life. Note, as examples, how Keleman was affected by his father's illness and how the young woman's life was affected by her running.

Do your work on the next page and continue on page 130 if you would like more room.

My Turning Points

High Points and Low Points

Some of us think of life as a staircase. Once we climb to the top—and get all those things we're striving for—we'll be happy (we think). But life to some seems to be more like a roller coaster. We go up and we go down. And we go up and we go down.

Abraham Maslow (1962) called attention to those moments when we are, so to speak, "up" on the roller coaster. He called these moments—instances of great happiness, ecstasy, or wonder—"peak experiences." A random sample of persons 16 years of age and older in five San Francisco Bay Area counties showed peak experiences to be relatively common: 82 percent reported the experience of being deeply moved by the "beauty of nature," 50 percent had experienced close contact with something "holy or sacred," and 39 percent had experienced being in "harmony with the universe." Furthermore, more than half of those who reported a peak experience said that it had had a deep and lasting effect on their lives (Wuthnow, 1978).

Psychologist Anthony D'Aguanno has been interested in "prolonged positive experiences"—experiences lasting a week or longer (possibly much longer), in which one feels "fully alive, fully healthy, functioning to the utmost of [one's] capabilities, and with an absence, or minimum, of conflict" (n.d., p. 10). The impact of a prolonged positive experience of his own brought his attention to this area—an incident that he describes in this way:

> About two years ago I had an experience that became a turning point in my life. It began when I left Los Angeles one Sunday morning, hitch-hiking my way up the Pacific Coast. I was leaving behind one of the most bizarre, intense, frightening, lonely, rich, challenging, tension-filled periods of my life. I had just completed a year's internship at a child guidance clinic as a prerequisite to obtaining my Ph.D. in clinical psychology.
>
> My year in Los Angeles was a year of pressure and conflict. I had never lived in a city before, and I found Los Angeles to be a totally new and, for the most part, alien environment. The work I was doing in the clinic was being continually observed, evaluated, and questioned—and I myself was questioning many of my own beliefs. Moreover, during that year, a long and intense relationship with a woman had been shattered.
>
> So, as I set out on my trip up the coast, I had a feeling of completion and a feeling of impatience to be free from the stifling surroundings of the city. Somewhere past Santa Barbara, I started experiencing a peace and calmness perhaps unknown at any other time in my life. I was happy, joyful, delighted at being alive. I was excited and bursting with energy—physical, mental, and emotional. I felt almost totally free and unrestricted. My actions seemed more spontaneous and "right," in the sense of being appropriate to the total situation. My thoughts were clearer, quieter, and less con-

flicted than usual. . . . My senses seemed sharper than normal; I felt that I was able to notice small details or subtleties that I normally might have missed. I had more appreciation of just being alive and of the entire universe, especially nature, than perhaps ever before.

The ways in which I met and experienced others were very different from what I was used to. I was able to relate to the most varied and diverse people, many of whom had certain qualities or traits which I would have normally disliked or even have found abhorrent, with an almost continuous positive feeling. I met people incredibly easily and seemed to be aware of cues (mostly nonverbal) I would have ordinarily missed. These provided "openings" in which might have appeared otherwise to be impregnable walls.

On the 24th day of my journey, I was conscious of having to make a decision—whether to prolong my trip or to return to the East Coast and a new job due to start soon. Somehow I knew my experience was over. I flew east that night.

Almost immediately upon my return I experienced the crash. I felt as though I were jolted back to earth with the harsh reality of everyday demands—finding a place to live, getting a car, the demands of my new job, the anxiety about my dissertation, the pain of seeing the woman I had formerly been living with, who was now with someone else. Gradually, however, I became resettled and began to notice that many of the positive effects of my experience were being carried over into my new life. Because of the impact of this experience on my life and because of my desire to discover something about this type of experience in the lives of others, I decided to do research on this very positive state of being. (n.d., pp. 9–10)

Consider your own life and recall a high point, a peak experience, or a prolonged positive experience. Write an account of this time below (add an additional sheet if you would like more space) and then turn to the next page.

In contrast to Maslow and D'Aguanno, who studied the upmost times of life, psychologist Peter Ebersole (1970) was interested in nadirs or low points. Ebersole defines nadir as "the most sorrowful or painful experience" of one's life. An example of a nadir experience or nadir period is vividly described by Jerry Rubin (1976) in his book about himself, *Growing (Up) at Thirty-Seven.* Here is a brief excerpt:

> In 1970, at the age of thirty-two, I had everything I thought I wanted in life. I was a leader of a powerful political movement struggling to transform our country's institutions. I loved and enjoyed the love of a warm woman. I had written a best-selling book and was a folk hero of rebellion to young people. My life was exciting, involved, relevant. I had satisfied all my childhood dreams. And then: crash.
>
> In two brief years the mass political movement disappeared and the woman left me. A group of young kids publicly retired me from the movement for being over thirty. My fame turned to notoriety and "Where is he now?" stories. Newspapers began describing me with adjectives like "erstwhile" and "aging." People began relating to me as an image, not as a human being. Worst of all, I myself believed the image; I forgot who I was. I felt dead at thirty-four. (pp. 1–2)

Consider your own life and recall a low point or nadir or a time of frustration, conflict, anxiety, pain, sorrow, or confusion. Write an account of this time below (add an additional sheet if you would like more space) and then turn to the next page.

Maslow noted that peak experiences may have very important consequences. After a peak experience, we may see ourselves or our world in a different and perhaps more positive way. D'Aguanno made a similar observation about the carryover of prolonged positive experiences. "Some of the common results included: more trust in the unconscious, less need for control, less anxiety about the future, feelings of security or strength not previously felt, the ability to be more clear on what one wants, the ability to be nicer to oneself, increased ability to accept reality without prejudging it, clearer thinking, renewed interest in learning, and alterations in the way of viewing reality" (p. 10). Thus, a high point in our life can also be a turning point.

Curiously, similar positive consequences have been noted after many nadir experiences or periods. In her study of victims of tragic events, Shelley Taylor (1989) found that many were caused to rethink their priorities and values and, as a consequence, came to lead more fulfilling lives. In Ebersole's study of nadirs and peaks in college students, many students indicated that their nadirs had positive effects, and some described their nadirs as more influential and enduring than their peaks. Perhaps nadir experiences, difficult as they are to live through, are necessary for growth or at least presage growth. Nadirs may be "little dyings" that permit us to be reborn or reconstituted in a different and better way. Following his "death" at the age of 34, Jerry Rubin wrote, "One day, as I was walking down the street in New York, an insight zapped me. I was being given an opportunity to grow. If I didn't stay stuck in old images, I could start my life all over, expand into new areas, reincarnate myself" (p. 2). Thus, a low point (as well as a high point) can be an auspicious turning point in our life.

In the space below (add another sheet if you would like more space), discuss the consequences of your high point and low point, indicating (1) what, if anything, you learned from them and (2) how, if at all, you changed or grew because of them.

Exploration

The Time Machine*

We can peer into the future from the present, or we can get into our "time machine" and project ourselves into the future; from that vantage point we can look back on the "past." For example, we can project ourselves into a time a few years from now and then look back on the events which occurred between that time and today. In the following passage, a 33-year-old woman visualizes her life three years from now:

> My thirty-sixth birthday last week. I finished my law degree with honors. Have been so busy that I haven't had time to write here for an entire year.
>
> I'm joining the Public Defender's office. Me—a trial lawyer. I can hardly believe it!
>
> The worst is over. I visited my daughter in Maine this summer. She's old enough to talk about what happened now. I think I was able to help her understand my decision. Oh, and my article on recidivism among middle-class women was published. So it's all worked out.

Projecting ourselves into the future is a useful way to explore alternative courses of action. Standing at a crossroad, we can project ourselves down one fork of the road and then the other, so that we can gain some perspective. For example, here a 24-year-old ballet dancer with a promising career and a decision to make about whether to marry her boyfriend projects herself down two roads (on the left, if she marries him, and on the right, if she doesn't marry at all):

I'm now forty years old, still in good shape and thinking about getting a facelift, but I'm afraid of an artificial look. How do I evaluate the past sixteen years with Jerry? It's been hard but worth it. Sometimes I've hated him, other times loved him intensely. It's never been boring, though often frustrating.

I never became really famous. I never set the world on fire, but I've done what I wanted, what interested me. All and all it's been good. It's the next ten years that worry me, forty to fifty. Will I pay now for having played it safe before? This is the time I had hoped to be most productive, to have my own dance troupe and be directing and choreographing. Now I know that won't happen. Unless I can do something earthshaking at this point, I will be disappointed in myself. I have no desire to grow into a pleasant matron. Glamour no longer attracts me.

Well, I've done what I set out to do. I have my own dance troupe which is world famous. We just finished the European and Soviet tour. Why I had to go it alone, without a man, I'm not sure. Women envy me and I resent their ignorant envy. A side of me has never been fulfilled, the girl-woman who needs to be loved and for whom the real proof would have been a lifetime of intimacy and devotion.

On the balance, I'm grateful for the specialized gratification I've had—freedom, the masculine pleasure of seeing my mind create form as dance and affect others at a deep level.

I'm sick right now over negotiations for the next season. Will I never be calm about this stage of it? I seem to work off my own stress. Even in production I can't say I *enjoy* it—not like one enjoys being held.

But my babies, my creations, seem worth it when it all comes together. There's the pleasure of marriage and birth with each new ballet.

* This exploration is adapted from the work of Tristine Rainer, and the two sets of case material are from her book *The New Diary* (1978).

From: *The Illuminated Life*, by Abe Arkoff. Copyright © 1995 by Allyn and Bacon.   135

After this woman had written and studied her two projections, she gained a deeper insight into the assumptions that she was making about career and marriage, and she saw that she needed to openly discuss her ambitions with her boyfriend. She wrote this further comment:

> I think what's interesting to observe here is that I set marriage and career as mutually exclusive options, as in a 1930s "woman's film." I see a place for some career within marriage, but strangely, no place for marriage within the career I really want. The work replaces both marriage and children. I suppose because I assume that any man—Jerry included—would be too threatened to live with a woman director-choreographer, and that I wouldn't want him to play the role of "wife" to me.

In this exploration, you are to project yourself into two realistic, definitely possible, but different futures—Future A and then Future B. You might, for example, project yourself several years into the future and see yourself if you start exercising and dieting (Future A) and then, for contrast, if you do not and simply continue as you are today (Future B). Or see yourself if you change your job or major (Future A) and also if you leave things as they are now (Future B). Or if you abandon or sever an important but troubled relationship (Future A) versus staying with it and working on it (Future B).

In Part I, begin this exploration by describing the two alternate futures or plans of action you are considering. Then board the Time Machine, travel to each future, and write up what happened in Part II. Afterward, turn to Part III.

Part I: Describe two realistic, definitely possible, but different futures or plans of action you are considering.

Future A:

Future B:

Part II: Write what happened when you chose and traveled to Future A and what happened when you chose and traveled to Future B.

Future A	**Future B**
Here I am _____ years later and this is what has happened:	*Here I am _____ years later and this is what has happened:*

Future A, continued   **Future B, continued**

Part III: Discuss your experience in the Time Machine, including any new or deepened insights and any conclusions or resolutions at which you have arrived.

Question 5

Significant Others

How Do I Relate to the Most Important Persons in My Life?

There may be times on life's journey when we feel very much alone, but usually we are on the path with others. Certain persons may be with us for the entire trip or nearly so. Others may join us for a while and then depart. Some who have gone remain with us in spirit or influence, while some who live with us may seem distant. And a few persons whom we have never met may somehow seem to guide our steps. The persons who have the most important effects on us are called *significant others.*

Significant others influence our lives in many ways. They may serve as models whom we pattern ourselves after, willingly or unwillingly, knowingly or unwittingly. They influence the assumptions we make about other people and the way we relate to or interact with them. They influence the way we think about and value ourselves.

Significant others may love us or hate us, or perhaps it is a combination of both emotions. They may nurture, comfort, support, and control us. They may help us grow or keep us from growing. They share our lives and we share theirs. For our part, we may love or hate or nurture or hamper them in return. Each of us is a significant other for a number of other individuals.

Most likely we consider each of our parents a significant other. One or more of our siblings may also be of considerable significance in our lives, as may be a grandparent, uncle or aunt, or cousin. Other very important individuals may include a lover, spouse, children of our own, a best friend, a teacher, or a mentor.

Human personality appears to be less a product of dramatic events than of countless daily events that shape us in a particular way. In trying to account for who we have become, we may recall a salient trauma, perhaps our failure to adjust to a new school or our parents' divorce. But, as Combs, Avila, and Purkey (1978) state, "What makes the difference in human personality is not the trauma itself, but the complex of other experiences that hammered and molded a person's meanings to a state later triggered into explicit expression by some traumatic event" (p. 25).

In the same way, the development of an individual's personality is influenced by a number of significant others. "It is rarely mother alone, father alone, schools alone, friends alone—any one factor alone—that shapes the destiny of the child. From birth onward, children are affected by a mosaic of forces. While one or another element may stand out in the case of a particular child, it is typically a combination of them that ultimately leaves its mark" (Segal & Yahraes, 1978b, p. 303). We are not riddles with a single answer; rather, we are puzzles whose every part must be fitted together. Segal and Yahraes explain:

> A caring mother's abiding presence early in the life of her child is clearly a source of strength and stability, yet her absence need not have a deleterious effect if the father or another substitute caretaker acts out of an equally strong commitment to the child's well-being. Erosions in the child's mental health induced by one wildly psychotic parent can be ameliorated by the other stable and healthy one. An eagerly anticipated child who enjoys warm and rewarding attachments during the first months of life may be protected against emotional problems—but not certainly; the benefits of early bonds can quickly come unglued in a harsh world of hunger and hate. And, as one more example, the flickering sense of self-confidence in a poor and persecuted child may be rekindled by a dedicated teacher who expects much and inspires greatly. (p. 303)

Both physical and psychological health are influenced by our larger social environments—most notably, by the networks provided by our families, peer groups, and workplaces. These networks support and empower us, give us a sense of belonging and identity, promote our self-esteem, and help buffer the impact of negative events. When these ties are disrupted, there may be a profound impact on our well-being. Of course, social networks also can be a negative influence, promoting illness or maladaptive behavior such as substance abuse (Rodin & Salovey, 1989).

Significant others can loom so large in our lives that we may be unable to look at them candidly or see them clearly. And our view of them may continually change. As psychiatrist-consultant Richard Robertiello told Nancy Friday, author of the widely read *My Mother/My Self:* "Like everyone else you keep changing your idea of your mother. One day she's good, kind, and loving. The next day, she's frightened, timid, and asexual. One day all you can see is your anger. Right now you want to go into a period of seeing her as all good. Either way, it means you are still avoiding the job of seeing her realistically" (Friday, 1978, p. 461). And in

IF ONLY I COULD RELATE TO THE PEOPLE I'M RELATED TO!

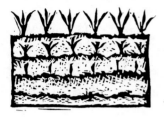

Significant Others: How Do I Relate to the Most Important Persons in My Life?

Seedthoughts

1. The meeting of two personalities is like the contact of two chemical substances; if there is any reaction, both are transformed.

   —*Carl Jung*

2. If the dead be truly dead, why should they still be walking in my heart?

   —*Winnenap, Shoshone medicine man*

3. Friend: one who knows all about you and loves you just the same.

   —*Elbert Hubbard*

4. It takes a long time to grow an old friend.

   —*John Leonard*

5. Don't walk in front of me,
   I may not follow.
   Don't walk behind me,
   I may not lead.
   Walk beside me,
   And just be my friend.

   —*Albert Camus*

6. Before you marry, keep both eyes open; after marriage shut one.

   —*Jamaican saying*

7. I believe that we all should wise up and recognize that a marriage is a small business and that married couples are business partners.

   —*David Hopkinson (clinical psychologist)*

8. Everybody comes from a crazy family.

   —*Kate Nelligan*

9. The first half of our lives is spoiled by our parents and the last half by our children.

   —*anonymous cynic*

10. When you have children, you begin to understand what you owe your parents.

    —*Japanese saying*

11. Pretend you are your father or mother and write a short composition on "The difficulties I had in raising my child."

    —*Martin Shepard*

12. It takes a whole village to raise a child.

    —*African saying*

the same connection Mark Twain wrote, "When I was a boy of fourteen, my father was so ignorant I could hardly stand to have the old man around. But when I got to be twenty-one, I was astonished to see how much he had learned in seven years."

Parents as Significant Others

As we begin to think of the persons who are most significant for us, probably our parents come immediately to mind. When we are very young, parents are giants in our lives; as we grow and as our world expands, they become more life-sized. But, for most of us, our parents continue to be a considerable force even though they may be far away or long since dead.

One way parents influence us is by serving as models. We imitate them and, to some extent, become like them, sometimes even without knowing it. Friday writes, "The older I get, the more of my mother I see in myself. The more opposite my life and my thinking grow from hers, the more of her I hear in my voice, see in my facial expression, feel in my emotional reactions I have come to recognize as my own. It is almost as if in extending myself, the circle closes in to completion. She was my first and most lasting model" (p. 45).

Sometimes our parents serve as negative models. We may decide we don't want to be like a particular parent—at least in some regard—and we make a determined effort to be the opposite. I remember hearing one young man say he wanted a son so he could show his father how a son should be brought up. He seemed determined to become the good father that, in his own estimation, he never had.

Occasionally we find to our surprise that we are more like a parent than we had intended to be. In dedicating a book to his own parents, psychologist Howard Halpern (1979) wrote, "Though you have been dead many years, I increasingly marvel at your continued existence in me, sometimes to my frustration and chagrin and often to my pleasure." Tongue in cheek (I think), Quentin Crewe observed that "children despise their parents until the age of forty, when they suddenly become just like them—thus preserving the system." One of the mothers Friday interviewed had a confirming experience:

> "I needed and loved my mother so intensely at times," says a young mother of a five-year-old daughter, "that I remember saying to her when I was eight, 'I will never love my child as much as you love me.' Now I know that I meant smother, not love. So many harmful ideas are hidden by the word love. My mother seemed so selfless, so giving. I remember dreading the thought of my mother dying. But I didn't want her to live for me. It piled too much guilt on me. And yet, I didn't dare ask for any space. It would have made me guilty. When I was seventeen I couldn't wait to get away from home. When I married and had a daughter of my own, I became just as possessive of her as my mother was of me. I was a working mother, and thought that meant I was giving my daughter the space I never had. But I used to telephone home all the time from work, and when I got home, guiltily made up for being away by smothering her. Just like my mother, I called every possessive, overprotective thing I did 'love.'" (p. 33)

A second way our parents influence us is by acting as guides and instructors. Our parents teach us manners and morals. They teach us their view of life and of the world. Their teachings may serve us well or serve us poorly. And we may chew on, digest, and assimilate their teachings or choke on them and throw them up.

Halpern (1976) makes an important distinction between "good enough" parents and parents who are "saints." Good enough parents allow us to become ourselves and teach us to question and make our own decisions. Saints know who

© Ashleigh Brilliant 1979. Reprinted by permission.

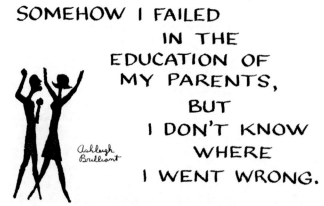

POT-SHOTS NO 1585.

SOMEHOW I FAILED
IN THE
EDUCATION OF
MY PARENTS,
BUT
I DON'T KNOW
WHERE
I WENT WRONG.

we should become (like them) and present us with a rigid system of shoulds and should nots, which they expect us to swallow whole (as they did).

If you have been "blessed" with saintly parents and are still trying to recover from this blessing, here are some questions Halpern suggests you ask yourself as you reappraise one of their injunctions—a rule that has been "nailed to the door of your mind":

Why am I following this injunction?
Does this way of behaving make sense to me now or am I adhering to it simply because that is what I was taught?
What are the consequences of continuing to follow this injunction?
What are the consequences if I break with this injunction?
If I break with the old rule, will somebody get hurt? Will I?
If I break with the old rule, will my life go better or worse?
Am I doing this only to rebel, or to get even with my parents for past injuries, or do I feel I really need to make this change to live more fully?
How much parental disapproval will result from this change? Can I bear their disapproval? Can I get them to be more accepting? (pp. 106–107)

Some of us have parents who themselves broke the rules in a way that caused considerable trauma in our lives. We may be survivors of extreme abuse: children of alcoholics or victims of incest or violence. Growing numbers of persons are joining self-help groups such as Adult Children of Alcoholics and Other Dysfunctional Families (ACOA). These groups have been helpful for many but have also been criticized for promoting "parent bashing" more than the acceptance of responsibility to make one's own adult life better (Blau, 1990).

More and more of us are raised in broken homes, perhaps scarcely knowing one of our parents, or in reconstituted families with a stepparent and possibly half-sibs. Recent research suggests that children are negatively affected by divorce and that its impact on them may persist indefinitely (Glenn, 1985; Wallerstein and Blakeslee, 1989). One problem, called "the sleeper effect," concerns the difficulty that some such children have in making later romantic attachments, and both males and females from broken homes are more likely to get divorced than those from intact families.

Although it is commonly assumed that older children weather the effects of parental divorce better than younger ones, a study of fifty college-age children whose parents divorced in midlife revealed that most of them (forty-seven) responded with a profound sense of loss, disillusionment, and negatively transformed attitudes toward love and marriage (Cain, 1990). Typical was this comment of one young man: "Since their divorce, I'm gun-shy about love and spastic about marriage. To me, getting married is like walking over a minefield, you know it's going to explode . . . you just don't know when!" (p. 54). Many students feared that they were destined to repeat their parents' mistakes, and they were determined not to. They still wanted to marry and have children, but what they hoped to recapture was the family of their innocent childhood.

There are two kinds of developmental stuckness, according to psychotherapist Martin Shepard (1976). Those of us who as adults are "child-stuck"—stuck in childhood—remain overly docile and dependent. If we are "adolescent-stuck," we relate to our parents—and perhaps other parentlike figures—in a perpetually rebellious and ill-tempered way. Shepard notes that, despite many exceptions, women are more likely to show child-stuckness and males are more likely to show adolescent-stuckness.

If we are stuck, the task is to get unstuck. As Shepard remarks, "You can't have a very good self-concept—can't very well consider yourself any person's equal—if you remain a child-at-heart in relationship to your parents" (p. 96).

Ram Dass (1971) writes that at every stage of our journey through life we need to keep our own relationships—especially our relationship with our parents—in order and leave no enemies behind.

> . . . if you never got on well with one of your parents and you have left that parent behind on your journey in such a way that the thought of that parent arouses anger or frustration or self-pity or any emotion . . . you are still attached. You are still stuck. And you must get that relationship straight before you can finish your work. And what, specifically, does "getting it straight" mean? Well, it means re-perceiving that parent, or whoever it may be, with total compassion . . . seeing him as a being of the spirit, just like you, who happens to be your parent. . . . Even if the parent has died, you must, in your heart and mind, re-perceive that relationship until it becomes, like every one of your current relationships, one of light. If the person is still alive you may, when you have proceeded far enough, revisit and bring the relationship to the present. For, if you can keep the visit totally in the present, you will be free and finished. (p. 56)

Several of my students who have been grievously hurt by a parent have told me they found Ram Dass's instructions extremely difficult—even impossible—to follow. Each of us may have to find our own way to bind our wounds and leave the past behind. Otherwise, we remain burdened by the past or stuck in it.

Shepard suggests the following axiom to help us see our own parents more realistically: "Grown-ups are merely children in aging skin." He recalls the approach taken by one of his therapeutical colleagues in treating a young man who was constantly fighting with his highly critical and irrational mother:

> My friend asked his patient the following question: "If you passed by a mental institution and saw your mother looking through the barred windows on one of the floors, and she was screaming the same things at you, as you passed by, that she now screams at you at home, would it still trouble you?" "No," said the young man. "I'd discount it, because I'd know she was crazy." "From now on, then, every time your mother gets on your nerves, I want you to recall that picture of her shouting from that hospital window." His patient did just that and found his aggravation and frustration subsiding. A device such as this is, I think, a useful tool for people who find themselves continuously fighting with a non-accepting parent. (pp. 97–98)

Eda LeShan (1988) recalls that in her mid-twenties, when she went to see a therapist, she started out by saying, "I don't understand how I could have any problems—I had perfect parents" (p. 473). It's doubtful that any of us had perfect parents any more than our parents had perfect children. And if we did have perfect parents, what then? I have a good friend who recalls her own childhood as nearly perfect, and yet her own life has not been an easy one; she is divorced and her relationship with her own children is not what she would like it to be.

I particularly like the evenhanded perspective taken by therapist Sheldon Kopp (1976) as he thought back on his own parents. He saw their virtues and flaws; but, more important, he saw how a parental flaw could provoke growth in a child as well as threaten it. He put this all in a nutshell in a dedication that appears in one of his books:

> For my dead parents, whom I often miss:
> My mother whose strength and ferocity nurtured me, almost did me in; and
>   taught me how to survive.
> And my father whose gentleness and passivity showed me how to love, let
>   me down often, and freed me to find my own way. (p. v)

I suggest that you stop reading now for a few minutes and imagine that you have just written a book. In the blank space below, write a dedication to your own parents—and perhaps in the same all-things-considered spirit as Kopp. In doing so, you might get a somewhat different perspective on your parents, their relationship to you, and their influence on you.

Dedication

Mothers as Significant Others

John Quincy Adams wrote, "All that I am my mother made me." And Abraham Lincoln is reputed to have said, "All that I am or hope to be, I owe to my angel mother." But Norman Douglas, seemingly a less fortunate or less charitable soul, wrote that "Nobody could misunderstand a boy like his own mother."

The importance of our relationship with our mothers can scarcely be overstated. It is, for many of us, our most enduring and salient human connection. Its effects on us may be incalculable, not only because they are so great but also because our perceptions of these effects may be so confused and changing.

Some psychoanalysts have suggested that in our marriages we attempt to restore the relationship we had as children with our own opposite-sex parent. They hypothesize that women tend to look for men who are like their fathers, and men tend to seek out women who are like their mothers. Whether this observation is true or not remains unproven, but one study, by psychologist Arthur Aron and his students (1974), presents some negative evidence. The responses of the persons studied—couples waiting in line to buy a marriage license—led to the conclusion that "both men and women seek to repeat in marriage the relationship they had with their mothers" (p. 22).

Other students of human nature have suggested that in our marital relationships some of us seek the mother we never had but always wanted. In the women she studied, Nancy Friday found marriages that failed because "the wife tried to turn the husband into the all-caring, protective mother she never had" (p. 32). Adrienne Rich (1977), in her book *Of Women Born,* recalls "lying in bed next to my husband, half-dreaming, half-believing, that the body close against mine was my mother's" (p. 246).

For women—and even for men—mothers can become important models. Our first and perhaps closest identification is with our mother or a mother surrogate. Although society supports this identification in girls, boys are soon under pressure to establish their masculinity by identifying with their fathers (or other male figures). But fathers are often absent or unsympathetic, so mothers continue to loom large in the lives of boys as well as girls.

Once a year, on Mother's Day, we honor mothers, but over the years mothers have come in for a good deal of criticism. In the 125 pertinent articles reviewed by psychologist Paula Caplan (1989) in her book *Don't Blame Mother,* mothers were blamed for seventy-two kinds of problems—ranging from learning problems and bed-wetting to schizophrenia—in their children.

A woman who regards her mother as unloving or "smothering" or as someone who has lived a life of compromise and self-effacement may seek to be as unlike her mother as possible. For example, her own housekeeping may be a negative image of her mother's style—"beds never made, dishes unwashed"—in contrast to the immaculately tended home from which she extricated herself (Rich, 1977). No such desire is present in Gretchen, age 16, a student interviewed by Anita Shreve (1987) for her book *Remaking Motherhood.* As Gretchen tells it, her own life tracks her mother's very closely:

> My mother is the director of admissions at a private boarding school in Tennessee. When she started working, and we were kind of on our own, she always said to me that she wanted me to be able to support myself. I think from her I've really gotten an idea of how society is changing. When I was little, the societal structure was for the husband to support the family, but I feel really strongly that in our generation it will be accepted that both parents work. When I was little and living with both parents, and my mother wasn't working, I had the expectation that when I grew up I would get married and stay home and be a mother. But after my parents got divorced, I think it was my mom who introduced me to the idea that women are equal to men and women should work and they are just as good or better than men. Since I've been in school, I think the culture also has really influenced me in terms of the people that I have met and other families that I have seen. I think none of us is really going to end up in the traditional structure of Mom stays home and Dad works. I think from my mom I've learned the importance of being a strong person, a strong woman especially, and how you shouldn't come to depend on your husband. You have to be your own person. (p. 44)

After years of interviewing women, Nancy Friday (1978) has concluded that whether "we [women] want our mother's life or not, we never escape the image of who she was." She notes that women who have created seemingly very different lives for themselves may overlook the fact that they have taken on their mother's anxieties, fears, angers, or patterns of relating. After a woman has told Friday that she is completely different from her own mother, her daughter in a separate interview may remark, "I'm always telling mom that she treats me just the way she said grandma treated her . . . ways she didn't like!" Or her husband may say, "The longer we're married, the more like her mother she becomes" (p. 22).

Box 5.2

Daughter to Mother: An Unsent Letter

Unsent letters are letters written with no intent of sending them. We sometimes imagine what we would like to say or to have said to someone—things that might be difficult, hazardous, or even impossible to convey; the unsent letter puts such thoughts into words. Such letters are sometimes written by people who keep personal journals, because the letters help them express, record, and examine their feelings; catharsis and a new or deepened insight may result. Three unsent letters appear in this chapter, and later in an exploration you will have an opportunity to write one of your own. The unsent letter below was written by Deborah Brink (1970) to her dead mother.

Dear Mother,

It is your birthday today, but there in the earth what is left of you does not know this. Bones and dust. And the rest of you, where did that go? Are you in some heaven somewhere, making up for all the joy you never had here on this earth? Or are you suffering in some hell somewhere for your sin of never having been the woman you could have been? For always having tried to placate (but succeeding mostly in annoying), for having been unable to give of yourself, unable to love? For never, I suspect, in joy having put your arms around the man, your husband, or even your children? For always, always having pulled back and having held yourself at bay?

But why should you be punished now for these things? Didn't you live your punishment every day of your life right here on this earth? Wasn't your life dry, and dull, and burdensome, and didn't you joylessly drag your feet from duty to duty—from reluctantly getting up in the morning to struggle with a cold, smoking woodstove at the dawn of day, to reluctantly with inner revulsion enduring the copulatory activities of your husband in bed at night? Remember telling me once that if you could have had children *any* other way, no matter how uncomfortable, you would have preferred it? Need any punishment be added to this? You married a lifelong punishment, but you dulled yourself against the pain of it. You never seemed to *hear* the scorn of impatience in his voice every time he spoke to you, as though you were some idiot child or some bereft and bungling slave he never should have bought. After he died others saw you as "blooming." It enraged me, but it was true. You had been married for 36 years (but not once had you celebrated a wedding anniversary), and your life, I guess, was Life to you—nothing else was possible. So your life went nowhere; it was a stalemate stirred to futile motion by the flow of time. And by long, long prayers at night and hoping for a heaven beyond the grave.

Well, is there one? Is that where you are now?

You can't answer me, and I'm not really asking. The fact is that your belief sustained you. Could you have endured otherwise for 36 years? But it also trapped you as securely as a steel cage. More so, because you could not know that you were trapped. With all your hopes on heaven and the hereafter, you never looked at yourself, or at him, and asked yourself if you might change; might you overcome your fears; might you become more loving; might you learn to play, to laugh, to hug, to enjoy; might you become more approachable, more human. But how *could* you have dared to ask with no one there to help you find all the answers?

You never knew, really, that I, from about the age of four, disowned you and would gladly have traded you in for almost any other woman as a mother. Or maybe you did know. When I was in my 40's you said to me once, with deep regret in your manner, that you had not been a good mother to me. And the saddest thing of it all is that you really were a good woman, a kindly, gentle, decent woman essentially. You were not mean, punishing, harsh, or full of hate. Just terribly, terribly frightened and ashamed of voluptuous life in the raw. It made you cringe and shudder and curl up and withdraw instead of going forth to *meet* it with eager breasts and arms extended.

"The sins of the fathers shall be visited upon the children." Yes, Mother, your sins and his were visited upon me, and upon my son, your grandchild, and they still are. Just as the sins of your forebears were visited upon you. I am almost 51 years old—almost 51!—and still do I live in a cage of fear and mistrust of the raw stuff that is me. But there is at least this difference between us; I cannot say to myself that my life is Life. I *do* know that there are other possibilities. I do know that it is different for some others, a few. I do know that people can and do change. I do know that I can and do change. The responsibility is mine.

And this is where I begin to drag my feet, and where I want to scurry back into the cage, join you in the grave, Mother. In the grave. No more doubts. No more exposure. No more shame. No more ridicule. No more cringing. No more effort. No more struggle. No more risks. No more failure. No more pain. Everything is resolved and settled for all eternity, perfectly. The pull of the grave at times is very strong because I, like you, am afraid of the raw imperfection, the full voluptuousness of Life. But—I am powerfully tempted to cast myself forward, as upon the heaving, tempestuous bosom of the ocean, and revel in sand and salt and sun. So this is where I stand today—poised . . .

Happy Birthday, Mother.

Your loving daughter,

Ora

Fathers as Significant Others

Out of the hundreds of interviews and questionnaires that Suzanne Fields (1983) gathered for her research on women's perceptions of their fathers, this central thesis emerged (her italics): *"Daddy hides and we forever seek him, only occasionally flushing him out of his hiding places.* We know where he hides. He hides behind his newspaper; he hides behind his wife; he hides behind his work; he hides behind his public image; he hides behind his authority. Most of all, he hides behind his fear of intimacy" (p. 9).

Shere Hite's (1981) survey of over 7,000 men revealed that they had a somewhat similar perception of their fathers. Almost none of her respondents said that they had been close to their fathers. Samuel Osherson's (1986) interviews with men in their thirties and forties produced similar results. Osherson concluded that "the psychological or physical absence of fathers from their families [is] one of the great underestimated tragedies of our time" (p. 4).

Fields describes the early importance a father can have for his young daughter:

> . . . a girl's first perception of the opposite sex comes through her daddy: he forever colors the eye through which a woman sees men. He shapes her expectations of male behavior. Did he hold our hands when we took our first faltering steps? Did he care when he watched us struggle through the multiplication tables? Was he comfortable showing us affection? Did he hold us close when we needed to be hugged, roughhouse with us when we wanted to play, punish us when we secretly yearned to be disciplined? Did he care how we looked? When our bodies began to change did he notice— or pretend not to? Was he pleased when we appeared in the living room all dressed up for a boyfriend? Whether at school, with our mothers, or with our first boyfriends, could we count on him to see us through those early, agonizing crises? As we got interested in the world around us, did he freely share his knowledge and perceptions? (p. 6)

In a similar way, Osherson, poet Robert Bly (who is at the forefront of a new men's movement), and others describe the special importance fathers have for their sons. At about the age of 3, boys begin to search for a masculine model to build their sense of self. In growing up as male, they are required to separate themselves psychologically from their mothers and identify and bond with their fathers. However, both Osherson and Bly note that many boys grow into manhood with a conflicted sense of masculinity rooted in their experience of their fathers as rejecting, incompetent, or absent.

If we were intimidated by a punitive father, our response to all authority figures may be influenced by that early memory. In this connection, psychoanalyst Willard Gaylin (1979) writes, "Regardless of how gentle and unchallenging the authority figure is, we may approach each teacher, each employer as though he had both the power and personality of that dominant father who once ruled our lives" (p. 22). Similarly, Fields notes that women with autocratic fathers "who criticized their every move and imposed harsh limits on their developing independence, complain of problems in their workplace and are unable to deal with any kind of authority without expressing overwhelming anger" (p. 28).

Anthropologist Corinne Nydegger (cited in Rubin, 1982) studied the way the fathering role changes as children grow up. She found that the father-son relationship is most often remembered as good when the son is of elementary school age. During the son's adolescence, the relationship often becomes worse but improves during his adult years. Psychologist Zick Rubin's (1982) interviews with fathers and sons corroborate Nydegger's last finding, indicating that there is often

a reunion or reconciliation between father and son when the son reaches his late twenties or early thirties.

This union or reconciliation may never come. Some of us are no better at emotional work than our fathers are. We are slow to speak, and then, when we find our voice, it is too late. Actor Patrick Swayze remembers his father (who died in his fifties) as a "man's man" but at the same time a very gentle, sensitive man who was always there for his son. In one of Swayze's movies, the script called for him to say good-bye to the person playing his father, and after some faulty takes the director said, "This time, Patrick, before you leave, tell your father you love him." Tears came to Swayze's eyes then and also as he recalled the incident. "You know," he said, "that's the one thing I would have liked to have told my father before he died" (Birnbach, 1990, p. 5).

Gaining insight into our relationship with our fathers and making that relationship what we want it to be are important tasks. Insight, forgiveness, and reform are all evident in the story of Rachel, one of the women studied by Fields. Rachel has been struggling with her feelings toward her 84-year-old father. She is making a sculpture of his head, and he is late for what may be their last visit together.

> "Annoyance became hysteria. The sculpture became therapy, not art. I raged at it, knocking the clay about in ways that I felt my father had knocked me about. I began to choke the slim neck, screaming at it: 'You bastard. You never gave me enough. You were never there for me except in your charm. You were never a father. You were a charmer, a charmer! I accepted that, too, but not again, not this time!'" Rachel broke down, sobbing, hurt, broken, angry, not only by her father, but by all the lovers who had treated her the way her father had done. "I idealize charming men, and they stand me up, just like my father. The men I go for are just like my father. They charm my pants off, literally, and then they disappoint me. They make promises they don't keep, and then I seethe with hysterical anger because I feel just like I did when I was a little girl, disappointed by my father." Eventually Rachel's father arrived, explaining with his usual insouciant charm that he had had to wait for the doctor; the examination took much longer than he had expected. She accepted his apology, and began to make a head, much more realistic than that she thought she wanted to make. The crisis had opened the way for her to work through some of her need to idealize him. "I need to lower my expectations of him and of my lover," she said, upon long and sober reflection. "I need to forgive my father for the wounds of my childhood. Most of all, I must learn to stop blaming my lover for those childhood wounds, too." (p. 259)

Box 5.3

Son to Father: An Unsent Letter

This is a letter that I wrote to my dead father.

September 22, 1982

Dear Dad,

I visited your grave when I had a chance to stop over in Iowa this summer. There you were—in the Jewish section of the cemetery—surrounded by all your old Jewish friends. I recognized the names, and each name brought back some memories.

Sitting there at your graveside I tried to hold a dialogue with you. The words came hard, just like some of those times when we tried to communicate, and our words went right past each other. Finally, the dialogue limped to a halt and I took out my pen and printed "Love" in small letters on the side of your footstone. Dear Dad, I love you.

Back in the days when I had a chance to put my arms around you and tell you that you were dear to me, I couldn't. I understood so little in those days—how much your religion meant to you (the religion I threw away as soon as I discovered science), how wrong your life's work was for you, how your brilliant mind was wasted, how your spirit was dragged down.

You worked so long and hard to provide us with a living, and we had what we really needed. But all I sometimes seemed to see was that you were a near-failure as a businessman, that you worked six and one-half long days each week in a little store, that you never took a vacation until you sickened and died, that you were an immigrant who never made it in the new world.

I'm glad that we kids—your children—did so well in school and debate and forensics. We all were determined to do well, and we did well. I know that you were proud of us.

Now I find in my mid-life—at the beginning of my old age really—that my science is inadequate nourishment and feeds my head better than my heart. Ironically, my new transpersonal interests have a lot in common with your religious pursuit. You had all along what I have sought and sought and still have not found.

Dad, this is your third-born child writing to you, my heart filled with emotion, with love, to say that I love you, that you are dear to me, that you matter, that your life mattered.

Aloha, shalom, love, your son,

Abe

Dinah Eng (1989) grew up in a Chinese-American family, one of seven daughters whose father had desperately wanted a son. She writes that he hasn't been a perfect father, and neither has she been a perfect daughter, but he is getting better—at least in one area—under her caring tutelage. Although her father's good-byes were always perfunctory and physically distant, she decided to reach out and hug him hello and good-bye each time they were together. She recalled that it was like hugging a log, but she never gave up, and then one day he hugged back. She was so moved that she cried. She writes, "Now, each visit, he reaches out to hug and kiss me." Eng's story suggests that it may never be too late to rear a father.

Siblings as Significant Others

For some of us, siblings become more significant significant others than parents. During childhood, we may spend many more hours in interaction with our sibs than with anyone else, and sibling interaction can be particularly intense and intimate. "Life among siblings," it has been said, "is like living in the nude, psychologically speaking" (Bossard & Boll, 1960, p. 90). And life among siblings can be rough: in a survey of 1,685 university students, almost 20 percent indicated that they had often fought violently with their sibs (Graham-Bermann, reported by Peterson, 1992).

© PEANUTS reprinted by permission of UFS, Inc.

Siblings teach each other and learn from each other. They hammer out their patterns of adjustment in the give-and-take of family existence. There is constant sibling cooperation and rivalry, sharing and preempting, alliance and disalliance.

Siblings serve parental functions. They nurture and dominate each other. They may provide each other with affection, belonging, and a sense of security.

Siblings serve as yardsticks to measure one's own status and achievement. They also serve as role models. Younger sibs, in particular, may shape their behavior from the examples of older ones. Children with opposite-sex siblings show more opposite-sex traits than do those without such sibs. The impact is even greater if the opposite-sex sib is older (Brim, 1958). In the two-child family, the younger child tends to be at a competitive disadvantage with the older and more powerful one (Forer & Still, 1976).

Sibling relationships appear to be influenced by several factors. The number of children in the family and their differences in age, sex, and personality—all are important considerations. Each child's relationship with her or his parents and with other important persons in the household must also be taken into account.

In a study of large families (six or more living children), the researchers found that each child tended to assume a particular personality role—a way of making her or his position in the family a special or meaningful one (Bossard & Boll, 1955, 1956). The roles appeared to be assumed in some sequence, with each succeeding child electing a role that had not already been preempted. Eight personality roles were identified, and these are listed below along with the child who usually or often had this role. (Note: Even those of us from small families may find that we indeed adopted or were cast in one of these roles. Can you find a role in the list that you played in your family?)

1. The responsible one (often the first-born child, especially if a daughter)
2. The popular one (second born or child following responsible one)
3. The socially ambitious one (mostly daughters, third, fourth, or fifth born)
4. The studious one (either son or daughter)
5. The family isolate (child separated by age or sex from the majority of siblings)
6. The irresponsible one (either son or daughter)
7. The sickly one (child with physical defect or chronic illness)
8. The spoiled one (last born or next to the last if the last born was unexpected or resented by mother)

Other investigators have noted additional roles, including that of "go-between"—the sib who becomes the mediator or peacemaker of the family (Bank & Kahn, 1975). One client told me that she became "the good child" to merit her parents' love because a sib, playing the role of "the bad child," had become an outcast. She said that, ironically, she played the role so well that she became too good for her own good.

Siblings can continue to influence each other throughout their lives. Since of all family linkages sib relationships are the most durable—some last seven or eight decades or more—the mutual impact can be considerable. And this impact appears even more pronounced as family size declines, divorce increases, and one-parent families become more common. Research with adult siblings indicates that a very large majority feel close or very close to each other. This closeness increases in later life as the siblings age and their parents die. Sisters contribute more to family solidarity than brothers do (Cicinelli, cited in Adams, 1981).

Solidarity is less common among adult sibs who were not close in their childhood years. It is also less common among sibs who were unable to work out or fight out their early differences. This lack of conflict resolution can occur if parents are ineffective mediators, perhaps rushing in too soon to resolve or forbid conflict. Some parents actually provoke or exacerbate conflict through invidious comparisons.

"Frozen images" and "frozen misunderstandings" can keep sibling relationships stuck or anchored in the past (Bank and Kahn, 1982). A frozen image pins or binds a sib indelibly and irrevocably to an old identity. The image of an idolized sib who died early may be frozen into sainthood, just as the image of a seemingly hostile sib may be unforgivingly cast as a devil. A frozen misunderstanding is a salient and lasting disparity in the recollection of certain shared childhood events. Such misunderstandings are more likely to emerge from chaotic and unhappy homes, "as if, in a sea of uncertainty, *positive certainty* about *something* or *someone*—even a negative person or thing—relieves tension, uncertainty, and anxiety" (Bank & Kahn, 1982, p. 75). Two sisters demonstrate their frozen misunderstanding in this brief recorded exchange:

Older Sister: We used to play in the living room, and we had a great time. You always used to like to read to me, pretending you were my older sister. I can still remember how great those evenings were—just you and me without a worry in the world.

Younger Sister: That's odd. I can't remember that at all. The thing that stands out is how you could be so unbelievably cruel to me. Just when I thought I could depend on you and trust you, you'd turn the tables on me, complaining to Mom about something I did, or dropping me cold to go play with your friends. (pp. 74–75)

Salient family problems can disrupt close sibling ties or knot them even tighter. A brother or sister's serious illness or marital, drinking, or psychological problem may cause a sib to protectively distance herself or himself or draw even closer to help. Providing care for aging, dependent parents can bring sibs together to cooperate or drive them apart if there is no agreement on what should be done and who should do it.

Rivalry is a common feature of sibling interaction, and it can continue throughout life. Of a group of sixty-five older persons (age 65 to 93) interviewed by Helgola Ross and Joel Milgrim (cited in Adams, 1981), 71 percent reported rivalrous feelings in childhood, and 45 percent indicated that these feelings continued to exist. Sibling rivalry was regarded as enjoyable and motivating by some, but more often it was considered destructive. Parental favoritism and invidious comparison were reported to be the chief sources of this rivalry.

What makes for the strongest and most lasting sibling bonds? These appear to form when siblings have plentiful access to and contact with each other in childhood and when there is insufficient parental influence and care. In such cases, siblings increasingly turn to each other for assistance and guidance (Bank & Kahn, 1982). In adulthood, intense sibling loyalty can be a great source of support, but it can also interfere with the development of outside relationships or with relationships to one's spouse and children.

Spouses and Lovers as Significant Others

I had a good friend—dead now—who married for the first and only time when he was far along in life. I had watched his progress through love relationships with three semisignificant others. I think it's only fair to say that he was poor pairing material at the beginning of those relationships, but each seemed to teach him something about love. By the time he met his wife to be, he had learned enough to make a remarkably good marriage. His three semisignificant others were not invited to his wedding, but I think they should have been there as the groom's maids of honor.

"Coupling changes us," writes Diane Vaughan (1986) in her book *Uncoupling*. She notes that when individuals couple, they are in a process of renegotiation.

> They restructure their lives around each other. They create common friends, belongings, memories, and a common future. They redefine themselves as a couple, in their own eyes and in the eyes of others, who respond to the coupled identity they are creating. They are invited out as a twosome, mail comes addressed to both, the IRS taxes them jointly. Single friends may hesitate to call, while the two people are readily incorporated into the social world of those who also are coupled. The coupled identity they create is constantly reaffirmed, not only by the words and deeds of others, but also by the way others come to take the relationship for granted. This continual public confirmation gives them a stable location in the social world and validates their identity. (p. 4)

In uncoupling, a reverse process occurs: the two partners disentangle their belonging and identities and become separate identities again. However, the separation may be slow to occur and may never be complete. Memories, shared loved ones (children, in-laws), properties, even unresolved anger and conflict may serve to keep the relationship alive. Vaughan writes that uncoupling leaves behind its traces just as a vanished glacier leaves its scars and deposit of boulders and debris.

Not everyone agrees that the coupling process is a fully mutual one. Sociologist Jessie Bernard (1971) observed that every marriage is in reality two marriages—*his* and *hers*. Letty Cottin Pogrebin (1983) agrees and goes on to say that *his* is better. "Contrary to common wisdom, married men are generally happier and healthier than bachelors, but single women are happier and healthier than married women" (p. 87). In Pogrebin's lectures around the country, often a woman in the audience will raise her hand to ask, "How can I get my husband to change?" "The honest answer," says Pogrebin, "is maybe she can't." In a marriage, it is the woman who is usually called upon to make the greater adjustment. She is expected to merge her identity with her husband's, taking his name and moving to where his job is. Even among two-career couples, it is the woman who commonly assumes (or winds up with) primary responsibility for household maintenance and child care. And it is usually the woman who is called upon to do what has been called "the invisible work" of the family—namely, the nurturing or emotional caretaking.

When a woman begins to grow or to redefine herself, the relationship itself may become challenged. As she begins to become more assertive, to enhance her self-image, to raise her career goals, the other members of the family are called upon to make accommodations. However, the challenge can cause the couple or family to grow as a unit and each member of the family to grow in new ways. This kind of growth is evident in the following account of a professor and his wife whose relationship changed when she decided she had a calling for the priesthood:

> "When she first came to me . . . and said, 'I really want to become an Episcopal priest'" [the professor says], "I replied, 'that's wonderful, dear,' in the most patronizing tone. I figured she'd get over that too." Five years of stormy transition followed: she began traveling, campaigning for women's ordination; he was teaching, directing, parenting, counseling students, entertaining—on his own. She applied to a seminary in Massachusetts; when she was accepted, he took a sabbatical and they moved up there with their children, then ages eight and 10. When she completed her studies, they returned to Houston, where she became a deacon and finally a priest, with a parish of her own. The professor continued to find it hard to adjust to his wife's new directions. "As each new demand was made of me, I would say 'no, I don't mind,'" he recalls, "but I could feel my face tightening. I remember lying in bed unable to sleep because my heart was pounding so hard. I guess it was a combination of conceptual adjustment and sheer physical overload. I also remember screaming at her: 'I'm a decent man. I make a decent living. We have a lovely home, wonderful kids. Why can't you be satisfied?'" Characterizing the first fifteen years as "uncomfortable—I stayed really busy with work to avoid dealing with her dissatisfaction"—and the next five as "trying beyond belief," he says the last seven years have been "fabulous—our marriage is more solid than it ever was." A major reason for their survival, he concedes, was her always taking time for the emotional caretaking function. "My instinct for nurturing, for knowing when one of my children needed attention, was always more highly developed than my instinct that it was time to vacuum the rug," she laughs. (Barrett, 1984, pp. 42, 111)

John Cuber and Peggy Harroff (1965) studied the marriages of over four hundred "significant Americans" (well educated, socially prestigious, vocationally successful). They found it possible to sort these marriages grossly into one of two styles: utilitarian and intrinsic. In the former, the relationship between the spouses is secondary to other considerations; in the latter, the relationship has priority.

In the utilitarian marriage, spousehood is or becomes peripheral to other matters. Close companionship, deep emotional involvement, joyful sex are not of major importance in this relationship. Rather, the marriage provides a necessary or convenient setting for other activities: careers for one or both spouses, the raising of children, and involvement in social or political activities. It permits a high degree of freedom and independence and provides stability and participation in the commonly expected family rituals of society.

Although some couples settle into a utilitarian marriage right after the honeymoon is over, such marriages usually emerge slowly as the spouses become more deeply aware of their needs, capabilities, limitations, propensities, and interests. For some couples it is a desired way of living; for others it is a compromise or an acceptance of the most that can be expected—at least at the time—given the circumstances.

In the account below, a woman describes what has happened to her own marriage; it is, in the words of Cuber and Harroff, "a common marital evolution." In early marriage this woman and her husband had enjoyed a full and vital relationship, but the intimacy had eroded and the focus changed.

At thirty-eight you're not old, yet you find that sex has gotten humdrum, the children fill your time with trivia—no stimulation, just fatigue. You hardly ever see your husband and when you do, he's preoccupied with other things. These all creep up on you and all of a sudden you realize that you're never going to be a couple again—not really! . . . But I got a perspective about it after a while—and it really wasn't anything so new—I knew it all along. I just couldn't give up. . . . That was six years ago. . . . Now we have it worked out perfectly. He travels—the whole southwest now that he's been promoted—and only gets home alternate weekends. And I teach—well, really, I'm the principal in a pretty exclusive girls' school. We've moved to the country now and Joey can have his horses and Ellen has her boating and swimming close by. At first it seemed like such a compromise—and I did consider a divorce, but that's foolish—you just get into the same bind again. Anyway, there's a lot of nothing between me and Bob—we might as well face it. When he comes home it's exciting at first but after a while. . . . Really, there's no sentiment or closeness there. I don't know whether he's got someone or something on the road—but what's the difference? I'm not losing anything. And he's had to forgive (or anyway not divorce me over) an affair or two. So you just balance it out. Anyway, we've worked it all out—equally and fairly. When we go to visit our families in the summer, we spend half the time with each set of grandparents—minus the time for travel. We work it out as exactly as we can. We both want to be fair about everything. And we have our beautiful new home now. The children have their own rooms. And I have my new car. (pp. 107–108)

In intrinsic marriage the intimate relationship between the spouses is primary. These couples may raise a family, and each may have a career, but these activities are kept subordinate to the spousal relationship. Such couples are somewhat less likely to participate in civic and even religious activities.

Some people in intrinsic couplings are escapees from the "deadly prose" of a past utilitarian marriage (just as some people in utilitarian marriages have escaped from "clinging vine," demanding relationships). In intrinsic relationships, activities (except for those pertaining to career) are shared and generally less formal and less standardized. Such couples tend to place a high degree of importance on sex and on the enjoyment of life.

A career woman in Cuber and Harroff's group provided a vivid contrast between utilitarian and intrinsic relationships by comparing her first marriage with her second, "marriage-type," marriage.

So many people—and me in my first marriage—just sort of touch on the edges of existence—don't really marry. It's funny, but my cookbook distinguishes between marinating and marrying of flavors. You know—the marinated flavors retain their identity—just mix a little—or the one predominates strongly over the other. But the married ones blend into something really new and the separate identities are lost. Well, a lot of people that I know aren't married at all—just marinated! (pp. 132–133)

Although even a marital marinade may be too much of a pickle for some of us, an enthusiastic case for intrinsic marriage is made by Clayton Barbeau (1988) in his discussion of fidelity. Fidelity, as Barbeau defines it, is more than sexual exclusivity. It is a relationship in which each person becomes for the other a truly significant significant other.

Fidelity is expressed in a relationship when each is aware that their relationship has priority over all other matters. The man who puts nearly all of himself into his work and leaves his wife only the leftovers is committing a form of adultery. Many a wife has commented: "He loves his job more than me." The woman who invests her greatest energies in housekeeping, her job, her children, and only gives her husband the remnants of her time and attention has likewise been unfaithful to her commitment. More than one husband, having succumbed to an "affair" because he was starved for the time and attention of his wife, has said: "She's married to the house and kids, not to me." Here one form of infidelity to the primary relationship of the couple has led to another form of infidelity to that same commitment.

My commitment in fidelity to you is diminished to the degree that I begin to condition my acceptance of you, to withhold myself unless you meet certain performance standards, to play roles, to close the doors of myself against you and permit our estrangement to grow. All of these are failures to live up to my commitment. Some of them can take forms much more seriously damaging to both of us than the act of sexual infidelity. For by permitting certain harmful patterns to grow in our relationship, letting estrangement between us solidify into a mere cohabitational arrangement, I'm slamming the doors on all that our relationship has to offer us in the way of our full growth as human beings and our full enjoyment of true intimacy in marriage. In doing so I am being unfaithful to our basic two-in-one relationship. (pp. 223–224)

Children as Significant Others

Parents raise their children. *And* children raise their parents. Wordsworth wrote that the child is father to the man. Reviewing the pertinent evidence, Julius Segal and Herbert Yahraes (1978a) conclude, "While we have some impact on our young, they shape *us* as well" (p. 90).

Infants show stable temperamental differences from the moment of their birth. Psychiatrists Alexander Thomas and Stella Chess (1977) found that two-thirds of the children they studied fell clearly into three categories: the "easy" child (whom parents found a pleasure to be around), the "difficult" child (whose vexing behavior tried the parents' patience), and the "slow-to-warm-up" child (whose withdrawing behavior and slow adaptation were also trying). Each kind of child behavior has a considerable influence on the parent, and this resulting parental behavior, in turn, influences the child. To some extent, children invite or provoke the kind of parental behavior they receive. (For more on how a mother's

Doonesbury   BY GARRY TRUDEAU

behavior influences her offspring, see the section headed "Love as Attachment" in Chapter 6.)

John Updike writes that "Society in its conventional wisdom sets a term to childhood; of parenthood there is no riddance." Once we become parents, we're Mom or Dad forevermore. Florida Scott-Maxwell, at the age of 82, wrote in her notebook (1968) that she kept looking for signs of improvement in her middle-aged children.

In his book *No Strings Attached* (1979), psychotherapist Howard Halpern describes some unfortunate "songs and dances" that parents get caught up in with their adult children. These include the following familiar routines:

1. The Guilt Gavotte. In this dance either the parent or the child—or most likely both—tries to control the other by proclaiming, "You are the cause of my suffering, so you owe it to me to make me feel better by doing what I want you to do." Whichever one can prove herself or himself the victim can claim the right to reparations.

2. The Fear Fandango. In this dance more likely the parent but possibly the child tyrannizes the other with fear. The fear provoker acts as if the other is there just to accede to his or her commands, which are backed up with a threatening "or else." "If you do this, I'll throw you out." "If you do that, I'll kill myself."

3. The Shame Shimmy. In this routine one of the parent-child pair (usually the parent) is a "Saint"—a person in touch with the Absolute Truth—and who knows how everyone should behave. The Saint tries to control behavior by shaming the other. Example: "I never thought a child of mine would ever do such a thing."

4. The Hootchy Kootchy. Romances involving a parent and the child of the opposite sex are a common feature of family living, but they are ordinarily outgrown before puberty. In this dance one parent is overly involved with the child, and the other parent is left out. If the romance persists into adolescence and adulthood, the relationship between all members of the family and the future relationships of the child can be seriously affected.

5. The Money Minuet. This dance can take many forms, but all basically involve the control and manipulation of the other through the use of money. You are dancing to the Money Minuet when (1) your grown-up child, in effect, manipulatively demands rather than realistically requests financial assistance, and you feel compelled to respond in a particular way, for example, having to give or having to refuse to give; or (2) you manipulatively and conditionally offer financial support to your children, and they feel compelled to comply with or defy or sabotage your demands on them.

What do parents caught up in such song and dances with their children need to do to stop the music? They can gain some insights from the behaviors of parents who have sidestepped these routines—parents who have healthy relationships with their adult children. According to Halpern, such parents have the following characteristics:

1. They see their children as separate from themselves and help their children to become independent.

2. They see their children as distinct from each other, and they appreciate and respond to their uniqueness even when it leads their children in directions different from their own.

3. They trust their children and their children's ability to find their own way.

4. They enjoy and are intrigued by the persons that their children are becoming.

5. Their concept of themselves is not based on the success or failure of their children; they don't need their children's accomplishments to give them status, nor are they brought down by their children's failures.

6. They have their own lives independent of their children's, and they pursue their own needs and potentials.

Friends as Significant Others

A friend, according to the *American Heritage Dictionary*, is a "person whom one knows, likes, and trusts," but there are various kinds of friends. We have best friends, close friends, good friends, and "just" friends. Best friends and close friends may play an important part in our lives and serve as very significant others.

Lillian Rubin (1985) writes that in a *best* friendship there's "a promise of mutual love, concern, protection, understanding and, not least of all, stability and durability" that distinguishes this relationship from all others. Best friendships embody "the best of all the important relationships in our lives—kin, mate and friend—along with the problems of all three." They "bring us both our greatest joys and our sorriest disappointments" (p. 175).

More often than not, our friends are persons like us—they are "our own kind"—and we share a common experience. This fact is highlighted in what Harlem resident Bernice Powell, a highly paid consultant, told Letty Cottin Pogrebin for the latter's book *Among Friends*. "My friends are women and men who are making something of themselves but who have never forgotten they're Black. They and I are at home in an all-white boardroom as in a Black church. We can talk Ivy League English or rap with the best of the brothers. We still make chitlins and sweet potato pie but we serve it on fine china." Powell and her friends spend large amounts of time and money helping the black community. She says, "Sharing those activities and having one foot in the ghetto and one foot in The Man's world can make people very close friends" (Pogrebin, 1987, p. 168).

Having friends of our own kind helps us affirm ourselves and what we stand for and keeps us from becoming lost in or engulfed by the larger society. We hold on to each other. Sociologist Maxine Baca Zinn explains the importance of compadres (close friends given the status of relatives) in her own Chicano society:

> Chicanos are a racial ethnic group, a people of color who have been colonized. We need ethnic friendship for cultural regeneration, for like-self affirmation of our roots, sometimes even for survival. Our *compadrazgo* system provides for godparents and co-parents, who have more social than religious significance. They are friends who will take care of you and your children in times of need when the rest of your family can't. I am a scholar and a modern woman, but in a crisis, what matters to me is being Mexican and having compadres. (Pogrebin, 1987, p. 174)

"Do you have a best friend?" This is a question that Rubin asked three hundred men and women (ages 25 to 55, working class and middle class) whom she interviewed for her research on friendship. Over three-fourths of the single women named a best friend, and this person was almost always a woman. In sharp contrast, fewer than one-third of the single men could identify a best friend, and those who were identified were much more likely to be a woman than another man.

Rubin's results showed that, at every age between 25 and 55, women had more friendships than men did, and the differences in quality were considerable. Women's friendships with each other rested on shared intimacies and emotional support. In contrast, friendships between men were based on shared activities and were much more emotionally constrained.

Other investigators have made similar observations. Levinson and his colleagues (1978), for example, found that "friendship was largely noticeable by its absence" in the American males they studied. This team tentatively generalized that a "close friendship with a man or woman is rarely experienced by American men" (p. 335).

As we begin to separate ourselves and grow away from our families in adolescence, friendships become more important to us as sources of support. However, in late adolescence and early adulthood, friendships can take a back seat to romantic relationships. Marriage can disrupt friendships; our interests change, and we begin to form relationships with other couples. In the same way, divorce can disrupt the friendships we formed as couples.

Like all important relationships, intimate friendships take work. They require us to open ourselves up, to trust, to share, to compromise, even to sacrifice. They involve caring—caring enough for another person so that her or his welfare becomes as important as our own, caring enough to go far, far out of our way to render help when it is needed.

Friendships also take time. Someone has said that the depth of a friendship can be gauged by the gallons of coffee (or beer or Diet Pepsi) shared together. When my father-in-law retired, he and my mother-in-law moved from the Midwest to Hawaii (my wife was their only child), but he never settled in. He greatly missed his hometown cronies who gathered each morning for coffee and recollection. As I write this, I am suddenly without my two closest friends—one died and one retired and moved far away—and I understand more fully my father-in-law's loneliness.

Teachers as Significant Others

When Miss Bessie died at the age of 85, hundreds of her former students mourned. Among them was columnist Carl Rowan, who later wrote her story. Bessie Taylor Gwynn was a short, slight, black woman, born in poverty and unable to afford a college education. Yet for forty-four years she taught hundreds of economically deprived black children much more than the three Rs. "Because of her inspiration," Rowan recalls, "I spent many hours squinting beside a kerosene lamp reading Shakespeare and Thoreau, Samuel Pepys and William Cullen Bryant. . . . Years later, her inspiration, prodding, anger, cajoling and almost osmotic infusion of learning finally led to that lovely day when Miss Bessie dropped me a note saying, 'I'm so proud to read your column in the Nashville *Tennessean*'" (1985, p. 125).

Many of us will recall a teacher who played a very significant role in our lives. Although I am not gifted with a prodigious memory, I remember with affection all my teachers at the grade school I attended about sixty years ago. They were truly dedicated, knowledgeable, and kindly women who introduced me to a world of learning that captured me completely. Because of their influence, I must have decided early never to leave school, and I never did; here I am retired and still teaching.

Mark Medoff, a professor as school-captured as I am, sat down a few years ago to recall and write about those who had taught him in the two decades that he had been a student. One of his college teachers, Medoff writes, "is still, aside

Box 5.4

Pupil to Teacher: An Unsent Letter

This is a letter (condensed) written to a dead high school teacher by Bel Kaufman (1975), who had herself become a teacher and also author of a best-selling book about teaching, *Up the Down Staircase*.

Dear Mr. Stock:

You probably wouldn't remember me, even if you were alive. I sat in the third row back in your English 512 class in South Side High School in Newark, New Jersey. You gave me an A minus for being unprepared.

You had asked us to write a composition in class about one of Hardy's heroines (was it Tess?), but I had neglected to read the book assigned. Caught off guard, I frantically described a young woman, the room she sat in, the beam of light from the high window, her hands in her lap, her thoughts in her head. I anticipated failure, worst of all—your disappointment. Instead, you gave me an A for something uniquely mine. Your scrawled comment in red ink on my paper read, "This isn't Hardy's character, but you've made yours very real."

Startled into gratitude, I became aware of my own possibilities. You *recognized* me.

I needed recognition. I was a shy, uneasy girl, too foreign, too intense. The English language, newly learned, lay clumsy on my tongue. Long sausage curls coiled down my shoulder blades—this, in the age of the shingle bob and spit curl. Instead of the scarlet Cupid's bow mouth, I was allowed but a pale touch of Tangee lipstick. How I longed for spike heels and gunmetal silk stockings. How I yearned for plucked eyebrows, flapping galoshes, a slicker with boy's initials painted on it, the boys themselves!

From the time I arrived in this country at 12 until skipping had brought me to the approximate age suitable for high school, I had been the oldest in the class, the last to be called, the least to be noticed. I was monitor of nothing.

I don't think you knew what you did for me, Mr. Stock. We teachers seldom know whom we influence. It was not my defects you emphasized, but my worth. For the first time I realized that what I had made up inside my mind could be real to someone else.

Other teachers dealt differently with us. One would silently, lips pursed, enter a meticulous zero into an ominous black notebook. Another, down the corridor from you, would review publicly and with exquisite sarcasm all our past misdeeds, of which the current one was the ultimate transgression. In Latin, the teacher made us sit quietly, hands on desk, eyes front. This was called "maintaining discipline." In history, our teacher perched on the windowsill, dangled his legs, and wooed us with false camaraderie.

You assumed one simple fact: If the lesson was interesting, we would be attentive. You did not try to charm or to beguile us. You never pretended to be a pal. You were a *teacher*. Your dignity was unassailable. Because you respected yourself and us, we were able to respect ourselves.

Memory is a selective sieve, which . . . No, you wouldn't like this. "Too literary," you would say, "simplicity is stronger." So I will say only that once you stopped at my desk and asked gently, "Stuck? Can't get started?" I nodded—and got started. Another time you called my handwriting distinctive. Did you say *distinctive* or *distinguished*? I no longer remember. What matters is how much that meant to me. In my skipping of grades, I had skipped right over the Palmer Method of ovals and strokes; consequently, my handwriting was different. But *distinctive*—imagine!

Somehow, you made everyone feel special. Once you quoted from Shakespeare: ". . . who can say more/Than this rich praise—that you alone are you?" I knew you meant me. And so did each of the 34 others in the room.

When one of us returned after an absence, you would say, "We missed you." When one was unprepared, you would shake your head: "Too bad; we were hoping to know what *you* think." When one came late, you assumed there was good reason for it that need not be asked. You treated us as adults, your equals, and so—in your class—we were. "Don't be captious," you would say, taking it for granted that we either knew the word or would look it up in one of several dictionaries you always left scattered around the room. We looked it up. Because you knew we were fine people, punctual attenders, conscientious homework doers, honorable test takers, devoted scholars, and responsible citizens, we were. For you, we were!

Teachers like you are not dead as long as there are children who can one day say, "I had a teacher once . . ." Perhaps at this very moment, someone, someplace, is saying this about one of us. That is our immortality.

Dear Mr. Stock, I see this has turned out to be a love letter to you. Well, there are times when a love letter needs to be written, even if it is never mailed.

Your Unforgetting Forever Pupil,

Bel Kaufman

from my parents, the single strongest influence in my life" (1986, p. 72). Medoff remembers returning to his high school after fourteen years and meeting his twelfth-grade English teacher again. "I want you to know," he hears himself say to her, "you were very important to me." On reflection, he decides those are the very words he would like to say to all the teachers who have become part of him and also the words he would like to hear one day from some returning student of his own.

In her autobiography, *The Story of My Life,* Helen Keller (1959) wrote, "The most important day I remember in all my life is the one on which my teacher, Anne Mansfield Sullivan, came to me. I am filled with wonder when I consider the immeasurable contrasts between the two lives it connects" (p. 25). Both lives she referred to were her own, but the first was that of a "wild and unruly" little girl deaf and blind and unable to speak. The second proved to be that of a world-famous author and humanitarian—symbol of courage and indomitable will. The relationship of Keller and Sullivan was to last forty-nine years, and its stormy and wondrous beginnings are dramatized in the play and film *The Miracle Worker.*

Mentors as Significant Others

A *mentor* is a wise or trusted counselor, coach, exemplar, or teacher. Such persons are generally somewhat older than oneself. Mentors are usually vocational figures with whom one develops a kind of apprentice-master relationship. This relationship is ordinarily a reciprocal and transitional one; both parties gain from it, and ultimately the apprentice moves beyond it.

Levinson and his colleagues (1978) write that we enter adulthood with a "Dream," which may be only poorly articulated. Our Dream can take dramatic form: perhaps we have a vision of ourself as a great artist, athletic or intellectual superstar, or business tycoon. Or our Dream may be more mundane but nevertheless inspiring and sustaining: we may see ourself as an accomplished craftsman, a certain kind of spouse or parent, or someone with a special status or place in our community.

A crucial function of a mentor is to support and guide us as we seek to realize our Dream. We grow]by following our mentor's instruction and by modeling our mentor's behavior until the time comes to move off on our own. The course of mentoring relationships is often rocky, and the endings are often painful (Levinson et al., 1978). Like any pair, mentor and protégé may be mismatched, and there may be manipulation, overdependence, jealousy, and unwanted emotional or sexual entanglement (Phillips-Jones, 1982).

Despite the potential benefits of a mentoring relationship, many adults have little experience of one (Levinson et al., 1978). However, eminent and successful persons often report such relationships. In her study of people of high or optimal well-being, Gail Sheehy (1981) found that most had a mentor and often more than one. In her study of women who were successful in business and industrial settings, Linda Phillips-Jones (1982) found that they commonly reported being mentored.

Women in education often report that they have benefited from a mentor relationship. A study of 113 female administrators revealed that over half had such a relationship, and some reported more than one. Mentors were credited with enhancing self-esteem and confidence in their protégés and with providing considerable emotional support and career assistance (Dodgson, 1987).

The successful, middle-aged male academics, businessmen, and scientists studied by George Vaillant (1977) often acknowledged that their mentors were father figures. However, they carefully differentiated these mentors from their real fathers. In over 95 percent of the cases, real fathers were seen as without influence or as negative examples. Seemingly, these males found in their mentors some of the fathering that had been missing in their lives.

Being a mentor can be as important as having a mentor. As Erik Erikson has noted (see Box 4.2 in Chapter 4), an important aspect of middle adulthood is "generativity" or the nurturance of the next generation. Having a protégé can be deeply satisfying because it allows the mentor to see her or his knowledge appreciated, put to use, and passed along—permitting a sense of connection to the future (Garfinkel, 1985).

In recent years, hundreds of formal mentor programs have been established for disadvantaged, disabled, and gifted children, and also for welfare mothers, teachers, managers, executives, and others. Many of these appear quite successful although some do not provide the one-on-one, close, long-term relationship that the term "mentoring" has traditionally implied (Hurley, 1988). A promising, fast-growing group of programs links inner-city youth with successful African-American adults, many of whom themselves grew up in inner-city neighborhoods (Freedman, 1993).

Other Significant Others

Many other persons can serve as significant others. A favorite aunt or uncle or grandmother or grandfather—all are likely candidates. Our relationships with our grandparents can be much less ambivalent and much more conflict-free than those with our parents. We do not see our grandparents as persons with their own agendas for us, or at least as having enforcement power, so we may be able to open ourselves more fully to them.

Jimmy Carter remembers as a significant force in his life a former boss, father of the U.S. nuclear fleet Admiral Hyman Rickover. Too feisty, prickly, and cantankerous to fit the role of mentor, Rickover sacked many an officer but not Ensign Carter, who went on to higher things. Carter (1975) writes, "He may not have cared or known it, certainly not at that time, but Admiral Rickover had a profound effect on my life—perhaps more than anyone except my own parents. He was unbelievably hardworking and competent, and he demanded total dedication from his subordinates. We feared and respected him and strove to please him" (p. 57).

For some persons, God as a person or a personal sense of God may serve as a significant other. In my own childhood, I remember a time when God seemed very present in my life. I felt watched and watched over by God. I prayed to God each night, and what God wanted—or at least what I thought God wanted—was an important consideration. And then I discovered science and sociology (psychology came later), and God as a person disappeared. This disappearance left me bereft, for although science can become one's god, it's not one that can be reified or one that invites communication.

Where significant others are sorely needed but not forthcoming, we may create them in fantasy. A lonely child may create an imaginary playmate—a friend, confidant, and even someone to take the blame when things go wrong. Adults may have a sense of an inner voice or a wise person within themselves whom they can call upon for assistance.

Anne Frank wrote that her reason for starting a diary was that she had no real confidant. Her diary was to become her friend; she called this friend Kitty and addressed her entries to her. "I hope," she wrote to Kitty, "I shall be able to confide in you completely, as I have never been able to do in anyone before, and I hope that you will be a great support and comfort to me."

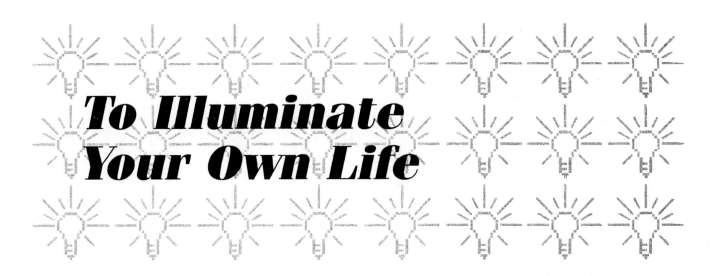

To Illuminate Your Own Life

*Anchor and Apply**

1. Who is the *most significant* significant other in your life? Why?

2. Discuss your parents as significant others. Also note whether your view of them has changed over the years.

3. In what ways are you like and in what ways are you different from your parents? In what ways would you want to be like them and in what ways would you want to be different?

4. Halpern contrasted "good enough" parents and parents who are "saints." How do you see your own parents in this regard?

5. Discuss your mother as a significant other. Also note how your view of her and your relationship to her have changed over the years.

6. Discuss your father as a significant other. Note whether he has been an absentee father or one who was or is very much there for you. Also note how your view of him and your relationship to him have changed over the years.

7. Discuss a sibling as a significant other. Also note how your view of this sib and your relationship to this sib have changed over the years.

8. If you are from a large family, identify and discuss the personality roles you and your sibs assumed in it.

9. Discuss your spouse, lover, boyfriend, or girlfriend as a significant other.

10. Cuber and Haroff contrasted "utilitarian" and "intrinsic" marriages. How utilitarian or intrinsic would you want your marriage (current or future) to be? Why?

11. If you are a parent, discuss your offspring as significant other(s).

12. Discuss a close friend, teacher, or mentor as a significant other.

---

* These "anchor and apply" items are designed to help you use the concepts of the chapter as stimuli to prompt new or deeper or clearer insights into yourself and your life. To respond to an item, first find the material in the chapter that is most relevant to the item *and* yourself; that's called "anchoring." Second, think about this material in relationship to yourself and your life and keep thinking about it until you arrive at a new or deeper or clearer understanding; that's the "apply" or application part. When you write or present your response to the item, be sure to include both parts, that is, both the anchor material and the application. You can know you are successful on an item if, in completing it, you truly learn something new or understand something better.

Exploration

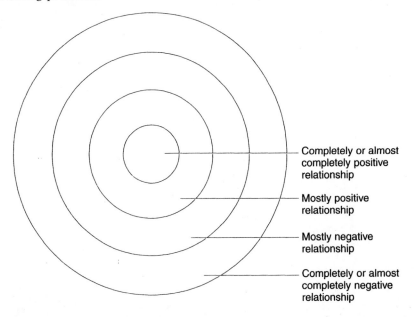

5A

Significant Riches

I remember attending a funeral of a very caring man. He had not advanced very far on the occupational ladder or acquired any wealth, but at one point in the eulogy the minister described him as "rich in people." It was an apt description. For many years this man and his wife had been foster parents to children and adolescents who had no place to go, and some of them had returned that day to say a tearful good-bye.

Are you rich in people? Is your life filled with significant others to help make it rich and full and good? Or is your life underfilled with those who might enrich it or overfilled with those who help make it poor? If you have learned how to be a "caring presence," you have a start toward a people-rich life.

1. Begin this exploration by calling to mind the significant others in your life with whom you are in current interaction. (Remember, *significant others* are those persons who have the most important effects on you.) Write the names of each of these persons in the appropriate circle below. The more positive your relationship or interaction with this person, the closer to the center this person's name will be. (Instead of the person's name, use initials or a pseudonym if you prefer.)

2. For each person in the circles for whom you are a caring presence, put a CP by that person's name, initials, or pseudonym. Be sure you truly qualify in each case by checking Box 1.4 in Chapter 1, which lists the four pledges made by a caring presence.

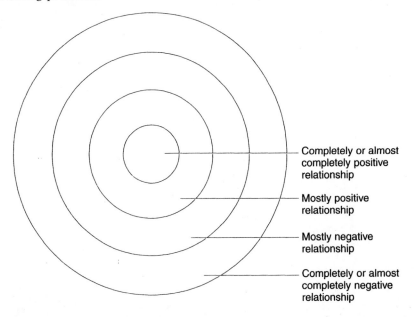

Completely or almost completely positive relationship

Mostly positive relationship

Mostly negative relationship

Completely or almost completely negative relationship

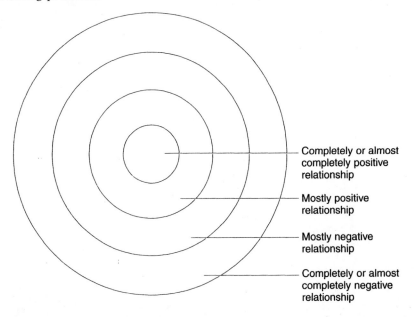

From: *The Illuminated Life*, by Abe Arkoff. Copyright © 1995 by Allyn and Bacon.

165

3. Is your life "rich in people"—that is, do you have the significant others you need to help make your life full and good? Answer this question and give your evidence in the space immediately below.

4. Are you skilled in fulfilling all four pledges made by a "caring presence"? Answer this question and give your evidence in the space immediately below.

5. Pick out one person in the circles with whom you can try to improve your relationship—possibly by becoming a caring presence to her or him or in some other way. (It isn't always possible to improve a relationship without the other's cooperation, but by trying you can improve yourself and take pride in yourself.) In the space immediately below, write up a plan to accomplish this goal and indicate the changes you will make in your behavior.

Significant Memories

Our relationships with the significant others in our lives have their ups and downs. We have had good times and bad times together, and we may hesitate to look back to recall the joy if with it comes pain or sorrow or regret. With our older, wiser eyes we can reminisce creatively about the past, gaining new perspective, accommodating what was bitter, celebrating what was sweet, and learning from both. Here are some bittersweet reminiscences of mine:

1 (a) *When I think of my childhood home, I like to remember* its wonderful setting. In the front yard was a huge cottonwood tree, around the sides and in the back fragrant lilacs, and also in the back a cherry tree and alley where all the kids gathered. One block away was a large playground where we played ball and not far beyond a woods and creek. My own grade school, the public library (where I spent much of my youth), and downtown with its five movie theaters (admission 10 cents) were just a few minutes' walk. Our house itself was modest and most unremarkable except for its single bathroom, which had three doors—one to a hallway, one to the kitchen, and one to the basement; it took some time to get properly locked in before going about one's business. Whenever my family has a reunion, that bathroom is recalled with amusement.

(b) *When I think of my childhood home, it hurts to remember* that there was a time when I was ashamed of it. It seemed so much more modest than the homes of my friends. It was a marginal house in a marginal neighborhood. We lived on Eighth Street. Seventh Street was clearly lower class, and the children who lived there went to one school. Ninth Street was safely middle class with a more highly regarded school. (Except for my oldest sib, we all managed to get ourselves to the latter school.) And we were a family on the margin of our world—orthodox Jewish in a very Catholic neighborhood in a very Christian Iowa town. Half the time I was proud to be one of "God's chosen people" and the other half I wished some other group had been given this honor.

(c) *When I look back with older, wiser eyes*, I see how lucky I was to grow up surrounded by so many things that make a childhood rich. Every set and scene a childhood needed were right there, in walking distance. And now I'm grateful for my marginality, which has given me a special empathy for people who are different or less favored or more troubled. Because of this empathy, I believe I'm a better person and a better psychologist.

2 (a) *When I think of my mother, I like to remember* her quiet, gentle strength. There were some very difficult times, but she was equal to them. She was never one to cause a stir; she just quietly did what needed to be done. I remember she would go about her work humming to herself. I sometimes

catch myself humming when I need to buoy myself up—almost as if I were invoking my mother's mantra.

(b) *When I think of my mother, it hurts to remember* that day she was brought home after major surgery. I returned from grade school and rushed in to see her. Coming home after school was always a treat; my mother was a world-class cook and baker, and wonderful things would be prepared or in progress in the kitchen. But this day she was in bed and barely stirred when I spoke to her. She seemed very weak and very tired and somehow far away.

(c) *When I look back with older, wiser eyes,* I see that my mother's illness was my first inkling that her strength and power had its limits and that she would not always be there as a bulwark against the world. I felt more vulnerable—more on my own. Still my mother's image remains very powerful for me. More than once in recent years when I have needed or received more than ordinary help or good fortune, the thought comes to me that my long-dead "sainted" mother will intercede or has interceded for me. I find this thought comforting but amusing since it is hardly in accord with my lack of belief in the supernatural. Perhaps the memory of her strength in adversity helps me summon my own.

3 (a) *When I think of my father, I like to remember* the close and light-hearted moments we had together. I remember making my own way to his store when I was very young to walk home with him. As we neared home, we got in step, and my father began to grin and march double quick in a military manner. "Mach shnehl [go fast]," he said. "Rekhts [right], links [left], rekhts, links." And we marched along—silly and happy—not caring what the neighbors might think.

(b) *When I think of my father, it hurts to remember* those final months of his life and his death from cancer. We seemed to be in a conspiracy to pretend that he wasn't fatally ill, so I missed my first chance to say good-bye to my father. I was across the state at college when I received word that my father was near death. Curiously, I missed my bus connection—a connection I had often made before—and didn't get home until the following morning. My father had died during the night, so I missed a second opportunity to say good-bye to my father. At the end of the funeral ceremony, our family was asked to rise and gather at the casket to view our father for the last time, but I was frozen to my chair and missed my third opportunity to say good-bye to my father.

(c) *When I look back with older, wiser eyes,* I see how important my father was and continues to be in my life. His illness and death overwhelmed me—they were more than I could bear—and I did everything I could to distance myself from them. The lingering memory of that time led to my later work with hospice patients and their families. I wanted to help them and help myself deal better with the painful final partings that are an intrinsic part of life.

In this exploration, you are to reminisce about three significant others or places or times. For each, first recall something you like to remember and then something it hurts to remember. You might recall two memories of your childhood home (as I did in my first set of reminiscences) or neighborhood or school. Your memories might concern your mother (as my second set of reminiscences did), father (as my third set of reminiscences did), grandparent, sibling, or some other salient figure. After each set of reminiscences, stop and think about what you see now as you look back on your recollections with older, wiser eyes.

Record your work on the next three pages in the spaces indicated.

1 (a)*When I think of _____, I like to remember . . .*

(b)*When I think of _____, it hurts to remember . . .*
         <small>same subject as 1(a)</small>

(c)*When I look back with older, wiser eyes . . .*

2 (a) *When I think of* _____, *I like to remember* . . .

(b) *When I think of* _____, *it hurts to remember* . . .
          same subject as 2(a)

(c) *When I look back with older, wiser eyes* . . .

3 (a) *When I think of _____, I like to remember . . .*

(b) *When I think of _____, it hurts to remember . . .*
           <small>same subject as 3(a)</small>

(c) *When I look back with older, wiser eyes . . .*

Significant Correspondence

Sometimes a person very central in your life—a *very significant* significant other—may be the one most difficult for you to communicate with. Many things may be left unsaid between the two of you. Perhaps you never could tell this person what you wanted to say, or you tried but it never got across. Perhaps there are things you would like to have heard from this person, but the words were never offered.

The person with whom your communication failed may now be dead or gone out of your life. Still, as the protagonist says in *I Never Sang for My Father* (Anderson, 1968), "Death ends a life but it does not end a relationship." There may be feelings still waiting to be expressed or words still waiting to be conveyed. There may be anger that needs to be expressed and defused, and forgiveness that needs to be offered.

Select one significant person in your life (present or absent, living or dead) with whom important things were left unsaid or unheard. In the space immediately below (and add as many more pages as necessary), write this person a letter to set forth all the things you would like to say. Then turn to the next page.

Dear _____ :

Earlier in this book (Box 1.4 in Chapter 1), we noted that one quality of a "caring presence" is the ability to put himself or herself in another's place and see the world through that person's eyes. A caring presence can get a sense of how the world must seem to this other person.

Now, for a few moments, put yourself in the place of the person to whom you just wrote your letter and look at the world through that person's eyes. (The more difficult this is for you to do, the more important it may be for you to try to do it.) As that person, write a reply to yourself in the space below (and add as many more pages as necessary). Then turn to the next page.

Dear _____ :

In the space below indicate (1) what you found most interesting, curious, or significant about this exchange of correspondence and (2) what you learned from it.

Question 6

Love

What Part Does Love Play in My Life?

Few persons dispute the importance of love in human existence. Love, we're told, makes the world go 'round. People fight for love. People even die for love.

But what is love? Few words in the English language have been used in so many ways or given so many meanings. "Love is a sickness full of woes/all remedies refusing," poetized Samuel Daniel. But many other poets—and songwriters— have seen love as the only cure to whatever it is that ails us.

Psychologists seem no more in agreement on love than the poets and songwriters. Hardly in a lyrical mood, the great behaviorist B. F. Skinner (1953) wrote that "love might be analyzed as the mutual tendency of two individuals to reinforce each other" (p. 310). But widely read counseling psychologist Wayne Dyer (1976) defines love as almost the opposite: "the ability and willingness to allow those that you care for to be what they choose for themselves, without any insistence that they satisfy you" (pp. 29–30).

What love is or isn't is of more than academic interest. Yale professor Robert Sternberg (1988b), a prominent theoretician and researcher on this subject, writes that one of the most common problems in loving relationships is that partners have different ideas about what love is. Each expresses love in her or his own way but not perhaps in one that the other expects, understands, or values.

What might be considered the final word about what love is was uttered by Henry Finck: "Love is such a tissue of paradoxes, and exists in such an endless

Box 6.1

Love: What Part Does Love Play in My Life?

Seedthoughts

1. When I think of all you have meant to me all these years, it is almost more than I can do, not to tell you.

    —*New England farmer to his mate of countless years*

2. Loving can cost a lot but not loving costs more.

    —*Merle Shain*

3. Love consists in desiring to give what is our own to another and feeling his delight as our own.

    —*Emanuel Swedenborg*

4. A common notion is that we "fall" in love—that we passively wait for the right person to come along and sweep us off our feet. . . . In contrast, I see love as being *active*, as something we ourselves create. *We make love happen.*

    —*Gerald Corey*

5. We must be our own before we can be another's.

    —*Ralph Waldo Emerson*

6. And stand together yet not too near together:
    For the pillars of the temple stand apart,
    And the oak tree and the cypress grow not in each other's shadow.

    —*Kahlil Gibran*, The Prophet

7. Love is unconditional—it makes no bargains, it trades with no one for anything, but conveys the feeling, the in-the-bones belief to the other that you are all for him, that you are there to give him your support, to contribute to his development as best you can, because the other is what he is, *not* because he is something you want or expect him to be, but because you value him for what he is.

    —*Ashley Montagu*

8. The secret is—don't marry anybody you love. You should marry someone you like, someone who is your best friend. Hot love doesn't last.

    —*Mickey Rooney, at the age of 70 and in his eighth and only durable marriage (fifteen years)*

9. It is not your love which sustains the marriage, but from now on the marriage that sustains your love.

    —*Dietrich Bonhoeffer, in a sermon written for the marriage of a young couple*

10. Fidelity is expressed in a [marital] relationship when each is aware that their relationship has priority over all other matters.

    —*Clayton Barbeau*

11. When you marry, you don't just marry the good. A person is a bushel of things, some good and some not so good. You can't just have the good. You can't throw out the bad like you would a rotten apple. It's all stuck together, so you accept each other the way you are.

    —*woman married to the same industrious, faithful, and consistently grouchy husband for nearly forty years*

---

variety of forms and shades, that you can say almost anything about it that you please, and it is likely to be correct." For some further but less than final words about love see the seedthoughts in Box 6.1, and for information about some of love's "variety of forms and shades" continue with the material that follows.

Love as Attachment

Here is a question to start you off: "What was your first love?" Stop reading for a moment and bring your answer to mind.

I remember the responses to this question gathered by a roving reporter. The passers-by recalled a grade school crush or a bout of puppy love, but deeper reflection might show that these loves were hardly first.

We human beings come into the world ready to love or to bond ourselves to our primary caregivers, who are usually our mothers. This is the first of a number of attachments we make as we move through life, and it can have a considerable effect on the bonds we later form (Bowlby, 1979). In fact, infant caregiver attachments and later romantic loves have a remarkable similarity. Infants and lovers both are intensely fascinated with their attachment objects, seek proximity and contact, become anxious when the relationship is not going well, are distressed by separation, and are joyful upon reunion. Infants and lovers both express their attachment by touching, smiling, laughing, clinging, cooing, and baby talk (Shaver, Hazan, & Bradshaw, 1988).

Here is a second question: "Which of the following best describes your feelings?"

- I find it relatively easy to get close to others and am comfortable depending on them and having them depend on me. I don't often worry about being abandoned or about someone getting too close to me.

- I am somewhat uncomfortable being close to others; I find it difficult to trust them completely, difficult to allow myself to depend on them. I am nervous when anyone gets too close, and love partners often want me to be more intimate than I feel comfortable being.

- I find that others are reluctant to get as close as I would like. I often worry that my partner doesn't really love me or won't want to stay with me. I want to merge completely with another person, and this desire sometimes scares people away.

The above item was one used in research by Phillip Shaver, Cindy Hazan, and Donna Bradshaw (1988). The first alternative describes secure adult attachment, the second avoidant, and the third anxious/ambivalent. This research team was interested in possible connections between adult and infant attachments. Earlier research (Ainsworth, Blehar, Waters, & Wall, 1978) had identified comparable attachments in infants and related them to these maternal behaviors:

Secure: Mother accessible and responsive. Infant secure with relatively less crying and distress at mother's absences.

Avoidant: Mother not very accessible or responsive and demonstrates more rejecting or rebuffing behavior, irritation, and anger. Infant defensively detached from or avoids mother.

Anxious/ Ambivalent: Mother slow or inconsistent in response or intrudes on or interferes with infant's desired activities. Infant cries more and explores less than secure infants, shows anger and anxiety, and is intensely distressed by mother's absence.

The Shaver team found that these three attachment types were distributed in adults in approximately the same proportions as they had been found in infants by an earlier research group (Campos et al., 1983).

	Infants	*Adults*
Secure	62%	56%
Avoidant	23	24
Anxious/Ambivalent	15	20

Here's a third and last question: "How does your present attachment style relate to your earlier attachment history?" That's a provocative but difficult question. We may never have thought about our "attachment style" or even been aware that we had one. One woman's hard-won insight: "For years my pattern was to look for men who were extremely hard to get at, hard to draw out—men like my father. I'm only now consciously trying to change that pattern" (Fleming, 1977, p. 42). About twenty-five centuries ago Greek lyric poet Sappho noted the resemblance of childhood and adult attachment styles in this quatrain:

> *Afraid of losing you*
> *I ran fluttering*
> *like a little girl*
> *after her mother*

In their research, the Shaver team employed two different samples: (1) a large and heterogeneous group, with a mean age of 36, who responded to a newspaper "love quiz" and (2) a smaller group of mostly freshmen with a mean age of 18. Their results await further confirmation but make considerable sense.

1. The most important love experience reported by secure adults was characterized by friendship, trust, and positive emotions. By contrast, the love experience of avoidant adults was marked by lack of trust and fear of closeness. Anxious/ambivalent adults had relationships marked by emotional highs and lows, desire for reciprocation, and jealousy.

2. On items administered only to the college sample, secure adults reported themselves as well liked and easy to get to know, and they saw others as good-hearted and well intentioned. By contrast, anxious/ambivalent adults described themselves as having self-doubts and as being underappreciated and misunderstood; they found others less able and willing than themselves to make commitments to a relationship. The avoidant adults fell between the other two groups, although they were closer to the anxious/ambivalent subjects; more than any other group, avoidant adults agreed with this statement: "I can get along quite well by myself."

3. In the newspaper sample (the comparable findings for the college students were generally similar but more complicated), the secure adults recalled warm childhood relationships with their parents and also warm relationships between their parents. Avoidant adults recalled their mothers as disrespectful, demanding, and critical and their fathers as uncaring and forceful. Anxious/ambivalent adults recalled their mothers as unfair and intrusive and their fathers as unfair and threatening.

4. In the newspaper sample, love relationships tended to last longer in the secure adults; they averaged 10.02 years. The relationships of the avoidant adults averaged 5.97 years and those of the anxious/ambivalent adults 4.86 years. (The average age of each of the three groups was the same—36 years.)

These results are presented here to start us thinking about love as attachment as well as about our own attachment style and that of those we attach to (or try to). However, the correlation between current attachment style and recollection of childhood parenting, although too large to be attributed to chance, was not very large. Furthermore, the correlation was stronger in the college students and in younger subjects generally, regardless of group. This finding led the investigators to conclude, "As distance from parents increases and adult love experiences accumulate, the effect of child relationships on adult . . . behavior decreases" (p. 84). Evidently, we are not necessarily captive to our early experience; at least, we need not remain that way. Every new and deepening relationship gives us an opportunity to observe ourselves and modify our ways of relating.

Love as Intimacy, Passion, and Commitment

> Snips and snails and puppy-dog tails.
> Sugar and spice and all things nice.
> Intimacy, passion, and commitment.

The first three ingredients are, as almost every little girl knows, what little boys are made of, and the second three are the components of their own sex. The last three, according to Robert Sternberg (1988a), are what bring and keep us together; they are the components of love. *Intimacy* refers to the closeness, bondedness, and warmth experienced in loving relationships. *Passion* subsumes romance, physical attraction, and sexual consummation. *Decision/commitment* consists of a short-term aspect of deciding one loves someone and a long-term aspect of committing oneself to maintaining that love.

Sternberg describes seven kinds of love in which these components are present, either alone or in various combinations. An eighth category is "non-love," in which all the components are absent. Sternberg calls his formulation "the triangular theory of love" because each of the three components can be viewed as one point of a triangle, and all seven kinds of love can be located somewhere on that triangle. Sternberg's triangle appears in Box 6.2, and his seven kinds of love are briefly described below.

Box 6.2

Sternberg's Triangle

Sternberg's triangular theory of love asserts that different kinds of love can be understood in terms of three components—intimacy, passion, and commitment—represented as the vertices of a triangle. Each kind of love is positioned on the triangle according to its combination of these components.

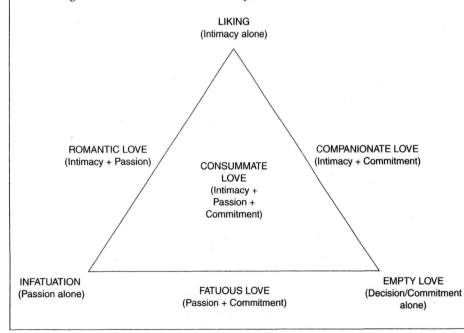

LIKING
(Intimacy alone)

ROMANTIC LOVE
(Intimacy + Passion)

CONSUMMATE
LOVE
(Intimacy +
Passion +
Commitment)

COMPANIONATE LOVE
(Intimacy + Commitment)

INFATUATION
(Passion alone)

FATUOUS LOVE
(Passion + Commitment)

EMPTY LOVE
(Decision/Commitment
alone)

Liking (Intimacy Alone)

Liking describes a relationship in which there is a feeling of warmth and closeness but one without passion or long-term commitment. Many friendships seem to fall within this category. Our friends are persons we like and to whom we feel close. As our friendships deepen, a sense of commitment may begin to grow, and a deep friendship may prove more durable than any other kind of love.

Nearly all of us need warm, intimate relationships, but not all of us know how to form and maintain them. Elaine Hatfield (1988) writes that a basic prerequisite for intimacy is independence (something that may erroneously be considered to be intimacy's opposite). Dependent individuals may not risk intimacy; they may not reveal their irritations, fears, and weaknesses lest these alienate the other. Independent individuals know they can make it on their own, so they can risk sharing their innermost thoughts and feelings and do not need to settle for partners who aren't responsive.

The couples who come to Hatfield for therapy are usually poor at relationships, and she teaches them intimacy skills. Here are four points she emphasizes in this training:

1. *Accept yourself as you are.* You don't need to be perfect. You're entitled to be who you are and to have the ideas and feelings you have. Of course, you still may need to better yourself, and you can do so by setting one small goal at a time and working to achieve it.

2. *Recognize your intimates for what they are.* You don't need to be perfect and neither does your partner. Learn to enjoy others as they are without trying to change them or fix them. In my own opinion, some of the best advice about love is contained in this simple statement by the poet John Ciardi: "If you will let people be wrong, most of whatever love is may begin."

3. *Express yourself.* You may be hesitant about sharing your ideas and feelings because of the possible effect on the relationship. Yet intimacy requires sharing, and with practice such sharing can become more skilled and graceful. Hatfield notes that "love and hate tend to flow together" and when you admit your irritations, your affection frequently increases; when lovers who think they are bored with each other or have fallen out of love begin to express themselves more fully, their love sometimes comes back in a rush.

4. *Deal with your intimate's reactions.* Your partners are apt to respond to your feelings by expressing their own. They may express hurt or anger or make you feel guilty. The important thing, says Hatfield, is not to apologize or back up or retreat. Her advice is to stay calm. Remind yourself that you are entitled to your thoughts and feelings, but listen carefully to what your partner is thinking and feeling, and keep trying to connect.

Infatuation (Passion Alone)

Infatuation has been said to be "love at first sight." The reason for this, some cynic has said, is that the second sight dispels it. Of course, if the second sight doesn't dispel it, infatuation may turn into something else; but until it does, infatuation is passion without the components of intimacy and commitment.

Sternberg notes three major problems that tend to be associated with infatuation. First, infatuation is based not on reality but on the idealization of the other. A deeper acquaintance may provide a more realistic second sight. A second problem is that infatuations tend to be obsessions. They can consume a person to such an extent that other pursuits are disrupted. Infatuations can also distress a partner who finds the intensity overwhelming or who perceives that he or she has become a figment of the other's fantasy needs. A third problem has to do with the asymmetry of infatuations. Lovers are often not equally smitten or equally blind to reality. Sometimes one is infatuated from afar, and the loved one may not know or care that he or she is the object of affection.

Two love researchers with a somewhat different view of infatuation are Elaine Hatfield (introduced earlier) and a colleague, G. William Walster (1985). When these researchers asked students at three universities to state the one thing they most wanted to know about love, with surprising frequency what these students wanted to know was the difference between love and infatuation. Their question was the same one that many have asked: "How can I know I'm truly in love—not just infatuated?"

Generally, students of love have proposed that infatuation is immediate, intense, and associated with surface qualities that have perhaps a special charm. By contrast, love or "true" love is likely to develop more slowly and is associated with deeper traits that have an enduring nature. Infatuation springs up suddenly and may just as readily subside. True love takes time but endures (Grant, 1976).

Hatfield and Walster regard this reasoned difference between infatuation and love as specious. To them, the solution to the love-versus-infatuation riddle is simple: there is no difference—at the time we are experiencing them. Lovers often use the term "romantic love" to describe relationships still in progress and the term "infatuation" for pairings that have terminated (Ellis & Harper, 1961).

"If love and infatuation are exactly the same thing, how come my mother—and my friends—keep insisting *they* can tell the difference?" This question keeps popping up, and here is Hatfield and Walster's answer: When parents and friends vehemently insist that we're "just infatuated" or grudgingly admit that we're "really in love," they are simply telling us whether they approve of our relationship. If they approve, it's love. If they don't, it's infatuation. "But," insist Hatfield and Walster, "*you* shouldn't get confused trying to make nonexistent distinctions between the two. It's exciting to come to deeply understand yourself and your emotions. It's important to realize that you love someone and to bask in that feeling, even though you are painfully aware that the relationship can come to nothing" (p. 53).

Empty Love (Commitment Alone)

Empty love, commitment without either intimacy or passion, describes a relationship long on duty or routine but short on magic. Empty love is what remains

© Ashleigh Brilliant 1983. Reprinted by permission.

© ASHLEIGH BRILLIANT 1983

POT-SHOTS NO 2887

Ashleigh Brilliant

IN SOME CASES, A BROKEN HEART PROVES TO BE ONLY A SUPERFICIAL WOUND.

in some long-term relationships after physical attraction has been lost and emotional involvement disappears.

Many familial relationships may be long on commitment but little else. All that maintains the bond is a sense of obligation. This bleak thought was expressed beautifully by a character in Robert Frost's poem "The Death of the Hired Man" when he defined a home as "the place where, when you have to go there,/ They have to take you in."

In our society, Sternberg (1988a) notes, empty love most frequently is seen as the end stage of a long-term relationship; it may be a relationship that has emptied out over the years until nothing but commitment is left. However, in some other societies, marriages are arranged and the spouses may be strangers as they join their lives; they begin with commitment and build from there.

Some empty love nests hold together because of the parents' sense of duty to the children. The time of crisis may come when the children grow up and move out, leaving the empty nest doubly empty.

Sometimes love empties only from one side of the relationship. One partner may have feelings for the other while the other retains only a sense of commitment. "Such asymmetrical relationships," Sternberg writes, "can be particularly difficult because of the added guilt felt by the less involved spouse at not being able to reciprocate the more involved spouse's feelings" (p. 125).

Fatuous Love (Passion + Commitment)

Fatuous (the word denotes smugness and stupidity) love involves passion and commitment in the absence of intimacy. Whirlwind courtships—some of which may be on the rebound from other failed relationships—are examples of fatuous love. What's missing is the intimate involvement that would provide some proof of common or compatible values or interests.

When passion fades from fatuous love, there is little left but commitment and perhaps not too much of that—since commitment, like intimacy, takes some time to deepen. Sternberg writes that fatuous lovers wind up feeling they have less than they bargained for, but their bargain included too much passion and too little intimacy.

Research supports the importance of intimacy to the success of a relationship, and a positive association has been found between the length of time spent in dating and subsequent marital happiness. With longer periods of acquaintance, unsuitable partners can be screened out. Furthermore, troublesome differences can be experienced, weighed, and worked on or accommodated (Grover, Russell, Schumm, & Paff-Bergen, 1985).

Romantic Love (Intimacy + Passion) and Companionate Love (Intimacy + Commitment)

Both romantic and companionate love include intimacy, but in the former it is paired with passion and in the latter with commitment. These two kinds of love have often been considered a basic division. Hatfield and Walster (1985) write that "passion is a fragile essence. It provides joy, excitement, delirium, and fulfillment—along with anxiety, suffering, and despair—for a short time. Companionate love is a heartier flower. It can provide gentle friendship for life" (p. 160).

Many love relationships begin romantically and then, if they survive, change gradually into more companionate arrangements: passion subsides while commitment builds. People differ as to the amount of romance they require in their lives, and the requirements may change in time.

The man who once thought he would sacrifice anything for passion may wake up one day to find that he's sick and tired of all the fuss. He wants what his friends have—a settled, companionate existence. The woman who has always cynically disdained passion and has opted for a routine, calm, and stable life may discover that—in middle-age—she's changed her mind. She may find herself wildly attracted to a young man and conclude that passion is underrated and success and marital stability are overrated. (Hatfield & Walster, 1985, pp. 171–172)

Romantic love, which is taken for granted in twentieth-century North America, is unknown in many cultures and has its defenders and detractors. Although passion is sometimes described as an ecstatic experience, passionate lovers know better. In one study of more than five hundred passionate lovers, almost all the subjects saw their love as decidedly bittersweet (Tennov, 1979). Passionate love, Hatfield writes, is made up of a roller coaster of experience: "euphoria, happiness, calm tranquility, vulnerability, anxiety, panic, despair" (p. 196). And, she adds, that the risks of romantic love add fuel to the fire.

Perhaps no one has described companionate love better than Robert Johnson (1985). He calls it "stirring-the-oatmeal" love. Two people love in this way when they "enter into the whole spectrum of human life together" (p. 19). They find value and beauty in simple things and meaning in such unromantic tasks as "earning a living, living within a budget, putting out the garbage, feeding the baby in the middle of the night" (p. 18). Johnson is impressed with a Hindu rite of marriage in which the bride and groom make this pledge to each other: "You will be my best friend." He writes, "Western couples need to learn to be friends, to live with each other in the spirit of friendship, to take the quality of friendship through the tangles we have made of love" (p. 20).

Consummate Love (Intimacy + Passion + Commitment)

Consummate love is the kind of love many people aspire to and strive for: to join with another and live not just happily, but intimately, passionately, and with commitment. The balance between the components of love may change, but all will continue to be present and an important part of the relationship. A study of happy, enduring marriages—they had lasted for 15 years or more whereas the average American marriage lasts 9.4 years—showed that they indeed were steeped in intimacy, passion, and commitment (see Box 6.3). Below is Sternberg's description of a couple who have attained consummate love (note that the relationship has had its stormy weather but outlasted it):

Harry and Edith seemed to all their friends to be the perfect couple. And what made them distinctive from many such "perfect couples" is that they pretty much fulfilled the notion. They felt close to each other, they continued to have great sex after fifteen years, and they could not imagine themselves happy over the long term with anyone else. Harry had had a few flings, none of them serious, and eventually told Edith about them, unaware of the fact that she already knew about them because he was so transparent. Edith, on the other hand, had had no extramarital affairs. But they had weathered their few storms, and each was delighted with the relationship and with each other. (1988a, p. 59)

Sternberg does not consider homosexual relationships, but research suggests that the relationships of gay and lesbian couples are not markedly different from heterosexual pairs (Duffy & Rusbult, 1985/1986; Leigh, 1989). Furthermore, reports of promiscuity among homosexuals have been exaggerated (Gordon &

Box 6.3

And So They Got Married and Lived Happily Ever After (or at Least for Fifteen Years)

What makes for an enduring and happy marriage? An answer to this question is what Jeanette and Robert Lauer (1985) sought in their survey of 351 couples married for fifteen years or longer. In 51 of these marriages, one or both partners were unhappily sticking it out for one reason or another. The partners in the 300 happy marriages individually set down the top reasons their marriage had thrived. Below are the results presented in order of diminishing frequency.

MEN	WOMEN
My spouse is my best friend.	My spouse is my best friend.
I like my spouse as a person.	I like my spouse as a person.
Marriage is a long-term commitment.	Marriage is a long-term commitment.
Marriage is sacred.	Marriage is sacred.
We agree on aims and goals.	We agree on aims and goals.
My spouse has grown more interesting.	My spouse has grown more interesting.
I want the relationship to succeed.	I want the relationship to succeed.
An enduring marriage is important to social stability.	We laugh together.
We laugh together.	We agree on a philosophy of life.
I am proud of my spouse's achievements.	We agree on how and how often to show affection.
We agree on a philosophy of life.	An enduring marriage is important to social stability.
We agree about our sex life.	We have a stimulating exchange of ideas.
We agree on how and how often to show affection.	We discuss things calmly.
I confide in my spouse.	We agree about our sex life.
We share outside hobbies and interests.	I am proud of my spouse's achievements.

(From Lauer & Lauer, 1985, p. 24)

Snyder, 1989). Promiscuity is rare among lesbians (Tripp, 1987). Although not uncommon in certain groups of gays, it was diminishing with the threat of AIDS (Connell et al., 1989; Siegel, Bauman, Christ, & Krown, 1988), but recent reports indicate a resurgence. Like heterosexuals, the great majority of gays and lesbians prefer consummate love—intimacy and passion with a stable, committed relationship (Macklin, 1987; Tripp, 1987); however, achieving such a relationship may be more difficult for homosexual couples because of the hostility of the larger society and the resulting need for secrecy, the lack of social and legal sanctions and support, and the more limited pool of eligibles.

Sternberg's seven kinds of love represent extremes, and most love relationships fit somewhere between these pure types. Living happily ever after, Sternberg notes, need not be a myth. To become a reality, however, it must be based on different configurations of components at different times, and consummate love never can be taken for granted. Sternberg tells us what many of us have already learned the hard way: "Relationships are constructions, and they decay over time if they are not maintained and improved. . . . we must constantly work at understanding, building, and rebuilding our loving relationships" (p. 138).

Love as an Exchange

In the estimation of psychiatrist Ari Kiev (1979), love is unconditional. "To be loving," he writes, "you must learn to accept others as they are without setting conditions for their behaviors" (p. 16). To Kiev, those who sustain love best are those who love "without the expectation of anything in return" (p. 3). The "unconditional lovers of the world are a notoriously blissful lot" (p. 21). Unconditional lovers don't seek love or gather love; they generate love from within. They look for the positive, not the negative.

Psychiatrist Gerald Jampolsky (1983) is in total agreement with Kiev. He writes, "Love is the total acceptance and total giving—with no boundaries and no exceptions" (p. xii). Jampolsky's work is inspired by *A Course in Miracles*, which is a kind of spiritual psychotherapy. One of the lessons taught by *A Course in Miracles* is based on "the law of Love," which states that "to give is to receive."

> Under this law, when we give our Love away to others, we gain and what we give we simultaneously receive. The law of Love is based on abundance; we are completely filled with Love all the time, and our supply is always full and running over. When we give our Love unconditionally to others with no expectations of return, the Love within us extends, expands and joins. So by giving our Love away we increase the Love within us and everyone gains. (Jampolsky, 1979, p. 51)

Eileen Cady, one of the founders of the Findhorn, the international personal growth center in Scotland, has spoken eloquently about what it means to love unconditionally. In her estimation, the unconditional lover is one who can answer "yes" to the following seven questions (as you will see, it's a tall order):

1. Can I be myself at all times and allow others to be themselves without judging, criticizing, or condemning?

2. Can I love and love and go on loving, asking nothing in return?

3. Can I love someone with the same depth and the same degree whether we are together or apart?

4. Can I still love someone when I do not approve of something they have said or done?

5. Can I love someone so much that I am willing to let them go because I know by doing so they will grow and mature?

6. Can I love someone enough that I can cease helping them because I know if I go on helping them I will hold up their growth and evolution?

7. Can I love someone enough to see that person leave me for someone else and hold no bitterness, resentment, or jealousy?

Is unconditional love possible? Eloquent as its proponents are, a formidable case has been made against it. Two anti-unconditionalists, William Griffitt and Elaine Hatfield (1985), write, "Men and women who insist they are capable of dispensing love with no thought of return are simply deceiving themselves. Those who expect such selfless love from their partners most assuredly are deceiving themselves. In fact, the more men and women are able to give another, the more they can expect in return" (p. 453).

What has been called "equity theory" suggests that in a relationship we seek a balance between what we are putting into it and what we are getting out of it. If we give more than we get, we may feel angry or exploited. If we get more than we give, we may feel guilty. We seem to have an internal bookkeeping system, and in time we try to balance the books in some way. Equity theory is in harmony with the idea of conditional love or a love that sets conditions.

What happens when a relationship is inequitable and the books are unbalanced? According to Hatfield and Walster, in such cases the partners generally will try to restore *actual equity* or *psychological equity* or move to end the relationship. To restore actual equity, the partner who is not getting a satisfactory exchange may demand more from the other, or the other—perceiving the inequity—may begin to provide more. To restore psychological equity, the partners may try to convince themselves or others that things are really more fair than they appear to be.

The evidence presented by Griffitt and Hatfield strongly supports equity theory. For example, in the pairing market, suitors with more desirable qualities attract the more desirable partners. Furthermore, men and women in equitable relationships—that is, those who said that they were getting and giving as much in their relationship as their partners—proved to be happier, more satisfied, and also had more stable relationships than other couples.

An intermediate position, between the unconditional and conditional love camps, holds that one gives unconditionally but only up to a point or that one gives without expecting an equal or immediate return. In the study of lasting marriages discussed earlier in Box 6.3, the couples generally were opposed to the conventional wisdom that marriage is a fifty-fifty proposition. A male in the study commented that marital success requires one to "give 60 percent of the time. You have to be willing to put in more than you take out." A wife, happily married for forty-four years, suggested that the formula for success was to give 70 percent and expect 30 percent in return. Others suggested that it was a mistake to look for equity in the short run but that giving and taking balanced out in the long run. One husband put it this way: "Sometimes I give far more than I receive, and sometimes I receive far more than I give. But my wife does the same. If we weren't willing to do that, we would have broken up long ago."

Another intermediate position is taken by those who advocate *unconditional love* for what a person *is* but not *unconditional acceptance* of everything that person *does*. According to this position, one can convey to another one's full love and commitment but not permit or accept certain behaviors. Parental discipline is necessary and acceptable to the child who has ample evidence of her or his parent's love. In fact, the discipline can show that the parent is not indifferent. Each act of discipline can be accomplished in a way that indicates it is the act—not the child—that is not wanted.

More than one of my students have told me that they thought of God's love in this way. This love is unconditional, but it does not include an unconditional acceptance of everything they do. The message on which they had been raised was this: "God loves the sinner but not the sin."

The Stages of Love

As every budding writer knows, the tried-and-true formula for a love story is (1) boy meets girl, (2) boy loses girl, and (3) boy gets girl. Love seems to have its acts or stages. In a research interview, one woman describes the progression of her marital relationship in this way: "We have been married for fifteen years. For several years we were passionate lovers. There was a lot of romance in our lives. Now there is less romance and very deep love and friendship. . . . We feel very warm, intimate and deeply trusting of each other" (Hawley, McGee, & Stanford, 1976, p. 55).

"When I fell in love with you, suddenly your eyes didn't seem close together. Now they seem close together again."

In observing the components of love in enduring relationships, Sternberg (1988a) notes that intimacy and commitment tend to increase gradually to a high point and then level off, while passion often rises quickly and then quickly declines. These rises, however, are seldom uninterrupted. More likely they reflect the truth of Shakespeare's observation that "the course of true love never did run smooth." In keeping with these observations, Daniel Goldstine and his colleagues suggest that there are three common stages of love: a first stage of passion or romance, a third stage of mutual acceptance or companionship, and an intermediate, in-between stage of, alas, disillusionment (Goldstine, Larner, Zuckerman, & Goldstine, 1977).

Stage I, "the sparkle," is the stage of falling in love. It's a heady, intense, and often fleeting phase. It can be a wonderful stage—one in which we find ourselves appreciated, cherished, trusted, and supported. And it can be an alarming stage, one in which we become vulnerable and fearful of rejection as we move beyond our usual restraints to declare our love and share our feelings. Not every couple go through this stage. Some never fall in love; they skip the agony and the ecstacy and instead grow together little by little.

Stage II, "disillusionment," is a time for dealing with differences and disappointments. In the first stage, partners treat each other with affectionate indulgence, ignoring faults and failures. In this early part of the relationship, there are enchantment, optimism, and goodwill. In the second stage, the enchantment fades away as the couple realize that they are not perfectly right for each other, that there are problems to be confronted and adjustments to be made. This can be a harsh time of mutual blame and disapproval.

In Stage III, "mutual acceptance," the couple have modified their expectations and have learned to accept and accommodate each other. Problems continue, as they will all through life, but they are not seen as a threat to the relationship, which is now taken for granted. The couple feel secure and at home with each other. This security, the Goldstine team writes, "accomplishes an indispensable function for the couple. They have each other to rely on, and the strength they exchange reassures them and reinforces them for their struggle through life. But best of all, that exchanged strength enriches their experience of life" (p. 417).

When Loving Fails

Psychoanalyst Reuben Fine (1985) writes, "Regardless of what problems a person comes to an analyst with, sooner or later it becomes clear that there is a lack in their love lives, and the problem cannot be satisfactorily resolved unless the love problem is remedied" (p. xi). The primary task of the therapist, as Fine sees it, is to teach patients how to love.

How do we learn to love? Fine argues persuasively that we learn to love by being loved. The more loving experiences we have as children, the greater our chances for becoming a loving adult. Sternberg's (1985) research suggests that loving tends to run in nuclear families, but also that such results do not necessarily generalize to relationships outside the family. Coming from a loving family does not guarantee that you will be successful in love; neither does coming from an unloving family necessarily predict that you will not form loving relationships elsewhere.

Families themselves are not what they used to be. They have a greater tendency to fall apart. These days there are more one-parent families and also more "reconstituted" families composed of parents who have been married before and children from earlier marriages.

In their book *In Search of Intimacy,* psychologists Carin Rubenstein and Phillip Shaver (1982) write, "Being a good parent (or a good lover) means being regularly available—physically and emotionally" (p. 43). Children whose parents are seriously inadequate in this regard may cling, be very anxious when separated from their parents, and have little confidence in themselves or others. More serious cases of rejection, abuse, or abandonment can result in children who are detached and aloof, keeping a self-protective distance from everyone (Rubenstein & Shaver, 1982). Related findings were presented earlier in this chapter, but this material is worth further discussion here as we consider how loving fails.[1]

Rubenstein and Shaver note that childhood clinging and detachment are related to adult clinging and evading patterns. Lonely college students often disclose too little or too much and also demonstrate other patterns that make others back away. Rubenstein and Shaver describe these patterns as follows:

> The overdisclosers or clingers are like clingy children, psychologically speaking. They want social contact so desperately that they can hardly wait to attach themselves, securely and permanently, to somebody. In the process, they overwhelm people with their eagerness for instant intimacy. The clinger's persistent needs and demands, even when accompanied by gifts, favors, and statements of concern, are more than most of us can handle, especially early in a friendship. We back away from the clinger, fearing for our independence and peace of mind. As the philosopher Friedrich Nietzsche observed: "The lonely one offers his hand too quickly to whomever he encounters."

> Underdisclosers, or intimacy evaders, in contrast with clingers, defend themselves against the pain of rejection by refusing to open up to other people for fear their deepest, most "real" self will be rebuffed. They come across as cool, aloof, disinterested, perhaps even snobby. They are actually desperate for contact and can fantasize about it incessantly but are too frightened, too well protected to take a chance on love. Unfortunately, love and friendship are inherently risky—there can never be an advance guarantee of acceptance between strangers. Because evaders rarely express their deepest needs to anyone, they are prone to self-administered anesthesia: solitary drinking or pill-popping, excessive television-viewing or eating. (p. 44)

---

[1]   I am greatly indebted to the work of Rubenstein and Shaver in the preparation of this section.

A student once told me that in his senior year in high school, which was the loneliest year of his life, he was voted the most popular student. Other students have shared similar stories. Despite the good show many of us put on in our teens and early twenties, this is in general the loneliest and least positive time of our lives.

Rubenstein and Shaver asked a group of college freshmen to review their high school romances. Satisfying relationships were reported by a few, but most clear were patterns of "pining" and "pseudoattachment." Piners were greatly attracted to someone but were either unable to make advances or let the other know how much they cared. Those who were "pseudoattached" were going with someone they little knew or for whom they little cared. They were going out just to go out.

Many teenage love affairs are unfulfilling because this is a time of generally low self-esteem and also of uncertain self-definition. Until we know and like ourselves, we are unable to make much of a commitment; and without such a commitment, mature intimacy isn't possible (Rubenstein & Shaver, 1982; Erikson, 1968).

One important reason for the high dropout rates in college appears to be that students are lonely and lack social support. Extreme loneliness is also a factor in campus suicides and alcoholism (Lamont, 1979). Carolyn Cutrona (1982) and her colleagues studied a group of new undergraduates at UCLA. Two weeks into the school year, 75 percent of these students had experienced at least occasional loneliness, and more than 40 percent reported loneliness of moderate to severe intensity. Follow-up showed that loneliness dropped significantly during the year, and at year's end only 25 percent reported that they had experienced loneliness in the previous two-week period.

Cutrona's data suggest that certain beliefs and attitudes play an important part in maintaining loneliness. Some students may have exaggerated notions of the extent of their peers' social relationships, and therefore are dissatisfied with their own. Students who remained lonely insisted upon romantic relationships as a solution, whereas students who recovered from their initial loneliness had built a network of friends. Persistently lonely students also attributed their loneliness to undesirable, unchangeable personal qualities in themselves; this attribution may have kept them from working to better their social lives, or perhaps it gave them an excuse not to try.

More people are electing to remain single these days, and most singletons try to establish some intimate ties or attachments. For some, this is the best of both worlds: intimacy but also independence. For most of us, however, enduring intimacy requires the commitment of marriage, and most of us sooner or later do marry.

Married persons are happier than single persons (Freedman, 1979). In married couples, the reported amounts of love and happiness are highly correlated. Of the married pairs studied by Rubenstein and Shaver, most happy were those in love with each other, next most happy were those no longer in love, and least happy were those who had never been in love with anyone.

Rubenstein and Shaver concluded that husbands generally get more out of marriage than wives do. Married men were less lonely than married women; by contrast, single and divorced males were more lonely than single or divorced females. Women seem to be better at living alone than men are. Women are better at caring for themselves and establishing social support systems. In our culture, most wives provide their husbands with the only intimate connection the latter have. Wives also do the "emotional work" within the family and maintain the ties with friends and relatives.

Marriage, of course, doesn't guarantee love. Rubenstein and Shaver write, "In most troubled marriages, psychological intimacy is the first to go, while daily routine—and sometimes uninspired sex—lingers on. Studies of divorced couples show that many remain together long after they have suffered an almost complete breakdown in communication and caring" (p. 98).

Divorce and death disrupt families, and both can cause severe repercussions. Grief for a dying marriage may need to be worked through just like grief over a death. Emotional attachments may remain even after bad marriages end, and there is almost always a mixture of other feelings to be sorted out.

Psychologists Judith Wallerstein and Joan Kelley (1980) studied a group of divorcing couples over a five-year period. These investigators were surprised by the length of time most of the persons required to recover. Loneliness persisted along with depression, hurt, and anger. After five years, only one-third of the women and two-fifths of the men felt that the divorce was no longer an issue in their lives.

Children, too, can suffer when their parents divorce, just as they can when parents remain together but are constantly in conflict. From their review of the literature, Rubenstein and Shaver conclude that the *quality* of home life and of other social supports is what is important. "Intense, long-term parental conflicts predispose children, especially young children, to later loneliness" (pp. 46–47). However, they emphasize the word "predispose" because not all children from high-conflict homes were found to be prone to loneliness as adults.

Few events in life are as traumatic as the death of a loved one, especially one who is very central in our lives. Many widows and widowers report loneliness. Among widows, loneliness and "husband sanctification" (idealization of the late husband) tend to go together. Americans who have lost a mate are particularly vulnerable to loneliness because of our society's emphasis on companionate relations (Lopata, Heinemann, & Baum, 1982).

It is commonly assumed that being old means being alone, being alone means being lonely, and therefore older adults are lonely adults. The first assumption is true; we are more likely to live alone as we grow old. But the second assumption is not supported by the research evidence. Quite the contrary: reported loneliness, which is most pronounced among adolescents, tends to decline with age (although it may increase again in those 80 years old and older). The typical old person living alone is not a notably lonely person (Peplau, Bikson, Rook, & Goodchilds, 1982).

One reason for the absence of self-reported loneliness in old persons is that these persons can find social support from friends. Research indicates that social contact with friends and neighbors is generally more important to an older person's well-being than contact with grown children or other relatives (Peplau et al., 1982). One group of investigators found that single old people living alone or with friends were less lonely than those who lived with relatives (Perlman, Gerson, & Spinner, 1978). There is an old saying that one can choose one's friends but not one's relatives, and apparently many older persons take advantage of this choice.

A second reason for the absence of loneliness in older adults may relate to their lower or more realistic expectations concerning social relations; older persons may have learned not to expect as much or demand as much as younger and perhaps more idealistic adults (Peplau et al., 1982). A third possibility is that older persons are reluctant to admit their loneliness; younger adults are members of a possibly more open and expressive generation.

Myths About Love

David Bricker (1978), Gerald and Marianne Corey (1993), Albert Ellis (1977c), and a number of other psychologists and psychiatrists have noted the many myths

about love that exist in our culture. Far from harmless, these misconceptions cause a good deal of mischief and unhappiness. Ellis writes that almost every day he sees a person in therapy with a problem related to one or more of these "superstitions." Following are five of these myths, synthesized from lists formulated by these psychologists.[2]

Myth 1. Love Is Mysterious

Some years ago, Wisconsin's Senator William Proxmire attacked a National Science Foundation's grant awarded for the study of the reasons that people fall in love. In a press release, the senator wrote that he objected because in his opinion the reasons for falling in love could not be determined scientifically, that whatever reasons were discovered would not be believed, and, further, that he and 200 million other Americans preferred that the whole matter remain a mystery. Columnist James Reston agreed with the senator that love would always be a mystery. "But," Reston added, "if the sociologists and psychologists can even get a suggestion of the answer to our pattern of romantic love, marriage, disillusions, divorce—and the children left behind—it [the grant] would be the best investment of federal money since Jefferson made the Louisiana purchase."

---

[2] The word "myth" is used here to mean something that isn't true. This use is different from that in the discussion of personal myths in Chapter 4.

As it turns out, the "mystery" of love lends itself quite well to scientific study. Since the 1950s, when scientists began to research various aspects of love, a lot has been discovered: "Taken all together, this information begins to shed some light on what love is, who finds it and who doesn't, and what causes love to flourish . . . or die" (Hatfield & Walstor, 1985 p. 2).

Myth 2. Love Is Forever/Love Is Fleeting

"I'll be loving you always, with a love that's true always," is an old song classic and also a great pledge—which often isn't kept. The belief that *our* love is forever can prove to be a dangerous myth *if* it lulls us into a false sense of security and prevents us from continuing the work that every worthwhile relationship requires. People change, and the love they feel for each other may change in quality or depth. Well-tended relationships deepen; commitment and shared experience produce a formidable bond. But people grow, and sometimes they grow irrevocably apart.

Some of us subscribe to an opposite myth—the belief that love is fleeting. We may not even be fully aware that we are influenced by this myth, but if we are the child of a broken marriage or have been around or involved in a number of failed relationships ourselves, we can develop a kind of cynicism or pessimism about love. We may be too quick to declare a struggling relationship dead or too slow to apply the first aid that could move a stuck or unsatisfying relationship to a better place.

Myth 3. Love Is Constant

Ellis writes, "Love, even when it is deepseated and intense, tends to be a distinctly intermittent rather than steady, incessant feeling" (p. 157)—especially, he adds, in love relationships that endure for a considerable length of time. Marshall Hodge (1967) agrees and notes that love itself does not come and go, but "our *experience* of love and our *expression* of love is intermittent" (p. 13).

Most persons can stand only so much closeness. There are times when we need to be in the company of others and times when we need to be apart. Periods of separation from a loved one can be healthy, and the inability to separate or to allow some separation may be a symptom of a deeper problem.

Some of the most eloquent words about love were written years ago by Anne Morrow Lindbergh in her classic book *Gift from the Sea,* and they cast light on both Myth 2 and Myth 3.

> When you love someone, you do not love him or her in exactly the same way, from moment to moment. It is an impossibility. And yet this is exactly what most of us demand. We have so little faith in the ebb and flow of life, of love, of relationships. We leap at the flow of the tide and resist in terror its ebb. We are afraid it will never return. We insist on permanency, on continuity, when the only continuity possible is in growth, in fluidity—in freedom. . . . The only real security in a relationship is not in owning or possessing, not in demanding or expecting, . . . but living in the present relationship and accepting it as it is now. (1965, pp. 108–109)

Myth 4. Love Is Exclusive

Some couples get wrapped up in themselves and let other friendships drop away. But it is not reasonable to expect one person to meet all our needs. Other people nurture us and encourage our growth in special ways, and when we are experiencing difficulties, these others can help us with support and understanding (Doress & Wegman, 1984).

Despite our love for and sexual attraction to our mate, it is normal to also feel an attraction to others. Someone who is attracted only to his or her mate and never interested in anyone else is "a most unusual and, very probably, abnormal individual" (Ellis, 1977c, p. 157). We may not do something about these interests, but it is almost impossible not to have them.

There are some aspects of love or of our thoughts and feelings that we may share only with our mate and some perhaps that we never share with her or him. Many couples choose to have sex only with each other; this to them is an essential commitment. Some women find it easier to share their innermost thoughts with a close woman friend or a continuing circle of friends rather than with their husbands; these friends may be able to share perspectives and experiences and respond in ways their husbands would never be able to.

Myth 5. Love Is Beyond Our Control

As was noted in the first chapter, a personality dimension called "locus of control" describes the measure of influence we believe we have over our lives. Some individuals, called "externals," believe that they lack control—that things happen to them. By contrast, others, called "internals," believe that they exercise control—that they make things happen. Of course, none of us is purely or completely one or the other. Many of us tend to be externals in some situations and internals in others.

Sometimes, the very language of love suggests that love is an arena over which we can exercise little control. For example, in describing the advent of a romantic relationship, we may say we "fell in love," as if we were the passive victim of overwhelming forces. We may say, "I wish I could get over my feelings for her" or "I wish I cared more for him," as if we were at a loss and unable to do anything about this aspect of our life (Bricker, 1978). Or we attribute our attraction to "chemistry" that is either right or wrong; if it's right, there's nothing that needs to be done, and if it's wrong, there's nothing that can be done (Bricker, 1978).

Many psychologists and other students of human behavior have taken strong exception to this notion of love. Their view is that love is not something that happens to us. Love is something we make happen. In this view, love is not passive; it is not a feeling that just comes over us. Love is active, and lovers are activators. "Love is as love does," writes M. Scott Peck (1978). "Love is an act of will—namely, both intention and an action" (p. 83). Or, to say it another way, when we love, we mean well and we do good.

Peck maintains that what is called "falling in love" is not love at all, because it is not an act of will. As he sees it, "falling in love" is a kind of genetic trick to get us to mate and enhance the survival of the species. Falling in love is a temporary and sexually motivated experience in which we are drawn beyond our usual restraints or defenses or boundaries. In this state, we wish to merge with the other. There are accompanying feelings of ecstasy and omnipotence, which, alas, disappear when reality with its everyday problems intrudes. We become individuals again and hardly omnipotent. At this point, we either say good-bye or we begin "the work of real loving."

The "work of real loving" is very much within our control. We take responsibility to make things good rather than waiting for good things to happen (Bricker, 1978). The analogy of love to "stirring the oatmeal" (presented earlier in this chapter) "means that two people take their love off the airy level of exciting fantasy and convert it into earthy, practical immediacy" (Johnson, 1985, p. 19). "The real relatedness between two people is experienced in the small tasks they do together: the quiet conversation when the day's upheavals are at rest, the soft word of understanding, the daily companionship, the encouragement offered in a difficult moment, the small gift when least expected, the spontaneous gesture of love" (p. 18).

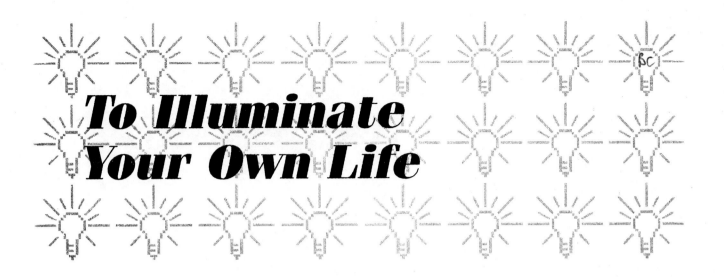

To Illuminate Your Own Life

Anchor and Apply*

1. Discuss your present attachment style and relate it to your earlier attachment history.

2. Using Sternberg's system, classify a love relationship you have or have had and discuss its intimacy, passion, and commitment.

3. Discuss your ability to form and maintain warm, intimate relationships.

4. Have you ever received unconditional love from another person? Have you ever given love unconditionally to another person? Or have all your love relationships been in accord with "equity theory"? Discuss this aspect of your experience with love.

5. Describe the stages (sparkle, disillusionment, mutual acceptance) as they have appeared or failed to appear in a love relationship you have had or have now.

6. Sternberg's research suggests that love runs in families. Does love run in your family? What effect has its absence or presence had on you?

7. Were your adolescent or high school friendships and/or romances satisfying? Why or why not?

8. Discuss the loneliness you have felt in any particular period of your life.

9. If you are from a broken family or one in which there was intense discord, discuss the effect this has had on you.

10. If the family you and your spouse established broke apart or suffered intense discord, discuss the effect this has had on you.

11. Of the love myths in the chapter, select one that your experience has taught you is truly a myth, and discuss this experience.

12. Of the love myths in the chapter, select one that you do not agree is completely a myth, and argue your point of view.

* These "anchor and apply" items are designed to help you use the concepts of the chapter as stimuli to prompt new or deeper or clearer insights into yourself and your life. To respond to an item, first find the material in the chapter that is most relevant to the item *and* yourself; that's called "anchoring." Second, think about this material in relationship to yourself and your life and keep thinking about it until you arrive at a new or deeper or clearer understanding; that's the "apply" or application part. When you write or present your response to the item, be sure to include both parts, that is, both the anchor material and the application. You can know you are successful on an item if, in completing it, you truly learn something new or understand something better.

Warm Fuzzies

As Claude Steiner (1974), who discovered them, noted, Warm Fuzzies come in a small, soft Fuzzy Bag. When you reach in your bag to get one, it is as small as a child's hand, but when it sees the light of day, it smiles and blossoms out into a large, shaggy Warm Fuzzy. When you lay it on a person's shoulder or lap, it snuggles up and makes the person feel good all over. "Warm Fuzzy" has become a metaphor for any manifestation of love that one person shows for another.

1. Suppose that one morning this week you were given a Fuzzy Bag filled with Warm Fuzzies and instructions to give one to every person you love. In the space below, write the name of each person to whom you would give a Warm Fuzzy and also why you would want to. (You may use initials or pseudonyms if you like instead of real names.) When you have finished, proceed to the second item.

2. Suppose that on the same morning this week every person in the world (not just you) was given a Warm Fuzzy Bag filled with Warm Fuzzies and the same instructions—to give one to every person they loved. In the space below, write the name of each person (or use initials or a pseudonym) who might give you a Warm Fuzzy and why he or she might want to. When you have finished, turn to the next page.

3. Are you sufficiently loving? Turn back to the first item in this exploration and put a star (*) by the name of each person to whom you have recently said something loving or clearly shown your love or positive regard. If there are enough listings (you decide how many are enough) and each now has a star, you are to be congratulated. By the way, did you give a Warm Fuzzy to yourself? If so, further congratulations are in order.

4. Are you sufficiently loved? Turn back to the second item in this exploration and put a plus (+) by the name of each person who has recently said something loving to you or clearly shown you her or his love or positive regard. If there are enough listings (again, you decide how many are enough) and each now has a plus, more congratulations are in order.

5. If you have been congratulated three times, great! Your work on this exploration is over. If not, what is one step that you could take right now to increase the Warm Fuzzies in your life? Will you take this step? Why or why not? Answer these three questions in the space below.

Love and Forgiveness

Begin this exploration by reading the following account (condensed) by Joseph M. Queenan (1987):

Three years ago, my recovering alcoholic father called me into my mother's kitchen to apologize for all the pain he inflicted on me for so many years. "One of the things I've learned through Alcoholics Anonymous is that you have to admit that you've hurt people and have to let them know how sorry you are," he explained to me. "Son, I'm sorry for anything I may have done to harm you." He then shook my hand.

"*May* have done" was the part I liked.

My father, a textbook alcoholic, beat his children, terrorized his wife, wrecked the house, went through an endless series of menial jobs and humiliated his family in front of friends. Like most alcoholics, he was a compulsive liar. Like many, he was lazy; I mean he didn't even bother to concoct new, more plausible lies. And at least three times a year he would explain disappearances of large sums of money by saying that his wallet had been stolen in the men's room at the North Philadelphia train station.

Like many alcoholics, my father behaved as though a thing hadn't happened if he couldn't remember it. Coming down to breakfast to find a window on the back porch broken, he would say that he was sorry, but he had no idea how it happened. About twice a year his rampages would become so violent that my mother would have to call the police, and my father would spend the night in the cooler. He wouldn't recall that in the morning, either.

At the age of 58, having no real contact with his children or grandchildren, having been thrown out of the house by my mother and having lost his job and pension, my father finally decided to do what we had been urging him to do for decades and give up drinking. After a fitful start, he's managed to go almost three years without a drink. My mother, who speaks with him occasionally (though she doesn't see him), says that he seems to be doing well, that he has a little job and lives in a little room. I wish him well, but I don't want to see him, either.

I hated my father for the first 20 years of my life. I don't hate him anymore—today I understand some of the roots of his behavior. That he had an alcoholic father; that he grew up during the Depression; that he was a high-school dropout; that he served an 18-month stint in an Augusta, Ga., military prison for going AWOL to his mother's funeral. And that he had four children that he couldn't support. There are enough mitigating circumstances in my father's life to make me feel sorry for him and for others like him and to applaud their efforts to salvage something of their ruined lives. But "to understand is to forgive" is one maxim I don't buy.

I understand but I won't forgive. And so a word about the etiquette of contrition. To all those who want to wipe the slate clean and launch brand-new relationships with those they *may* have harmed during their binges, stupors and rages, I would urge caution. If you're trying to pull your life together at a very late date—terrific. If you're genuinely sorry for whatever you've done and whomever you've harmed, tell them so. If feeling good about yourself is the only way to stay away from the bottle, feel free to feel good about yourself. Just don't think that a belated apology makes everything even-steven.

And don't go sticking your hand out waiting for someone to shake it. Keep it to yourself.

Answer the questions that follow in the space indicated.

1. (a) Do you agree or disagree with the position taken by Queenan? Why? (b) Do you believe Queenan is helped or hurt by the position he has taken? Why?

2. Recall something for which you haven't forgiven another—preferably something that happened some time ago. (a) What was it? (b) Why haven't you forgiven this person? (c) Are you helped or hurt by the position you have taken? Why? (If you can't recall something for which you haven't forgiven another, recall something that you have forgiven—preferably something that was hard to forgive. Then answer the same three questions, but change the "haven't" in the second question to "have.")

3. Recall something for which you haven't forgiven yourself—preferably something you did some time ago. (a) What was it? (b) Why haven't you forgiven yourself? (c) Are you helped or hurt by the position you have taken? Why? (If you can't recall something for which you haven't forgiven yourself, recall something for which you have forgiven yourself—preferably something that you very much regretted. Then answer the same three questions, but change the "haven't" in the second question to "have.")

4. (a) What connection do you see between your ability to forgive others and your ability to forgive yourself? (b) What connection do you see between your ability to forgive and your ability to love?

Exploration

A Friendly Inner Voice

A number of psychologists and psychiatrists have written about the importance of self-love. Specifically, they note, those of us who accept ourselves tend to accept others as well; similarly, if we are able to respect and love ourselves, we are better able to love others.

Psychoanalyst Erich Fromm (1963) maintains that our love for ourselves is inseparably connected to our love for others. Both selfish persons and those who seemingly can only love others are really incapable of love. Selfish persons love themselves not too much but, rather, too little; their behavior serves as compensation for their failure to care for themselves. Concerning those who seemingly can only love others, Fromm writes, "If an individual is able to love productively, he loves himself too; if he can *only* love others, he cannot love at all" (p. 50).

Leo Buscaglia, who is probably the leading exponent of love in the United States today, agrees with Fromm. Buscaglia (1972) states, "To love others you must love yourself" (p. 135). Some of us have trouble loving ourselves because we fall short of who we want to be, and we are more accustomed to putting ourselves down than raising ourselves up. Buscaglia insists we love ourselves as we are: "Loving yourself . . . involves the knowledge that only you can be you. If you try to be anyone else, you may come very close, but you will always be second best. But you are the best you. It is the easiest, most practical, most rewarding thing to be" (p. 143).

Some of us are uncomfortable with the idea of loving ourselves; we may think of self-love as conceit or egotism. And the idea may be confusing: exactly what would it mean to love oneself? It may be easier to consider the possibility of being a friend to ourselves. We know how friends treat each other.

George Bach and Laura Torbet (1983) have written that if we listen very carefully within, we can become aware of how we talk to ourselves or think to ourselves or regard ourselves. Listening carefully, we may hear the same inner voice again and again. It may be what Bach and Torbet call an "ally voice"—one friendly and helpful. Or it may be an "enemy voice"—unfriendly and hurtful. Some enemy voices mean well, but they can be hurtful nevertheless. In Box 6.4 are some examples of ally and enemy voices.

Begin your work on this exploration by recalling and listing in the left column on page 208 five events or incidents that have occurred in your life in the past few days or weeks. Try to recall some times when you were successful or doing well and some times when the reverse was true. As you recall an event, recall what you said to yourself at the time *or* listen to what you are saying to yourself now about the event *or* decide what would be in character for you to say about it. If you hear something friendly or helpful or possibly an ally voice, write it down in the middle column. If you hear something unfriendly or hurtful or possibly an enemy voice, write it in the right-hand column. Or if you can't hear anything or even

Box 6.4

Ally and Enemy Voices

"You idiot!" Have you ever heard yourself say that—and at a time when you were the only person around? In their book *The Inner Enemy,* George Bach and Laura Torbet (1983) write that we have self-critical, hurtful, negative "enemy voices" within us that drag us down. We may not be fully aware of these "enemy voices" or of their destructive power unless we listen carefully within ourselves.

Ally Voices

The Optimist: To the Optimist the world is an OK place, life is good, and everything is going to work out all right. The Optimist won't let you get bogged down in gloomy predictions, negative scenarios; it won't let you give up. This voice keeps you thinking positively about your work, your friends and family, and especially yourself. During difficult times the Optimist convinces you that you will prevail and that a good solution will be found.

The Adventurer: When you want to try something new, to make a change, to explore, the Adventurer is right with you. It helps you not get bogged down in unproductive doubts, groundless fears, endless questioning. The Adventurer enjoys trying new food, meeting new people, learning new things. It reassures you of the benefits and rewards of success and the pleasures of trying. It encourages you to go out on a limb, to take the risks—however grand or humble—that will help you get where you want to go.

The Fan: In the eyes of the Fan, you are something special. The Fan is a loyal supporter who sees all the good, strong, positive traits in you and points them out at every opportunity. "You remember so much of what you read." "Your new girlfriend is going to love it when you play the piano for her." "Your will power on this diet is impressive." "It's great that you painted the kitchen." The Fan believes in you and what you can do, and its cheers and compliments can overcome the doubts and criticisms of powerful enemies.

The Good Buddy: This voice is the companion and confidant of your inner life. It understands you and wants the best for you, is sympathetic to your dreams, your feelings, your concerns. It is this voice to whom you confide day-to-day issues and major undertakings; it is your companion when you mull over a problem, try to reach a decision. The Good Buddy will talk back to enemies and critics.

The Comforter: When you are having a hard time, when you have made a mistake or failed at something, the Comforter will soothe your frazzled nerves and reassure you that you're all right. The Comforter rescues you from self-recrimination. The Comforter licks your wounds when you've been hurt. It helps you take care of yourself, go easy on yourself, get over what's troubling you and move on.

Fortunately, there may also be self-supporting, helpful, positive "ally voices" that come to our assistance. Bach and Torbet maintain that by identifying and modifying enemy voices while finding or creating and strengthening ally voices, we can change the course of our lives. Below are some examples of these two kinds of voices. Have you heard some of these voices within yourself?

Enemy Voices

The Pessimist: This is the voice of doom and gloom, a bottomless well of frightening predictions and bad news. It never expects anything good to come of anything or anyone. You will never get out of debt. You son will probably flunk out of school and end up a bum. There will be no snow when you go skiing next weekend. The bus will be late. The new neighbors will turn out to be bores. You won't enjoy the movie. Aside from stealing your rightful pleasures in life, the Pessimist serves the function of giving you an excuse *not* to do, *not* to care, *not* to count on, *not* to want things.

The Scaredy-Cat: This character is afraid of everything. Afraid you'll get sick. Afraid you'll fall down. Doesn't want you to take that long drive. Afraid it'll rain. Afraid to buy a house if there's a chance that real-estate values will fall. Afraid to call a new friend to make a date. Afraid there's going to be a war. It's a sure thing that listening to this voice will raise your anxiety level and keep you sticking close to home.

The Belittler: This is the voice that turns your dreams and accomplishments to ashes. "So you finally got up the nerve to tell Allan that he should share the housework. Big deal. You should have done it a long time ago." "What in the world do you want to study acting for? You'll starve. It'll take years before you get any parts. You're not exactly a natural." "At your age you should be making more money." "You call that a soufflé?" "Why do you waste your time with such a useless hobby?" The Belittler makes it hard to take pride in your abilities and discourages your interests in trying new things.

The Doubter: "You'll never be able to do that." "You're getting in over your head." "That's just too difficult." The Doubter has a very low opinion of your abilities. It's a wonder you can get through the day without making a terrible blunder. It's a wonder you have any friends, that you can keep your job. In the names of caution and reason, this voice will keep you from attempting anything new on the grounds that you just aren't up to it, or that it doesn't want to see you hurt. Listen to this voice enough and you'll stay stuck right where you are, until you're afraid to try anything new—even something exotic on a restaurant menu.

Box 6.4

Ally and Enemy Voices

The Spoiler: This voice is the wet blanket of the group. It can be counted on to show up when you're having a good time—too good a time, it thinks. This voice is a pleasure stealer. When you're on vacation, finally, and are winding down from the pace of your hectic life, it reminds you of things you forgot to do, or itemizes the work waiting for you at home, or it worries that the house will burn down. As you shed your cares at a party with friends, you are suddenly overcome by a feeling of dread, a premonition of some unnameable disaster. When you receive a promotion, the Spoiler pipes up with all sorts of reasons why you don't deserve it. When you win a race, complete a difficult task, enjoy a new friend's company, when things are going just too well, the Spoiler will come along to take the fun out of it.

decide what would be in character for you, write nothing in the middle and right-hand columns.

Here are some examples that may be of assistance. Suppose you failed the written test when you went to renew your driver's license. Maybe an inner unfriendly voice remarked, "How dumb!" or "This is really embarrassing." Or perhaps a friendly inner voice offered some reassurance: "Just need to study harder, that's all" or "Not so bad—almost passed."

Another example: Suppose you played what was for you a super game of tennis. A friendly inner voice might have said, "That's great!" Or an unfriendly voice might have told you, "It must have been a fluke, so don't feel too good about it."

One last example: Suppose you had a fight with someone important to you. A friendly inner voice would understand: "That really hurt, didn't it?" And try to help: "Give it a few days; it will blow over." An unfriendly voice: "You'll never learn to keep your big mouth shut!"

Five Recent Events	Friendly/Helpful/Ally Voice	Unfriendly/Hurtful/Enemy Voice

1. For each event for which you made no friendly/helpful/ally entry, think of such a response now—perhaps something a good friend might have said to you—and write it in the appropriate place in the middle column as practice for the future. <u>Draw a bold line under this friendly/helpful/ally entry to emphasize that this is a voice that will be making itself heard more and more!</u>

2. Start practicing your friendly/helpful/ally voices today. They will soon begin to pipe up without prompting. To complete this exploration and to start your practice, select one of the ally voices in Box 6.4, and in this voice (or with the attitude and in the mood of this voice) write yourself a letter or memo below, telling yourself something that it would be good for you to hear at this time in your life.

Question 7

Ultimate Point

What Is the Meaning of Death to My Life?

In our lives we move through many turning points. Some are small and taken in stride. Others are large and very affecting. And then one day we reach a point whose immensity cannot be disputed: death. Death is the ultimate turning point.

Why Death Is Important to Life

Why is the consideration of death and dying so important as we seek to illuminate our lives? Death is a turning point that casts its influence far in advance of its occurrence. How differently we might lead our lives if we knew we would never die. How differently some of us lead our lives as we pretend we never will.

For ten years (1980–1990), I was a volunteer working with hospice patients and those with life-threatening illness. I have also given workshops on preparation for death. I call these workshops "Dying Readiness/Freedom to Live"—an apt title, I think, because those of us who face our mortality and prepare for it free ourselves to live more fully. In getting our house in order and readying ourselves for death, we ironically open wider the door to life. Following are some reasons that this is so.

1. The full realization that we are mortal makes life precious.

Suppose there was an account into which $1,440 was deposited every day for you to spend. However, at the end of the day, the unspent portion is forfeited because no balance can be carried forward. Furthermore, you are given no idea when the account will be closed. How much of your account would you leave unspent?

We each have an account—a true one, not a fantasy. Each day there is a deposit of 24 hours or 1,440 minutes. At the end of the day, all the wasted minutes are forfeited because no time can be carried forward to the next day. Furthermore, you can never know for sure when the account will be closed. How much of this account do you forfeit, waste, and throw away?

211

The full realization that we are mortal, that we will die one day, and indeed might die at any moment makes life more precious. Persons who have been very near death but recovered frequently report a new appreciation for life and even the smallest joys of life. In a letter written while he was recovering from a heart attack, Abraham Maslow eloquently expressed this idea:

> The confrontation with death—and the reprieve from it—makes everything look so precious, so sacred, so beautiful that I feel more strongly than ever the impulse to love it, to embrace it, and to let myself be overwhelmed by it. My river never looked so beautiful. . . . Death and its ever present possibility makes love, passionate love, more possible. I wonder if we could love passionately, if ecstasy would be possible at all, if we knew we'd never die.

2. The full realization that we are mortal makes life purposeful.

Suppose you knew you were going to live forever. What would you get busy and do right now? There might not be much point in getting a move on if you had until the end of time—which is how long death-denying folks seem to think they have. Elisabeth Kübler-Ross (1975) writes, "It is the denial of death that is partially responsible for people living empty, purposeless lives; for when you live as if you would live forever, it becomes too easy to postpone the things that you must do" (p. 164).

Never-ending life has been given considerable attention by writers of imaginative and science fiction. Merritt Abrash (1985) reviews these writings in an essay entitled "Is There Life After Immortality?" and concludes that immortality "would not be merely undesirable for various social and philosophical reasons, but a curse upon the so-called beneficiaries" (p. 26). Immortality destroys life's pleasure, creativity, and significance and as such, ironically, becomes "a fate worse than death."

Suppose you knew you probably had no more than six months of life to live. What would you get busy and do right now? This supposition is not so far-fetched. Quite a number of us will be seated in a doctor's office one day and learn—if our physician is candid—that we probably have little time to live. The question that opened this paragraph is sometimes asked in workshops dealing with death and dying. Many folks respond by saying that with only six months to live, they would get busy and do some things they were letting slide or planning to do some indefinite day. The knowledge that they had only six months to get things done filled them with purpose, made them shake a leg and get busy.

Kübler-Ross writes that when we awaken each morning, we might do well to tell ourselves that that day may be the last day we have. This understanding or thought could be especially helpful on those days when we have trouble getting a move on. Not forever, not six months, just twenty-four hours. What is it you are going to do today for sure, knowing that this is the only day you have for sure?

3. The full realization that we are mortal gives us a useful perspective.

There is a saying that goes, "I complained that I had no shoes until I met a man who had no feet." Large matters give us some useful perspective on small ones. There is much in life to fuss and fret about until we separate what is petty or trivial from what is important. One sign of maturity is that we have experienced enough of life so that we are able to tell the difference between the two.

Nothing gives us a better perspective on life than death. In the presence of death, unimportant things indeed seem unimportant, and important things are more easily given their due. "When I thought I might be terminally ill, I thought, my God, how much I love my wife and kids," a man told me, "and I realized how screwed up my values were since I spent so little time with them." Further tests were fortunately negative; he's still alive and living his life more lovingly.

Nobody has written more eloquently or usefully about this matter than Carlos Castaneda. In *Journey to Ixtlan* Castaneda (1972) describes a conversation concerning death with his mentor, don Juan, a Yaqui medicine man:

> "Death is our eternal companion," don Juan said with a most serious air. "It is always to our left, at an arm's length. . . . It has always been watching you. It always will until the day it taps you. . . . The thing to do when you're impatient," he proceeded, "is to ask advice from your death. An immense amount of pettiness is dropped if your death makes a gesture to you, or if you catch a glimpse of it, or if you just have the feeling that your companion is there watching you. . . . Death is the only wise adviser that we have. Whenever you feel . . . that everything is going wrong and you're about to be annihilated, turn to death and ask if that is so. Your death will tell you that you're wrong; that nothing matters outside its touch. Your death will tell you, 'I haven't touched you yet.'" (pp. 54–55)

In my own life, I have found don Juan's image of death at arm's length a very powerful one. With death the measure, cataclysms become tremors, whirlwinds whispers, and much pettiness does indeed fall away.

4. The full realization that we are mortal allows us to make the most of the end of our lives.

"To everything there is a season, and a time for every purpose under heaven." These are familiar words from Ecclesiastes, and, indeed, every season of life has its special reasons for being. To have a full life, one would want to live each season fully.

Kübler-Ross titled one of her books *Death: The Final Stage of Growth*. Sometimes when I talk about dying as an important stage of life, someone will say something like "No thanks. I would just as soon skip it. I'm hoping to depart suddenly as the result of a massive heart attack at the age of 85." But every stage of life offers us an opportunity to grow, and none more so than the stage called "dying." When I first began to work with terminally ill patients, I thought that my visits would be filled with talk of dying and death. Instead, I found my patients more occupied with living and life. Some of them seemed to be living life more fully (if more effortfully) than ever before.

I came to see that dying folks who openly confronted their approaching deaths had freed themselves to live and grow. They were free to regard this part of their lives as a completion to be lived rather than a catastrophe to be denied. They were free to get their house in order, to catch up on all the things that need-

---

Box 7.1

Ultimate Point: What Is the Meaning of Death to My Life?

Seedthoughts

1. John Quincy Adams is well but the house in which he lives at the present time is becoming dilapidated. It's tottering on its foundations. Time and the seasons have nearly destroyed it. Its roof is pretty well worn out. Its walls are much shattered and tremble with every wind. I think John Quincy Adams will have to move out of it soon. But he himself is quite well, quite well.

   —*John Quincy Adams, to a friend who inquired about him*

2. A good working formula is: the more unlived life, or unrealized potential, the greater one's death anxiety.

   —*Irvin Yalom*

3. Death destroys a man; the idea of Death saves him.

   —*E. M. Forster*

4. Expect an early death—it will keep you busier.

   —*Martin Fischer*

5. Death is not the greatest of ills; it is worse to want to die and not be able to.

   —*Sophocles*

6. Death is really nothing, for so long as we are, death has not come, and when it has come we are not.

   —*Epicurus*

7. Our preoccupation with immortality has something pathological about it. . . . Many men today are quite content to be just dead when they die.

   —*Lin Yutang*

8. I do not know what I believe about life after death; if it exists, then I burn with interest, if not—well, I'm tired.

   —*Florida Scott-Maxwell, at the age of 82*

9. To fear death, gentlemen, is nothing other than to think oneself wise when one is not; for it is to think one knows what one does not know. No man knows whether death may not even turn out to be the greatest of blessings for a human being, and yet people fear it as if they know for certain that it is the greatest of evils.

   —*Socrates, just before drinking the hemlock poison*

10. To die will be an awfully big adventure.

    —*J. M. Barrie,* Peter Pan

11. To be born twice is no more amazing than to be born once.

    —*author unknown*

12. I feel the flowers growing over me.

    —*John Keats, last words*

---

ed to be done, and to say good-byes. They were free to realize the preciousness of each remaining day.

I remember visiting a man who had cancer throughout his body. When we began to work together, he seemed to be nearing death but managed to hang on and even get a little better. As we sat together, enjoying our cups of hot chocolate, he said to me, "I'm grateful. That may seem strange to hear from a man who has had my troubles the past few years. But my wife and I are closer than we have ever been. I'm still working on my relationship with my sons, but at least I have some time to work on it. I like myself better. I'm a lucky man."

The Dying-Readiness/Freedom-to-Live Test

As indicated earlier, my work has led me to believe that those of us who ready ourselves to die also free ourselves to lead our lives more fully than ever before. Typically, in my workshops on dying readiness, I administer my Dying-Readiness/Freedom-to-Live Test. I give it item by item, discussing each item as I go, so that the participants may have some basis for their answers.

POT-SHOTS NO. 3851   Ashleigh Brilliant

I'm still
not sure
whether
the end of
my life
will be
a landing
or a
taking-off.

©ASHLEIGH BRILLIANT 1985.

The ten items of the test are presented in the material that follows, and each item is briefly delineated. You are invited to take the test now. After you have read each item and its delineation, return to the item and answer it by drawing a circle around "Yes" or "No," as is appropriate in your own case. If your answer isn't clearly "yes" or "no," circle the question mark.

Yes   ?   No   1. I have allowed myself to think deeply about death and my own death and to experience the feelings that this thought engenders.

Edna St. Vincent Millay wrote a beautiful poem about death that has these lines:

Childhood is the kingdom where nobody dies.
Nobody that matters, that is.

Distant relatives die. But mothers and fathers don't die, and any thought of our own death is far away. But the innocence of childhood is soon lost as we grow and develop an increasing acquaintance with death. We come to know that we too will die. How do we deal with that awesome knowledge?

J. Williams Worden, a psychologist who has worked with many dying patients and their families, has concluded that many of the problems we face in life stem from our inability to confront the simple fact that we will one day die. Worden's concept of "personal death awareness," or PDA for short, describes the extent to which we are mindful of our mortality, accepting of it, and living our life in accordance with this mindfulness and acceptance (Worden & Proctor, 1976).

Although it is possible to be overly preoccupied with death, Worden believes that most people's PDA is too low because they tend to shy away from thoughts of their own mortality; they tend to deny that their lives will end. People who *willingly* increase their PDA and face their mortality, Worden has found, seldom want to go back to their former state of low awareness.

Worden believes there are two main reasons we keep our PDA at a low level. The first is that we find it anxiety-provoking to think about our own death. Second, we believe it's useless to think about death because there's nothing we can do about it. "That's where you're wrong," Worden says, and he is right: there's a lot we can do about death. The choices and options open to us will become apparent as we proceed with our test.

Your response to this chapter may be a good indication of the level of your PDA. If as you read along you find you're a bit anxious or if you wish it hadn't been included, your PDA may be on the low side. If you ordinarily avoid talking about death (except to joke) or visiting persons near death or attending funerals, that avoidance may be a further indication of a low PDA.

At this point, go back and answer Item 1 by circling the alternative that best describes your situation. Each of the succeeding items will encourage you to think a little more deeply about your own death and to experience the feelings that thoughts of death engender. If in all honesty, you now have to answer Item 1 "no," perhaps by the end of this test you will be a little closer to answering it "yes."

Yes   ?   No   2. I have made out a will.

Picasso left a huge fortune in art works, real estate, investments, and bank accounts, but he left no will. He predicted that after his death there would be a scramble among his legitimate heirs and illegitimate children and children's children. He said, "It will be worse than anything you can imagine." And it was.

Why don't people make out wills? One important reason is that a will is associated with the idea of our death. As was already indicated, thoughts of our mortality can be anxiety-provoking, and whatever provokes anxiety may be pushed aside or avoided.

Some of us find it comforting to assume a kind of immortality for ourselves— or at least a nonmortality—and this is inconsistent with making out a will. Somerset Maugham once wrote that if one were small, one might hope to be overlooked by death. For some, making out a will is like registering to die, and signing a will is like signing a death certificate or, at least, a promissory note. By not making out a will or not signing it, we feel we haven't put ourselves in jeopardy.

A second reason for not completing a will is that we assume it can be delayed. Because we don't expect to die soon (if at all), why bother now? We can take care of this when we're old and gray.

A third reason is that we assume we are not leaving much of value. (But if you die a "wrongful death," you may be worth a lot more dead than alive—and who gets it?) A fourth reason is the wishful thought that somehow things will work out all right and that those who should inherit will inherit; because making out a will is an expense and bother, why not just hope for the best?

Dying without a will may save you some effort and momentary anxiety, but it creates problems for those you leave behind. If you die without leaving a valid will, you are said to have died "intestate." Here is what David Larsen (1980), an attorney specializing in wills, trusts, and estate planning, has to say about intestacy:

> The main problem with intestacy is, of course, that you have no say where your property goes. Your spouse, your children, your adopted children, your parents—all of them may get more, or less, of your property than you might have expected or wanted. That special heirloom may go to a person whom you'd rather not have it. Your funeral and burial wishes may not be carried out. (Will anyone know what they are?) If you and your spouse both die so that your minor children are orphans, the court-appointed "guardian of the person" and "guardian of the property" may be people you'd rather not have watching after your children and their property. The executor of your estate may be some person you wouldn't want. Your executor and the guardian of your children's property may have to post bond, thereby costing your estate money, meaning that your heirs get less. You could end up paying a lot more in death taxes than you need to: the federal government and the [state] can steamroller your estate because you didn't put up any tax-saving defenses. Finally, dying intestate shows a lack of planning, meaning more than likely that your affairs will be a mess when you die. And who's left to straighten out your mess when you're gone? Your family—and at just the time when they are least able, emotionally, to do it. (p. 12)

It seems a bit curious that folks who care for their loved ones and who also care about their own hard-earned or carefully acquired possessions would leave both in limbo upon death. Making out a will shows that you care. It also shows that you weren't afraid to face your own demise. It's an important step in getting your house in order. Before proceeding further, answer Item 2 by circling one of its three alternatives.

Yes   ?   No   3. I have made known my choice between having and not having my life extended through artificial or heroic measures in the event that there is no reasonable expectation of my recovery from physical or mental disability. (Or I have made out a living will or executed a durable power of attorney.)

Medical science is my shepherd:
  I shall not want.
It leadeth me beside the marvels of
  technology.
It restoreth my brainwaves;
It maintaineth me in a persistent vegetative
  state for its name sake.
Yea, though I walk through the valley of
  the shadow of death,
I shall find no end to life;
For thou art with me;
Thy respirator and heart machine,
  they sustain me.
Thou preparest intravenous feeding for me
In the presence of irreversible disability;

Thou anointest my head with oil;

My cup runneth on and on and on and on
and on.

Surely coma and unconsciousness shall
follow me all the days of my continued
breathing;

And I will dwell in the intensive-care unit
forever.

—Reverend Robert Fraser

The case against maintaining life at all costs is vividly made in the Reverend Robert Fraser's adaptation of the 23rd Psalm that appears above. Advances in medicine often make it possible to delay death in terminally ill patients and to keep nonterminal but irreversibly comatose patients indefinitely alive. Sometimes the days that technology adds are of little use or quality, and the additional time is purchased at considerable cost and discomfort.

Competent adults have the right to refuse life-sustaining treatment, but what happens if one becomes incompetent to make her or his wishes known? In this litigious age, physicians run into few problems if they continue to treat a patient, but there can be considerable danger in stopping treatment. In the absence of specific instructions, it is unlikely that life-support systems would be withdrawn.

By planning ahead, we can have a say about artificial or heroic measures that might be used to prolong our own lives. Various advance directives can be employed for this purpose, but the two most important are the living will and the durable power of attorney for health care. Living wills are now recognized by statute in more than half the states, although provisions vary considerably. All states and the District of Columbia have statutes recognizing durable powers of attorney, and in most states such powers can be worded to create a document covering (and limited to) health care. (Unlike an ordinary power of attorney, which terminates if the principal becomes incapacitated, a *durable* power of attorney continues despite the principal's condition.)

A *living will* (not to be confused with a living trust) is a written, signed, witnessed, and possibly notarized declaration that specifies your wishes concerning the use of life-sustaining procedures in your own case if you become terminally ill and incompetent. A *durable power of attorney for health care* is a written, signed, witnessed, and possibly notarized document in which you (the principal) give another (the agent) the legal authority to make health-care decisions on your behalf if you become terminally ill and incompetent. Because some living wills also provide for a health proxy, who, in effect, can serve as an agent, and some durable powers of attorney also specify your health-care wishes, there can be a great deal of overlap in these two approaches. State laws vary, so it is important that a local attorney or some other knowledgeable authority be consulted for assistance as you weigh your options and devise your own plan.

Answer Item 3 before reading further.

Yes	?	No	4. I have planned my own funeral or planned to dispense with a funeral and made these plans known.
Yes	?	No	5. I have chosen and made known a plan for the disposal of my body after death.

Although we don't plan our entrance into this world, we have an opportunity to plan our departure. In our plans, we will want to consider our own wishes and also the needs of our survivors and what would be helpful and convenient for them. Careful planning can avoid a situation like this one described by Robert Kavanaugh (1974):

> Not long ago I attended a funeral of incredible ugliness. The minister kept referring to the deceased by the wrong name, totally unaware of frantic cues from the pews, mistaking our winces and near groans for tears of muffled grief. The eulogy by this insensitive last-minute hireling had obviously been canned for any occasion. His suavity hinted he could be speaking to any luncheon club anywhere, except for his rude and impertinent insistence on forcing his religious assumptions on the semireligious friends of a dead nonbeliever.
>
> I wondered then and still wonder what purpose such a funeral was thought to serve. Who needed it? Nearly everyone departed in humiliation and anger, pitying the family too distraught to accept our sympathies. I wondered about that man of God who could be paid to talk so glibly about death without touching a single unifying spark in his saddened congregation beyond anger for himself. I wondered why the family needed this hollow and decrepit ritual and why anyone allowed them to put themselves through such a travesty after six months of watching their daughter die. (pp. 187–188)

Here, in sharp contrast, is a recollection of a member of the Older Women's League:

> I'd like to tell you about a memorial service I once attended at a senior center. I didn't know the woman who had died. I was visiting a friend in another city and she invited me to go to the senior center for a memorial service for one of the active members. There was nothing solemn about the occasion—the feeling of the group was warm and friendly. The group leader started by telling about the deceased—some of her special contributions and a couple of amusing anecdotes illustrating her lively character. Another person told a similar story, and soon the conversation was moving along, bringing laughter and an occasional tear. Family members talked of what she had meant to them. One person sang a song, another read a brief poem. A display of pictures and a few clippings were on the wall. The service lasted about 45 minutes, followed by much hugging and then refreshments.
>
> I felt privileged to have heard this re-creation of a remarkable woman's life, told by those who had shared it. The loss was evident, but the group was healing itself and would carry on, with their deceased friend living in their hearts and memories.

What will your funeral or memorial service be like? Or do you want a service at all? Are you leaving this all up to others? In making our own final plans, we help ourselves in that (1) we can contemplate making a departure appropriate to our own wishes and the wishes of our survivors, (2) we can pre-experience this departure just as we pre-experience a well-planned trip, and (3) we can gain a sense that we have done what needs to be done and therefore are free to go on to the business of living.

In our final planning we also help those we leave behind. First of all, our survivors will not be forced to make decisions at the very time when they might be least able to make them; they won't have to guess at what we would have wanted, and they won't have to argue among themselves. Second, we may ameliorate a common tendency of bereaved persons to overspend on funeral arrangements.

Simplicity is what London schoolmaster Ken James sought in his final arrangements. When he died of cancer, he left an estate of $40,800 but no funds for a funeral. In his will, he wrote, "I specifically forbid a conventional funeral. There must be no ceremony of any kind, religious or otherwise, no floral tributes or mourners or any fuss whatsoever. My ashes are not to be buried or sentimentally scattered, but are to be inconspicuously deposited in any convenient dustbin for refuse collection in the usual way." (That proved to be a bit much for the officials; they had James's ashes buried under a bed of flowers at the crematorium.)

For those of us who wish simplicity and economy in our final disposition (but perhaps not quite so simple and economical as Ken James's), joining a memorial society is a good option. These societies are cooperative, democratically run, nonprofit organizations that contract with funeral directors on behalf of their members. By practicing simplicity and by bargaining collectively, the members of the society save 50 to 75 percent of usual funeral costs. These memorial societies have low fees to join (rarely over $25), sell no services of their own, and should not be confused with private companies that call themselves societies. For a directory of cooperative societies, contact their national organizations: Continental Association of Funeral and Memorial Societies, 6900 Lost Lake Road, Egg Harbor, WI 54209, or the Memorial Society of Canada, Box 96, Station A, Weston, Ontario M9N 3M6.

Benevolence is what poet Robert Test seeks in his final disposition. As a last act, he wants to give himself away:

> The day will come when my body will lie upon a white sheet neatly tucked under four corners of a mattress located in a hospital busily occupied with the living and the dying. At a certain moment a doctor will determine that my brain has ceased to function and that, for all intents and purposes, my life has stopped.
>
> When that happens, do not attempt to instill artificial life into my body by the use of a machine. And don't call this my deathbed. Let it be called the Bed of Life, and let my body be taken from it to help others lead fuller lives.
>
> Give my sight to the man who has never seen a sunrise, a baby's face or love in the eyes of a woman. Give my heart to a person whose own heart has caused nothing but endless days of pain. Give my blood to the teenager who was pulled from the wreckage of his car, so that he might live to see his grandchildren play. Give my kidneys to someone who depends upon a machine to exist from week to week. Take my bones, every muscle, every fiber and nerve in my body and find a way to make a crippled child walk.
>
> Explore every corner of my brain. Take my cells, if necessary, and let them grow so that, someday, a speechless boy will shout at the crack of a bat and a deaf girl will hear the sound of rain against her window.
>
> Burn what is left of me and scatter the ashes to the winds to help the flowers grow.
>
> If you must bury something, let it be my faults, my weaknesses and all prejudice against my fellow man.
>
> Give my sins to the devil. Give my soul to God.
>
> If, by chance, you wish to remember me, do it with a kind deed or a word to someone who needs you.
>
> If you do all I have asked, I will live forever.

Those of us who, like Test, would like to give ourselves away can do so by completing a Uniform Donor Card, which is a binding legal document in every state through laws based on the Uniform Anatomical Gift Act. This card permits us upon death to make one or more of our body organs available for transplantation or research. For a card or further information, call the nearest organ and tissue bank (look in the phone book yellow pages under "Organ & Tissue Banks"). Some states offer you the opportunity to complete a card when you are applying for or renewing your driver's license. If you wish to donate your body for medical education, call a school of medicine.

Before proceeding, return to questions 4 and 5, and answer them.

Yes   ?   No   6. I have made out a survivor's guide.

Dear Ann:

I am perplexed by a problem that I have run across three times in the past few years—secretive husbands.

In one case, an older cousin's husband died and the woman had no idea of the state of their finances. He always provided her with plenty of household and pocket money, but became apoplectic when asked about financial matters, even after he became terminally ill. When he died, his widow was unable to find any assets.

In the second case, a successful physician is unwilling to share information about the family finances. His wife (my sister) has no inkling of their financial status. He has a highly successful practice, is chief of staff of the community hospital and a pillar of the medical community, but totally secretive about financial matters. They have recently reconciled after nearly breaking up over this situation. My sister is a successful professional person in her own right and has had to run the household with her own funds, not paying much attention until recently when it became a bone of contention.

The third example is a sister-in-law. Her husband died suddenly last December. She was unable to find any resources except a small stock account and an apartment in London, which was in both names. He never spoke of business matters, even though they appeared to have a solid marriage.

What do you have to say about such peculiar behavior? How can a woman protect herself against a man who is secretive?

Perplexed In The West

Dear Perp:

It is hard to imagine a woman being so ignorant and passive about family finances in this day and age, especially since so many females are knowledgeable and involved in business.

Any wife who reads this and does not know what she can count on if her husband dies before her (and most of them will) should open the subject before another day goes by. If her husband refuses to talk about it, she should tell him he owes her that consideration and if he persists in being uncooperative, she will be forced to see a lawyer. She should not hesitate to make good her threat.

The same goes for men whose wives control the purse strings. They, too, have a right to know what goes on. A marriage in which such information is withheld indicates a serious lack of trust and mutual respect.

Ann Landers

There is often much that needs to be done when a person dies, and the people who need to do it may be in shock or upset and scarcely able to manage. Sometimes it may even be impossible to complete everything that needs doing because vital information is incomplete or unavailable. And yet much of this work could have been easily done long before death by the subject person herself or himself.

The problem noted in the letter written by "Perplexed in the West" is only one of many that a person can avoid by filling out a survivor's guide (sometimes called a family guide). This guide is simply a listing of the data that a survivor will need in order to handle funeral, obituary, legal, financial, and tax matters upon and after your death. You are the best person to gather your own data. You can do in a relatively short period of time what your survivors may be able to do only with difficulty or perhaps not at all.

Survivor's guides take various forms. A typical guide contains information relative to your death certificate and obituary, desired funeral arrangements, will, safety deposit box, insurance, Social Security benefits, pensions, annuities, checking accounts, property, and other financial assets and liabilities.

Some funeral homes or mortuaries will provide you with a complimentary survivor's or family guide. To receive a copy of a guide by mail, send $2.00 to the Continental Association of Funeral and Memorial Societies, Inc., 6900 Lost Lake Road, Egg Harbor, WI 54209. Answer Item 6 before continuing on to the next item.

Yes   ?   No   7. I have made my relationships with "significant others" current by "clearing the past."

We want, of course, to be treated fairly. We want our world to be just. We want what is due to us. We want to get as good as we give. We want others to treat us as nicely as we treat them, and to pay us back for all we've done for them.

Alas, our world is not always just, and the people in it who are most important to us—our "significant others"—are not always fair. When we are treated unfairly, unjustly, we may build up a good deal of anger and resentment. The raw deals, the things that others did to us and shouldn't have, the things they didn't do but should have—these may fester in our minds and memories.

It is important to distinguish between two kinds of wrongs. There are the wrongs to work on and the wrongs to let go of. It takes some wisdom to know the difference.

Some of us become resentment collectors. We are unable to forgive the wrongs done to us. This kind of collecting accomplishes nothing and can become self-destructive. Our resentment consumes energy and keeps us stuck in the past. Like other persistent negative emotions, resentment can have corresponding physiological reactions with adverse effects.

Why do we sometimes choose the heavy burden of resentment rather than the liberation that comes with forgiving? What do we get out of it?

Some persons don't forgive because they confuse forgiveness with condonation. They think that to forgive is to condone or overlook or even give approval to a wrong. By being unforgiving, they continue to bear witness to the wrong. They keep the offender on the hook (and perhaps themselves as well). But to forgive does not require one to overlook or approve a wrong. Forgiveness notes that there is something to be forgiven and also something to be gained by letting go and moving along.

Some persons don't forgive because no retribution has been made. There appears to have been no punishment, no repayment. To pardon the offender might set a bad example. Or would it present a good model? In any case, what may be more important is the effect of forgiveness on the forgiver and on the relationship of the forgiver to the one forgiven.

If we forgive others, we find it easier to forgive ourselves for what we may have done in the past, whether wittingly or unwittingly. If others don't have to be perfect, we don't have to be perfect either. If others can be forgiven, we can forgive ourselves.

The solution to the burden of resentment is forgiveness. When we forgive, we "clear the past" and write off all outstanding emotional debts. We let go of our resentment and let go of the past. In doing so, we free ourselves to come fully into the present and to make the most of it.

In his wise and helpful book *Forgive and Forget*, Lewis Smedes (1986) presents a fable, "The Magic Eyes." Such eyes allows one to see things in a new light, so that hurts flowing from the wounds of yesterday may heal. This fable is presented in Box 7.2.

Smedes asks, "What do you do when you forgive someone who hurts you? What goes on? When is it necessary? What happens afterward? What should you expect it to do for you? *What is forgiving*?" Here are his answers:

> The act of forgiving, by itself, is a wonderfully simple act; but it always happens inside a storm of complex emotions. It is the hardest trick in the whole bag of personal relationships.
>
> So let us be honest with each other. Let us talk plainly about the "magic eyes" that are given to those who are ready to be set free from the prison of pain they never deserved.
>
> We forgive in four stages. If we can travel through all four, we achieve the climax of reconciliation.
>
> The first stage is *hurt*: when somebody causes you pain so deep and unfair that you cannot forget it, you are pushed into the first stage of the crisis of forgiving.
>
> The second stage is *hate*: you cannot shake the memory of how much you hurt, and you cannot wish your enemy well. You sometimes want the person who hurt you to suffer as you are suffering.
>
> The third stage is *healing*: you are given the "magic eyes" to see the person who hurt you in a new light. Your memory is healed, you turn back the flow of pain and are free again.
>
> The fourth stage is *the coming together*: you invite the person who hurt you back into your life; if he or she comes honestly, love can move you both toward a new and healed relationship. The fourth stage depends on the person you forgive as much as it depends on you; sometimes he doesn't come back and you have to be healed alone. (p. 18)

I would make two amendments to what Smedes has written. First, I don't think it is necessary to forget wrongs. In fact, not forgetting the hurt of a wrong done to us may keep us from inflicting similar hurt onto others. But it is necessary for us to remember the wrong differently—perhaps with sadness rather than anger or with a generosity that is above revenge and resentment. Second, with "magic eyes," we may see the person who hurt us in a new light, but these eyes may also help us to see ourselves differently. We may respect ourselves more as generous, forgiving persons than as vengeful, resentful ones, and also find ourselves easier to live with.

When we have done all the necessary emotional work and "cleared the past," our house is in better order. We are ready to die—and we are free to live our lives without the burden of resentment. Answer Item 7 before continuing on.

Box 7.2

The Magic Eyes
A Little Fable

by Lewis B. Smedes

In the village of Faken in innermost Friesland there lived a long thin baker named Fouke, a righteous man, with a long thin chin and a long thin nose. Fouke was so upright that he seemed to spray righteousness from his thin lips over everyone who came near him; so the people of Faken preferred to stay away.

Fouke's wife, Hilda, was short and round, her arms were round, her bosom was round, her rump was round. Hilda did not keep people at bay with righteousness; her soft roundness seemed to invite them instead to come close to her in order to share the warm cheer of her open heart.

Hilda respected her righteous husband, and loved him too, as much as he allowed her; but her heart ached for something more from him than his worthy righteousness.

And there, in the bed of her need, lay the seed of sadness.

One morning, having worked since dawn to knead his dough for the ovens, Fouke came home and found a stranger in his bedroom lying on Hilda's round bosom.

Hilda's adultery soon became the talk of the tavern and the scandal of the Faken congregation. Everyone assumed that Fouke would cast Hilda out of his house, so righteous was he. But he surprised everyone by keeping Hilda as his wife, saying he forgave her as the Good Book said he should.

In his heart of hearts, however, Fouke could not forgive Hilda for bringing shame to his name. Whenever he thought about her, his feelings toward her were angry and hard; he despised her as if she were a common whore. When it came right down to it, he hated her for betraying him after he had been so good and so faithful a husband to her.

He only pretended to forgive Hilda so that he could punish her with his righteous mercy.

But Fouke's fakery did not sit well in heaven.

So each time that Fouke would feel his secret hate toward Hilda, an angel came to him and dropped a small pebble, hardly the size of a shirt button, into Fouke's heart. Each time a pebble dropped, Fouke would feel a stab of pain like the pain he felt the moment he came on Hilda feeding her hungry heart from a stranger's larder.

Thus he hated her the more; his hate brought him pain and his pain made him hate.

The pebbles multiplied. And Fouke's heart grew very heavy with the weight of them, so heavy that the top half of his body bent forward so far that he had to strain his neck upward in order to see straight ahead. Weary with hurt, Fouke began to wish he were dead.

The angel who dropped the pebbles into his heart came to Fouke one night and told him how he could be healed of his hurt.

There was one remedy, he said, only one, for the hurt of a wounded heart. Fouke would need the miracle of the magic eyes. He would need eyes that could look back to the beginning of his hurt and see his Hilda, not as a wife who betrayed him, but as a weak woman who needed him. Only a new way of looking at things through the magic eyes could heal the hurt flowing from the wounds of yesterday.

Fouke protested, "Nothing can change the past," he said. "Hilda is guilty, a fact that not even an angel can change."

"Yes, poor hurting man, you are right," the angel said. "You cannot change the past, you can only heal the hurt that comes to you from the past. And you can heal it only with the vision of the magic eyes."

"And how can I get your magic eyes?" pouted Fouke.

"Only ask, desiring as you ask, and they will be given you. And each time you see Hilda through your new eyes, one pebble will be lifted from your aching heart."

Fouke could not ask at once, for he had grown to love his hatred. But the pain of his heart finally drove him to want and to ask for the magic eyes that the angel had promised. So he asked. And the angel gave.

Soon Hilda began to change in front of Fouke's eyes, wonderfully and mysteriously. He began to see her as a needy woman who loved him instead of a wicked woman who betrayed him.

The angel kept his promise; he lifted the pebbles from Fouke's heart, one by one, though it took a long time to take them all away. Fouke gradually felt his heart grow lighter; he began to walk straight again, and somehow his nose and chin seemed less thin and sharp than before. He invited Hilda to come into his heart again, and she came, and together they began again a journey into their second season of humble joy.

(From Smedes, 1986, pp. 13–15)

WHAT'S THE GOOD OF BEING FORGIVEN, IF I HAVE TO PROMISE NOT TO DO IT AGAIN?

Yes   ?   No   8. I keep my relationships with "significant others" current by manifesting my love.

Immediately following are instructions for an exercise you can administer to yourself.[1] Pause after reading each paragraph, and imagine or simply think about yourself as being in that situation. Answer the questions to yourself. Then go to the next paragraph and continue in the same way until you have completed the exercise.

You are seated in a doctor's office. You are waiting for the doctor to come in with the results of your medical examination. It has been rather a long wait. Take a little time to imagine how the office looks or just think about how it looks. How does it smell? What thoughts are going through your mind? What do you feel? (Pause)

The doctor comes in and sits down. There are a number of laboratory reports and some X rays. You wait for the doctor to speak up. Why doesn't the doctor speak up? Finally, the doctor starts to go over the medical findings with you. You begin to realize that the findings are serious, very serious. You must check into the hospital immediately for more tests. What is going through your mind now? What are you feeling? To whom do you want to talk? Or be with? What would you say to them? (Pause)

Some months have gone by. You are at home and in bed. You are aware that you have only a short time to live. Your body is wasted and weak, but your mind is lucid and you can communicate with others. What are you thinking? What are you feeling? With whom do you want to be? What do you want to say to them? (Pause)

You are back in the hospital. There is only a little time left. People have come to see you and be with you, but the nurse has suggested only one or two approach you at a time. Whom do you want to see the most? Imagine or think of them standing there by your bed. What is being said? (Pause)

And now you have died. Your body remains on the hospital bed. Although the medical staff has left, some people have stayed to be with you a little longer. Who are they? If you could speak to them now, what would you say? (Pause)

[1]This visualization is adapted from Perlin, 1982.

In one of his newspaper columns, Charles McCabe (1975) wrote movingly about a dear friend who had died the previous week. McCabe deeply regretted that he had never been able to tell this friend how much he loved him. McCabe added, "I do not know how common this affliction is, this inability to express love. I know that it has been with me nearly all my life, and has caused me many moments of regret."

Many of us are like McCabe. After completing the preceding exercise, many persons report that somewhere in the process they expressed their love and appreciation to a number of significant others—something they had not done recently, very much, or at all. They did not want to die without manifesting their love. But why—if the declaration of love is so important—were they living without manifesting it?

Marshall Hodge (1967) points out in his book *Your Fear of Love* that we fear emotional closeness because it involves vulnerability. Hodge writes, "When we open ourselves and permit another person to know that we love him, we risk being hurt. And because we know how it feels to be hurt, this risk is frightening" (p. 7).

Some of us have trouble in expressing our love because we have grown up in cold or undemonstrative families and have never learned how. Some consider love a kind of reward to be administered only when someone performs up to standards. Some are wary of love because it can interfere with independence.

Hodge writes that although love seems to ebb and flow like the ocean, it is not caring itself but rather the *experience* of love and the *expression* that are intermittent. Moments of love are followed by periods of withdrawal. To keep our relationships with others as current as possible, we need to keep tabs on our "accounts payable (love division)" and not let them get too far overdue.

It will be helpful to run a check on yourself now. In the space below, make a list of all the people in your life whom you love (names, initials, or symbols will do). Then cross out the name of everyone to whom you haven't manifested your love in the past half year. (My dictionary says that *to manifest* means to make clearly apparent to sight or understanding; obvious. So just knowing they know that you love them doesn't qualify.)

These are the persons whom I love:

Now, based on the preceding exercise and everything else you know about yourself, answer Item 8. Then continue with remaining two items.

Yes   ?   No   9. I have learned to die my "little deaths" in preparation for my "big death."

Plato, on his death bed, gave this advice to a visiting friend: "Practice dying." Life gives us plenty of opportunity for this practice because life is filled with a number of little deaths. These are the times when we lose not life but something very important to it. Perhaps someone dear to us dies or we are permanently disabled or we lose a relationship or position of many years or we suffer a great financial reversal or we come to the realization that something we have dreamed of and hoped for will never come to pass.

In Chapter 4, we noted Keleman's conception of life as a migration through many little dyings. In each dying, something old is lost, and something new is born. "Growth, change and maturing occur by deforming the old and forming the new. In these little dyings we can learn how to live our big dying" (Keleman, 1974, p. 26).

Keleman believes that big dying—death itself—is similar to little dying. If we want to know how we will face big death, we can review our little deaths, those events in our lives involving major loss or other misfortune. If we find we haven't "died" well or learned from our little dyings, we can change the way we live our dying and better prepare ourselves for big death.

How can we manage our little dyings better? An answer lies in the research and writing on mourning, which, according to psychiatrist George Engel, is like healing. If we do our "grief work" properly, we are healed and become healthy. Psychiatrist Will Menninger spoke of troubled people who healed so well that they became "weller than well." In effectively managing our little deaths, we can become sturdier than sturdy—more and more able to face and manage big death or the prospect of it.

William Worden (1982) has identified four tasks involved in mourning or in the adaptation to loss. The first task is to accept the reality of the loss. One of the primary responses to loss is denial. We refuse to believe that what has happened has happened. Or we deny that it is irreversible. Or we minimize the full meaning of the loss. Our first task requires us to face the facts and realize what has happened, to know it can't be undone, and to acknowledge its full importance to us.

The second task is to experience the pain of the grief. In grieving we may feel shock, anger, sadness, guilt, anxiety, loneliness, helplessness, depression, or a combination or alternation of these states. Instead of acknowledging our grief, we may try to deny it, shut it off, and busy ourselves with other matters. Friends and relatives may support our tactics, encouraging us to keep a stiff upper lip and look on the bright side. Various authorities on mourning believe that bereaved persons have to go through the pain of grief. If we avoid this pain, the course of mourning is prolonged. Some bereaved persons constrict their lives in an effort to prevent painful memories from arising.

The third task of mourning or adaptation to loss is to adjust to the new reality. We need to pick ourselves up and make a go of it with whatever we have left. This may be enormously difficult—to face life without whoever or whatever it was that made life worth living. But what choices do we have? Judith Viorst (1987) minces no words as she spells out our alternatives when a loved one dies: "To die when they die. To live crippled. Or to forge, out of pain and memory, new adaptations" (p. 295). Picking ourselves up may mean setting new goals, learning new skills, or playing new roles. Very often it means compromise. But there is also an opportunity for growth and development that otherwise might not have occurred.

A fourth task is to detach the energy we have invested in an emotional attachment and reinvest it in new relationships or enterprises. It is not easy to let go of old attachments. We do not want to appear disloyal, or we may feel that nothing can replace what we have lost. And we may fear that what was lost once and with so much pain might be lost again.

What little deaths have you suffered? And how have you managed them? What have you learned? Have you learned to accept the reality of your losses? Can you allow yourself to feel the pain of your griefs? Are you able to accommodate your deprivation? Have you invested your emotional energy anew? Consider your responses to these questions and answer Item 9 before you continue.

Yes   ?   No   10. I make it a point to appreciate and deeply enjoy the little joys of life.

There is a national organization for persons with life-threatening illness and their families called "Make Today Count." It encourages these persons to live each day as fully as possible—to make today count, since one cannot count on tomorrow.

None of us—whether seriously ill or seemingly hale—can count on endless tomorrows. Our lives could end at any moment. Are we fully living our lives? Or are we saving our lives to be lived at a later date?

If we don't think of ourselves as mortal, if it's inconceivable to us that we will ever die, then we have forever. What's one day if we have forever? We can throw it away. What's a little joy if we have forever? We can keep pursuing big joys, whatever they may be.

As we learned earlier in this book, one notion of life is that it is a staircase. We climb up step by step, and when we get to the top, we can be happy. If we are not happy at the top, maybe it isn't the top—maybe it's just a landing—so we need to resume climbing until we get to some place where happiness is.

Hermann Hesse wrote of the "little joys" available to us as we make our daily rounds. These are small things to which we may pay little notice but which can give us some moments of delight if we give them their due: a flower, a stretch of sky, a piece of fruit, children's laughter. His advice was that we seek out each day as many as possible of these small joys. "It is the small joys first of all that are granted us for recreation, for daily relief and disburdenment, not the great ones" ([1905] 1988, p. 271).

Happiness, according to painter-photographer Jacques Henri Lartigue, is not an elusive bird that requires work to catch. Instead, happiness is an element like air, which is everywhere. If "you don't run after it too hard and too long, you'll find it right there, within reach, all the time . . . waiting for you to take it."

When we are ready to die, we are not so focused on large and distant pleasures. We do not primarily pursue the two elusive birds in the distant bush; we attend the one within reach or earshot. We take time to delight in the little joys that present themselves here and now.

Take a moment to recall the little joys you have delighted in today. How about yesterday? What about the day before? Do the memories of little joys come easily to mind or are you drawing a blank? What about your life as a whole? Are you waiting for some Big Joy to make it all worthwhile? Think about this, and answer Item 10 before you go on. (It would be hard to overemphasize the importance of little joys, so there is more about them later in this book; turn to Chapter 10, Exploration 10A, if you want to peek ahead.)

Take a few moments to review your response to all ten items of the test. In your own estimation (there is no exact passing score), do your responses indicate you are ready to die? If so, congratulations: your house is in order and you are free to live. If your answers indicate you have more work to do, get busy and do it—not for death's sake but for life's sake.

Kenneth Woodward wrote that "there is no such thing as a good death except for those who have achieved a good life." And to M. V. Kamath the art of living and the art of dying are not different; neither can they be separated, for one flows into the other: "He who has mastered the art of living has already mastered the art of dying; to such, death holds no terrors."

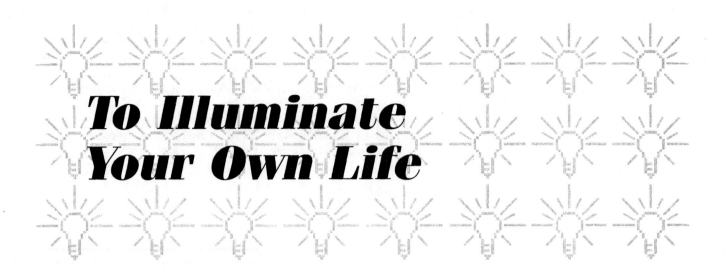

To Illuminate Your Own Life

Anchor and Apply*

1. Is your personal death awareness (PDA) at an optimal level? How does your personal awareness of death affect the way you live your life?

2. Have you made out a will? Why or why not? To whom would you want to leave personal items or property with sentimental value or special meaning? Why did you select these people? Have you ensured that they will receive the items you want them to receive? If damages might be paid your estate because of your "wrongful death" (for example, through accident), whom would you like to inherit this money? Why them? Have you ensured that they will inherit it?

3. Are there any conditions under which you would consider measures to prolong or shorten your life if you were terminally ill or irreversibly comatose? What have you done to ensure that your wishes in this regard are respected?

4. What plans for funeral or memorial services or for the disposal of your body after death do you prefer? Why? What have you done to ensure that your wishes in this regard are respected?

5. Have you made your relationship with "significant others" current by "clearing the past"? If so, give your proof. If not, why not?

6. Do you keep your relationships with "significant others" current by manifesting your love? If so, give your proof. If not, why not?

7. How have you dealt with a little death—that is, some great loss or misfortune in your life? What did you learn from this experience?

8. Do you make it a point to appreciate and deeply enjoy the little joys of life? If so, give your proof. If not, why not?

---

* These "anchor and apply" items are designed to help you use the concepts of the chapter as stimuli to prompt new or deeper or clearer insights into yourself and your life. To respond to an item, first find the material in the chapter that is most relevant to the item *and* yourself; that's called "anchoring." Second, think about this material in relationship to yourself and your life and keep thinking about it until you arrive at a new or deeper or clearer understanding; that's the "apply" or application part. When you write or present your response to the item, be sure to include both parts, that is, both the anchor material and the application. You can know you are successful on an item if, in completing it, you truly learn something new or understand something better.

My Own Death

What is your conception of your own death? What—if anything—do you believe awaits you after you die? In the space below, write a brief essay (one to three paragraphs) describing your conception on your own death. If you prefer, instead of an essay you may write a poem, make a collage, or draw or paint something that represents your conception of your own death. (Afterward, there are three items for you to complete at the end of this exploration.)

Be careful to note that your work on this exploration is not to concern your dying—only what follows when you are dead.

What awaits us when we die? Is there *new* life? A life after life. Is there *no* life?
Nothingness. Many conceptions of death appear to fall within the following categories: death as new life or transition, death as no life or extinction or completion, and death as mystery.

Death as New Life or Transition

The majority of Americans believe death is a transition to a new and different kind
of existence, although some believe they will be reborn to another life in this
world. Approximately three of every four Americans believe there is life after
death (Gilbert, 1988; Greeley, 1989), and about one in four believes in reincarnation (Woodward, 1989). A 1989 national survey of adults showed that 77 percent of the respondents believe there is a heaven, and 76 percent think that they
have good to excellent chance of getting there. By contrast, only 58 percent
believe there is a hell, and only 6 percent rate their chances for admission as
(unfortunately) good or excellent. Concerning what it might be like in heaven,
91 percent think it will be peaceful, 83 percent expect to be with God, and 77 percent expect reunion with people they have known (Woodward, 1989).

It has been argued that a belief in heaven can prevent a person from demanding more or making the most of life on earth. Hence these lines in an early labor
movement song: "Work and pray, live on hay,/ You'll get pie in the sky when you
die." Social scientist-priest-novelist Andrew Greeley rejects the notion that the
promise of heaven interferes with fulfillment in this life. His survey data indicate,
he says, that "those who believe in life after death lead happier lives and trust
people more. The people who believe in [heaven] are just as committed to this
world as those who don't. Belief in personal survival is not the coward's way out"
(quoted in Woodward, 1989, p. 53).

Death as No Life or Extinction or Completion

A considerably smaller number of Americans think of death as the absolute end.
For some it may be a welcomed end, for some a feared end, and for others a necessary end. I remember watching a televised interview with an eloquent man
(whose name I unfortunately did not catch) who said he thought death was the
end and hoped it would be the end because to him eternal life would be unbear-
ably tedious.

Philosopher Bertrand Russell conceived of his own death as no-nonsense extinction. He wrote, "When I die, I shall rot and nothing of my ego will survive." Mary Stoneman Douglas agreed that death is final, but she saw it more softly—as completion rather than extinction. In her autobiography, this remarkable woman, who led a sixty-year fight to save the Everglades, wrote, "I think that death is the end. I believe that life should be lived so vividly and intensely that thoughts of another life or a longer life are not necessary."

Death as Mystery

For some, death is shrouded in mystery, and they believe there is no way to know or guess what lies beyond the grave. At the age of 82 and in poor health, Florida Scott-Maxwell (1968) wrote, "I do not know what I believe about life after death; if it exists, then I burn with interest, if not—well, I'm tired" (p. 75). (I like that as a kind of win-win philosophy—you win whatever happens.)

Socrates was another who looked upon death as mystery. Just before drinking hemlock poison and thus ending his own life, he said, "To fear death, gentlemen, is nothing other than to think oneself wise when one is not; for it is to think one knows what one does not know. No one knows whether death may not even turn out to be the greatest blessing for a human being, and yet people fear it as if they know for certain that it is the greatest of evils."

As this discussion shows, death can have a number of meanings, and its meaning for any one of us relates to and varies with our life circumstances. Thanatologist Richard Kalish (1985) wrote, "Developing a coherent concept of what death means can be very useful but it is often not possible. We are entitled to be inconsistent about what death means to us at any given time, since it is so immense and so complex that its meanings are often in flux—changing at the very moments that we try to grasp them" (p. 57).

To complete this exploration, answer the three questions below.

1. How does your conception of your own death sit with you; that is, is it comforting, upsetting, or what? Discuss this aspect of your concept.

2. How firm, unchanging, coherent, and consistent is and has been your conception of death? Discuss this aspect of your concept.

3. How does your conception of death influence the way you live your life? Discuss this aspect of your concept.

E x p l o r a t i o n

7B

The Epitaph

An epitaph is an inscription on a tomb or monument commemorating a person. Or it can be a brief poem or writing in praise of someone deceased. Some persons have written their own epitaphs; for example, publisher Malcolm Forbes chose these words for his tombstone: "While alive, he lived." Economist-educator-author John Kenneth Galbraith said he "yearned" to have these words as his epitaph: "He Comforted the Afflicted and Afflicted the Comfortable." Ann Richards (who, as I write this, is governor of the state of Texas) recalled that in her former doldrums as a housewife she came to realize what she *didn't* want for an epitaph: "I didn't want to have on my tombstone 'Boy, did she keep a clean house!'" On the monument below, write your name and your epitaph—that is, what you would like to be remembered for. And add anything else you wish. Then turn to the next page.

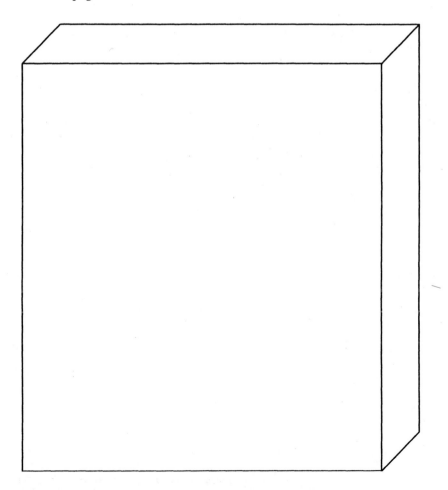

Life may seem to stretch out endlessly ahead, but death can come at any moment. Are you living your life so that you will be remembered for what you want to be remembered? What are you doing in your life right now to earn your epitaph? What could you do—what *will* you do—beginning now to better earn it? Write your answers to these questions in the space below. Be specific!

A Remembrance Will

When someone dear to us dies, we sometimes think of what we would like to have said to that person but somehow never did. When we die, we may leave some important words unsaid to those we leave behind. In fact, there may be some important unsaid words in our lives right now, and thinking of what they might be may prompt us to convey them in little ways if not in words.

A Remembrance Will that may be helpful has been begun for you below. Write the name of someone you love or feel very close to in the blank and then complete the message in as many words or sentences as you like. And, if you like, in your message you can bequeath to the person something of sentimental value or of special significance or just recall the memory of something you two shared. When you have finished your message, sign your name and record the date. Repeat this procedure for each of the others who are dear to you (continue on the next page and add more sheets of paper as necessary).

Important! When you have completed all your messages, write a paragraph summarizing your experience in writing your Remembrance Will.

Dear _____, in case I never get around to telling you this, I want you to know . . .

Question 8

Potentiality

What's Possible for Me?

Imagine yourself in this situation: You are an illegitimate 6-year-old child. Your mother is a deaf-mute. You have spent most of your life with your mother in a dark room separated from the rest of your mother's family. What kind of person would you be and become?

Isabelle (a pseudonym) actually spent the first part of her life in the condition just noted. When she was discovered at the age of 6, she appeared to be half infant and half wild animal. The professionals who examined her concluded she was feeble-minded and uneducable. Fortunately, they decided to try. A year and a half later Isabelle had blossomed into a "very bright, cheerful, and energetic little girl." At the time of the last report, she was 14, doing well, and had just passed the sixth grade (Davis, 1940a, 1947).

There appears to be a strong impulse to grow in every person (as indeed there was in Isabelle). We desire to be more than we are. Each of us will have our own idea of what we wish to become: perhaps better informed and more knowledgeable, or more understanding and loving, or more capable and creative, or more joyful and serene.

On the path of growth, sometimes we trudge and sometimes we leap ahead. We occasionally have a growth spurt when we make rapid progress and have an exhilarating sense of being more than we were. It may be a particular summer or year when everything seems to be going just right, or it may involve a particular relationship in which we find an enlarged sense of ourselves.

Just as there is a strong impulse to grow, there are strong impediments to growth. Rarely are they as complete and obvious as in the case of Isabelle. But there are growth blocks or impasses in which we are frustrated and seem unable to progress at all. There are even growth reversals—times when we appear to regress and give up hard-earned gains.

Personal growth, as it is defined here, is simply change in a desired or valued direction. Values, of course, vary from person to person. I may feel I have grown when I have freed myself from dependence on my parents. You may experience personal growth when you change your conception of yourself and begin to respond to the world in a new and freer way. My parents, however, may not agree that my newfound autonomy is growth, and your spouse may be threatened by your new self-definition and put pressure on you to revert to the person you were.

Box 8.1

Potentiality: What's Possible for Me?

Seedthoughts

1. Many men build as cathedrals are built, the part nearest the ground finished, but the part that soars toward the heaven—the turrets and the spires—forever incomplete.

    —*Henry Ward Beecher*

2. Compared with what we ought to be, we are only half awake. Our fires are damped, our drafts are checked. We are making use of only a small part of our possible mental and physical resources.

    —*William James*

3. The outstanding thing about the human organism is not its limitations but its potentials. It is characteristically overbuilt! When an engineer builds a bridge, he designs it with a built-in "safety factor"—a degree of sturdiness many times stronger than he expects the structure will need to withstand. People are like that, too. Most of us, in the course of our daily lives, use but a small portion of what is possible for the physical organism.

    —*Arthur Combs, Donald Avila, and William Purkey*

4. Your body is a three million year old healer. Over three million years of evolution on this planet it has developed many ways to protect and heal itself.

    —*Mike Samuels and Hal Bennett*

5. . . . never underestimate the capacity of the human mind and body to regenerate—even when the prospects seem most wretched.

    —*Norman Cousins*

6. Come to the edge, he said.
    They said: We are afraid.
    Come to the edge, he said.
    They came.
    He pushed them . . . and they flew.

    —*Guillaume Apollinaire*

7. [There is a] drive in living matter to perfect itself.

    —*Albert Szent-Gyoergyi*

8. If you deliberately plan to be less than you are capable of being, then I warn you that you'll be deeply unhappy the rest of your life.

    —*Abraham Maslow*

9. I would like to be able to fly if everyone else did, but otherwise it would be kind of conspicuous.

    —*12-year-old girl quoted by David Riesman*

Potentiality refers to inherent capacity for growth. What's possible for us? What can we become? What can keep us from becoming all we wish to become? How can we find a path of growth that's right for us? These are some of the questions we will consider in the material that follows.

The Potential for Growth

A Russian scientist has estimated that with our brain working at only half capacity, we could learn forty languages with no difficulty (Otto, 1972). Many of us, however, find it something of a struggle to learn more than one. From this perspective, we certainly seem to be less than we could be.

What is now called the "human potential movement" began during the 1960s and was dedicated to helping people make the most of their capacities. An underlying assumption—sometimes called "the human potential hypothesis"—was that most people function at only a small fraction of their potential. A further assumption was that by proceeding in certain ways they can realize much more of this potential.

Nearly a century ago William James, one of the earliest American psychologists, estimated that humans, on the average, functioned at about 10 percent of their capacity. Later, anthropologist Margaret Mead put this figure at 6 percent. Human potentialist Herbert Otto's original estimate of average fulfillment was a

"Well, whatever it is we change into, it can't come soon enough for me."

modest 5 percent, which he later reduced to 4 percent. The estimated percentage has been decreasing, he writes, because "we are discovering that every human being has more powers, resources, and abilities than we suspected ten years ago, five years ago" (1972, p. 14).

A trio of psychologists, Arthur Combs, Donald Avila, and William Purkey (1978), maintain that human beings are "overbuilt": "One of the most exciting discoveries of this generation is the idea that human capacity is far greater than anything ever thought possible. The fascinating thing about human beings is *not* their limitations, but their immense capabilities.... From everything we can observe, it seems clear that few of us ever remotely approach the potentialities for effective behavior that lie within us. Most of us use but a small fraction of our capabilities" (pp. 69–70, 71).

Norman Cousins administered his own recovery from a supposedly incurable illness. From this experience, he learned "never [to] underestimate the capacity of the human mind and body to regenerate—even when the prospects seem most wretched" (1977, p. 5). Later, in looking back on his entire life, he wrote:

> What, then, have I learned? The most important thing I think I have learned is that human capacity is infinite, that no challenge is beyond comprehension and useful response. I have learned that the uniqueness of human beings is represented by the absence of any ceiling over intellectual or moral development. In this sense, the greatest gains achieved by the species are not connected to the discovery of nuclear fission or the means by which humans can be liberated from earth gravity. The greatest gains are related to expanding knowledge about the human brain itself. (1980, p. 10)

Some evidence concerning regenerative capacity is provided by George Vaillant's study (1977) of a group of Harvard students. Vaillant followed this group from college age to about age 50 and found that their lives were "full of surprises" and even "startling change and evolutions" (p. 372). Quite notable was a subset of men in the study who had very serious psychological problems, which they dealt with by themselves to arrive at quite satisfactory patterns of adjustment.

One of the most optimistic of the human potentialists is Will Schutz (1979). "As human beings," he writes, "we are without limit" (p. 25). In his opinion, the limits we experience are "limits of belief" but not "limits of the human organism." He points out that there are pragmatic advantages to assuming that one is limitless: "If indeed I am truly limitless, and I assume I am, then I may discover that limitlessness. On the other hand, every limit I assume I have prevents me from discovering whether that limit is in fact real" (p. 26). Claim a limit, Richard Bach says, and it's yours.

Despite these enthusiastic voices, optimism about human potentiality is not widespread. Psychiatrist Cornelis Bakker (1975) attributes the deep sense of pessimism in some quarters to "the myth of unchangeability." It is a myth to which some persons in mental health subscribe when they see dramatic improvements that somehow do not last. It is a myth held by parents who look at their adult child and see what appears to be almost the same personality that was present at age 7 or 8. It is a myth any one of us might tend to embrace as we see ourselves wrestling with seemingly the same basic problems year after year or decade after decade.

We do have certain basic tendencies or dispositions that tend to stabilize between the ages of 21 and 30. Even though we continue to grow and change, these enduring dispositions remain (Costa & McCrae, 1992). Often, they seem so salient and so identifying that the changes that do occur may not be given their due. Consider, for example, an aggressive person who sees ambiguous cues as hostility and responds in kind. When this person is taught to view these cues more benignly, the hostility is not triggered; this change can make a crucial difference in the person's life without greatly affecting the underlying disposition (Kazdin, 1992).

Not all students of human nature are convinced that the myth of unchangeability is fully a myth. Psychologist Bernie Zilbergeld (1983), for example, believes that "people are very difficult to change" and that "there are limits to how much each of us can change." In his opinion, "the limits of human malleability are much closer to the ground than they are to the sky" (p. 247). Therefore, he adds, we may have to question utopian notions and give up our ideas about what is possible for humans.

However, there is a silver lining to Zilbergeld's dark cloud. Although he believes that human beings are difficult to change, he also concludes that there is not as much need for change as is commonly thought. He makes a strong case that many of the most creative and productive persons—Charles Darwin, Abraham Lincoln, Goethe, William James, August Strindberg, Virginia Woolf, Vincent van Gogh, Albert Einstein, etc.—were laden with personal problems and far from "normal."

Zilbergeld believes that people don't need fixing as much as they need to change their unrealistic notions of what life can be: "Much of what we think of as problems—things that ought to be altered and for which there are solutions—are not so much problems as inescapable limits and predicaments of life" (p. 251). Leslie Nipps (1992) agrees: "The two guarantees of taking on the mantle of personhood are mortality and fallibility, a potent combination that produces lifelong joy and sorrow" (p. 4). Much more could be said on this subject, and more is presented in Chapter 14, in the discussion of personality changes to be expected during the adult years.

The Impulse to Grow

A point emphasized by the human potentialists is that we have not only a considerable potential for growth but also a powerful impulse to make the most of this potential. Albert Szent-Gyoergyi, a research biologist who twice was awarded the Nobel Prize, has written that the data he had observed were explainable only if one assumed that there is an "innate drive in living matter to perfect itself" (1974, p. 14). A number of personality theorists have similarly hypothesized an "actualizing tendency" in humans—that is, a drive toward growth, enhancement, and perfection.

Carl Rogers (1975) wrote that each living organism has "an inherent tendency to develop all his/her capacities in ways that serve to maintain or enhance the organism." And, he added, each organism has an inherent wisdom that allows it to differentiate between experiences that do or do not further the actualization process.

Abraham Maslow (1970) put it succinctly when he wrote that what we *can* be, we *must* be. We must be true to ourselves—to our basic nature. Our capabilities are a promise that begs to be kept. Even if all our basic needs are met, we develop a restlessness, a discontent, unless we are keeping that promise: "A musician must make music, an artist must paint, a poet must write, if he is to be ultimately at peace with himself" (p. 46).

The Burden of Growth

Is the impulse to grow a blessing or a burden? Little Linus in a "Peanuts" comic strip once lamented his own situation, saying "there is no heavier burden than a great potential." Maslow (1972) cautioned his own students: "If you deliberately plan to be less than you are capable of being, then I warn you that you'll be deeply unhappy the rest of your life" (p. 36). Jungian analyst Florida Scott-Maxwell (1968) writes of our need to "live our strengths." She recalls that a client once told her: "I don't mind your telling me my faults, they're stale, but don't tell me my virtues. When you tell me what I could be, it terrifies me" (p. 22).

In her book *Smart Girls, Gifted Women*, Barbara Kerr (1986) takes gifted women to task for not achieving their full potentiality. She maintains that women "are too well adjusted for their own good. They are great at adjusting resourcefully and congenially to whatever situation is handed to them" (p. 5). Kerr herself was criticized for not accepting the women's own choices, but she stuck to her guns, suggesting that self-actualization is more than a right—it is a responsibility.

The human potentialists and, indeed, the entire field of psychotherapy have been criticized for tending to make people dissatisfied with themselves. Like some other industries that sell their products by convincing people they are not all they should be or can be—that they don't look right or smell right or are not always free of aches and anxieties—potentialists may create or exacerbate the very conditions or dissatisfactions they seek to correct.

Schutz (1979) disagrees with those who see potential as a burden. He understands that his own assumption of "human limitlessness" contains an implied demand that one live up to one's potential. But, he maintains, one has no obligation to be everything one is capable of being. "If I wish," he writes, "I can choose to feel inadequate because I have not realized myself fully. But it is not inherent in the assumption of limitlessness that failure to achieve all that is possible must lead to feelings of guilt and depression" (p. 26).

Those who have been stuck on life's path—at impasses, up blind alleys, forever marking time, caught up in low-level enterprises, getting by perhaps but not getting anywhere—will know the despair that comes with not growing. Those who have gotten themselves unstuck and who then are able to make more—maybe much more—of their lives will know the exhilaration that comes as growth resumes.

Success and Failure in Growth

Not long ago, one of my friends was telling me about an old acquaintance who was going to visit him soon. It was someone with whom he had gone to college but who afterward never seemed to make very much of his life. This acquaintance had never married and had moved from job to job in the same industry, but none of the jobs was different from or better than the others. From the outside at least, this man's life did not seem to add up to much.

A character in Anne Tyler's novel *Breathing Lessons* is taken aback when her daughter asks her, "Mom? Was there a certain conscious point in your life when you decided to settle for being ordinary?" Do any of us prepare ourselves for an "ordinary" life? What would you have answered if someone at your high school graduation asked if you would be willing "to settle for being ordinary"?

Thinking it over, I wonder how my friend's acquaintance regarded his life. Did he see it as disappointingly ordinary? Comfortably ordinary? Or not ordinary at all—which is the way Tyler's character responded as she recalled the incident with a friend: "It got to me," she said. . . . "I mean, to *me* I'm not ordinary." Ordinary may imply a lack of distinctive quality and a kind of failure. However, many of us happily, or at least willingly, lead an ordinary life and settle for its pleasures.

I have never been to a high school or college reunion, but more faithful alumni have told me that one of the attractions is learning what one's classmates have done with their lives. How high have they climbed on the ladder of success? What have they accomplished? Whom have they married? How much have they changed? (One woman told me she went to see how much hair had gone from the heads of her ex-beaus and how much flesh had gathered on the hips of her old rivals.)

Two better alumni than I, Michael Medved and David Wallechinsky, made a study of their high school class ten years after graduation. They published it in 1976 as *What Really Happened to the Class of '65?* The class happened to be the one *Time* magazine featured in its cover story "Today's Teenagers," who were said to be then "on the fringe of a golden era." Instead, the ten years proved to be a sad and turbulent decade that included assassinations of Robert Kennedy and Martin Luther King, Jr., drugs, the draft, and the Vietnam War.

During the decade, some alumni continued to blossom, some were transformed, and others met with tragedy. The alumna who had been voted "the most outstanding woman" of the class got her doctorate and a professorship at Princeton. The young man voted "most reserved" earned a degree in engineering and became a Krishna devotee. The quarterback of the football team, "an athletic ladies' man," became a Hollywood masseur. "The grind" went on to graduate from Stanford, drop out of graduate school at UCLA, and then was under intensive care at a state psychiatric institution. And the member of the class voted "most popular"—an all–Western League end and baseball team captain—committed suicide.

Ten years later Wallechinsky did a second survey on the class of '65, but this time not just his own high school class. He traveled all over the country and surveyed a varied sample of his generation of age peers. Out of this survey came a book, *Midterm Report* (1986), which includes a report card on his generation midway in life. How do you judge a whole generation? Wallechinsky's criterion: "Did they leave the world in a better condition than they found it?" After considering what the generation had done for culture, education, freedom, peace and security, technology, environment, and standard of living, he awarded it the midterm grade of B. But, as he pointed out, the final grade—which was still to be determined—is the more important one.

Continuing the matter of "midterm" grades, Gail Sheehy (1981) reviewed the lives of some of history's greats and found that they often seemed to be and thought themselves to be failures at some time in their lives. Lord Randolph Churchill described the career of British statesman Benjamin Disraeli as "failure, failure, partial success, renewed failure, ultimate and complete triumph." Robert Rhodes James titled his biography of Winston Churchill *Churchill: A Study in Failure* because Churchill's career appeared to have ended in complete failure before it renewed and outdid itself. Golda Meir failed as a wife and was far from a model mother but became the mother figure of Israel.

Meir was a failure as a homebody but a success as a public person, and many of society's or history's greats were notable failures in one or more aspects of their personal lives. Charles Darwin, Lord Byron, Shelley, and Tennyson were all hypochondriacs. Ernest Hemingway, Jack London, Edgar Allan Poe, F. Scott Fitzgerald, John O'Hara, William Faulkner, Edwin Arlington Robinson, Eugene O'Neill, James Joyce, Sinclair Lewis, Jack Kerouac, Raymond Chandler, and Thomas Wolfe were alcoholics. Virginia Woolf, Sylvia Plath, George Eastman, Vincent van Gogh, and also Hemingway and London took their own lives (Zilbergeld, 1983).

Some say that the memory of Martin Luther King, Jr., has been tarnished by posthumous revelations of promiscuity and plagiarism, but King was highly critical of himself. In one sermon, he said, "You don't need to go out this morning saying that Martin Luther King is a saint. I want you to know this morning that I am a sinner like all of God's children, but I want to be a good man and I want to hear a voice saying to me one day, 'I take you in and I bless you because you tried.'" Neither we nor those who inspire us will be without failure and flaws, but the weeds in our gardens need not choke out the flowers. Speaking of King, Ellen Goodman (1990a) writes, "Here was a man, an ordinary man, with human strengths and weaknesses. But when the time came and much was demanded of him, he found the greatness within himself . . . and he changed the world we live in" (p. A16).

Inspiration for Growth

Much of our learning as children is through observation and modeling. We learn by watching others and patterning our behavior after them. We are especially influenced by those who are important in our lives or who are receiving rewards we covet or who have qualities we admire. The persons we pattern ourselves after are *role models*. These models give us a sense of what's possible for us and who we can become. For example, we can grow up and be like our mother or father and do what she or he does. Some models, however, convey a sense of the limits and fallibilities of human beings. If they somehow haven't amounted to much, maybe we can't or won't either.

The words "role model" and "hero" or "heroine" are sometimes used interchangeably, but a useful distinction can be made between them. Our role models are those we aspire to be like or who at least have qualities we seek. Heroes and heroines are those who make the world better, but they are not necessarily those we want to be like or even feel we could be like. "Hero" and "heroine," as terms, were once reserved for mythical figures and later for real but larger-than-life personages, but these terms are increasingly used to describe those we greatly admire.

Our first role models and heroes and heroines are likely to be our parents and, a little later, our teachers. When psychologist Frank Farley had 340 University of Wisconsin students rank their top five heroes and heroines, the run-away winners were the students' parents. Moms did best, gathering six times more first-place votes than any other heroine. Dads received twice the first-place votes of any other hero (Stark, 1986).

"What man living today in any part of the world do you admire most?" Stop for a moment and arrive at your answer. When you have it, ask yourself who is the woman you most admire. In national polls that have posed this question over the years, nearly half of the male heroes have been presidents or other American political leaders, and similarly nearly half the women have been first ladies or other American political figures. Foreign political leaders and religious leaders were also high in the rankings for both sexes (Smith, 1986).

When *Newsweek*'s Charles Leerhsen (1990a) asked adolescents at five very different schools (an Indiana military academy, a Bronx eighth grade, a Dallas girls' school, a Midwestern high school, a South Dakota Indian reservation school) to write down their heroes, he got something of a shock. Most frequently mentioned: basketball star Michael Jordan. A number of commentators on the recent scene have lamented that there is an absence of true heroes. Instead we have cult celebrities: sport figures, rock stars, movie idols (Walden, 1986; Roche, 1988). These figures exalt competition, winning, success, power, and prestige, but not sacrifice, valor, and commitment to some larger good or purpose.

To my friend sociologist Earl Babbie, a hero is somebody who willingly assumes responsibility for working on a public problem. In his book *You Can Make a Difference*, Babbie (1985) points out the extraordinary efforts of ordinary people to make this world a better place to live in. Among Babbie's heroes are Candy Lightner, who formed MADD (Mothers Against Drunk Drivers) after her daughter was killed by a drunk driver; Helen Caldicott, whose Physicians for Social Responsibility has become a mainstay of the movement against nuclear weapons; and 11-year-old Trevor Ferrell, who became for a while a special person on the streets of Philadelphia by initiating and leading a drive to provide food, clothing, and shelter for local street people. Babbie believes each of us can make a difference. We each have hero potential.

Obstacles to Growth

Why don't we make more of ourselves and our lives? Why don't we realize more of our potential? These are important questions, and ones that many philosophers and psychologists, and stuck, bewildered souls have pondered.

A Diminished Conception of Ourselves. One reason we don't make more of ourselves is that we may have a diminished view of who we are and what we can become. To some extent, we are who we think we are, and some of us may not think we're much. Although research suggests we are more likely to overestimate than underestimate ourselves, psychologists Ellen Langer and Carol Dweck (1973) believe that "there are few, if any, of us who have a truly satisfying self-concept. People occasionally put on a good show and seem to others to be on top of it all, but these very same people often think: 'if they only knew the real me'" (p. 29).

The basic goal of many personal growth programs and psychotherapies is to get the individuals concerned to enhance their self-concept and to accept, love, and prize themselves more. A basic goal of some transpersonal approaches is to inspire persons with awe or reverence for themselves and their place in the universe. As such individuals come to see more in themselves, they attempt and accomplish more; and accomplishing more, they further enhance their conception of themselves.

The following true story (recalled by a woman psychologist from her prepsychology days) indicates how important an obstacle a negative self-concept can be, and how a positive self-concept can both instigate and stem from growth:

"I was living out in San Francisco at the time. While coming home from work one day I got involved in an accident and required the attention of a doctor. A friend of mine mentioned the accident to his friend, an eager, but not yet established, young lawyer. The lawyer contacted me, and then proceeded to persuade me that I had a case and that he was the one to handle it.

"That was the way I met Hank. The impression I got of him after talking over the phone for the next week or so was that he was enthusiastic, good humored, and sort of charming. When he came over to my house to discuss the case further, I had to add unattractive to the list of adjectives.

"After we concluded our discussion of business matters, we got involved in a friendly and rather personal conversation. Hank had recently come to San Francisco from New York. He was divorced and was eager to tell me about the marvelous changes in his life. It seemed that his ex-wife had constantly told him how ugly he was. I thought that that was both cruel and accurate—but kept the latter thought to myself. Hank explained how inhibited this made him with other people. 'I had little confidence in myself and was enormously shy.' I said I couldn't believe that he was ever shy. He recounted some experiences he had had at parties and with clients to convince me. He was successful in gaining my sympathy.

"Then he told me how different he was now. He had traveled across the country with the thought that he just might not be as homely looking as she said—so he took some risks. He gradually improved his opinion of himself. He put this a little differently though: 'I slowly started to recognize how wrong she was. Now I know I'm good looking. When I walk into a room people take notice of me and believe it or not (I didn't) the girls are all over me at parties.' We talked some more, and then a horn starting honking outside. He said it was his new girlfriend picking him up. We went over to the terrace to see if it were she—it was, and she was simply beautiful. For a moment I couldn't believe the whole episode. What was even more bewildering was that I started finding him attractive."

Although Hank's somewhat dramatic tale is not unique, most people with negative self-concepts never bother to test out other hypotheses about themselves, as he did. While at first he accepted his wife's opinion as indisputable truth, he later formulated an alternative positive view, "I am *not* ugly," and set out to confirm it. Now Hank tells people how to respond to him. His new manner has an air of confidence, and the subtle and not so subtle cues are effective. It is not surprising that most people listen. (Langer and Dweck, 1973, pp. 40–42)

A Fixed Conception of Ourselves. A second reason we don't grow as much as we might is that we fix our conception of ourself. We begin to think, "Well, I've always been this way." We each begin to think of ourself as a person who can do this but can't do that. In this situation, growth concedes to "destiny."

To find out where our "I've always been this way" originated, Bloomfield and Kory (1980) recommend that we quiz the significant others of our childhood days. How did they see us? What labels did they apply to us? We may hear from their lips the same labels we have come to apply to ourselves. If we announce we're going to change, how do they respond? Does their response seem to say: "Lots of luck and you'll need it because 'you've always been this way'"? For illustration, here is a case presented by Bloomfield and Kory:

> John, a college student, complains, "I can count the number of dates I've had on one hand and not run out of fingers." He's obviously got a sense of humor, but he is afraid to be himself around women. "I'm shy," he says. "That's my nature." John recalls his mother telling people that he was "the shy one." He never realized that his mother had an emotional investment in keeping him tied to her apron strings. John spent his childhood and adolescence living up to the family label of "the shy one." No doubt he had a tendency to be shy as a little boy, but with their labeling, his parents helped him develop that tendency into a full-blown personality characteristic. The question is whether John is going to continue justifying his fears of women with the rationale: "Shyness is my nature." (p. 167)

A fixed notion of who we are can easily result when we continue to move around in the same old subenvironments that call forth the same old response. We can develop a kind of comfort in leading our familiar life and in being our familiar self. To change and grow might bring welcome hope and pleasurable excitement, but it might also bring unwelcome anxiety. More about this in the material that follows.

The Need for Safety. A third obstacle to growth concerns an unwillingness to leave safe places. Maslow (1968) hypothesized that, in addition to growth forces, each person also has safety forces; and these two sets work in opposition to each other. Maslow noted that the conflict between these forces can block the individual. He diagrammed this process as follows:

Safety ◄────────■ *PERSON* ■────────► *Growth*

Elaborating on these opposing forces, Maslow wrote:

> Every human being has *both* sets of forces within him. One set clings to safety and defensiveness out of fear, tending to regress backward, hanging on to the past, *afraid* to grow away from the primitive communication with the mother's uterus and breast, *afraid* to take chances, *afraid* to jeopardize what he already has, *afraid* of independence, freedom and separateness. The other set of forces impels him forward toward wholeness of Self and uniqueness of Self, toward full functioning of all his capacities, toward confidence in the face of the external world at the same time that he can accept his deepest, real, unconscious Self. (p. 46)

Both safety and growth, Maslow noted, have drawbacks and attractions for the individual. The person grows when the drawbacks of safety and the attractions of growth are greater than the attractions of safety and the drawbacks of growth. Parents, teachers, and therapists sometimes are able to step in to change the weight of safety and growth vectors. As our conception of ourselves is enhanced, safety becomes less attractive and necessary, and growth becomes more attractive and even irresistible.

When I consider the lives of my mother and father, it is easier for me to think of my mother's life as a success. Both my parents were immigrants, my mother from Latvia, my father from Russia. Both were looking for better lives in a new land; and both made their way to a small Midwestern city, where they found each other, married, and raised five children. Success in life, according to Freud's bare-bones set of criteria, requires success in loving and working. I think that my mother found fulfillment as a wife and mother and, during her widowhood, as a caring resident landlady of a modest fourplex, but I never felt that my father found his true work or calling. He became quite depressed for a while in his late middle years—his response, I believe, to his inability to move his life along. My father was a brilliant, scholarly, and spiritual man who might have been fulfilled as a rabbi or teacher. Instead, for almost all of his adult life, he spent six and a half long days a week in a little store, an occupation for which he exhibited little zest or talent. In a book my brother Sam wrote about his own remarkably fulfilling life as a Hollywood producer, he recalls that my father would sit in the back of the store reading. Sam continues, "The regular customers knew to shout, 'Louie,' which would prompt my father to set down his books and come forward to sell a pair of overalls or shoes" (1992, p. 9).

Some years ago I went back to my home town just to wander again around old boyhood places. My parents were long since dead, and no relatives or close friends remained, but I found a man who had known my father quite well. We had coffee together and talked about the old days. He remembered that my father had been a force in the usually rabbi-less Jewish community and took it upon himself to round up ten mostly reluctant men so that a Friday-night sabbath prayer meeting could be held. "But," my father's friend added, "one thing about your father, he wasn't willing to take a chance."

I wondered about that: my father, a man who went AWOL from the Czar's army and came to a far-away land whose language and culture was completely strange to him, who fell in love, married, started a business, had five children, became a pillar of his religious community. He had taken chances, made commitments, achieved. What had happened to him along the way? How had he gotten so mired, so stuck? (One of my Elderhostel students, a woman of my age, took exception to this evaluation of my father's life. She said that the story of my father was the story of her father, too, but what could they do, they had to earn a living. And she added, "Your father's five children turned out well. You don't think that's success?")

In her book *Pathfinders* Gail Sheehy (1981) describes a group of "people of high well-being"—those who successfully negotiate the crises of life. She concludes that the "master quality" possessed by pathfinders is their willingness to take risks. In her study of lives, she found that a continuing sense of well-being generally requires a continual willingness to risk change. Similar findings came out of a longitudinal study of men and women by social scientists at the University of California at San Francisco (Lowenthal, 1980). The researchers expected to find the greatest sense of well-being among those adults who showed a strong sense of continuity in values and goals; instead, those who showed the greatest sense of well-being were those who demonstrated change.

The Fear of Growth. A fourth obstacle to growth concerns fear of what growth may bring. A number of students of human nature have noted an absolute fear of growth in some individuals. Why should some of us fear to grow? One reason may be that we fear the unknown. Even if we do not like or are not comfortable

with who we are, at least we are accustomed to ourselves. We hesitate to risk what we have (even though it's not all we want) when we may end up with something less or worse.

A second reason we fear growth is that it might bring responsibilities we will be unable to meet. If we succeed, more will be expected of us, and we may doubt our ability to continually meet these expectations. "The higher you climb, the harder you fall," we tell ourselves, "so maybe it's better not to reach too high."

There is a third fear of growth that Maslow (1972) called "the Jonah Complex." This complex (named after Jonah, who wound up in the whale when he ran from a mission he had been given from on high) refers to our fear of our own greatness. Maslow hypothesized that in the presence of very special individuals (saintly persons, geniuses, beauties, etc.), we may tend to feel uneasy, envious, or inferior and therefore countervalue (or depreciate) them or their qualities. If we could bring ourselves "to love more purely the highest values in others," Maslow suggests, we would become better able to discover and love and make the most of these qualities in ourselves.

Some Arenas of Growth

Every arena of life offers opportunity for growth and development. Among the more notable or more scrutinized are college, psychotherapy, and self-help organizations.

Personal Growth in College

Considerable study has been made of the personal growth that occurs during the college years.[1] This growth is not necessarily due to college itself, since gifted adults might continue to grow whether or not they continue academic work past high school. However, the college experience can act as a catalyst or facilitator, accelerating changes that would have occurred anyway, but at a slower pace.

Intellect, Knowledge, and Learning. Students continue to grow intellectually during their time in college. For example, general verbal and quantitative skills improve during the college years. Seniors are superior to freshmen in speaking and writing. Seniors are also more able to think critically (weigh evidence and distinguish

---

[1]   This section is largely based on a review by Pascarella & Terenzini, 1991. Other sources include Arkoff, 1968; Kuh, Krehbiel, & Macay, 1988; and Perry, 1981.

between weak and strong arguments) and make reflective judgments (use reason and evidence to decide controversial issues). Seniors also demonstrate more intellectual flexibility (see different sides of complex issues).

The longer students attend college, the more knowledgeable they become. The more courses they take in a particular area of knowledge, the higher their score on tests of knowledge in that area. It's reassuring that not everything disappears after the final exams.

Educational Values. Notable changes in attitudes and values take place as students progress through their undergraduate years. They begin to value education for its own sake rather than as simply an avenue to a vocation or higher standard of living, and they place more value on the intrinsic rewards promised by a career (challenge, autonomy, adventure, etc.) and less on extrinsic ones (job security, compensation, perquisites, etc.).

Liberal education is increasingly appreciated as students move through college. They become more interested in arts and humanities—that is, in subjects such as classical music, theater, creative writing, philosophy and history.

Autonomy and Internality. Autonomy and internality grow during college. Students become more independent of their parents, although not necessarily more independent of their peers. A number of my commuter students have told me that as freshmen they relied considerably on their parents and a continuing circle of high school friends; but as the semesters went by, they became increasingly detached from both of these sources of influence.

Students become more internal in their locus of control; that is, they see themselves as more able to influence outcomes and produce results. They feel increasingly in charge of their own lives and responsible for what happens in them. They become more their own persons.

Some students welcome the increased responsibility; others see it as something imposed on them and the necessity for it comes as a shock. Freshmen find that college provides less structure than high school, and no one keeps after them to do what must be done. Financial assistance may be limited or absent, making students largely or wholly responsible for their own support.

Relations to Oneself and Others. With an increase in self-sufficiency comes an increase in self-esteem. As students proceed in college, they develop a surer and more positive image of themselves, and scores on tests measuring anxiety and neuroticism recede. Relationships with others, including those of the opposite sex, become more mature.

Some of the increasing and more positive sense of self comes from a growing academic efficacy. Later semesters are generally less difficult than early ones. Early semesters can be bruising as students struggle to learn the ropes or to find purpose or direction. One of my students who is a junior told me recently that when he began college, studying was all he did and just to keep his head above water. But now, in addition to his study time, there is job time, exercise time, and leisure time.

Moral and Ethical Reasoning. Moral reasoning or judgment matures during the college years. Specifically, there is some shifting from "conventional" judgment to "postconventional" judgment. Conventional judgments are those made according to the expectations of others and the rules or laws of society. Postconventional judgments are made according to moral principles and override agreements, rules, or laws; these principles are selected by individuals themselves but are assumed to have universal applicability. Postconventional judgments take into account the uniqueness, dignity, and well-being of the individual.

Many students come to college expecting to learn what is right or true. As they progress, they learn that there is not always a right answer, that different views can be taken, and it may seem that nothing is certain. Ultimately, students see that they must make up their own minds about certain matters but must also be open to new evidence that presents itself (Perry, 1981). As one student put it, "It took me quite a while to figure out that if I was going for something to believe in, it had to come from within me" (Perry, 1981, p. 92).

Authoritarianism and Dogmatism. Along with an increasing interest in and exposure to liberal education, students become more liberal in their social and political attitudes. The college experience causes students to mull over previously unchallenged and unexamined ideas in these areas. The greater the exposure to dissimilar thoughts and beliefs, the greater the challenge.

Generally, students become less narrow-minded, less authoritarian and dogmatic. *Authoritarianism* refers to attitudes that are antidemocratic and anti-intellectual and that favor submission to authority; students become more critical of authority and more favorable to democratic and intellectual process. *Dogmatism* refers to belief systems that are closed and not receptive or responsive to change or to nonconforming or conflicting beliefs; students become more open to the consideration of new and different beliefs as they proceed through college.

Prejudice. Prejudice decreases during the college years. *Ethnocentrism*—considering one's own ethnic group as superior to others—diminishes. Students become less likely to resort to stereotypes in evaluating a person of another class or culture or race. They are more likely to consider this person an individual on her or his own merits. Both males and females move away from sex-role stereotypes and become more sensitive to the expanding roles the sexes may play in modern-day society.

Religiosity. There is generally a lessening of religious belief and practice during the college years—especially, as might be expected, at institutions without a religious affiliation. There is some movement away from doctrinaire religious views and a greater tolerance for the religious views of others. Students living away from home show the greatest change; those remaining at home are more insulated from the potentially challenging views of other students and more likely to continue familial religious patterns.

General Change. The college years are both broadening and leavening. Pascarella and Terenzini (1991) note that the progress made in college is "away from a personal perspective characterized by constraint, narrowness, exclusiveness, simplicity, and intolerance and toward a perspective with emphasis on greater individual freedom, breadth, inclusiveness, complexity, and tolerance" (pp. 559–560). These observers further note an increasing "other-person orientation" and a concern for individual rights and human welfare.

Factors Influencing Personal Growth in College. The greater a student's involvements in all aspects of college life, the greater the opportunity for personal growth. Much of what one learns at college is the result of out-of-class experience. New peer relationships, relationships with faculty, and cocurricular activities are of considerable importance in promoting growth along with the acquisition of knowledge.

A sense of belongingness is vital to many students' satisfaction, academic success, and personal growth. This sense is more easily provided by small than large institutions, and small institutions also provide proportionally more opportunities for meaningful involvement. Commuter students who have not distanced themselves from their parents or high school friends are less challenged to reconsider their beliefs. Also, commuter students and part-time students are less likely than those residing on campus to become involved in a wide range of campus activities that provide opportunities for growth; however, some nonresidential students are heavily involved in growth-provoking activities off campus.

Personal Growth in Therapy

I have been a therapist many years, and I have been in therapy myself three times during my life. The first time was in graduate school, when each of us students entered counseling as a didactic or educational exercise. The second occasion was in my thirties, when I seemed to be stuck and unable to move my personal life along. The third involved my whole family and came at a time when my wife and I were at our wits' end and ready to put our adolescent children out for adoption. Thinking back on this experience, I see that I grew quite a bit in the first, very little in the third (except in humbleness), but greatly in the second—when that particular experience was complete, I was in some ways a crucially different human being.

There are so many different kinds of therapy and therapists and so many different reasons for entering therapy that it is difficult to generalize about the amount and kind of growth that occurs. It has been estimated that two out of every three people who undergo therapy benefit from it (Garfield, 1983). (That is somewhat in accord with my story, since I entered therapy three times and benefited twice.) For many the gains are modest, but for some people therapy can be the doorway to a fuller, richer life.

Carl Rogers (1961), one of the most eminent of all psychologists and therapists, has described how his clients have grown in therapy. His description seems relevant to the growth many of us experience, whether or not it is within a formal therapeutic relationship. Like Rogers' clients, we seem to be asking these two questions: "Who am I?" "How can I become myself?"

The first change Rogers noted in the persons he helped toward growth was that they became more open to their experience. They became less defensive and more able to put aside their masks. They became more aware of their own feelings and attitudes and could respond to the world around them without distortion or preconception.

A second change that Rogers observed in his clients was a growth of trust in themselves, which relates to and stems from the increased openness:

> When a client is open to his experience, he comes to find his organism more trustworthy. He feels less fear of the emotional reactions which he has. There is gradual growth of trust in, and even affection for, the complex, rich, varied assortment of feelings and tendencies which exist in him at the organic level. Consciousness, instead of being the watchman over a dangerous and unpredictable lot of impulses, of which few can be permitted to see the light of day, becomes the comfortable inhabitant of a society of impulses and feelings and thoughts, which are discovered to be very satisfactorily self-governing when not fearfully guarded. (p. 119)

A third change was that individuals in therapy increasingly accepted responsibility for making judgments about what was happening in their lives and for determining the directions their lives were to take. They depended less and less on others for approval or disapproval or for standards to live by or for choices and decisions. To see that one is responsible for one's own life, Rogers wrote, is both a frightening and an invigorating realization.

The final change concerned the willingness to be a process rather than a finished, perfected product. Rogers noted that when persons entered therapy, they were likely to want to arrive at some fixed state of being or a place where their problems were fixed once and for all. In therapy, they came to accept the fact that they were fluid—not static entities—and capable of dealing with whatever arose in their lives. Rogers' clients replaced their need for fixity with the realization that they were and always would be in a "process of becoming."

Personal Growth in Self-Help Endeavors

"God helps them who help themselves." This familiar saying appears to be a proverb in all languages. For Americans who need additional help in helping themselves, a vast array of self-help organizations and publications stand at the ready.

Self-Help Organizations. Almost everyone must know about Alcoholics Anonymous, an organization developed and conducted by alcoholics to help themselves attain and retain sobriety. It is just one of many organizations designed so that persons with a particular problem or interest can help each other. In these organizations, help comes from the inside, so to speak—from those who experience the problem or concern—rather than from outside experts or professionals. Much of this help is from the support and understanding that only persons who share a problem can give each other.

The number of self-help organizations has grown rapidly in the last decade. At present there are approximately 500,000 such organizations in the United States with a membership of 15 million (Leehrsen, 1990b). In his review of self-help organizations, Thomas Powell (1987) writes that there are such organizations "for nearly every conceivable personal problem or problematic life situation" (p. 20).

Self-help chapters are usually small, simple, and informal with a shared and often revolving leadership. They manifest a strong optimism about people's ability to change and about the power of lay individuals to help themselves, to help others like themselves, and to be helped by helping. The emphasis is on taking life one day at a time and doing the best one can that day (Riessman, 1987).

Self-help organizations are directed primarily at four main types of problems (Leehrsen, 1990b): (1) addictive behavior (for example, Alcoholics Anonymous, Gamblers Anonymous, Kleptomaniacs Anonymous, Compulsive Shoppers); (2) physical and mental illness (Parkinson's Support Group, Depressives Anonymous, Schizophrenics Anonymous); (3) transition or crisis (Compassionate Friends, Widow to Widow, Parents Without Partners, Incest Survivors); (4) problems faced by relatives and friends of persons with problems (Toughlove, Adult Children of Alcoholics and Other Dysfunctional Families, Al-Anon, Alateen).

Despite the growth of these organizations, many modest-sized communities do not have chapters. However, in such situations a few residents can unite and form their own group. To find out if there is an organization with a local chapter relevant to your need, call or write the National Self-Help Clearinghouse, 33 West 42nd Street, New York, NY 10036, (212) 642–2944. This referral service is free.

What to me seems notably missing from the self-help scene is an organization for persons who are not occupied with a salient problem but who are interested in their own personal growth—persons who would like to understand themselves and others more fully and who would like to make the most of their lives. This is an organization I am currently developing. It's called "The Illuminated Life," or TIL for short, and anybody anywhere can form a chapter. All that's needed is one other similarly motivated person, although two or three or four others would be preferable. If you're interested, read Box 8.2.

Self-Help Books. Brian Kiley tells a story about a man who went to a bookstore and asked a clerk where the self-help section was. "If I told you," the clerk replied, "that would defeat the whole purpose."

As a visit to your local bookstore or a glance at the best-seller lists will quickly show, the world is awash in self-help books—not to mention a growing wave of self-help audiotapes and video programs. However, do-it-yourself materials in this field have been severely criticized. At best they are held to be inane "psy-

Box 8.2

The Illuminated Life (TIL) Group

As many persons in self-help organizations have discovered, it can be very helpful to share our lives with others and to have them share their lives with us. Human beings are storytellers, but the stories of our own lives are often untold or poorly understood. In sharing our lives, we can come to understand ourselves better, affirm ourselves, get out of stuck places, and move ourselves along. As we share, we obtain the support of others, feel more deeply connected and less alone.

For those who would like to participate in this kind of sharing, I suggest you form or join a TIL group. Four or five persons is a good size for such a group, but a group might be as small as two or quite large if it broke into small subgroups for sharing. Your group might be made up of persons who have a good deal in common, perhaps all of particular age or stage of life, the same sex, or those who share a special concern. It can be best not to have persons who are well acquainted in the same group or subgroup if this acquaintanceship would act as a restraint on sharing.

Your group might meet each week or once or twice each month for a total of fourteen meetings. (Or the group might meet seven times and then decide whether to continue for a second seven meetings.) Each meeting would be devoted to the pursuit of one "life question." Before a meeting, each person would pursue the question by reading the appropriate chapter of the book *The Illuminated Life* and completing all or a selection of the chapter's explorations. An application item (a set is included with each chapter) might be completed in lieu of an exploration.

In the meeting, each person would have an allotted time (perhaps ten or fifteen minutes, depending on the size of the group) to be the "caring discloser" (see Chapter 2, Box 2.4); the caring discloser would begin by giving her or his answer to the question and then would ask for the group's response. Until asked for their response, the others would simply listen *without speaking,* each being a "caring presence" (see Chapter 1, Box 1.4). One person would be appointed to chair or "keep watch" at a meeting, to ensure that each person had equal disclosure time and that appropriate roles and rules were observed. (These rules are explained more fully in Appendix B.)

Although someone would take the initiative to organize a group, the group would be leaderless; no one would be in the position of expert or authority. There would be no fee. The group might meet on a round-robin basis at the homes of the members and possibly begin with a potluck meal. When the group completed all of the units, it could decide whether to continue and on what basis. At that time, some of the members might decide to organize and participate in a new group to extend this work and keep themselves working on their own lives.

---

chobabble" and to promise far more than they deliver. At worst, they are faulted for proposing untested or tested-and-found-wanting procedures and some that if misapplied may be harmful (Rosen, 1987).

A recent survey of thirty-four studies of the use of self-help books, videotapes, and audiotapes on a variety of disorders showed these materials to be generally helpful (Clum & Gould, reported by DeAngelis, 1991). Furthermore, according to surveys made by Steven Starker (1988), many psychologists find self-help books of use and recommend them to their clients, although such books are not considered an alternative to professional help for those with serious problems. Most frequently prescribed are books on parenting, and second are books on personal growth and relationships. Other areas include assertiveness, sexuality, and stress.

A number of current self-help books are written by eminent psychologists and psychiatrists. To find out who the author is and what he or she is promising, read the biographical note and preface or foreword and ignore the sales pitch on the cover, about which the author probably had little say. I have found a number of self-help books worth reading and recommend them to those with whom I work. A brief current list is presented in Box 8.3. I think these can provide some helpful insights, although I do not agree with everything in them. I do agree with the psychologists surveyed by Starker that such books are not a substitute for professional help for those in need of it.

Box 8.3

A Brief List of Recommended Self-Help Books

Book, Author, Publisher	Comment
Feeling Good: The New Mood Therapy by David D. Burns. Publisher: Avon.	Helpful information on how we think ourselves into depressed and unhappy moods and how we can think ourselves back out of them.
The Feeling Good Handbook: Using the New Mood Therapy in Everyday Life by David D. Burns. Publisher: Plume.	Further helpful information on a wide range of problems, including depression, anxiety, fears, and phobias.
How to Stubbornly Refuse to Make Yourself Miserable About Anything—Yes, Anything! by Albert Ellis. Publisher: Lyle Stuart/Carol Publishing Group.	The author, one of America's most influential, honored, and forceful psychologists, believes that we largely create our own misery and that we can learn not to.
Love Is Never Enough by Aaron T. Beck. Publisher: HarperCollins.	A prominent psychologist tells how to correct the failures in communications that cause marriages to fail.
Honoring the Self: The Psychology of Confidence and Respect by Nathaniel Branden. Publisher: Bantam Books.	Why the judgment we pass on ourselves is the most important of all judgments and how we can grow in self-confidence and self-respect.
How to Raise Your Self-Esteem by Nathaniel Branden. Publisher: Bantam Books.	More information and guidance on strengthening self-confidence and self-respect.
Self-Directed Behavior: Self-Modification for Personal Adjustment (6th ed.) by David L. Watson and Roland G. Tharp. Publisher: Brooks/Cole.	Scientifically based instruction in modifying our own behavior to improve our lives.
Your Perfect Right: A Guide to Assertive Living (6th ed.) by Robert E. Alberti and Michael L. Emmons. Publisher: Impact.	Written by two pioneers in assertiveness training, this book is a manual in how to stand up for oneself without denying the rights of others.
Anger: The Misunderstood Emotion (rev. ed.) by Carol Tavris. Publisher: Touchstone/Simon & Schuster.	The uses and abuses of this important, troubling, and misunderstood emotion.
In the Mind's Eye: The Power of Imagery for Personal Enrichment by Arnold Lazarus. Publisher: Guilford Press.	The author, a prominent psychologist, shows how to use imagery and fantasy to overcome negative emotions and habits and to enhance enjoyment of life.
Creative Visualization by Shakti Gawain. Publisher: Bantam Books.	The use of imagination and affirmation to help create what one wants in life.
Necessary Losses: The Loves, Illusions, Dependencies, and Impossible Illusions That All of Us Have to Give Up in Order to Grow by Judith Viorst. Publisher: Fawcett Gold Medal.	The author's subtitle says it all. Wise and witty.
Healthy Pleasures by Robert Ornstein and David Sobel. Publisher: Addison-Wesley.	The pleasure-loving, pleasure-seeking, pleasure-creating route to health.

Pathways to Growth

All of life is concerned with growth, and all of this book is as well. It would be impossible and unnecessary here to review every pathway to growth that has been proposed or pursued. But it may be helpful to distinguish between two main paths that have aroused some controversy.

One path to growth is an individual way. Its emphasis is on oneself and involves developing one's own potentiality and making the most of one's life and spirit. It is an essentially inner path, although it may move out like a widening spiral to encompass more than oneself.

A second path is an outer and collective path—one of social activism and change. It involves finding ways to change the institutions of society—for example, the home and school and marriage—to enhance the lives of all people. It involves taking responsibility for the betterment of everyone everywhere, especially those less fortunate than oneself.

Some advocates of the second path have called the first a "narcissistic" one because they view it as a selfish pursuit. To them, it is a kind of self-absorption when the times call for social change and the reconstruction of social agencies. They fear that in frustration, people are "searching within" when they should be "reaching out."

Proponents of the first path vigorously disagree. They feel that personal growth or enhancement is a necessary first step—that one cannot reach out if one's center is hollow. If one wants a better world, the way to begin is to make oneself a better or fuller person. They ask how those who do not and cannot respect and love and help themselves hope to relate to and help others.

Roberts Samples (1977) calls the first path "self*ness.*" This is "the state in which self is celebrated in a non-exploitative mode." It is distinct from self*ish*, the exploitation of others for the benefit of oneself, and is also distinct from self*less*, the exploitation of oneself for the benefit of others.

> The search for self, alone and in the quiet of one's own skills of introspection, is never done at the expense of the whole. A person who looks inward is no more a deviant from the whole than is a cloud from rivers and seas when one contemplates the water cycle. When one looks inward, it is difficult to avoid coming back more whole, more intact. Of course, here I exclude that small fringe group who look inward and stay there. When those who come back choose to enter a relationship, a community or a culture, they seldom bring a more despotic, more deficient human back into the action. Such people, with a fuller knowledge of their own strengths and limitations, are richer and closer to being psychically balanced and complete.
>
> It is these balanced humans who can be counted on to exercise the most basic kind of morality. I call it *selfness.* From this point, growth and being become a celebration of one's own person and the purity of all that is called humanness is then extended outward to the whole community of humankind. The extension of this process one day will hopefully eliminate the social and cultural inequities that currently exist—inequities nourished by leaders and followers whose psychic selves are empty. (Samples, 1977, p. 2)

There is, it seems, nothing essentially incompatible in the two paths. Service to others is a time-honored avenue to transcendence, and so is the deep inner pursuit of oneself. One can grow from the inside out or from the outside in or both ways at once. There are many kinds of growth and many routes—each of us can find our own way.

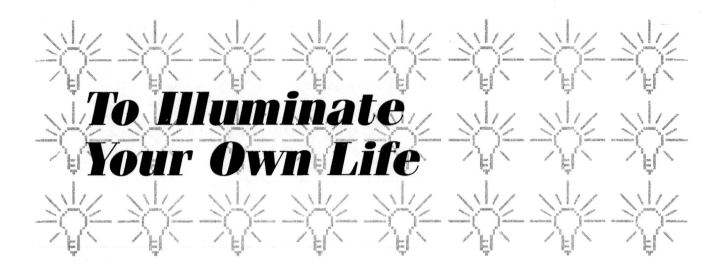

To Illuminate Your Own Life

To the Reader. You are now just past the halfway mark in this book, and you may have noticed that, in your responses to the application and exploration items for the first seven chapters, you have been occupied with certain central concerns in your life. Each succeeding chapter gives you an opportunity to pursue these concerns in a new and different way and to arrive at new and deeper insights. If you find that you are repeating old responses to new items, you are not taking advantage of this opportunity, and—let's face it—you are wasting your time. A human life is endlessly complex, and pursuing a life has been compared to peeling an onion—there is always another layer and another layer under that. There may be some tears along the way, but the end result is well worth the effort.

Anchor and Apply*

1. Do you believe or have you ever believed "the myth of unchangeability"? If so, give your reasons and indicate the effect of this myth on you.

2. Do you have any sense of a drive within yourself toward growth, enhancement, or perfection? Discuss this aspect of yourself.

3. Have you felt any guilt because of your failure to make more of yourself or a nostalgia for the person you might have become? Discuss this aspect of yourself.

4. Would you be willing to settle for an "ordinary life"? Why or why not? If not, what would it take to make your life acceptably "extraordinary"?

5. Consider the various areas of your life—home, school, work, recreation, social relationships, community services, spirituality, and so on. In which areas are you growing and in which are you stuck or failing to grow? Why?

6. For older students: Have you attended any of your class reunions? If so, what did you learn about the growth of the class members?

7. Discuss your own role models, heroes, or heroines and indicate their influence on you.

* These "anchor and apply" items are designed to help you use the concepts of the chapter as stimuli to prompt new or deeper or clearer insights into yourself and your life. To respond to an item, first find the material in the chapter that is most relevant to the item *and* yourself; that's called "anchoring." Second, think about this material in relationship to yourself and your life and keep thinking about it until you arrive at a new or deeper or clearer understanding; that's the "apply" or application part. When you write or present your response to the item, be sure to include both parts, that is, both the anchor material and the application. You can know you are successful on an item if, in completing it, you truly learn something new or understand something better.

8. What obstacles to growth have you found in yourself and how have they affected your life?

9. Are you a risk taker or a security seeker? What are the relative strengths of safety and growth forces in your life? Discuss this aspect of yourself.

10. Describe the personality change or personal growth you have noted in yourself during your high school and/or college years.

11. If you have been in therapy, discuss the changes or growth that took place in yourself during and/or after this process.

12. If you have been or are now in a self-help group, discuss the help you have received and provided.

The Growth Garden

Some poets have likened the human personality to a garden, and it may be helpful for you to think of yourself in this way. Imagine that you are a garden divided into various plots or sections, some larger, some smaller, and each representing some area of your life (family or relationships, work, school, recreation, religious or spiritual pursuits, etc.). What parts of you are growing well—nicely planted, cared for, and blooming? What parts are growing badly—full of weeds, untended, or perhaps not even sown? What parts crowd out or overwhelm the others?

Draw your garden below, and divide or section and label it any way you like to describe the growth you've achieved and the growth you need. Then turn to the next page. (Instead of a garden, you may imagine yourself to be a tree, a building, a river, or anything else that serves the purpose of this exploration.)

In the space below, describe your garden (or other image) and indicate what it says or suggests about (1) the growth you have achieved, (2) the growth you still need, and (3) the steps you can take—beginning today—to attain that needed growth.

The Growth Dialogue

Abraham Maslow (1968) wrote that within each of us "safety" and "growth" forces oppose each other. On one hand, there is the desire and impulse to grow—to reach out, take risks, and make the most of ourselves and our capacities. On the other, there is the desire to be safe—to stay put, avoid risks and the anxiety that comes with them. When these two sets of forces are of approximately equal strength, we feel blocked and frustrated.

Although we like to be integrated and have all aspects of ourselves working together, it can be helpful to purposefully disintegrate ourselves and examine the separate parts or forces. In doing so, we can give each a voice, create a dialogue between these separate forces, and perhaps gain some new insights. "Inner" dialogue of this nature is a feature of some kinds of psychotherapy, dream analysis, and personal journal work.

Below, as a brief illustration of inner dialogue, is a young man's statement of his conflict and the very beginning of a dialogue (only the first three interchanges) between his growth and safety forces:

Conflict

My relationship with my girlfriend has been close, but we seem to disagree on so many things. I feel that I should break off the relationship so that I can be free to find a more compatible one. Yet I don't seem to be able to do this. I seem to be afraid to let go.

Inner Dialogue

Growth Force	Safety Force
I've got to end this. It's just dragging on and on.	*Is it really all that bad? This is the closest relationship you've ever had.*
But it's one hassle after another. I want something more than this.	*Relationships were never your strong point. Don't you remember all those lonely times?*
I'm stronger now. I've grown. I'm ready for a new kind of relating.	*You scare me when you talk like that. Let's not do anything rash.*

In this exploration you are to consider one personal area or pursuit in which your growth has been impeded or blocked—where there is conflict between growth and safety forces. Begin by writing a statement or description of your conflict in the space indicated at the top of the next page.

From: *The Illuminated Life*, by Abe Arkoff. Copyright © 1995 by Allyn and Bacon.

My Conflict

Now, in your mind's eye, visualize an image to represent your safety force and another image to represent your growth force. The safety image can be you, but dressed, speaking, and conducting yourself in a very conservative way; you might model this image after a time when you felt very cautious or reluctant to risk or change. The growth force can be you dressed and conducting yourself in a way that symbolizes action and development; you might model this image after a time when you felt yourself expanding and surging ahead.

When you have an image of each force, your inner dialogue is ready to begin. First speak as your growth force, and in the left column write what this force has to say about your conflict. Then speak or answer as your safety force, and write this response or reply in the right column. Remember to shift your image and mind-set as you move from one force to another. Make each speech brief, but keep speaking (writing) back and forth until the conflict is resolved in some way or until you arrive at a new or deepened insight. Begin your dialogue below, continue on the next page, and add more pages if you need them. When you are finished, turn to the final page of this exploration.

My Inner Dialogue

My Growth Force	My Safety Force

My Inner Dialogue
(continued)

My Growth Force   My Safety Force

In the space below, indicate what your inner dialogue taught you about (1) your conflict and (2) the safety and growth forces within you.

The Growth Fantasy*

Human adults tend to be specialists. By the time we are full grown, we have learned that some of what we might like to do is all right or rewarded or practical while some is not. We have to make our way in life, get along, and earn a living, so we take our heads out of the clouds and put our shoulders to the wheel. We narrow down our lives, and some of what we could be we never become.

In growing all the way up to adulthood, we also learn that we do some things well and others not so well. We tend to stick to the things we are good at, and we get better and better at fewer and fewer things. (Someone defined an expert as a person who knows more and more about less and less.) We tend to shy away from things that we might not do well or that might embarrass us, or that others around us don't seem to be doing.

Robert Fulghum (1990) has lamented the radical difference between what kindergartners and college students think they can do.

> Ask kindergartners how many can draw—and all hands shoot up. Yes, of course we draw—all of us. What can you draw? Anything! How about a dog eating a firetruck in a jungle? Sure! How big you want it?
>
> How many of you can sing? All hands. Of course we sing! What can you sing? Anything. What if you don't know the words? No problem, we can make them up. Let's sing! Now? Why not!
>
> How many of you dance? Unanimous again. What kind of music do you like to dance to? Any kind! Let's dance! Now? Sure, why not?
>
> Do you like to act in plays? Yes! Do you play musical instruments? Yes! Do you write poetry? Yes! Can you read and write and count? Soon! We're learning that stuff now.
>
> Their answer is Yes! Again and again and again, Yes! The children are large, infinite and eager. Everything is possible. (p. 88)

When Fulghum tries the same questions on a college audience, the result is very different. When he asks college students who can draw or paint or sing or dance or play an instrument, only a few hands go up. Often those whose hands are up want to qualify their response; for example, if they admit they sing, it's only in the shower. Fulghum writes, "College students will tell you they do not have talent, are not majoring in art or have not done any of these things since about third grade. Or worse, they are embarrassed for others to see them sing or dance or act" (pp. 88, 90). Almost any group of adults would respond in the same way.

This exploration seeks to put you in greater touch with some of your less explored or developed potential. What is there in you that longs for expression

*This exploration is derived from the work of Don H. Parker.

but is largely or wholly unexpressed? What part of you is uncultivated or severely pruned? What part is dark continent, rich in resources, but undeveloped third world?

To continue this exploration, get into a comfortable posture and relax. Then read slowly through the numbered instructions below and think about what you are reading as you are reading it. It is not necessary to visualize the material, but if you wish to do so you might have someone read it to you or you can tape and listen to it. Another option: you can read the material several times and then close your eyes, relax, and recall it.

If you are a member of a class or group, the instructor of the class or a member of the group can slowly read the material to the others while they are deeply relaxed. Or have someone record the material in advance, so that all can participate. If the material is being administered in a class or group, your responses—instead of being written—can be shared orally in the group as a whole or in smaller subgroups.

1. Imagine or simply think of yourself resting very, very comfortably in a very pleasant place. You feel snug and cozy. You feel wonderfully relaxed and at ease. You are neither fully awake nor asleep. You are in that in-between state: half awake, half asleep, half way into a dream.

2. As you relax more and more deeply, you feel yourself descending gently, gently into a very deep and secret place. Gently, gently, deeper and deeper into a very secret place.

3. You find that you are in a place filled with clothes and costumes of every description. Racks and racks of clothes. Shelves and shelves of clothes. Piles and piles of clothes. Drawers and drawers of clothes.

4. There are clothes and costumes of every period of history and prehistory. Clothes from long ago. Clothes for today. Clothes for centuries far into the future. Clothes for every walk of life and every role in life. And every set of clothes is complete from head to foot.

5. Wander about and look at all the clothes and costumes. Find three sets of clothes that help you express some very deep part of yourself that longs for more expression. Or let the clothes find you; they may know you better than you know yourself.

6. You'll know the right three sets of clothes not by how they look but, rather, by what you think and feel and do when you put each of them on. Each of the three sets will help you express some very deep part of yourself that longs for more expression. Dress up in each set and see what you think and feel and do when you have it on.

7. When you are finished, get back into your street clothes and come back from this very deep and secret place. Then, feeling fully awake, rested, and relaxed, complete the instructions that follow.

On any blank sheets of paper (use the blank pages in earlier chapters if you wish), provide the following for each of your three sets of clothes: (1) describe the set of clothes or draw it (with you in it, if you like), (2) describe what you thought and felt and did when you put the set of clothes on, and (3) indicate what the set of clothes told you about yourself and especially about that part of yourself longing for greater expression.

Question 9
Values
What's Important to Me?

I s a meaningless life worth living?[1]

Imagine a happy group of morons who are engaged in work. They are carrying bricks in an open field. As soon as they have stacked all the bricks at one end of the field, they proceed to transport them to the opposite end. This continues without stop and every day of every year they are busy doing the same thing. One day one of the morons stops long enough to ask himself what he is doing. He wonders what purpose there is in carrying the bricks. And from that instant on he is not quite as content with his occupation as he had been before. I am the moron who wonders why he is carrying the bricks. (Quoted in Cantril & Bumstead, 1960, p. 308)

Is a meaningless life worth living? "No," was the answer of the 28-year-old man who wrote the above note. He killed himself.

Is that all there is?

Is that all there is?

If that's all there is my friends

Then let's keep dancing,

Let's get out the booze

And have a ball,

If that's all there is . . .

Is a meaningless life worth living? Some years ago Peggy Lee sang a song, a fragment of which appears above. Some of us lead lives like that. We go from day to day without joy or purpose, trying to distract ourselves from our despair.

The world is so full of a number of things,

I'm sure we should all be as happy as kings.

[1] In preparing this chapter I was greatly aided by Irvin Yalom's discussion of meaning and meaninglessness in his book *Existential Psychotherapy*. Anyone—psychotherapist or lay person—who is interested in the human condition will enjoy Yalom's wise and beautifully written book.

Box 9.1

Values: What's Important to Me?

Seedthoughts

1. Let us now consider what we can do if a patient asks what *is* the meaning of his life. I doubt whether a doctor can answer this question in general terms. For the meaning of life differs from man to man, from day to day, and from hour to hour. What matters, therefore, is not the meaning of life in general, but the specific meaning of a person's life at a given moment.

    —*Viktor E. Frankl*

2. I was never taught to listen within myself. Instead I was taught to listen to the outside—to parents, teachers, Boy Scout leaders, professors, bosses, the church, the government, psychologists, science— almost any outer source of instruction in how to live my life. . . . So now when I came to listen to myself, there were so many stations jamming the signal that it turned out to be very hard to discern my own voice. I would not even know that I had such a voice were it not that thousands of hours of listening to the people who come to me demonstrated beyond question that it exists in each of us and that our task is to reclaim this, our birthright, which has been partly or wholly covered over.

    —*James F. T. Bugental*

3. If a man does not keep pace with his companions, maybe it is because he hears a different drummer. Let him step to the music he hears, however measured and far away.

    —*Henry David Thoreau*

4. Money never made a man happy yet nor will it. There is nothing in its nature to produce happiness. The more a man has, the more he wants. Instead of filling a vacuum, it makes one.

    —*Benjamin Franklin*

5. I don't know anyone who wished on his deathbed that he had spent more time at the office.

    —*Peter Lynch, investment superstar, on quitting his fourteen-hour-a-day position*

6. As a result of our misunderstanding of what we are on the earth for, we have brought ourselves very near to the edge of doom. I regard most people as dead, simply as creatures wandering around, having no realization of why they are on this earth. They have no idea that the only reason for being on this earth is to live to love.

    —*Ashley Montagu*

7. Only a life lived for others is worthwhile.

    —*Albert Einstein*

8. Please congratulate me. I have been given a splendid opportunity to die. . . . I shall fall like a blossom from a radiant cherry tree. . . . How I shall appreciate this chance to die like a man! . . . Thank you, my parents, for the twenty-three years that you have cared for me and inspired me. I hope that my present deed will in some small way repay what you have done for me.

    —*kamikaze pilot, in a letter to his parents*

9. [Our] energies are consumed in making living, and rarely in living itself. It takes a lot of courage for a man to declare, with clarity and simplicity, that the purpose of life is to enjoy it.

    —*Lin Yutang*

10. I used to trouble about what life was for—now being alive seems sufficient reason.

    —*Joanna Fields*

Is life meaningful? Is life worth living? Most of us think it is. Indeed, as Robert Louis Stevenson poeticized, the world is full of a number of things to facilitate happiness or—more to the point—to engage us. What is it that we find or create to give meaning to our lives? What is it that we value most? These are the questions that we will turn to now.

The Meaning *of* Life and Meaning *in* Life

What is the meaning of life? What meaning do I find in my life? These are two important but very different questions (Kalish, 1985).

SHOE

The Meaning *of* Life

What is the meaning of life? Posed in this way, the question asks why we were put here on this earth. It suggests that there is some cosmic or ultimate plan which describes how we should live our lives and why we should live them in that way. Various religions have held that there is such a plan and that it is divinely ordained. For example, one view is that we should fulfill God's will as it is revealed in the Scriptures. Another and related view is that we should emulate God, who represents perfection, by striving for perfection ourselves. A third view holds that it is most important to have faith because we cannot know God's mind with certainty.

This approach is exemplified by Rabbi Harold Kushner (1986) in his book *When All You've Ever Wanted Isn't Enough*. He writes, "Our souls are not hungry for fame, comfort, wealth, or power. These rewards create almost as many problems as they solve. Our souls are hungry for meaning, for the sense that we have figured out a way to live so that our lives matter" (p. 18). We find meaning, Rabbi Kushner says, in living up to the moral obligation that God imposes on us: "Our lives become important because we are here on earth not just to eat, sleep, and reproduce, but to do God's will" (p. 180).

In contrast to Western religions that pose a duality (God above, human beings below), some Eastern religions regard all things as aspects of the One. The Chinese philosophy known as Taoism holds that there is a unifying principle to which everything in the world relates or a flow of nature of which everything is a part. When we do not oppose nature but instead come into effortless harmony with it, we derive a special power or efficaciousness. "Returning to the Tao" (complying with nature's meaning) is comparable to "finding the Kingdom of God" (complying with God's meaning) (Bolen, 1979, p. 98).

In Hinduism, the goal of life is to achieve a spiritual perfection that will lead to absorption in the world-soul or Brahman. Hinduism teaches that, although the body dies, the soul continues to be reborn. A good life leads to reincarnation in a higher state, a bad life to reincarnation in a lower one. With perfection, there is escape from the wheel of rebirth to the highest level of existence.

Meaning *in* Life

What meaning do I find in my life? When we ask the question in this way, we do not imply that there is a cosmic or ultimate plan that applies to all lives. The question asks what it is that makes our own lives purposeful or worth living. Of course, if we believe that there is a given meaning *of* life or some cosmic plan, then our purpose may largely be to live our lives in accordance with that plan.

Box 9.2

The Meaning of Life

David Friend and the editors of *Life* magazine (1990, 1992) asked a number of persons to answer this question in 250 words or less: What is the meaning of life? Below is a sampling of the responses. (A space is provided at the end, No. 6, so that you can add your own response to this question.)

1. Since age two I've been waltzing up and down with the question of life's meaning. And I am obliged to report that the answer changes from week to week. When I know the answer, I know it absolutely; as soon as I know that I know it, I know that I know nothing. About seventy percent of the time my conclusion is that there is a grand design. I believe that the force that created life is betting that human beings will do something quite wonderful—like live up to their potential. I am influenced largely by Blaise Pascal and his wager. Pascal advises us to bet on the toss of a coin that God is. If we win, we win eternity. If we lose, we lose nothing.

    I'm looking out a large window now and I see about forty dogwood and maple and oak and locust trees and the light is on some of the leaves and it's so beautiful. Sometimes I'm overcome with gratitude at such sights and feel that each of us has a responsibility for being alive: one responsibility to creation, of which we are a part, another to the creator—a debt we repay by trying to extend our areas of comprehension.

    —*Maya Angelou, writer and actress, is the author of* I Know Why the Caged Bird Sings.

2. We human beings are only one small part of creation. Sometimes we act as if we were the whole rather than merely a part of creation. There are other worlds besides the human world. The plant world and the animal world are equally important parts of this creation.

    The meaning of life is to live in balance and harmony with every other living thing in creation. We must all strive to understand the interconnectedness of all living things and accept our individual role in the protection and support of other life forms on earth. We must also understand our own insignificance in the totality of things.

    —*Wilma Mankiller, chief of the Cherokee Nation, is the first woman to lead a large Native American tribe.*

3. Awhile back, my son and I were hunting up at Pumpville. There is an old railroad stop there. It was late in the season. Hunting was tough. It got down to 10 degrees, one of the coldest days of the year. We had the option of staying in a heated trailer with some other hunters. But my son said, "No Dad. Let's stay in the tent. Let's rough it."

    Well, we practically froze to death. We had a fire going, and we let it die down, and then we went to bed. He woke up in the middle of the night. His sleeping bag was wet because his breath was freezing right there close to his face. So he got up and unzipped the tent and stepped outside, and he said, "Dad, Dad. Get up. You've got to see this. This is beautiful." He said, "I can see all the stars."

    I just stuck my head out of the sleeping bag because I knew what he was talking about. The stars were extremely bright, and it looked like they had come down to be a little closer to us. It was absolutely beautiful. The embers were glowing, and the fire was ringed with limestone rocks. It was all framed beautifully.

    That, to me, was life. That happiness that night was what life is all about. It just doesn't get any better. Money could not have bought me what we felt. We were together in a sort of hardship situation, even though we had asked for it. There was beauty. There was companionship. There was wonder in his voice.

    —*Sylvestre Sorola is a wildlife biologist.*

4. The Old Testament Book of Micah answers the question of why we are here with another question: "What doth the Lord require of thee but to do justly, and to love mercy, and to walk humbly with thy God?"

    We are here to witness the creation and to abet it. We are here to notice each thing so each thing gets

But if we have not been given meaning, we are faced with the task at arriving at our own set of purposes or meanings.

Some philosophers have held that there are no meanings divinely ordained or naturally imposed. In their view, rather than relying on God's meaning or nature's meaning, we must invent our own meanings and commit ourselves fully to them. If we want something to live for, it's up to us to create it.

Viktor Frankl (1979, 1985), whose work was introduced in the first chapter, believes there is no one meaning that is true for all lives or even a meaning that

Box 9.2

noticed. Together we notice not only each mountain shadow and each stone on the beach but, especially, we notice the beautiful faces and complex natures of each other. We are here to bring to consciousness the beauty and power that are around us and to praise the people who are here with us. We witness our generation and our times. We watch the weather. Otherwise, creation would be playing to an empty house.

According to the second law of thermodynamics, things fall apart. Structures disintegrate. Buckminster Fuller hinted at a reason we are here: By creating things, by thinking up new combinations, we counteract this flow of entropy. We make new structures, new wholenesses, so the universe comes out even. A shepherd on a hilltop who looks at a mess of stars and thinks, "There's a hunter, a plow, a fish," is making mental connections that have as much real force in the universe as the very fires in those stars themselves.

—*Annie Dillard, Pulitzer Prize–winning essayist, poet and teacher, is the author of* Pilgrim at Tinker Creek.

5. I figure life is like a glide-through. You shouldn't have to work at it.

I seen a lot of people like my stepdad. He worked up to the day he died. Sixty-seven years old. Dead. For what? He wasn't having any fun. He had all that money in the bank. All he was worried about was his job, fretting about how supplies weren't getting there on time. I think you ought to go through life having fun, trying not to mess people over, making as many friends as possible and getting by, not getting rich.

I give people art. If they ride a Harley-Davidson, they get that on there. If they have a friend die, they've got that on there, and they can point to their arms for different periods of their life and say, "I was doing this here, and this guy gave it to me." It's like reading the book of their life.

I really don't think that much about what life is all about. I go through scrapes, I lose old ladies, or get in motorcycle accidents. I just heal and go on. I fig-

ure if I'm busy contemplating the whys and the wherefores of life, I don't have time for anything else. That's why I have this job. I just go along slow and easy.

—*Michael Metzen is a tattoo artist.*

6. (In this space, you may write your answer to the question "What is the meaning of life?")

is always true for one life. Each of us is unique and each of us changes, and as we do, the meaning we will find for our lives changes too. In brief, it is up to each of us to find—and keep finding—our own meaning.

We change as we age, and what was meaningful for us at one stage may not be meaningful at another. In his work with older persons, Carl Jung noted that some entered their middle years with the false assumption that what had been meaningful would continue to be so. Older persons, he wrote, "cannot live the afternoon of life according to the program of life's morning; for what was great in

the morning will be little at evening, and what in the morning was true will at evening become a lie." "The afternoon of life," he continued, "must have a significance of its own and cannot be merely a pitiful appendage of life's morning" ([1930] 1971, p. 17).

No one expressed the sometimes meaninglessness of life better than Shakespeare when he had Hamlet declare "How weary, stale, flat, and unprofitable, / Seem to me all the uses of this world!" Some of my therapy clients have expressed the same sentiments although less eloquently. By contrast, one of my students wrote she found it incredible that some people found nothing meaningful, because everything in her life had meaning for her, and she didn't have to look to find it. To her, "serving burritos at Chi Chi's" (a place she worked as a waitress) was meaningful. The pen she was writing with—she liked its design and grace—was meaningful. Every person she met interested her and lent meaning to her life. She continued, "Questions like 'What makes your life meaningful?' throw me off. The answer is *everything*. What do I value? Everything and everyone—everything!"

This student happened to be a young woman very much *engaged* in life: married, taking a full schedule of courses, and holding down three part-time jobs. In the view of psychotherapist Irvin Yalom (1980), engagement—rather than the pursuit of meaning as such—is the antidote or therapeutic answer to meaninglessness: "the more rationally we seek [meaning], the less we find it; the questions we pose about meaning will always outlast the answers" (p. 482). His solution is engagement or profound involvement in life: to work, to love, to serve, to create, to build, and to remove any obstacle that keeps all this from happening.

Meaning and Values

What meaning do I find in my life? Another way of posing this question is to ask what is it that I value? A *value* is simply the degree of worth attached to something, and our *system of values* is the relative worth we place on the various things of life. Few of us will have a value system as dramatic as Patrick Henry's "Give me liberty or give me death!" To Sir Edmund Stockdale, money was clearly most important: "Money isn't everything—but it's a long way ahead of what comes next." But to William Thackeray, love was both first and second in importance: "To love and win is the best thing; to love and lose, the next best."

© ASHLEIGH BRILLIANT 1988   *Ashleigh Brilliant*   POT-SHOTS NO 4508.

IF MY LIFE
CAN'T HAVE
BOTH COMFORT
AND MEANING,
I'D PREFER
MEANINGLESS COMFORT
TO
UNCOMFORTABLE MEANING.

General Values

What most of us value most, according to some state and national surveys, is family. In a national survey conducted by the National Opinion Research Center, 97 percent of the respondents reported that their own families and children were important to them. Career or work was second, with 87 percent indicating it was important to them. In third place was religion and church, with 75 percent (*General Social Surveys,* 1982). In a 1991 national survey, respondents were asked to rate twenty-nine values, and the results (see Box 9.3) taken as a whole indicate again that what is generally valued most is one's family. Being responsible for one's own actions was also a top-rated value (*1991 American family values study,* 1991).

In the 1992 national election, "family values" became an important issue, but there was far from perfect agreement on what such values were. The proponents of such values mainly lauded the two-parent (one of each sex) traditional family; they directed their fire at homosexuality, abortion, unmarried mothers, and married mothers who were more dedicated to their careers than to their home-maker role. Interestingly, when respondents in the 1991 survey (noted above) were asked which of twenty-nine items were family values, they indicated essentially the same ones they had rated important; in fact, the more important a value was, the more it was considered a family value.

Another meaning for family values might be "values that are learned in the family," since the 1991 survey respondents indicated that their family was the chief source of their own values—a far more important source than teachers, friends, religion, books, movies, or television. When the respondents were asked who *should have* the most influence on young people's values today, the great majority said "parents," but when they were asked who *does have* the most influence, they rated "television entertainment programs and movies" as most influential, and "other young people" edged out parents for second in influence. Although most of the respondents were satisfied with their own family life, a majority rated American family life in general as only "fair" or "poor." The surveyors write, "In general, Americans are quite concerned about the decline in family life and family values, yet a [survey of a] random cross-section of American people finds few who say their own family reflects these trends" (p. 19).

Moral Values

Some of our most difficult value conflicts concern moral behavior. *Moral behavior* is behavior that is considered right or good, behavior in line with certain declared or established codes of conduct.

Box 9.3

What Values Are Most Important to You?

A national random sample of adults (18 years of age or older) who participated in a survey concerning values (*1991 American family values study*, 1991) were asked to rate twenty-nine values on a five-point scale: 5 = one of the most important values you hold, 4 = very important, 3 = somewhat important, 2 = not too important, and 1 = not at all important. The values are identified in the left col-

umn below. The second column shows the percentage of the respondents who indicated that a particular item was one of their most important values. The third column presents the mean of the ratings of all respondents for a particular item. You can rate the items yourself in the fourth column.

Value	Percent giving item a rating of 5	Mean rating	My rating
Being responsible for your actions	46	4.45	_____
Being able to provide emotional support for your family	43	4.39	_____
Respecting one's children	43	4.38	_____
Respecting other people for who they are	40	4.36	_____
Having a happy marriage	41	4.33	_____
Being able to communicate your feelings to your family	38	4.29	_____
Respecting one's parents	47	4.27	_____
Leaving the world to the next generation in better shape than we found it	38	4.27	_____
Taking care of one's parents in their old age	36	4.27	_____
Having faith in God	45	4.24	_____
Respecting authority	29	4.16	_____
Living up to my full potential	28	4.12	_____
Following a strict moral code	30	4.10	_____
Being physically fit	27	4.07	_____
Being married to the same person for life	36	4.04	_____
Having a rewarding job	23	4.01	_____
Being financially secure	23	3.92	_____
Being well-educated and cultured	23	3.92	_____
Being independent	23	3.91	_____
Earning a good living	20	3.90	_____
Having good relationships with your extended family including aunts, uncles, and cousins	20	3.86	_____
Having children	23	3.79	_____
Helping your community or neighborhood	14	3.77	_____
Being married	22	3.71	_____
Having leisure time for recreational activities	14	3.71	_____
Being in favor of prayer in school	22	3.46	_____
Opposition to abortion	18	3.08	_____
Having nice things	6	3.01	_____
Being free of obligations so I can do whatever I want to	7	2.61	_____

We learn very early that some behaviors are considered right and some are considered wrong. We also learn that establishing a consistent system of moral values is not a simple matter. We may be taught one thing but observe another. We witness a good deal of moral hypocrisy—persons professing a particular standard but not holding to it themselves. We find that behavior we have been taught is bad sometimes pays off. Moreover, our own values clash with each other or prove inexpedient. "Always tell the truth," we may be taught. "Always be nice to others." But sometimes it's nicer not to tell the truth, and often it's more expedient.

The 1980s were looked upon as a time of moral disarray. Comparisons of the moral values of Midwestern college students in 1958, 1969, and 1988 showed the last group to be the least severe. The 1988 group, in particular, was less harsh in its judgment of selfishness and misrepresentation for financial gain. Seemingly, students were becoming more mercenary and affected by examples of corruption in politics and business (Bovasso, Jacobs, & Rettig, 1991).

In a 1989 national survey of the general population, three quarters of the respondents said that American society was becoming less ethical and honest (Groller, 1989). And in the more recent national survey by James Patterson and Peter Kim (1991)—referred to earlier in this book as one designed to get at what people really believe—the letdown in moral values was considered the number one problem facing the country. The consensus of the respondents was that the United States lacked moral leadership and had become a meaner, greedier, more selfish and uncaring place.

According to Patterson-Kim data, six out of every ten Americans have been the victims of a major crime. One in every six was physically abused as a child and one in seven sexually abused. Two out of every ten women in the survey reported being raped by their dates.

Not only have we suffered at the hands of others, but we haven't been too saintly ourselves. About nine of every ten Patterson-Kim respondents reported that they lied regularly, and only three in ten believed that honesty is the best policy. In a separate survey of more than six thousand college students, at least 90 percent in each institution surveyed agreed that it is wrong to cheat; nevertheless, 76 percent reported that they had cheated in high school and/or college. Men consistently reported more cheating behavior than women, and both sexes cheated considerably more in high school than in college (Davis, Grover, Becker, & McGregor, in press). Concerning other kinds of cheating: in a recent poll of one thousand adults, 25 percent said they know someone who cheated on taxes, and 59 percent know someone who cheated on his or her spouse (Vox Pop, 1992).

Patterson and Kim asked their respondents if in the previous year they had done anything they were truly ashamed of. About one in four admitted to such an act, and most commonly mentioned were sexual misbehaviors: adultery/affair, 18 percent; fornication/premarital sex, 14 percent. Other dishonorable mentions: lying, 11 percent; illegal drug use, 10 percent; stealing, 10 percent; cheating/taking advantage of others, 6 percent; drunkenness, 5 percent; abortion, shoplifting, wicked thoughts, 3 percent; and verbal cruelty, masturbation, stealing from work, kinky sex, and pornography, 2 percent each.

In this same survey, respondents were asked to recall "the worst sin" they had ever committed. Here is a sampling of the "worst sins" reported:

"Killed other humans in war."—a post office clerk from the West Coast, forties, Baptist, not a churchgoer.

"Got into a fistfight with my father. I knocked my father down twice."—a truck driver . . .

"I shot two people once and almost killed them."—a man in his thirties . . .

"Hit my mother."—a single man in his late twenties.

"Allowed former spouse to physically abuse me without seeking help."—an Hispanic secretary in her early twenties.

"I once convinced a rich person to invest money in my company and we used it for living."—a real estate agent from the Southwest.

"Stealing over $500 worth of material from the hospital that I didn't really need."—a registered nurse from the Midwest.

"Stealing from my uncle, and I am very sorry."—a bank teller from the Northeast.

"Selling drugs to high-school kids."—a single man from New England, in his early twenties.

"Being jealous of my next-door neighbor's new car."—a housewife, in her early fifties, churchgoing Catholic.

"Playing sexually with little girls."—a single man in his late thirties.

"Having a child out of wedlock."—a sixty-five-year-old woman from the . . . South.

"The most serious sin I have committed is not being able to quit drinking and writing bad checks."—a single man, in his late thirties, Lutheran.

"I had an abortion when I was a very young girl."—a thirty-year-old woman, now divorced and unemployed.

"Five abortions."—a woman in her late thirties, churchgoer from the South.

"Stealing and, though not controllable by me, sex with my brothers."—a saleswoman, single, Jewish, attends services regularly.

"Tried to commit the ultimate sin, suicide."—a disk jockey from the Midwest, single man, Catholic, doesn't attend church regularly.

"Attempted suicide."—a divorced man in his thirties from New England, Baptist, not a churchgoer.

"Euthanasia. I helped my sister to die."—a secretary from the Northeast, in her forties, graduated from parochial school, attends church irregularly. (pp. 203–204)

From all of their data, Patterson and Kim concluded that women are morally superior to men. (Both sexes appeared to agree with this conclusion.) Women reported themselves as more responsible, trustworthy, and truthful. On the job, they are less likely to drink, use drugs, steal, malinger, leave early, goof off, or lie to their boss. (It's ironic: for this exemplary behavior, women are generally paid less than men.)

Patterson and Kim might be faulted for being more attentive to America's faults than to its virtues (which would have less shock appeal). Since they asked what truly shameful thing the respondent had done in the past year, for balance they might also have asked what truly nice thing he or she had done. Since they asked the respondent to recall her or his worst sin, it would have been fair to ask also for a recollection of the respondent's most noble act or finest hour.

Value Gaps

Our system of values becomes second nature to us. We may be scarcely aware of what our values are until we run up against someone whose values are very different from our own or whose values challenge our own. The discrepancy between two sets of values is called a *value gap*. Such gaps can occasion conflict and require us to defend our values or to change or compromise them.

The Generation Gap

The conflict in values between parents and their children—especially adolescents—has been well documented and even given a name: the generation gap. It has been argued that in a family there is an inevitable conflict between youthful idealism and adult realism, the latter born of hard experience (Davis, 1940b). Parents can be regarded as jaded or cynical because they show little enthusiasm for the goals that their children feel are well within reach (Csikszentmihalyi & Larson, 1984).

University dean Carolyn Lewis has two "unprodigal sons" who went off to lead simple, rural lives completely unlike her own. She writes, "Plainly what my sons want and need is something different—something smaller, simpler and more manageable. They march to a different drummer, searching for an ethic that recognizes limits, that scorns overbearing competition and what it does to human relations, and that says simply and gently, enough is enough." Not all parents are as understanding as Lewis, who puts their common accusation in a nutshell: "We gave him everything, and he chooses to weave blankets in Maine" (1982, p. 11).

Part of the generation gap results from differences in salient experiences, and part is a difference that comes with age. A generation that has lived through a great depression, a world war, or crushing prejudice may develop values quite different from the value of a generation without this experience. Older feminists, for example, lament the rejection of feminist militancy and the feminist label by younger women who have reaped the benefits of their pioneering. Nancy Gibbs (1990) writes, "Few daughters remember the barriers their mothers faced when applying for scholarships, jobs, and loans—even for a divorce" (p. 12).

Ogden Nash wrote this definition: "Middle age: when you're sitting at home on Saturday night and the telephone rings and you hope it isn't for you." Similarly, J. B. Priestley wrote that one of the delights beyond the grasp of youth but well known to age is the enjoyment of "not going." Research suggests we come to value different things as we make our way through the seasons of life. Young adults (age 20–40) place a high value on making their mark in the world: getting things, having things, achieving things. People in the middle years (age 40–65) greatly value self-respect, respect for others, and good relations with others. In the later years (age 65+), values center around security, ease, contentment, and satisfaction (Bee, 1987).

Every year since 1966, the Cooperative Institutional Research Program has surveyed a national sample of full-time students entering their freshman year at two-year and four-year colleges and universities. These data now permit a comparison of approximately two generations of college students. One of the most striking generational differences concerns the value placed on two "life goals." In 1967, 83 percent of the freshmen considered it essential or very important to develop a meaningful philosophy of life, but this percentage has steadily shrunk over the years—to only 43 percent in 1991. By contrast, in 1967, only 44 percent considered it essential or very important to be very well off financially, but this percentage has steadily grown, reaching 74 percent in 1991. Over the years, some of the largest increases have concerned the value placed on power and status as well as money, while some of the largest declines have concerned the importance attached to altruism and matters of social concern (Astin, Green, & Korn, 1987; Astin, Dey, Korn & Riggs, 1992).

The Spouse Gap

The values conflict between spouses—the spouse gap—is well known to every marriage counselor. Research and common sense indicate we are drawn to those who share our own attitudes, beliefs, and values (Berscheid & Walster, 1978). However, sometimes we pair or marry only to find that our values are not as similar or complementary as we had supposed, or that they are becoming increasingly dissimilar as the months and years and arguments go by. Differences in valuing the display of affection are frequently mentioned as a problem by couples seeking counseling: one (usually the wife) wants more, while the other is willing to take love for granted. The value placed on saving money also is a prominent issue, with one wanting to spend it while the other believes in stashing it away. Many a pair have proved to be an "odd couple," one valuing appearance with everything in its place, while the other, let's face it, is a slob.

Ellen Goodman (1990b) wryly describes the spouse gap (neatness division) in her own marriage. She begins by posing this question: Which makes a marriage happier? (a) The simultaneous orgasm. (b) The single standard of cleanliness. The answer, she writes, is of course (b), although it's much harder to achieve. She continues:

> How do I know this? Let me put it this way. My husband believes, as a matter of deep moral conviction, that clothes should be turned right side out BEFORE they go into the washing machine.
>
> In the days before our two families blended their laundry, he lived in an apartment that could be described (by me) as Spartan-Japanese. I lived in a home that could be described (by him) as Early Childhood Chaos. With dog.
>
> His kitchen had surfaces. Mine had them too, of course, although they hadn't made an appearance for some time. He regarded the dishwasher as something to be run. I thought of it as a convenient storage space. He liked the refrigerator clean (without anything to eat). I liked it full (of mold).
>
> When these opposites attracted more than dust, I got weekly cleaning help. He cleaned up for the cleaning help.
>
> We had made compromises, of course. But he still cannot understand how any human being—let alone one he loves—can walk up the stairs without picking up the shoes on the landing. I cannot believe that anyone—let alone someone I love—cares whether a pair of shoes is on a landing or in a closet.
>
> Deep in the hearts of couples like us who share space but not standards, each sees this difference as a character flaw. (p. A12)[2]

The Gender Gap

What are often called "marital differences" sometimes prove to be gender differences. Men and women tend to value different things. They even tend to speak different languages. Linguist Deborah Tannen (1991) notes that male conversation is more likely a negotiation to achieve and maintain status or to keep the upper hand. For women, conversation is more likely a negotiation for closeness and consensus. No wonder that bickering lovers often complain, "You just don't understand" (which happens to be the title of Tannen's eminently readable book).

---

[2] Copyright 1993, The Boston Globe Company. Reprinted with permission.

Gender differences in values are clearly discernible in the findings of the national freshmen survey noted earlier. This item is an example: "It is all right for two people who really like each other to have sex even if they've known each other for a very short time." In 1991, 65 percent of the men agreed with this statement, but only 37 percent of the women did. In previous years, an item concerning living together before marriage also elicited more support from males than from females.

Some of the value differences in men and women can be seen most easily in what each has been found to fear. Men value strength and success more than women do. Therefore, men fear appearing physically or emotionally weak or any appearance of failure or inadequacy. Women value love and relationships more than men do. Therefore, women fear being unattractive or loveless or estranged from or unable to assist those they love (Eisler, reported by Goleman, 1992).

What if women ran the country? That's a question the Gallup Organization pursued for *Life* magazine in a 1992 national survey. About one out of three respondents believed that would make for a better country—one kinder and gentler. There is a joke that if women ran America, there would be no more war—just intense negotiations every twenty-eight days. Although this might sound like a put-down, it also sounds like a better way to run a world.

The Culture Gap

One of the problems with the world is the gap between what various cultures and subcultures hold important. Individuals moving from one country to another sometimes find these differences sharply upsetting—a condition called "culture shock." Understanding each other's values is a prerequisite to getting along.

Immigrants raising their children in their new country often find their brought-along values at sharp variance with those their children are introjecting. One Japanese immigrant to Hawaii quite poignantly described her feelings toward her Hawaii-born and -raised children. She said that she was "a goose who had laid duck eggs" (Ogawa & Grant, 1985, p. 19).

"Ducks" who have hatched from such eggs have poignant feelings of their own as they find how different they are from their "mother goose." In her book *The Organization Woman,* my sister, Edith Highman (1985) describes just such a difference between herself and our immigrant mother. She writes, "I grew up an only girl with four brothers. I must have been seven years old when I informed my mother that I was probably smarter than my brothers[3] and I didn't see why I was the one who had to help with the household chores just because I was the girl. Of course it didn't do me much good. My mother was of the old school, and quite horrified" (p. 16).

Within the larger American culture are a number of subcultures, some with sharply different values. In the larger culture, land is a commodity to be developed and exploited. In traditional Native American or Indian culture, land is sacred. A Shoshone Indian, Joe Sanchez, explains:

> For most Americans, land is a dead thing. It means nothing. But to disconnect from land is unthinkable to Indians. It's where the ancestors' spirits live. It is not a commodity that can be bought or sold, and to rip it open to mine it is deeply sacrilegious to all Indian people. Nowadays most Americans live in or near cities. They have no connection with the land, the earth. They have no way of identifying with the most essential feelings that define Indian experience and values. (quoted in Mandler, 1992, p. 223)

---

[3] The author of the present book believes this assumption to be correct but would prefer that it not be announced to the world.

Criteria for Judging Values

There is an old Latin proverb that there can be no disputing about tastes and another that one man's meat is another man's poison. So how can we know whether our value system is a good one? Some criteria that can prove useful in judging the soundness of a value system are its explicitness, consistency, flexibility, realism, and the extent to which it produces satisfaction.[4]

Explicitness

The first criterion is explicitness and concerns the extent to which a value system is defined and understood. Since the learning of values is a gradual and even subtle process, we can come to prize something without being fully aware of it. When we are in close association with someone whose value system is very different from ours, we may become more fully aware of some of our own values. For example, when we are paired with somebody who couldn't care less about appearances, we may realize for the first time how important our concern for appearances is. Or when our mate is someone who loves to spend dollars, we may realize how compelling our need to pinch pennies is. Knowing what our values are can keep us out of difficult situations, although an opposing system can help us rethink and perhaps modify our own.

What is important in your life? You might find that your answer to this question is clear, ready, and sure—that your values are well formulated and well understood. This sureness is seen in Norman Podhoretz's candid introduction to himself in his book *Making It:*

> Let me introduce myself. I am a man who at the precocious age of thirty-five experienced an astonishing revelation: It is better to be a success than a failure. Having been penetrated by this great truth concerning the nature of things, my mind was now open for the first time to a series of corollary perceptions, each one as dizzying in its impact as the Original Revelation itself.
>
> Money, I now saw (no one, of course, had seen it before), was important: it was better to be rich than to be poor. Power, I now saw (moving on to higher subtleties), was desirable: it was better to give orders than to take them. Fame, I now saw (how courageous of me not to flinch), was unqualifiedly delicious: it was better to be recognized than to be anonymous.
> (1967, p. xi)

By contrast, some of us might find this question a very difficult one. We may not have formulated an explicit or coherent system of values. We may still be struggling to decide what is important and what we can believe in. This uncertainty is well illustrated in this statement by a young woman in therapy:

> I was thinking about this business of standards. I somehow developed a sort of knack, I guess, of—well—habit—of trying to make people feel at ease around me, or to make things go along smoothly. There always had to be some appeaser around, being sorta the oil that soothed the waters. At a small meeting, or a little party, or something—I could help things go along nicely and appear to be having a good time. And sometimes I'd surprise myself by arguing against what I really thought when I saw that the person in charge would be quite unhappy about it if I didn't. In other words I just

---

[4] This discussion of the criteria of a sound value system is partly based on Coleman, Morris, & Glaros, 1987.

wasn't ever—I mean, I didn't find myself ever being set and definite about things. Now the reason why I did it probably was I'd been doing it around home so much. I just didn't stand up for my own convictions, until I don't know whether I have any convictions to stand up for. I haven't been really honestly being myself, or actually knowing what my real self is, and I've been just playing a sort of false role. (Quoted in Rogers, 1961, p. 109)

And there are those of us who find that our seemingly explicit and well-formulated value systems have come undone. We thought we knew what was important and what we wanted, but we find that, somehow, it wasn't all it was cracked up to be. In this connection, James Michener wrote, "Many a father who has spent the years from 22 to 52 in a mad race to accumulate now finds himself powerless to answer his children who ask, 'Why did you do it, Pop? What good did you get out of it? What have you got to show for the rat race except two cars and three picture windows?' These are terrifying questions to throw at a man in his 50's."

Consistency

The second criterion for judging a value system is consistency. If our values are inconsistent, we will be at cross-purposes with ourselves. If we value security but also excitement, we may be hard pressed to find a lifestyle that accommodates both (although a secure job and an adventurous avocation may be a compromise). If we value a carefully controlled life but also hunger for love, we may be in for some interesting problems, since intimate associations have a way of upsetting old patterns.

We need to expect a certain amount of inconsistency in our values because we have been exposed to diverse persons and forces. As we grow up, we frequently discover that our significant others have significant differences concerning what is good or bad. Our mother may have one set of values, our father a somewhat different set, and our friends a third set.

The drama and agony of intrapersonal value conflict have been eloquently described by Barry Stevens (1971). In the beginning, she notes, she was just one "I"—that is, of one mind with one set of values. Then, listening to outside authorities, she became several "I's" with conflicting values. Stevens' advice to us is to make our own choices and form our own values no matter what anybody says is good or bad. In the condensation that follows, she shows the difficulty she has had in following her own advice. She says, "The one person the world seems hell-bent on my not living with is *me*" (p. xi).

In the beginning was I, and I was good.

Then came in other I. Outside authority. This was confusing. And then other I became *very* confused because there were so many different outside authorities.

Flush the toilet at night because if you don't it makes it harder to clean. DON'T FLUSH THE TOILET AT NIGHT—you wake people up! Always be nice to people. Even if you don't like them, you mustn't hurt their feelings. Be frank and honest. If you don't tell people what you think of them, that's cowardly.

The most important thing is to have a career. The most important thing is to get married. The hell with everyone. Be nice to everyone. The most important thing is sex. The most important thing is to have money in the bank. The most important thing is to have everyone like you. The most important thing is to dress well. The most important thing is to be sophisticated and say what you don't mean and don't let anyone know what you feel. The most important thing is to be ahead of everyone else. The most important thing is to be clean. The most important thing is to always pay your debts. The most important thing is to love your parents. The most important thing is to work. The most important thing is to be independent. The most important thing is to speak correct English. The most important thing is to be dutiful to your husband. The most important thing is to see that your children behave well. The most important thing is to go to the right plays and read the right books. The most important thing is to do what others say. And others say all these things. . . .

So both I's have a house and a husband and children and all that, and friends and respectability and all that, and security and all that, but both I's are confused because other I says "You see? You're lucky," while I goes on crying. "What are you crying about? Why are you so ungrateful?" I doesn't know gratitude or ingratitude, and cannot argue. I goes on crying. Other I pushes it out, says "I am happy! I am very lucky to have such a fine family and a nice house and good neighbors and lots of friends who want me to do this, do that." I is not reasonable, either. I goes on crying.

Suddenly: "What am I doing?" "Am I to go through life playing the clown?" "What am I doing, going to parties that I do not enjoy?" "What am I doing, being with people who bore me?" "Why am I so hollow and the hollowness filled with emptiness?" A shell. How has this shell grown around me? Why am I proud of my children and unhappy about their lives which are not good enough? Why am I disappointed? Why do I feel so much waste?

I refuses to play the clown any more. Which I is that? "She used to be fun, but now she thinks too much about herself." I lets friends drop away. Which I is that? "She's being too much by herself. That's bad. She's losing her mind." Which mind? (pp. 1–3)

Flexibility

Flexibility is the third criterion. A sound value system can bend a bit and form some compromises. This may be a bit hard to swallow. After all, if something is very important, it shouldn't be compromised, should it?

Unfortunately, very important things have a way of conflicting with other very important things. Suppose you are a woman of 40 finally making it big in the business world. And suppose your biological clock says it's now or never for that child you've wanted. What do you do?

Even if our value system proves internally consistent, it may conflict with that of the larger society or of persons important to us. Young persons may greatly value independence but because of economic circumstances have to bend a little and form some accommodations with their parents. On the other hand, in order to keep some peace in the family, parents may have to modify the values they are trying to push onto a resisting offspring.

Realism

Fourth, a sound value system is responsive to the realities of a situation. There are a number of things that for us would be ideal. Knowing the difference between ideals that are possible and ideals that are impracticable, that's the trick. Reinhold Neibuhr's prayer (adopted by Alcoholics Anonymous) is instructive here: "God grant me the serenity to accept the things I cannot change, courage to change the things I can, and wisdom to know the difference."

As was noted earlier, realism appears associated with age. Youthful idealism is modified by experience and instruction in the art of what's possible. John Galsworthy suggested that the closer one gets to a problem, the less idealistic one becomes. Still, credit must be given to a scattering of efficacious idealists who through the years made a difference when others said it could not be made.

Edgar Howe wrote, "Some people never have anything except ideals." Impossibly high ideals can provide an excuse for inaction: if only the impossible is acceptable, then why try? And, if we try, impossibly high ideals can leave us frustrated and demoralized.

Satisfaction

Last, the proof of a sound value system is the extent to which it helps us achieve satisfaction. Robert Potter (1988) has made an important distinction between "the standard of living" and "the quality of life." To put it in a nutshell, the first refers to the material aspects of life and the second to the satisfaction life provides. Of his own life at the time, Potter wrote that his standard of living was higher than it had ever been while the quality of his life was getting lower. His life was moving at such a frantic pace that he had time for few of the simple pleasures that make it all worthwhile.

It may seem strange that a person can learn to value and avidly pursue something that does not bring satisfaction in the end. How does this come about? Carl Rogers (1964) has pointed out that infants clearly show their values. For example, they value food when they're hungry, dry diapers when they're wet, and being held and loved. But as they grow, they introject the values of the significant others in their lives in order to merit approval, affection, and esteem.

I remember a young woman who came to see me in the student counseling center just before her graduation with a degree in education. She was from a family of teachers—mother, father, aunt. She had never really thought through her decision to follow in their footsteps. But her semester of practice teaching had awakened her to the realization that she was on the wrong path and didn't enjoy the classroom. It was a reluctant awakening because it meant starting over and without the support of her family.

And I remember a young assistant professor in my department who had applied for promotion and tenure, which he would have certainly received. But then, at the last moment, he withdrew his application and resigned because, as he said, he wasn't sure the academic life would be satisfying and he wanted to be free to try some other paths. It took some courage for him to give up the position he had attained and go beyond the value system that had so captured his academic colleagues.

It can be a difficult task to turn our lives around and make them more satisfying. Potter asked himself why he continued on with a lifestyle that provided less and less satisfaction:

> Then why don't I stop? Why don't I do something else? Why don't I turn back the clock and live like it was even five short years ago? Surely no one has chained me to my desk and to the routine of my life. Or is that so sure? The chains are there. And what is worse, I'm not alone.
>
> My personal confession can be matched by most [people], I fear. Our chains are much like those of Jacob Marley. We are chained by the demands that our advanced standard of living has placed upon us. We cannot afford to give up the good job—how else can we make payments on the mortgage?

We can't afford to slow down—other people are depending on us to come up with certain papers by deadlines which they set and over which we have no control.

We dare not relax and take it easy—our Puritan consciences, schooled carefully, would prick us most uncomfortably. And so we plunge on, "living more now but enjoying it less," to paraphrase the cigarette commercial. (p. 463)

The Pursuit of Meaning

As Freud indicated, love and work are central to life. For many of us, those we love and the work we do are what make life worth living; life lacks meaning for us when we lack love or work that is satisfying, and we will need to remedy these lacks or find other pursuits to enhance our existence. Below are some other pursuits that have provided purpose or meaning.

Religious or Spiritual Pursuit

For many persons, religious or spiritual pursuit makes their lives meaningful. And many turn to religion with new or renewed dedication when they find that their lives lack purpose or when the purposes they have set themselves to are threatened. As noted in the first chapter, Tolstoy turned to religion when he found his life devoid of meaning and as he pondered his relationship to the infinite.

The novelist and playwright Christopher Isherwood (1968) movingly describes his own search for meaning. Baptized in the Church of England, he lost his faith after confirmation; or, to be more exact, he found he never had any. Calling himself an atheist, he found two substitutes for religion, his devotions to the writer's art and to social reform, but neither provided the meaning he was desperate for. He ultimately found this meaning in the guru-disciple relationship provided in Vedanta, a system of Hindu philosophy. Of this relationship Isherwood writes, "It is the one reality of which I am never in doubt, the one guarantee that I shall ultimately surmount my own weakness and find knowledge of eternal peace and joy. If having found this relationship, I could in some terrible way be deprived of it again, then my life would become a nightmare of guilt, boredom and self-disgust" (pp. 135–136).

Although religion has been reputed to be on the wane in the United States, the considerable survey data reviewed by Greeley (1989) do not show a notable secularization or weakening of religion during the past half-century. Most Americans are born into a religious heritage and continue in that heritage. Although fewer than half of them regularly attend religious services, most declare that religion is very important to them (Gilbert, 1988).

Dedication to a Cause

A second important source of meaning is dedication to a cause that takes us beyond personal concerns and allows us to identify with something larger than ourselves. Irvin Yalom (1980) takes note of historian-philosopher Will Durant's book *On the Meaning of Life*, in which eminent persons state their ideas on this subject. A pervasive theme is working for a cause, and this also is Durant's personal position. In his estimation, the meaning of life lies in the opportunity to contribute to something greater than ourselves, something that will lift us out of ourselves and make us a "cooperating part of a larger scheme."

The particular cause a person dedicates herself or himself to apparently does not matter. It is the courage of one's convictions, not the content, that counts. Bertrand Russell (1930) in an irreverent mood pointed this out years ago:

> Belief in a cause is a source of happiness to large numbers of people. I am not thinking only of revolutionaries, socialists, nationalists in oppressed countries and such; I am thinking also of many humbler kinds of belief. The men I have known who believed that the English were the lost ten tribes were almost invariably happy, while as for those who believed that the English were only the tribes of Ephraim and Manasseh, their bliss knew no bounds. I am not suggesting that the reader should adopt this creed, since I cannot advocate any happiness based upon what seem to me to be false beliefs. For the same reason I cannot urge the reader to believe that men should live exclusively upon nuts, although, as far as my observation goes, this belief invariably ensures perfect happiness. But it is easy to find some cause . . . and those whose interest in any such cause is genuine are provided with an occupation for their leisure hours and a complete antidote to the feeling that life is empty. (p. 92)

Creativity

I remember a conversation with a fellow professor whom I have known for a long time. He has produced many books and continued to do so far into retirement. At one point in the conversation, I asked him why he continued to write, and he answered, "For the same reason I've always written; I have to have something meaningful to do when I wake up in the morning." To write—to create—gave meaning to his life.

Yalom (1980) hypothesizes that a number of creative artists have suffered "from a crisis of meaninglessness and, with a ferocity born of desperation, plunged into creative efforts" (p. 435). He notes that Beethoven was kept from suicide only by his composition. In despair because of deafness, Beethoven wrote, "Little kept me back from putting an end to my life. Art alone held me back. Alas, it seems to be impossible for me to leave the world before I have done all that I feel inclined to do, and thus I drag on this miserable life."

Yalom emphasizes that the creative road to meaning is not limited to artists. "A creative approach to teaching, to cooking, to play, to study, to bookkeeping, to gardening adds something valuable to life" (p. 436). Business ventures for some are a creative activity. I read recently of a man who retired after many years of manufacturing cookware. Unsuccessful at retirement, looking for new meaning, and inspired by the troubles his arthritic wife was having with kitchen gadgets, he started a new manufacturing business based on an easy-to-grip gadget handle. He said, "I need to be making and selling things" (Palmeri, 1992).

Pleasure

A fourth important source of meaning is the pursuit of pleasure. The age-old doctrine of hedonism holds that pleasure is the only thing intrinsically good, and pain is the only thing intrinsically evil; therefore, the purpose of life is to maximize pleasure and minimize pain. A latter-day restatement of hedonistic philosophy was made several decades ago by Hugh Hefner in his "Playboy Philosophy." To be a "playboy," Hefner wrote, one needs to possess a certain point of view. "He must see life not as a vale of tears, but as a happy time. [He must be] a man sensitive to pleasure, a man who—without acquiring the stigma of the voluptuary or dilettante—can live life to the hilt" (quoted in Banowsky, 1969, p. 38). A recent report suggests that the Playboy Philosophy may be aging along with Hefner, and that the "feckless, reckless" rabbit will become a "more sensitive, ruminative" rabbit (Levine, 1992).

Strong cases for pleasure have been made recently by the psychologist-physician team of Robert Ornstein and David Sobel (1989) and by George Leonard (1989). In their book *Healthy Pleasures,* Ornstein and Sobel hold that puritan and work ethics have made us feel bad about feeling good. It is their observation (and their italics) that *"the healthiest people seem to be pleasure-loving, pleasure-seeking, pleasure-creating individuals"* (p. 7). Leonard agrees that pleasure is a good prescription. He notes that pleasure can lead one astray, "but, properly harnessed, it remains an effective guide for good living and good health" (p. 154).

Service to Others

As was noted earlier in this chapter, depression and meaninglessness have been attributed to the rise of individualism with a weakening of commitment to the common good. To help, nurture, or serve others provides meaning for many individuals. In one study, subjects who increased their helping behavior for just one week also increased their belief that life was meaningful (Sappington, 1989).

Altruistic persons are happier than those who are selfish (Rimland, 1983). Helping others removes us from preoccupation with our own concerns. Helping attenuates feelings of separateness or isolation and gives us a sense of connection or belonging.

There is mounting evidence that doing good is good for us not only spiritually but also physically and emotionally. In one study, more than 70 percent of 246 women volunteers reported that their helping experience produced such sensations as a "helper's high," greater strength or energy, warmth, calmness, lessened depression, greater self-worth, and fewer aches and pains. Harvard cardiologist Herbert Benson says, "For millennia, people have been describing techniques on how to forget oneself, to experience decreased metabolic rates and blood pressure, heart rate and other health benefits. Altruism works this way, just as do yoga, spirituality and meditation" (quoted in Luks, 1988, p. 42).

Self-Actualization

A sixth source of meaning comes from actualizing ourselves or fulfilling our potential. We find meaning by making the most of ourselves and becoming what

SELF-ACTUALIZER

we can be. When we fail to make full use of our endowment, we feel stagnant and discontent.

We humans appear to be impelled to grow—to enhance and perfect ourselves. We may recall some growth-spurt periods in our lives—times when we were growing rapidly, enhancing ourselves, becoming more competent at something, feeling ourselves fuller, better persons. At such times we probably did not stop to ask ourselves about the meaning of our lives, because our lives were filled with meaning.

Self-actualization can proceed at the expense of commitment to the common good, but individualistic and collectivist values are not inherently opposed to each other (Schwartz, 1990). As noted in the last chapter, there is nothing necessarily antagonistic between service to self and service to others, and one may assist the other. A participant in a study of self-actualizing individuals saw her own fulfillment in this way; it was paramount but also a precondition to helping others.

> I guess the responsibility to self is to me the highest religious calling, to live out life. We were created for God's pleasure, and I see his pleasure in our living out all the possibilities created in us and for us. So that becomes an act of worship. Becoming most wholly and truly what the blueprint or design was for our lives and to not fall short of the creation.

> There is a kind of self-absorption that doesn't go any place. You really meet a lot of people that are at that point. In my own situation, there is a sense that I am enacting a larger program in my own self-growth. As I fulfill this blueprint for my life, I feel that the end result down the line is that I will more effectively make the contribution to the purpose of the world—to other people's growth. (Brennan & Piechowski, 1991, p. 55)

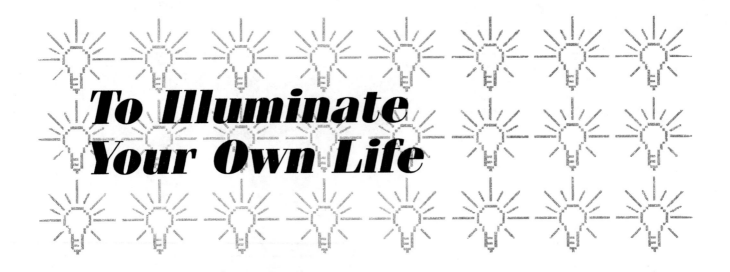

To Illuminate Your Own Life

Anchor and Apply*

1. What is the meaning of life? What meaning do I find in my life? Think through and write down your personal answer to these two questions.

2. Has there ever been a time when you felt your life was aimless or senseless? If so, discuss this time and what you did or are doing in response to it.

3. What do you value most in life? Why? How has your value system changed over the years? What accounts for this change?

4. What, to you, is a "good" person? Do you qualify according to your own definition or set of criteria? Why or why not?

5. Describe a moral conflict or problem you face or have faced and indicate your resolution or response.

6. Discuss a value gap that exists between yourself and a very significant other—for example, your parents (or one of them), your children (or one of the them), or your spouse, lover, or girlfriend or boyfriend.

7. Judge the soundness of your value system, using the criteria presented in the chapter.

8. Compare your own "standard of living" with your "quality of life." What changes have you seen in each of them in the past few years? What changes do you expect in the foreseeable future?

9. What compromises have you had to make in the pursuit of your highly valued goals?

10. Are spiritual or religious pursuits important to you? If so, discuss the effects of these pursuits on your life.

11. Are creative, altruistic, or self-actualizing pursuits important to you? If so, discuss the effects of one of these pursuits on your life.

---

* These "anchor and apply" items are designed to help you use the concepts of the chapter as stimuli to prompt new or deeper or clearer insights into yourself and your life. To respond to an item, first find the material in the chapter that is most relevant to the item *and* yourself; that's called "anchoring." Second, think about this material in relationship to yourself and your life and keep thinking about it until you arrive at a new or deeper or clearer understanding; that's the "apply" or application part. When you write or present your response to the item, be sure to include both parts, that is, both the anchor material and the application. You can know you are successful on an item if, in completing it, you truly learn something new or understand something better.

12. Are you dedicated to a cause? If so, discuss the meaning that this dedication adds to your life.

13. Are you "pleasure-loving, pleasure-seeking, pleasure-creating"? If so, discuss the meaning that the pursuit of pleasure adds to your life.

What's Important to Me?

Below are a number of incomplete sentences. Complete each sentence as thoughtfully as you can and go on to the next. Then turn to the next page.

1.   *To me, what is most important in life . . .*

2.   *One thing I'd like said about me when I die . . .*

3.   *Something that (seems/seemed) very important to my mother . . .*

4.   *I'll consider my life a failure if . . .*

5.   *"The good life," as I see it, . . .*

6.   *If I had to state one rule for living . . .*

7.   *I doubt that life is worth living if . . .*

8.   *Most people live their lives as if . . .*

9.   *What makes my life worth living . . .*

10.   *Something that (seems/seemed) very important to my father . . .*

11.   *I'll consider my life a success if . . .*

12.   *I would say a life is wasted if . . .*

13.   *As I see it, the purpose of life . . .*

Many philosophers and others have wondered and written about the meaning of life. Psychiatrist Viktor Frankl maintains that the "will to meaning" or the search for meaning is life's primary force. In his estimation, there is no one meaning true for all lives; each of us has to discover what can give our life meaning, and this may change over time.

Frankl believes that many of us are frustrated in our will to meaning. We struggle to find something of value—some purpose or something to make life worth living—but without success. Our lives seem petty or boring or futile. We live in what Frankl labels an "existential vacuum" (existential = pertaining to life or existence, and vacuum = emptiness), and we suffer from "noogenic neurosis" (noos = spirit or soul, and genic = origin), which is spiritual distress rather than mental disease.

Study your responses to the incomplete sentences on the preceding page. (Your responses will probably overlap or show some consistency or patterning.) Is your life meaningful? Why or why not? What in your present stage of life is meaningful or important to you? Why? Answer these questions in the space below.

Two Kinds of Values*

A *value* is the degree of worth we attach to something, and our *system of values* is the relative worth or importance we place on the various things of life. Some things that are highly valued by many people are a challenging or secure job, good health, a happy marriage, a satisfying family life, a nice home, a pleasant city or place to live in, good friends, a sustaining religious faith or philosophy, relaxing hobbies or avocations, travel, a comfortable amount of money, freedom to do what one wants, justice or equality under the law, and peace in the world.

Immediately after the three dots of each incomplete sentence below ("I value . . .), write something in life you value—something that is important to you. When you have completed all six incomplete sentences (but not before), turn to the next page. Be careful not to write *in* the boxes; you will be writing *on top of* the boxes.

1. *I value . . .*

2. *I value . . .*

3. *I value . . .*

4. *I value . . .*

5. *I value . . .*

6. *I value . . .*

*This exploration is adapted from Arkoff, 1988.

An important distinction can be made between two kinds of values. One kind, "announced values," refers to those things *we say* are important. A second kind, "committed values," refers to those things *our behavior says* are important.

Generally, our values guide our actions, but this is not always the case. We may announce that something is important to us, but never commit our energies and resources to it. For example, we may say that we value a particular career, but do little to make it a reality. Or that we value our health, but fail to care for it. Or that we value loving relationships, but spend little time in making our relationships loving. Conversely, we may give a lot of ourselves to something we don't profess to value, such as watching television or drinking. And occasionally we are forced by necessity or by powers greater than our own to devote ourselves to things on which we place little value.

Sometimes we don't pursue a valued end because we feel it is beyond us, or we don't see any way to reach it. For example, we may value serenity in ourselves or peace in the world, but we doubt that either we or the world will ever be tranquil. Or a particular goal may appear to require more time, money, and effort than we are willing to allot to it. Sometimes two valued ends conflict with each other, and we must decide between them or arrive at some compromise.

Consider each of the valued things you listed on the previous page. If you are truly committing the energy, money, and other resources its importance merits, write "Therefore" above the underscoring in the box and indicate the evidence for your commitment. For example, "I value becoming a lawyer. *Therefore,* I don't let anything interfere with my studies." Or "I value my health. *Therefore,* I have given up smoking and junk food, and I jog every day."

If you aren't making the necessary commitment, write "However" above the underscoring in the box and indicate how your commitment falls short. For example, "I value a satisfying family life." "*However,* I spend too much time golfing and not enough time with my family." Or "I value peace in the world." "*However,* I still haven't joined that peace organization, and I haven't contributed any money to it either."

When you have finished with your "therefores" and "howevers," turn to the next page.

Daniels and Horowitz (1984), on whose work this exploration is based, suggest that the more your values and actions are congruent with each other, the more whole or genuine you will feel. And the more that valued ends have been achieved or seem achievable through the efforts you are making, the more contented or at peace with yourself you will be. In other words, the more "therefores" and the fewer "howevers" you have written in the boxes on page 295, the more genuine and contented you should feel.

In the space below, answer these two questions: (1) How do your therefores and howevers relate to your feelings of genuineness and contentment? (2) What are you able and willing to do right now to change each of your howevers into a therefore? (If you had no howevers, congratulations! Therefore, you may disregard the second question.)

The Values Gap

Begin this exploration by reading the following letter written to a newspaper columnist:

Dear Ann:

I am a person of simple taste. I don't need much to make me happy. A can of beer, two good baseball teams, a freeway and a tank full of gas.

A sunny day in early June. A brisk run at sunrise. A pretty girl who smiles when I look her way. A short story by William Faulkner.

None of these will pay the rent so I have to work—which I hate, but I realize a person must be practical.

What I need to know is why should I kill myself to meet someone else's definition of success.

To me, success is having enough money to prepare tomorrow's meal. Since I was old enough to talk I was told I was brilliant and would make a lot of money and have the world on a string.

So here I am at 23, not earning very much, but I'm genuinely happy and don't want for a thing.

My father (who has ulcers) is ashamed of me. My mother (her life is the beauty salon and clothes) thinks I'm a disgrace.

I respect your opinion and would appreciate your opinion of my lifestyle. Am I wrong? Are they right? Where do you stand?

Jerry in Yonkers

Assume that the columnist is on vacation and you are asked to write a reply to this young man. Write your reply below (or on any sheet of paper) and then—but not before—go on to the next page.

People differ and so do their values. When individuals with very different values are locked together in a relationship or cross paths, the conflict can be irritating or worse. The spouse gap (neatness division) is wryly illustrated by Ellen Goodman on page 280 of this chapter and is well known to every marriage counselor. Value differences have also been noted between families with children and those without them ("the family gap"), between the sexes ("the gender gap"), between cultures or subcultures ("the culture gap"), and between generations ("the generation gap").

The letter on the previous page was written, of course, to Ann Landers and her reply appears below:

Dear Jerry:

The most revealing part of your letter can be found in four words, "work—which I hate."

Why does a smart guy like you hate work? Don't you realize money is only one of the benefits of labor?

If you hate your job and view it as something you must do so you can eat the next day, you are wasting your time and probably ripping off your employer.

This country wasn't built by men who wanted nothing more out of life than a can of beer, a tank full of gas and a story by Faulkner.

And it's a good thing, because if everyone thought as you do we'd still be living in caves.

There would be no progress in the sciences or the arts—or in any of the areas that separate us from primitive people.

As a person who has worked very hard for many years (and I didn't need the money) I can tell you, my young friend, that work can be tremendously rewarding and wonderful fun.

My idea of hell would be a life of leisure. The happiest people I know are the busiest. The most miserable are the idle rich.

I'm sorry about your dad's ulcers but I'll bet your relationship with him has a lot to do with why you hate work. Anything HE likes, you probably hate.

Too bad you didn't get that problem resolved earlier. Since you are only 23, it's not too late.

In the space below (or on any sheet of paper), compare Ann Landers' reply with your own and discuss any gap you see between her values and yours.

In the space below, consider your own system of values in relation to that of some significant other in your life whose values are quite different. This significant other might be your parents (or one of them), a lover or spouse (or an ex-lover or ex-spouse), a friend, or one of your children. First, compare what you consider important in life to what he, she, or they consider important. Second, indicate the effect of this gap or difference in your two sets of values. Third, discuss your efforts to deal with, close, or bridge this gap.

Question 10
Goals
What Do I Seek?
What Do I Find?

I had a conversation with a man who had recently retired from a job he had held for many years. To keep busy, he had made up a list of things he had wanted to do around the house. "Well," he told me, "I finished the whole list in two weeks, and then I proceeded to go nuts. I had no reason to jump out of bed in the morning."

As a sometime counselor in a student counseling center, I have had many conversations with students who were floundering in college. One told me she was just getting required courses "out of the way." "Out of the way for what?" I asked. "That's what I don't know," she answered. "I don't know what I want to do. That's why I am here in your office."

A life without goals—what would that be like? For many of us, it is scarcely imaginable. Or tolerable. We need our goals to give direction to our lives. We need goals to inspire us and move us along.

A story is told about a man who died and found himself in a place where his every desire was quickly satisfied. At first he was elated, but he soon became desperately bored. He sought out the person who seemed to be in charge and told him he couldn't stand heaven, that he would rather go to hell. "My dear fellow," came the reply, "wherever do you think you are? This is hell."

On Setting Goals

I remember part of a song that went "We don't know where we're going, but we're on our way!" And I also recall a saying: "If you don't know where you're going, you may wind up somewhere else." One of the reasons we don't reach important goals is that we don't know how to set them. Below are some questions that it may be helpful to ask ourselves.

1. What exactly do I want?

It is helpful to be clear, specific, and concrete in setting goals. When our goals are exact, we know exactly what to steer toward, and we know when we've truly

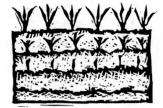

Box 10.1

Goals: What Do I Seek? What Do I Find?

Seedthoughts

1. The Great Way is not difficult for those who have no preferences.

    —*Sengstan, third Zen patriarch*

2. There is no greater sin than desire,
    No greater curse than discontent.
    No greater misfortune than wanting something for oneself.
    Therefore he who knows that enough is enough always has enough.

    —*Lao-tsu*

3. Basically, the essence of Buddhism is not trying to find something one doesn't have, but simply to recover what one does have but doesn't know it.

    —*Yeshi Dhonden*

4. There are two things to aim at in life; first, to get what you want; and, after that, to enjoy it. Only the wisest of mankind achieve the second.

    —*Logan Pearsall Smith*

5. When first my way to fair I took
    Few pence in purse had I,
    And long I used to stand and look
    At things I could not buy.

    Now times are altered: If I care
    To buy a thing, I can;
    The pence are here and here's the fair,
    But where's the lost young man?

    —*A. E. Housman,* Last Poems

6. I want the magnificent American dream: a wife, a dog, a house, a bathroom.

    —*Laotian refugee*

7. I have to tell you that our generation has to sacrifice for the next generation. We have our dreams, but we cannot make ours come true. We pass our dreams to the next generation and ask them, push them, help them to make it.

    —*Vietnamese immigrant, father of five*

8. . . . the self-renewing man never feels that he has "arrived." He knows that the really important tasks are never finished—interrupted, perhaps, but never finished—and all the significant goals recede before one.

    —*John W. Gardner*

9. To get to a place you have never been, you must go by a road you have never taken.

    —*David Ansen*

arrived. In their book *Overcoming Your Barriers*, Gerald Piaget and Barbara Binkley (1985) write, "Since most people find it easier to gripe about what they don't have and don't want than to specify exactly what they *do* want—and because setting specific goals is often threatening—we often leave our goals vague. Unfortunately, vague and general goals are a lot more difficult to achieve than clear, specific ones" (p. 48).

2. Why do I want it?

An important reason for knowing just why we seek something is that if the goal we set proves unattainable, we can set another goal that provides the something we need. Or we can design a part-goal that gets us some of what we need while we are on our way to a fuller goal. In their book *Wishcraft: How to Get What You Really Want*, Barbara Sher and Annie Gottlieb (1979) encourage their readers to determine the *touchstone* of their goals; a *touchstone* is what one wants and needs from a goal. This may be creative fulfillment, the chance to help people, love, money, public notice, closeness to nature, etc. Identifying the touchstone will help us design the best route to the goal and also alternate goals if the original seems impossible. The sooner we get some of what we want, the more energy we'll have to pursue the rest of it.

POT-SHOTS NO. 571
Ashleigh Brilliant

ONE POSSIBLE REASON
WHY THINGS
AREN'T GOING
ACCORDING
TO PLAN

IS THAT
THERE NEVER
WAS A PLAN.

© BRILLIANT ENTERPRISES 1974

3. Do I believe I can get it?

Wishing won't make it so, but believing in our ability to make it so is a good beginning and not believing is a bad one. If we see ourselves in a negative light, we may set ourselves for failure. We may avoid pursuing our goals or pursue them only half-heartedly. Why waste the time and energy, we think, if we're going to fail? On the other hand, if we have a high regard for our assets and aptitudes (or our ability to persist and make the most of whatever we have) and if we believe we can succeed, we will likely act in ways consistent with our expectations (Langer & Dweck, 1973).

4. What do I need to do to reach my goal?

What competencies do I need to acquire to get me where I want to go? What certification, degrees, licenses? What personal qualities should I develop more fully? How much time, energy, and money will be required? How can I get necessary help and support? If any goal is a rather distant one, it may be well to establish some part-goals along the way with appropriate pauses and rewards.

5. What other needs or goals will conflict with this one?

Alas, our goals are sometimes incompatible with each other, or they compete for our limited resources. When there is a conflict between goals, we may be able to arrange a compromise. For example, we may need to balance the time we spend in the pursuit of our career with the time we spend with our family. Sometimes we will need to consider which of our goals are most important to us. Lakein (1973) suggests that, in order to decide what to attend to in our busy daily schedule, we stop and ask ourselves, "What is the best use of my time right now?" This

is a good question to consider when we find ourselves caught up in too many things, or when we are distracted or running out of steam.

6. When will I begin? When will I arrive?

It can be important to set up a timetable—a time to begin, a period of achievement, and a deadline for completion. "Procrastination may not be the biggest single barrier pattern in everyone's life, but for many of us it comes close. It is natural to avoid that which we find uncomfortable—and one of the simplest ways to avoid things is to put them off" (Piaget & Binkley, 1985, p. 34). Our timetable can specify the times we are to arrive at each station or part-goal, so that we know whether we are on schedule.

7. Can I accept the goal?

This may seem like a rather strange question—not accept a goal we work to achieve? Although we strive for success, we can also fear success. Success can establish a precedent—a standard to be lived up to—and bring on new responsibilities. Success can make others jealous or hostile. In her book *The Impostor Phenomenon*, Pauline Rose Clance (1985) writes about high achievers who behind their false front of confidence are filled with doubt about themselves; despite their success, they remain unsatisfied, reject all praise, and attribute their achievements to almost everything except their own abilities.

On Not Setting Goals

Paradoxically, our goals can get in the way of our progress. For example, college freshmen are frequently under considerable pressure from their parents and themselves to set a vocational goal. But it is a mistake to assume that students entering college are able to make a satisfactory choice, since few know enough about themselves or the vocational world to do so. Research indicates that only a relatively low proportion of students manage to implement their initial career plans (Astin, 1977). Responding to pressure, students may make a vocational commitment prematurely, and if their choice proves not to be a good one, they feel they have failed or wasted their time (Berger, 1993).

The early college years are best regarded as a time for exploration—a time to pursue and test one's interests and to discover new interests, a time to test one's abilities in various courses. A student's conception of her or his abilities is likely to be based on high school experience, but the standards set by high schools and colleges vary widely (Berger, 1993).

Writer James A. Michener (1988) has made an eloquent plea for "wasting time" and for not setting important goals too soon. He spent a good deal of his early adult years knocking around the world and trying to find out what he believed in. He doubts that it is possible for young people to waste time, since all experience can be of use. In his opinion, one has until age 35 to decide on what one wants to do. Something of a laggard himself, he wrote nothing at all until he was 40.

On Resetting Goals

In a fortune cookie I found this sage observation: "Life is what happens while you are making other plans." Experience suggests we consider holding goals lightly, remaining open to modifying or resetting them as circumstances dictate.

Life is full of surprises. Unplanned children appear. Jobs suddenly end. Great opportunities rise before us. Relationships take unexpected turns. The stock market crashes. Our company really takes off. Illness and accidents happen. We constantly are called upon to reconsider our goals and reset them to accord with our changing, waning, waxing fortunes.

Some of our once-in-a-lifetime goals wind up two-timing us. Our marriage vows—"till death do us part"— endure on the average 9.4 years. (We get time off for bad behavior.) But most divorced persons remarry. And if they get divorced again, they remarry again. Current statistics show that about three out of every four divorced women and five out of six divorced men try their marital luck again.

We may spend a lot of time and money for our "lifetime" career, but most of us don't stay in one job till retirement. On the average we shift jobs between five and ten times, although these jobs may still be within the same field (Toffler, 1970). However, a study of one hundred men who were followed from high school to their middle thirties showed that 30 percent had shifted vocational fields completely (Super, 1985).

The setting of goals, or at least long-term goals, becomes a somewhat dubious business in a rapidly changing world. At best, such goals must be considered tentative destinations. When a group of women of the University of Michigan class of 1967 were interviewed before graduation and then again in 1981, they were found to be living lives very different from their original plans. Compared to their expectations, far more were working and had obtained advanced degrees; more were unmarried, and those who did marry had much smaller families than they had expected (Tangri & Jenkins, 1986).

A number of observers on the American scene have noted that our lives, which in earlier generations were "linear," are becoming increasingly "cyclical." The progression of our lives used to be more straightforward: complete our education, get a job, marry, "settle down," raise kids, pay off the mortgage, and ultimately retire. Now people often go back to school in mid-life to train for a new career, or after retirement they go back to get the liberal education that is supposed to be the chief fare of freshmen and sophomores. More about this in the last chapter of this book.

A Hierarchy of Needs or Goals

Abraham Maslow (1970) held that human needs or goals can be arranged in a hierarchy according to their power or prepotence. This hierarchy has five levels: physiological, safety, belongingness or love, esteem, and self-actualization. Ordinarily, the lower, more basic needs must be satisfied before higher ones can emerge (see Box 10.2).[1]

Most prepotent of all requirements are those involving physiological needs. Until these needs are met, we are seldom free to pursue higher ones. As Maslow points out, when we are dangerously hungry, nothing is important except food.

As physiological needs are met, safety needs, which are at the next level of the hierarchy, can emerge. We begin our search for an orderly environment, one in which unpredictable events cannot happen. We employ safeguards and take precautions against danger. We attempt to make ourselves stronger than any adversary, present or potential. Maslow indicates that in our culture most adults feel relatively safe, but needs at this level are expressed in such activities as seeking jobs with tenure, opening savings accounts, and taking out insurance of all kinds.

---

[1] This section is adapted from Arkoff, 1968.

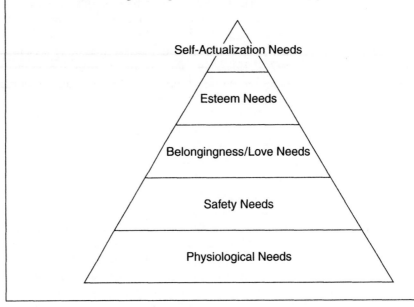

Maslow's Hierarchy of Needs

Abraham Maslow (1970) conceived of human needs or goals as being arranged in a hierarchy according to their power or prepotence. The lower, more basic needs ordinarily must be satisfied in some degree before higher ones can be attended to, and the lower needs are generally better satisfied than the higher ones are.

Self-Actualization Needs

Esteem Needs

Belongingness/Love Needs

Safety Needs

Physiological Needs

Following the satisfaction of physiological and safety needs, love needs may be expressed and attended to. Almost everyone wants to give and to receive affection. We want to be a member of an affectional group and to know and be assured of our place in this group. We need people around us who are important to us and to whom we are important: parents and friends, sweethearts, and then a family of our own.

Esteem needs can emerge when physiological, safety, and love needs have achieved some satisfaction. Esteem needs involve our desire to respect ourselves and to have the respect of others around us. Each of us needs to feel that he or she is a worthy person, one who is well thought of by others. In part, our self-appraisal is based on the opinions of others; it is difficult to respect ourselves if others refuse to take us seriously, laugh at us, or hold us in contempt.

Finally, with the satisfaction of our more basic requirements, the need for self-actualization or fulfillment can find expression, perhaps in such higher-order pursuits as knowledge, truth, justice, and beauty. The patterning of this need varies, depending on the potentialities that each of us has. We may strive for fulfillment in education, athletics, parenthood, art or music, or many other areas.

Generally, as we satisfy our needs at one level of the hierarchy, we may move up and attend to our needs at the next. But one level of need does not have to be completely satisfied before the next-higher need can be attended to. At any particular time, we are likely to be partially satisfied and partially unsatisfied at each level of the hierarchy. The lower the level, the greater our satisfaction is likely to be: at the bottom of the hierarchy our physiological requirements are comparatively well met, but at the top our need for self-actualization is seldom well realized.

As Maslow notes, there are a number of important exceptions to the hierarchy. For example, if early personal relationships are painful, we may attempt to insulate ourselves against love needs. One who has suffered a good deal of deprivation may attempt to live safely and according to minimum essentials. Another person may give little attention to more basic needs as he or she assiduously pursues higher ones. A number of individuals throughout history have sacrificed comfort and safety and even life itself for a particular cause or for other people who were important to them.

Maslow's theory has been widely reported and sometimes uncritically accepted, but there is little clear or consistent supporting evidence (for relevant research and comment, see Mathes, 1981; Mathes & Edwards, 1978; Sappington, 1989; Wahba & Bridwell, 1983). Certainly his theory is provocative, and some questions may come immediately to mind as we think of our own lives in terms of the need hierarchy. Are we living too low in the hierarchy, perhaps slighting love in favor of safety? Are we able to take pride in ourselves? Do we feel fulfilled, and are we making the most—or at least much—of our potentialities? If not, why not? What can we do to move up the hierarchy and make more of our lives?

Dreams as Goals

Mary Groda-Lewis's story is one of those inspirational stories that pop up now and then in such magazines as the *Reader's Digest,* where it indeed appeared some years ago (Blank, 1986). Its title was "Mary's Impossible Dream." Her dream—to become a doctor like one who befriended her—did seem impossible. What she had been was an elementary school dropout, a street fighter, and an inmate of two institutions for juvenile delinquents. What she was, on the brink of adulthood, was dyslexic and unable to read or write and also the unmarried mother of two children. Following the birth of her second child, she suffered five cardiac arrests and a stroke that nearly killed and greatly incapacitated her. Yet (to greatly shorten a remarkable story) she relentlessly pursued her dream, graduated from medical school, and in the process won four awards.

But then there is the quite different story of Uncle Harry, whose account never appeared in any magazine. Uncle Harry (not his real name but some families have a real one) was a dreamer, but none of his dreams managed to come true. Head in the clouds, one failed grand plan after another. His wife took in sewing to support the family. And then one day he died without getting anywhere, and people said how sad but what could you expect from such a dreamer?

How much of a dream dare we dream? How high should we set our goals? Is the sky the limit? Indeed, Ralph Waldo Emerson wrote, "Hitch your wagon to a star." And in the same vein, Robert Browning announced, "Ah, but a man's reach should exceed his grasp/Or what's a Heaven for?" But by contrast there is the Hungarian proverb that says, "Where ambition ends, happiness begins." And Henry Wadsworth Longfellow had a similar thought when he wrote, "Most people would succeed in small things if they were not troubled by great ambitions."

Wendell Johnson (1946) identified a common condition he called the IFD Disease. This is a three-stage disorder of idealization, frustration, and demoralization. It begins with the struggle toward an ideal highly valued but perhaps not very well spelled out or attainable. Failing to attain our ideal and being unwilling to relinquish it, we feel great frustration, and continued frustration brings demoralization. Johnson (who happened to be one of my professors but who, I trust, didn't have me in mind) felt that the IFD disease was particularly high among college students. He noted a study showing that about two out of every three students enrolled at a large Midwestern university were setting out to become doctors or lawyers or to enter some comparable profession. "The crucial fact is," he wrote, "that only one out of 16 university students *can* achieve such an ideal in our society" (p. 10).

In contrast to Johnson, Abraham Maslow (1972) was concerned about our failure to dream and to set high goals. As was noted earlier in this book, Maslow held that many of us fear our highest possibilities; they overwhelm us and make us feel presumptuous. People who have accomplished great things may awe us and make us resentful; we feel inferior by comparison. When we get to know them, we see how very human they are. Maslow believed that if we can undefensively value high qualities in others, we will be able to find and value what's best in ourselves.

We may aim too low because we fear appearing presumptuous or arrogant. But to invent something or create something, Maslow noted, requires a touch of arrogance or at least a considerable pride in oneself, although the pride must be gracefully integrated with humility. There is a relevant Hasidic saying that each person must have two pockets and as necessary reach into one or the other. In one pocket will be the words: "For my sake the world was created!" And in the other: "I am but dust and ashes" (Kopp, 1971).

Many of us enter adulthood with a dream, and this dream or vision of our own future can be a vitalizing force in our development. Levinson and his colleagues (1978), who have been studying the seasons of adult lives, concluded that the individuals under investigation suffered when they moved off in a direction that conflicted with their dreams.

> A man may be pushed in [this conflicting] direction by his parents, by various external constraints, such as lack of money or opportunity, and by various aspects of his personality, such as guilt, passivity, competitiveness and special talents. He may thus succeed in an occupation that holds no interest for him. The conflict may extend over many years, evolving through various forms. Those who betray the Dream in their twenties will have to deal later with the consequences. Those who build a life structure around the Dream in early adulthood have a better chance for personal fulfillment, though years of struggle may be required to maintain the commitment and work toward its realization. (p. 92)

Although dreams are profoundly important, they can be mixed blessings. A dream may promise undying happiness if it is realized and total disaster if it isn't, but neither is likely to be the case. As we go through life, we may rework our dreams, keeping their inspiring qualities but making them more reality-based. Other problems arise when the dreams of several persons whose lives are intertwined are not harmonious. Levinson writes that acknowledging and managing dream disparities are crucial problems in the relationship between lovers and spouses. If in supporting the dream of one, they deny the dream of the other, both may later pay a price.

Certainly life without a dream can be a drab thing. But life with a truly impossible dream can be devastating. A dream can enslave us or guide us or inspire us. A dream can be a substitute for action or a prelude to action. Voltaire lamented, "My life's dream has been a perpetual nightmare." But George Bernard Shaw wrote, "You see things; and you say 'Why?' But I dream things that never were; and I say 'Why not?' "

No one was more moved by a dream than was Martin Luther King, Jr., and his dream—so eloquently expressed—moved many others. "I have a dream," he told 200,000 people assembled at the Lincoln Memorial one August day in 1963. "I have a dream that one day this nation will rise up and live out the meaning of its creed: 'We hold these truths to be self-evident; that all men are created equal.' "

> ### Box 10.3
>
> # The American Dream
>
> As a reachable goal, the American Dream of happiness and prosperity, liberty and equality has been more myth than reality for many throughout the years of our republic, but it is still very much alive. In a survey conducted by the Roper Organization for the *Wall Street Journal* in 1987, two out of every three respondents reported that the American Dream was more than a phrase and had real meaning for them. Furthermore, most believed that the Dream was largely attainable; with the Dream anchoring 10 on a 1 to 10 scale, the respondents, on the average, estimated themselves currently at 5.8 and anticipated eventually getting to 8.2. The persons were also asked to indicate which items on a list were very much a part of what they understood the Dream to mean or sort of what it meant or not what it meant. The list below shows the percentage of the respondents who indicated an item was "very much" what the Dream meant to them.
>
> | | |
> |---|---|
> | 84% | To be able to get a high school education |
> | 80 | To have freedom of choice in how to live one's life |
> | 78 | To own a home |
> | 77 | To be able to send one's children to college |
> | 68 | To be able to get a college education |
> | 64 | To be financially secure enough to have ample time for leisure pursuits |
> | 61 | To do better than one's parents did |
> | 58 | To be able to start a business on one's own |
> | 52 | To be able to rise from clerk or worker to president of a company |

In his speech, Reverend King said that his dream was deeply rooted in the American Dream. The American Dream—what is that? Traditionally it has meant happiness and prosperity, liberty and equality. To learn what the American Dream more specifically means to Americans today, see Box 10.3. And then, for some information about the American *Day*dream, see Box 10.4.

Barbara Sher is a therapist who encourages people not to give up their "impossible" dreams. In her book *Wishcraft* (written with Annie Gottlieb), she advises, "If you're deeply in love with a goal you're sure is impossible, don't become bitter about 'what might have been' and consider your life wasted. Ask yourself, *what is the touchstone?* Why do I want this goal?" (1979, p. 75). The touch-

© BRILLIANT ENTERPRISES, 1974   POT-SHOTS NO 572
                                       Ashleigh
                                       Brilliant

TO BE SURE
OF HITTING
THE TARGET,

SHOOT FIRST

AND, WHATEVER YOU HIT,
CALL IT THE TARGET.

Box 10.4

The American Daydream

Daydreams may be flights of fancy, satisfying in themselves, or they can be a preliminary part of our goal-setting, goal-reaching behavior. A Roper survey conducted in 1989 presented the respondents with a list of daydreamable items and asked them to designate those that were subjects of their daydreams or thoughts. The percentage of the respondents designating each item is shown below (multiple responses were accepted).

49%	Being rich
44	World travel
32	Being smarter
32	Seeing your future
29	Having a better job
24	Things in the past
23	Living in another part of the world
23	Having an important person back
19	Living a different life
18	Living in past time
16	Being great artist, etc.
16	Being famous
14	Knowing more people
13	Being friends with someone you admire
11	Being handsome/beautiful
11	Romance with handsome/beautiful star
11	Having power/influence
10	Being a great athlete
9	Being involved with media
8	Getting even with someone
4	Being elected to office

stone (a concept presented earlier in this chapter) is what one needs from the goal. Once you understand the touchstone, you can design a reachable goal that will provide you with what you need. And you can start with what Sher calls a "first target," "a smaller goal that's both a step on the road to your ultimate destination and a little triumph in its own right" (p. 71).

Psychologists have studied the varying effects of distal (far) and proximate (near) goals. Our dreams generally concern a distant future, and they may be too far removed in time to provide effective incentive. By establishing more proximate subgoals—targets with rewards along the way—we motivate ourselves and also provide ourselves with measures of progress and proof of capability.

As we achieve one subgoal and then another, our confidence in our ability rises, and our larger goal will appear more and more achievable. Even if we never realize our ultimate dream, we may achieve much more than we otherwise might have achieved (Bandura, 1989a). Ironically, in this way we may fall short of our dream but still attain more than we dreamed we could.

Many persons are defeated before they start because they focus on their end or far goal (for example, becoming a physician), which indeed seems dim and distant, instead of focusing on the next subgoal (perhaps raising the grade point average this semester) and celebrating it when it is reached. There is an account of a bright but unmotivated college dropout who was working as a hospital orderly. He decided to become a doctor but was dismayed when an academic counselor outlined the required steps. "My God," the dropout said. "I'm 25 now. I'll be 27 when I finish my undergraduate work, 31 when I get my medical degree, 32 when I finish my internship, and 35 by the time I complete my residency." He sighed and then said again, with emphasis, "I'll be 35!" "Well," asked the counselor in a gentle voice, "how old will you be in ten years if you don't become a doctor?"

Why Goals Fail

There is an old saying, "Be careful what you wish for, you might get it." Not infrequently we work hard and reach a goal only to find it's not what we thought it would be. Somehow it doesn't provide the satisfaction or happiness we expected. We got the job we worked for or the mate we sought or the home we wanted, and we were supposed to be happy ever after, weren't we? Below are some reasons that our goals sometimes fail.

Goals in Fantasy Don't Match Goals in Reality

We frequently feel a letdown after reaching an earnestly longed-for and fervently sought goal. Instead of being on top of the world, we may feel curiously unmoved, maybe even down in the dumps. One of the reasons is that the goal close up is somehow not what we thought it would be or fantasized it would be.

We create our fantasies to suit ourselves and invest them with considerable power. In fantasy we can create goals without flaws, goals that contain the solution to all our problems. We think to ourselves, "Everything will be all right once I get into graduate school, or get my new nose, or get a place of my own, or land this great job, or get married, or get divorced, or survive cancer five years, or maybe after I've had therapy." Then we get into that graduate school (or get that new nose) only to find it's not the great happy ending but only the beginning of a new set of problems—although perhaps a better set than the last one. Psychotherapy, we find, won't solve our problems, although it can help us deal more effectively with them. Maybe we had expected to be rescued from a larger predicament and saved once and for all, but real-life rescues more often put us back on shore rather than on top of the mountain, and they hardly match our fantasies.

Recall the seedthought in Chapter 4 (Box 4.1) concerning major lottery winners. Winning huge amounts of money appeared to produce no significant gains in happiness (although no winner offered to give back the money). Yet what fantasies we spin as we buy our lottery tickets or fill out the incessant flow of win-five-million-dollars coupons (or is it ten million?) from *Reader's Digest* or the Publishers Clearing House. We think once we win this lottery or once our name is picked in this drawing . . .

Just as goals once attained may disappoint us because they fail to match our fantasies, fears that become realities often prove to be not as bad as they were imagined. The research team that studied the lottery winners also studied a group of paraplegics who had been paralyzed in accidents. When these paraplegics were asked to rate their present happiness on a scale running from 0 ("not at all") to 5 ("very much"), with a midpoint of 2.5, they achieved a mean of approximately 3. This score did not match the happiness ratings of a control group or those of the lottery winners (both achieved a mean of approximately 4), but it was considerably higher than might have been expected (Brickman, Coates, & Janoff-Bulman, 1978). Taken together, these findings suggest that the roses in real life come with thorns and that among the thorns of life we may find some roses.

Explicit Goals Don't Meet Implicit Needs

A second reason our goals fail to satisfy us is that they don't meet our *implicit needs,* those that are not clearly defined or even fully understood. Since we may be largely unaware of these needs, we do not consider them in our goal-setting processes. Many of us have never been taught or given permission to do something about what we want for ourselves. Instead, we have been impressed by what we should want or what others want for us.

Barbara Forisha (1978) presents the case of "Edward," a young man who was "persuaded" to be someone other than who he was and to pursue goals that were not his own. An only boy in a family of three children, he learned to read early and was fascinated by books, but his parents were concerned because he was so quiet and had no inclination toward sports. His father was delighted when Edward became a "sports freak" in the fourth grade. Edward's story, in part, appears below:

> I found I liked to play and I was good at it. You should have seen my father eat it up. At last he had that son to play catch with! I don't think anything was so strongly reinforced as my enthusiasm for sports. My coaches and my father worshipped victory. To win was the only acceptable outcome of competition. To lose was to be damned, to be weak, to be less of a man. My grade-school football coach was the biggest blowhard of this crap I have ever met; his quest for victory was an obsession and his fear of defeat was neurotic. He kicked and ranted, he raved and all but killed us, but we won. Thank God!

> The competitive ethic learned in sports was carried into the academic and the social spheres in high school. We were taught to thrive on competition and achievement. Failure was not to be tolerated. I was taught the school conception of what it is to be a man. I was to be intelligent and extremely logical in all circumstances. I was to be a leader who helped those less fortunate. I was to be strong and support the weak. I was to strive continually for mental, physical, and spiritual greatness. In short, I was to be godlike.

> A man also was supposed to be a great lover and to have good-looking girlfriends. He was also supposed to be able to kick the shit out of anyone who crossed him. Great respect was given to the victor of a fight.

> A lot of emphasis was placed on the future acquisition of status symbols such as Eldorados, mansions, and of course a harem of the world's most desirable women. . . .

> I was sucked into this achievement vacuum of my own volition. I could feel its pull, which received extensive positive reinforcement from my family, my girlfriend, her parents, and my peer group. I am now slowly fighting the suction power of this vacuum and beginning to surface with a clearer, more autonomous outlook on life. . . . Right now I feel light, almost high, as if weight has been taken off my mind and body. I don't feel pressured anymore to be "masculine," to be a Rock of Gibraltar, a pillar of strength, aggressive, logical, analytic, argumentative, competitive. . . . I feel like a baby discovering himself for the first time. (pp. 14–15)

Forisha commented that Edward's life had been ruled by an ethic stressing achievement at any cost. It was an ethic shaped for him by others. She adds, "Now at last he . . . is beginning to determine his own needs and to discover who he is" (pp. 14–15).

Our *explicit needs*—those that are clearly defined and understood—are often those on which there is general accord. If everyone I know is planning to go to college, or planning not to go to college, well then, that must be what I want to do. If almost everyone seems attracted to the opposite sex . . . If almost everyone wants a spouse, home, and children . . . If almost everyone retires at 65 . . .

Besides being generally shared, our explicit goals are frequently supposed-to-do or ought-to-do goals. But off-the-rack and one-size-fits-everyone goals are often a poor fit. To quote again the sadder-but-wiser participant in Warren Farrell's men's group quoted in Chapter 3: "I feel like I've spent 40 years of my life working as hard as I can to become someone I don't even like."

It's surprising how uninformed our explicit goals sometimes are. For example, many college students have little information about the actual hour-by-hour, day-by-day activities of the occupations for which they are preparing. In one study, for example, undergraduates were asked to state specifically what they would do in the occupation for which they were preparing, and many were unable to do so. The students offered such hazy statements as: "I will talk with people." "I will deal with people." "I will attend committee meetings." "I will help people and answer the questions they bring to me." When the interviewers attempted to get more specific information, the students expressed embarrassment, annoyance, and hostility (Beardslee & O'Dowd, 1962; O'Dowd & Beardslee, 1960).

One way to begin to test our explicit goals is to live them out in our imagination (Sher & Gottlieb, 1979; Kriegel & Kriegel, 1984). If you would like to explore this method, begin by getting into a relaxed posture. Close your eyes and take three deep breaths, holding each succeeding breath a little longer than the last. As you let out each breath, tell yourself "Relax." When you feel relaxed, imagine you have reached your goal. In your mind's eye, picture yourself (or just think of yourself) as having attained what you seek. Where are you? How do you look? Who are you with? What are you doing? How does it feel? Don't try to create the scene; just let it create itself. Watch it as if you were watching a movie or a play unfold. See what your imagination has to say to you about the goal.

The Ability to Achieve Exceeds Ability to Enjoy

A third reason why goals fail is that we can be better at setting and reaching them than at enjoying them. We may be future-captured beings, always trying to get ourselves to a better place and then a better place. We can't stop to enjoy the goal, because it is just a way station on the climb to a better goal. And then, of course, there is a better goal after that—somewhere in the future.

If we are captured by the future, we can work so hard on "getting there" that we are scarcely "here." Focused on tomorrow, we may lose today. The trick is to get "there" while being "here." To quote again the anonymous philosopher whose "rules for being human" were presented in Chapter 3 (Box 3.8), " 'There' is no better than 'here.' When your 'there' has become a 'here' you will simply obtain another 'there' that will, again, look better than 'here.' "

If we are not future-captured, we may be security-captured beings—always needing a little bit more and then a little bit more in order to feel safe. How can we enjoy what might be lost or taken away? In order to have enough, we must have too much, but almost no amount may be too much.

Others of us may be guilt-ridden. We don't feel we really deserve what we achieve. How can we enjoy what we don't deserve? Or our success may make us anxious as we stand apart and above the crowd. Others may snipe at us or expect too much of us or be delighted to see us fail next time. After all, the higher you climb, the farther you fall.

Hardscrabble living turns some of us into expert strugglers, and struggling can become a way of life. We expect life to be hard, and we find it hard, or we make it hard. Banished from the Garden of Eden, we expect to eat our bread in the sweat of our brows, and we are not surprised that there is never jam today.

Hardscrabble living can also turn some of us into expert non-enjoyers. Psychologist Dorothy Rowe (1982) recalls asking one of her clients if she thought she deserved to be happy. "Happy," it appeared, was not in her client's vocabulary: she replied, "I don't think I ought to be comfortable." Another of Rowe's clients, when asked how she had enjoyed a family party in which everything had gone well, replied, "I didn't enjoy it as much as I ought to have enjoyed it." She at least sensed something was missing in her response to life (p. 176).

The Pursuit of Relief Doesn't Lead to Delight

A fourth reason goals fail to satisfy us—or, better yet, fail to delight us—is that we have not put ourselves on the road to delight.[2] Maybe the most we expect to get in life is occasional relief. Frank Dougherty (1988) has made a useful distinction between the pursuit of relief and the pursuit of delight. In pursuing relief, we overcome a deficit in some area and bring ourselves up to zero, while the pursuit of delight starts at a zero and can be a blast-off into higher reaches of joy.

When we are caught up in the pursuit of relief, we are busy (as college students often seem to be) getting required things "out of the way," or putting things in order, or making sure everything is in its place or under control or taken care of. And when everything is in order or in its place or under control or taken care of, do we feel delight? No, only relief—we've gotten ourselves out of the minus zone but only up to zero.

To be fair, there are times, as Dougherty notes, "when relief is both necessary and rewarding—even vital!" (p. 267). Eating when you are very hungry, drinking when you are very thirsty, relieving yourself after a long wait to get to the restroom—these acts can be accompanied by a surge of pleasant sensation. But this sensation is short-lived and soon replaced by bland zeroness.

When we are caught up in the pursuit of delight, our mind-set is entirely different. We have set ourselves to appreciate and relish and enjoy. We can find things to enjoy everywhere—maybe the very things the person seeking relief is doing but with a very different mind-set. It can be as simple as the difference between wolfing down our food or taking time to enjoy it, or the difference between ignoring the flowers as we rush to a destination or letting their beauty move us.

The healthiest people not only seek pleasure; they also expect and create it. They simply anticipate that there will be pleasure in much of what they do. For such people, pleasure proves twice rewarding: first, enjoyment, and second, better health (Ornstein & Sobel, 1989).

An illustration of the difference between the pursuit of relief and the pursuit of delight was given by one of my students in his recollection of a recent group backpacking trip. Each night a particular member of the group was always first to get to the place where they would camp. One evening the group was discussing some of the breathtaking vistas of the day, and this person finally spoke up and said, "All I really saw today was the top of my shoes."

Here's the bad news and the good news according to Dougherty. Bad news first: no amount of relief will produce delight. "Solve every problem in your life, satisfy every need, and soon as one is relieved another takes its place. There's no end to it. You can't get to delight from relief" (p. 268). Now the good news: problems need not be a barrier to delight. Delight has to do with the space the mind is in—with one's point of view—not with external conditions. Persons on the road to delight handle their relief problem more easily and simply as they bounce

---

[2]   This section is adapted from Arkoff, 1988.

Box 10.5

The Pursuit of Relief and the Pursuit of Delight

When we pursue relief, we perceive a deficit in some area, and our goal is to correct it. In effect, we start at some minus point and get ourselves up to zero. Sometimes there may be a burst of release or excitement above zero as we accomplish our goal, but it doesn't last very long.

When we pursue delight, we are in a different mind-set entirely. We start at zero, and the sky's the limit. If things don't work out, there may be a burst of disappointment, but we're soon back to zero and ready to look up again. Some of us live our lives as if relief were the only reality. We focus on the endless weeds that must be picked (when they are, we give a sigh of, yes, relief) but seldom take time to delight in the flowers.

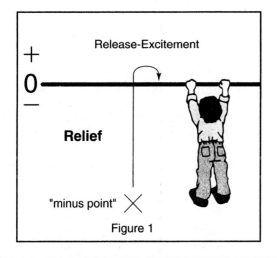

Figure 1

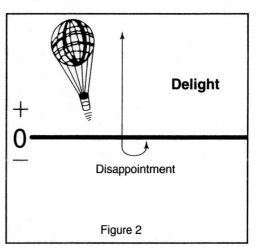

Figure 2

(Source: Frank Dougherty, 1988)

along. Children have the ability to make the most of life's pleasures. Dougherty's advice is that we reawaken the little kid in ourselves.

The Ultimate Goal

When we consider our goals, we often think first of what we want to *have* or *do* rather than what we want to *be*. We think that once we *have* enough money, we will be able to *do* what we want, and then we will *be* happy. Or once we *have* our degree and license, we will be able to *do* the work we want to do, and then we will *be* all set and secure.

Happiness, security, and peace of mind are commonly desired states of "being" and it's commonly thought that one brings them about by "having." These states, we may think, await us at the top of life's staircase—that place where we finally have enough—and we climb up step by step to reach them. But some who arrive at what seems to be the top find themselves no happier or more secure than before. And some find joy or peace of mind without taking a step.

My wife leads tour groups to China. Most of the persons in her groups are retired folks who have waited and saved all their lives to do some extended traveling. Most prove to be happy travelers, but there are a few who fuss and stew and don't seem to be able to enjoy anything. I suspect the happy folks were happy

before—they had learned how to *be* happy—while the fussy folks had practiced their fussiness during much of their traveling through life.

Individuals can make themselves miserable almost without regard for what they have or don't have. And, in the same way, they can make themselves unmiserable and beyond that—happy. They can create their state of mind. At every moment of our waking day, we have the opportunity to practice how we want to be by the thoughts we choose to think, the beliefs we choose to adopt, and the attitudes we choose to take. Does it make sense to go out in *frantic* pursuit of those things we believe will ultimately make us more *serene?* Does it make sense to create an *unhappy* life for ourselves as we seek to accumulate those things we believe someday will make us *happy?*

We find it difficult to remain unaffected by what we do. Our means and ends are so entangled that in changing one we change the other. In narrating his own life, Ken Wilber (1982) writes, "I used to think that one adopted a path just to get to a goal. I have learned better: The true path is itself the ultimate goal" (p. 89).

Carlos Castaneda's Indian mentor, don Juan, told him much the same thing, and we noted that earlier in this book. Rather than "true path," don Juan used the term "path with a heart." If we are on a path with a heart, he said, we would have a joyful journey; if not, we would come to curse our life.

How can you know if your path is true? How can you know if your path has a heart? It has a heart if in your travels each day you are the person you want to be. It has a heart if each evening you can say to yourself, "I like who I was today." It has a heart if each evening—regardless of your progress or lack of it since morning—you can say to yourself, "I traveled well today."

Jesus said, "For what is a man advantaged, if he gain the whole world, and lose himself, and be cast away?" (Luke 9:24–25). The ultimate goal, then, is not to lose ourselves along the way. The ultimate goal is to be who we want to be as we become who we want to become as we live our lives. Walk a true path, a path with a heart.

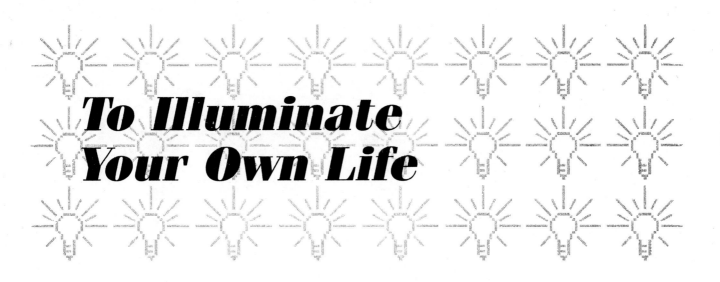

To Illuminate Your Own Life

*Anchor and Apply**

1. Concerning one of your most important goals, ask and answer the seven questions in the section of the chapter on setting goals.

2. Make (a) a list of your important goals, (b) identifying the "touchstone" of each (see pp. 304 and 311–312) and (c) also, if possible, in each case suggesting a substitute goal that might provide some of the same satisfaction.

3. Describe any seemingly aimless periods of your life or any "knocking around" you have done. Was this wasted time? Why or why not?

4. Describe your own life in terms of Maslow's hierarchy of needs or goals. How satisfied are you at each level of the hierarchy? What are you doing to increase your satisfaction?

5. Do you have a dream or vision of your future that serves as a vitalizing force for you? If so, discuss this aspect of your life.

6. What does the "American Dream" mean to you? How much of this Dream have you achieved? How much do you expect to achieve? Why?

7. Describe your daydreams and the part they play in your life.

8. Test one of your explicit goals by living it out in your imagination and writing down the results, including what you learned from this exercise. (See instructions on p. 315.)

9. How much of your life is a pursuit of relief? How much is a pursuit of delight? Discuss this aspect of your life and your satisfaction or lack of satisfaction from it.

10. Does your current path in life "have a heart"? Discuss this aspect of your journey through life.

* These "anchor and apply" items are designed to help you use the concepts of the chapter as stimuli to prompt new or deeper or clearer insights into yourself and your life. To respond to an item first find the material in the chapter that is most relevant to the item *and* yourself; that's called "anchoring." Second, think about this material in relationship to yourself and your life and keep thinking about it until you arrive at a new or deeper or clearer understanding; that's the "apply" or application part. When you write or present your response to the item, be sure to include both parts, that is, both the anchor material and the application. You can know you are successful on an item if, in completing it, you truly learn something new or understand something better.

Little Joys

In reading the Talmud (a collection of comments on Hebrew laws and teachings), one expects to be reminded of one's sometimes heavy obligations. However, I was rather startled to find in one place the reminder that I had a duty to enjoy myself. There, indeed, some sage had written what has become my favorite warning: "Man will be called to account in the hereafter for all the God-given pleasures that he failed to enjoy."

One of the most sought-after or wished-for goals is happiness. When people are asked what they want in life, they frequently answer that they want to be happy or to have the things that will bring happiness. When they are asked what they want for those they love, they often answer in the same way: they want their loved ones to be happy or to find happiness.

Life is filled with opportunities for happiness, and many of these opportunities cost little or nothing. In an essay "on little joys," written in 1905, Hesse pointed out that these little joys are liberally scattered throughout our daily rounds if we pause to take advantage of them. The enemy of these joys is the hurried pace of life, including, ironically, the frantic pursuit of entertainment. Although written at the turn of this century, Hesse's words seem remarkably appropriate for today.

George Leonard (1989) recommends the Zen strategy for finding joy in the commonplace. What this strategy requires is not a change of activity but, rather, a change of attitude. "You might think that the value of Zen practice lies in the unwavering apprehension of the present moment while sitting motionless. But a visit to a Zen retreat quickly reveals that potentially, *everything* is a meditation—building a stone wall, eating, walking from one place to another, sweeping a hallway" (p. 156).

Psychologist Ed Diener (quoted in Adler, 1989) found that people who experience frequent little joys (positive emotions) tend to be happier than those who experience an occasional big joy (*intense* positive emotions). Intense emotions apparently do not promote a general sense of well-being because they occur infrequently, are often purchased at the price of past unhappy events, and can serve to diminish one's pleasure in less intense positive events. Thus, Diener, Leonard, and Hesse agree that the key to well-being is to fill one's days with little joys.

The Chinese philosopher Lin Yutang (1975) passionately described the little joys that made his own life joyful. Indeed, there were many, and in his enthusiasm he gave a number of them first place on his list. For example, he wrote, "If there is a greater happiness than lying in the sun, I'd like to be told." But then he noted, "If a man will be sensible and . . . count on his fingers how many things give him enjoyment, invariably he will find food is the first one." But again, seemingly to settle the matter, he set down the final truth: "If one's bowels move, one is happy, and if they don't move, one is unhappy. That is all there is to it."

Boyd Ray's (Mountain City, Tenn.) Joy List

These are the things I deeply enjoy.

1. Watching the sunrise
2. Watching the sunset
3. Watching it rain
4. Watching it snow
5. Watching the fire in my fireplace
6. Sitting on the patio and watching the fields and valleys and mountains change with the shadows as the sun moves across the sky
7. Making love to a lovely woman
8. Reading poetry, fiction, history, science, politics, religion
9. Watching news on TV
10. Watching a few programs on TV
11. Looking at good quality cattle
12. Having a spirited conversation with a knowledgeable person on a subject of interest to both of us
13. Sitting on the patio in the evening with a companion—preferably a woman
14. Giving a flower to a lovely woman and watching her eyes light up
15. Looking at the flowers on my kitchen table
16. Browsing antique shops
17. Walking around the shopping mall with a friend and just looking
18. Cooking—sometimes
19. Mowing the lawn
20. Riding out in the fields and checking my cattle
21. The view from the hill in the back of my farm
22. The cozy heat from the wood stove in the basement on a cold winter day
23. Mowing hay
24. Looking at—and feeling proud of—the many afghans and quilts my mother made and gave to me
25. Driving a good, responsive car on a curvy mountain road
26. Watching football and basketball on TV
27. Watching the Olympics on TV (I get so proud of our talented youngsters)
28. Listening to the crows fuss and call from the woods and fields
29. Listening to good music—piano, mood, country, classical
30. Taking an interesting woman to dinner and the theatre
31. Sitting on the couch in front of the fireplace (with a fire in it) and holding hands and rubbing noses with a lovely woman
32. Keeping my farmstead up—mending buildings, fences, roads, etc., making it look good
33. Talking to my children on the phone and finding them all right
34. Attending high school and college reunions

Sol Gordon (1975) tells us that we can be happy in an unhappy world if we can intensely or deeply enjoy at least the number of things equal to our age. His own list of fifty-one items, drawn up when he was 51 years old, contains such items as Mozart, nature (but not too much at a time), walks, reading slowly the good novelists, sex, and remembering his mother's expressions like "How can good food be bad for you?" A list constructed by a 64-year-old man in one of my Elderhostel workshops (a program for persons age 60 and above) is presented in Box 10.6; it's quite a remarkable list and not only because the word "chocolate" does not appear in it once. My oldest and indeed most lively and full-of-joy student was 91 years of age when she was in a workshop with me, and she had no trouble constructing a list of ninety-one items.

One of my very dear friends was a man whom I met when we were both working as volunteers with hospice patients. When he became terminally ill himself, he asked me to work with him, which I did until he died. We taught each other a lot, and one of the things he taught me was a poem that had come to be

35. Going to see plays, concerts, etc. at the local area college and university

36. Drawing house plans for especially interesting building sites

37. Construction of buildings—houses, barns, etc.

38. Eating at church suppers or dinners on the grounds

39. Going to the grocery store (supermarket) and bumping into old friends and making new ones

40. Flirting with the pretty girls at the cash registers and counters at the supermarkets and stores

41. Telling after-dinner jokes at banquets, dinner programs, etc.

42. Taking an afternoon nap on the couch

43. Wearing my cowboy boots

44. Wearing my cowboy hat

45. A good songfest

46. Playing bridge—sometimes

47. Driving through the country roads and just looking at the countryside

48. Sitting *alone* on the patio and thinking

49. Joining a group such as Elderhostel once in awhile

50. Standing on a bridge and watching the water run under it

51. Watching the moon rise on a clear, cold night in the fall when the moon is full

52. Watching the herd of deer in the back fields of my farm

53. Watching the flock of Canadian geese, raised by my neighbor, fly around and hearing them honking

54. Talking and visiting with my son and grandson

55. *Taking* presents to friends at Christmas time (it's much more personal than sending them by mail)

56. Being a part of the community life by serving on the Industrial Commission and taking square dance lessons and attending the annual dinners of the Chamber of Commerce and other such programs

57. Eating popcorn at a movie or, for that matter, while at home watching football on TV

58. Encouraging people to tell me more about themselves

59. Sidewalk art exhibits

60. Craft shows

61. Standing in the barn and listening to the rain fall on the metal roof

62. Standing in the barn loft—after feeding hay to about 100 cattle—and listening to them crunch or munch the hay

63. Looking at the frost on a cold autumn morning and then watching the fields turn green again as the sun melts the frost away

64. After a hard, tiring day outside, a drink of good straight bourbon sour mash whiskey, mixed with a little 7-Up and cranberry juice

Calvin and Hobbes   by Bill Watterson

very meaningful to him. He didn't know the poet, and I'm not sure I remember the poem correctly, but it went something like this:

> Once little cares annoyed me
> (When little cares were few),
>
> And one fly in the ointment
> Would make me fret and stew.
>
> Now my life has taught me
> Each little joy to prize,
>
> And I delight to find some ointment
> In my little jar of flies.

What joys has life taught you to prize? What are the things that you deeply enjoy? This is your opportunity to call them to mind. As you do, write them down as indicated on the next page.

My List of Joys

Below are the things I deeply enjoy. (Number each item as you list it, and don't stop until you have at least as many items as you are years old. Add another page if you need more room. When your list is complete—but not before!—turn to the next page.)

Go through your joy list and put a check (✔) in front of each item you have actually enjoyed in the past thirty days. (What good is an opportunity for joy if you don't take advantage of it?) Then, in the space immediately below, answer these questions: (1) How important a goal is joy or happiness for you? (2) Are you satisfied with the amount of joy in your life? Why or why not? (3) What did you learn from constructing and checking your joy list?

Little Dream, Big Dream

Wendell Johnson (1946), in his book *People in Quandaries,* identified an ailment he called the IFD disease. He lamented that many of us use a high degree of *idealization* in setting our goals. When we find we can't achieve our ideals, we suffer *frustration,* and constant frustration ends in *demoralization.* Thus: Idealization → Frustration → Demoralization.

By contrast, Abraham Maslow (1972) suggested that many of us do not dream a large enough dream. In his estimation, we fear our own greatness and run away from our best talents:

> We are generally afraid to become that which we can glimpse in our most perfect moments, under the most perfect conditions, under conditions of greatest courage. . . . I have found it easy to demonstrate this to my students simply by asking, "Which of you in this class hopes to write the great American novel, or to be a Senator, or Governor, or President? Who wants to be Secretary-General of the United Nations? Or a great composer? Who aspires to be a saint, like Schweitzer, perhaps? Who among you will be a great leader?" Generally everybody starts giggling, blushing, and squirming until I ask, "If not you, then who else?" Which of course is the truth. And in this same way, as I push my graduate students toward these higher levels of aspiration, I'll say, "What great book are you now secretly planning to write?" And then they often blush and stammer and push me off in some way. But why should I not ask that question? Who else will write the books on psychology except psychologists? So I can ask, "Do you not plan to be a psychologist?" "Well, yes." "Are you in training to be a mute or inactive psychologist? What's the advantage of that? That's not a good path to self-actualization. No, you must want to be a first-class psychologist, meaning the best, the very best you are capable of becoming. If you deliberately plan to be less than you are capable of being, then I warn you that you'll be deeply unhappy for the rest of your life. You will be evading your own capacities, your own possibilities." (p. 36)

A dream can be a substitute for action or it can be a prelude to action. "The Secret Life of Walter Mitty"—James Thurber's classic short story—describes a life that substitutes imagination for action. Mitty escapes his trivial, boring, henpecked existence in his daydreams. In this "secret life" he becomes a heroic figure and triumphant in the most extreme situations. A real-life person who made her dream a prelude, goad, and guide to action is Francie Berger. Fascinated by Lego building bricks as a child, she built bigger and bigger houses of them and even tried to get the manufacturer to sell her two million standard red blocks. She later majored in architecture and upon graduation prevailed upon the Lego company to hire her for a job that didn't exist. Now she is doing just what she dreamed of—designing and building Lego models (and also supervising a staff of assistants).

Below are five areas of life concerning which we sometimes have a dream or goal. For each of these areas, now dream a little dream and a BIG DREAM. The little dream might be what you can realistically expect to attain in this area. The BIG DREAM might represent the most you can hope for or imagine when, indeed, you stretch your hopes and imagination to their absolute limits. After you have dreamed your dreams and written them in the spaces indicated, turn to the next page.

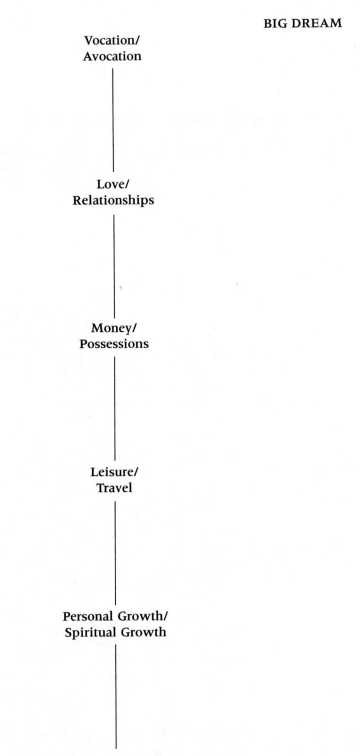

little dream   BIG DREAM

Vocation/
Avocation

Love/
Relationships

Money/
Possessions

Leisure/
Travel

Personal Growth/
Spiritual Growth

In the space below, indicate (1) what you learned from your little dreams and BIG DREAMS and (2) the effect of your dreams (or the absence or abandonment of them) on your life.

Five Lives

If you had five lives, how would you live each of them? Note that this doesn't necessarily mean who would you be if you could be five different people. It means who would you be if you could be five different versions of yourself—you five times over—each time developing some interest, need, talent, or potentiality to its fullest.

Barbara Sher, whose book *Wishcraft* (written with Annie Gottlieb, 1979) provides this exploration, has this to say about the five lives she would choose for herself: "In one of my lives, I'd be exactly what I am. In one I'd be nineteenth-century botanist and spend all my time painting flowers. In another I'd be a theoretical physicist. In my fourth, I'd be Judy Garland—no, something a little less intense and tragic: a musical-comedy star! In my fifth, I'd be a hermit and live alone on an island and write" (p. 84).

In the space below, describe the five lives you would choose for yourself, and in each case indicate why. Then turn to the next page. (You can choose fewer than five lives or more than five if you wish.)

According to Sher, if we each plan our one life well, no important interest, need, talent, or potentiality would go unfulfilled. We could roll all five lives into one. We might, for instance, adopt sequential goals—going from life to life, so to speak, having one vocation or lifestyle and then moving along to a very different one. Or we might try time sharing; an example would be the business woman who spends her evening and weekends painting. Another possibility would be alternating pursuits, such as taking a sabbatical now and then from one's regular work to do something very different. Some of us might be able to blend all our interests into a single pursuit.

In the space below, devise a plan that would allow you to incorporate all the important aspects of your five lives into the one life you are now leading—that is, a plan rolling all five lives into your present one.

Question 11

Coping

How Do I Manage Stress, Threat, and Challenge?

Somewhere in my office files, there is a cartoon that—like so many things I've carefully saved—I can't seem to locate again (except occasionally by mistake). Anyway, as I recall, it shows two drivers who have bashed fenders, and one driver is shaking a fist at the other, who calmly replies: "My wife just ran off with my best friend, the IRS says I owe them more money than I made last year, my doctor tells me I have to give up alcohol and tobacco and lose 40 pounds, and when I came home last night, my dog bit me. And now you say that *you* are going to make trouble for me!"

"Life," Kathleen Norris says, "is easier to take than you'd think; all that is necessary is to accept the impossible, do without the indispensable and bear the intolerable." That's a pessimist speaking, but there's no doubt that life is filled with stress. *Stress* refers to any event in which the demands made upon us tax our ability to cope (Monat & Lazarus, 1985). The demands (or *stressors*, as they are sometimes called) may be environmental—for example, a flood or the insistence of another person, group, or institution that certain requirements be met. Or the demands may be internal: a runner's attempt to beat his own record or a student's efforts to get a high grade point. In many situations, there is a complex interweaving of environmental and internal demands: the student sets out to get high grades to maintain her self-esteem (internal) and to keep her scholarship (external).

Coping refers to our efforts to manage or master stressful situations. When Rose Kennedy was asked how she managed to keep going despite the considerable tragedies her family had suffered, she replied, "I cope" (Kleinke, 1991). We cope as we try to overcome our frustrations and reach our goals. We cope as we move to resolve our conflicts so that we can get out of stuck places. We cope as we wind our way through a daily welter of hassles.

Our lives are frequently filled with stress, and stress can wear us out or wear us down. Stress has been held to be the main cause or the major contributing cause of 75 percent of all illness (Brown, 1984).

Although "stress" is a word that frequently receives bad press, not all stress is bad. In fact, a life without stress would be scarcely imaginable or even worth

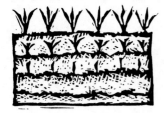

Box 11.1

Coping: How Do I Manage Stress, Threat, and Challenge?

Seedthoughts

1. What on earth would a man do with himself if something did not stand in his way?

    —*H. G. Wells*

2. Bad times have a scientific value. These are occasions that a good learner would not miss.

    —*Ralph Waldo Emerson*

3. It may be that when we no longer know what to do that we have come to our real work, and when we no longer know which way to go we have begun our real journey. The mind that is not baffled is not employed. The impeded stream is the one that sings.

    —*Wendell Berry*

4. To the ordinary man, everything that happens to him is either a curse or a blessing. To a warrior, each thing is a challenge.

    —*Carlos Castenada*, The Teachings of Don Juan

5. What doesn't kill me, makes me stronger.

    —*Friedrich Wilhelm Nietzsche*

6. The worst obstacle is our own self-limiting beliefs.

    —*Jean Bolen*

7. If you sometimes get discouraged, consider this fellow:
    He dropped out of grade school.
    Ran a country store.
    Went broke.
    Took 15 years to pay off his bills.
    Took a wife. Unhappy marriage.
    Ran for House. Lost twice.
    Ran for Senate. Lost twice.
    Delivered speech that became a classic.
    Audience indifferent.
    Attacked daily by the press and despised by half the country.
    Despite all this, imagine how many people all over the world have been inspired by this awkward, rumpled, brooding man who signed his name simply
    A. Lincoln.

    —*author unknown*

8. We have met the enemy, and he is us.

    —*Pogo*

living. We make demands of ourselves and put ourselves in demanding situations. These demands rouse us and compel us to make the most of our abilities.

Hans Selye, who pioneered research in this area, writes that we are "built for work" (1983, p. 19). He makes a distinction between understress and overstress and between good stress and bad stress. Understress leads to boredom and lack of fulfillment, whereas overstress leads to various physical and psychological ills. Good stress is associated with generally pleasant experiences, usually those we seek out and think of as challenges. Bad stress is associated with generally unpleasant experiences, those we seek to avoid and think of as threats. We cannot, of course, run away from every unpleasant experience, and many situations are a mixture of good and bad. Our goals, according to Selye, should be (1) to strike a balance between understress and overstress and (2) to maximize good stress and minimize bad stress.

Ingenious as we humans are, we find many ways to cope. One investigator was able to identify twenty-eight different coping strategies (McCrae, 1984). Even this number hardly does justice to human ingenuity, for we may combine strategies or vary them as we continue to deal with a particular problem. However, we come to favor certain patterns even though they may not all serve us well.

Psychological investigators have been interested in determining the advantages and disadvantages of various coping strategies. One research team recently

CATHY   **by Cathy Guisewite**

YOU WENT OUT AND GOT DRUNK BECAUSE YOU WERE JEALOUS? THAT WAS STUPID. / HOW IS THAT ANY MORE STUPID THAN YOU EATING WHEN YOU'RE JEALOUS?	IRVING, I EAT WHEN I'M **DEPRESSED**. I BUY **SHOES** WHEN I'M JEALOUS. I BREAK THE TELEPHONE WHEN I'M ANGRY...	I MANGLE MY FINGERNAILS WHEN I'M LONELY...I THROW THINGS ALL OVER THE HOUSE WHEN I'M HURT...AND I WASTE MONEY ON MAKE-UP WHEN I'M FRUSTRATED.	MEN JUST DON'T KNOW HOW TO COPE.

fashioned an instrument—appropriately named COPE—that measures fourteen relatively distinct and clearly focused ways of coping with stress. They administered it to groups of undergraduates along with measures of various personality dimensions, including anxiety, self-esteem, optimism-pessimism, and hardiness. Hardiness itself is composed of these qualities: (1) internal control (a belief in one's ability to influence the situations in which one finds oneself), (2) commitment (deep involvement in what one is doing), and (3) challenge (being stimulated rather than intimidated by stress). Box 11.2 shows the coping strategies and the personality dimensions associated with them. For example, persons who used active coping as a strategy tended to be optimistic, hardy, high in self-esteem, and low in anxiety. Individuals making use of denial and behavioral disengagement tended to be just the opposite: pessimistic, low in hardiness and self-esteem, and high in anxiety.

In his recent book *Coping with Life Challenges,* which is recommended for those who would like to pursue this subject further, Chris Kleinke (1991) reviews research studies on coping. He found that the investigators generally agreed on the differences between successful copers and unsuccessful ones.

Coping Strategies and Their Personality Correlates

Carver, Scheier, & Weintraub (1989) have developed an inventory called COPE, which measures fourteen coping strategies or ways of responding to stress. Significant relationships have been found between these strategies and certain personality dimensions in undergraduates. In general, coping strategies considered to be functional were linked to personality qualities regarded as desirable; less functional strategies were inversely associated with these qualities. Four of these qualities (optimism, self-esteem, hardiness, and anxiety) and the strategies they were related to appear below. The strategies are numbered, and

immediately following each strategy are the items that were dispersed in the inventory to assess it.

Note that undergraduates using "positive interpretation & growth" and "active coping" as strategies tended to be optimistic, hardy, high in self-esteem, and low in anxiety. Undergraduates making use of "behavioral disengagement" and "denial" tended to be just the opposite: pessimistic, low in hardiness and self-esteem, and high in anxiety. Some strategies were correlated with fewer than four qualities or with none at all.

Optimism, Self-Esteem, Hardiness, Low Anxiety

1. Positive reinterpretation & growth

   I look for something good in what is happening.

   I try to see it in a different light to make it seem more positive.

   I learn something from the experience.

   I try to grow as a person as a result of the experience.

2. Active coping

   I take additional action to try to get rid of the problem.

   I concentrate my efforts on doing something about it.

I do what has to be done, one step at a time.

I take direct action to get around the problem.

Optimism, Self-Esteem, Hardiness

3. Planning

   I try to come up with a strategy about what to do.

   I make a plan of action.

   I think hard about what steps to take.

   I think about how I might best handle the problem.

Optimism, Low Anxiety

4. Restraint coping

   I force myself to wait for the

right time to do something.

I hold off doing anything about it until the situation permits.

I make sure not to make matters worse by acting too soon.

I restrain myself from doing anything too quickly.

Optimism

5. Acceptance

   I learn to live with it.

   I accept that this has happened and that it can't be changed.

   I get used to the idea that it happened.

   I accept the reality of the fact that it happened.

Successful copers respond to life challenges by taking responsibility for finding a solution to their problems. They approach problems with a sense of competence and mastery. Their goal is to assess the situation, get advice and support from others, and work out a plan that will be in their best interest. Successful copers use life challenges as an opportunity for personal growth, and they attempt to face these challenges with hope, patience, and a sense of humor.

Unsuccessful copers respond to life challenges with denial and avoidance. They either withdraw from problems or they react impulsively without taking the time and effort to seek the best solution. Unsuccessful copers are angry and aggressive or depressed and passive. They blame themselves or others for their problems and don't appreciate the value of approaching life challenges with a sense of hope, mastery, and personal control. (p. 11)

The material that follows offers some insights and makes some suggestions concerning coping strategies.

6. Turning to religion
   I seek God's help.
   I put my trust in God.
   I try to find comfort in my religion.
   I pray more than usual.

7. Seeking social support for instrumental reasons
   I ask people who have had similar experiences what they did.
   I try to get advice from someone about what to do.
   I talk to someone to find out more about the situation.
   I talk to someone who could do something concrete about the problem.

(no correlates)
8. Seeking social support for emotional reasons
   I talk to someone about how I feel.
   I try to get emotional support from friends or relatives.
   I discuss my feelings with someone.
   I get sympathy and understanding from someone.

9. Suppression of competing activities
   I put aside other activities in order to concentrate on this.
   I focus on dealing with this problem, and if necessary let other things slide a little.
   I keep myself from getting distracted by other thoughts or activities.
   I try hard to prevent other things from interfering with my efforts at dealing with this.

Pessimism
10. Alcohol-drug disengagement
    I drink alcohol or take drugs, in order to think about it less.

Pessimism, High Anxiety
11. Focus on and venting of emotions
    I get upset and let my emotions out.
    I let my feelings out.
    I feel a lot of emotional distress and I find myself expressing those feelings a lot.
    I get upset, and am really aware of it.

12. Mental disengagement
    I turn to work or other substitute activities to take my mind off things.
    I go to movies or watch TV, to think about it less.
    I daydream about things other than this.
    I sleep more than usual.

Pessimism, Low Self-Esteem, Low Hardiness, High Anxiety
13. Behavioral disengagement
    I give up the attempt to get what I want.
    I just give up trying to reach my goal.
    I admit to myself that I can't deal with it, and quit trying.
    I reduce the amount of effort I'm putting into solving the problem.

14. Denial
    I refuse to believe that it has happened.
    I pretend that it hasn't really happened.
    I act as though it hasn't even happened.
    I say to myself "this isn't real."

How to Cope: Positive Reinterpretation

The story is told (in fact, it is an old story that has been told and retold in many ways) about two little boys who have inadvertently locked themselves into their grandfather's barn. There appears to be nothing there but a huge pile of manure. One little boy begins to cry and pound on the door while the other happily grabs a shovel and begins to dig. When their grandfather arrives on the scene a little while later, the second boy explained why he hadn't been upset: "With all that manure, I figured there must be a pony."

If we see a situation as a threat, we respond in one way, but if we see it—or can come to see it—as benign or as a challenge, we respond in quite another way. Our appraisal of a situation is not necessarily fully conscious, so sometimes we may not fully understand our response. Generally, our appraisals take into account the characteristics of the situation and also our own coping resources and strategies. Appraisal itself—or reappraisal—is an important strategy for coping. Sometimes we need do little more in a stressful situation than alter our perception of the situation or ourselves.

In the COPE study, the strategy "positive reinterpretation and growth" was found to be associated with positive personality characteristics. *Positive reinterpretation* refers to the appraisal or reappraisal of a stressful situation so that it becomes more of a positive force in our lives. Below are a number of suggestions concerning how we can positively reinterpret or rethink the problems or obstacles that seemingly block our way.

Obstacles as Adversities to Be Used

"Who would have known Hector, if Troy had been happy? The road to valor is built by adversity." So wrote Ovid, and many others have written that adversity—or, more specifically, our mastery of adversity—builds character. Those whom we admire most are frequently those who have suffered much and overcome much.

Nehru used his time in jail to write his best book. Wendell Johnson was a world authority on stuttering; he became interested in stuttering because he stuttered. Paul Sheriff, confined to a wheelchair, found his store-bought clothes highly impractical; he designed new clothes for himself and then began a whole new industry making clothes for other wheelchaired folks.

Laura Archera Huxley (1974) maintains that we should be constantly ready to use misfortune instead of having misfortune use us. She writes:

> We cannot guarantee ourselves against misfortune, but we can do something to transform the evils that afflict us into a less painful, even a creative reality. We can do this by asking ourselves the question:
>
> *How can I use this?*
>
> "This" can be anything that is in the process of using us. It can be anything from an annoyance to a catastrophe, from a twinge of disgust to an access of desperation. I have become the victim of "this." How can I turn the tables? Instead of being used by "this," how can I make use of it? (p. 70)

One of my students said she preferred the phrase "What good can come of this?" rather than "How can I use this?" She recalled reading about a minister who had just rear-ended the car in front. A fellow passenger was startled and impressed to hear the minister say as he got out to approach the other driver: "Well, let's see what good can come of this."

Obstacles as Self-Imposed

Many of the obstacles that appear to confront us are really self-imposed. They are projections of our inner resistance to an undertaking. This brings to mind the story of the seemingly unhappy little boy who was seated on the curb in front of his house; when asked what he was doing there, he replied that he was running away from home but wasn't allowed to cross the street. Snell and Gail Putney (1964) call these self-imposed barriers "cherished obstacles."

> There are some obstacles which people seek out and claim for their own. These are external circumstances which they use to rationalize their self-doubts, and if such obstacles were to suddenly evaporate, they would be panic-stricken. But if the obstacles are to serve the function for which they are valued, people must believe these barriers are not of their own choosing. To strengthen this illusion, they engage in a great deal of ritualistic griping about these cherished obstacles. (pp. 170–171)

©ASHLEIGH BRILLIANT 1982   POT-SHOTS NO 2500.

**LORD, HELP ME TO MEET
THIS SELF-IMPOSED
           AND TOTALLY
               UNNECESSARY
                   CHALLENGE.**

Ashleigh
Brilliant

The Putneys argue that except in very unusual circumstances, we encounter few obstacles that can't be surmounted. If we are blocked, it is because we wittingly or unwittingly cooperate with whatever it is that appears to be blocking us. We choose what we will do and what we will keep ourselves from doing. Say the Putneys: "Those restraints that are effective are self-imposed, and those barriers that are insurmountable are ones which [we choose] not to surmount" (p. 175).

The ways we impose obstacles upon ourselves may be rather subtle or complicated. For example, a person may insist he has not chosen to be lonely or she has not chosen to be shy or uncomfortable with other people. However, in the first case it may be the person's scorn and disdain for others that has isolated him (Yalom, 1980). In the second instance, the person's belief that she should always say bright, intelligent, and witty things—something she finds impossible to do—may be responsible for her shyness (Greenwald, 1988). We sometimes say of a person: "He's his own worst enemy." Such persons create problems for themselves and need to understand and take responsibility for the predicaments in which they place themselves.

Obstacles as Gateless Gates

Some of the barriers that loom large in our lives simply do not exist. They are phantoms that appear to menace us in the distance but disappear if we dare approach. But if we remain in the distance, we never learn they aren't real.

Vincent and April O'Connell (1974) describe the Zen concept of the "gateless gate":

What that concept means is that before you get to an achievement, you perceive before you a gate, or a barrier: a doorway that you feel you need to enter upon and cross. Many times traversing that pathway seems an impossible task, and so we often hold back from the act of stepping forward into the doorway because our present pattern of conditioning says it is impossible. Yet, when you have passed through the doorway and look around, you see that there was actually no barrier there, after all. It was a gateless gate—a barrier to our growth only before we passed through it, the realization that the barrier existed only in our own perception. Once we acknowledge its existence and dared to encounter it the barrier to growth disappeared. (p. 438)

Returning to college was a gateless gate for one of my undergraduate students, a woman 37 years old. She had begun college upon graduation from high school, but her freshman year was a disaster, and she dropped out to become a barber. In the years that followed, she got married, divorced, remarried, and also tired of cutting hair. Still, the memory of her earlier academic difficulties and also the fear that she was too old to become a student again kept her from coming back to college. Finally, she decided that she had to do something about her vocational life. She returned to college, is making good grades, and sees that the gate she thought was closed to her was gateless after all.

An example of a *double* gateless gate (double in that it was an obstacle for two persons) is provided by Harry Browne (1974) in his book *How I Found Freedom in an Unfree World*. Browne remained in an unhappy marriage for a number of years and wouldn't consider divorce because his wife seemed helpless without him. He feared she might even commit suicide if he left. When he did decide to leave (after preparing for every dire possibility), his wife at first resisted but in two weeks became self-sufficient, doing things neither thought possible. Browne notes, "One of the most meaningful compliments I've ever received came years later when my wife thanked me for making her freedom possible" (p. 363).

Obstacles as Blessings in Disguise

Writes cardiologist Robert Eliot in his book (with coauthor Dennis Breo) *Is It Worth Dying For?* "It sounds strange, but my heart attack was the best thing in the world for me" (1984, p. 6). Before the attack, Eliot drove himself to make a success of his career, and there was no time to care for his body or his family or for anything but work. During three months of recuperation, he rethought his life and rearranged his priorities. Years later, his wife told him, "You know, Bob, if you had died from your heart attack, I don't think the kids and I would have missed you. We never really knew you. If you were to die now, we would miss you very much" (p. 7).

There is an old and provocative saying, "Every gift a burden and every burden a gift." It hypothesizes a kind of poetic justice in the world, in which each rose is accompanied by thorns and, to be fair, each set of thorns is accompanied by a rose. Or each stroke of good fortune carries with it the possibility of an unhappy outcome, while each misfortune presents an opportunity.

This poem, a prayer written by an unknown Confederate soldier, beautifully states the case for obstacles as blessings in disguise:

> I asked God for strength, that I might achieve,
>
> I was made weak, that I might learn humbly to obey . . .
>
> I asked for health, that I might do greater things,
>
> I was given infirmity, that I might do better things . . .
>
> I asked for riches, that I might be happy,
>
> I was given poverty, that I might be wise . . .
>
> I asked for power, that I might have the praise of men,
>
> I was given weakness, that I might feel the need of God . . .
>
> I asked for all things, that I might enjoy life,
>
> I was given life, that I might enjoy all things . . .
>
> I got nothing I asked for—but everything I had hoped for,
>
> Almost despite myself, my unspoken prayers were answered.
>
> I am among all men, most richly blessed.

Obstacles as Prices to Be Paid

As was noted in Chapter 10, many problems can be overcome, but at a price—often one that is higher than we want to pay. The price may have to be paid in money, time, or effort. It may involve confronting and working through an unpleasant situation. It may mean giving up something we don't want to give up or accepting something we don't want to accept.

All the things in life that are worth getting seem to come with a price. There is a Greek proverb with this message from on high: "God says take what you want and pay the price." Consider, for example, love. Love worth getting requires commitment. That's a price up front. Then there is the maintenance fee—the continual work any real relationship requires. And don't forget the crushing cost that may be exacted at the other end—the grief when the loved one dies. We get stuck because we don't want to pay the price; it seems too high, unfair, too much to pay.

Almost every major change we want to make in our lives carries a sizable price. The price may be relinquishing a business we've built from scratch or setting aside years of professional training to start anew. The price may be selling a house we love and giving up custody of our children. The price may be emotional upheaval for ourselves and others.

Harry Browne (1974) maintains that no matter how many mistakes we've made, how many knots we've woven into our lives, there is always a way out if we are willing to pay the price.

> Never feel that your life is frozen in its present routine and that it's hopeless to want anything better. No matter how complicated your life has become, there's a way to unravel it. No matter how many boxes you may be in, there's always a way to pay a price and get out. . . . Pay the price. Don't be so afraid of sudden, sharp discomfort that you willingly tolerate chronic, continual, deadening pain the rest of your life. If you refuse to undergo temporary discomfort, you're resigning yourself to a lifetime with little happiness. The chronic pain can deaden your senses, destroy your love of life, and make you bitter. You won't avoid the price by staying where you are. Instead, you'll pay it every day of your life as you stand on the sidelines and watch exciting alternatives pass you by. And the longer you put off the confrontation, the greater the price to be paid eventually. (pp. 350, 358–359)

Obstacles as Insoluble Problems to Be Outgrown

Sometimes, our problems seem truly insoluble. We wrestle and wrestle with them and make no progress. Carl Jung (1962) wisely saw that some problems which resisted solution could simply be outgrown. This "outgrowing," as Jung describes it, consists of a "new level of consciousness." We develop higher or wider interests, our view widens, and the particular problem loses urgency or importance. For example, her husband's absorption in his career may devastate a young wife, but as her own interests develop and as she finds confidantes among others, the problem fades in importance.

As we grow in maturity and wisdom, we become better able to manage our insoluble problems. We "rise above" situations that formerly dragged us down. In rising to a higher level, we are, to use Jung's description, above the storm instead of in it.

I know families in which parents and one or more of their adolescent children were in constant battle. In some of these families, considerable effort (including professional therapy) was expended to resolve differences, but with little success. But then, some years later, when all were adults, a reconciliation occurred. They seemed somehow to outgrow their problems, or perhaps they all grew up.

Obstacles as Questions to Be Lived

Clients often come into therapy with questions that perplex them. And they urgently seek answers. Why, they ask, do I feel the way I do? Why am I having the thoughts I think? What is the meaning of the things I'm led to do?

The formation of insight in therapy is a process that cannot be rushed. The best insights are formed by the clients themselves and come out of intensive inner exploration. "The wise therapist," psychotherapist James Bugental writes, "knows no one can *give* a client insight" (1978, p. 57).

In all of life, important questions are not easily answered. Life is a complicated business—full of confusion and ambiguity—and there can be a powerful temptation to ignore a problem or seize a simple solution. Instead, it may be better to stay with the problem and enhance our skill in dealing with it. Rather than rushing to an answer, we arrive at it little by little as we occupy ourselves with the question; or, as Rainer Maria Rilke suggested in his *Letters to a Young Poet*, we "live the question":

> Be patient with all that is unsolved in your heart
> and try to love the questions themselves
> like locked rooms and like books that are written
> in a very foreign tongue.
> Do not seek the answers, which cannot be given you
> because you would not be able to live them.
> And the point is, to live everything.
> Live the questions now.
> Perhaps you will then gradually, without noticing it,
> live along some distant day into the answer.

A poignant example of living the question is provided by psychotherapist Sheldon Kopp (1976) as he writes about his own life made difficult by an ineradicable brain tumor. (Kopp was introduced on the first page of this book.) This passage, although long, has been shortened from Kopp's fuller account, which is well worth reading:

> Last summer came close to being my final pilgrimage to the sea. The winter preceding it I had undergone the tortured ordeal of brain surgery during which I almost died, and after which I was psychotic for a time. I was grateful to have survived, though part of the tumor could not be removed and my future was ominously uncertain. My hearing in one ear was lost. I was left with precarious physical balance that I experience as a loss of grace as I move through the world. And pain had become my unwelcome companion, dogging me with two or three headaches every day. If only I could have one day without the pain, it would be like coming up for a gulp of sweet, fresh air, after having been submerged too long beneath the water's surface. . . .
>
> Fear that the remaining sliver of tumor would begin to grow again left me feeling that, rather than someday simply dying, I was to be killed off. Or, worse yet, I felt the terror that I might not die, that instead I would become paralyzed. What would it be like to be trapped alive, imprisoned for

years in a dead body? What if I could do nothing for myself, and if no one else would be there to bother to do for me, except out of burdensome pity?

I felt deeply sorry for myself. It seemed to me that I could not stand being so out of control of my life. My wife was there, with her own pain, and sorely open to mine. She later described it as "the summer we cried on the beach." But I was so into myself, so frightened, so determined to reassert my will and to have my own way that nothing else seemed to matter.

I spent many hours huddled on the empty beach, alone and brooding. Again and again, I decided that this was to be my final meeting with the sea, that I would swim out as far as I could, leaving my painful life, like a bundle of old clothes on the shore. And each time, I chose not to kill myself, explaining to myself that my wife and children needed me, would miss me too much. But it was not out of any sense of fairness to them that I did not drown myself. In my nearness to suicide, I really cared about nothing but escape from my own helplessness and anxiety. Recalling what I was up to, even now I still feel ashamed.

When we left the island to go home, I was still very depressed, unsure as to whether I was fit to help anyone else. It was time for me to get some help. But it was so very hard to face. I was feeling so down that the idea of going back into therapy as a patient once more made me feel like my life had been a fraud and a failure. And yet, if I would not go and ask for something for myself, then everything I had tried to offer my own patients was a lie.

There was an older therapist in town—a man whom I trust. He had supervised my work years ago, during a period when my father was dying. I used to go for supervision and cry every time. He had helped me then, and I hoped he would be able to help me again.

I phoned and told him briefly about my illness, and how bad I finally realized I was feeling, hoping that he might have free time to see me. I was grateful and deeply moved when he told me he would "make time." The day I went to his office, I felt frightened, but was grimly determined to work things out. I told him my story in a detailed and well-organized account, and stated that I wanted to get to work right away, to get past this depression, to get back on my feet. Though sympathetic to the pain of my ordeal, his wry answer to my impatience was: "How come a big, tough guy like you is thrown by a little thing like a brain tumor?"

That lovely bastard turned me around in a way that helped me to laugh at myself for thinking that I should be able to handle anything, without sorrow, rest, or comfort. He put me in touch with my own longings when he pointed out that I had resisted going through with drowning myself, *not* because my family needed me, but because *I needed them.* He said softly: "If you kill yourself, you'll never see your wife or your kids again, never. Think how much you'd miss them."

After much crying, and some raging, I came to accept how sick I'd been. This tumor was no existential challenge. I had been cut down, without reason. I was in some ways helpless, and perhaps still in danger, but I was alive, and could have what I could have if only I would surrender to things as they were.

This summer I have returned to the sea, no longer feeling any temptation to swim out and never return. I enter the water to play at fighting the great torrents. My balance remains impaired and my stamina is limited, but my courage has returned. Soon I go with the power of the surging seas, happily body-surfing, allowing each newly breaking wave to return me to the shore where I belong. I merge with the sea only briefly, knowing that I am from the water but not of it. The sea renews me with its dark powers, but I am I, and She is She. My pilgrimage of repeated return to the sea will not end so long as I live. And now I know that I *shall* live, for as long as is given to me. And should my body be battered even more, then I will live as I can, enjoying what I might, having what joy is available to me, and being what I may to the people whom I love. I must continue my pilgrimage, for it is my only way of remaining open to this vision. It is to this end that I must struggle for the remainder of that pilgrimage that is my life. (pp. 210–214)

Obstacles as Imperfections to Be Accepted

It's an imperfect world filled with imperfect people—all going about their lives in imperfect ways. If we can't accept some imperfection in ourselves, others, and the world beyond, we're in for a miserable time. Consider, for example, the plight of the raccoon in these lovely lines by Kenneth Rexroth:

The raccoon wears a black mask,
And he washes everything
Before he eats it. If you
give him a cube of sugar,
He'll wash it away and weep.
Some of life's sweetest pleasures
Can be enjoyed only if
You don't mind a little dirt.

One of my students, a young woman 21 years old, recalled learning to accept her own imperfect body. She has scoliosis (an abnormal lateral curvature of the spine), which has made her considerable interest in sports difficult and painful to follow. In high school, she made friends with the fact that some activities would be twice as hard for her and truly a challenge. "I totally accepted it," she said, "and learned to deal with it." Currently she has taken to the water, has a part-time job as a lifeguard, and enjoys aqua jogging—two activities that are less exacting on her back and knees.

In his book *Feeling Good*, psychiatrist David Burns (1980) challenges his readers to be average. "Dare to be average!" he writes, and he explains why it is important that we accept his dare:

"Perfection" is man's ultimate illusion. It simply doesn't exist in the universe. There is no perfection. It's really the world's greatest con game; it promises riches and delivers misery. The harder you strive for perfection, the worse your disappointment will become because it's only an abstraction, a concept that doesn't fit reality. Everything can be improved if you look at it closely and critically enough—every person, every idea, every work of art, every experience, everything. So if you are a perfectionist, you are guaranteed to be a loser in everything you do. (pp. 300–301)

In his second book, *The Feeling Good Handbook,* Burns (1990) notes that he is not opposed to high standards, since without them there might be few achievements in the sciences or the arts; but he distinguishes between "perfectionism" and "the healthy pursuit of excellence." Perfectionists strive for perfection and fear failure, for it makes them feel like failures as human beings. Perfectionists believe they must be special in order to merit their own esteem and the accep-

© ASHLEIGH BRILLIANT 1985.   POT-SHOTS No.3191.

It's only because I want everything I do to be perfect that I never actually do anything.

Ashleigh Brilliant

tance and love of others, but their accomplishments never satisfy them. Those who pursue excellence in some area are not afraid to fail or to fall short. They don't believe they have to earn their own esteem or that they have to impress others, and their efforts give them satisfaction even when they prove less than excellent.

How to Cope: Active Coping

As was noted earlier, the first step in coping is appraisal. It might also be all the subsequent steps in some cases, because in our appraisal and reappraisal or positive reinterpretation we may do all we need to do about a problem. However, frequently we will be required to do more. We may need to confront the problem, holding ourselves back from premature or impulsive actions, suppressing competing activities so that more attention can be focused on this one, gathering information, devising and carrying out a plan, and seeking assistance and support.

In the COPE study, active coping (like positive reinterpretation) was associated with positive personality characteristics. Planning, restraint, and seeking support for instrumental reasons also had some positive associations. Since the latter activities are frequently associated with active coping, let's broaden our use of the latter term to include them: *active coping* refers to all efforts designed to directly

© BRILLIANT ENTERPRISES 1974   POT-SHOTS NO 702

IF YOU CAN'T LEARN TO DO IT WELL,

Ashleigh Brilliant

LEARN TO ENJOY DOING IT BADLY.

remove, overcome, or circumvent the stressor or to ameliorate its effects. An effective active-coping approach might include the five steps noted below (Carver, Scheier, & Weintraub, 1989; Coleman, Morris, & Glaros, 1987; Weiten, Lloyd, & Lashley, 1991).

Ascertain the Problem

The first step in dealing with a problem systematically is to determine what the problem is. Human life is often complex and ambiguous; it may be difficult to determine the true cause of distress in a particular instance. Marriage counselors, for example, frequently note that spouses take very different views of their conflicts and culpability. A wife may feel deserted by a workaholic husband, while he sees his devotion to his work as necessary and in the best interests of his family.

Constructive coping implies that we minimize distortions and blind spots and make an accurate appraisal of our problems. Cameron and Meichenbaum (1988) write, "Although there may be some situations in which distortion is adaptive, it seems probable that interpretations consistent with available evidence generally will be more adaptive in the long run" (p. 699). They present several reasons why this is so. If we misperceive a benign situation as threatening, we subject ourselves to unnecessary stress. And if we misperceive a harmful situation as benign or if we underestimate its danger, we may not take the appropriate action.

The help of others may be useful and even necessary as we appraise a problem. Others may be more experienced or more objective than we are. At least, they may provide another view for us to consider along with our own.

Formulate Some Alternative Courses of Action

Once we understand the problem, the next step is to consider various ways of dealing with it. Sometimes we may not be able to think of more than one approach (or even one). Perhaps a particular approach is clearly better than any other that occurs to us. Frequently, however, we will be able to generate a number of plans, each with its own pluses and minuses. Again, we may want to seek the help of others.

Sometimes the minuses associated with a possible course of action seem so imposing that we discard it without giving it its due. And we can get into a critical or despairing mind-set that kills every idea almost before it is born. In situations like these, brainstorming—a process ordinarily used by groups—can be helpful for an individual. To *brainstorm* is to produce without evaluation or clarification as many alternatives as possible for dealing with a situation. The idea is to create a climate in which there is an unhampered flow of ideas, which may then be used to create a useful plan.

In brainstorming, clarification is suspended and both negative and positive evaluations postponed, because these processes thwart creativity. "Killer" phrases (such as "That won't work." "That was already tried." "That's a crazy idea.") are not permitted. "Booster" phrases (such as "That's terrific." "That's it!") aren't permitted either, since they imply that the other ideas aren't so good or that further ideas aren't necessary.

Evaluate the Alternatives and Select One

Once we have generated a number of possible plans, we must choose one of them. Our choice should be based on certain specified criteria. Coleman, Morris, and Glaros (1987) suggest that, to arrive at a final selection, we weigh the probability of success, satisfaction, and cost.

Weighing the Odds. How realistic is a plan? What are the chances it will work and have the desired effect? We won't be able to answer these questions without some previous experience or relevant information. We tend to have favorite solutions that can prove poor in the long run. For example, we may use violent bursts of anger to cower unruly family members. It's possible we will need someone more objective and uninvolved than we are to help us answer this question.

Weighing the Satisfactions. A number of plans may seem workable, but some will promise greater levels of satisfaction than others. Satisfaction and the probability of success need to be considered together. A plan that promises the most satisfaction for us may have little chance of success.

Weighing the Costs. Almost every plan will cost something. It will take time or money or effort. It may require giving up something we don't want to lose or accepting something we don't want to accept. It also means giving up the other alternatives.

In selecting a course of action, we hope to find a plan that will work, produce a high level of satisfaction, and not cost too much, but we usually settle for less of a bargain. We are willing to pay more or sacrifice more if we are encouraged by the prospects.

Take Action

The fourth step is to put the plan into action. This is a step we may fail to take except in fantasy. Of course, it is not a bad idea to rehearse the plan in our heads and consider all the possibilities, including the possibility that something unexpected may occur. "The best laid schemes of mice and men go aft awry," wrote Robert Burns, but many more are aborted.

A particularly desirable course of action may be closed to us if we lack the ability to bring it off. For example, we may lack skill in communication when lack of communication is at least part of our problem. Or we may be unable to assert ourselves and defend our rights. In such cases, our first course of action may be to acquire the skills basic to the solution or amelioration of the problem.

Timing is often a crucial matter in the execution of a plan. Just as we may greatly delay action as we debate one possibility and another, we may be carried away and act impulsively or without sufficient restraint. Hasty action sometimes provides a momentary catharsis but leaves us worse off than before.

Maintain Flexibility and Utilize Feedback

As we carry out a plan, we need to observe what is successful and what isn't. Although we give our plan a good go, we maintain some flexibility, so that we can make some adjustments as we proceed. We learn from our errors as well as our successes; and the more we learn, the more successful we will be next time.

How to Cope: Managing Emotions

Many problem situations are attended by emotion. Perhaps we feel anxious or depressed, and such emotional responses themselves can become our problem or a large part of it. We can become so anxious that our coping efforts become ineffective, or we become so depressed that we can't stir ourselves to get busy and do something. In situations such as these, some or even all our efforts may need to be focused on relieving or managing our emotional response, but the COPE study suggests that certain emotion-focused strategies are of dubious value. Four of the

POT-SHOTS NO 4482.

**PLEASE
DON'T TELL ME
THERE'S NO
NEED TO
WORRY ~**

IT'S
THE ONLY
THING
I'M ANY
GOOD AT.

© ASHLEIGH BRILLIANT 1988

most frequent emotional responses to stress are anxiety, guilt, anger, and depression.[1]

Anxiety

Anxiety is a state of arousal caused by threat to well-being.[2] When we are anxious, we feel endangered or challenged in some way. We are tense or uneasy and ready to act or respond.

"Fear" is a term used almost interchangeably with "anxiety," but a useful distinction can be made between them. Anxiety is an emotion while fear is an ideation; that is, *fear* is the idea that a particular stimulus or set of conditions will produce the emotion anxiety. The term "phobia," rather than "fear," is used when the fear is irrational, persistent, and there is a compelling desire to avoid the aversive stimulus. And the term "worry" is used if our fear concerns a possible future or anticipated event.

One could have a fear but avoid anxiety by avoiding the stimulus that triggers it. For example, one could fear heights but have no anxiety as long as one stayed at low elevations. In the same way, if one fears being in crowds, enclosed places, or certain social situations, one could keep anxiety in check by avoiding such places. Of course, such avoidant behavior would restrict one's life.

Sometimes we become anxious without knowing why, and some of us may have a good deal of chronic anxiety without fully understanding what there is that we find so threatening. *Anxiety attacks*—or *panic attacks*, as they are sometimes called—are sudden bursts of anxiety that rapidly mount to a peak and then fade away. Stage fright is a kind of anxiety attack that many of us have experienced.

Anxiety is a familiar companion because we are seldom free from threat of some kind in our lives. Too much anxiety can disorganize our efforts and even paralyze us. But moderate amounts can rouse us and prompt us to do what we need to do.

Anxiety is both a sign and the price of growth. We become anxious when we leave comfortable plateaus—when we leave our comfort zone—and begin an ascent to higher reaches. So anxiety is not necessarily the enemy. It can be a good—though sometimes painful—friend and helper.

Albert Ellis (1990b) makes an important distinction between healthy and unhealthy anxiety. Healthy anxiety is mild and often manifests itself as concern,

---

[1]　Grief, another common emotional response, was discussed in Chapter 7.
[2]　This section is adapted from Arkoff, 1988.

caution, or vigilance. This kind of anxiety is necessary to keep us out of trouble. Unhealthy anxiety is more severe and manifests itself as overconcern, dread, or panic. This kind of anxiety gets us into trouble by making us freeze up or fall apart and act incompetently.

According to Ellis, we usually go from concern to overconcern when, instead of *preferring* that something happen or not happen, we begin to believe that this something *must* happen or *must not* happen. To say it another way, we create severe anxiety when we shift from inclination to "*must*urbation." Ellis gives this example:

> If you *prefer* to perform well and *want* to be accepted by others, you are *concerned* that you will fail and be rejected. Your healthy concern encourages you to act competently and nicely. But if you devoutly believe that you absolutely, under all conditions, *must* perform well and that you *have* to be accepted by others, you will then tend to make yourself—yes, *make* yourself—panicked if you don't perform as well as you supposedly *must*. (p. 17)

Albert Ellis's *How to Stubbornly Refuse to Make Yourself Miserable About Anything—Yes, Anything!* and David Burns's *The Feeling Good Handbook* are recommended for those who would like to understand and work on their own anxiety, fears, and phobias. Where professional assistance is desired or indicated, psychotherapy can be very helpful, especially cognitive therapies that teach new ways of thinking about one's symptoms, oneself, and one's life. Special group therapy approaches are available for individuals with various phobias, such as a fear of flying or driving.

Human beings vary widely both in their ability to tolerate anxiety and in the ways they respond to it. One of the most common methods used to reduce anxiety is drugs, including alcohol, barbiturates, and tranquilizers. If nothing is done to deal with one's problems, antianxiety drugs may provide little more than temporary escape; indeed, such drugs may compound problems by leaving them unattended or by reducing one's image of oneself as a person who can deal with these problems. Injudicious and long-term use of some antianxiety drugs can create serious dependency or addiction problems as well as adverse side effects (High anxiety, *Consumer Reports*, 1993).

Various psychological techniques have been proposed to help those persons whose general levels of anxiety or tension are inappropriately high. These methods include yoga, autohypnosis, biofeedback, and numerous forms of meditation and relaxation. Instruction in these methods is provided by various self-help manuals or through group or individual instruction.

Guilt

Guilt is remorse over wrongdoing. When we feel guilty, we feel we have violated some moral or ethical code. In brief, we feel we have been bad.

Some philosophers have written that our choice is always between anxiety and guilt. If we stay secure within our safety zone, we experience *existential guilt* because of our failure to make more of our existences or lives; we feel guilty because of our undeveloped potential or because of our unused, wasted opportunities to grow. If we venture beyond our safety zone, we experience *anxiety*, which is triggered by our fear of the unknown and unmastered.

"An uneasy conscience," Mark Twain wrote, "is a hair in the mouth." What is a "healthy conscience"? It could be defined as a conscience that elicits guilt commensurate with our misdeeds and one that serves to dissuade us from such acts.

Some persons lack the capacity to feel guilt, and others are too easily made to feel guilty. Judith Viorst (1987) notes that she is one of the latter—that she can muster up guilt about almost anything. She writes that she could easily list several hundred items that provoke guilt in her, including the following examples:

> I feel guilty whenever my children are unhappy.
> I feel guilty whenever one of my houseplants dies.
> I feel guilty whenever I fail to floss after eating.
> I feel guilty whenever I tell the whitest of lies.
> I feel guilty whenever I step on a bug deliberately—all cockroaches excepted.
> I feel guilty whenever I cook with a pat of butter that I have dropped on the kitchen floor. (p. 132)

Viorst points out that one cause of excessive guilt is failure to distinguish between forbidden thoughts and forbidden deeds. Some of us feel as guilty for what we are tempted to do as for what we actually do. But if each of us were incarcerated for every forbidden thought, there would be few folks outside of prison walls.

Another reason given by Viorst for excessive guilt is a cherished illusion that somehow—between our efforts and God's—everything is or can be brought under control. We would rather feel guilty than helpless. We would rather feel guilty for what we did or didn't do than face the fact that we live in a world where bad things sometimes happen to good people.

Benjamin Disraeli, in writing about a political enemy, said this man made his conscience his accomplice instead of his guide. Some of us are deficient in our capacity for guilt or in our ability to take responsibility for our transgressions. There are certain "sociopathic personalities" who seem incapable of remorse or restraint, but, as history inexorably records, there are situations in which "good people" hush their consciences or turn their moral responsibilities over to others (Viorst, 1987).

Psychiatrist David Burns (1980) suggests a distinction between "healthy remorse" and "unhealthy guilt." We feel remorseful or regretful when we have behaved in a way that has violated our personal moral or ethical standards; we have done something bad. By contrast, we feel guilty when we assume that this bad behavior shows we are a bad person. "To put it in a nutshell," he writes, "remorse or regret is aimed at behavior, whereas guilt is targeted toward the 'self' " (p. 177).

Some of us get caught up in a patterning of guilt that goes like this: I've done something bad (or I'm tempted to do something bad). Therefore, I'm a bad person and deserve to suffer. Or to fail. Or not to amount to anything. Psychotherapist Samuel Warner (1966) writes that "the guilt-laden individual welcomes the heavy hand of fate" because he or she has a "quota of suffering" to fulfill. Such individuals are not free to succeed; if good fortune is thrust upon them, they may be, as Freud said, "wrecked by success."

Unpleasant though guilt feelings are, some people seem very attached to them and are loath to give them up. Why should this be so? Here are some reasons why guilt feelings might persist or be valued or provide some hidden payoffs (Bloomfield and Kory, 1980; Dyer, 1976; Marecek, 1985):

1. Our guilt can be an expected companion in life. Some of us have grown up believing that life is a terribly difficult and serious business and that pleasure needs to give way to hard work and responsibility. Whenever our lives seem not to be extracting the price we expect to pay or whenever we're tempted to indulge ourselves a bit, we can be assaulted by waves of guilt. An anonymous poet has written: "The Puritan through life's sweet garden goes/To pluck the thorn and cast away the rose." When we've grown up thorn-expectant, winding up with a bouquet of roses can be a bit unsettling.

2. Our guilt is our way of paying off our transgressions. Guilt can become a kind of exoneration through self-mortification when we do wrong as children. We're often made to confess our guilt or to appear sorry; then we may be punished or pardoned or "paroled." We can continue this patterning into adulthood, where our guilty feelings serve us as a combination of penance and punishment, after which we're free—perhaps to transgress again.

3. Our guilt is a way of keeping ourselves passively in the past rather than confronting the future. Changing one's behavior can be hard and even risky work. We may find it easier to ruminate about the "should haves" of the past (because one can't do a "should have") than to get busy with the "will do's" of today and tomorrow.

4. Our guilt proves to others that we know what is right and keeps them off our case. By indicting and convicting ourselves, we keep control of the situation. We show others that we know what we should do even though we haven't done it. We administer our own discipline in a way that may be more to our liking.

How can we get rid of self-defeating feelings of guilt? First, we need to see how we may be using our guilt in the ways just discussed. It is especially important to become aware of the misuse of guilt that keeps us mired in the past rather than moving along into the present and future.

Second, we need to reconsider our system of "shoulds" and "should nots." Our guilt arises from the shoulds we don't do and the should nots we do (or are tempted to do). Some of these doubtless relate to our irrational beliefs—for example, the belief that we should always observe standards of behavior few humans attain.

Third, we can become aware of how others manipulate us into feeling guilty. Wayne Dyer (1976) identifies a kind of "leftover guilt"—a guilt or propensity to guilt left over from childhood. Some of us had parents who were expert in making us feel guilty, and we can carry this vulnerability to guilt into our adulthood, where it is triggered by others who also wield some power over us or whom we feel a need to please.

Fourth, we can learn to accept ourselves, including those things others may not value. If we approve of ourselves, we don't need to have the approval of others. If we approve of ourselves, we don't feel guilty for being who we are.

Fifth, we need to distinguish carefully between remorse for something we've done and guilt for who we are. Remorse can be a helpful prod to making amends and a guide to future behavior—to creating a better next time. Guilt for who we are is self-defeating and destructive.

Anger

When our goal-seeking behavior goes well, we are pleased. When it doesn't go well, one of our primary responses is anger. *Anger* can be simply defined as feelings of displeasure. These feelings may be openly expressed or they may be kept hidden within ourselves or perhaps even from ourselves.

Anger, as a term, is frequently confused with aggression and assertiveness. *Aggression* is hurtful behavior. We can express our anger without being deliberately hurtful. For example, we could express our anger by informing a group that we are displeased with the way they treated us, or we could become aggressive and tell them how awful they are for treating us that way. However, some persons may respond to even a mild expression of anger as if it were an aggressive act.

Assertiveness refers to behavior that protects our own rights without infringing on the rights of others. When we are being assertive, we ordinarily state simply

Box 11.3

Assertiveness, Nonassertiveness, and Aggressiveness

Assertiveness refers to the expression of one's rights without infringing upon the rights of others. When we are assertive, we stand up for ourselves and express our thoughts and feelings directly, honestly, and appropriately. We show respect for ourselves, but at the same time we demonstrate respect for those with whom we are involved.

By contrast, *nonassertiveness* refers to the failure to express one's rights. When we are nonassertive, we hold back and fail to present our thoughts and feelings. Or we express ourselves in such half-hearted, roundabout, or self-effacing ways that we can be misperceived or disregarded. In nonassertion we do not show respect for ourselves, and although we sometimes rationalize that we hold ourselves back for altruistic reasons, we may have an implicit disrespect for others and their ability to stick up for themselves and deal with their own problems and disappointments.

Aggression is frequently confused with assertive behavior but is very different in its manifestations and effects. *Aggressiveness*, broadly defined, is hurtful behavior; it can be used to express one's rights but at the expense of another person. When we are aggressive, we lash out verbally or physically, directly or indirectly, in the attempt to belittle or overpower others or put them down. When we use aggression, we do not show respect for others, and we may show a simultaneous lack of respect for our own capacities in that we have found it necessary to resort to such tactics.

Consider, for example, this situation: Your neighbor is having a very noisy party and in response to your phone call says that everyone will probably be going home pretty soon. How would you respond? Nonassertive response: Well, all right, as long as it won't be too long. Aggressive response: You're so damn inconsiderate; I'm calling the cops! Assertive response: The noise has got to stop right now; if it doesn't, I'll call the police.

We can be assertive in nonverbal as well as in verbal ways. It's not just what we say, but also how we say it. Vocal tone, inflection, and volume are all important factors. So are facial expression, eye contact, gestures, and body posture, and in a particular situation we may be able to express and assert ourselves eloquently without saying a word. When we are being assertive, our general behavior lends support and emphasis to what we are saying. When we are being nonassertive, our general behavior frequently suggests weakness, uncertainty, and anxiety. When we are being aggressive, our verbal and nonverbal behavior may combine to threaten, dominate, or put someone down.

Is assertiveness important? People who complete assertiveness training generally report some personal gains. For one thing, skill in assertion improves our relationship with ourselves. Typically we gain respect for ourselves, and we have more confidence in and control over our behavior. We are better able to express ourselves, pursue our goals, and meet our needs. A second area of gain comes in our relationships with others. Asserting ourselves and sharing our thoughts and feelings seem vital to true intimacy. Our assertions and disclosures can encourage others to respond similarly and open themselves to us. By contrast, nonassertion can lead others to disrespect us or look upon us with pity or disgust, while aggression can disrupt relationships and encourage others to retaliate or withdraw.

This does not mean, of course, that all assertiveness leads to improved relationships, especially when it disrupts what another feels is a desirable status quo. However, when relationships are disrupted, they sometimes can be reconstructed in a way that allows all parties to grow. An assertive person can be a fuller person and lead a richer life, and those with whom he or she interacts can similarly benefit.

(Adapted from Arkoff, 1988)

and specifically (1) what was done, (2) why this was a problem, and (3) the correction to be made. If we tell the clerk how mad we were when this supposedly preshrunk shirt shrank after washing, that's anger. If we carry on about what a lousy store this is to have such lousy merchandise, that's aggression. But if we say the shirt shrank, now it's too small to wear, and we want our money back, that's assertiveness. (See Box 11.3.)

What should we do when we feel anger? Is it better to express or suppress our angry feelings? According to one point of view, it is unhealthy to bottle up angry feelings, and we best get rid of them by expressing them. However, angry feelings, even if unexpressed, generally dissipate in time. When we begin to express our anger, we frequently stimulate ourselves to even greater anger. When we begin to talk out our anger, we may *rehearse* rather than reduce it; we build up our anger all over again. And expressing our anger can compound our problems as others respond in kind or find their own ways to retaliate.

In her helpful book *Anger: The Misunderstood Emotion*, Carol Tavris (1989) writes that *suppressing* anger can be harmful if its effect is to continue a stressful situation, and *expressing* anger can be harmful if it makes a stressful situation worse. Her advice is to keep quiet if we want our anger to go away and have the association in question remain congenial; however, we should keep talking if we want to stay angry and use our anger. For the small indignities of life, she recommends the former strategy (along with watching a Charlie Chaplin movie, since you can't laugh and be angry at the same time). For the larger indignities, she recommends we fight back. "And, most important," she writes, "learn the difference."

Let's ask the question again: "Is it better to express or suppress our angry feelings?" David Burns (1980) suggests we have a third option—to stop creating our anger. Burns maintains that anger, like all emotion, is created by our thoughts. A particular event doesn't make us angry; we make ourselves angry in the way we think about that event or the meaning we attach to it. The same seemingly frustrating event may affect two individuals quite differently—one may blow up while the other remains quite calm.

Burns distinguishes between "hot" thoughts and "cool" thoughts. When we think "hot" thoughts, we provoke ourselves. When we think "cool" thoughts, we calm ourselves. An example of a hot thought is "He can't talk to me that way!" Rephrased as a cool thought, it might be "He must be really upset to talk that way."

Sue, one of Burns's patients, was a 31-year-old woman whose husband, John, had a teenage daughter, Sandy, from a prior marriage. Sue felt anger, jealousy, and resentment (and ultimately guilt because of these feelings) because of Sandy's selfish manipulations of her father. As an assignment, Sue wrote down her "hot" thoughts and "cool" thought replacements (see Box 11.4).

As Sue substituted cool thoughts for hot thoughts, she felt better and had less need to try to control John. Sue still believed that John was wrong to allow himself to be manipulated, but she gave him the right to be wrong. John began to feel less pressured, and their relationship greatly improved. Burns notes that it was not only Sue's cool thoughts that led to success, but still they were a "necessary and gigantic first step."

Depression

When nothing appears to be going right in our lives and we seem unable to do anything about it, we may feel blue or downcast or depressed.[3] *Depression* is a condition in which we are preoccupied with negative thoughts about ourselves and our world or life situation, and our future—to us—seems hopeless (Beck, 1976). When we are depressed, we have little zest for life. We lack energy, and we lose interest in usual life pursuits. We may have little appetite and considerable difficulty in sleeping. We may have trouble being attentive or concentrating.

When we are depressed or in despair, life may seem hardly worth living, and major depression or deep despair is prominent among the multiple causes of suicide (Holden, 1992). Suicidologists have identified despair as one of the precursors of suicide in young adults ages 15 through 24. The other signs include use of alcohol or drugs, low self-esteem, a tendency toward isolation, and progressive withdrawal from relationships and favored activities. A group of adolescents ages 15 through 18 independently arrived at a similar set of signs (Firestone & Seiden, 1990).

---

[3] This discussion does not include bipolar depression—(a state in which depression alternates with mania (an elated, expansive, and irritable mood); the discussion is limited to the much more common unipolar depression (depression without mania).

Box 11.4

Cool Thoughts for Hot Thoughts

Sue wrote down her "Hot Thoughts" when her husband acted like a soft touch in response to his teenage daughter's selfish manipulations. When Sue substituted less upsetting "Cool Thoughts," her jealousy and resentment diminished.

Hot Thoughts	Cool Thoughts
1. How dare he not listen to me!	1. Easily. He's not obliged to do everything my way. Besides he *is* listening, but he's being defensive because I'm acting so pushy.
2. Sandy lies. She says she's working but she's not. Then she expects John's help.	2. It's her nature to lie and to be lazy and to use people when it comes to work and school. She hates work. That's her problem.
3. John doesn't have much free time and if he spends it helping her, I will have to be alone and take care of my kids by myself.	3. So what. I like being alone. I'm capable of taking care of my kids myself. I'm not helpless. I can do it. Maybe he'll want to be with me more if I learn not to get angry all the time.
4. Sandy's taking time away from me.	4. That's true. But I'm a big girl. I can tolerate some time alone. I wouldn't be so upset if he were working with my kids.
5. John's a schmuck. Sandy uses people.	5. He's a big boy. If he wants to help her he can. Stay out of it. It's not my business.
6. I can't stand it!	6. I can. It's only temporary. I've stood worse.
7. I'm a baby brat. I deserve to feel guilty.	7. I'm entitled to be immature at times. I'm not perfect and I don't need to be. It's not necessary to feel guilty. This won't help.

(From Burns, 1980, p. 152)

The vast majority of depressions cannot be attributed to identifiable medical causes or genetic influence. Self-reported depressive symptoms are most closely related to adverse life experience (Antonuccio, 1993). All of us suffer losses, failures, disappointments, and rejections, but we needn't become depressed by these adversities. Depressed individuals may have more than the usual adversity in their lives, but they may also help fashion the bleak world they inhabit. Seligman (1991) believes that pessimism is at the root of depression. He writes, "People who have a pessimistic explanatory style and suffer bad events will probably become depressed, whereas people who have an optimistic explanatory style and suffer bad events will tend to resist depression" (p. 77). Rumination, or the tendency to continue to mull over one's problem, seems to be a necessary ingredient in the depressive stew. Pessimists who don't brood tend to avoid depression.

The pessimistic explanatory style consists of three kinds of explanation for bad events: (1) *personal*—believing oneself at fault for the situation, (2) *permanent*—believing the situation will never get any better, and (3) *pervasive*—believing the situation will adversely affect every part of one's life. For example, if a love relationship goes sour, pessimists may tell themselves they are to blame (personal), they never again will find anyone to love (permanent), and, therefore, any happiness for them is out of the question (pervasive).

Here is a perfect example of a pessimistic explanation for a failed event: "I always do everything wrong." *I* (personal) *always* (permanent) do *everything* (pervasive) wrong. Try saying "I always do everything wrong" over and over with

---

Box 11.5

What Do You Do When You Are Feeling Down?

Check how often you do each of the following things when you are feeling down:

	Never	Rarely	Sometimes	Often
1. I seek out friends for support.	_____	_____	_____	_____
2. I blame myself.	_____	_____	_____	_____
3. I watch TV.	_____	_____	_____	_____
4. I work out a plan to make myself feel better.	_____	_____	_____	_____
5. I take tranquilizers.	_____	_____	_____	_____
6. I sleep, daydream, or try to escape.	_____	_____	_____	_____
7. I engage in some sort of activity, such as reading, music, art, or sports.	_____	_____	_____	_____

The preceding items have been adapted from the Depression Coping Questionnaire, which Chris Kleinke and his associates have administered to a large and varied group of persons (Kleinke, 1984, 1988; Kleinke, Staneski, & Mason, 1982). Interesting differences have been found between the coping strategies of depressed and nondepressed persons. When nondepressed persons felt down, they tended to get busy, seek support, and engage in problem solving. By contrast, depressed persons were more likely to become passive, withdraw, blame themselves, and take tranquilizers. In reviewing the evidence, Kleinke (1991) concludes that depression and passivity feed on each other and that depressed persons could make themselves feel better if

---

conviction and see if you don't feel a bit down. We'll have more to say about pessimism in the last chapter when we discuss its opposite, optimism.

People often use the words "sadness" and "depression" interchangeably, but there is an important difference between these concepts. To be sad is to be low in spirits or sorrowful, but it does not imply negativity toward oneself, one's world, and one's future. For example, if we lose someone who is dear to us, we will doubtless be sad or low in spirits. But if we think we are nothing because we have lost this person and we can never be happy again and we have no future, then we are better described as depressed (Burns, 1980).

Although we usually speak of depression as something that seems to descend on us ("She's suffering from a depression." "He fell into a depression."), a case could be made that we depress ourselves, not only by the explanatory style we adopt but also as an effort to get our lives under control. Psychiatrist William Glasser (1985) contends that, although we are largely unaware of it, we choose most of the misery we suffer, because misery or depression almost always serves a purpose at the time. For example, without being aware that we are making a choice, we might depress ourselves because depression attracts help, or gives us control over others, or excuses our unwillingness to get a move on and do something more effective.

We are more vulnerable to depression if we lack certain skills that provide assistance in adversity (Heiby, 1991). One such skill is self-reinforcement—that is, the ability to reward ourselves (see Box 2.5); another is the ability to cope actively with our problems when we are feeling down (see Box 11.5).

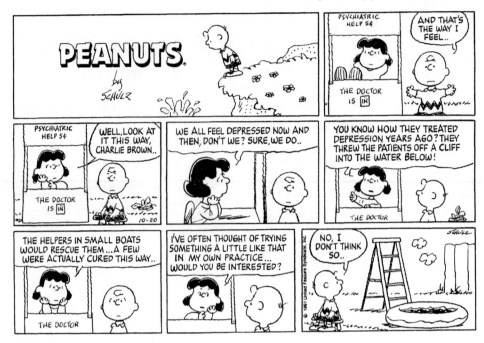

Those of us who seek professional help in dealing with depression may be given antidepressant medication or psychotherapy or both. Because of the assumption that depression is a "medical illness" and because of aggressive marketing, medication is the most popular treatment in the United States (Antonuccio, 1993). However, analysis of the relevant research suggests that psychotherapy is generally more effective or as effective as medication (Antonuccio, 1993; Greenberg & Fisher, 1989). Furthermore, antidepressant medications cannot be considered benign treatments; they can have unpleasant and harmful side effects (Antonuccio, 1993).

Not all psychotherapies are effective in the treatment of depression. Cognitive and behavioral therapies appear to be among the best approaches (Antonuccio, 1993). Cognitive therapies work to change maladaptive thinking patterns, for example, by modifying the person's pessimistic explanatory style or by helping the person replace irrational thoughts with rational ones (see Chapter 3). Behavioral therapies may involve training in various skills, for example, in problem solving, decision making, social interaction, communication, assertiveness, and self-control.

Most depressive episodes are relatively short in duration and are managed or lived through without professional assistance (Flanagan, 1990). What can we do when we are making ourselves depressed or at least contributing to our depression? We can work to reverse, undo, or correct what's gone wrong or isn't right.

1. We can listen carefully to what we are saying to ourselves about ourselves, our lives, and our futures. We can stop self-defeating thoughts and substitute self-enhancing ones. We can distract ourselves from and refuse to ruminate on thoughts that bring us down.

2. We can observe ourselves and gain insight into the mileage we get out of our depressed moods. For example, do we use them to control others or make them concerned about us and pay attention to us and help us? Do we use them to excuse our unwillingness to get a move on and shape up our lives?

3. We can act to reduce the stress in our lives. For instance, we can work on important relationships; learn needed social skills, such as those involved in problem solving, communication, and assertiveness; or set new and more attainable goals.

4. We can make ourselves be active, scheduling places to go, engaging in sports, exercising. Exercise has been shown to be both a good antidote and a preventive for depression—possibly because exercise stimulates the brain's natural opiates and the body's neurotransmitters, which carry messages between the nerves.

5. We can build more pleasant events into our lives and focus on those that do occur. For example, we can give ourselves a reward (compliment, candy, drink, movie, new shirt, etc.) when we have successfully completed some step to combat depression. Or we can take advantage of the little joys that present themselves throughout our daily rounds. And we can continually load up with humorous books, videocassettes, and audiocassettes to add laughter to massage our innards, reduce stress, ease pain, and brighten our outlook on life (Cousins, 1989).

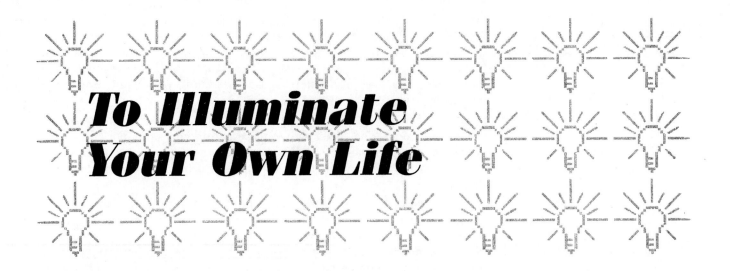

To Illuminate Your Own Life

Anchor and Apply*

1. Make a list of the major stressors or sources of stress in your life at present and indicate how and how well you manage each of them.

2. Make a list of your personal attributes and resources that help you manage stress in your life at present and indicate how each has been of assistance.

3. Describe the coping strategies you used or are using in working on a recent or present problem and indicate their effect.

4. Positively reinterpret or rethink one of your current obstacles or problems by using one of the eight appraisal or reappraisal techniques given in this chapter.

5. Make up a plan for solving a problem you now face by completing at least the first three of the five steps given in the section on active coping.

6. Describe your own experience with anxiety, fear, or worry.

7. Describe your own experience with guilt.

8. Describe your own experience with anger.

9. Describe your own skill or lack of skill in assertiveness.

10. Describe your own experience with depression.

* These "anchor and apply" items are designed to help you use the contents of the chapter as stimuli to prompt new or deeper or clearer insights into yourself and your life. To respond to an item, first find the material in the chapter that is most relevant to the item *and* yourself; that's called "anchoring." Second, think about this material in relationship to yourself and your life and keep thinking about it until you arrive at a new or deeper or clearer understanding; that's the "apply" or application part. When you write or present your response to the item, be sure to include both parts, that is, both the anchor material and the application. You can know you are successful on an item if, in completing it, you truly learn something new or understand something better.

Coping Strategies

In a comic strip earlier in this chapter, Linus tells Charlie Brown that no problem is so big or so complicated that it can't be run away from. A woman in therapy with me took a somewhat different view: she said that in her life no problem was too small for her to try to escape. She said it with a smile, and indeed it wasn't completely true because she had come to confront her problems and do something about them.

Although running away from problems—whether large or small—is a popular response, it is only one of the many coping strategies we humans use. Fourteen coping strategies are presented in Box 11.2. Doubtless each of us had made use of a number of these strategies. In dealing with one problem, we may use one strategy or set of strategies; in dealing with another, we may use a different set. We may vary our strategies as we continue to confront an obstinate problem.

We humans tend to be creatures of habit, and we have our habitual or favorite ways of responding to problem situations. Some of our preferred strategies may be gender-linked; in the study reported in Box 11.2, men reported more alcohol or drug use, and women reported more use of social support and more focus on and venting of emotions.

1. To begin this exploration, recall the problems that you have faced in the recent past and the coping strategies you have used to deal with these problems. In the space immediately below, write the answers to these questions: (a) Which three or four of the fourteen coping strategies have you used the most? (b) Have these most-used strategies served you well? Why or why not?

2. To complete this exploration, consider a problem in your life at present.[4] In the space immediately below, write the answers to these questions: (a) What is the problem? (b) Which of the fourteen coping strategies are you using to deal with this problem? (c) How are you using these strategies (be specific, give examples)? (d) How successful are these strategies? What other strategies might be successful or more successful? Why?

---

[4] Occasionally, someone working on this part of this exploration says that he or she has no problems. If you don't have a problem and you still want to complete this exploration—well, then, that's the problem.

Stumbling Blocks and Stepping Stones

Think of some circumstance in your life that you have come to regard as a hindrance to your happiness or development. Describe this circumstance in the space immediately below. Then—but not before—continue with material that follows.

All learning involves some degree of frustration; and frustration, itself, is an important source of new patterns of response. Mark May (1961) writes that "the thwarting of a goal response is precisely a prime condition that gives rise to thinking" (p. vii). Every obstacle provokes thought and presents us with an opportunity to grow and enlarge ourselves.

The Chinese word for *crisis* is made up of two characters. One may be translated "danger" and the other "opportunity." A crisis we find ourselves in or an obstacle we face may endanger or frighten us; at the same time, it may present us with an opportunity for mastery and growth. We can emerge sturdier or wiser than we were (Shapiro, 1978).

Some of the persons we find most admirable are those who have mastered the most difficult obstacles: personal handicaps or personal circumstances that would have defeated many. Some became what they were *despite* their obstacles, but others *because* of them.

Martha Crampton (1974), on whose work this exploration is based, suggests we turn our obstacles into stepping stones by seeing them as opportunities for growth rather than as reasons for lament and self-pity. According to Crampton, the obstacles that confront us serve a useful purpose, and each obstacle contains the key to its overcoming. When we find the key, we can change what might have been a stumbling block into a stepping stone. The key is frequently some quality we enhance in ourselves, perhaps determination, forbearance, patience, or understanding.

Addressing a recent commencement audience, Circuit Judge Marie Milks recalled an obstacle in her academic path. A professor wrote a letter to the graduate school of her choice remarking that "Marie Nakanishi [her maiden name] had a sunny disposition" but not the stuff required for graduate work. Her determination to prove this professor wrong got her through the rough times in law school. "Today," she told her audience, "I am most grateful for the letter he wrote. It has been my inspiration" (Tanahara, 1992, A3).

Reflect on the circumstance or obstacle you described on the previous page until you find the key to overcoming it. The key will be some quality within yourself that you must employ or develop in order to deal constructively with the obstacle. This quality may help you change outer circumstances if that seems possible and advisable, or it may help you change yourself or the way you perceive or respond to these circumstances. The prayer of Reinhold Niebuhr, adopted by Alcoholics Anonymous, is relevant in this connection: "God grant me the Serenity to accept the things I cannot change, Courage to change the things I can, and Wisdom to know the difference."

What is the key to your obstacle? How does this obstacle provide you with an opportunity for personal growth? Reflect on these two questions and write your answers below (add another sheet of paper if you would like more space for your response).

The Fable

Sometimes we can't find the solution to a problem or even get some needed perspective because we are so close to it. If we establish some "psychological" distance—that is, back away from the problem—we can get a different view and perhaps a better idea of what to do about it. Or we come to see and accept what we were trying hard not to see.

One way of putting some psychological distance between ourselves and a problem is to write about it as though it were happening to someone else or to some thing (perhaps an animal, a plant, or even an inanimate object). To remove it even more, we can write it as a fable that took place in a distant time and place. A fable I wrote when I was trying without success to get my adult children to follow in my footsteps and go to college is presented in Box 11.6. Read it before continuing on.

Begin your part of this exploration (which is based on the work of Michael Mayer) by thinking of one of the most difficult problems you now have or one of the worst obstacles you now face. To gain the most psychological distance, write a fable about this problem or obstacle, but write it as though it were happening to someone else or some thing and in some faraway time and place.

Box 11.6

Abe's Fable

Once upon a time, far, far away there lived an old chipmunk. He was (he thought) a master gardener, and many chipmunks came to work with him and then went off to start gardens of their own. He believed everyone would want to be a gardener, but, alas neither his daughter nor his son showed the slightest interest.

It would seem impossible to work this out because the more the old chipmunk boosted gardening, the more the little chipmunks resisted. The daughter chipmunk said that one of her friends who had graduated in gardening was now catching beetles for minimum wage and another was digging tunnels for rabbits, which is exactly what he did before he learned gardening. The son chipmunk said nothing at all and just went off to gather wild berries, which he ate or gave away.

Then one day the old chipmunk's wife gave him some seedlings to plant. The old chipmunk was amused (because after all *he* was the master gardener) and later irritated because they grew so slowly. Sometimes he would pull on them so that they would get the idea although he always taught his gardening students not to do this. One morning his wife called him over to inspect the new plants more closely, and he saw that indeed each was delicately formed and quite lovely except for the bruised places where he had pulled on them. They are not like I thought they'd be, he said to his wife. I guess they decided to be themselves, she answered. Chipmunks aren't all alike either, she added.

And the message of this story is listen to the lessons you teach others because you may need to learn them yourself. Or old chipmunks are as blind as moles when there is something they prefer not to see. Or there are lots of ways to grow; if you want to help, help each individual to find his or her own way.

From: *The Illuminated Life,* by Abe Arkoff. Copyright © 1995 by Allyn and Bacon.

Your fable is to be in four parts. For each part you are given a phrase to start you off, but you can alter it if you like. In Part 1, introduce and describe your problem. In Part 2, dwell on the problem and make it as vivid and formidable and impossible as you can. In Part 3, resolve the problem. In Part 4, state the moral or larger truth of your fable. Finish one part before going to the next. Now turn to the first part and begin.

Part 1 (in which your fable introduces and describes your problem)

Once upon a time, far, far away . . .

Part 2 (in which your fable dwells on the problem and makes it vivid, formidable, and seemingly impossible to solve)

It would seem impossible to work this out because . . .

Part 3 (in which your fable arrives at a solution or resolution of the problem, possibly by seeing yourself or the problem in a new light)

Then one day . . .

Part 4 (in which you state the moral or larger truth of your fable)

And the message of this story is . . .

Question 12

Assets

What Do I Have Going for Me?

There are times in our lives when everything seems to be going just right; things fall into place of their own accord, and we are scarcely aware of making an effort. And there are times when nothing seems to go right, and we face massive obstacles; at these times, we may have to summon all our resources to move along or just to survive.

What personal resources do we have at our disposal? What personal strengths or assets can we count on and mobilize to help us enjoy life and deal with its problems? What are we worth?

Some time ago, a professor of anatomy estimated that the average human body is worth about $7.28; that's the value of its minerals and trace elements. At that price, we average out at about 5 cents a pound, and there may indeed be moments in our lives when we feel about as worthless.

More recently another anatomy professor calculated that a live person is worth $6 million, with hormones and DNA included. Think about that! I've heard people in an exuberant mood say, "I feel like a million!" Imagine feeling like your true worth—six million!

We humans have enormous powers and are capable of wonderful things. For $7.28 or even $6 million, we're considerable bargains. According to psychologists Arthur Combs, Donald Avila, and William Purkey (1978) "The outstanding thing about the human organism is not its limitations but its potentials. It is characteristically overbuilt!" And they continue:

When an engineer builds a bridge, he designs it with a built-in "safety factor"—a degree of sturdiness many times stronger than he expects the structure will need to withstand. People are like that, too. Most of us, in the course of our daily lives, use but a small portion of what is possible for the physical organism. . . . In less physically related behavior the scope of human potential is even more impressive. People can learn to read a page at a glance and to perform prodigious feats of memory and perception. Human creativity goes on and on. Scientists continue to discover, painters paint, and poets write. There seems literally no limit to the possibilities for

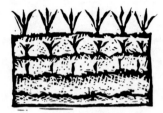

Box 12.1

Assets: What Do I Have Going for Me?

Seedthoughts

1. Up the mountain went the Little Blue Engine. And all the time she kept saying, "I think I can, I think I can, I think I can. . . ."

   —*Watty Piper,* The Little Engine That Could

2. I don't know how anyone can work with their need-to-improves without ready access to their strengths. I don't know how we can be effective, fully functioning persons without full ownership and use of our strengths, men or women.

   —*Theodora Wells*

3. People are designed to be able to weather all kinds of beatings by life and still come up smiling.

   —*Gilbert Brim*

4. [Superkids] deal with an excellence and an adaptive capacity that don't seem to come from anywhere, as if they had carved out these qualities by themselves. We think, here's this awful home; here are these awful parents, here's this awful upbringing, and, we expect, here is this awful result. But, instead, here's a really remarkable child—contrary to everything one might think possible.

   —*E. James Anthony, psychiatrist who works with the children of psychotic parents*

5. Actualizing one's strengths is possible only when one has the capacity for experiencing weaknesses as well. The person who knows that his capacity to express anger is the same capacity that motivated another person to commit murder can say, "There, but for the grace of God, go I."

   —*Everett L. Shostrom*

6. There are two kinds of weakness, that which breaks and that which bends.

   —*J. R. Lowell*

7. I am not a perfect servant. I am a public servant doing my best against the odds. As I develop and serve, be patient. God is not finished with me yet.

   —*Jesse Jackson*

8. Happiness is not the end of life: character is.

   —*Henry Ward Beecher*

9. Think of what you have rather than of what you lack. Of the things you have, select the best and then reflect how eagerly you would have sought them if you did not have them.

   —*Marcus Aurelius*

10. All of you is worth something, if you will only own it.

    —*Sheldon B. Kopp*

thinking, feeling, loving, hoping, seeking and the behaviors they produce. People are always rising to new occasions. (pp. 70–71)

After forty years of intensive research on school learning, Benjamin Bloom (1985b) concludes that almost all persons are potentially talented. He writes, "What any person in the world can learn, *almost* all persons can learn *if* provided with appropriate prior and current conditions of learning" (p. 4). Bloom excludes only the bottom 2 or 3 percent, who have severe difficulties that impair learning, and the top 1 or 2 percent, who are so capable that they can learn regardless of the conditions. The remaining 95 percent of us are reservoirs of talent—developed or neglected.

We are not only "overbuilt" but we are commonly "self-repairing." Some of us get the idea we're fragile vessels (and maybe we are if we think we are), but we're tough old birds. In *The Well Body Book* Mike Samuels and Hal Bennett (1973) remind the reader: "Your body is a three million year old healer. Over three million years of evolution on this planet, it has developed many ways to protect and heal itself" (p. 1).

"Overbuilt" and "self-repairing," we have a lot going for us as we go about our lives. We need to know our strengths, to own or acknowledge them, to develop them, and to make the most of them. More will be said about this in the material that follows.

Know Your Strengths

As was pointed out in Chapter 2, an important way to improve our relationship to ourselves is to get to know ourselves better. It is hard to relate to something unknown. And it is hard to put to use personal strengths that we aren't aware of. We need to know the extent of our capacities. There may be dramatic moments in our lives when we might not survive without this knowledge. We would hardly want to scale a difficult peak without a sense of ourselves as mountaineers. But life is filled with metaphoric mountains from which many a "mountaineer" has fallen or tumbled, or (as large a pity) from which many capable souls disqualify themselves.

Psychologist Duane Schultz (1977) reviewed what seven famous psychologists and psychiatrists (Gordon Allport, Viktor Frankl, Erich Fromm, Carl Jung, Abraham Maslow, Fritz Perls, and Carl Rogers) had to say on the question "What is a healthy personality?" Schultz found considerable disagreement among these men, but one point on which they concurred was that healthy personalities know themselves—their strengths and also their weaknesses, their virtues and their vices.

Abraham Maslow (1968) wrote that we need to know but we can also fear knowing. We grow by acquiring knowledge, and our knowledge makes the world more predictable and manageable. Knowledge reduces anxiety, but knowledge may also increase anxiety. We want to think well of ourselves, so we may fear knowledge that might lower our self-esteem. Through denial, repression, and other psychological mechanisms, we defend ourselves against such unwelcome facts. But we can also fear knowledge of our capacities and potentialities. Knowledge and action tend to be linked, so knowing what we can do may require us to do it or to feel guilty if we don't.

How can we get more information about our strengths? One way is to try many things, to see what we enjoy and what we do well. We can begin by junking the old saying that "Anything that is worth doing is worth doing well." It can be replaced with a new saying: "Most things that are worth doing aren't worth doing well." Having to do things perfectly (or having to do well at everything we do) can keep us from trying and finding out what we like and can do well. Many stories of success have early chapters of failure after failure. "A failure," Elbert

Hubbard wrote, "is a man who has blundered, but is not able to cash in the experience."

Liberal arts colleges generally require course work in a variety of fields, and in this way students receive a broad education and also have an opportunity to see where their interests and capacities lie. However, some students can be under pressure from themselves or their families to make vocational decisions before they have sufficient knowledge of themselves or the vocational world. Vocational counselor Emmanuel Berger (1993) insists that all vocational choices in college should be considered tentative rather than committed ones. "Then," he writes, "the task becomes one of discovering, testing, confirming whether or not the choice was a good one in much the way a scientist goes about testing a hypothesis. Students do not have to defend the presumption that they knew all they needed to know about themselves and the field they chose at the time they chose it, before they had any opportunity to confirm their choice by experience" (p. 443).

As Berger sees it, persons who change majors or fields or jobs on the basis of what they are learning haven't failed. Rather, this is just the "error" part of a trial-and-error process involved in the solution of any difficult problem. We arrive at the correct choice by eliminating inappropriate ones.

Berger points out that since we and our world are constantly changing, we may never be free of the necessity for reconsidering our vocational choice. If we think of vocation in its broadest sense—that to which we are called—we may periodically need to reconsider the directions and pursuits of our lives.

I remember a political candidate who said he was not worried so much about what his opponent didn't know. No, what worried him was what his opponent *knew for sure* that wasn't so. Some of our "certain" knowledge of ourselves or our world may be simply wrong or out of date. Are we open to the possibility of amending it?

Sometimes it takes challenge and adversity to show us we have strengths we never suspected we had. I remember when I was called into the army and entered basic training in the midsummer Texas desert. Short, slight, bookish, nonathletic, I thought I wouldn't survive, but three months later I was still answering roll call. I found I was a lot tougher than I thought.

A case was made in the second chapter that we generally take a positive view of ourselves—that we create positive (but not outlandish) illusions concerning who we are and what we can do. It was noted then, and again in this section, that we protect ourselves against unfavorable information. Consequently, we can come to know our strengths better than those areas where we need to build strength, and getting to know the latter can be the greater challenge.

In our culture there appears to be a taboo against the admission of weakness, especially for males. To allow oneself to be vulnerable is an important human quality and one that makes intimate human relationships possible. One reason females are better at forming friendships is that they are better at allowing themselves to be vulnerable and at confiding their problems.

Toughness is not necessarily a sign of strength—it can be brittleness. And vulnerability is not necessarily a sign of weakness—it can be strength. Ironically, as we allow ourselves to be more vulnerable—not blunting our sensitivity or defending ourselves against it—we become stronger, not weaker, and more fully human.

Own Your Strengths

When we "own" something, we acknowledge that it is ours. When we own (or "own up to") a shortcoming, we face up to it. When we own a strength, we take credit for it and pride in it.

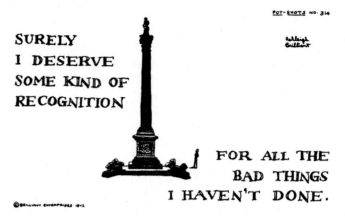

Why aren't some of us better at owning our strengths? One reason may be that we have been taught as children to be humble and modest (Shostrom, 1976). We may have been taught not to brag, but we were not taught the essential difference between bragging and just feeling good about what we can do and what we have done. In our society, women especially may have trouble in this area. Feminist Theodora Wells (1980) writes that one of the things women learn from their role is that they must never claim their strengths. To do so isn't "nice." "Nice girls are modest, never brag, never become conceited." As was noted earlier in this book, women are slower than men to take credit for something good but quicker to shoulder the blame for something bad.

Women also are more likely than men to "deceive down" rather than to "deceive up" (Hartung, 1988). When we deceive up, we delude ourselves that we are more than we are; when we deceive down, we delude ourselves that we are less. We may deceive ourselves down to enhance our ability to act subordinately toward perhaps an employer or spouse in order not to jeopardize the relationship. This is not the same as "playing dumb," in which we seek to deceive another but not ourselves. In deceiving down, we convince ourselves we are less than we are to make a situation tolerable. Unfortunately, as we convince ourselves we are less, we may become less.

In working with older people, I've noted a number of women who have blossomed after a divorce they hadn't sought or after the death of a spouse of many years. Some of this blossoming came about because they had to take more active management of their lives, but in some cases I am convinced that the transformation took place because the person no longer needed to deceive herself down into a subordinate role.

In writing about her own childhood in a small Southern town, Mary Ellen Snodgrass (1989) recalls that there were no female role models for any leadership positions "that really mattered." In her church, women were "keepers of the nursery, singers in the choir, leaders of endless circle meetings, teachers of Sunday school . . . bakers of angel bread." Snodgrass recalls, "The message was clear to my eight-year-old-mind: women were not meant to think too hard, and certainly not to lead menfolk in prayer and worship" (p. 66). She writes that her early conditioning influenced her to seek supportive rather than leadership roles, and she never has found a proper niche for her talents.

Psychologist Martin Seligman (1975) has shown that dogs subjected to shock which they cannot avoid demonstrate a "learned helplessness." When later placed in a two-sided chamber where they can escape from shock by jumping a barrier, they do not try. Instead, they run around frantically and then lie down and whine. This same kind of helplessness has been observed in other species, including human beings.

Seligman has also shown how learned helplessness can be unlearned and prevented. If the barrier is removed and the leashed dog is dragged from the shock side of the chamber to the other side, it eventually learns to escape the shock by itself; and if the dog is taught to escape shock before encountering the unescapable shock, it is "immunized" and doesn't later lapse into helplessness. Another important finding: dogs raised in cages where almost nothing is under their control prove much more subject to helplessness than other dogs.

Seligman's research suggests that the way to teach persons to own their strengths or to learn they have power is to provide them with early and continuing experiences involving mastery. All of us need to be continually taught and shown that what we do makes a difference, that the environment responds to our efforts.

Persons who feel powerless give up, and sometimes they waste away and die. In some cultures, for example, a person who has been hexed and feels powerless to escape the spell or curse, becomes ill and dies. By the same token, individuals who regain power may show remarkable improvement. For example, a group of nursing home elderly who were encouraged to take responsibility for changing their environment, deciding their activities, and making their complaints known became healthier and happier than a group who remained totally cared for. Furthermore, eighteen months later, the death rate of the people in the empowered group was about half the rate of the other group (Langer & Rodin, 1976).

Develop Your Strengths

In Chapter 8, we noted the hypothesis that most persons function at a fraction of their potential. How can we develop more of ourselves? There are as many ways to develop a strength as there are ways to grow. Some salient ways are described in the material that follows.

Imaging

One way to develop a strength is to have a clear and compelling image or mental picture of oneself as a person who has that strength or is acquiring or able to acquire it. Professor Richard Weaver (1991) holds that self-fulfillment begins with an image, which we then nurture into being. He tells his own story—about growing up in Ann Arbor on the doorstep of the University of Michigan, where he coasted through his freshman year with dismal results. The next year he traveled with his parents, who were on Fulbright grants, and learned how impressed people around the world were with his university.

> When I realized what I *really* had on my doorstep, I came to realize how silly I was being. I wasn't working up to my potential; I wasn't fulfilling my abilities; I wasn't taking advantage of the opportunity that was being given to me. . . . I gained an entirely new *image* of myself—an image of me, Richard Weaver, identified with this great institution. And it was that *image* that directed and guided my behavior after that. . . . I *was* a University of Michigan student; now all I had to do was get my life in order to achieve the self-fulfillment of that image—the me *I* wanted to be. (p. 217)

Some of our assets or strengths can be considered "harvest" qualities. They are strengths that are part of our repertory or armory. They are fully developed, usable, and used. Other assets might be considered "seeds," since they are waiting to be developed or they are tender sprouts in need of attention. One way of developing a seed strength is to imagine it as ready for harvest; that is, to see ourselves as already having the quality we wish to have and then act accordingly. This "as if" process—playing a part in order to test and develop it—is commonly used by adolescents as they seek to determine who they are, and it has been used by many famous people. One of these was Theodore Roosevelt, who wrote about it in his autobiography (this passage was partly quoted in an early exploration, but it's worth extending here):

> I was, as a young man, at first both nervous and distrustful of my own prowess. I had to train myself painfully and laboriously not merely as regards my body but as regards my soul and spirit. . . . When a boy, I read a passage in one of Marryat's books which always impressed me. In this passage, the captain of some small British man-of-war is explaining to the hero how to acquire the quality of fearlessness. He says that at the outset almost every man is frightened when he goes into action, but that the course to follow is for the man to keep such a grip on himself that he can act just as if he were not frightened. After this is kept up long enough, it changes from pretense to reality, and the man does in very fact become fearless by sheer dint of practicing fearlessness when he does not feel it. . . . This was the theory upon which I went. There were all kinds of things of which I was afraid at first, ranging from grizzly bears to "mean" horses and gun fighters; but by acting as if I was not afraid I gradually ceased to be afraid. Most men can have the same experience if they choose. ([1913] 1946, p. 52)

Psychologist Sidney Jourard wrote, "When we come into the world, we are the embodiment of incredible possibilities" (1975, p. 5). But we are soon persuaded to become a particular kind of person by our families, peers, mass media, schools, and other agents of socialization. In this process, certain of our possibilities are nurtured while others are allowed to remain undeveloped. However, the unsprouted seed qualities remain, and if we wish one to grow, we can begin by rediscovering a quality in ourselves and visualizing it in full blossom.

The "as if" process involves two phases: seeing ourselves as having the quality we desire, and behaving as though we did. By visualizing a quality, we can inwardly rehearse it before outwardly acting it. The deliberate and systematic use of fantasy can have a considerable effect on us, and the image of an event may sometimes have the same effect on us as the actual event itself. Psychologist Arnold Lazarus (1977) calls the practice of a skill in one's imagination "goal rehearsal" and illustrates its use in the following case of a 25-year-old man who was unable to assert himself in his work with his father:

> The father was a powerful, dictatorial individual who shouted down any new ideas his son tried to introduce. At my instigation, the son practiced goal rehearsal. He imagined suggesting to his father that a new line of merchandise be introduced. He would then picture his father's typical reaction—ranting and raving. I instructed the son to keep picturing the image, to keep on trying to find a way to get through to his father in the image. It took him more than a week of imagery practice to picture himself outdoing his father's tirade. In his mind's eye he saw himself banging the desk with his fist and yelling, "The only way to get heard in this place is to yell louder than you can." In real life, the son was inclined to be quiet and withdrawn and he had never raised his voice to his father. I encouraged him to act out his fantasy. "I can't do it!" he protested. This is where goal rehearsal came into force. I asked him to rehearse in his mind the shouting scene over and over again.

BABY BLUES by Jerry Scott and Rick Kirkman. By permission of
Jerry Scott, Rick Kirkman and Creators Syndicate.

It took yet another week, during which time the son pictured himself outdoing his father's vituperation hundreds and hundreds of times. He rehearsed this image so thoroughly that it began to feel like second nature to him. Two days later he called me to report that it had been put to good use. "My dad was yelling and carrying on and quite suddenly, almost by complete surprise, it came out of me. . . . Just as I had done so many times in my image I pounded the desk, and shouted at the top of my lungs that I was sick of being treated like a child, sick of being yelled at, sick of being overruled. . . . My father was nonplussed. . . . For the first time in my life, as far back as I can remember, my dad backed down and gave in to me." As the reader can well imagine, the upshot of this interaction was a new-found respect between father and son, and a greater feeling of self-confidence in a formerly timid and inhibited young man. (pp. 62–63)

A similar kind of rehearsal is recommended by Tristine Rainer (1978) to those of us who are diarists or journal keepers. Rainer calls this technique "second chance." When we are dissatisfied with the way we have behaved in a particular interaction, we are encouraged to visualize ourselves in the same situation but behaving in a way we wish—behaving with more of our seed strength: perhaps more patient or more assertive. Then we write this revision of our behavior in our journal as a rehearsal for the future.

Affirmation

Affirmation is another useful technique for developing strengths. To affirm means to declare positively or firmly or to assert that something is true. An *affirmation*, as we are using the term here, is a positive declaration about ourselves. Two famous examples of affirmation are "Every day in every way I'm getting better and better," and "Black is beautiful."

You may recall some spontaneous affirmations of your own. Perhaps you were having momentary trouble doing something, and you said to yourself, "I know I can do it. I just know I can do it." Or perhaps someone put you down, and you reassured yourself that you weren't all that bad; in fact, you were all right!

One night Madeleine L'Engle wrote in her journal, "I'm a writer. That's who I am, even if I'm never published again." She had sold several books before she was 30, but only two books in the next twelve years, and she was getting one rejection slip after another. Yet, as her journal entry showed, she never stopped affirming herself, and soon afterward she wrote *A Wrinkle in Time*, which won a medal for children's literature and was made into a motion picture (Gellman & Gage, 1985).

A nearly constant inner monologue goes on inside our heads. We are constantly telling ourselves things, saying what's good and what's bad, saying what we should be doing or not doing. This "mind chatter" is what we try to turn off when we seek repose or when we are in meditation; but, as beginning meditators find, it is not an easy thing to do. Some of this mind chatter is outmoded and negative and serves to bring us down or keep us down. For example, we may continually tell ourselves we're ugly or dumb or we can't do something or we'll never be able to do something. One way to bring ourselves up is to replace the negative chatter with material that is more positive and helpful, and we can do this through the use of affirmations.

The affirmations that work the best for us may be the ones we create for ourselves. Here are some guidelines for making affirmations: (1) Affirmations are stated positively. For example: "I am a patient person." Not: "I am not impatient." (2) Affirmations are stated in the present tense, as if they are already achieved; in making such a statement, we are not lying but, instead, are creating a blueprint for what we are in the process of building. (3) Affirmations are short, simple, and worded in a way that is appropriate for the affirmer. (4) Affirmations are said with belief.[1]

The simplest use of affirmation is to write over and over or tell ourselves over and over whatever it is we wish to affirm. For example, "I am an assertive person" (repeated). Or "I, [*your name*], am an assertive person" (repeated).

An interesting variation—a test really—is to write an affirmation and then listen to see if there is an echo, perhaps one of disbelief or question or growing belief. Don't argue with the echo; simply listen to what it has to say and go on adhering to your affirmation.

Below is an example of the use of this technique employed by "Julia," a 31-year-old attractive, intelligent woman. After being deserted in two relationships, she needed to see herself as worthy and deserving of love.

I, Julia, deserve love. *No, I don't.*

I, Julia, deserve love. *Not me.*

I, Julia, deserve love. *Who would love me?*

I, Julia, deserve love. *Not really.*

I, Julia, deserve love. *I'm ugly.*

I, Julia, deserve love. *Selfish, selfish, selfish.*

I, Julia, deserve love. *Can't believe that.*

I, Julia, deserve love. *Maybe I'm not so ugly.*

I, Julia, deserve love. *This is silly.*

I, Julia, deserve love. *From whom?*

I, Julia, deserve love. *From myself?*

I, Julia, deserve love. *From my dad?*

I, Julia, deserve love. *Maybe I do.*

I, Julia, deserve love. *Can I say so?*

I, Julia, deserve love. *Do I dare?*

I, Julia, deserve love. *Perhaps I do.*

I, Julia, deserve love. *I do.* (Bloomfield & Kory, 1980, pp. 122–123)

---

[1] These guidelines are adapted from Gawain, 1978.

Elevation, Degradation

You may remember that on Sheldon Kopp's laundry list or philosophy of life these two points appeared:

> All evil is potential vitality in need of transformation.
> All of you is worth something, if you will only own it.

There is an old saying that you can't make a silk purse out of a sow's ear, but within each of us is much that we can make either good or bad. Not long ago I read about a man who was making a good living as a security consultant. He gave advice on how to make places burglar-proof. He seemed eminently well qualified because he had a very long history of burglary, for which he had served very little time. Evidently it was enough time to get him to elevate what society considered a weakness into what it agreed was a considerable and even marketable strength.

Some of our personal qualities have the potential for being strengths or liabilities, depending upon how they are used. We can elevate (or upgrade) them into assets or degrade (or downgrade) them into liabilities (Ferrucci, 1982). As an example, consider the sense of humor: it can be a considerable asset in coping, but humor can also be used destructively to attack others or to deprecate ourselves; sarcasm is a form of wit used to taunt or wound another. Or consider a critical facility: it is necessary for evaluating any performance and it can be an important form of help, but it can be degraded into a destructive force without any redeeming constructive quality, tearing down without helping to rebuild. Those of us with hypercritical attitudes may find nothing good enough. Our impossible standards can become two-edged swords, cutting down others and ourselves as well.

Compensation

In Chapter 2 (Box 2.2), compensation was introduced as a defense mechanism; it was defined as a response to threat in which we use achievement in one area to make up for a deficit in another. In doing so, we protect and perhaps even enhance our image of ourself. Compensation might be more broadly defined as a "coping mechanism" because, with or without threat, we often try to find areas of success to offset or counterbalance areas of failure or weakness.

Comedienne Carol Burnett recalled that her sense of comedy came to her assistance as she was growing up. She felt that she was unattractive—especially in comparison to her parents, who were "beautiful people"—and remembers joking and clowning around "just to get over the fear of not being liked because I was poor and not very pretty" (quoted in Zimbardo, 1977, p. 74). Interestingly, a research team has found that professional comedians, despite their considerable intelligence, generally did poorly in school with its emphasis on discipline and decorum; to compensate—to prove they were somebody—they developed their comic skills and made the classroom laugh (Fisher & Fisher, 1981).

In compensating, we ordinarily develop one personal asset or strength to offset a quality that is less promising or completely unpromising; sometimes, however, through persistent effort, we become strong in the very area in which once we were weak. A case in point is Theodore Roosevelt, who was mentioned earlier, in the section on imaging. When Roosevelt was young, he was asthmatic and frail, and his physical weakness led him to embark on a program of rigorous exercise. He became very successful in strengthening himself and in leading a robust life that included distinguished leadership of the Rough Riders (a calvary regiment) in the Spanish-American War.

Knowing when to keep trying to develop some resistant area of strength in ourselves and when it is better to develop some other strength—that's the trick. We admire those who never give up at something until finally they succeed, but we deplore those who never give up at something and never succeed. It's also important to know when a personal asset or strength has been eroded or lost, so that we can move on to make more of what we have left or what we can yet to develop.

At the age of 21, Paul Sheriff was in an automobile accident that left him paralyzed from the waist down. Paul, who has spoken to my classes and is a most inspiring person, knew at that point he had to make something different of his life. Wrestling with clothes that poorly accommodated his wheelchair status, he decided to design and manufacture special clothes for other persons like himself. He was doing well when a national company overtook him and put him out of business. Nothing daunted, he started all over again, and now has a consulting firm that shows companies how to adapt their premises to accommodate handicapped persons.

At the age of 18, Larry Alford was among America's top junior golfers. Then, in an automobile accident that nearly killed him, he lost his left arm just below the elbow. He refused to give up golfing and started practicing with one arm. An innovative prosthetic "golf hand" especially designed for him has allowed him to resume tournament play with success, and, as I write this, he is a member of the golf team of Sam Houston State University. Speaking to a group of young amputees, he said, "Don't think of your missing limb as something that makes you a lesser person. Think of it as something that can make you stronger. I would love to be the first pro golfer with a prosthetic hand. But I also know that if I don't succeed, I won't be a failure. We only fail when we don't try—when we don't dream" (Pekkanen, 1993, p. 96).

Practice

All human strengths are skills that can be improved through practice. Thomas Edison, a genius, once defined genius as "1 percent inspiration and 99 percent perspiration." A study of 120 of the nation's top athletes, artists, and scholars suggests that Edison was right (Bloom, 1985a). The researchers concluded that it was not great natural talent but determination and drive that produced success. They had expected to find that these outstanding persons had great natural gifts. Instead, mothers often reported that another child seemed more talented. The persons themselves often made an inauspicious and far from outstanding entry to their field. But what was outstanding was their unceasing effort and dedication. The finding reminded the director of the research, Benjamin Bloom, of the joke concerning a young man lost on the streets of New York City. Finally this man stops and asks an elderly lady, "How do I get to Carnegie Hall?" And she looks up at him and replies, "Practice, young man. Practice" (Savage, 1985).

Direction, determination, and practice are required to develop any strength or talent. To know what we want to do or who we want to be, to be determined to do it or be it, and then practice, practice.

It is also helpful to make a record of our progress (or retrogress) by observing ourselves carefully and writing down what we see. As we note wanted behavior increasing or unwanted behavior diminishing, we'll know we're on the right track. For example, we tally each time we respond to a trying situation with the forbearance or patience we are developing in ourselves; and, to be fair, we note each time the old angry response reasserts itself. We look for an increase in the former and a decrease in the latter.

Watson and Tharp (1993) note that when a behavior is under scrutiny, it often changes. "Undesirable behaviors tend to diminish, and desired behaviors tend to increase *because you are observing and recording them*" (p. 88). It appears to be more effective to record an *undesired* behavior *before* performing it and a *desired* one *after* its performance. For example, if you're cutting down on angry responses, tally anger before you express it (and you'll be less likely to do so). And if you show forbearance or patience, tally it afterward (as a pat on the back).

At one point in his life, Benjamin Franklin carefully observed and recorded his own behavior in order to develop his strengths. He began by listing and defining thirteen virtues:

1.	Temperance	Eat not to dullness: drink not to elevation.
2.	Silence	Speak not but what may benefit others or yourself; and avoid trifling conversation.
3.	Order	Let all things have their places, let each part of your business have its time.
4.	Resolution	Resolve to perform what you ought; perform without fail what you resolve.
5.	Frugality	Make no expense but to do good to others or yourself; i.e., waste nothing.
6.	Industry	Lose no time; be always employed in something useful; cut off all unnecessary actions.
7.	Sincerity	Use no hurtful deceit; think innocently and justly, and, if you speak, speak accordingly.
8.	Justice	Wrong none by doing injuries, or omitting the benefits that are your duty.
9.	Moderation	Avoid extremes; forbear resenting injuries so much as you think they deserve.
10.	Cleanliness	Tolerate no uncleanliness in body, clothes, or habitation.
11.	Tranquillity	Be not disturbed at trifles, or at accidents common or unavoidable.
12.	Chastity	Rarely use venery but for health or offspring, never to dullness, weakness, or the injury of your own or another's peace or reputation.
13.	Humility	Imitate Jesus and Socrates.

© Ashleigh Brilliant 1985. Reprinted by permission.

Box 12.2

Benjamin Franklin's Record of Faults

Here is a page from Benjamin Franklin's notebook, the first week he devoted to improving his virtues. This was the week he concentrated on temperance. Each "spot" shows a fault committed against a particular virtue on that day. (See the text for the name of the virtue corresponding to each letter.) As can be seen, Franklin did well on temperance but poorly on order, the area in which he proved most "incorrigible." However, "something, that pretended to be reason" suggested to him that he shouldn't be too vain about his morals, that a benevolent man allowed himself a few faults so as not to show up his friends, and "that a perfect character might be attended with the inconvenience of being envied and hated" ([1784] 1904, p. 198). Thus, wise to his own ways and somewhat tongue in cheek, he got himself off the hook.

TEMPERANCE.							
EAT NOT TO DULLNESS; DRINK NOT TO ELEVATION.							
	S.	M.	T.	W.	T.	F.	S.
T.							
S.	*	*		*		*	
O.	* *	*	*		*	*	*
R.			*			*	
F.		*			*		
I.			*				
S.							
J.							
M.							
C.							
T.							
C.							
H.							

Franklin ruled pages of his notebook into seven columns, one for each day of the week, and into thirteen rows, one for each virtue. Each week he would concentrate on one virtue, and each evening he would record any fault committed that day against any virtue (see Box 12.2). (He would have done better to record the fault before its occurrence.) He hoped especially to keep the featured virtue fault-free and to continue it fault-free as he went on to the next virtue the next week; then continue both fault-free as he went on to the third virtue; and so on.

Summing up his experiment, Franklin wrote, "I was surpis'd to find myself so much fuller of faults than I had imagined; but I had the satisfaction of seeing them diminish. . . . On the whole, tho' I never arrived at the perfection I had been so ambitious of obtaining, but fell far short of it, yet I was, by the endeavor, a better and happier man than I otherwise should have been if I had not attempted it" ([1784] 1904, 197–198, passim).

Use Your Strengths

Observing a developing infant, you soon see how eager it is to put each new capacity to use. It wants to do what it can do. It wants to make things happen. It shows its pleasure when it does. For example, in one experiment involving 2-month-old babies and an overhead mobile, infants who controlled the movement of the mobile by turning their heads smiled more than infants who saw the mobile but didn't affect its movements (Watson & Ramey, 1972).

Psychologist Gilbert Brim (1988) observes that 2-year-olds being tested "smile when they solve a difficult problem but go deadpan when they solve an easy one" (p. 48). Not just youngsters, but almost all of us at every age smile more when we are making things—and especially important things—happen in our lives. "Young or old," Brim observes, "we want to be challenged" (p. 48). Growth, challenge, and mastery are central to our sense of well-being. Sometimes we may want to test our limits and sometimes we need to rest on our oars, but usually we seek challenges of what psychologist Nicholas Hobbs calls "just manageable difficulty." These challenges require most but not all of our capacity; we hold something back to use just in case it's required.

Brim notes that winning leads us to raise our sights and losing to lower them. But losing can also challenge us to learn from our failure, to make more and better use of our strengths and redouble our efforts.

As we grow, more and more is asked of us, and we ask more and more of ourselves. We become increasingly competent, developing our aptitudes, skills, and talents and putting them to use. What we want to do and what we are able to do change as we move through life. We are faced with a continual gap between "want" and "can"—the "achievement gap," Brim calls it—and how we manage this gap is central to our sense of well-being.

Brim tells a story about his father to illustrate what it means to manage the achievement gap successfully and to make the most of whatever one has. It's worth retelling here:

My Father's Windowbox

My father was 103 when he died the summer before last. He grew up on a farm in Ohio, was the only one of seven children to leave farming, found his way through some complicated paths to Harvard and to Columbia, doing his Ph.D. with John Dewey (on rural education) and taught at Ohio State University until he was 60. Then he and my mother bought an old, abandoned farm of several hundred acres in northwest Connecticut, remodeled the house and moved there to live.

He set about to clean the fence rows and to clear the woods the way he had been taught to do as a boy in Ohio. For many years he roamed the hillsides and mountaintop, thinning trees, trimming brush and taking pride in looking up from the porch at his clean and tidy mountain. As he grew older, his legs and back would tire earlier in the day; sometimes he'd get a friend or a young hired man to help him keep up the place.

Over the years, hardly with any notice, the upper part of the mountain was no longer within range, and gradually his level of aspiration lowered, coming down the hillside, so to speak, into the trees around the house and a new and large investment of energy in gardening—both vegetables and flowers. At one time he had plots of asparagus and rows of raspberries and fields of gladioli and would supply his friends throughout the northwest corner of Connecticut with armloads of "glads." He cultivated these with a power tiller, much like a lawnmower. Later, as it became harder for him to bear down on the handles to lift the tiller's front end to turn, the width between the rows grew larger. On his 90th birthday he bought a small riding tractor.

One year he did not plant the gardens and his attention turned to the little border flowers around the house and to four large window boxes at eye level when he stood; they required no knee bending to cultivate. The window boxes served well for years, but then his failing sight and muscular strength meant that even these were not tended without great effort. But he focused on a new activity: listening to "talking books"—novels, biographies of great poets and a good sampling of the world's drama.

After a few minor strokes during his 102nd year, he could not see well enough to deal with television or hear well enough to use the talking books. His window boxes were still there, and he would go outdoors to see them, dimly. He felt the soil and watered them when needed. Although planted by someone else, they still were his achievements. He would file his garden tools, especially his hoe, to keep them sharp; it was easy to do by touch. Having seen the scope of his life shrink dramatically to its narrow compass ("There's so little left of me," he said) he told me he would like to leave—but not through his own action; he was waiting and hoping.

This man was as happy and fulfilled at 101 as he was at age 60. He spontaneously used some of the most important principles that modern psychology has uncovered for living well with the changes and challenges we confront in the course of life: In dealing with the gaps between his aspirations and achievements, he altered his methods, such as adding help, both personal and mechanical; he lowered his level of aspiration, being willing to settle for less; and he shifted goals as he grew older. An unyielding drive for growth and mastery, a rational mind and a capacity for change determined my father's methods, his levels of aspiration and his goals in his later years. But my father's way of managing reality was not unique to him—it is part of every naturally dynamic, striving human being. (p. 51)

The difference between who we are and who we could be can be a negative, destructive force, filling us with self-contempt (Horney, 1950). Or it can be a positive, constructive force, motivating us to get a move on and make more of ourselves (May, 1967). It can provide us with the clue that we have lost our way. It can be a guide, letting us know when we are back on the path (Yalom, 1980).

Why don't we use more of our strengths? Some answers to this question lie in what was written earlier in this chapter. We may not use our strengths because we have inadequate or inaccurate knowledge of them or we fear to know them. We may not use them because we have disowned them to somehow keep our place or perhaps because life has taught us to be helpless and passive. Or perhaps we just never learned how to develop them or we settled for a lesser bargain.

Another set of reasons why we might not make use of our strengths has to do less with the individual than with society (although, of course, we have had a hand in creating it). Carl Rogers (1980) has written eloquently about the "person of tomorrow." This "new person" he describes will live in a "new world"—one that prizes the individual and encourages the development of all the strengths of mind and spirit. But until tomorrow comes, we live in this "old world"—or a part of it—that may not encourage us to use all our strengths. In fact, it may discourage or even punish us for making the most of some of what we have.

Recent research indicates that the achievement of American students compares unfavorably with that of students in a number of other nations (Ravitch, 1989), and studies of U.S. adolescents show that, although there is peer pressure to graduate from high school, there is also pressure against outstanding academic achievement. Being a "brain" can be closely associated with being a "nerd," and a strategy to keep from being labeled a nerd is to deliberately underachieve. Educators B. Bradford Brown and Laurence Steinberg (1990) (who document these findings) write that "it is frightening that many of the most intellectually capable high school students strive to be *less* than they can be in order to avoid rejection by peers" (p. 60).

Brown and Steinberg note that women and blacks are especially vulnerable to peer pressure against achievement. Researchers Signithia Fordham and John Ogbu (1986) found an antiacademic ethos among students in a Washington, D.C., all-black high school. High achievers were accused of "acting white," ostracized and labeled "brainiacs," excluded from peer activities, or even assaulted.

Two anthropologists, Dorothy Holland and Margaret Eisenhart (1990), followed the lives of twenty-three women students at two Southern state-funded, nonelite colleges, one historically black and the other predominantly white. The students were interviewed in their sophomore year, at graduation, and later in their lives. College for most of these women was a narrowing rather than a broadening experience—one in which they were "mobbed by romance." They pursued and found Mr. Right instead of ideas, scaled down their ambitions, and wound up with marginal careers.

Robert Brannon (1985) notes that one of the central requirements of the American male sex role is to avoid anything considered feminine. "No sissy stuff" is a rule little boys learn early, and it's a rule that remains in full force all through life. Unfortunately included in the proscribed behavior are some highly important human qualities, such as emotional expressiveness, without which truly intimate relationships are difficult. Brannon writes that the qualities assigned to our sex roles are imposed on us even if we have little interest in or aptitude for them. "Traditionally sex roles come in just two large and unwieldy packages: masculine and feminine. (We don't even get to choose which one fits us best.) What this arbitrary assignment discourages most of all is the option of choosing what sort of characteristics we want to have" (p. 312).

Women have traditionally been defined as expressive, emotional, sentimental, and supportive and also as dependent and interpersonally oriented. Men, by contrast, have been defined as inexpressive, rational, unsentimental, and also independent, competitive, and achievement oriented (Balswick, 1988).

Brannon concludes that sex roles "are neither necessary nor beneficial" and that "life after sex roles" would be more diverse, more interesting, and happier. We are a long way from being a society without sex roles, but there is some movement toward redefinition. The new definition calls for a greater flexibility, interchangeability, and sharing of roles to permit better use of our strengths. For women, this new definition calls for the expansion of the current female role to include extrafamilial positions of power and prestige traditionally occupied by men. For men, the definition calls for such preeminent qualities traditionally associated with women as nurturance, tenderness, and expressiveness (Balswick, 1988).

To Illuminate Your Own Life

Anchor and Apply*

1. Describe the trial-and-error process you have gone through in school, at work, or in any area of life in which you have come to know more about your strengths.

2. Have you had difficulty in owning your strengths? Have you "played dumb" or "deceived down"? Describe your experience in this regard.

3. Has your experience in life empowered you or given you a "learned helplessness"? Discuss your life in this regard.

4. Describe the way you developed a specific strength or skill in yourself.

5. Describe any use you have made of imaging, acting "as if," "goal rehearsal," or "second chance" in developing a strength.

6. Describe any use you have made of affirmation in developing a strength.

7. Describe your experience in elevating a quality so that it became a strength rather than a liability.

8. Describe any use you have made of compensation in developing a strength.

9. Discuss the difference between who you are and who you could be. Is this difference a positive or negative force in your life? Give your evidence.

10. Describe the pressure you have felt from your family, peers, school, or other institutions in your development and use of your strengths.

11. Spend a few days or a week working on a strength or "virtue" (to use Benjamin Franklin's term). Record your efforts at the end of each day, and summarize your progress when you conclude your work.

---

* These "anchor and apply" items are designed to help you use the concepts of the chapter as stimuli to prompt new or deeper or clearer insights into yourself and your life. To respond to an item, first find the material in the chapter that is most relevant to the item *and* yourself; that's called "anchoring." Second, think about this material in relationship to yourself and your life and keep thinking about it until you arrive at a new or deeper or clearer understanding; that's the "apply" or application part. When you write or present your response to the item, be sure to include both parts, that is, both the anchor material and the application. You can know you are successful on an item if, in completing it, you truly learn something new or understand something better.

Personal Accomplishments

Research workers and clinicians have noted that happy and productive persons see themselves and their world in a positive way. By contrast, persons in therapy often have shrunken notions of themselves, and they frequently underrate their abilities and accomplishments. A prominent goal of therapy is to help these persons accept and appreciate themselves and see themselves in a more favorable light.

All of us need to appreciate, affirm, and take pride in ourselves. Although pride of another sort has achieved the unenviable position of first on the list of the seven cardinal sins, reference is not being made here to arrogance or conceit but rather to self-respect and a sense of one's value and dignity as a human being. This essential pride was described earlier in Exploration 2C. It is not a noisy "pride" that needs to announce itself to the world, nor is it an embarrassed "pride" that is self-conscious and disconcerted. It is a simple, confident, quiet pride.

In this exploration, you are asked to list all of your accomplishments that come to mind. Put down all the things you look back on with pride, all the things you have created, achieved, developed, learned, overcome, or won. Note that these accomplishments do not need to be of championship proportions, such as winning a gold medal, silver cup, or blue ribbon (although these should certainly be listed); they may include such everyday heroics as overcoming a fear, getting along with a difficult relative, learning a skill, adjusting to a misfortune, getting a college degree, building a business, or raising two great children. Be as specific as you can.

Begin your list below, numbering each item as you go, and add additional pages as needed.

---

* The three explorations for this chapter form a progression; each succeeding exploration builds on what has gone before.

Read and reread your list of accomplishments until you feel very, very positive about yourself—keep reading and adding items until you do. Then give yourself an award for all you have accomplished. The award can be a medal or ribbon, a plaque or trophy, a certificate or scroll, a badge, garter (order of), belt (black or any color), or anything. Create your award in any way you like or draw a picture of it in the space below. Be sure the award is suitably inscribed or has an accompanying message to indicate why it was given.

Personal Strengths

As was noted earlier in this chapter, we humans are "overbuilt" and "self-repairing" and have a lot going for us. We need to be aware of our strengths, to own or acknowledge them, to develop them, and to make the most of them.

Some of our strengths can be referred to as "harvest" qualities. These are personal qualities that are well developed and put to good use in our lives. Other strengths can be called "seed" qualities if they are not well developed and if our lives are less than they might be on this account.

To illustrate, "assertiveness" may be one of our harvest qualities if we can stand up for ourselves and maintain our rights without infringing on the rights of others and if we make good use of this quality in our lives. By contrast, assertiveness would need to be considered a seed quality if we have difficulty in this area and if we need to nurture or develop this quality to make more of our lives.

In completing the previous exploration, you wrote down a number of accomplishments in which you take pride. In arriving at each of these accomplishments you must have demonstrated one or more personal qualities. For example, in getting along with a difficult relative, you may have shown a good deal of patience, perseverance, or a sense of humor. Perhaps one of these strengths also was instrumental in some of your other accomplishments; if so, it probably is one of your harvest qualities.

Perhaps there is something you wish you could have accomplished but were unable to because one (or more) of your personal qualities isn't as fully developed as it might be. For example, you may not have accomplished something because you are not sufficiently independent; this then may be a seed quality for you.

Study the list of accomplishments you prepared in the previous exploration and also the list of personal qualities in Box 12.3. On the latter list, find five qualities that are well represented in your accomplishments and that for you are harvest qualities. Write each of these qualities in the spaces indicated below. (No doubt you have more harvest qualities, but for this exercise choose just five.)

Find one quality on the list of personal qualities that for you is a seed quality—one that is not well represented in your list of accomplishments but that will improve your life in some way as you make it sprout, grow, and blossom. Write this quality in the space indicated below. If one or more of your important harvest or seed qualities is not on the list, write it in at the end of the list and in the appropriate space below.

Harvest Qualities	Seed Quality
1. _____	1. _____
2. _____	
3. _____	
4. _____	
5. _____	

From: *The Illuminated Life,* by Abe Arkoff. Copyright © 1995 by Allyn and Bacon.

Box 12.3

Personal Qualities

1. *Acceptance.* To be favorably disposed toward others and yourself.
2. *Achievement.* To work to accomplish difficult, rewarding, or worthy goals.
3. *Assertiveness.* To maintain your own rights and the rights of others.
4. *Caringness.* To be deeply concerned about the welfare of others.
5. *Commitment.* To stand by and be faithful to your pledges and vows, and stated courses of action.
6. *Cooperativeness.* To work well with others toward common ends.
7. *Courage.* To face danger and adversity with confidence and firmness of purpose.
8. *Curiosity.* To desire to know or learn about new or different things.
9. *Empathy.* To be able to enter into another's world of feelings and meanings.
10. *Enthusiasm.* To be greatly interested in, excited by, and responsive to what is present in your life.
11. *Expressiveness.* To communicate fully, concretely, and unambiguously.
12. *Flexibility.* To accommodate changing conditions.
13. *Friendliness.* To form warm, comforting, and trusting relationships.
14. *Generativity.* To be devoted to the welfare of generations succeeding your own.
15. *Generosity.* To be willing to give and share.
16. *Gentleness.* To be considerate and kindly.
17. *Happiness.* To be in good spirits, finding joy and pleasure in living.
18. *Helpfulness.* To nurture, assist, and protect others.
19. *Honesty.* To be truthful, sincere, and genuine.
20. *Hopefulness.* To believe that desired outcomes are possible.
21. *Imagination.* To be able to deal creatively with reality.
22. *Independence.* To be self-reliant.
23. *Insightfulness.* To be able to discern the true nature of things, including yourself.
24. *Integrity.* To have a sense of coherence and wholeness.
25. *Internality.* To believe in your ability to control your own life.

26. *Intuitiveness.* To be able to gain knowledge directly and without the use of rational process.
27. *Intelligence.* To have a considerable facility for learning and applying knowledge.
28. *Lovingness.* To be affectionate and devoted to others.
29. *Optimism.* To believe that desired outcomes are likely.
30. *Orderliness.* To be methodical and systematic.
31. *Patience.* To have the capacity for calm endurance.
32. *Playfulness.* To be lighthearted and full of fun and good spirits.
33. *Perseverance.* To keep at something until it is accomplished.
34. *Presence.* To be fully attentive—totally in a situation in mind, body, and spirit.
35. *Self-disclosure.* To allow others to know you as you are; to share your inner thoughts and feelings.
36. *Sense of humor.* To perceive, express, and enjoy the funny or comical side of things.
37. *Sensitivity.* To be attuned to subtle expressions and nuances of meaning and be able to adjust your behavior accordingly.
38. *Sensuousness.* To be susceptible to and appreciative of the pleasures of the senses.
39. *Serenity.* To have a tranquility of nature relatively impervious to agitation or turmoil.
40. *Simplicity.* To be without affectation, pretension, or artificiality.
41. *Stability.* To be constant in character and purpose.
42. *Talentedness.* To have one or more special aptitudes or abilities.
43. *Tolerance.* To allow or respect the beliefs and behaviors of others.
44. *Trustworthiness.* To be dependable, reliable, and worthy of another's confidence.
45. *Understanding.* To grasp clearly and completely what is being conveyed.
46. *Venturesomeness.* To be daring and bold.
47. *Warmth.* To communicate feelings of closeness and affection.
48. *Wisdom.* To have sound judgment and the ability to apply to good effect what you have learned.
49. _____.
50. _____.

In the space below, with quiet pride, discuss each of the five harvest qualities on your list, indicating how it helped you in one or more of your accomplishments.

In the space below, with earnest determination, discuss the seed quality you listed, indicating (1) how you will make it sprout, grow, and blossom, and (2) how it will then help you in accomplishing something you want to accomplish.

Personal Worth

How much are you worth? This is not just an academic question, because its answer relates to the amount of money your survivors might collect if you died a wrongful death or how much should be spent in cleaning up the atmosphere or improving the safety of your work environment or modes of transportation or in medical treatment. Some years ago the Environmental Protection Agency put a price on a human being of from $400,000 to $7 million. The Federal Aviation Administration came up with a tag of $650,083; the Occupational Safety and Health Administration, $3.5 million (Doan, 1985).

Suppose a witch or wizard who dealt in personal strengths asked to buy your five harvest qualities—the five you identified in the previous exploration. Once you sold a quality, you wouldn't have it anymore and would have to live your life without it. Write the names of your harvest qualities below and opposite each the amount of money for which you would sell it. Then turn to the next page.

Harvest Quality	Sales Price
1. _____	$ _____
2. _____	$ _____
3. _____	$ _____
4. _____	$ _____
5. _____	$ _____

In the space below, write your answers to these two sets of questions: (1) Do you have some harvest qualities that you would hate to lose or would refuse to sell at any price? Why? What difference would their absence make in your life? (2) Have you been sufficiently mindful in the past that you possess these valuable qualities? How does your recognition that you possess these valuable qualities influence your attitude toward yourself now?

Question 13

Commitment

What Will I Do to Move My Life Along?

Commitments are the glue that holds us together and the propulsion that gives momentum and direction to our lives. Commitment is necessary to preserve life from chaos. We come to rely on the promises we make to each other.

We make commitments or promises to each other, and we also make promises to ourselves. We dedicate ourselves. We resolve. We set ourselves on perhaps long and arduous journeys that lead us to where we want to go.

Commitment has been defined as "whatever it is that makes a person engage or continue in a course of action when difficulties or positive alternatives influence the person to abandon the action" (Brickman, 1987, p. 2). Commitments involve a bonding of several elements, one positive (a "want to") and one negative (a "have to") (Brickman, 1987). We are pledged to take the bad with the good. For example, traditional marital vows (when they are taken at their word) require a pair to forsake all others and bind them for worse as well as for better, for poorer as well as for richer, and in sickness as well as in health. "One advantage of marriage," writes Judith Viorst, "is that when you fall out of love with him or he falls out of love with you, it keeps you together until you fall in again."

When we make a commitment, we are not free to change or, at least, we are resistant to change. We find reasons to support this commitment and reasons why we should not break it. We work to reduce any cognitive dissonance or internal discord raised by doubts that we have made the wrong decision; we justify what we have done and persuade ourselves we are right.

Some of our commitments are explicit; they are precise and clearly defined. We pledge allegiance to the flag. We sign a contract. We exchange marriage vows. We take out a mortgage or sign a promissory note. We adopt a child. Other commitments are more implicit and perhaps accrue little by little while we're scarcely aware of what's happening. One couple told me that when they moved in together, some things were "hers" and some were "his," but more and more things became "ours." When the question of marriage later arose, it was not "Will you?" or "Shall we?" but rather "When?"

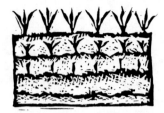

Box 13.1

Commitment: What Will I Do to Move My Life Along?

Seedthoughts

1. Sometimes a person will say he had made a decision to change but has trouble carrying it out, even though he uses a lot of will power. If anybody says that, it means he has made a wish, not a decision. A decision is something that results in action. If you haven't taken any action, it's only a wish.

   —*Harold Greenwald*

2. When you have to make a choice and don't make it, that is in itself a choice.

   —*William James*

3. I am my choices.

   —*Jean-Paul Sartre*

4. Life is Act, and not to Do is Death.

   —*Lewis Morris*

5. I learned at least this by my experiments. That if one advances confidently in the direction of his dreams, and endeavors to live the life he has imagined, he will meet with a success unexpected in common hours. He will put something behind and will pass an invisible boundary.

   —*Henry David Thoreau*

6. The important thing is this: to be able at any moment to sacrifice what we are to what we could become.

   —*Charles Du Bois*

7. This is the true joy in life, the being used for a purpose recognized by yourself as a mighty one.

   —*George Bernard Shaw*

8. I am only one.
   But still I am one.
   I cannot do everything.
   But still I can do something;
   And because I cannot do everything;
   I will not refuse to do the something that I can do.

   —*Edward Everett Hale*

9. One definition of insanity: When you keep doing the same old things and expect a change.

   —*source unknown*

10. There are many times when one feels an urge to make a decision when, upon calmer reflection, it becomes clear that it is not the right, or only, moment to decide. This can happen, for example, when important facts that bear on a problem are not available, when the person is not psychologically "strong" or clear-headed enough to take the plunge, or when events may reasonably be expected to fall into place if one just waits a while. Deciding not to decide for the time being is often the most responsible thing to do in such circumstances, provided the individual is ready to bear any consequences which may follow from this self-chosen delay. A process of "creative stalling" can be useful in these conditions when, after reasonable prudence in exploring the major facets of a decision, we realize we simply do not know what to do.

    —*Stephen Bendich*

Among the most notable characteristics of individuals who have achieved eminence are that they believed in themselves and their goals and they were committed to achieving them (White, 1982). Many outstanding authors and artists underwent years of rejection but refused to give up. The American novelist William Saroyan received several thousand rejection slips before one of his works was accepted. Vincent Van Gogh—one of whose paintings recently brought $75 million, not including a 10 percent auction house commission—managed to sell only one work in his lifetime. Frank Lloyd Wright, now considered America's foremost architectural genius, was ignored or disparaged during most of his career except by a select following (Bandura, 1989a).

Trying times may help us clarify what our commitments truly are or need to be. In the highly acclaimed movie *Kramer vs. Kramer* (refashioned from Avery Corman's novel), a man whose first commitment is to his work and who hardly knows his 6-year-old son is forced to reconsider his priorities when his wife abandons the two of them. Eighteen months later, when his wife returns to claim the boy, father and son have bonded, and there is no doubt about the father's top priority.

A librarian here at the University of Hawaii at Manoa told me about an incident that occurred while she and her husband were on appointments to a university in Beijing during the student protests. At the height of the conflict, they were given thirty minutes to pack and leave, but they decided to stay. They hoped there would be a large enough foreign presence to dissuade the troops from committing further atrocities against the Chinese students and faculty. Their action ultimately proved futile as the other nationals were ordered out by their countries, but the moment when they had decided to stay was for her and her husband "a moment of truth." At that moment they saw the depth of their commitment to their Chinese students and colleagues.

Overcommitment, Undercommitment, and Broken Commitments

Some of us are heavily committed. We may be deeply immersed in a few pursuits or considerably involved in almost too many. Living life to the hilt can be enriching. I had an uncle (a hard-working and caring man although prone to retell his favorite jokes) who used to say he was busy twenty-six hours each day. How did he manage this? By borrowing two hours.

Variety is the spice of life, and multiple commitments can indeed add flavor. For example, more and more women these days value and elect marriage, motherhood, and a career. And, of course, the list of commitments may not end there: there may be a circle of friends; one or more aged parents to care for; and some school, religious, political, neighborhood, or community activities, not to mention an avocation.

The more numerous our commitments, the greater the demands on our time, energy, and management skills. Sometimes we find we are overcommitted, we have to cut down, set some priorities, or seek more help. When we divide ourselves among too many pursuits, all may suffer and none be attended to in any depth. Furthermore, scattering our finite resources can be a strategy for not committing ourselves at all. We spread ourselves thin so we don't get ourselves in too deep anywhere, and our seeming overcommitment is really a lack of any real dedication.

John Haughey (1975) writes of a special kind of overcommitment—one that "occurs when people pursue a commitment so exclusively that their lives become brittle and their horizons narrow" (p. 55). Such overcommitments may involve a relationship, vocation, organization, or ideology. In such overcommitments, Haughey notes, one's identity is merged into, rather than developed by, the commitment. Such commitments can make for narrow lives, but, to be fair, they also may produce a Thomas Alva Edison and a Mother Teresa.

Some of us are heavily committed, some overcommitted—and some of us lack commitment. We have trouble forming commitments, or those we seem to form prove fragile. Possibly, we fear commitments and back away from them or manage to sabotage those that begin to grow.

A life without commitment—what would that be like? To simply drift without a sense of purpose or direction. This kind of life is well illustrated by Biff in Arthur Miller's *Death of a Salesman*. At one point in the play, Biff sums up his failure of commitment when he says to his mother, "I just can't take hold, Mom. I can't take hold to some kind of life."

We may seek casual sex and relationships without strings attached. We look for jobs instead of vocations. I know of someone who worked a long time for a temporary-help agency. He went from job to job, and some of these were offered

to him on a permanent basis. He refused them all because that would have been a commitment.

Not all commitments are kept. Treaties are broken. Marriage vows are ignored or retracted. Priests and nuns withdraw from religious life. The courts are filled with cases concerning broken contracts and other failures to perform as promised.

Keeping commitments is more difficult in a rapidly changing society. We are less rooted to a place and less committed to that place and also less rooted and committed to a job or a clan. We move about and in doing so weaken old commitments (Haughey, 1975).

As society changes and as we change and grow, we see the need to revise our commitments. Sometimes the very act of growing makes old commitments impossible to maintain. In Henrik Ibsen's classic play *A Doll's House*, the protagonist, Nora, lives a marital malaise until in a crisis she comes to understand the commitment she must make to herself. She sees that she has been her father's doll-child, her husband's doll-wife, and that she is passing her doll-identity down to her daughter. Her husband, Helmer, is outraged when she announces she is leaving and accuses her of running out on her "most sacred vows."

Nora:	What do you think are my most sacred vows?
Helmer:	And I have to tell you that! Aren't they your duties to your husband and children?
Nora:	I have other duties equally sacred.
Helmer:	That isn't true. What duties are they?
Nora:	Duties to myself.
Helmer:	Before all else, you're a wife and mother.
Nora:	I don't believe that anymore. I believe that, before all else, I'm a human being, no less than you—or anyway, I ought to try to become one. ([1879] 1978, pp. 192–193)

Identity and Commitment

Late adolescence and the early adult years are especially important in the formation of identity and the making of commitments (Erikson, 1982).[1] College stu-

---

[1] This discussion of identity and commitment is based on Marcia, 1980, and especially McAdams, 1985. The findings are largely paraphrased from McAdams, and the four rubrics are his apt titles for the four categories of students described by Marcia.

dents can be placed in one of four categories on the basis of their exploration of and commitment to a vocation and an ideological stance (system of values or philosophy of life). These categories include identity achievement, moratorium, foreclosure, and diffusion (Marcia, 1980).

Identity Achievement (Exploration: yes. Commitment: yes.)

This category includes students who have made significant vocational and ideological explorations and arrived at some basic commitments. These are individuals who know who they are and what they believe and who are pursuing self-chosen goals. Such students are generally at an advantage over those in the other three categories; identity achievers are more academically inclined and earn higher grades (Cross & Allen, 1970). Women in this category choose more difficult majors (Marcia & Friedman, 1970). Friendships and love relationships are highly satisfactory for both men (Orlofsky, Marcia, & Lesser, 1973) and women (Tesch & Whitbourne, 1982). Identity achievers tend to have positive although somewhat ambivalent relationships with their parents, and they are less concerned than students in other categories with winning their parents' love (Jordan, 1971; Josselson, 1973).

Moratorium (Exploration: yes. Commitment: no.)

Included in this category are those students who are in the midst of exploration but who have not arrived at a set of commitments. These are persons who do not fully know who they are or what they believe, and they are aware that they do not know. In relative advantage, they are next to those in the identity achievement group, which they may join as they clarify their beliefs and make commitments. Moratoriums tend to be uncertain and anxious (Marcia, 1967; Oshman & Manosevitz, 1974; Podd, Marcia, & Rubin, 1970). They also tend to have highly ambivalent relationships with their parents, from whom they may be seeking greater psychological distance (Erikson, 1959).

Foreclosure (Exploration: no. Commitment: yes.)

These students have forgone exploration and made premature ideological and vocational commitments. They have introjected the values and beliefs with which they grew up, with little questioning. Such students tend to be low in anxiety (Marcia, 1967; Marcia & Friedman, 1970), low in autonomy (Orlofsky, Marcia, & Lesser, 1973), and high in submission to authority (Marcia, 1966, 1967; Marcia & Friedman, 1970; Schenkel & Marcia, 1972). Foreclosures tend to be well behaved (Donovan, 1975; Marcia, 1980), keep regular hours, and study diligently (Donovan, 1975). They are very close to their parents, whom they typically see as accepting and encouraging (Jordan, 1971).

Diffusion (Exploration: no. Commitment: no.)

These students make up a relatively small group who have not explored or made ideological or vocational commitments. They feel socially isolated, approach others warily, and are out of place in the world. They tend to withdraw from stressful situations (Bob, 1968). These students see their parents as distant and misunderstanding, and they are not captives to their familial past (Donovan, 1975). Concerning this group, McAdams (1985) concludes: ". . . with few strong allegiances to the past and fewer explicit commitments to a particular future, these young men and women appear afloat in a sea of ambiguity, without anchor to a bygone yesterday nor anticipated tomorrow" (p. 46).

William Perry (1981) has traced the typical journey of students as they look for answers about life's problems during their college years. In the beginning, many are caught up in a black-white dualism that divides everything into two realms: good-bad, right-wrong, success-failure, we-they. In this position, students believe the authorities have an answer for every problem.

These absolutistic and authoritarian beliefs are challenged by the diversity of ideas found in college, and students come to see that there are areas without right answers or in which answers depend on contexts. Ultimately, in maturity, they accept the task of constructing sets of answers that are right for themselves—answers that will serve to guide their lives but not shut off future modification or respect for the differing answers of others.

In this pursuit of answers, students typically begin at the position on the left below. If all goes well and they don't get stuck along the way or make a retreat, they arrive at the position on the right (this is a journey many of us make, whether students or not):

"Authorities know, and if we work hard, read every word, and learn the Right Answers, all will be well."

"I must be wholehearted while tentative, fight for my values yet respect others, believe my deepest values right yet be ready to learn. I see I shall be retracing this whole journey over and over—but, I hope, more wisely." (p. 79)

Changing Commitments over the Life Span

To be "wholehearted while tentative" and to "believe my deepest values right yet be ready to learn" make for a tall order. Commitments bind us to a course of action—one resistant to change—but over life's long trajectory our commitments change. We change as persons, our values change, and the things that capture and occupy us change.

Early adulthood is usually a time of commitment to launching a career and establishing a marital bond and a family. Some of us delay either a vocational or a familial commitment in favor of the other or in favor of developing ourselves. More of us these days are electing to marry later or not have children or to have only one child.

What has been called the midlife crisis is often a crisis of commitment. It is a time when we may feel blocked in our work, bored or "burnt out," and questioning our career path. It is a time when children may be off on their own (or nearly so), the nest is empty, and there seems little to keep the spouses together. It is a time when life suddenly doesn't seem endless, a time to get busy, but busy at what?

In early adulthood, American men are generally high in achievement motivation or mastery and highly committed to their careers. Young women—although not without vocational ambition—tend to be high in affiliative needs and show a considerable interpersonal commitment. But as men move beyond their middle years, they often become less aggressive and ambitious and more affiliative and nurturant. Women somewhat reverse this patterning, becoming more aggressive, assertive, or managerial (Fiske, 1980).

Changing commitments over the span of life can be a source of conflict in couples. The great psychologist Carl Jung wrote that "these changes are accomplished by all sorts of catastrophes in marriage, for it is not hard to imagine what will happen when the husband discovers his tender feelings and the wife her sharpness of mind" ([1930] 1971, p. 16). On the basis of his observations, Jung pleaded for greater accommodation of these changes.

Why Is It So Hard to Make Commitments?

"They are decided only to be undecided, resolved to be irresolute, adamant for drift, all-powerful for impotence." So spoke Sir Winston Churchill in eloquent contempt for a set of adversaries, but although history likes to portray great leaders as unwavering, many have been consumed by doubts (Kolbert, 1991). All of us have wrestled with difficult decisions, and in such moments many have felt indecisive, irresolute, and impotent. Why is it so difficult to make commitments?

Lack of Experience

One reason we may find it hard to commit ourselves is that we have lacked models for or experience with commitment. In his widely read book *The Road Less Traveled*, psychiatrist M. Scott Peck (1978) writes that problems of relational commitment "are a major, inherent part of most psychiatric disorders" (p. 141). If our parents failed to make a meaningful commitment to us and we grow up without this experience, we will tend to form shallow attachments ourselves. If we received a commitment of love as children, but this commitment was interrupted or lost, the resultant pain can cause us to dread new attachments.

We require commitment in our relationships and the assurance that we can disagree and struggle over issues without destroying the attachment. Those of us who have lacked this kind of early commitment can be healed by more satisfying later ones. Commitment, Peck notes, is the cornerstone of long-term psychotherapy: "For basic healing to take place it is necessary for the psychotherapist to bring to his or her relationship with a new patient the same high sense and degree of commitment that genuinely loving parents bring to their children" (pp. 141–142).

Wandering from cause to cause, from job to job, from relationship to relationship, from marriage to marriage can be dismaying. Merilyn Jackson, a woman interviewed by Ralph Keyes (1985) for his book *Chancing It*, quit her job to buy a store of her own. After seven years of eighty-hour weeks, she was forced to sell it at a loss. However, she was grateful for the experience and for what her experience taught her about commitment. (She had two failed marriages and commitment had not been her strong suit.) She put it this way:

I was never really committed to anything in my life, except my children. Commitment is not something I'm good at. My pattern in the past has been that when things got rough, when I had a failure, I ran. Owning my own business taught me the elements of commitment—that commitment has in it "for better or for worse," not just "for better." It taught me that commitment means sticking through the worst times. I think that was an important lesson for me to learn. (p. 215)

A friend once told my wife that had she (the friend) worked as hard at her first marriage as she was currently working at her second, there would never have been a divorce. The difference was that she had learned what commitment was and what it required, and she was now committed to making marriage a success.

Freedom and Responsibility

Some of us avoid commitments because we see them as a loss of the freedom that we prize. Don't fence us in! At first glance, freedom might seem to be in conflict with commitment. If we make a commitment, then we are not as free as before. But part of this freedom is the freedom to choose and decide, and what good is this freedom if it is never exercised?

Haughey (1975) writes, "To attempt to live one's life in a state of indetermination is the surest way of becoming unfree, because then one will be determined by forces outside oneself" (p. 33). For example, if we refuse to commit ourselves to a participation in political matters, we will have no say in such matters when they directly affect us. If we insist upon keeping all our relationship options open, we may limit ourselves to shallow relationships or to relationships with those similarly unwilling or unable to love deeply or to put love before autonomy.

At conception or birth, each of us is given a life. At death, that life is taken away. What we make of the time between these two events is up to us. We are *responsible.* Although we are not necessarily the cause of all that happens in our lives, we are responsible for what we make of what happens. Rarely are circumstances just what we want them to be, and sometimes they are greatly adverse. But, as Josh Billings wrote, "Life consists not in holding good cards but in playing those you do hold well."

We take for granted that it is good to be free. But if we are truly free to live life, then we must decide, make choices, and be responsible for these decisions and choices. There's the rub. Bernard Shaw said it well in his *Maxims for Revolutionists:* "Liberty means responsibility. That is why most men dread it."

In the first chapter of this book, a distinction was made between persons who see a causal relationship between what they do and what happens to them and those persons who see little relationship between their efforts and outcomes. The former, called "internals," accept responsibility for their lives (or, at least, certain areas of it) while the latter, called "externals," do not. Reviewing the relevant psychological literature, Herbert Lefcourt (1982) concludes that internals and externals confront many life experiences in markedly different ways. Internals show greater signs of what Lefcourt calls "vitality"—an active grappling with important life events and a greater commitment. Externals show greater apathy and withdrawal. In grappling with life, internals are more likely to be successful, since their belief in their ability to control outcomes increases their efforts to try, along with their chances to succeed or at least to find success in the results.

Irwin Yalom (1980), to whose work I am greatly indebted in writing this chapter, has gathered some pertinent data concerning responsibility. These data suggest that effective psychotherapy helps the patient become more aware of personal responsibility for life. For example, when patients in several research studies were asked to select items describing particularly useful aspects of therapy, this item was very often chosen: "Learning that I must take ultimate responsibility for the way I live my life no matter how much guidance and support I get from others" (p. 265). This item is particularly noteworthy because human beings can go to great lengths to avoid responsibility. Yalom himself wrote that no therapist finishes a work day without encountering several examples of responsibility-avoiding defenses—among such defenses are denial and displacement.

Denying Responsibility. One way we try to avoid responsibility is to deny we are responsible or free. "I've always been this way." "You can't fight city hall." These are common rationalizations of persons who deny responsibility for their lives. They think of themselves as unchangeable and set in their ways. Or they see so many or such formidable external obstacles that it is pointless to oppose them.

Psychologist Albert Ellis writes that in the course of one of his working days he often sees about twenty therapy clients individually and another twenty in a group situation. Most of these clients, he notes, believe to some degree that "they *have* to behave in a certain disturbed way because of previous conditioning or early influences" (Ellis & Harper, 1975, p. 168). Ellis teaches his clients to think of their pasts as handicaps but not blocks. He reminds them that their present constitutes their past of tomorrow; by changing their way of thinking in the present, they can radically change tomorrow's behavior.

Displacing Responsibility. Another way we avoid responsibility is to surrender to some person or system. In his widely acclaimed book *Escape from Freedom*, Erich Fromm (1941) theorizes that totalitarian governments are attractive to some individuals because such systems make it unnecessary for the individual to take personal responsibility for her or his life. In blind obedience to a political system or charismatic leader, a person can trade away freedom to get freedom from freedom.

Peck (1978) believes that most persons who seek therapy have a "sense of impotence," of not being able to cope, but they have to some degree attempted to escape the pain of freedom and given their power away. "Sooner or later, if they are to be healed, they must learn that the entirety of one's adult life is a series of personal choices, decisions. If they can accept this totally, then they become free people. To the extent they do not accept this, they will forever feel themselves victims" (p. 44).

Valery Klever was one of fifty Soviet émigrés to the United States who decided to return to their homeland in 1987. Klever and his wife are painters who emigrated so that they would be free to express themselves in their art. But, as Klever explained in an interview with Hal Piper (1987), he found that freedom was having to "worry about your life and your apartment, your bills every month, everything." As Piper noted, Klever learned that freedom was having to make choices, and Soviet citizens—at that time—were spared that burden; decisions were made for them. Subsequent events may have caused the Klevers yet another change of mind.

Yalom notes that his clients commonly try to displace personal responsibility onto another—perhaps onto him. Some clients look to the therapist to rescue them, just as some worshippers seek rescue in answer to their prayers. Both believe in an ultimate rescuer—a belief they may be very reluctant to relinquish. But Yalom holds that the assumption of personal responsibility is a prerequisite for change. Benjamin Franklin held much the same view and expressed it tersely: "God helps those who help themselves."

Cost

A third reason we balk at commitments is that they cost something. Commitments come with a price and perhaps a very high one. The price may be to renounce something we are not ready or willing to give up. Or it may involve incurring an obligation we are not ready or willing to take on.

Making an important choice—electing something—often means giving up something else. What might our lives be like if we take the other job offer? Get married to X instead of Y? Not marry at all? Have children? Not have children?

Frost ends his poem "The Road Not Taken" by noting that at the choice point he took the road "less traveled by" and "that has made all the difference." Some of us get stuck at every crossroad because so much seems at stake, and we think our choice may make all the difference. A contrary view is taken by psychiatrist Theodore Rubin (1985) in his book *Overcoming Indecisiveness*. "The Big Fact," according to Rubin, is this: *"In very few instances is one decision actually better than another"* (his italics). Rubin holds that most of our choices can prove to be good ones if they are accompanied by commitment. He writes:

1. . . . in most issues, very few options would make "bad" decisions. There are exceptions, of course, but few choices are discarded because they represent "bad" choices. Some choices become discarded choices not because they are "bad" but because no matter who we are, we simply cannot have it all. An option becomes a discard through the process of our withdrawing our investment—ourselves—from it.

2. By the same token, an option becomes a decision through the process of our dedicating ourselves to it and investing ourselves in it. Our loyalty and commitment to the decision is what this core of decision-making is all about. Aside from grossly inappropriate decisions, pseudodecisions and coercive decisions, it is not the choice itself that makes or breaks the decision. The decisionmaker makes or breaks the decision according to the strength or weakness of commitment and loyalty to the choice.

3. You make it work! It almost always is the decisionmaker and not the particular choice that makes the decision work. If it doesn't work, the problem almost always lies with the decisionmaker, and the decision will not succeed regardless of which choice is made. I repeat the salient point: *The failure of the decision has little or nothing to do with the choice. The failure is directly traceable and proportional to lack of dedicated commitment.* Most choices or options have their good and bad points. Choices are good only if we make them good. Some require increased adaptation effort, but our loyalty to them will make this effort possible. This devotion of our time, energy, hope and struggle to the cause at hand is crucial. (p. 77)

In making commitments we not only give up some things; we take on others. Every commitment requires an expenditure of time or energy or money or all of these. Some commitments are for a lifetime or nearly so and continue to make demands all the while.

Someone has said, "a child is forever"; someone else has said (in jest, I think) that the first half of our lives is ruined by our parents and the second half by our children. In her notebook, written when she was 82, Florida Scott-Maxwell wrote, "No matter how old a mother is she watches her middle-aged children for signs of improvement" (p. 16). However, Barry Stevens decided to become a "former mother" to her "ex-son": "When I don't think of myself as mother, parent, guardian or whatever, and don't think of my child as 'my' somethingorother, I am more free" (1976/77, p. 70).

These days some persons—women mostly—have found themselves with a double parenting commitment. Called "the sandwich generation," they find that while parenting their own children (perhaps for many more years than they expected) they are also called upon to parent their own aged and frail parents.

Some find it necessary to parent their grandchildren when their own children are unable to do so.

Most familial commitments—even those disrupted by divorce or alienation or death—continue to affect one and impose a cost, if only in memory, lament, or nostalgia. Other kinds of seemingly renounced or abandoned commitments also leave their indelible marks: financial obligation, a history that can't be lived down, a reputation or identity that clings.

Although commitments cost, not making commitments also exacts a cost and often a higher one. This is the lesson learned too late by George Gray, who is one of the persons buried and "sleeping on the hill" in Edgar Lee Masters' classic *Spoon River Anthology*. Masters has each character come back to life to recite his or her own epitaph, and these are Gray's poignant words:

> I have studied many times
> The marble which was chiseled for me—
> A boat with a furled sail at rest in a harbor.
> In truth it pictures not my destination
> But my life.
> For love was offered me and I shrank from its disillusionment;
> Sorrow knocked at my door, but I was afraid;
> Ambition called to me, but I dreaded the chances.
> Yet all the while I hungered for meaning in my life.
> And now I know that we must lift the sail
> And catch the winds of destiny
> Where ever they drive the boat.
> To put meaning in one's life may end in madness,
> But life without meaning is the torture
> Of restlessness and vague desire—
> It is a boat longing for the sea and yet afraid. (1931, p. 65)

Lucinda Matlock, another character in *Spoon River Anthology*, is someone who paid a high price for her commitment and never doubted that it was worth it. She is the polar opposite of George Gray and a critic of all those like him, and here is the epitaph Masters has her compose for herself:

> I went to the dances at Chandlerville,
> And played snap-out at Winchester.
> One time we changed partners,
> Driving home in the moonlight of middle June,
> And then I found Davis.
> We were married and lived together for seventy years,
> Enjoying, working, raising the twelve children,
> Eight of whom we lost
> Ere I had reached the age of sixty.
> I spun, I wove, I kept the house, I nursed the sick,
> I made the garden, and for holiday
> Rambled over the fields where sang the larks,
> And by Spoon River gathering many a shell,
> And many a flower and medicinal weed—
> Shouting to the wooded hills, singing to the green valleys.
> At ninety-six I had lived enough, that is all,
> And passed to a sweet repose.
> What is this I hear of sorrow and weariness,
> Anger, discontent and drooping hopes?
> Degenerate sons and daughters,

Life is too strong for you—
It takes life to love Life. (p. 229)

Risk

A fourth reason it is difficult to make commitments is that the changes they entail involve risk. We cannot know for sure the consequences of our decisions or how favorable or adverse they may be. "At its simplest," Ellen Siegelman (1983) writes, "any change brings a loss of the known" (p. 36). Any large change threatens our sense of ourselves. Siegelman notes that we will go to great lengths to maintain our continuous sense of selfhood, even if it means repeating old and familiar self-defeating patterns.

Psychologist Daniel Kahneman (Cordes, 1984) observes that most people are "loss averse." That is, their response to loss is more intense than their response to a suitably matched gain. In contemplating a change involving risk, they are conservative because the possibility for loss looms larger than that for gain.

James and Elizabeth Bugental (1984) make a similar point. According to the Bugentals, we construct a life for ourselves doing the best we can. The best may not be very good, but we do not readily give it up. It is all we know, and it is what we think was meant to be. The Bugentals offer this parable to illustrate their point:

The man wakes to find himself swimming in the sea. As far as he can see in any direction there is nothing but the uneasy plain of waves and troughs, of moving water; no landmark, no distant shore to guide his efforts. He treads water, then swims for a time in one direction, but he cannot be certain he is not circling. He begins to tire; no relief seems likely.

Now he discerns a more solid shape some distance away on the waves. Renewed by the sight, he swims to it and soon grasps a plank that has been carried on the water. Gratefully he throws an arm over the plank and eases his pain-filled muscles. He half-rides, half-swims and looks about for more flotsam. And he finds more. A hatch cover floats a short distance away trailing a length of rope. Soon it is tied to the plank. So it goes. Slowly, with great struggles at times, with fortuitous ease at others, the man collects and puts together what he finds until eventually he can climb onto his crude raft and rest.

Now a squall is on the horizon, and the water grows choppy. He must hang on to the raft to survive and to try to hold it together. When the storm hits, the man loses parts; hard-won supports are swept away. For a brief, terrifying moment, he almost loses it all back to the endlessly grasping water.

When the squall is past, he finds some, but not all, of the lost pieces. After a bit the sun comes out, and new gifts arrive from the sea. Now the man builds a more stable vessel. The next squall takes a smaller toll, and he grows more confident in his emerging boat.

In time other castaways float by on their rafts, and the man merges his construction with theirs. The vessel becomes larger and more dependable. At times great storms play havoc with it, but mostly it is possible to preserve the central portion and to rebuild adequately.

As days turn into years, the man and his children lose their memories of how the rafts came to be. The big raft on which they live they name "the world," and they are certain that their life is the way life is really meant to be. (pp. 543–544)

Although we tend to hang on to what we have rather than risk it for something new, we seem to be at our best when we are challenged. Research on nat-

THE SAFEST PLAN IS NEVER TO DO ANYTHING FOR THE FIRST TIME.

ural catastrophes such as floods and earthquakes indicates that these events aren't followed by widespread mental illness but, rather, have some positive effects. From her research on responses to disasters, sociologist Verta Taylor (1977) concludes that mental health is a dynamic state that is reenergized when one responds to challenges; moreover, the experiences of coping with and mastering the personal crises associated with the disaster may enhance one's psychological well-being.

One of the first qualities Gail Sheehy (1981) discovered in her "pathfinders"—people who show a high degree of well-being—was their willingness to take risks. Ironically, she found that playing it safe could be dangerous. Her unhappiest men and women were generally those who had been resistant to change or not confident they could change.

In interviewing people for his book *Chancing It: Why We Take Risks,* Ralph Keyes (1985) found that the greatest regret was not expressed by those who had risked and lost. These persons, he writes, invariably "felt proud for having dared, and even educated in defeat. The real regret, bordering on mourning, came from those who hadn't taken chances they'd wanted to take and now felt it was too late" (p. 274). He concludes that "the case is for taking risks."

Successful Risking

"How does one go about taking a personal risk successfully?" This is a question posed by Siegelman (1983) and answered in her book *Personal Risk,* which is recommended for anyone contemplating a major life change. Since risk is an important deterrent to commitment, her seven-step or stage risk-reduction process deserves careful attention. Siegelman notes that the stages may not occur in precise order, and a person may have to pass through some stages more than once in dealing with a particular risk.

Stage 1. Becoming Aware of Negative Feelings. The first stage of successful risk taking is becoming aware that something is critically wrong with our lives. At the outset, our clues may be little more than visceral. We may not feel right, or we may not feel well. Instead, we feel vaguely ill, bored, burned out, or trapped. There is no joy in our relationships or in our work or other pursuits. And more than that, there may be continuing crisis or irritation. We find we don't like ourselves or the persons we are becoming or we can't abide one or more aspects of the lives we are leading.

Stage 2. Recognizing the Need to Change. In the second stage, feelings of dissatisfaction become translated into impulses toward action. We begin to think we would like to quit what we're doing and get on to something new. Or that we want to move out or move away. Or that we must face up to something we've been avoiding or confront our problems and do something about them. The danger at this stage, says Siegelman, is that we will abort our wistful thoughts, our yearnings, and our fantasies along with the kernel of hope they contain. Siegelman encourages us to pay attention to our fantasy life because it often embodies very deep but unmet needs.

> When we spell out our fantasies, we can use them to make the transition from "If I only could" to the determined "By God, I will"—I will approach my boss, I will start my own business, I will move to California, I will make my marriage work, I will learn to live alone, I will quit this research job I loathe, I *will . . .*" (pp. 132–133)

Stage 3. Experiencing Ambivalence. The resolve to do is often followed by anxiety and doubt. "I will!" fades into "But can I?" The push toward the hoped-for future frequently is followed by a pull back to the familiar past. There is so much to gain *and* so much to lose. One day or one moment we feel one way and the next just the opposite: "Of course, I can move there. No, it won't work. I don't know anybody there. It will all be so strange. It's not good here, but at least I know the problems. Too many problems. I can't take this any longer. I've got to do something." (And so the battle continues back and forth.)

Too much or too little anxiety should give us pause. Pervasive, persistent anxiety may be a signal that the undertaking is too threatening—more threat or change than we can manage. Our bodies may find a way to let us know what our minds are reluctant to admit. As Siegelman writes, a "peptic ulcer can counterbalance a host of theoretical pluses" (p. 134). If our anxiety is minimal, there may be little risk, or the push to get out of an intolerable present situation may be so great that we have little choice but to proceed. Or minimal anxiety may mean we are denying danger. Siegelman emphasizes that it is *necessary* to experience the push and pull and the fear and hope of our ambivalence in taking a big step. She writes (her italics), *"When fear is balanced by a sense of excitement and purpose, it offers an emotional preparation for the risk we are undertaking"* (p. 137).

Stage 4. Reducing the Risk through Preparation. Siegelman suggests a number of ways to reduce the risk involved in a new enterprise. First, we can often reduce the urgency involved in such situations. The deadlines imposed by others are often not sacrosanct and can be extended. We may be the culprit, imposing harsh deadlines upon ourselves because of an internal taskmaster or our inability to tolerate a state of indecision. If we learn to allow ourselves incubation time, we may well find that resolution will come "in a mysterious, almost effortless way" (p. 140). (More about this later on.)

Second, Siegelman suggests we reduce the uncertainty of change by seeking information and rehearsing or sampling what we're getting into. The more we can learn about our own capabilities and the demands of what's before us, the less fearful and difficult a change will be. The fear and difficulty are further reduced if we practice in advance; for example, having a trial separation as prelude to a possible divorce or cultivating—before we retire—interests that may occupy us later on.

A third way to reduce risk or the anxiety it engenders is to seek support. The support may come from family members, friends, spiritual advisers, or professional counselors. A support group of people who share our experience or who have already been through what now confronts us can be particularly helpful.

Fourth, we can reduce anxiety by changing our perception of the seeming irreversibility of a change or decision. In some situations that seem irreversible, hard and creative thought will produce a way out or a retreat position or a plan to cut one's losses. Perhaps we can arrange to take a leave instead of quitting; the thought of returning may be a bit humbling, but the thought that one can return may help reduce the anxiety surrounding a move and help ensure its success.

A fifth tactic is to reduce the scale of the risk by restructuring it. In restructuring, we recast the risk or see it in a new and less anxiety-provoking perspective. For example, we can come to see that the possibility of failure is not catastrophic—that we can learn and gain a great deal regardless of an outcome. The immensity of a task may stagger us, but we can break it down and focus instead on separate parts. The Chinese sage Lao-Tsu wrote, "A journey of a thousand miles begins with a single step." We can begin by focusing on that step instead of boggling at the thousand miles.

Stage 5. Letting It Be. Much of what we do in making a decision seems to be a conscious, effortful process. Sometimes the more effort we apply, the more perplexed we become. When we pause for a while and then return, we often see the situation in a new way. During the pause, less conscious processes continue to work, and new insight or impetus may suddenly emerge. Letting the process be is not a procrastination to make us feel guilty; it is not a shutting down but, rather, as Siegelman writes, "a poised readiness" for the something to come.

Stephen Bendich (1979) refers to this stage of letting be as "creative stalling." When we are putting "unreasonable and unproductively strong pressure" on ourselves, it is reasonable and productive to engage in "some old-fashioned lollygagging procrastination or sludge-gudgery" (p. 53). Creative stalling is not to be confused with "stalling pure and simple"; instead, a period of creative stalling is a time of incubation, a time in which we decide not to decide until we acquire more facts, or we are more clearheaded, or certain events fall into place.

Stage 6. Taking the Plunge. Siegelman writes that despite our preparation, there is always something that remains unknown both in the situation and in ourselves. Ultimately, acting on faith, we take the plunge—we make the leap. If we have prepared well, the risk is calculated, and it may seem less at this point than earlier in the process. Along with the plunge may come "a heady sense of relief" as we put stewing and planning behind and get the show on the road.

Stage 7. Evaluating the Outcome. Our evaluation of each risky pursuit will influence our future risk-taking behavior. Siegelman points out that every evaluation has two aspects—an outer and an inner. The outer evaluation concerns the seeming success of the pursuit. Did it apparently work out? The inner concerns how the risker felt about the outcome. Sometimes a pursuit that is apparently successful proves unsatisfying while an ostensible failure is nevertheless gratifying: we are pleased we tried and gave it a good go, and we welcome what we have learned about the pursuit and ourselves.

Spiritedness and Commitment

"Spirit" is a word that seldom appears in psychological thinking and writing, but it is frequently used by the man and woman on the street. We say that someone is spirited or in high spirits. Or that his spirits fell or her spirit was broken. If so, we may do something to help raise their spirits. Or maybe they get busy on their own, liven up, and we say, "That's the spirit!"

Psychologist Sidney Jourard (1971) proposed the concept of a spirit-titre—the concentration or amount of spirit in a person. The titre might vary between zero and 100. Most of us most of the time would fall within an intermediate range. During peak experiences and other very positive times, our titre would be high. During sad and depressed states or in states of pessimism or hopelessness, our titre would go down.

Elizabeth and James Bugental (1984) have written that dispiritedness results when we are unable to bring our intentions or wishes to fruition or actuality. We are blocked or stuck in neutral. Our titre is low. Similarly, Robert and Marilyn Kriegel (1984) describe three performance zones, each encompassing a different behavior, a different degree of commitment, and a different relationship of challenge to mastery. The Kriegels' three performance zones are diagrammed in Box 13.2.

Box 13.2

The Kriegels' Three Performance Zones

The Kriegels describe three performance zones, each with a different degree of commitment, a different relationship of challenge to mastery, and a different behavior. In the Drone Zone, we are uncommitted; there is not enough challenge, too much mastery, and boredom. In the Panic Zone, the situation is reversed. The winning combination of commitment, confidence, and control in the C Zone relates to the balance of challenge and mastery. What zone are you in at this time in your life?

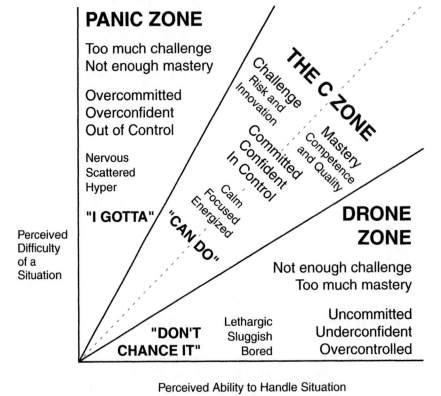

(From Kriegel & Kriegel, 1984, p. 20)

If we are in the C Zone, we move back and forth between mastery and challenge. In the mastery subzone, we feel competent, confident, and in control. With this solid footing, we can take some calculated risks, innovate, and stretch ourselves a little. Our stretch puts us in the challenge subzone, where we take some time to get new footing, hunker down a little, and gain new mastery. When this mastery comes, we are ready to take the next step—risking again for the sake of growth.

We can do our best and be our best in the C Zone. We are energized, but we are also focused and in control. Willie Unsoeld, who was the first American to reach Everest's summit, told the Kriegels:

> You need an element of risk, a challenge to perform at your peak. The right amount of risk throws you into a state of total concentration where there is nothing but the moment. You feel as if you have more time and more strength to accomplish things than you ever thought possible. But before you take that risk you've got to master the fundamentals and become competent in the technical aspects of what it is you are doing. (p. 9)

If we are in the Panic Zone, there is too much challenge and not enough mastery. We have gone beyond our competence; we are over our heads and not fully in control. We are trying to do too much in too little time or with not enough skill or resources. As a result, we feel nervous, scattered, or frantic. In the Panic Zone, we are subject to a good deal of stress and become less effective. We are vulnerable to stress-related diseases. This stress has a physical effect on us, but it also affects the way we think and feel and relate to others.

In the Drone Zone, by contrast, there is too much mastery and not enough challenge. Ironically, drone zoners may perform poorly despite their competence because they are bored and unstimulated. Therefore, this zone may be relatively safe, but it's not stress-free. In the Drone Zone, we feel dull, sluggish, and lethargic. We may also feel stuck if we are afraid to risk moving our lives along. We may feel guilty and disappointed in ourselves.

In an interview with Barbara Walters, then world heavyweight champion Michael Tyson said frankly that boxing bored him. To get his interest up for a bout, he waited until the last possible moment (maybe even longer) to begin training; then, challenged, or challenging himself really, he felt energized to do what needed to be done. He scared himself up out of the Drone Zone. (That may explain his loss of the championship to relatively unknown James Buster Douglas: Tyson saw no reason to scare himself.)

© BRILLIANT ENTERPRISES 1973   POT-SHOTS NO. 436

IF YOU'RE CAREFUL ENOUGH, NOTHING BAD OR GOOD WILL EVER HAPPEN TO YOU.

Ashleigh Brilliant

Commitment, the Good Life, and Mental Health

Philosophers and many other persons have wrestled with the notion of "the good life," but there is little agreement on what it is. For some, the good life is a happy and comfortable life, but others have taken rigorous exceptions to this notion. In the second edition of his widely acclaimed book *Excellence,* John W. Gardner writes (his italics): *"The best kept secret in America today is that people would rather work hard for something they believe in than live a life of aimless diversion"* (1984, p. 155). It's erroneous, he holds, to think that happiness necessarily involves ease, comfort, and tranquility or arriving at a state where all our wishes are satisfied. Happiness, in his estimation, comes from striving toward meaningful goals. "I believe," Gardner states, "that most Americans would welcome a new burst of commitment" (p. 155).

G. Marian Kinget (1975) points out that a good life is highly gratifying but is not necessarily marked by pleasure: "Few would deny that a fair share of the goodness of life fell to such persons as Abraham Lincoln, Gandhi, Louis Pasteur, Albert Schweitzer, Dorothea Dix, Dietrich Bonhoeffer, Pope John XXIII, Martin Buber, and Martin Luther King. Hardly anyone, however, would say that these persons' lives were marked by lots of fun" (pp. 227–228). What these lives were marked by is commitment. To know these persons is to know at once what each stood for and worked for.

George Bernard Shaw wrote that the true joy of life was being used for a "mighty" purpose, and Charles de Gaulle noted that France was at her best only when she was engaged in a "great enterprise." These observations can help you assess the sufficiency of commitment in your life. Are you being used for a mighty purpose? Are you engaged in a great enterprise?

The mighty purposes of societies are rarely fully achieved, and great enterprises are frequently compromised. Gardner (1964) writes that those who are dedicated to achieving such goals as promoting good government or eliminating human misery can win small victories but never the war because there is always something more to be done. Tasks of overriding importance are never finished, but it is necessary to pursue them.

Just as philosophers have argued about "the good life," psychologists have debated about the criteria of mental health. Philip Brickman and Dan Coates (1987) hold that commitment is a necessary condition for mental health, but it is not a sufficient one. Commitment is a process that enhances psychological adjustment when it goes well, but commitment can go wrong: consider the Jonestown tragedy, in which over nine hundred Peoples Temple followers perished in a mass suicide-murder, and the more recent disastrous events at Waco, Texas, involving federal agents and members of the Branch Davidian cult.

According to Brickman and Coates, commitment furthers psychological adjustment in three ways. First, it promotes subjective well-being: "People who are engaged in what have traditionally been recognized as overarching, lifetime commitments are generally happier than those who are not" (p. 225). According to the evidence they muster, happiness is a durable marriage, a satisfying occupation, or an embraced set of religious beliefs—or nonbeliefs. When it comes to beliefs, apparently commitment or conviction but not specific content is what counts, because there is no evidence that one religion is more beneficial than another (Batson & Ventis, 1982; Cutler, 1976). And in one study, women who described themselves as very religious or not at all religious or even antireligious were happier and healthier than those who were moderately or slightly religious (Safran, 1977).

Second, commitment enhances the ability to cope. Earlier in this book, we noted that hardiness in the face of stress is a composite of commitment, a sense of control, and the propensity to see a problem as a challenge rather than a threat.

When we are committed to a pursuit, we are better able to tolerate the negative aspects of a situation because they are connected to and balanced off against stronger positive ones and they are both a part of a meaningful enterprise. Furthermore, our commitments usually provide us with networks of support that come to our assistance in stressful times.

Third, commitment keeps us working on tasks and relationships that are not immediately or fully rewarding. Our commitment gives us a reason to bear up and go on. It keeps us on track; and rather than questing for ideal solutions, we settle for adequate ones and then convince ourselves that what we have is right for us.

In his book *The Prophet,* Kahlil Gibran writes:

> When you are joyous, look deep into your heart and you shall find it is only that which has given you sorrow that is giving you joy.

> When you are sorrowful, look again in your heart and you shall see in truth you are weeping for that which has been your delight. (1923, p. 29)

We put so much of ourselves into our commitments, and they bring both joy and sorrow. Commitment furthers psychological adjustment, as was just indicated, but Brickman and Coates also note that it increases the possibility of jealousy, guilt, and depression.

The more deeply we are committed to a relationship, the greater the possibility of jealousy if we see ourselves being supplanted by another. Jealousy has traditionally been considered more likely in persons who are insecure or low in self-esteem. In their survey, Brickman and Coates found evidence supporting this view—especially for men. The more deeply we are committed to a relationship or enterprise, the greater the possibility of guilt if we see that our inclinations or actions threaten that pursuit. Guilt may arise when one important commitment steals time, energy, or resources from another important commitment—if, for example, work demands are in fierce competition with familial demands. Guilt also may arise when stated or implied promises, duties, or obligations are not observed—for example, when a parent finds difficulty in loving a particular child or when a spouse engages in or is tempted to engage in an affair.

The more deeply we are committed to a relationship or pursuit and the more dependent we are on it, the greater the possibility of deep sadness or depression if it is lost. Brickman and Coates note that depressed persons differ from those with other diagnoses in that they have suffered more "exit events," that is, losses of important relationships. Such losses heighten the possibility of suicide unless there are other supporting commitments—parents, a spouse, a close friend, or a sustaining religious faith or occupation.

The Power of Commitment

In her work on the risk-taking process, Siegelman (1983) found that the preaction stages were generally the most frightening. One of her research subjects put this finding into words: "Just deciding to take the risk is the most risky thing most of the time" (p. 137). Siegelman cites a study of the anxiety recalled by sport parachute jumpers: their most frightening moment generally came when they were still on the ground deciding whether to go aloft to jump—not when they were about to step out into space, for by that time they were set in their decision.

Once we put doubt aside, make a commitment, and launch ourselves into a new pursuit, we move ahead more quickly than we thought possible. Later we may look back and wonder why we were so apprehensive, why we delayed so long, why we wasted so much time.

Commitment has a power of its own. Henry David Thoreau followed his inner bent, took unconventional stands on public issues, and expressed his convictions in dramatic actions. He wrote that if one advances confidently in the direction of one's dreams and endeavors to live that imagined life, then that person will pass "an invisible boundary" and meet with unexpected success ([1854] 1947, p. 562).

Goethe was of much the same opinion. His life was rich with commitment and accomplishment. He wrote:

> Until one is committed, there is hesitancy, the chance to draw back, always ineffectiveness, concerning all acts of initiative (and creation). There is one elementary truth the ignorance of which kills countless ideas and splendid plans: that the moment one definitely commits oneself, then providence moves too. All sorts of things occur to help one that would never otherwise have occurred. A whole stream of events issues from the decision, raising in one's favour all manner of unforeseen incidents and meetings and material assistance which no man could have dreamed would have come his way. Whatever you can do or dream you can, begin it. Boldness has genius, power and magic in it. Begin it now.

Commitment has the power to move our lives along, but it also gives our lives stability. In a sermon written for the marriage of a young couple, the German theologian Dietrich Bonhoeffer wrote, "It is not your love which sustains your marriage, but from now on marriage that sustains your love." Love creates commitment, but once made, commitment provides a safe, sure harbor in which love can prosper and grow (Barbeau, 1988).

We commit ourselves to the things that are important to us, and then they are important because we have committed ourselves to them. In Antoine de Saint-Exupéry's story *The Little Prince,* the prince has a rose he cherishes, the only rose, he thinks, in the whole universe. Then he finds thousands of roses in a single garden. He is saddened to think his rose is common and therefore he is not a very great prince. But he comes to see that his rose is special and more important than all the other roses because he has dedicated himself to her. She is the rose he has watered, put under a glass globe, and sheltered behind a screen. She is the rose he has listened to when she grumbled or boasted or said nothing. She is special because, as he explains, "She is *my* rose." She is the rose to which he has made his commitment.

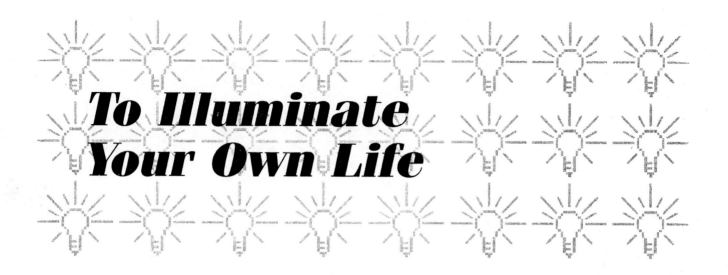

To Illuminate Your Own Life

Anchor and Apply*

1. Are you undercommitted or overcommitted? Discuss this aspect of your life.

2. Discuss a commitment that you broke or abandoned.

3. Discuss your experience in and/or travel through any or all of these identity states: identity achievement, moratorium, foreclosure, and diffusion.

4. How have your commitments changed during your life or a particular time of it?

5. Have you taken full responsibility for your life? If not, why not? If so, how so?

6. Describe a commitment you have or have had some trouble in making (getting a degree or certificate, starting a business, getting engaged or married, having a child, tackling a new career, and so on). Why is it or was it so hard for you to make this commitment?

7. Using Siegelman's seven steps, describe a personal risk you successfully undertook.

8. In which of the Kriegels' three performance zones do you currently fall? Discuss this aspect of your life.

9. What, for you, would be "the good life"? Describe what you have done or are doing to attain it.

10. Describe how your commitments contribute to your mental health or psychological well-being.

11. Describe how a commitment (or its failure or loss) has contributed to your jealousy, guilt, or depression.

12. Are you being used for a "mighty" purpose? Are you engaged in a "great enterprise"? Discuss this aspect of your life.

---

* These "anchor and apply" items are designed to help you use the categories of the chapter as stimuli to prompt new or deeper or clearer insights into yourself and your life. To respond to an item first find the material in the chapter that is most relevant to the item *and* yourself; that's called "anchoring." Second, think about this material in relationship to yourself and your life and keep thinking about it until you arrive at a new or deeper or clearer understanding; that's the "apply" or application part. When you write or present your response to the item, be sure to include both parts, that is, both the anchor material and the application. You can know you are successful on an item if, in completing it, you truly learn something new or understand something better.

13. "Commitment has the power to move our lives along, but it also gives our lives stability." Apply this insight to a commitment you have made.

Small Terrors, Secret Heroics

Although we may think of "terror" and "heroics" as large or dramatic acts, Amy Gross (1993) writes eloquently about the little terrors that quietly fill our everyday lives, challenging us to perform our own secret heroics. She writes that to others these small terrors may appear silly and the heroics they call for may seem like small acts. "The fact that they require enormous courage," she continues, "is known only to the protagonist" (p. 204).

Among the small terrors given as examples by Gross are speaking in public, initiating a conversation with a stranger across the room, arguing a grade, and, under some circumstances, asking for something we want or announcing that there is something we deserve. Gross cites the case of a woman who, after painting many years, takes her work to a gallery. "Risking being told she's no good, risking her hope that she is saying something unique with her paints, that *she* is unique—that's a very great risk" (p. 204).

Gross tells of another woman who has been living with a man simply to keep from being alone. This woman argues that she hasn't found anyone better, and if she left this man, she would be adrift and might be alone forever. Gross is saddened by this woman's inability to open herself to the possibility of something better, but she understands the woman's dread of being alone: "If she were to let go of her man—clearly and crisply—it would be an ostensibly small act. In my eyes, at least, it would be heroic" (p. 245).

Psychologist Arnold Lazarus and psychiatrist Allen Fay (1975) advise us to take at least one "psychological risk" every day: "The wise individual will obviously avoid dangerous or harmful situations, but the risks to which we are referring do not fall into this category. Taking calculated *psychological* risks (such as accepting a new job, telling someone off, going out on a blind date, asking a favor, expressing an opinion, or offering advice) tends to change an everyday existence into an exciting life" (p. 69).

Psychologist Ellen Siegelman (1993) has written a book, *Personal Risk,* for persons who want to take risks but are afraid to. This might describe almost all of us at almost any time in our lives. There is almost always something we are drawn toward, something that might make our lives better, but we hold ourselves back, wondering "Can I?" "What if I make a mess of it?"

On the following three pages is an exercise, adapted from Siegelman's book, to help you get some insight into a psychological or personal growth risk you considered and might have taken but didn't, a risk you did take, and a risk you now might take. To complete the exercise, write your response for each item or question in the space provided for it.

A Personal Growth Risk I Might Have Taken but Didn't Take

1. What was the risk?

2. Why was the risk appealing? What might you have gained?

3. Why was the risk frightening? What might you have lost?

4. What was the worst thing that might have happened if you had taken the risk and it turned out badly?

5. If the worst thing happened, what good might have come of it?

6. Looking back and considering all your answers above, how do you feel about the fact that you didn't take the risk? Why?

A Personal Growth Risk I Did Take

1. What was the risk? What was the outcome?

2. Why was the risk appealing? What might you have gained? What did you gain?

3. Why was the risk frightening? What might you have lost? What did you lose?

4. What was the worst thing that might have happened if things had turned out badly?

5. If the worst thing happened, what good might have come of it?

6. Looking back and considering all your answers above, how do you feel about the fact that you took this risk? Why?

A Personal Growth Risk I Might Take

1. What is the risk?

2. Why is the risk appealing? What might you gain?

3. Why is the risk frightening? What might you lose?

4. What is the worst thing that might happen if you take the risk and it turns out badly?

5. If the worst thing happened, what good might come of it?

6. Considering all your answers above, and also those on the previous two pages, how do you feel about taking this risk? Why?

A Persistent Personal Problem

Think of a personal problem you have had for a long, long time—a problem that has hung on and on that maybe you could have done something about but haven't done much about in any lasting way. Maybe it's something within yourself that has needed working on or an external situation that has needed attention, but somehow you haven't done very much about it. When you have thought of such a problem, write it in the place indicated below, and then—but not before—continue with the material that follows.

A personal problem I have had for a long, long time . . .

Now, with reference to the personal problem you described above, indicate why you don't like this problem, how this problem hurts you or affects your life in a negative way. Complete the incomplete statement immediately below, and then—but not before—continue with the material that follows.

I don't like this problem because . . .

Now, with reference to the personal problem you described, think of why you like this problem, how this problem helps you or affects your life in a positive way. These further instructions may seem ridiculous. We generally think of problems as being all bad. But maybe this problem isn't all bad. Maybe it has some hidden advantage or payoff. Think about this and complete one of the two incomplete statements immediately below; then proceed to the next page. If you can't think of anything to write below (after you have thought and thought about it), go directly to the next page.

I like this problem because . . .
I don't like this problem, but it's not all bad because . . .

One of my friends, Andre Auw, who is a psychotherapist, told me that people sometimes come to him with a problem but resist giving it up. It often turns out to be, he says, their "precious problem"—one they would hate to lose. Upon analysis, it turns out that these problems have a positive as well as a negative side: without realizing it, the person gets some mileage out of the problem, although at a considerable cost.

Other therapists have made similar observations. William Glasser (1985) writes that, painful as depression is, we may unknowingly depress ourselves because we have learned to use our depression to control others and to get them to pay attention to us, sympathize with us, and help us. Depression may seem to be our problem, but it may also be our solution.

Patricia Jakubowski and Arthur Lange (1978) encourage people to become more assertive, but they find that some people are reluctant to give up their passive ways. Clearly, although there are definite disadvantages to acting nonassertively—such as losing respect for oneself, not getting one's needs met, and becoming resentful—there may be advantages as well:

> [When you present] yourself as helpless and unable to act in your behalf, other people may act for you. Nonassertive behavior can help you to perpetuate certain public images. For example, by not asking for the information you need, you can appear all-knowing; by not expressing irritation, you can appear to be very understanding and accepting of other people; by not expressing controversial opinions, you can appear to be in agreement with other people. (pp. 65–66)

In his widely read book *Your Erroneous Zones*, Wayne Dyer (1976) writes that we are responsible for our own feelings, we choose the way we feel, and there are psychological payoffs for choosing guilt and worry. For example, guilt keeps us focused on the past, about which we can do nothing, rather than on the harder task of working on ourselves in the present; also, professions of guilt win pity from others or at least keep them from getting on our case. Worry keeps us focused on the future and also gives us an excuse for not getting busy with what we could be doing now; worry can also elicit sympathy from others and prove to them that we are concerned, caring persons.

This chapter poses the question "What will I do to move my life along?" By gaining insight into the advantages or hidden payoffs of persistent problem behavior, we can understand better why we continue it and what we would have to give up in order to change. Were you able to think of some reasons why you like the personal problem you described earlier in this exploration? If not, see if you can think of some reasons now, and write them down on the previous page. Or perhaps the discussion above brings to mind a different persistent personal problem that might have some hidden payoffs for you; if so, redo the exploration, focusing on this latter problem.

As a last step in this exploration, write down what you have learned from it in the space below, and add another page if you would like more space.

The Self-Contract

A *psychological contract* is a written statement that specifies what you agree to do in order to bring about some improvement in your life and what the consequences will be if you succeed or fail. A *self-contract* is a psychological contract you make with yourself. In a self-contract, you set down in words exactly what it is you promise yourself you will do.

Psychological contracts have been found helpful in modifying various problem behaviors (Kanfer & Gaelick, 1986). Self-contracts have proved useful in various self-change projects; compared to persons who were not asked to sign such contracts, those who were asked and did so increased their chance for success (Griffin & Watson, 1978; Seidner, 1973). There seems to be something about putting our names on the dotted line that impresses us, or maybe we don't put our names on the dotted line until we are impressed. Perhaps Samuel Goldwyn was right when he said, "A verbal contract isn't worth the paper it's written on."

Legal documents are sometimes signed in the presence of witnesses or a notary public, and psychological contracts seem to be more effective when there is some kind of public commitment or witnessing. It can be helpful to sign a self-contract in front of a relative, friend, class, or group of associates—not so that they can nag us later (although they might), but so that they can remind us of our resolve, offer their support, and help us celebrate our success.

If we are making a public commitment, we must be careful that we don't get carried away and promise too much in order to impress those in attendance. If we promise too much and fall short, we may want to avoid our witnesses (Kanfer & Gaelick, 1986). Through projection, we may see in their eyes the criticism we really have for ourselves.

To be most effective, the provisions of a contract need to be spelled out in detail: exactly what are you agreeing to do; exactly how will you do it; exactly how will you know it is done? There needs to be some provision for reward upon the completion of the contract and perhaps some penalty for failure. It is good to have a fairly limited and short-range goal; smaller or part-goals can be strung together as they are completed, to move us along to larger and more distant goals.

Consider a change you would like to make in your life right now, one you are ready to make, one you are committed to making. Perhaps you would like to improve your relationship to yourself by saying self-enhancing rather than self-defeating things. Perhaps you have an irrational belief or an always-never rule that needs modification. Maybe you would like to demonstrate more forgiving behavior or manifest your love more for a particular person. Is there a personal habit that might be changed for the better? Is there a relationship to which you could devote more time or show more consideration or in which you could practice being a caring presence?

What about your priorities? Do they need adjusting, with more time given over to things you really value? Maybe you have a low personal death awareness and haven't taken all the steps you might in order to ready yourself to die so that you can free yourself to live? Perhaps you could practice letting down your defenses, disclosing yourself more, and letting others know what you are thinking and feeling. What could you do to add more breadth to your life? What might you begin to do that you have avoided because you might not do it well?

On the page that follows, there is a self-contract for you to complete. Be careful: this is a legal document (well, almost). Be resolute but not foolhardy; avoid anything that could be harmful or dangerous. When you have filled out your part of the contract, make a public commitment by sharing what you have written with three other people (one by one or all together). Then have each of them sign as a witness.

Self-Contract

I, the undersigned, being of sound mind, firm purpose, and earnest commitment to grow and keep growing—in return for promise or promises made to me, whose receipt is hereby acknowledged—do hereby promise, vow, and declare that I will, in the interest of my personal growth, take tangible, concrete, and explicit actions consistent with what is set forth below.

1. This is exactly what I will do (what, when, how, etc.) . . .

2. This is exactly how my life will be made better by the actions I will take . . .

3. This is exactly how (a) my efforts might be sabotaged and (b) how I will prevent this sabotage . . .

4. These are exactly the personal resources (or harvest qualities) within myself and/or the support from others I will summon to help me . . .

5. This is exactly how I will know I have been successful (deadline date, results to be manifested) . . .

6. This is exactly how I will reward myself upon my success (in addition to the quiet pride I will take in my achievement) . . .

Dated this _____ day of _____, A.D. _____.

_____
Promissor

_____
Promisee/Witness No. 1

_____
Promisee/Witness No. 2

_____
Promisee/Witness No. 3

Question 14
Threshold
What's Ahead for Me?

At the beginning of this book, we took our bearings by seeking an answer to this question: "Where am I now in my life?" Now, having pursued our lives through thirteen questions, we are ready to ask our last question, which concerns our future. The question is: "What's ahead for me?"

On the Threshold

Each day in our lives is a bridge between all that has gone before and all that is yet to come. Each day could be thought of as a threshold we traverse—the past at our back and the future before us. On the threshold we can look back and gain insight and perspective. We can look ahead to get a sense of where we are going and who we are becoming. And on the threshold we must be careful that we are not so captured by the past or so drawn to the future that we do not live each moment of the present.

Remembering the Past

The Chinese sage Confucius said, "Study the past if you would divine the future." And philosopher-poet George Santayana wrote, "Those who cannot remember the past are condemned to repeat it." We cannot escape the past because it is lodged in memory and woven into our patterns of thinking, feeling, and acting.

We can easily become a captive of the past. It may be a past that was too good to leave ("the good old days"). Or it may be a past too bad to forget or forgive or too powerful (we think) to overcome.

We can more easily find our way out of the past if we illuminate it rather than keeping it in the dark. The repressed, suppressed, half-accommodated past is more likely to intrude upon the present than the past that has been explored, understood, and affirmed or forgiven.

As we illuminated the past by answering the questions posed by this book, probably we recalled some events we liked to remember, and some we recalled with quiet pride. There were probably some it hurt to remember, and some that we needed to forgive.

Each time we looked back on the past, we had an opportunity to do so with older, wiser eyes. Through creative reminiscence, we had a chance to clear the past and to deal with denial, regret, and unfulfilled dreams. And we had a chance to commemorate and celebrate the past, making the most of what was good.

Whatever our past has been, we have an opportunity to create a great one for ourselves. Today will be our past tomorrow. We can make the most of today and each today. Then in some distant tomorrow each of us can look back and say, "What a great past I made for myself."

Living in the Present

Only the present—this moment—exists. We can live in it or let it slip away. Time is precious, we say, but we "kill time" and "pass the time away" waiting for a better moment to get here. Life is short, we say, but we may let our days go by unlived while we are waiting for the main event.

The playwright Thornton Wilder was very concerned with this matter. He said that he wrote *Our Town* (which proved to be his most famous work) as "an attempt to find a value above all price for the smallest events in our daily life." In this play he shows what is extraordinary about the ordinary and commonplace.

In *Our Town*, Emily, who died in childbirth, finds she can return to relive a day of her life. She is warned not to return; and then, because she is determined,

she is cautioned, "At least, choose an unimportant day. Choose the least important day in your life. It will be important enough." She selects her twelfth birthday but finds her experience, from the vantage point of death, too precious, too poignant, and in sharp contrast to the living, who move matter-of-factly through the day. Overcome, she returns to death, and Wilder has her say to the audience and to the stage manager (who narrates the play):

> Good-by, good-by, world. Good-by, Grover's Corners . . . Mama and Papa. Good-by to clocks ticking . . . and Mama's sunflowers. And food and coffee. And new-ironed dresses and hot baths . . . and sleeping and waking up. Oh, earth, you're too wonderful for anybody to realize you.
>
> *She looks toward the stage manager and asks abruptly, through her tears:*
>
> Do any human beings ever realize life while they live it?—every, every minute? ([1938] 1985, p. 100)

To be present in the present—this is not always an easy task. Even when we have freed those parts of ourselves that had been stuck in the past, and have reclaimed those parts that had been caught up by the future, the present may elude us.

There may be times when we are not fully present anywhere because we are everywhere at once—we're scattered, fragmented, in bits and pieces. We can't seem to get ourselves and our acts together. The Buddha said, "When you are walking, walk. When you are standing, stand. When you are sitting, sit. Don't wobble" (Easwaran, 1978, p. 132). Some of us are expert wobblers.

There may be times when we seem to be nowhere at all—we feel distant, removed, apart from everything. We're not "with it." Food has no taste; colors are muted; nothing is enjoyable. At times like these, we feel as though we're not truly living life.

To be completely *in* a situation doesn't mean we can attend to everything at once. There is often a "too-muchness" about life that requires us to select or focus ourselves, because otherwise the overload would be unbearable (Murphy, 1975). One goal of meditation is to train the mind to be "one-pointed," that is, to focus purposefully on a single subject. We learn to live in the moment but also to choose the reality for that moment, as is aptly illustrated in this Zen story:

> A man was fleeing, pursued by a tiger. He came to the edge of a precipice, the tiger right behind. In desperation he climbed over the edge down a long

© ASHLEIGH BRILLIANT 1981   POT-SHOTS NO 2254

Ashleigh Brilliant

The only difference between yesterday and tomorrow is: Today.

vine. Above him the tiger roared. Below him lay a thousand-foot drop into raging rapids. Further, two mice, one white and one black, had begun gnawing through the vine. Suddenly, the man noticed a luscious strawberry growing just within reach. Holding onto the vine with one hand, with the other he plucked the strawberry. How delicious it tasted. (Reps, 1958, pp. 22–23)

In such a situation there are a number of compelling stimuli on which to focus. There are the roaring tiger above, the raging rapids below, the gnawing mice, the vine within his hands. Yet he chooses the one thing in the situation that can give him a moment of pleasure: he plucks the strawberry and pops it into his mouth (Shapiro, 1978).

There is no real way to save time. Our only choice concerns how to spend it, how to make the most of each moment. On a sundial, dated 1695, there is this inscription: *Tenere non potes, potes no perdere diem*—It is not possible to hold the day; it is possible not to lose it.

Envisioning the Future

I remember a conversation I had with one of my academic colleagues. (His life reminded me a little of my own.) When he was in high school, he studied hard so that he could get into a good college. When he was in college, he burned the midnight oil so that he could get into graduate school. Graduate work was slavery, but he was determined to finish and get a good appointment. Now he had it, but he couldn't relax because his research grant was up for renewal and he was also coming up for promotion and tenure. And, of course, there would be the promotion beyond that and the promotion beyond that.

You may remember a children's chant that goes:

> One for the money
> Two for the show
> Three to get ready
> Three to get ready
> Three to get ready . . .

Of course, it really ended: "And four to go!" But some of us never get to go. We live a lifetime of getting ready.

Erving and Miriam Polster (1974), a pair of Gestalt therapists, recall this chant as they write of a common tendency to slight the present because of a concern

© Brilliant Enterprises 1975. Reprinted by permission.

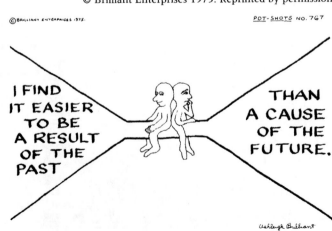

© BRILLIANT ENTERPRISES 1975.   POT-SHOTS NO. 767

for the future. The Polsters note that many of us get stuck in stage number three—getting ready and getting ready and getting ready for events that never come or, if they do, find us too worn out or still too future-oriented to make the most of them.

Living in the future and living in the present are very different approaches to life, and, as the Polsters indicate, the first can interfere with the second. When individuals with a strong future orientation reach a goal, they often seem unable to enjoy it. Instead, they set off on another goal and then another. Whether it's money, fame, or power, or simply getting one's work done, they never seem to reach a stopping and enjoying place. And to live in the future appears to be an awful waste. If we're living in the future, we're not living in the present. Victor Daniels and Laurence Horowitz (1976) write, "If I'm hurrying to get *there*, I'm not being *here*. My mind is filled with where I'm going, and I'm blind to where I am" (p. 143).

This is not to say that we should never focus on the future. It is to our advantage sometimes to look ahead, make plans, and create visions to inspire us. But to have a *concern for* the future is not the same as to *live in* the future. The first kind of futurity need not inundate the present, while the latter is at the expense of the present. The trick is to keep every "unpresent" in proper perspective. When we launch ourselves into the future, we do so consciously and constructively, and then return ourselves safely to the present (Shapiro, 1978).

How we look ahead to the future is of prime importance. As we stand on the threshold, on the brink of the rest of our lives, what is the future we see for ourselves? How optimistic are we that our lives will be good—that we will be able to

---

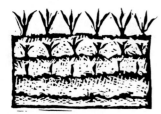

Box 14.1

Threshold: What's Ahead for Me?

Seedthoughts

1. Today is the first day of the rest of your life.

   —pop saying

2. There are only two ways to live your life. One is as though nothing is a miracle. The other as though everything is a miracle.

   —Albert Einstein

3. Expect a miracle.

   —bumper sticker

4. All difficult things have their origin in that which is easy, and great things in that which is small.

   —Lao-tsu

5. It is better to light one candle than to curse the darkness.

   —old saying

6. Two men looked out through the same bars.
   One sees mud, and one sees stars.

   —Frederick Langbridge

7. No plain not followed by a slope.
   No going not followed by a return.

He who remains persevering in danger
Is without blame.
Do not complain about this truth;
Enjoy the good fortune you still possess.

   —I Ching

8. Surrender the idea that the past remains all-important and that because something once strongly affected your life it must do so indefinitely. While considering your past history seriously and doing your best to learn valuable lessons from it, realize that your present constitutes tomorrow's past, and that working to change the present may enable you to create a radically better future.

   —Albert Ellis and Robert A. Harper

9. Ask, and it shall be given you; seek, and you shall find; knock, and it shall be opened unto you.

   —Matthew 7:7

10. Grow where you are planted.

   —cross-stitching on an old sampler

make them good? How much change can we anticipate for ourselves? How much ferment? How much constancy? These are some questions we will pursue in the material ahead.

An Optimistic or a Pessimistic Life?

"Facts do not cease to exist because they are ignored," Aldous Huxley wrote. But Mark Twain wasn't so sure; he said, "Get your facts first and then you can distort them as much as you please." We humans are good at denying the facts or, at least, putting a good spin on them. More about this as we look at some facts about denial, optimism, and pessimism.

Denial

The second chapter noted the strong case made by Shelley Taylor for "positive illusions" (1989). Taylor argues that it can be helpful and healthful for us to mute or blunt the facts and interpret them in the best possible light. However, she makes a firm distinction between our everyday use of positive illusions and the defensive use of denial, in which we refuse to admit a fact, or repression, in which we hide it from ourselves.

Richard Lazarus (1985), one of the foremost investigators in the area of stress and coping, makes a case for the judicious or selective use of denial. After examining research studies in which denial seemed to have constructive outcomes and those in which the results were damaging, Lazarus formulated some tentative principles concerning the benefits and limitations of denial.

1. If direct action is essential or useful in changing a threatening or damaging situation, denial is destructive. If direct action is useless to alter the situation, denial may help reduce stress and allow for the shifting of attention and energy to other matters.

   > This principle also allows us to extrapolate to other damaging circumstances, for example, illnesses such as kidney failure and diabetes. Control of these illnesses depends on vigilant attention to diet and exercise, and to behavioral and bodily signals of the need for dialysis or insulin. To the extent that successful denial of fact or damaging implications pushes the person to overlook such signals and therefore to evade suitable actions, it is counterproductive and could even be fatal. However, depression and disengagement are also enemies of efforts to stay alive and functioning well, and to mobilize the necessary vigilance over a long time requires relatively good morale and the feeling of hope. It could be argued, therefore, that some positive thinking in the face of a severe hardship might also prove of value and even be necessary. (p. 171)

2. If a given kind of stress must be dealt with again and again, denial would have negative value because it would serve to prevent ultimate mastery. It is best to face early what must be faced sooner or later.

3. Denial can be of positive value at an early state of coping when a person's resources are overwhelmed or insufficient. Denial in such instances serves as a temporary preservative.

   > Severely injured patients gain from denial when their life hangs in balance, when they are too weak or shocked to act constructively and so

need to be supported by others. Thus, the patient with spinal cord injury is helped for a while by believing that bodily functions that have been lost will return, or that the incapacitation is not as severe as it seems. Only later will the person be strong enough to come to terms with the reality of the condition and ultimately struggle to cope in a practical, problem-focused sense. (p. 172)

4. Some kinds of denial have value while others are useless or dangerous. The use of denial which is partial, minimal, or tentative is less likely to pose a problem because it does not close off the truth so tightly or completely. Denial of what is clear and unambiguous is more likely to be dangerous than denial of that which cannot be known for certain, because the latter does less violence to reality. Denials can be positive if they help us see an adversity as a challenge rather than as a threat and ourselves as able to perform adequately under the circumstances.

A case for selective denial was made by Norman Cousins (1979), who told his dramatic story in *The Anatomy of an Illness as Perceived by the Patient*. Faced with a life-threatening illness from which the chance of full recovery was said to be 1 in 500, he devised his own treatment (laughter promoted by classic comedy films, massive doses of Vitamin C, and a full range of positive emotions, including love, hope, faith, and a fierce will to live) and made a remarkable recovery. Said Cousins, "You never deny the diagnosis, but do deny the verdict that goes with it." Medical statistics are based on the average case, but—in his view—with appropriate denial, determination, and hope, one can beat the average.

Calvin and Hobbes   by Bill Watterson

Calvin and Hobbes   by Bill Watterson

Optimism and Pessimism

Pollyanna, the memorable child heroine of a book written by Eleanor Porter, was noted for her propensity to play the "Glad Game." She found something to be glad about in every seeming misfortune, and in doing so transformed her own life and helped others transform theirs.

The dictionary on my worktable defines "Pollyanna" as a "foolishly or blindly optimistic person," but Pollyanna's relentless optimism, although blind, served her and others well—it made good things happen. And recent research on optimism generally suggests that the "Glad Game" is still worth playing, although not blindly.

Reviewing the evidence, Margaret Matlin and David Stang (1978) conclude that there is a "Pollyanna Principle" evident in our language, memory, and thought. We understand pleasant information more quickly and accurately than that which is unpleasant; we spend more time thinking pleasant thoughts than we do thinking unpleasant thoughts; and if an event is unpleasant, it will tend to fade or even lead to the Glad Game as we come to see it in a different light.

As was noted earlier, we humans generally are optimistic about our future—sometimes more so than reality supports. But our optimism generally is not blind Pollyannaism. Instead, it "shows a patterning that corresponds quite well to the objective likelihood of events, to relevant experience with events, and to the degree to which one can actively contribute to bringing events about. Positive events are simply regarded as somewhat more likely and negative events as somewhat less likely to occur than is actually the case" (Taylor, 1989, p. 37).

While optimists expect happy happenings, pessimists expect unhappy ones. Pollyanna had the good fortune to "live" before the discovery of Murphy's Law, which declares "If anything can go wrong, it will." Pessimists uphold this law except for those most hard-core pessimists who think it is too optimistic and should read: "Anything will go wrong whether it can or not."

Research suggests that optimists tend to do better and behave differently than pessimists in stressful situations. Optimists are more likely to remain focused on the problem, try different strategies, and seek the help of others. Pessimists are more likely to disengage themselves from the goal and focus on the emotion that has been aroused (Scheier & Carver, 1985; Scheier, Weintraub, & Carver, 1986).

From his review of hundreds of studies, Seligman (1991) found that, compared to pessimists, optimists are happier, healthier, and may even live longer. Optimists are superior in school and college and also at work and on the playing field. Optimists exceed what might be predicted from their aptitude scores, and when they run for office, they are more likely to win. Seligman concludes, "There can be no doubt about it: Optimism is good for us" (p. 291). And, as Seligman notes, it is more fun.

Norem and Cantor (1986), in their study of optimists and pessimists, noted a particular kind of pessimism—"defensive pessimism"—in which persons set unjustifiably low expectations to prepare for potential failure and motivate themselves to avoid that failure. As an example, these investigators point to straight-A students who insist they are going to "bomb" an exam: "Nothing their friends can say reassures them; indeed, reminding them of their past successes seems only to lead to more anxiety or confusion. These persons proceed to rush home, drink gallons of coffee, study furiously throughout the night, and annoyingly, but not surprisingly, receive the highest score in the class" (p. 1209). Exhorting these defensive pessimists to think positively or optimistically may not be useful or helpful; in fact, when such encouragement was provided by Norem and Cantor, it led to impaired performance.

This pair of investigators followed groups of defensive pessimists and optimists in an honors college from their freshman through their junior year and found that pessimism had some long-term costs (Cantor & Norem, 1989). Although the two groups did not differ in grade point average (GPA) or on measures of life satisfaction and stress in their freshman and sophomore years, by the third year the defensive pessimists were significantly higher in stress and lower in GPA and life satisfaction; they also showed more physical and psychological symptoms. One hypothesis was that overpreparing can be exhausting and also perhaps somewhat dismaying as one sees that one's all-out efforts and worry are usually unnecessary.

Summing up the evidence against pessimism, Seligman (1991) offers these generalizations:

1. Pessimists tend to make gloomy prophecies of failure that are self-fulfilling.
2. Pessimists tend to give up or withdraw in the face of setbacks.
3. Pessimists tend to feel bad (blue, worried) regardless of the circumstance—whether they're right and things turn out wrong or they're wrong and things turn out right.
4. Pessimists are prone to depression and poor physical health.

Seligman finds that being a pessimist is not all pits; there are some cherries. Depressed persons—most of whom are pessimists—are more realistic than are nondepressed persons—most of whom are optimists. In various laboratory situations depressed and pessimistic persons prove to be better judges of reality; for example, they are better judges of the amount of control they have over various

---

Box 14.2

Are You an Optimist?

Indicate the strength of your agreement or disagreement with each of the items below by placing a check in the appropriate column.

	Strongly agree	Agree	Neutral	Disagree	Strongly disagree
1. In uncertain times, I usually expect the best.	____	____	____	____	____
2. If something can go wrong for me, it will.	____	____	____	____	____
3. I always look on the bright side of things.	____	____	____	____	____
4. I'm always optimistic about my future.	____	____	____	____	____
5. I hardly ever expect things to go my way.	____	____	____	____	____
6. Things never work out the way I want them to.	____	____	____	____	____
7. I'm a believer in the idea that "every cloud has a silver lining."	____	____	____	____	____
8. I rarely count on good things happening to me.	____	____	____	____	____

The preceding items have been included in a research instrument (the Life Orientation Test) to measure the extent to which persons are optimistic or expect favorable outcomes. Agreement with Items 1, 3, 4, and 7 and disagreement with the remaining items are indicative of optimism. Disagreement with Items 1, 3, 4, and 7 and agreement with the remaining items are indicative of pessimism (Scheier & Carver, 1985). These items, as they are presented here, cannot be considered a definitive test of your degree of optimism or pessimism, but they can help you think about this aspect of your orientation to life.

laboratory processes and the amount of skill they demonstrate on them. Pessimists also are less likely to interpret information in self-protective ways; therefore, they are better monitors and perhaps quicker to take the measures required by a situation (Cantor & Norem, 1989). They are more likely to see their dentists every six months, watch their blood pressure, and get their mammograms on schedule. They expect the worst and prepare for it; they are not likely to be overconfident and more likely to be ready should things go wrong.

Flexible Optimism. On Seligman's balance sheet, full-blown pessimism gets no respect, and the merits of the everyday, garden variety lag behind those of optimism. However, he notes that there are times when a bit of watch-out pessimism is necessary to damp all-out optimism; there can be a useful dynamic tension between the two, with each continually correcting the other. Optimism helps us dream and carry on, while a touch of pessimism keeps us from being rash and foolhardy.

Cantor and Norem emphasized the importance of a flexible response to stress, which allows one to devise optimistic or pessimistic strategies for handling stress, as a situation dictates. Seligman, in agreement, makes a case for "flexible optimism," which he describes as "optimism with its eyes open" (p. 292). He adds, "We must be able to use pessimism's keen sense of reality when we need it, without having to dwell in its dark shadows" (p. 292).

When is it good to use optimism as a strategy? When should optimism be avoided? According to Seligman, we should mainly consider the cost of failure in a given instance. If the cost is high, optimism is wrong. Examples of the wrong times to be optimistic: a motorist deciding whether his failing brakes will last a little longer or whether he needs to buckle up for just a short ride or whether he can drive home after a stop at a bar. Good times to be optimistic: a shy person deciding to start a conversation, a salesperson deciding on one more call, a passed-over-for-promotion executive deciding to put out some job feelers. In addition to the matter of cost, here are three situations in which to use optimism and three in which to avoid it, according to Seligman:

- If you are in an achievement situation (getting a promotion, selling a product, writing a difficult report, winning a game), use optimism.
- If you are concerned about how you feel (fighting off depression, keeping up your morale), use optimism. . . .
- If you want to lead, if you want to inspire others, if you want people to vote for you, use optimism. . . .
- If your goal is to plan for a risky and uncertain future, do not use optimism.
- If your goal is to counsel others whose future is dim, do not use optimism initially.
- If you want to appear sympathetic to the troubles of others, do not begin with optimism, although using it later, once confidence and empathy are established, may help. (pp. 208–209)

Learning Optimism. We can increase our optimism by modifying our explanatory style or the way we habitually account for the events in our lives. The pessimistic explanatory style was introduced in Chapter 11 in the discussion of depression and will be extended here with reference to optimism. Our explanations, according to Seligman, can be measured along three dimensions: permanence, pervasiveness, and personalization.

Pessimists, depressed persons, and those who give up easily tend to believe that their bad events have a *permanence*—that these events will persist, never go away, always affect their lives. Optimists, nondepressed persons, and those who resist helplessness believe the causes of such events to be temporary. For example: The pessimist fails at a task and says, "I'll never be able to do this." The optimist might say, "I'm a bit tired," leaving the door open to success after a bit of rest. Further example after a bad day in Las Vegas: The pessimist says, "I always am unlucky." The optimist says, "I wasn't lucky today."

For good events the situation is just reversed. The pessimist sees these as transient in causation, perhaps due to a mood or special effort or circumstance unlikely to be repeated. The optimist, by contrast, sees good events as having permanent causes, perhaps related to traits or abilities. The pessimist: "I had a lucky day." Or "Things went just right for once." The optimist: "I'm a lucky person." Or "I'm pretty good at this."

The second dimension distinguishing pessimists from optimists concerns *pervasiveness*—whether something is universal or specific. Pessimists find universal explanations for bad events and specific explanations for good ones. When something goes wrong, pessimists take this as evidence that everything is wrong, and when something goes right, it is evidence that only that one thing is right. Optimists reverse this pattern. Optimist: "I'm not good at math." Pessimist: "I'm not good at anything." Optimist: "I'm not attractive to him." Pessimist: "I'm just not attractive." Or for good events, optimist: "I'm smart." "I'm attractive." Pessimist: "I'm smart *at math*." "I was attractive *to him*."

The third explanatory dimension is *personalization*—whether or not the person is responsible. Optimists take the credit but not the blame, while pessimists take the blame but not the credit. Optimists are internalizers for good events—they believe that they have made such events happen—but externalizers for bad events, which they regard as beyond their control. Pessimists reverse this pattern. Pessimist: "It's my fault." Optimist: "It's bad luck." Or for a good event, pessimist: "It was a lucky break." Optimist: "I got a clear shot and made the most of it."

Snyder and Higgins (1988) conclude that although we are taught not to make excuses, some excuse making may have positive benefits, raising self-esteem and lowering anxiety and depression. In many of our excuses, we don't shift blame outside ourselves but only to a less threatening and less central aspect of self. For example, we say, "I got a low score because I didn't study" rather than "I got a low score because I'm stupid." Philosopher J. L. Austin (1970) observes that "Few excuses get us out of it completely; the average excuse, in a poor situation, gets us only out of the fire into the frying pan—but still, of course, any frying pan in a fire" (p. 177).

Seligman notes that there are obvious advantages to teaching persons to see bad events as temporary and specific. On the other hand, he warns that teaching people to externalize the causes of these events might erode personal responsibility, and, after all, we will not change for the better if we do not assume this responsibility. However, he does encourage such externalization for depressed persons, because these individuals assume too much responsibility for adverse events.

To Seligman, becoming more optimistic is just a matter of ABC; that is, using Albert Ellis's system (presented in Chapter 3) to change self-defeating beliefs. (Actually, it involves a bit more of the alphabet: ABCDE.) This system stresses that adverse Activating events (A) do not cause adverse Consequences (C) such as depression and other miseries; rather, our pessimistic Beliefs (B) or explanations bring about these miseries. To go from pessimism to optimism, we monitor our beliefs or explanations to determine those that produce pessimism, and then we Dispute (D) and replace them with beliefs that will enhance optimism. Distraction (D)—if we don't mind another D—is also a useful technique to keep ourselves from ruminating or brooding. The result: a new optimistic Effect (E) or outcome.

Seligman advises that in disputing beliefs, we scan all possible causes and focus on those that are changeable (for example, we were not well enough prepared), specific (this particular competition was a tough one), and nonpersonal (the judging left something to be desired). Seligman writes, "You may have to push hard at generating alternative beliefs, latching onto possibilities you are not fully convinced are true. Remember that much of pessimistic thinking consists in just the reverse, latching onto the most dire possible belief, not because the evidence supports it, but precisely because it is so dire" (p. 222). Those of us who tend to arrive at pessimistic permanent, pervasive, and personal explanations for adverse events need to become skilled at generating alternatives. Here is Seligman's example of a student (Judy) disputing her beliefs, arriving at alternative explanations, and brightening her despair:

Adversity: I recently started taking night classes after work for a master's degree. I got my first set of exams back and I didn't do nearly as well as I wanted.

Belief: What awful grades, Judy. I no doubt did the worst in the class. I'm just stupid. That's all. I might as well face facts. I'm also just too old to be competing with these kids. Even if I stick with it, who is going to hire a forty-year-old woman when they can hire a twenty-three-year-old instead? What was I thinking when I enrolled? It's just too late for me.

Consequences: I felt totally dejected and useless. I was embarrassed I even gave it a try, and decided I should withdraw from my courses and be satisfied with the job I have.

Disputation: I'm blowing things out of proportion. I hoped to get all As, but I got a B, a B+, and a B–. Those aren't awful grades. I may not have done the best in the class, but I didn't do the worst in the class either. I checked. The guy next to me had two C's and a D+. The reason I didn't do as well as I hoped isn't because of my age. The fact that I am forty doesn't make me any less intelligent than anyone else in the class. One reason I may not have done as well is because I have a lot of other things going on in my life that take time away from my studies. I have a full-time job. I have a family. I think that given my situation I did a good job on my exams. Now that I took this set of exams I know how much work I need to put into my studies in the future in order to do even better. Now is not the time to worry about who will hire me. Almost everyone who graduates from this program gets a decent job. For now I need to concern myself with learning the material and earning my degree. Then when I graduate I can focus on finding a better job.

© Ashleigh Brilliant 1980. Reprinted by permission.

Outcome: I felt much better about myself and my exams. I'm not going to withdraw from my courses, and I am not going to let my age stand in the way of getting what I want. I'm still concerned that my age may be a disadvantage, but I will cross that bridge if and when I come to it. (pp. 218–219)

The Optimistic World of Yes. Optimists live in far richer worlds than pessimists, and as we bring more optimism into our lives, we enhance them. In other words, pessimists live in a world of no and optimists in a world of yes. The poet E. E. Cummings expressed this point eloquently and simply:

> Yes is a world
> & in this world of
> yes live
> (skillfully curled)
> all worlds

A Cyclic or a Linear Life?

If you were born in 1776, the year this country was born, your life expectancy would have been a short 35 years. By contrast, children born today can expect to reach the age of at least 75 years. Life expectancy has more than doubled during the lifetime of this country (Dychtwald & Flower, 1989).

We are living longer, and the pattern of our lives is becoming more complicated. In the old and not-so-old days, when few people lived to be very old, lives were rigidly linear: education in youth, work and child rearing in maturity, and possibly leisure and retirement in old age. Lives were relatively short and often not so sweet. (But hardly as sour as proclaimed by a bumper sticker I saw recently: "Life's a bitch and then you die.")

The linear life was run by a loud-ticking "social clock" that told people when the various events of life should occur. There was a time to go to school, a time to settle in your life's work, a time to marry, a time to have children, a time to retire (if you lived that long or could afford to). Every individual was aware of the clock, and if he or she forgot, there were plenty of others and traditions, rules, and regulations as reminders.

In his book *Flexible Life Scheduling: Breaking the Education-Work-Retirement Lockstep*, Fred Best (1980) argues that life would mean more to us if we could break out of this lockstep. Some of us—even without the institutional change and support that Best advocates—have managed to do so.

Present generations have more years of life to live and more opportunity to live a less linear existence. There is not just one time for something. Formal education increasingly doesn't necessarily end in the late teens or twenties; it's seen as a lifelong process. Look inside some college classrooms, and you will see students of every age, 18-year-olds right out of high school and persons of more years than three score and ten. Many have come back to school after a hiatus devoted to work or raising a family or just knocking about.

Living longer makes "until death do us part" a longer and harder-to-keep promise, and we are more likely to take that vow more than once. We marry later and have fewer children; and therefore can devote more of our adult years to other pursuits and relationships. However, since our parents also live longer and our children may take longer to establish themselves, we can find ourselves a member of the "sandwich generation"—sandwiched between our still-dependent adult children and our increasingly dependent aging parents.

Families these days are not only constituted; they are likely to be reconstituted and made up of one or two parents who have been married before and one or more children from a previous marriage or marriages. Speaking of cycles, sociologists Andrew Cherlin and Frank Furstenberg, Jr., believe that it will be rather common for children of this decade to whirl through this sequence:

with both parents several years →
with mother after parents divorce →
with mother and stepfather →
alone for a time in early adulthood →
with someone of the opposite sex without marrying →
married →
divorced, alone again →
remarried →
alone once more when spouse dies

Clearly it won't be all merry, but it will be a go-round.

Living longer, we have time enough for more than one career or calling. I recently asked one of my older students if he was retired. "Retired?" he answered. "I've retired three times." And sabbaticals are not just for professors; others as well take leaves to recharge themselves.

It's less of a crime these days to take some time off after high school or in the middle of college or to find a "not-forever" job while you're learning who you are and tending your other wishes and needs. Novelist James Michener (1988) writes that we have until the age of 35 to decide on what we want to do, and the years we "waste" may turn out to be the most creative and productive. Something of a slowpoke himself, he wrote nothing at all until he was 40. He notes that if he had made a vocational commitment at the age of 18 as he was encouraged to do, any choice would have had to be wrong.

Fred Best (1980) recommends that employees, employers, unions, and the government work together to facilitate life-cycle planning. He foresees a pattern that might resemble the following:

Student Years:	Part-time work and extended time for education and leisure.
Single and Non-offspring Years:	Longer workweeks of 45 to 50 hours with annual vacations ranging from 8 to 14 weeks and some sabbaticals.
Early Child Rearing Years:	Shorter workweeks of 25 to 40 hours with moderate vacations of two to four weeks.
Late and Post Child Rearing Years:	Moderate to long workweeks of 40 to 45 with long annual vacations of five to eight weeks and extended sabbatical leaves.
Old Age:	Short to moderate workweeks of 25 to 40 hours and long vacations and sabbatical leaves. (pp. 17–18)

Best concludes that a good life requires continual alternation between action and renewal:

With due recognition for the diversity of the human species, it seems that the fullest and most productive lives are those in which individuals fluctuate through periods of action and accomplishment—which expand our awareness and solidify our sense of self—and rest and reflection—which integrate our sense of self and the world. In this way, action becomes more than reaction to an endless treadmill of unchosen challenges, and reflection more than stultifying repetition of old thoughts and experiences. The actualization of this cyclic relationship between action and renewal is essential to human growth and fulfillment, and it requires that there be a better balance of learning, work, and leisure through all stages of our lives. (p. 175)

A Consistent or a Changing Self?

In Chapter 8, there was a discussion of the potential for growth and the impulse to grow. The following material considers the personal growth and other personality changes to be expected during the adult years.

How much does our personality change over our lifetime? How different are we now from what we have been? How different will we be in the years to come? When we attend our fiftieth or sixtieth high school reunion, what will we find? Will the person voted most likely to succeed have proven to be a success? Will the person voted most popular be as likable? Will the class clown still be hamming it up?

In 1951 I received my doctoral degree from the University of Iowa and made my way out to Hawaii, where I have lived to this day except for some sabbatical semesters. Now and then, someone I knew back in the Midwest visits the Islands, and we meet again after fifty or more years apart. Almost every time, I have thought how much like their old selves they still were despite the wrinkles, added pounds, and graying and/or balding tops. Yes, I think, that's Nick! Or same old Annie! On the other hand, as a clinical psychologist I have worked with persons who were trying to mend their lives or get themselves unstuck. They begin to grow, do things they were unable to do before, be persons they were afraid to be before. And I think to myself, wow, how they've changed, how much they've grown.

There is the instance of my own life. How stuck I was in my bachelorhood in my middle thirties, with my personal life caught up in cul-de-sacs and blind alleys. Then long months of therapy from which I emerged to quickly marry, father two children, and catch up with my social clock. How much I changed. How much my life changed. And much for the better. And yet I seem to be in some ways stubbornly my same old self: workaholic, achievement oriented, and unable to get through a three-day holiday without working on or planning a project.

Both change and stability characterize development all through life. We want to change, and yet we want to remain the same. Brim and Kagan (1980) write that on one hand there is "a powerful drive to maintain the sense of one's identity, a sense of continuity that allays fears of changing too fast or of being changed against one's will by outside forces." They note the heroic efforts of political prisoners and prisoners of war to maintain their identity under great stress, isolation, and torture. But Brim and Kagan continue, "On the other hand, each person is, by nature, a purposeful, striving organism with a desire to be more than he or she is now. From making simple new year's resolutions to undergoing transsexual operations, everyone is trying to become something that he or she is not but hopes to be" (pp. 17–18).

During our adult years we may note periods of rapid change—sometimes too much change. At other times nothing seems to be happening, and this inaction may be comforting or boring. There are also periods when much of our life seems to be stable, but one area—perhaps our work or marriage or our relationship to our children or a child—is in considerable ferment.

Some changes appear quite predictable. There are changes that may be expected with every new social role (Perlmutter & Hall, 1985); for example, we assume that people who marry will "settle down." Liberals not infrequently become more conservative as they grow older. In advanced age people may be expected to cut down on some of their activities.

Other changes are quite unpredictable. Perlmutter and Hall pose this question: "Does knowing that a man is a stockbroker, married and the father of five children at the age of 35 allow us to predict his profession and family status eight years later?" Their answer: "Not always. If the year is 1883, the place is Paris, and the stockbroker is Paul Gauguin, in 1891, he will be alone in Tahiti, devoting himself to painting" (p. 22).

A brief survey of our own acquaintances can supply other examples of unpredictable or dramatic change: persons who embrace a new religion and greatly alter their lives, alcoholics who become teetotalers, seemingly cautious and responsible persons who throw caution or prudence to the wind.

As was noted in Chapter 8, we have certain basic tendencies or dispositions that tend to stabilize in young adulthood (Costa & McCrae, 1992). For example, our relative standing on certain elements of social or emotional style, such as anxiety and introversion-extroversion (whether we are in-dwelling or outgoing), seem relatively constant over the years. (If we are introverted as young adults, we are likely to be even more introverted in old age, since introversion itself appears to increase with age.) Constancy has also been found for "neuroticism," which includes anxiety, depression, hostility, and impulsiveness. Reviewing the evidence, psychologist Zick Rubin (1981) writes, "Neurotics are likely to be complainers throughout life. They may complain about different things when they get older—for example, worries about love in early adulthood, a "midlife crisis at about age 40, health problems in late adulthood—but they are still complaining" (p. 23).

Other aspects of personality appear to undergo important changes over the course of life. There seem to be significant changes in some values and attitudes in the adult years (Glenn, 1980). The change is greater in young adults than in older ones, but Brim and Kagan (1980) conclude that "many attitudes of older adults, including some that reflect 'basic values,' do not become highly resistant to change" (p. 11). For example, these days later-life romantic attachments increasingly involve nontraditional patterns of sexual behavior and living together.

Significant differences have been found in the life attitudes of young adults, middle-aged adults, and elderly ones. Young adults show a considerable need to achieve new goals and to have new and different experiences, but this need diminishes with age. Elderly persons report more satisfaction with life as well as more acceptance of death (and less fear of death) than middle-aged and younger adults (Reker, Peacock, & Wong, 1987; Gesser, Wong, & Reker, 1987–88).

New environments may prompt change while old environments retard it. When we are constantly in the company of the same people or groups, we may feel compelled or encouraged to remain the same predictable person. We can continue to earn the reputation we gained early in life (the "black sheep," "the brain," the "spoiled brat"). If we have broken away from our old home environment and way of being, we may find some old personality patterns reasserting themselves when we return to visit. We start behaving again as we promised ourselves we wouldn't, and then—to our horror or amusement—we're told we haven't changed a bit (Whitbourne, 1986).

A number of older widows have told me how much they and their lives have changed since their husbands died. Often it's been a change for the worse—especially during the year following bereavement, when increased rates of depression, disease, and death are found (Bee, 1987). However, more than one widow has reported a burst of growth, a blossoming out, or the advent of something new in their lives.

Age cohorts (that is, people of the same age or generation) become less and less alike as they grow older, because each individual falls under the influence of specific or special events or circumstances and thus is influenced to change in ways differing from the others (Perlmutter & Hall, 1985). Some of these influences are pleasant (a distinguished career, a best-seller, a happy marriage, talented children, financial success, robust health), and some are unpleasant (loss of work, a failed enterprise, divorce, a problem child, bankruptcy, accident, disease). As we become less and less like each other, Bernice Neugarten (1964) suggests, we become more and more like ourselves. We develop a stable set of coping strategies and become dedicated to a central core of habit patterns. At the same time, we build a network of social relationships that both support us and lock us in.

Each new generation enters a stream of history different from that of every other generation. No generation will live the same life course as another (Brim & Kagan, 1980). According to some futurists, present generations have some breathtaking changes in store for them. These changes will considerably alter what it means to be a young adult, middle-aged, or old. In their book *Age Wave* Ken Dychtwald and Joe Flower (1989) point to a coming social revolution brought on by three demographic phenomena: the increase in older persons, the decrease in younger persons, and the aging of the post–World War II baby-boom generation.

1. *The senior boom.* We Americans are living longer, and the older generation is more numerous, healthier, wealthier, more active, and more influential than any previous older generation.

2. *The birth dearth.* We Americans are generally not oriented to having large or even what used to be called middle-sized families. The fertility rate in America is now the lowest it has ever been. American women average about 1.8 births, which is less than half the rate of their mothers.

3. *The aging of the baby boom.* Births boomed following World War II. One-third of all living Americans were born in the eighteen-year period between 1946 and 1964. "Likened to a 'pig moving through a python,' this generation has dominated American culture for four decades" (p. 13). As the boomers become the older generation, their numbers and influence will produce an historic shift in America.

Here are some of the ways that, according to Dychtwald and Flower, these three factors will work to change you, the life you will lead, and the environment you will live it in:

You will live longer than you might now expect—possibly much longer—as future science brings the aging process under control. It is likely that you will grow old more slowly than did members of previous generations, with greater health, energy, dynamism, and direction. You may even benefit from long-sought-after breakthroughs in life extension that will allow many people to live to 100, and some even to 120. And as science learns more about the aging process, you will be able to take advantage of the continual discovery of new drugs, foods, therapies, and health programs that will cause your body to age at a slower pace.

You will change the way you love, whom you love, and how long you will love them. Marriage will change, as "till-death-do-us-part" unions give way to serial monogamy. In an era of longer life, some people will have marriages that last 75 years, while others will have different mates for each major stage of life. You may find yourself falling in love later in life, and in more unusual ways, than you now expect. Older women will deal with the shortage of older men by turning increasingly to unconventional relationships, such as dating younger men or sharing a man with other women.

You will change your conception of family life and the ways in which you relate to your parents and children. The child-focused, nuclear family will become increasingly uncommon and will be replaced by the "matrix" family, an adult-centered, transgenerational family bound together by friendship and choice as well as by blood and obligation. The physical environment you live in will change. Because the man-made world we inhabit is now designed for youth, the form and fit of everything will be redesigned. To fit the pace, physiology, and style of a population predominantly in the middle and later years of life, the typeface in books will get larger, and traffic lights will change more slowly; steps will be lower, bathtubs less slippery, chairs more comfortable, and reading lights brighter. Neighborhoods will be safer, and food will be more nutritious.

You may never retire, or you may retire several times. You may stop working one or more times in your thirties, forties, or fifties in order to go back to school, raise a second (or third) family, enter a new business, or simply to take a couple of years to travel and enjoy yourself. You may go back to work in your sixties, seventies, or even eighties. You may find that the traditional framework of life—with youth the time for learning, adulthood for nonstop working and raising a family, and old age for retirement— will come unglued, offering you new options at every stage. A cyclic life arrangement will replace the current linear life plan as people change direction and take up new challenges many times in their lives. (pp. 1–3)

Such a future is not without problems, but you can consider them challenges and opportunities for personal growth. You can meet them head-on with optimism and with your coping skills, your harvest qualities, and your determined commitment.

All the best to you on your path ahead. It promises to be an interesting time. Whatever comes, know you're in charge, you will manage, good will come to you, and you will do good and make good out of that which comes.

Aloha,

Abe Arkoff

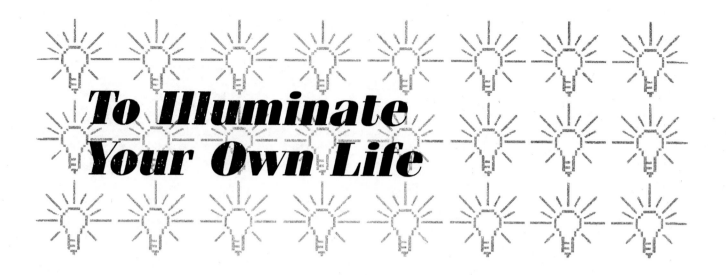

To Illuminate Your Own Life

Anchor and Apply*

1. Discuss the extent to which you are "captured by the past" or "live for the future" and/or are "fully present in the present." Be specific, give examples, and indicate the effect of this orientation on your life.

2. Give examples of the use you have made of denial and indicate how helpful or hurtful this use has been.

3. Are you an optimist? A flexible optimist? A pessimist? A defensive pessimist? Discuss this aspect of yourself and include a consideration of how well your attitude serves you.

4. Using Ellis's ABCDE system, dispute one of your self-defeating beliefs and write an account following Seligman's example on pages 436–437.

5. How linear or cyclic has your life been? How linear or cyclic do you expect it to be in the future? Discuss this aspect of your life.

6. How much has your personality changed? How different are you now than you have been? What changes do you expect in yourself in the future? Discuss the consistency and/or change you have noted and expect in yourself.

7. Do you welcome the changes that Dychtwald and Hall foresee? Why or why not?

---

* These "anchor and apply" items are designed to help you use the concepts of the chapter as stimuli to prompt new or deeper or clearer insights into yourself and your life. To respond to an item, first find the material in the chapter that is most relevant to the item *and* yourself; that's called "anchoring." Second, think about this material in relationship to yourself and your life and keep thinking about it until you arrive at a new or deeper or clearer understanding; that's the "apply" or application part. When you write or present your response to the item, be sure to include both parts, that is, both the anchor material and the application. You can know you are successful on an item if, in completing it, you truly learn something new or understand something better.

Past Gleanings

"Know thyself" is an ancient injunction, but this is not an easy task. Cervantes wrote, "Make it thy business to know thyself, which is the most difficult lesson in the world." Cicero claimed that each person is least known to himself, and François Villon agreed, writing, "I know all save myself alone."

Sigmund Freud, the founder of psychoanalysis, began analyzing himself as a young man and continued to do so all his life. He took his self-analysis very seriously and reserved the last half hour of each working day for this purpose. Few people can claim to have made such a thorough study of themselves or to have arrived at such deep insights as Freud.

During your journey through this book, you have been studying yourself. What are the most important things you have observed in yourself as you worked your way through the fourteen questions posed by the chapters? What new or deepened insights have you formed? In effect, you have been enrolled in a course in which you have been the subject. What have you learned about this subject?

Below, write down ten things you have learned about yourself during your journey through the fourteen questions:

1.

2.

3.

4.

5.

6.

7.

8.

9.

10.

Learning about ourselves—forming new insights and deepening old ones—can be an important aspect of personal growth. Some of our insights help transform us; seeing ourselves and our worlds differently, we become different. But personal growth also involves commitment and effort; we work to change ourselves and to move our lives in the direction we want them to go.

Some of the ten things you recorded on the previous page may involve not only insight but also change in a positive direction. And, as you look back again on your journey through the fourteen questions, you may think of some other positive changes you have made or are beginning to make. Perhaps, before your journey, you weren't a caring presence because you imposed your solutions on others, but now you listen while they find their own solutions. Or perhaps you weren't a caring discloser because you kept everything inside, but now you are beginning to share your feelings. Perhaps you were your own worst enemy and critic, but you are becoming an ally and friend to yourself.

Maybe you used to have trouble in managing your anger, but now you are getting better at thinking hot thoughts or cool thoughts as you choose. Maybe you were threatened or defeated by a particular obstacle, but increasingly you see it as a challenge. Maybe you are shifting out of a coping strategy that never served you very well. Maybe you are becoming better at forgiving and loving.

It is important for us to take note of and to feel good about even little positive changes, because that's typically how growth occurs. The previous chapter took note of Lao-tsu's observation: "A journey of a thousand miles begins with a single step." Sometimes, it's two steps forward and one step back, but we can still feel good about our progress even if it isn't always in a straight line.

Use the blanks below to acknowledge three positive changes you have made or you began to make during your journey through the fourteen questions. These may or may not be items that you noted on the previous page. After you finish each item, tell yourself you've grown. Let yourself know it! Then tell yourself you will keep growing. And, with determination and commitment, you will!

1. *I used to* _____

_____

_____.

That wasn't good because _____

_____

_____.

I have grown! Now, instead of what I used to do, I _____

_____

_____.

This is good because _____

_____

_____.

I have grown! I'll keep growing!

2. *I used to* _____
_____
_____.

That wasn't good because
_____
_____.

I have grown! Now, instead of what I used to do, I _____
_____
_____.

This is good because _____
_____
_____.

I have grown! I'll keep growing! _____

3. *I used to* _____
_____
_____.

That wasn't good because _____
_____
_____.

I have grown! Now, instead of what I used to do, I _____
_____
_____.

This is good because _____
_____
_____.

I have grown! I'll keep growing!

Future Doings

In an expansive moment Robert Louis Stevenson rhymed, "The world is so full of a number of things,/I'm sure we should all be as happy as kings."[1] Seemingly in the same mood, Edna St. Vincent Millay wrote, "O world, I cannot hold thee close enough!" Indeed, there are many wonderful things to do in this world.

What do you look forward to? What would you like to do before you die? What ten things in particular seem important to you? Complete the list below, and then turn to the next page.

Ten things I would like to do before I die:

1.

2.

3.

4.

5.

6.

7.

8.

9.

10.

[1] I know I've quoted these lines earlier in this book, but they're favorites out of my long-past childhood.—Abe

When I was working with hospice patients, I got to know one who told me that it seemed as if he had spent his whole life getting ready to live. He said he had never done much of what he wanted to do because he was saving up to do it all when he retired. He had great things planned. Then, just before it was time for him to retire, he became terminally ill. On his tombstone it could have been written: "In memory of all the things I was going to do tomorrow."

We need to get busy and make the things we want to happen happen. In one investigation, elderly persons were asked to indicate all the positive events they were anticipating. They also indicated the extent of their confidence that each event would take place, and the investigators classified each event as self-initiated or other-initiated. In a follow-up study two years later (and with the effects of initial levels of health partialed out), physical and psychological well-being was significantly better in those who might be called "determined optimists"—those who expected good things *and* were taking steps to bring them about (Reker & Wong, 1983).

Study the list of ten things you would like to do before you die. Which of them are you *determined* to do? Print a C (for commitment) in front of each of these. Which of them are just wishes? Print a W (for wish) in front of each. Which one would you regret most if you never did it? Print R (for regret) in front of it.

In the space below, discuss what to you seems most notable or important about your list of items as you have written, studied, and marked it.

Exploration

14C

The Threshold*

The future may seem dim or uncertain to us, but our *immediate* future, of course, is almost here. At this moment we stand on the threshold of what's to come. What do we see in the next few years ahead?

　　For a moment, close your eyes, relax yourself as deeply as you can, and visualize yourself (or simply think of yourself) in front of an opening door—the door to your immediate future. In your mind's eye, step through that doorway and see (or think about) what lies before you in the next few years. Then open your eyes and, in the space below (or on any piece of paper), draw what you saw or thought. When you have finished your drawing, turn to the next page.

---

* This exploration is suggested by the work of Ira Progoff (1975). For an alternate exploration, see Appendix A.

To complete the second part of this exploration, pose this question to yourself: "What's ahead for me?" In the space below, begin your answer in this way: "I am entering a time when . . ." When you are through, turn to the next page.

What's ahead for me? I am entering a time when . . .

Consider the immediate future you see for yourself. Are you looking out through optimistic rose-colored glasses or pessimistic dark-colored glasses? What are you doing/what can you do/what will you do to make your immediate future the future you want? Write your answers to these questions below.

The Class Reunion*

If you have worked your way through this book as a member of a class or group, imagine that you are having your first reunion. The reunion may be taking place any number of years in the future—let the group decide. Because you are such a great, growing group, you have scattered to the four corners of the earth and are much too busy to come together in one place. So you have decided to write a letter to let each other know how you have grown. Continue your letter from this beginning (and also use the next page if you would like more space):

Date _____
(Exactly ____ or 5 or 10 or 25 or 50 years from today)

Dear Class/Group:

Since last we met, _____ years have gone by. They have been really great, growing years. What I am most pleased to report to you is . . .

---

* This exploration may be used instead of Exploration 14C. Or it may be used as a final class/group exercise: simply finish the regular agenda of the last meeting a little early, declare the class/group ended, say good-bye, board your time machines (for which practice was provided in Exploration 4C, but none is really necessary), travel to the time the class/group has selected for the reunion, look back on what has happened, write your letters, and share them in any way you wish. Another way to use this exploration is for a real letter reunion: exchange permanent addresses, and on the agreed-on date, write and mail your reunion letters.

From: *The Illuminated Life*, by Abe Arkoff. Copyright © 1995 by Allyn and Bacon.   455

Ground Rules for Sharing in Small Groups

Sharing in small groups proceeds best when each member fulfills in turn the roles of "caring presence" (see pp. 14–15) and "caring discloser" (see p. 47). The ground rules presented below can be helpful in promoting these two roles.

1. The purpose of the small group is to allow each member to share what he or she wishes to share from the assignment.

2. When the small group has formed, one member volunteers to be the chair, or the group selects one member for this role. The chair's duties are simply to ensure that (a) the roles of caring discloser and caring presence are observed, and (b) each caring discloser receives an equal amount of the available time.

3. After the chair is designated, one member volunteers to be the first caring discloser and to present whatever he or she wishes from the assignment. The other members become caring presences and say nothing until the caring discloser indicates he or she is ready for the group's response. Then all may join in until the first person's time is up.

4. A second member volunteers to be the caring discloser, and the group continues as before. This procedure is followed until all have had a turn.

5. To highlight the rule that caring presences are to saying nothing until explicitly invited to participate, use is made of a small card marked "Talker Ticket—Admit One." The chair will hand this ticket to each member when he or she assumes the role of caring discloser—thereby signaling that only this person is permitted to speak. When the caring discloser is ready for the group's response, he or she will return the ticket to the chair as a signal that all may now join in. The talker ticket idea is based on the Native American (American Indian) talking stick. You may cut out and use the talker ticket below or design your own ticket or talking stick.

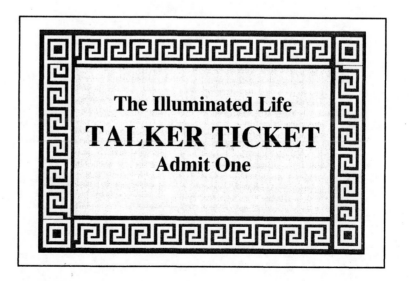

The Illuminated Life
TALKER TICKET
Admit One

References

Abrash, M. (1985). Is there life after immortality? In C. B. Yoke and D. M. Hassler (Eds.), *Death and the serpent: Immortality in science fiction and fantasy* (pp. 19–27). Westport, CT: Greenwood Press.

Adams, V. (1981, June). The sibling bond: A lifelong love/hate dialectic. *Psychology Today,* pp. 32, 34, 36–41, 43–47.

Adler, J. (1992, February 17). Hey, I'm terrific! *Newsweek,* pp. 46–51.

Adler, T. (1989, August). For happiness, it's quantity that counts. *Monitor,* p. 13.

Ainsworth, M. D. S., Blehar, M. C., Waters, E., & Wall, S. (1978). *Patterns of attachment: A psychological study of the strange situation.* Hillsdale, NJ: Erlbaum.

Alberti, R. E., & Emmons, M. L. (1990). *Your perfect right: A guide to assertive living* (6th ed.). San Luis Obispo, CA: Impact.

Allen, B. P. (1990). *Personality, social and biological perspectives on personal adjustment.* Pacific Grove, CA: Brooks/Cole.

Allen, J. R., & Allen, B. A. (1988). Scripts and permissions: Some unexamined assumptions and connotations. *Transactional Analysis Journal, 18*(4), 283–293.

Allport, G. W. (1961). *Pattern and growth in personality.* New York: Holt, Rinehart & Winston.

The American dream: A national survey conducted for the "Wall Street Journal" by the Roper Organization. (1987). New York: Dow Jones.

Anderson, A. J. (Ed.). (1975). *Lin Yutang: The best of an old friend.* New York: Mason/Charter.

Anderson, R. (1968). *I never sang for my father.* New York: Random House.

Andrews, F. M., & Withey, S. B. (1976). *Social indicators of well-being: Americans' perception of life quality.* New York: Plenum Press.

Ansen, D. (1980, August 4). The great impersonator. *Newsweek,* pp. 43–44.

Antonuccio, D. (1993, August). *Psychotherapy vs. medication for depression: Challenging the conventional wisdom.* Paper presented at the annual convention of the American Psychological Convention, Washington, DC.

Argyle, M. (1987). *The psychology of happiness.* London and New York: Methuen.

Arkoff, A. (1968). *Adjustment and mental health.* New York: McGraw-Hill.

Arkoff, A. (1988). Anxiety. In A. Arkoff (Ed.), *Psychology and personal growth* (3rd ed., pp. 229–232). Boston: Allyn & Bacon.

Arkoff, S., with Trubo, R. (1992). *Flying through Hollywood by the seat of my pants.* New York: Birch Lane Press.

Aron, R., Ain, R., Anderson, J. A., Burd, H., Filman, G., McCallum, R., O'Reilly, E., Rose, A., Stichman, L., Tamara, Z., Wawro, J., Weinberg, L., & Winesauker, J. (1974). Relationships with opposite-sex parents and mate choice. *Human Relations, 27*(1), 17–24.

Astin, A. W. (1977). *Four critical years.* San Francisco: Jossey-Bass.

Astin, A. W., Dey, E. L., Korn, W. S., & Riggs, E. R. (1992). *The American freshman: National norms for fall, 1991.* Los Angeles: Higher Education Research Institute, Graduate School of Education, University of California, Los Angeles.

Astin, A. W., Green, K. C., & Korn, W. S. (1987). *The American freshman: Twenty year trends, 1966–1985.* Los Angeles: Higher Education Research Institute, Graduate School of Education, University of California, Los Angeles.

Austin, J. L. (1970). *Philosophical papers* (2nd ed.). New York: Oxford University Press.

Babbie, E. (1985). *You* can *make a difference.* New York: St. Martin's Press.

Bach, G. R., & Torbet, L. (1983). *The inner enemy: How to fight fair with yourself.* New York: Morrow.

Bakker, C. B. (1975). Why people don't change. *Psychotherapy: Theory, Research and Practice, 12*(2), 164–172.

Baldwin, C. (1977). *One to one: Self-understanding through journal writing.* New York: M. Evans.

Balswick, J. (1988). *The inexpressive male.* Lexington, MA: Lexington Books/Heath.

Bandura, A. (1982). The psychology of chance encounters and life paths. *American Psychologist, 37*(7), 747–755.

Bandura, A. (1989a). Human agency in social cognitive theory. *American Psychologist, 44*(9), 1175–1184.

Bandura, A. (1989b). Self-regulation of motivation and action through internal standards and goal systems. In L. A. Pervin (Ed.), *Goal concepts in personality and social psychology* (pp. 19–85). Hillsdale, NJ: Erlbaum.

Bank, S. P., & Kahn, M. D. (1975). Sisterhood-brotherhood is powerful: Sibling subsystems and family therapy. *Family Process, 14*(3), 311–337.

Bank, S. P., & Kahn, M. D. (1982). *The sibling bond.* New York: Basic Books.

Banowsky, W. S. (1969). *It's a playboy world.* Old Tappan, NJ: Fleming H. Revell.

Barbeau, C. (1988). Fidelity: The creative vow. In A. Arkoff (Ed.), *Psychology and personal growth* (3rd ed., pp. 221–225). Boston: Allyn & Bacon.

Barber, B. R. (1985, May 20). United States of anomie. *New Republic,* pp. 33–34, 36.

Baron, P. (1974). Self-esteem, ingratiation, and evaluation of unknown others. *Journal of Personality and Social Psychology, 30,* 104–109.

Barrett, K. (1984, June). Two-career couples: How they do it. *Ms.,* pp. 39–42, 111, 114.

Barron, F. (1968). *Creativity and personal freedom.* Princeton, NJ: Van Nostrand.

Baruch, G., Barnett, R., & Rivers, C. (1983) *Lifeprints: New patterns of love and work for today's women.* New York: New American Library.

Batson, C. D., & Ventis, W. L. (1982). *The religious experience.* New York: Oxford University Press.

Beardslee, D. C., & O'Dowd, D. D. (1962). Students and the occupational world. In N. Sanford (Ed.), *The American college* (pp. 597–626). New York: Wiley.

Beck, A. T. (1976). *Cognitive therapy and the emotional disorders.* New York: International Universities Press.

Beck, A. T. (1985). Theoretical and clinical aspects. In A. T. Beck, G. Emery, with R. Greenberg, *Anxiety disorders and phobias: A cognitive perspective* (pp. 3–164). New York: Basic Books.

Beck, A. T. (1989). *Love is never enough.* New York: HarperCollins.

Beck, J. (1992, February 28). More self-esteem, fewer "lifts." *Honolulu Advertiser,* p. A14.

Bee, H. L. (1987). *The journey of adulthood.* New York: Macmillan.

Bendich, S. (1979). Creative stalling in decision making. *Voices, 15*(3), 51–53.

Berg, J. H. (1987). Responsiveness and self-disclosure. In J. H. Berg & V. J. Derlega (Eds.), *Self-disclosure: Theory, research, and therapy* (pp. 101–130). New York: Plenum Press.

Berg, J. H., & Derlega, V. J. (1987). Themes in the study of self-disclosure. In J. H. Berg & V. J. Derlega (Eds.), *Self-disclosure: Theory, research, and therapy* (pp. 1–8). New York: Plenum Press.

Berger, E. (1952). The relation between expressed acceptance of self and expressed acceptance of others. *Journal of Abnormal and Social Psychology, 47,* 778–782.

Berger, E. M. (1993). Vocational choices in college. In A. Arkoff (Ed.), *Psychology and personal growth* (4th ed., pp. 442–446). Boston: Allyn & Bacon.

Bernard, J. (1971). The paradox of the happy marriage. In V. Gornick and B. K. Moran (Eds.), *Woman in sexist society* (pp. 85–96). New York: Basic Books.

Berne, E. (1961). *Transactional analysis in psychotherapy.* New York: Grove Press.

Berne, E. (1964). *Games people play.* New York: Grove Press.

Berne, E. (1972). *What do you say after you say hello? The psychology of human destiny*. New York: Grove Press.

Berscheid, E., & Walster, E. H. (1978). *Interpersonal attraction* (2nd ed.). Reading, MA: Addison-Wesley.

Best, F. (1980). *Flexible life scheduling: Breaking the education-work-retirement lockstep*. New York: Praeger.

Birnbach, L. (1990, April 8). "The things I wanted to say to him." *Parade*, pp. 4–5.

Birnbaum, J. A. (1975). Life patterns and self-esteem in gifted family-oriented and career-committed women. In M. Mednick, S. Tangri, & L. Hoffman (Eds.), *Women and achievement* (pp. 396–419). New York: Halsted Press.

Blank, J. P. (1986, July). Mary's impossible dream. *Reader's Digest*, pp. 77–82.

Blau, M. (1990, July/August). Adult children: Tied to the past. *American Health*, pp. 57–58, 60–62, 64–65.

Bloom, B. S. (Ed.). (1985a). *Developing talent in young people*. New York: Ballantine Books.

Bloom, B. S. (1985b). The nature of the study and why it was done. In B. S. Bloom (Ed.), *Developing talent in young people* (pp. 3–18). New York: Ballantine Books.

Bloomfield, H. H., & Kory, R. B. (1980). *Inner joy: New strategies to put more pleasure and satisfaction in your life*. New York: Wyden.

Bob, S. (1968). *An investigation of the relationship between identity status, cognitive style, and stress*. Unpublished doctoral dissertation, State University of New York at Binghamton.

Bolen, J. S. (1979). *The Tao of psychology: Synchronicity and the self*. San Francisco: Harper & Row.

Bossard, J. H. S., & Boll, E. S. (1955). Personality roles in the large family. *Child Development, 26*(1), 71–78.

Bossard, J. H. S., & Boll, E. S. (1956). *The large family system*. Philadelphia: University of Pennsylvania Press.

Bossard, J. H. S., & Boll, E. S. (1960). *The sociology of child development* (3rd ed.). New York: Harper & Row.

Bovasso, G., Jacobs, J., & Rettig, S. (1991). Changes in moral values over three decades, 1958–1988. *Youth and Society, 22*(4), 468–481.

Bower, S. A., & Bower, G. H. (1991). *Asserting yourself: A practical guide for positive change* (updated ed.). Reading, MA: Addison-Wesley.

Bowlby, J. (1979). *The making and breaking of affectional bonds*. London: Tavistock.

Bradburn, N. M. (1969). *The structure of psychological well-being*. Chicago: Aldine-Atherton.

Branden, N. (1985). *Honoring the self: The psychology of confidence and respect*. New York: Bantam Books.

Branden, N. (1987). *How to raise your self-esteem*. New York: Bantam Books.

Brannon, R. (1985). Dimensions of the male sex role in America. In A. G. Sargent (Ed.), *Beyond sex roles* (pp. 296–316). St. Paul: West.

Brennan, T. P., & Piechowski, M. M. (1991). A developmental framework for self-actualization: Evidence from case studies. *Journal of Humanistic Psychology, 31*(3), 43–64.

Bricker, D. (1978). Myths of romantic love. *Rational Living, 13*(1), 31–35.

Brickman, P. (1987). Commitment. In P. Brickman et al., *Commitment, conflict, and caring* (pp. 1–18). Englewood Cliffs, NJ: Prentice-Hall.

Brickman, P., & Coates, D. (1987). Commitment and mental health. In P. Brickman et al., *Commitment, conflict, and caring* (pp. 222–276). Englewood Cliffs, NJ: Prentice-Hall.

Brickman, P., Coates, D., & Janoff-Bulman, R. (1978). Lottery winners and accident victims: Is happiness relative? *Journal of Personality and Social Psychology, 36*(8), 917–927.

Bridges, W. (1980). *Transitions: Making sense of life's changes*. Reading, MA: Addison-Wesley.

Brim, G. (1988, September). Losing and winning. *Psychology Today*, pp. 48, 50–52.

Brim, O. G., Jr. (1958). Family structure and sex role learning by children: A further analysis of Helen Koch's data. *Sociometry, 21*(1), 1–16.

Brim, O. G., Jr., & Kagan, J. (1980). *Constancy and change in human development.* Cambridge, MA: Harvard University Press.

Brink, D. (1970, Fall). A letter to the dead. *Voices,* pp. 106–107.

Brown, B. B. (1984). *Between health and illness: New notions on stress and the nature of well being.* Boston: Houghton Mifflin.

Brown, B. B., & Steinberg, L. (1990, March). Academic achievement and social acceptance. *Education Digest,* pp. 57–60.

Browne, H. (1974). *How I found freedom in an unfree world.* New York: Avon Books.

Bugental, E. K., & Bugental, J. F. T. (1984). Dispiritedness: A new perspective on a familiar state. *Journal of Humanistic Psychology, 24*(1), 49–67.

Bugental, J. F. T. (1976). *The search for existential identity: Patient-therapist dialogues in humanistic psychotherapy.* San Francisco: Jossey-Bass.

Bugental, J. F. T. (1987). *The art of the psychotherapist.* New York: Norton.

Bugental, J. F. T., & Bugental, E. K. (1984). A fate worse than death: The fear of changing. *Psychotherapy, 21*(4), 543–549.

Burns, D. D. (1980). *Feeling good: The new mood therapy.* New York: Morrow.

Burns, D. D. (1990). *The feeling good handbook: Using the new mood therapy in everyday life.* New York: Plume.

Buscaglia, L. (1972). *Love.* Greenwich, CT: Fawcett.

Cain, B. S. (1990, February 18). Children and divorce. *New York Times Magazine,* pp. 26–27, 50, 54–55.

Cameron, R., & Meichenbaum, D. (1982). The nature of effective coping and the treatment of stress related problems: A cognitive-behavioral perspective. In L. Goldberger & S. Breznitz (Eds.), *Handbook of stress: Theoretical and clinical aspects* (pp. 695–710). New York: Free Press.

Campbell, J. (1968). *The hero with a thousand faces.* Princeton, NJ: Princeton University Press.

Campbell, J. (1971). Editor's introduction. In J. Campbell (Ed.), R. F. C. Hull (Trans.), *The portable Jung* (pp. vii–xxxii). New York: Penguin.

Campos, J. J., Barrett, K. C., Lamb, M. E., Goldsmith, H. H., & Sternberg, C. (1983). Socioemotional development. In M. M. Haith & J. J. Campos (Eds.), *Handbook of child psychology.* Vol. 2: *Infancy and psychobiology* (pp. 783–915). New York: Wiley.

Cantor, N., & Norem, J. K. (1989). Defensive pessimism and stress and coping. *Social Cognition, 7*(2), 92–112.

Cantril, H. (1965). *The pattern of human concerns.* New Brunswick, NJ: Rutgers University Press.

Cantril, H., & Bumstead, C. H. (1960). *Reflections on the human venture.* New York: New York University Press.

Caplan, P. (1989). *Don't blame mother: Mending the daughter-mother relationship.* New York: Harper & Row.

Carter, J. (1975). *Why not the best?* Nashville, TN: Broadman.

Carver, C. S., Scheier, M. F., & Weintraub, J. K. (1989). Assessing coping strategies: A theoretically based approach. *Journal of Personality and Social Psychology, 1989, 56*(2), 267–283.

Castaneda, C. (1968). *The teachings of Don Juan.* Berkeley: University of California Press.

Castaneda, C. (1972). *Journey to Ixtlan.* New York: Simon & Schuster.

Chernin, K. (1985). *The hungry self: Woman, eating, and identity.* New York: Times Books.

Chung, S. (1991, April 8). Students confident with school work. *Ka Leo O Hawai'i,* pp. 1, 3.

Clance, P. R. (1985). *The imposter phenomenon: The fear that haunts your success.* Atlanta: Peachtree.

Coleman, J. C. (1979). *Contemporary psychology and effective behavior* (4th ed.). Glenview, IL: Scott, Foresman.

Coleman, J. C., Morris, C. G., & Glaros, A. G. (1987). *Contemporary psychology and effective behavior* (6th ed.). Glenview, IL: Scott, Foresman.

Coleman, L. M., & Antonucci, T. (1983). Impact of work on women at midlife. *Developmental Psychology, 19*(2), 290–294.

Coles, R. (1989). *The old ones of New Mexico* (rev. ed.). Albuquerque: University of New Mexico Press.

Combs, A. W., Avila, D. L., & Purkey, W. W. (1978). *Helping relationships: Basic concepts for the helping professions* (2nd ed.). Boston: Allyn & Bacon.

Comstock, G. W., & Patridge, K. B. (1972). Church attendance and health. *Journal of Chronic Diseases, 25,* 665–672.

Connell, R. W., Crawford, J., Kippax, S., Dowsett, G. W., Baxter, D., Watson, L., & Berg, R. (1989). Facing the epidemic: Changes in the lives of gays and bisexual men in Australia and their implications for AIDS prevention strategies. *Social Problems, 36,* 384–402.

Coopersmith, S. (1967). *Antecedents of self-esteem.* San Francisco: W. H. Freeman.

Cordes, C. (1984, December). Kahneman: Loss looms large. *Monitor,* p. 26.

Corey, G., & Corey, M. S. (1993). *I never knew I had a choice* (5th ed.). Pacific Grove, CA: Brooks/Cole.

Cornell, G. (1992, March 14). Pollster finds clergy most attuned to people's thinking. *Honolulu Advertiser,* p. A6.

Cornell, W. F. (1988). Life script theory: A critical review from a developmental perspective. *Transactional Analysis Journal, 18*(4), 270–282.

Costa, P. T., Jr., & McCrae, R. R. (1980). Still stable after all these years: Personality as a key to some issues in adulthood and old age. In P. B. Baltes & O. G. Brim, Jr. (Eds.), *Life-span development and behavior,* vol. 3 (pp. 65–102). New York: Academic Press.

Costa, P. T., Jr., & McCrae, R. R. (1992, August). *"Set like plaster?" Evidence for the stability of adult personality.* Paper presented at the annual convention of the American Psychological Association, Washington, DC.

Cousins, N. (1977, May 28). Anatomy of an illness (as perceived by the patient). *Saturday Review,* pp. 4–6, 48–51.

Cousins, N. (1979). *Anatomy of an illness as perceived by the patient: Reflections on healing and regeneration.* New York: Norton.

Cousins, N. (1980, September). Capacity and control. *Saturday Review,* p. 10.

Cousins, N. (1989). *Head first: The biology of hope.* New York: Dutton.

Crampton, M. (1974). Psychological energy transformations: Developing positive polarization. *Journal of Transpersonal Psychology, 6*(1), 39–56.

Cross, H., & Allen, J. (1970). Ego identity status, adjustment, and academic achievement. *Journal of Consulting and Clinical Psychology, 34,* 288.

Csikszentmihalyi, M., & Larson, R. (1984). *Being adolescent: Conflict and growth in the teenage years.* New York: Basic Books.

Cuber, J. F., & Harroff, P. B. (1965). *The significant Americans: A study of sexual behavior among the affluent.* New York: Appleton-Century.

Cummings, E. E. (1978). *No thanks* (G. J. Firmage, Ed.). New York: Liveright.

Cutler, S. J. (1976). Membership in various types of voluntary associations and psychological well-being. *The Gerontologist, 16,* 335–339.

Cutrona, C. E. (1982). Transition to college: Loneliness and the process of social adjustment. In L. A. Peplau & D. Perlman (Eds.), *Loneliness: A sourcebook of current theory, research and therapy* (pp. 291–309). New York: Wiley.

D'Aguanno, A. (n.d.). Prolonged positive experiences. *Personal Growth,* No. 24, 9–27.

Daniels, V., & Horowitz, L. J. (1976). *Being and caring.* Palo Alto, CA: Mayfield.

Daniels, V., & Horowitz, L. J. (1984). *Being and caring: A psychology for living* (2nd ed.). Palo Alto, CA: Mayfield.

Davis, K. (1940a). Extreme social isolation of a child. *American Journal of Sociology, 45,* 554–565.

Davis, K. (1940b). The sociology of parent-youth conflict. *American Sociological Review, 5,* 523–535.

Davis, K. (1947). Final note on a case of extreme isolation. *American Journal of Sociology, 52,* 432–437.

Davis, S. F., Grover, C. A., Becker, A. H., & McGregor, L. N. (in press). Academic dishonesty: Prevalence, determinants, techniques, and punishments. *Teaching of Psychology.*

DeAngelis, T. (1991, June). Self-help books no joke in easing panic disorder. *Monitor,* p. 16.

DeStefano, L. (1990, January). Church/synagogue membership and attendance levels remain stable. *Gallup Poll Monthly,* pp. 32–34.

Doan, M. (1985, September 16). What a life is worth: U.S. seeks a price. *U.S. News & World Report,* p. 58.

Dodgson, J. (1987, January). Do women in education need mentors? *Education Digest,* pp. 26–28.

Donovan, J. M. (1975). Identity status and interpersonal style. *Journal of Youth and Adolescence, 4,* 37–55.

Doress, P. B., & Wegman, P. N. (1984). Working toward mutuality: Our relationships with men. In *Our bodies, ourselves* (3rd ed., pp. 123–140). New York: Simon & Schuster.

Dougherty, F. E. (1988). How come you're not running everywhere, anymore? In A. Arkoff (Ed.), *Psychology and personal growth* (3rd ed., pp. 266–268). Boston: Allyn & Bacon.

Driscoll, R. (1982, July). Their own worst enemies. *Psychology Today,* pp. 45–49.

Duffy, S. M., & Rusbult, C. E. (1985/1986). Satisfaction and commitment in homosexual and heterosexual relationships. *Journal of Homosexuality, 12*(2), 1–23.

Dukakis, K. (1990). *Now you know.* New York: Simon & Schuster.

Dychtwald, K., & Flower, J. (1989). *Age wave: The challenges and opportunities of an aging America.* Los Angeles: Tarcher.

Dyer, W. W. (1976). *Your erroneous zones.* New York: Funk & Wagnalls.

Easwaran, E. (1978). *Meditation.* Petaluma, CA: Nilgiri Press.

Ebersole, P. (1970). Effects of nadir experiences. *Psychological Reports, 27,* 207–209.

Ehrenreich, B. (1986, August). Night terrors of a middle-class sort. *Ms.,* p. 34.

Eliot, R. S., & Breo, D. L. (1984). *Is it worth dying for? A self-assessment program to make stress work for you, not against you.* New York: Bantam Books.

Ellis, A. (1957). Outcome of employing three techniques of psychotherapy. *Journal of Clinical Psychology, 13,* 344–350.

Ellis, A. (1973a). The A-B-Cs of rational-emotive therapy. In A. Ellis, *Humanistic psychotherapy: The rational-emotive approach* (pp. 55–67). New York: McGraw-Hill.

Ellis, A. (1973b). The value of a human being: A psychotherapeutic appraisal. In A. Ellis, *Humanistic psychotherapy: The rational-emotive approach* (pp. 17–29). New York: McGraw-Hill.

Ellis, A. (1977a). The basic clinical theory of rational-emotive therapy. In A. Ellis & R. Grieger (Eds.), *Handbook of rational-emotive therapy* (pp. 3–34). New York: Springer.

Ellis, A. (1977b). Psychotherapy and the value of a human being. In A. Ellis & R. Grieger (Eds.), *Handbook of rational-emotive therapy* (pp. 99–112). New York: Springer.

Ellis, A. (1977c). *Sex without guilt.* North Hollywood, CA: Wilshire.

Ellis, A. (1990a). How to maintain and enhance your rational-emotive therapy gains. In W. Dryden (Ed.), *Rational-emotive counselling in action* (pp. 96–102). London: Sage.

Ellis, A. (1990b). *How to stubbornly refuse to make yourself miserable about anything—yes, anything!* New York: Lyle Stuart/Carol Publishing Group.

Ellis, A. (1992). Secular humanism and rational-emotive therapy. *The Humanistic Psychologist, 20*(2–3), 349–358.

Ellis, A., & Harper, R. A. (1961). *Creative marriage.* New York: Lyle Stuart.

Ellis, A., & Harper, R. A. (1975). *A new guide to rational living.* Englewood Cliffs, NJ: Prentice-Hall.

Eng, D. (1989, June 17). How a difficult father shaped his daughter's life. *Honolulu Star-Bulletin,* p. A6.

Erikson, E. H. (1959). *Identity and the life cycle.* New York: International Universities Press. (Reissued by Norton, 1980)

Erikson, E. H. (1963). *Childhood and society* (2nd ed.). New York: Norton.

Erikson, E. H. (1968). *Identity: Youth and crisis.* New York: Norton.

Erikson, E. H. (1982). *The life cycle completed: A review.* New York: Norton.

Erikson, E. H., Erikson, J. M., & Kivnick, H. Q. (1986). *Vital involvement in old age.* New York: Norton.

Farrell, W. (1984, June). Male mid-life crisis. *AHP Newsletter,* pp. 18–19.

Feinstein, D., & Krippner, K. (1988). *Personal mythology: The psychology of your evolving self.* Los Angeles: Tarcher.

Ferguson, A. (1990, October 17). Kitty and Bill, singing the blues. *Wall Street Journal,* p. A14.

Ferrucci, P. (1982). *What we may be: Techniques for psychological and spiritual growth.* Los Angeles: Tarcher.

Festinger, L. (1957). *A theory of cognitive dissonance.* Stanford, CA: Stanford University Press.

Fields, S. (1983). *Like father, like daughter: How father shapes the woman his daughter becomes.* Boston: Little, Brown.

Fincher, J. (1975, November). Dialogue in a journal. *Human Behavior,* pp. 17–23.

Fine, R. (1985). *The meaning of love in human experience.* New York: Wiley.

Firestone, R. W., & Seiden, R. H. (1990). Psychodynamics in adolescent suicide. In L. C. Whitaker & R. E. Slimak (Eds.), *College student suicide* (pp. 101–123). New York: Haworth Press.

Fisher, S., & Fisher, R. L. (1981). *Pretend the world is funny and forever: A psychological analysis of comedians, clowns, and actors.* Hillsdale, NJ: Erlbaum.

Fiske, M. (1980). Changing hierarchies of commitment in adulthood. In N. J. Smelser & E. H. Erikson (Eds.), *Themes of work and love in adulthood* (pp. 238–264). Cambridge, MA: Harvard University Press.

Flach, F. F. (1974). *The secret strength of depression.* Philadelphia: Lippincott.

Flanagan, C. M. (1990). *People and change: An introduction to counseling and stress management.* Hillsdale, NJ: Erlbaum.

Fleming, A. T. (1977, July). What do you still want—that you're not getting—from your father? *Redbook,* pp. 42, 45–46.

Folkman, S., Lazarus, R. S., Gruen, R. J., & DeLongis, A. (1986). Dynamics of a stressful encounter: Cognitive appraisal, coping, and encounter outcome. *Journal of Personality and Social Psychology, 50,* 992-1003.

Fordham, S., & Ogbu, J. U. (1986). Black students' school success: Coping with the burden of "acting white." *Urban Review, 18*(3), 176–206.

Forer, L. K., & Still, H. (1976). *The birth order factor: How your personality is influenced by your place in the family.* New York: McKay.

Forisha, B. L. (1978). *Sex roles and personal awareness.* Morristown, NJ: General Learning Press.

Frank, A. (1953). *Anne Frank: The diary of a young girl.* New York: Pocket Books.

Frank, R. N. (1977). If I had infinite courage. *Voices, 13*(3), 55–56.

Frankl, V. E. (1972). The feeling of meaninglessness: A challenge to psychotherapy. *American Journal of Psychoanalysis, 32*, 85–89.

Frankl, V. E. (1979). *The unheard cry for meaning: Psychotherapy and humanism.* New York: Touchstone/Simon & Schuster.

Frankl, V. E. (1985). *Man's search for meaning* (rev. ed.). New York: Washington Square Press. (Original work published 1946)

Franklin, B. (1904). *Autobiography.* In J. Bigelow (Ed.), *The works of Benjamin Franklin* (Vol. 1, pp. 31–313). New York: Putnam's. (Original work published 1784)

Freedman, J. L. (1979). *Happy people.* New York: Harcourt Brace Jovanovich.

Freedman, M. (1993). *The kindness of strangers: Adult mentors, urban youth, and the new voluntarism.* San Francisco: Jossey–Bass.

Friday, N. (1978). *My mother/my self.* New York: Dell.

Friedman, M. (1967). *To deny our nothingness: Contemporary images of man.* London: Macmillan.

Friedrich, O., & McDowell, J. (1989, January 16). Flashy symbol of acquisitive age. *Time,* pp. 48–54.

Friend, D., & Editors of *Life.* (1990). *Meaning of life: Reflections in words and pictures on why we are here.* Boston: Little, Brown.

Friend, D., & Editors of *Life.* (1992). *More reflections on the meaning of life.* Boston: Little, Brown.

Fromm, E. (1941). *Escape from freedom.* New York: Holt, Rinehart & Winston.

Fromm, E. (1963). *The art of loving.* New York: Bantam Books.

Fulghum, R. (1989). *All I really need to know I learned in kindergarten.* New York: Ivy Books.

Fulghum, R. (1990, Fall/Winter). A bag of possibles and other matters of the mind. *Newsweek,* pp. 88, 90, 92.

Gallup, G., Jr., & Newport, F. (1990, June). More Americans now believe in a power outside themselves. *Gallup Poll Monthly,* pp. 33–38.

Gardner, J. W. (1964). *Self-renewal: The individual and the innovative society.* New York: Harper Colophon.

Gardner, J. W. (1984). *Excellence: Can we be equal and excellent too?* (rev. ed.). New York: Norton. (1st ed. published 1961)

Garfield, S. L. (1983). *Clinical psychology: The study of personality and behavior* (2nd ed.). New York: Aldine.

Garfinkel, P. (1985). *In a man's world: Father, son, brother, friend, and other roles men play.* New York: New American Library.

Gawain, S. (1978). *Creative visualization.* Berkeley, CA: Whatever Publishing.

Gaylin, W. (1979). *Feelings.* New York: Harper & Row.

Gellman, M., & Gage, D. (1985). *The confidence quotient.* New York: World Almanac Publications.

General Social Surveys, 1972–1991: Cumulative codebook. (1991). Chicago: National Opinion Research Center, University of Chicago.

Gergen, K. J. (1972, May). The healthy, happy human wears many masks. *Psychology Today,* pp. 31–35, 64, 66.

Gesser, G., Wong, P. T. P., & Reker, G. T. (1987–88). Death attitudes across the life-span: The development and validation of the Life Attitude Profile (DAP). *Omega, 18*(2), 113–128.

Gibbs, N. (1990, Fall). The dreams of youth. *Time,* pp. 10–14.

Gibran, K. (1923). *The prophet.* New York: Knopf.

Gilbert, D. M. (1988). *Compendium of American public opinion.* New York: Facts on File Publications.

Gillett, R. (1992). *Change your mind, change your life*. New York: Fireside.

Ginzberg, E., Ginsburg, S. W., Axelrad, S., & Herma, J. L. (1951). *Occupational choice: An approach to a general theory*. New York: Columbia University Press.

Glasser, W. (1985). *Control theory: A new explanation on how we control our lives*. New York: Perennial Library.

Glenn, N. D. (1980). Values, attitudes, and beliefs. In O. G. Brim, Jr., and J. Kagan (Eds.), *Constancy and change in human development* (pp. 596–640). Cambridge, MA: Harvard University Press.

Glenn, N. D. (1985, June). Children of divorce. *Psychology Today*, pp. 68–69.

Goffman, E. (1955). On face-work: An analysis of ritual elements in social interaction. *Psychiatry: Journal for the Study of Interpersonal Process, 18*, 213–231.

Goldstine, D., Larner, K., Zuckerman, S., & Goldstine, H. (1977). *The dance-away lover*. New York: Morrow.

Goleman, D. (1992, July). Gender fears. *Self*, p. 73.

Goodman, E. (1979). *Turning points*. Garden City, NY: Doubleday.

Goodman, E. (1990a, November 16). King and all those "P-words." *Honolulu Advertiser*, p. A16.

Goodman, E. (1990b, November 13). Perils of the neatness gap. *Honolulu Advertiser*, p. A12.

Goodman, G., & Esterly, G. (1988). *The talk book: The intimate science of communicating in close relationships*. New York: Ballantine Books.

Gordon, S. (1975, January–February). Creative infidelity: On being happy in an unhappy world. *The Humanist*, pp. 25–26.

Gordon, S., & Snyder, C. W. (1989). *Personal issues in human sexuality* (2nd ed.). Boston: Allyn & Bacon.

Gorsuch, R. L. (1980). An interactive, multiple model approach to illicit drug use. In D. J. Lettieri (Ed.), *Theories of drug use* (pp. 18–23, 383–385). Washington, DC: National Institute of Drug Abuse.

Goulding, M. M., & Goulding, R. L. (1982). *Changing lives through Redecision Therapy*. New York: Grove Press.

Graham, T. W., Kaplan, B. H., Cornoni-Huntley, J. C., James, S. A., Becker, C., Hames, C. G., & Heyden, S. (1978). Frequency of church attendance and blood pressure elevation. *Journal of Behavioral Medicine, 1*(1), 37–43.

Grant, V. W. (1976). *Falling in love*. New York: Springer.

Greeley, A. M. (1989). *Religious change in America*. Cambridge, MA: Harvard University Press.

Greenberg, R. P., & Fisher, S. (1989). Examining antidepressant effectiveness: Findings, ambiguities, and some vexing puzzles. In S. Fisher & R. P. Greenberg (Eds.), *The limits of biological treatments for psychological distress* (pp. 1–37). Hillsdale, NJ: Erlbaum.

Greenwald, A. G. (1980). The totalitarian ego: Fabrication and revision of personal history. *American Psychologist, 35*(7), 603–618.

Greenwald, H. (1988). Decision therapy. In A. Arkoff (Ed.), *Psychology and personal growth* (3rd ed., pp. 354–358). Boston: Allyn & Bacon.

Griffin, D. E., & Watson, D. L. (1978). A written, personal commitment from the student encourages better course work. *Teaching of Psychology, 5*, 155.

Griffitt, W., & Hatfield, E. (1985). *Human sexual behavior*. Glenview, IL: Scott, Foresman.

Groller, I. (1989, June). Is society morally bankrupt? *Parents*, p. 35.

Gross, A. (1993). Small terrors, secret heroics. In A. Arkoff (Ed.), *Psychology and personal growth* (4th ed., pp. 203–206). Boston: Allyn & Bacon.

Grover, K. J., Russell, C. S., Schumm, W. R., & Paff-Bergen, L. A. (1985). Mate selection processes and marital satisfaction. *Family Relations, 34*, 383–386.

Halpern, H. M. (1976). *Cutting loose: An adult guide for coming to terms with your parents*. New York: Simon & Schuster.

Halpern, H. M. (1979). *No strings attached: A guide to a better relationship with your grown-up child*. New York: Simon & Schuster.

Hamachek, D. E. (1978). *Encounters with the self* (2nd ed.). New York: Holt, Rinehart & Winston.

Hamachek, D. E. (1992). *Encounters with the self* (4th ed.). Fort Worth, TX: Harcourt Brace Jovanovich.

Hartung, J. (1988). Deceiving down: Conjectures on the management of subordinate status. In J. S. Lockard & D. L. Paulhus (Eds.), *Self-deception: An adaptive mechanism?* (pp. 170–185). Englewood Cliffs, NJ: Prentice-Hall.

Hatfield, E. (1988). Passionate and companionate love. In R. J. Sternberg & M. L. Barnes (Eds.), *The psychology of love* (pp. 191–217). New Haven, CT: Yale University Press.

Hatfield, E., & Sprecher, S. (1986). *Mirror, mirror . . . The importance of looks in everyday life*. Albany: State University of New York Press.

Hatfield, E., & Walster, G. W. (1985). *A new look at love*. Lanham, MD: University Press of America.

Haughey, J. C. (1975). *Should anyone say forever? On making, keeping, and breaking commitments*. Garden City, NY: Doubleday.

Hawley, N. P., McGee, E. A., & Stanford, W. C. (1976). Sexuality. In *Our bodies, ourselves* (2nd ed., pp. 38–62). New York: Simon & Schuster.

Heiby, E. M. (1981). Depression and the frequency of self-reinforcement. *Behavior Therapy, 12,* 549–555.

Heiby, E. M. (1983a). Assessment of frequency of self-reinforcement. *Journal of Personality and Social Psychology, 44,* 1304–1307.

Heiby, E. M. (1983b). Depression as a function of the interaction of self-and environmentally controlled reinforcement. *Behavior Therapy, 14,* 430–433.

Heiby, E. M. (1983c). Toward the prediction of mood change. *Behavior Therapy, 14,* 110–115.

Heiby, E. M. (1991, September). *Some implications of recent multivariate theories for the assessment of depression*. Paper presented to the Third National Congress on Psychological Assessment, Barcelona, Spain.

Hesse, H. (1988). On little joys. In A. Arkoff (Ed.), *Psychology and personal growth* (3rd ed., pp. 270–271). Boston: Allyn & Bacon. (Original work published 1905)

High anxiety. (1993, January). *Consumer Reports*, pp. 19–24.

Highman, E. L. (1985). *The organization woman: Building a career—an inside report*. New York: Human Sciences Press.

Hite, S. (1981). *The Hite report on male sexuality*. New York: Knopf.

Hodge, M. B. (1967). *Your fear of love*. Garden City, NY: Dolphin/Doubleday.

Hoffer, E. (1951). *The true believer*. New York: Harper & Brothers.

Holden, C. (1992). A new discipline probes suicide's multiple causes. *Science, 256,* 1761–1762.

Holland, D. C., & Eisenhart, M. A. (1990). *Educated in romance: Women, achievement, and college culture*. Chicago: University of Chicago Press.

Horney, K. (1950). *Neurosis and human growth: The struggle toward self-realization*. New York: Norton.

Hugick, L. (1992, March). Satisfaction with U.S. at ten-year low. *Gallup Poll Monthly*, pp. 47–50.

Hunt, M. M. (1993). The limits of intimacy. In A. Arkoff (Ed.), *Psychology and Personal Growth* (4th ed., pp. 271–272). Boston: Allyn & Bacon.

Hurley, D. (1988, May). The mentor mystique. *Psychology Today*, pp. 38–39, 42–43.

Huxley, L. A. (1974). *You are not the target*. North Hollywood, CA: Wilshire.

Ibsen, H. (1978). *A doll's house.* In R. Fjelde (Ed. and Trans), *The complete major prose plays of Ibsen* (pp. 119–196). New York: Farrar, Straus, & Giroux. (Original work published 1879)

Ingram, R. E. (1990). Self-focused attention in clinical disorders: Review and a conceptual model. *Psychological Bulletin, 107*(2), 156–176.

Ingram, R. E., & Smith, T. W. (1984). Depression and internal versus external focus of attention. *Cognitive Therapy and Research, 8*(2), 139–152.

Isherwood, C. (1968). What Vedanta means to me. In B. Dixon (Ed.), *Journeys in belief* (pp. 125–136). London: Allen & Unwin.

Jakubowski, P., & Lange, A. L. (1978). *The assertive option: Your rights and responsibilities.* Champaign, IL: Research Press.

James, M., & Jongeward, D. (1971). *Born to win.* Reading, MA: Addison-Wesley.

Jampolsky, G. G. (1979). *Love is letting go of fear.* Millbrae, CA: Celestial Arts.

Jampolsky, G. G. (1983). *Teach only love: The seven principles of attitudinal healing.* New York: Bantam Books.

Janoff-Bulman, R. (1989). Assumptive worlds and the stress of traumatic events: Applications of the schema construct. *Social Cognition, 7*(2), 113–136.

Janoff-Bulman, R. (1992). *Shattered assumptions: Toward a new psychology of trauma.* New York: Free Press.

Jay, K., & Young, A. (1979). *The gay report.* New York: Summit Books.

Johnson, D. W. (1993). *Reaching out: Interpersonal effectiveness and self-actualization* (5th ed.). Boston: Allyn & Bacon.

Johnson, R. (1985). Stirring the oatmeal. In J. Welwood (Ed.), *Challenge of the heart* (pp. 18–20). Boston: Shambala.

Johnson, W. (1946). *People in quandaries.* New York: Harper & Row.

Jordan, D. (1971). *Parental antecedents and personality characteristics of ego identity statuses.* Unpublished doctoral dissertation, State University of New York at Binghamton.

Josselson, R. L. (1973). Psychodynamic aspects of identity formation in college women. *Journal of Youth and Adolescence, 2,* 3–52.

Jourard, S. M. (1968). *Disclosing man to himself.* Princeton, NJ: Van Nostrand.

Jourard, S. M. (1971). *The transparent self* (rev. ed.). New York: Van Nostrand.

Jourard, S. M. (1975, January). On being persuaded who you are. *AHP Newsletter,* pp. 5–7.

Jung, C. G. (1959). Concerning the archetypes, with special reference to the anima concept. In H. Read, M. Fordham, E. G. Adler (Eds.), R. F. C. Hull (Trans.), *The collected works of C. G. Jung* (Vol. 9, Part I, pp. 54–74). New York: Pantheon. (Original work published in *The archetypes and the collective unconscious,* 1936)

Jung, C. G. (1962). Commentary. In R. Wilhelm & C. G. Jung, *The secret of the golden flower: A Chinese book of life* (pp. 79–137). New York: Harcourt, Brace & World.

Jung, C. G. (1966). The relations between the ego and the unconscious. In H. Read, M. Fordham, G. Adler, & W. McGuire (Eds.), R. F. C. Hull (Trans.), *The collected works of C. G. Jung* (2nd ed., Vol. 7, pp. 123–241). Princeton, NJ: Princeton University Press. (Original work published in *Two essays on analytical psychology,* 1928)

Jung, C. G. (1966). *The practice of psychotherapy.* In H. Read, M. Fordham, G. Adler, & W. McGuire (Eds.), R. F. C. Hull (Trans.), *The collected works of C. G. Jung* (2nd ed., Vol. 16). New York: Pantheon. (Original work published 1958)

Jung, C. G. (1971). The stages of life. In J. Campbell (Ed.), R. F. C. Hull (Trans.), *The portable Jung* (pp. 3–22). New York: Penguin. (Original work published 1930)

Justice, B. (1988). *Who gets sick: How beliefs, moods, and thoughts affect your health.* Los Angeles: Tarcher.

Kahn, M., Kroeber, T., & Kingsbury, S. (1988). The staircase and the roller coaster. In A. Arkoff (Ed.), *Psychology and personal growth* (3rd ed., pp. 285–288). Boston: Allyn & Bacon.

Kalish, R. A. (1985). *Death, grief, and caring relationships* (2nd ed.). Monterey, CA: Brooks/Cole.

Kanfer, F. H., & Gaelick, L. (1986). Self-management methods. In F. H. Kanfer & A. P. Goldstein (Eds.), *Helping people change: A textbook of methods* (pp. 283–345). Elmsford, NY: Pergamon Press.

Kaufman, B. (1975, March–April). Letter to a dead teacher. *Today's Education*, pp. 20–23.

Kavanaugh, R. E. (1974). *Facing death*. Baltimore: Penguin.

Kazantzakis, N. (1952). *Zorba the Greek*. New York: Simon & Schuster.

Kazdin, A. E. (1992, August). *Does psychotherapy change personality?* Paper presented at the annual convention of the American Psychological Association, Washington, DC.

Keen, S., & Valley-Fox, A. (1989). *Your mythic journey: Finding meaning in your life through writing and storytelling*. Los Angeles: Tarcher.

Keleman, S. (1974). *Living your dying*. New York: Random House/Bookworks.

Keller, H. (1959). *The story of my life*. London: Hodder & Stoughton.

Kelton, N. (1984, November). I'm divorced, thank you. *Redbook*, p. 220.

Keniston, K. (1983, June). Remembering Erikson at Harvard. *Psychology Today*, p. 29.

Kenkel, W. F. (1985). The desire for voluntary childlessness among low-income youth. *Journal of Marriage and the Family, 47*(2), 509–512.

Kerr, B. (1986). *Smart girls, gifted women*. Columbus: Ohio Psychology Publishing Co.

Keyes, R. (1985). *Chancing it: Why we take risks*. Boston: Little, Brown.

Kiev, A. (1979). *Active loving: Discovering and developing the power of love*. New York: Crowell.

Kinget, G. M. (1975). *On being human: A systematic view*. New York: Harcourt Brace Jovanovich.

Kleinke, C. L. (1984). Comparing depression coping strategies of schizophrenic men and depressed and nondepressed college students. *Journal of Clinical Psychology, 40*, 420–426.

Kleinke, C. L. (1988). The Depression Coping Questionnaire. *Journal of Clinical Psychology, 44*, 516–526.

Kleinke, C. L. (1991). *Coping with life challenges*. Pacific Grove, CA: Brooks/Cole.

Kleinke, C. L., Staneski, R. A., & Mason, J. K. (1982). Sex differences in coping with depression. *Sex Roles, 15*, 585–600.

Kobasa, S. C., & Maddi, S. R. (1977). Existential personality theory. In R. J. Corsini (Ed.), *Current personality theories* (pp. 243–276). Itasca, IL: Peacock.

Kohn, A. (1989, December). Do religious people help more? Not so you'd notice. *Psychology Today*, pp. 66, 68.

Kohn, A. (1990). *The brighter side of human nature: Altruism and empathy in everyday life*. New York: Basic Books.

Kolbert, E. (1991, February 10). The state of the governor. *New York Times Magazine*, p. 38.

Kopp, S. B. (1970). The laundry list. *Voices, 6*(2), 29.

Kopp, S. B. (1971). *Guru: Metaphors from a psychotherapist*. Palo Alto, CA: Science and Behavior Books.

Kopp, S. B. (1976). *If you meet the Buddha on the road, kill him!* New York: Bantam Books.

Kopp, S. B. (1987). *Who am I—really? An autobiographical exploration on becoming who you are*. Los Angeles: Tarcher.

Kriegel, R. J., & Kriegel, M. H. (1984). *The C zone: Peak performance under pressure*. Garden City, NY: Anchor Press/Doubleday.

Kübler-Ross, E. (1975). *Death: The final stage of growth*. Englewood Cliffs, NJ: Prentice-Hall.

Kuh, G. D., Krehbiel, L. E., & Macay, K. (1988). *Personal development and the college student experience: A review of the literature*. Unpublished manuscript, prepared for the College Outcomes Evaluation Program, New Jersey Department of Higher Education, Trenton, NJ. Bloomington, IN: Department of Educational Leadership and Policy Studies, School of Education, Indiana University.

Kushner, H. S. (1981). *When bad things happen to good people.* New York: Schocken Books.

Kushner, H. S. (1986). *When all you've ever wanted isn't enough.* New York: Summit Books.

Lakein, A. (1973). *How to get control of your time and your life.* New York: Wyden.

Lamont, L. (1979). *Campus shock.* New York: Dutton.

Landers, A. (1986, July 1). Share financial data. *Honolulu Advertiser,* p. D2.

Langer, E. J., & Dweck, C. S. (1973). *Personal politics: The psychology of making it.* Englewood Cliffs, NJ: Prentice-Hall.

Langer, E. J., & Rodin, J. (1976). The effects of choice and enhanced personality for the aged: A field experience in an institutional setting. *Journal of Personality and Social Psychology, 34,* 91–98.

Larsen, D. C. (1980). *Who gets it when you go?* Honolulu: University Press of Hawaii.

Lauer, J., & Lauer, R. (1985, June). Marriages made to last. *Psychology Today,* pp. 22, 24–26.

Lauer, R. H., & Lauer, J. C. (1989). *Watersheds: Mastering life's unpredictable crises.* New York: Ivy.

Laughlin, H. (1979). *The ego and its defenses.* New York: Aronson.

Lazarus, A. (1977). *In the mind's eye: The power of imagery for personal enrichment.* New York: Rawson Associates.

Lazarus, A., & Fay, A. (1975). *I can if I want to.* New York: Morrow.

Lazarus, R. S. (1985). The costs and benefits of denial. In A. Monat & R. S. Lazarus (Eds.), *Stress and coping: An anthology* (2nd ed., pp. 154–173). New York: Columbia University Press.

Leerhsen, C. (1990a, Summer/Fall Special Issue). This year's role model. *Newsweek,* pp. 44–47.

Leerhsen, C. (1990b, February 5). Unite and conquer. *Newsweek,* pp. 50–55.

Lefcourt, H. M. (1982). *Locus of control: Current trends in theory and research* (2nd ed.). Hillsdale, NJ: Erlbaum.

Lefcourt, H. M. (1983). *Research with the locus of control construct.* Vol. 2: *Development and social problems.* New York: Academic Press.

Lefcourt, H. M. (1984). *Research with the locus of control construct.* Vol. 3: *Extensions and limitations.* New York: Academic Press.

Leigh, B. C. (1989). Reasons for having and avoiding sex: Gender, sexual orientation, and relationship to sexual behavior. *Journal of Sex Research, 26*(2), 199–209.

Leonard, G. (1989, May). The case for pleasure. *Esquire,* pp. 153–154, 156.

Lerner, M. J. (1980). *The belief in a just world: A fundamental delusion.* New York: Plenum Press.

LeShan, E. J. (1988). In search of myself and other children. In A. Arkoff (Ed.), *Psychology and personal growth* (3rd ed., pp. 473–478). Boston: Allyn & Bacon.

LeShan, L. (1989). *Cancer as a turning point: A handbook for people with cancer, their families, and health professionals.* New York: Plume.

Levine, J. (1992, February 17). The rabbit grows up. *Forbes,* pp. 122, 127.

Levinson, D. J. (1986). A conception of adult development. *American Psychologist, 41*(1), 3–13.

Levinson, D. J., with Darrow, C. N., Klein, E. B., Levinson, M. H., & McKee, B. (1978). *The seasons of a man's life.* New York: Knopf.

Lewis, C. (1982, May 10). My unprodigal sons. *Newsweek,* p. 11.

Lin, Y. (1975). *Lin Yutang: The best of an old friend.* Ed. by A. J. Anderson. New York: Mason/Charter.

Lindbergh, A. M. (1965). *Gift from the sea.* New York: Random House, Vintage Trade Books.

Lopata, H. Z., Heinemann, G. D., & Baum, J. (1982). Loneliness: Antecedents and coping strategies in the lives of widows. In L. A. Peplau & D. Perlman (Eds.), *Loneliness: A sourcebook of current theory, research, and therapy* (pp. 310–326). New York: Wiley.

Lowenthal, M. F. (1980). Changing hierarchies of commitment in adulthood. In N. J. Smesler & E. H. Erikson (Eds.), *Themes of work and love in adulthood.* Cambridge, MA: Harvard University Press.

Luks, A. (1988, October). Helper's high. *Psychology Today,* pp. 39, 42.

Lynd, H. M. (1958). *On shame and the search for identity.* New York: Harcourt, Brace.

Macklin, E. D. (1987). Nontraditional family forms. In M. B. Sussman & S. K. Steinmetz (Eds.), *Handbook of marriage and the family.* New York: Plenum Press.

Maddi, S. R. (1989). *Personality theories* (5th ed.). Pacific Grove, CA: Brooks/Cole.

Madison, P. (1969). *Personality development in college.* Reading, MA: Addison-Wesley.

Mandler, J. (1992). *In the absence of the sacred: The failure of technology and the survival of the Indian nations.* San Francisco: Sierra Club Books.

Marcia, J. E. (1966). Development and validation of ego identity status. *Journal of Personality and Social Psychology, 3,* 551–558.

Marcia, J. E. (1967). Ego identity status: Relationships to change in self-esteem, "general maladjustment," and authoritarianism. *Journal of Personality, 35,* 119–133.

Marcia, J. E. (1980). Identity in adolescence. In J. Adelson (Ed.), *Handbook of adolescent psychology* (pp. 159–187). New York: Wiley.

Marcia, J. E., & Friedman, M. L. (1970). Ego identity status in college women. *Journal of Personality, 38,* 249–263.

Marecek, M. (1985). *Let go of guilt.* Somerville, MA: Author.

Markus, H., & Kunda, Z. (1986). Stability and malleability of the self-concept. *Journal of Personality and Social Psychology, 51(4),* 858–866.

Markus, H., & Nurius, P. (1986). Possible selves. *American Psychologist, 41(9),* 954–969.

Maslow, A. H. (1962). Lessons from the peak-experience. *Journal of Humanistic Psychology, 2(1),* 9–18.

Maslow, A. H. (1968). *Toward a psychology of being* (2nd ed.). New York: Van Nostrand Reinhold.

Maslow, A. H. (1970). *Motivation and personality* (2nd ed.). New York: Harper & Row.

Maslow, A. H. (1972). *The farther reaches of human nature.* New York: Viking.

Masters, E. L. (1931). *Spoon River anthology.* New York: Macmillan. (Original work published 1915)

Mathes, E. W. (1981). Maslow's hierarchy of needs as a guide for living. *Journal of Humanistic Psychology, 21(4),* 69–72.

Mathes, E. W., & Edwards, L. L. (1978). An empirical test of Maslow's theory of motivation. *Journal of Humanistic Psychology, 18(1),* 75–77.

Matlin, M. W., & Stang, D. J. (1978). *The Pollyanna principle: Selectivity in language, memory, and thought.* Cambridge, MA: Schenkman.

May, M. A. (1961). Foreword. In J. Dollard, L. W. Doob, N. E. Miller, O. H. Mowrer, & R. R. Sears, *Frustration and aggression* (pp. vii–viii). New Haven, CT: Yale University Press.

May, R. (1967). *Art of counseling.* Nashville, TN: Abington Press.

McAdams, D. P. (1985). *Power, intimacy, and the life story: Personological inquiries into identity.* Homewood, IL: Dorsey Press.

McCabe, C. (1975, September 16). Love untold. *San Francisco Chronicle,* p. 35.

McCarthy, K. (1990, October). People presume women and men differ; do they? *Monitor,* p. 33.

McCrae, R. (1984). Situational determinants of coping responses: Loss, threat and challenge. *Journal of Personality and Social Psychology, 46(4),* 919–928.

Medoff, M. H. (1986, November 9). In praise of teachers. *New York Times Magazine,* pp. 72–75, 89, 104, 108–109.

Medved, M., & Wallechinsky, D. (1976). *What really happened to the Class of '65?* New York: Random House.

Michener, J. A. (1988). On wasting time. In A. Arkoff (Ed.), *Psychology and personal growth* (3rd ed., pp. 529–530). Boston: Allyn & Bacon.

Miller, A. (1970). *The death of a salesman.* New York: Penguin. (Original work published 1949)

Miller, A. (1980, November 13). "People invest a whole lifetime in falsehood." *The Listener.*

Monat, A., & Lazarus, R. S. (Eds.). (1985). *Stress and coping: An anthology* (2nd ed.). New York: Columbia University Press.

Moody, R. A., Jr. (1975). *Life after life.* Atlanta: Mockingbird Books.

Morris, C. G. (1990). *Contemporary psychology and effective behavior* (7th ed.). Glenview, IL: Scott, Foresman/Little, Brown, Higher Education.

Morrison, E. S., Starks, K., Hyndman, C., & Ronzio, N. (1980). *Growing up sexual.* New York: Van Nostrand.

Morrow, L. (1991, April 29). The trouble with Teddy. *Time*, pp. 24–27.

Murphy, G., with Leeds, M. (1975). *Outgrowing self-deception.* New York: Basic Books.

Myers, D. G. (1992). *The pursuit of happiness: Who is happy—and why.* New York: Morrow.

Neugarten, B. L. (1964). Summary and implications. In B. L. Neugarten, Berkowitz, H., Crotty, W. J., Gruen, W., Gutmann, D. L., Lubin, M. I., Miller, D. L., Peck, R. F., Rosen, J. L., Shukin, A., & Tobin, S. S., *Personality in middle and late life: Empirical studies* (pp. 188–200). New York: Atherton Press.

Neugarten, B. L., & Neugarten, D. A. (1987, May). The changing meaning of age. *Psychology Today*, pp. 29–30, 32–33.

Nichols, R. G., & Stevens, L. A. (1957). *Are you listening?* New York: McGraw-Hill.

1991 American family values study: A return to family values. (1991). Springfield, MA: Massachusetts Mutual Life Insurance Company.

Nipps, L. (1992, June). Letter. *AHP Perspective*, p. 4.

Noonan, P. (1990). *What I saw at the revolution: A political life in the Reagan era.* New York: Random House.

Norem, J. K., & Cantor, N. (1986). Defensive pessimism: Harnessing anxiety as motivation. *Journal of Personality and Social Psychology, 51*(6), 1208–1217.

O'Connell, V., & O'Connell, A. (1974). *Choice and change: An introduction to the psychology of growth.* Englewood Cliffs, NJ: Prentice-Hall.

O'Dowd, D. D., & Beardslee, D. C. (1960). *College images of a selected group of professions and occupations.* Cooperative Research Project No.562(8142), U.S. Office of Education. Middletown, CT: Wesleyan University Press.

Ogawa, D. M., & Grant, G. (1985). *To a land called Tengoku: One hundred years of Japanese in Hawaii.* Honolulu: Mutual Publishing of Honolulu.

O'Neil, J. M., Helms, B. J., Gable, R. K., David, L., & Wrightsman, L. S. (1986). Gender-role conflict scale: College men's fear of femininity. *Sex Roles, 14*, 335–350.

Orlofsky, J. L., Marcia, J. E., & Lesser, I. M. (1973). Ego identity status and the intimacy versus isolation crisis of young adulthood. *Journal of Personality and Social Psychology, 27*, 211–219.

Ornstein, R., & Sobel, D. (1989). *Healthy pleasures.* Reading, MA: Addison-Wesley.

Osherson, S. (1986). *Finding our fathers: The unfinished business of manhood.* New York: Free Press.

Oshman, H., & Manosevitz, M. (1974). The impact of the identity crisis on the adjustment of late adolescent males. *Journal of Youth and Adolescence, 3*, 207–216.

Otto, H. A. (1972). New light on human potential. In College of Home Economics, Iowa State University, *Families of the future* (pp. 14–25). Ames: Iowa State University Press.

Oyserman, D., & Markus, H. (1986). *Possible selves, motivation, and delinquency.* Unpublished manuscript, University of Michigan.

Palmeri, C. (1992, February 17). I need to be making and selling things. *Forbes*, p. 97.

Pascarella, E. T., & Terenzini, P. T. (1991). *How college affects students: Findings and insights from twenty years of research.* San Francisco: Jossey-Bass.

Patterson, D. (1983). Introduction to L. Tolstoy, *Confession* (pp. 5–9). (D. Patterson, Trans.) New York: Norton. (Original work published 1882)

Patterson, J., & Kim, P. (1991). *The day America told the truth.* New York: Prentice Hall Press.

Pearlin, L. I., & Lieberman, M. A. (1979). Sources of emotional distress. In R. G. Simmons (Ed.), *Research in community and mental health,* (Vol. 1, pp. 217–248). Greeenwich, CT: JAI Press.

Pearlin, L. I., & Schooler, C. (1978). The structure of coping. *Journal of Health and Social Behavior, 19,* 2–21.

Peck, M. S. (1978). *The road less traveled.* New York: Simon & Schuster, Touchstone Books.

Pekkanen, J. (1993, August). Drive of a champion. *Reader's Digest,* pp. 91–96.

Pennebaker, J. W. (1990). *Opening up: The healing power of confiding in others.* New York: Morrow.

Pennebaker, J. W., & Beall, S. K. (1986). Confronting a traumatic event: Toward an understanding of inhibition of disease. *Journal of Abnormal Psychology, 95,* 274–281.

Pennebaker, J. W., Kiecolt-Glaser, J. K., & Glaser, R. (1988). Disclosure of traumas and immune function: Health implications for psychotherapy. *Journal of Consulting and Clinical Psychology, 56*(2), 239–245.

Peplau, L. A., Bikson, T. K., Rook, K. S., & Goodchilds, J. D. (1982). Being old and living alone. In L. A. Peplau & D. Perlman (Eds.), *Loneliness: A sourcebook of current theory, research, and therapy* (pp. 327–347). New York: Wiley.

Perlin, S. (1982). Death visualization: A teaching and learning device. *Death Education, 6,* 294–298.

Perlman, D., Gerson, A. C., & Spinner, B. (1978). Loneliness among senior citizens: An empirical report. *Essence, 2*(4), 239–248.

Perlmutter, M., & Hall, E. (1985). *Adult development and aging.* New York: Wiley.

Perry, W. G., Jr. (1981). Cognitive and ethical growth: The making of meaning. In A. W. Chickering (Ed.), *The modern American college* (pp. 76–116). San Francisco: Jossey-Bass.

Pesmen, S. (1977, October 23). Jill Kinmont: The other side of the story. *Sunday Star-Bulletin & Advertiser* (Honolulu).

Peterson, K. S. (1992, August 19). Psychologists on lying, violence, body image. *Honolulu Star-Bulletin,* p. B3.

Phillips, G. M., & Metzger, N. J. (1976). *The study of intimate communication.* Boston: Allyn & Bacon.

Phillips-Jones, L. (1982). *Mentors and protégés.* New York: Arbor House.

Piaget, G. W., & Binkley, B. (1985). *Overcoming your barriers: A guide to personal reprogramming.* New York: Irvington.

Piper, H. (1987, January 20). Why Soviets leave the U.S.: The insupportable burden of freedom. *Honolulu Star-Bulletin,* p. A15. (Reprinted from the *Baltimore Sun*)

Pirot, M. (1986). The pathological thought and dynamics of the perfectionist. *Journal of Individual Psychology, 42*(1), 51–58.

Podd, M. H., Marcia, J. E., & Rubin, B. M. (1970). The effects of ego identity and partner perception on a prisoner's dilemma game. *Journal of Social Psychology, 82,* 117–126.

Podhoretz, N. (1967). *Making it.* New York: Random House.

Pogrebin, L. C. (1983). *Family politics: Love and power in our intimate frontier.* New York: McGraw-Hill.

Pogrebin, L. C. (1987). *Among friends: Who we like, why we like them, and what we do with them.* New York: McGraw-Hill.

Polster, E., & Polster, M. (1974). *Gestalt therapy integrated: Contours of theory and practice.* New York: Brunner/Mazel.

Possible selves. (1987, Spring/Summer). *ISR Newsletter,* pp. 5–7.

Potter, R. E. (1988). The quality of life within the rat race. In A. Arkoff (Ed.), *Psychology and personal growth* (3rd ed., pp. 531–533). Boston: Allyn & Bacon.

Powell, T. J. (1987). *Self-help organizations and professional practice*. Silver Spring, MD: National Association of Social Workers.

Prather, H. (1970). *Notes to myself*. Moab, UT: Real People Press.

Progoff, I. (1975). *At a journal workshop*. New York: Dialogue House.

Putnam, F. W. (1984). The psychophysiological investigation of multiple personality disorder: A review. *Psychiatric Clinics of North America, 7*(1), 31–39.

Putney, S., & Putney, G. J. (1964). *The adjusted American: Normal neuroses in the individual and society*. New York: Harper Colophon.

Queenan, J. M. (1987, August 31). Too late to say, "I'm sorry." *Newsweek*, p. 7.

Ragghianti, M. (1988, August 14). You can look at your bars, or through them. *Parade*, pp. 4–5.

Ragghianti, M. (1989, May). The life my mother chose. *Reader's Digest*, pp. 7–9, 11.

Rainer, T. (1978). *The new diary*. Los Angeles: Tarcher.

Ram Dass. (1971). *Be here now*. San Cristobal, NM: Lama Foundation, New York: Crown.

Rankin, P. T. (1939). Listening ability. In *Proceedings of the Ohio State Educational Conference*. Columbus: Ohio State University Press.

Ratner, R. (1984). Heal, body, heal: Invocations to hope and health. In M. Kaminsky (Ed.), *The uses of reminiscence: New ways of working with older adults* (pp. 85–105). New York: Haworth Press.

Ravitch, D. (1989, March 6). Back to basics. *New Republic*, pp. 13–15.

Regier, D. A., Narrow, W. E., Rae, D. S., Manderscheid, R. W., Locke, B. Z., & Goodwin, F. K. (1993). The de facto US mental and addictive disorders service system: Epidemiologic catchment area prospective 1-year prevalence rates of disorders and services. *Archives of General Psychiatry, 50*, 85–94.

Reker, G. T., Peacock, E. J., & Wong, P. T. P. (1987). Meaning and purpose in life and well-being: A life-span approach. *Journal of Gerontology, 42*(1), 44–49.

Reker, G. T., & Wong, P. T. P. (1983). *The salutary effects of personal optimism and meaningfulness on the physical and psychological well-being of the elderly*. Paper presented at the 29th annual meeting of the Western Gerontological Society, Albuquerque, NM.

Reps, P. (1958). *Zen flesh, Zen bones*. Rutland, VT: Charles Tuttle.

Rich, A. (1977). *Of woman born: Motherhood as experience and institution*. New York: Bantam Books.

Riessman, F. (1987). Foreword. In T. J. Powell, *Self-help organizations and professional practice* (pp. vii–x). Silver Spring, MD: National Association of Social Workers.

Rimland, B. (1983). The altruism paradox. *Psychological Reports, 51*, 521–522.

Roche, G. (1988, November). A world without heroes. *USA Today*, pp. 57–59.

Rodin, J., & Salovey, P. (1989). Health psychology. *Annual Review of Psychology, 40*, 533–579.

Rogers, C. R. (1961). *On becoming a person: A therapist's view of psychotherapy*. Boston: Houghton Mifflin.

Rogers, C. R. (1964). Toward a modern approach to values: The valuing process in the mature person. *Journal of Abnormal and Social Psychology, 68*(2), 160–167.

Rogers, C. R. (1975). Client-centered psychotherapy. In A. M. Freedman, H. I. Kaplan, & B. J. Sadock (Eds.), *Comprehensive textbook of psychiatry* (Vol. 2, pp. 1831–1843). Baltimore: Williams & Wilkins.

Rogers, C. R. (1980). *A way of being*. Boston: Houghton Mifflin.

Rokeach, M. (1960). *The open and closed mind*. New York: Basic Books.

Roosevelt, T. (1946). *Theodore Roosevelt: An autobiography*. New York: Scribner's. (Original work published 1913)

Roper Organization. (1987, February). *The American dream: A national survey by the "Wall Street Journal."* Princeton, NJ: Dow Jones.

Roper Organization. (1989, February). *Most common daydreams.* Study 89–3. Princeton, NJ: Dow Jones.

Rosen, G. M. (1987). Self-help treatment books and the commercialization of psychotherapy. *American Psychologist, 42*(1), 46–51.

Rosenberg, M. (1979). *Conceiving the self.* New York: Basic Books.

Rosenfeld, A., & Stark, E. (1987, May). The prime of our lives. *Psychology Today,* pp. 62–64, 66, 68–72.

Rowan, C. (1985, March). Unforgettable Miss Bessie. *Reader's Digest,* pp. 123–126.

Rowan, J. (1990). *Subpersonalities: The people inside us.* New York: Routledge.

Rowe, D. (1982). *The construction of life and death.* Chichester, England: Wiley.

Rubenstein, C., & Shaver, P. (1982). *In search of intimacy.* New York: Delacorte.

Rubin, J. (1976). *Growing (up) at thirty-seven.* New York: M. Evans.

Rubin, L. B. (1985). *Just friends: The role of friendship in our lives.* New York: Harper & Row.

Rubin, T. I. (1985). *Overcoming indecisiveness.* New York: Harper & Row.

Rubin, Z. (1981, May). Does personality really change after 20? *Psychology Today,* pp. 18–24, 26–27.

Rubin, Z. (1982, June). Fathers and sons: The search for reunion. *Psychology Today,* pp. 23, 25–26, 28–30, 32–33.

Russell, B. (1930). *The conquest of happiness.* New York: Liveright.

Ryff, C. (1989). Happiness is everything, or is it? Explorations on the meaning of psychological well-being. *Journal of Personality and Social Psychology, 57*(6), 1069–1081.

Safran, C. (1977). How religion affects health, happiness, sex, and politics. *Redbook,* pp. 216–224.

Saint-Exupéry, A. de (1943). *The little prince* (K. Woods, Trans.). New York: Harcourt, Brace & World.

Samples, R. (1977, May). Selfness: Seeds of a transformation. *AHP Newsletter,* pp. 1–2.

Samuels, M., & Bennett, H. (1973). *The well body book.* New York and Berkeley: Random House/Bookworks.

Santoli, A. (1990, April 8). You can find the courage. *Parade,* pp. 6, 8–9.

Sappington, A. A. (1989). *Adjustment: Theory, research, and personal applications.* Pacific Grove, CA: Brooks/Cole.

Sappington, A. A. (1990). The independent manipulation of intellectually and emotionally based beliefs. *Journal of Research in Personality, 24,* 487–509.

Savage, D. G. (1985, February 17). Drive, not talent, found key to achievement. *Sunday Star-Bulletin & Advertiser* (Honolulu), p. A16.

Schaar, J. H. (1970). " . . . and the Pursuit of Happiness." *Virginia Quarterly Review, 46*(1), 1–26.

Scheier, M. F., & Carver, C. S. (1985). Optimism, coping, and health: Assessment and implications of generalized outcome expectancies. *Health Psychology, 4*(3), 219–247.

Scheier, M. F., Weintraub, J. K., & Carver, C. S. (1986). Coping with stress: Divergent strategies of optimists and pessimists. *Journal of Personality and Social Psychology, 51*(6), 1257–1264.

Schenkel, S., & Marcia, J. E. (1972). Attitudes toward premarital intercourse in determining ego identity status in college women. *Journal of Personality, 3,* 472–482.

Schlossberg, N. K. (1987, May). Taking the mystery out of change. *Psychology Today,* pp. 74–75.

Schlossberg, N. K. (1989). *Overwhelmed: Coping with life's ups and downs.* Lexington, MA: Lexington Books.

Schultz, D. (1977). *Growth psychology: Models of the healthy personality.* New York: Van Nostrand.

Schutz, W. (1979). *Profound simplicity.* New York: Bantam Books.

Schwartz, S. H. (1990). Individualism-collectivism: Critique and proposed refinements. *Journal of Cross-Cultural Psychology, 21*(2), 139–157.

Scott-Maxwell, F. (1968). *The measure of my days.* New York: Knopf.

Segal, J., & Yahraes, H. (1978a, November). Bringing up mother. *Psychology Today,* pp. 90, 93–94, 96.

Segal, J., & Yahraes, H. (1978b). *A child's journey: Forces that shape the lives of our young.* New York: McGraw-Hill.

Seidner, M. L. (1973). *Behavior change contract: Prior information about study habits treatment and statements of intention as related to initial effort in treatment.* Unpublished doctoral dissertation, University of Cincinnati.

Seligman, M. E. P. (1975). *Helplessness: On depression, development, and death.* San Francisco: W. H. Freeman.

Seligman, M. E. P. (1991). *Learned optimism.* New York: Knopf.

Selye, H. (1983). The stress concept: Past, present, and future. In C. L. Cooper (Ed.), *Stress research: Issues for the eighties* (pp. 1–20). New York: Wiley.

Shapiro, D. H., Jr. (1978). *Precision nirvana.* Englewood Cliffs, NJ: Prentice-Hall.

Shaver, P., Hazan, C., & Bradshaw, D. (1988). Love as attachment: The integration of three behavioral systems. In R. J. Sternberg & M. L. Barnes (Eds.), *The psychology of love* (pp. 68–99). New Haven, CT: Yale University Press.

Sheehy, G. (1976). *Passages: Predictable crises of adult life.* New York: Dutton.

Sheehy, G. (1981). *Pathfinders.* New York: Morrow.

Shepard, M. (1976). *The do-it-yourself psychotherapy book.* New York: Dutton.

Sher, B., with Gottlieb, A. (1979). *Wishcraft: How to get what you really want.* New York: Viking.

Shippam, E. (1968). Twice born. In B. Dixon (Ed.), *Journeys in belief* (pp. 191–198). London: Allen & Unwin.

Shorr, J. E. (1977). *Go see the movie in your head.* New York: Popular Library.

Shostrom, E. L. (1976). *Actualizing therapy: Foundations for a scientific ethic.* San Diego, CA: Edits.

Shreve, A. (1987). *Remaking motherhood: How working mothers are shaping our children's future.* New York: Viking.

Siegel, K., Bauman, L. J., Christ, G. H., & Krown, S. (1988). Patterns of change in sexual behavior among gay men in New York City. *Archives of Sexual Behavior, 17,* 481–497.

Siegelman, E. Y. (1983). *Personal risk: Mastering change in love and work.* New York: Harper & Row.

Skaalvik, E. M. (1986). Sex differences in global self-esteem: A research review. *Scandinavian Journal of Educational Research, 30*(4), 167–179.

Skinner, B. F. (1953). *Science and human behavior.* New York: Macmillan.

Smedes, L. B. (1986). *Forgive and forget: Healing the hurts we don't deserve.* New York: Pocket Books.

Smith, T. W. (1986). The polls: The most admired man and woman. *Public Opinion Quarterly, 50*(4), 573–583.

Snodgrass, M. E. (1989, March). Growing up Baptist. *Ms.,* pp. 66–67.

Snyder, C. R., & Higgins, R. L. (1988). Excuses: Their effective role in the negotiation of reality. *Psychological Bulletin, 104*(1), 23–25.

Spilka, B., Hood, R. W., Jr., & Gorsuch, R. L. (1985). *The psychology of religion: An empirical approach.* Englewood Cliffs, NJ: Prentice-Hall.

Stark, E. (1986, May). Mom and dad: The great American heroes. *Psychology Today*, pp. 12–13.

Starker, S. (1988). Do-it-yourself therapy: The prescription of self-help books by psychologists. *Psychotherapy, 25*(1), 142–146.

Steinem, G. (1992). *Revolution from within: A book of self-esteem*. Boston: Little, Brown.

Steiner, C. (1974). *Scripts people live*. New York: Grove Press.

Sternberg, R. J. (1985, April). The measure of love. *Science Digest*, pp. 60, 78–79.

Sternberg, R. J. (1988a). *The triangle of love: Intimacy, passion, commitment*. New York: Basic Books.

Sternberg, R. J. (1988b). Triangulating love. In R. J. Sternberg & M. L. Barnes (Eds.), *The psychology of love* (pp. 119–138). New Haven, CT: Yale University Press.

Stevens, B. (1971). Curtain raiser. In C. R. Rogers and B. Stevens (Eds.), *Person to person: The problem of being human* (pp. 1–3). New York: Pocket Books.

Stevens, B. (1976/77). Reflections on unparenting. *Voices, 12*(4), 68–71.

Stevens, J. O. (1971). *Awareness: Exploring, experimenting, experiencing*. Moab, UT: Real People Press.

Super, D. E. (1985). Coming of age in Middletown: Careers in the making. *American Psychologist, 40*, 405–414.

Swann, W. B., Jr. (1984). Quest for accuracy in person perception: A matter of pragmatics. *Psychological Review, 91*, 457–477.

Szent-Gyoergyi, A. (1974). Drive in living matter to perfect itself. *Synthesis, 1*, 14–26.

Tanahara, K. M. (1992, August 10). "Make a difference," UH grads told. *Honolulu Advertiser*, p. A3.

Tangri, S. S., & Jenkins, S. R. (1986). Stability and change in role innovation and life plans. *Sex Roles, 14*(11/12), 647–662.

Tannen, D. (1991). *You just don't understand: Women and men in conversation*. New York: Ballantine Books.

Tavris, C. (1985, August). *Pride and prejudice*. Paper presented at annual convention of the American Psychological Association, Los Angeles.

Tavris, C. (1989). *Anger: The misunderstood emotion* (rev. ed.). New York: Simon & Schuster, Touchstone Books.

Tavris, C., & Wade, C. (1984). *The longest war: Sex differences in perspective* (2nd ed.). San Diego, CA: Harcourt Brace Jovanovich.

Taylor, S. E. (1989). *Positive illusions: Creative self-deception and the healthy mind*. New York: Basic Books.

Taylor, S. E., & Brown, J. D. (1988). Illusion and well-being: A social psychological perspective on mental health. *Psychological Bulletin, 103*(2), 193–210.

Taylor, V. (1977, October). Good news about disaster. *Psychology Today*, pp. 93–94, 124, 126.

Tennov, D. (1979). *Love and limerence: The experience of being in love*. New York: Stein & Day.

Tesch, S. A., & Whitbourne, S. K. (1982). Intimacy and identity status in young adults. *Journal of Personality and Social Psychology, 43*, 1041–1051.

Thomas, A., & Chess, S. (1977). *Temperament and development*. New York: Brunner/Mazel.

Thoreau, H. D. (1947). *Walden: or, Life in the woods*. New York: Viking. (Original work published 1854)

Toffler, A. (1970). *Future shock*. New York: Random House.

Tolstoy, L. (1978). Confession. In J. Bayley (Ed.), *The portable Tolstoy* (pp. 666–731). New York: Penguin. (Original work published 1882)

Tripp, C. A. (1987). *The homosexual matrix*. New York: Meridian.

Turner, R. H., & Vanderlippe, R. H. (1958). Self-ideal congruence as an index of adjustment. *Journal of Abnormal and Social Psychology, 57*, 202–206.

Turner, T. (1991, January/February). Humanism's fighting chance. *The Humanist*, pp. 12–14.

Vaillant, G. E. (1977). *Adaptation to life*. Boston: Little, Brown.

Vargiu, J. G. (1980). Subpersonalities. In A. Arkoff (Ed.), *Psychology and personal growth* (2nd ed., pp. 22–27). Boston: Allyn & Bacon.

Vasconcellos, J. (1989). Preface. In A. M. Mecca, N. J. Smelser, & J. Vasconcellos (Eds.), *The social importance of self-esteem* (pp. xi–xxi). Berkeley: University of California Press.

Vaughan, D. (1986). *Uncoupling: Turning points in intimate relationships*. New York: Oxford University Press.

Viorst, J. (1987). *Necessary losses*. New York: Fawcett Gold Medal.

Vox Pop. (1992, February 10). *Time*, p. 15.

Wahba, M. A., & Bridwell, L. G. (1983). Maslow reconsidered: A review of research on the need hierarchy theory. In R. M. Steers & L. W. Porter (Eds.), *Motivation and work behavior* (3rd ed., pp. 34–41). New York: McGraw-Hill.

Walden, D. (1986, January). Where have all our heroes gone? *USA Today*, pp. 20–25.

Walen, S. R., DiGiuseppe, R., & Wessler, R. L. (1980). *A practitioner's guide to rational-emotive therapy*. New York: Oxford University Press.

Wallechinsky, D. (1986). *Midterm report: The class of '65—chronicles of an American generation*. New York: Viking.

Wallerstein, J. S., & Blakeslee, S. (1989). *Second chances: Men, women, and children a decade after divorce*. New York: Ticknor & Fields.

Wallerstein, J., & Kelley, J. (1980). *Surviving the break-up: How children actually cope with divorce*. New York: Basic Books.

Walster, E. (1965). The effect of self-esteem on romantic liking. *Journal of Experimental Social Psychology, 1*, 184–197.

Warga, C. (1988, September). You are what you think. *Psychology Today*, pp. 54–58.

Warner, S. J. (1966). *Self-realization and self-defeat*. New York: Grove Press.

Watson, D. L., & Tharp, R. G. (1993). *Self-directed behavior: Self-modification for personal adjustment* (6th ed). Pacific Grove, CA: Brooks/Cole.

Watson, J. B. (1928). *The ways of behaviorism*. New York: Harper & Brothers.

Watson, J. S., & Ramey, C. T. (1972). Reactions to response-contingent stimulation in early infancy. *Merrill-Palmer Quarterly, 18*(3), 219–227.

Watts, R. J., Milburn, N. G., Brown, D. R., & Gary, L. E. (1985, November). *Epidemiological research on blacks and depression: A sociocultural perspective*. Paper presented at the annual meeting of the American Public Health Association, Washington, DC.

Weaver, R. L., II (1991, January 15). Self-fulfillment through imaging. *Vital Speeches of the Day*, pp. 216–218.

Weiten, W., Lloyd, M. A., & Lashley, R. L. (1991). *Psychology applied to modern life: Adjustment in the 90's* (3rd ed.). Monterey, CA: Brooks/Cole.

Wells, T. (1980). Psychology of woman. In A. Arkoff (Ed.), *Psychology and personal growth* (2nd ed., pp. 84–95). Boston: Allyn & Bacon.

Welwood, J. (1980). Reflections on psychotherapy, focusing, and meditation. *Journal of Transpersonal Psychology, 12*(2), 127–141.

Whitbourne, S. K. (1986). *Adult development* (2nd ed.). New York: Praeger.

White, J. (1982). *Rejection*. Reading, MA: Addison-Wesley.

Wilber, K. (1982). Odyssey: A personal inquiry into humanistic and transpersonal psychology. *Journal of Humanistic Psychology, 22*(1), 57–90.

Wilder, T. (1985). *Our town*. New York: Harper & Row. Perennial Library Edition. (Original work published 1938)

Williams, J. E., & Best, D. L. (1982). *Measuring sex stereotypes: A thirty-nation study*. Beverly Hills, CA: Sage.

Woodward, K. L. (1989, March 27). Heaven. *Newsweek*, pp. 52–55.

Woollams, S., & Brown, M. (1979). *TA: The total handbook of transactional analysis*. Englewood Cliffs, NJ: Prentice-Hall.

Worden, J. W. (1982). *Grief counseling and grief therapy*. New York: Springer.

Worden, J. W., & Proctor, W. (1976). *PDA: Personal death awareness*. Englewood Cliffs, NJ: Prentice-Hall.

Wrightsman, L. S. (1988). *Personality development in adulthood*. Newbury Park, CA: Sage.

Wuthnow, R. (1978). Peak experiences: Some empirical tests. *Journal of Humanistic Psychology, 18*(3), 59–75.

Yalom, I. D. (1980). *Existential psychotherapy*. New York: Basic Books.

Zarin, C. (1990, July 30). A part in the play. *New Yorker*, pp. 37–45, 48–54.

Zilbergeld, B. (1983). *The shrinking of America: Myths of psychological change*. Boston: Little, Brown.

Zimbardo, P. G. (1977). *Shyness: What it is, what to do about it*. Reading, MA: Addison-Wesley.

Zuckerman, D. M., Kasl, S. V., & Ostfeld, A. M. (1984). Psychosocial predictors of mortality among the elderly poor. *American Journal of Epidemiology, 119*(3), 410–423.

Name Index

Note: Pages numbers in *italics* refer to text in boxes.

Credits

Question One (Bearings)

Question Two (Self)

Question Three (Beliefs)

Question Four (Turning Points)

Question Five (Significant Others)

Question Six (Love)

Question Seven (Ultimate Point)

Excerpt from "Childhood is the Kingdom Where Nobody Dies" by Edna St. Vincent Millay. From *Collected Poems,* HarperCollins. Copyright 1922, 1934, 1950, 1962 by Edna St. Vincent Millay and Norma Millay Ellis. Reprinted by permission of Elizabeth Barnett, literary executor.

Adaptation of the 23rd Psalm by the Reverend Robert Fraser. Reprinted by permission of the Reverend Fraser.

"To Remember Me" by Robert Noel Test. Reprinted by permission of the poet. Copyright 1980 by Robert Noel Test.

Ann Landers letters, *Honolulu Advertiser,* July 1, 1986, D-2. Permission granted by Ann Landers and Creators Syndicate.

Excerpts from *Forgive and Forget* by Lewis B. Smedes. Copyright (c) 1984 by Lewis B. Smedes. Reprinted by permission of HarperCollins Publishers.

Question Eight (Potentiality)

Excerpt from *Personal Politics: The Psychology of Making It* by Ellen J. Langer & Carol S. Dweck, pp. 40–42, (c) 1973. Reprinted by permission of Prentice Hall, Englewood Cliffs, New Jersey.

Question Nine (Values)

Excerpt from the song "Is That All There Is?" by Jerry Lieber and Mike Stoller, (c) 1966, 1969 Jerry Lieber Music and Mike Stoller Music. All rights reserved. Used by permission.

Individual responses to the question "What is the meaning of life?" are used by permission of Maya Angelou, Wilma Mankiller, Sylvestre Sorola, Annie Dillard, and Michael Metzen, respectively.

MassMutual survey data are used by permission of MassMutual.

Excerpt from the book *The Day America Told the Truth* by James Patterson and Peter Kim. (c) 1991. Used by the permission of the publisher, Prentice Hall Press/A Division of Simon & Schuster, New York.

Excerpt from Ellen Goodman's column, "Perils of the Neatness Gap," November 13, 1990. (c) 1993, The Boston Globe Company. Reprinted with permission.

Condensation of "Curtain Raiser" by Barry Stevens in *Person to Person: The Problem of Being Human* by Carl R. Rogers and Barry Stevens. (c) 1967. Used by permission of the publisher, Real People Press.

Ann Landers letters, *Honolulu Advertiser,* August 1, 1977, B2. Permission granted by Ann Landers and Creators Syndicate.

Question Ten (Goals)

Excerpt from *The Collected Poems of A. E. Housman.* Copyright (c) 1922, 1965 by Holt, Rinehart and Winston, Inc. Copyright (c) 1950 by Barclays Bank, Ltd. Reprinted by permission of Henry Holt and Company, Inc.

Condensation from *Sex Roles and Personal Awareness* by Barbara Lusk Forisha. Used by permission of the author.

Relief and delight figures from "How Come You're Not Running Everywhere, Anymore?" by Frank E. Dougherty, *A.R.C. Linkletter,* Vol. 1, No. 2, pp. 3–4. Used by the permission of the author.

Boyd Ray's Joy List is used by permission of Boyd Ray.

Question Eleven (Coping)

Excerpts from *If You Meet the Buddha on the Road, Kill Him!* by Sheldon B. Kopp. By permission of the author.

Excerpt from the poem "Raccoon" from *Kenneth Rexroth: Selected Poems.* Copyright (c) 1978 Kenneth Rexroth. Reprinted by permission of New Direction Publishing Corporation.

COPE inventory items adapted from "Assessing Coping Strategies: A Theoretically Based Approach" by C. S. Carver, M. F. Scheier, & J. K. Weintraub, *Journal of Personality and Social Psychology,* 1989, *56*(2), 267–283. Used by permission of the senior author.

Cool Thoughts for Hot Thoughts. Figure 7–3 (pg. 152) from *Feeling Good: The New Mood Therapy* by David D. Burns, M.D. Copyright (c) 1980 by David D. Burns, M.D. Reprinted by permission of William Morrow & Company, Inc.

Depression Coping Questionnaire items from *Coping with Life Challenges* by C. L. Kleinke. Copyright (c) 1991 by Wadsworth, Inc. Reprinted by permission of Brooks/Cole Publishing Company, Pacific Grove, CA 93950.

Question Twelve (Assets)

"My Father's Windowbox" by Gilbert Brim, reprinted with permission from *Psychology Today* Magazine. Copyright (c) 1988, Sussex Publishers, Inc.

Excerpt from *In the Mind's Eye* by Arnold Lazarus. Reprinted with the permission of Rawson Associates, an imprint of Macmillan Publishing Company. Copyright (c) 1977 Arnold Lazarus, Ph.D.

Question Thirteen (Commitment)

Paraphrase from *Power, Intimacy, and the Life Story* by Dan P. McAdams, copyright (c) 1985, by permission of Brooks/Cole Publishing Company, Pacific Grove, CA 93950.

Excerpt from *Overcoming Indecisiveness* by Theodore Rubin, M.D. Copyright (c) 1985 by Theodore Isaac Rubin, M.D. Reprinted by permission of HarperCollins Publishers.

Excerpt from "A Fate Worse than Death" by J. F. T. Bugental & E. K. Bugental, *Psychotherapy,* 1984, *21*(4), 543–549. Reprinted by permission of *Psychotherapy.* Copyright (c) 1984.

Diagram from *The C Zone* by Robert J. Kriegel and Marilyn Harris Kriegel. Reprinted by permission of Doubleday, a division of Bantam, Doubleday, Dell Publishing Group, Inc.

Excerpt from *The Prophet* by Kahlil Gibran. Copyright 1923 by Kahlil Gibran and renewed 1951 by Administrators C.T.A. of Kahlil Gibran Estate and Mary G. Gibran. Reprinted by permission of Alfred A. Knopf, Inc.

Question Fourteen (Threshold)

Items from the Life Orientation Test by permission of Charles S. Carver.

Excerpts from *Learned Optimism* by Martin E. P. Seligman. Copyright (c) 1991 by Martin E. P. Seligman. Reprinted by permission of Alfred A. Knopf, Inc.

Lines from "love is a place" from *No Thanks* by E. E. Cummings, edited by George James Firmage, by permission of Liveright Publishing Corporation. Copyright (c) 1935 by E. E. Cummings. Copyright (c) 1968 by Marion Morehouse Cummings. Copyright (c) 1973, 1978 by the Trustees for the E. E. Cummings Trust. Copyright (c) 1973, 1978 by George James Firmage.

Excerpts from *Age Wave* by Ken Dychtwald and Joe Flower. Reprinted by permission of The Putnam Publishing Group for *Age Wave* by Ken Dychtwald and Joe Flower. Copyright (c) 1989 by Ken Dychtwald.